Shakespeare and Higher Education—
A Global Perspective

SHAKESPEARE AND HIGHER EDUCATION– A GLOBAL PERSPECTIVE

Edited by
Sharon A. Beehler
and
Holger Klein

A Publication of the Shakespeare Yearbook
Volume 12

The Edwin Mellen Press
Lewiston•Queenston•Lampeter

Shakespeare and Higher Education–A Global Perspective.
　　Edited by Sharon A. Beehler and Holger Klein.
　ISBN 0-7734-7262-2

Copyright　©　2001　The Edwin Mellen Press

All rights reserved. For information contact

　　　　　　The Edwin Mellen Press　　　　The Edwin Mellen Press
　　　　　　　　　Box 450　　　　　　　　　　　　Box 67
　　　　　　　Lewiston, New York　　　　　　Queenston, Ontario
　　　　　　　USA 14092-0450　　　　　　　CANADA L0S 1L0

　　　　　　　　　The Edwin Mellen Press, Ltd.
　　　　　　　　　Lampeter, Ceredigion, Wales
　　　　　　　　UNITED KINGDOM SA48 8LT

　　　　　　　　Printed in the United States of America

EDITORIAL ADDRESSES:
The Edwin Mellen Press
PO Box 450
Lewiston, NY 14092, USA

General Editor	**Reviews Editor**
Holger Klein	C. N. Smith
Institut für Anglistik	School of Modern Language
und Amerikanistik	and European Studies
Universität Salzburg	University of East Anglia
A-5020 Salzburg, Austria	Norwich NR4 7TJ, UK
Fax: 0043-662-8044-167	Fax: 01603-250599

The *Shakespeare Yearbook* is an annual dealing with all aspects of Shakespeare and his period, with particular emphases on theater-oriented, comparative, and interdisciplinary studies. From Volume IV (1993) onwards each volume has a main theme, but there will always be space for some independent contributions on other issues. As a rule, articles are double-read before acceptance.

Members of the Editorial Board
Dimiter Daphinoff (Fribourg)
Péter Dávidházi (Budapest)
James Harner (Texas A&M)
Joan Hartwig (Lexington)
André Lorant (Paris)
Jean-Marie Maguin (Montpellier)
Michele Marrapodi (Palermo)
Peter Milward, S.J. (Tokyo)
Ann Thompson (King's College, London)
Helen Wilcox (Groningen)
Simon Williams (Santa Barbara)
Linda Woodbridge (Pennsylvania State)
Rowland Wymer (Hull)

Contributions: Please type 60 digits per line, use line-spacing 1.5, employ MLA style and send in hard copy plus a disk (MS DOS, Word 6 or 7 for Windows, or WordPerfect, *both geared to IBM*). **Reviews** (not usually longer than 1000 words; one hard copy plus disk): **send to** Dr. C. N. **Smith**, University of East Anglia, School of Modern Languages and European Studies, Norwich NR4 7TJ, England, Fax: 01603-250599, Tel. 01603-56161. **Articles** (under 30 pages including notes; two hard copies needed plus disk): **send to** Professor H.M. **Klein**, Institut für Anglistik und Amerikanistik, Universität Salzburg, Akademiestraße 24, A-5020 Salzburg, Austria. Fax: +43-662-8044-167: The General Editor also welcomes **announcements, ideas** and **suggestions**.

Published annually. Subscription price $ 49.95 (hardcover). To order please contact the Order Fulfillment; The Edwin Mellen Press; P.O. Box 450; Lewiston, NY 14092-0450; (716) 754-2788; FAX: (716) 754-4056.

CONTENTS

SHARON BEEHLER
Introduction   1

REX GIBSON
Teaching Shakespeare in Schools   5

DALYA EL-SHAYAL
A 'Sea of Troubles': Teaching Shakespeare to Egyptian Students   26

DANIELA RHINOW
Dealing With Shakespeare With Foreign Language Students:
An Experience in Brazil   46

ARTHUR KINCAID
How to Have the Shakespeare Cake and Eat it Too   51

ANDRÉ LEMMER
Shakespeare among South African Schoolchildren   66

GREGORY MAILLET
On Teaching (and Being Taught) Shakespeare in China and Canada   77

HUGH MACRAE RICHMOND
Multivalent Shakespeare: The Spanish Connection   108

LAURA RAIDONIS BATES
"Here Is Not a Creature But Myself":
Shakespearean Reception in Solitary Confinement   122

MICHELLE EPHRAIM
The 'Play' Within the Play: Teaching Shakespeare to Engineers   131

CHRIS HASSEL
On Teaching Shakespeare to 'This Distracted Globe' 143

CHARLES H. FREY
Teaching a Sense of Shakespeare to Heterogeneous Classes 158

EDNA Z. BORIS
Teaching Shakespeare in the Multi-Cultural Classroom 176

LLOYD EDWARD KERMODE
Tempo/Tempest: The Timeliness of Shakespeare in the Diverse Classroom 197

JAMES R. ANDREAS
Rewriting Race Through Literature: Teaching Shakespeare's African Plays 215

JANE CARDUCCI
"And That's True Too": Teaching the Conflicts in Shakespeare's Works" 237

C.W. GRIFFIN
Reading and Teaching Shakespeare's Plays 252

JOYCE SUTPHEN
Remembering the Way Into Shakespeare 275

RANDAL ROBINSON
Shakespeare's Language and the Goals of Teaching 284

MICHAEL W. SHURGOT
Live from the Coast: It's Shakespeare Tonight! 298

LAURIE OSBORNE
Shakespeare and the Construction of Character 312

JOAN MENTO
"Suit the action to the word, the word to the action": Using Performance
Pedagogy to Activate Multiple Intelligences   332

EDWARD L. ROCKLIN AND SARAH INNERST-PETERSON
Examining *Measure for Measure* Through Performance   356

MARY Z. MAHER
Teaching Shakespeare Through Performance – "I Know My Course"   371

MICHAEL J. COLLINS
An Approach to Teaching *Romeo and Juliet*   386

CHRISTOPHER L. MORROW
"Shakespeare and Pedagogy" – A Bibliography   398

OTHER CONTRIBUTIONS

RODNEY STENNING EDGECOMBE
Two Textual Notes on *The Taming of the Shrew*   447

REVIEWS

Lorna Flint, *Shakespeare's Third Keyboard:
The Significance of Rime in Shakespeare's Plays*. (Clive Scott)   450

Michele Marrapodi and Giorgio Melchiori. *Italian Studies in
Shakespeare and his Contemporaries.*
Michele Marrapodi, et al. *Shakespeare's Italy: Functions of
Italian Locations in Renaissance Drama*. (Sandra Clark)   453

Andrew Gurr and Mariko Ichikawa. *Staging
in Shakespeare's Theatres*. (David Gwyn Harris)   456

Charles Edelman. *Shakespeare's Military Language:
A Dictionary*. (Christopher Smith)   460

Romeo and Juliet, 1597. Ed. Jill L. Levenson and Barry Gaines. (Christopher Smith)   463

The Cambridge Companion to Shakespeare on Film. Ed. Russell Jackson. (Val Taylor)   465

William Shakespeare, *King Henry VIII, Or All Is True*. Ed. Jay L. Halio.
William Shakespeare, *King Henry VIII (All Is True)*. Ed. Gordon McMullan. (Dermot Cavanagh)   469

Lawrence Danson. *Shakespeare's Dramatic Genres.* (Richard Willmott)   473

INTRODUCTION

Sharon A. Beehler
(Montana State University)

In choosing the topic for this volume of *Shakespeare Yearbook*, the editors were anxious to invite a global conversation about the ways and beliefs of teaching Shakespeare. In past years several collections of outstanding essays on the subject of Shakespearean pedagogy have been published, from three special issues of *Shakespeare Quarterly* to separate books published in the United States and overseas. These collections have tended to remain focused upon specific strategies rather than upon the settings and audiences within which the ideas are practiced. For scholars and teachers this focus has proven very valuable, but what has become apparent is that we find ourselves, when reading these articles and chapters, thinking, "That's great, but it would never work with my students" or "I really like that idea, but in my part of the world, it would be inappropriate". A sharing of these different global experiences seems called for, so this volume seeks to address that need.

The one notable exception to the past trend is Michael Yogev's essay on teaching Shakespeare in Israel that appeared in the Summer 1995 issue of *Shakespeare Quarterly*. In this essay the author describes the parallels between Elizabethan England and contemporary Israeli culture that emerged for the him while teaching Arab and Jewish students. In the essay Yogev demonstrates the thought-provoking work that international colleagues can do concerning Shakespeare and education. The present volume asks the question, "what in the world is going on?" when it comes to teaching Shakespeare. The collected articles range widely over the issues and strategies practiced globally and their implications for teachers in far-reaching parts of the world. The essays have been chosen with an eye to showing the extraordinary diversity among the situations in which individuals teach and to introducing methodologies suitable for adaptation in a wide variety of settings with students of different sorts.

The essays by Rex Gibson, Dalia El-Shayal, Daniela Rhinow, Arthur Kincaid, Andre Lemmer, and Greg Maillet share the experiences of scholars teaching in worldwide settings outside the U.S. The stories they tell of working with Shakespeare in South Africa, in China and Canada, in Estonia, in Great Britain, in Brazil, and in Egypt introduce us to conflicts and issues that are only guessed at by most Shakespeareans. Gibson describes the "radical transformation" of Shakespeare instruction in England since 1980. El-Shayal describes her experience helping Egyptian students, accustomed to rote memorization, to find a personal involvement with the plays. Rhinow shows us that non-English speakers in Saõ Paolo gradually came to an appreciation of Shakespeare and his culture through an effort to perform Tom Stoppard's *The Fifteen Minute Hamlet*. Kincaid shares his experiences helping students in Estonia create a "Shakespeare Day" that engaged students in competitive activities, including performance, based on Shakespeare's plays. Lemmer addresses the disenchantment of South African students encountering Shakespeare only as an examination text. And Maillet compares the teaching of Shakespeare in China and Canada, pointing out that careful questioning can bring students of diverse backgrounds to a shared cross-cultural engagement with fundamental topics of human interest.

Essays that concern unusual teaching circumstances in the U.S. are offered by Hugh Macrae Richmond, Laura Radonis Bates, Michelle Ephraim, and R. Chris Hassel, Jr. From Hispanic students in California to imprisoned felons, to engineers, to immigrants from China, India, and Ghana, the students faced by these writers are among the most challenging Shakespeareans attempt to teach. Richmond demonstrates the cultural connection that can be used to draw Hispanic students to Shakepeare's 'Spanish' plays. Bates opens our eyes to the conditions of teaching Shakespeare in a maximum security prison where even the most hardened criminals find connections to *Richard II*. Ephraim tells us about her engineering students who found the study of Shakespeare to be "a way of engaging with everyday life more profoundly and imaginatively". Hassel shares

Introduction

with us the written responses to Shakespeare of his non-native students who struggle to assimilate Shakespeare as well as the conditions of their new home.

The essays by Charles H. Frey, Edna Z. Boris, and Lloyd E. Kermode deal with the issue of multicultural/heterogeneous classes. Frey's essay explores the rich diversity beyond that of multicutural and multi-ethnic interests, calling for ways to access and encourage that diversity among students of Shakespeare. Boris builds on Frey's account by sharing exercises and techniques that engage a diversity of response. Kermode also seeks to engage diversity, and he does so through "an interrogation of the concepts of the 'foreign' and the 'alien'".

The group of essays that focus on specific suggestions for teaching include those by Jim Andreas, Jane Carducci, C. W. Griffin, Joyce Sutphen, Randal Robinson, Michael W. Shurgot, and Laurie Osborne. Andreas focuses on a method of "teaching race issues [...] straightforwardly" through Shakespeare's African plays. Carducci advocates teaching the conflicts in Shakespeare, through issues ranging from gender to authorship to textuality. Griffin's essay describes a process of gauging and improving reading skills that can help students connect better with Shakespeare. Sutphen argues for having students memorize lines from Shakespeare's plays, working to speak with understanding and emotional commitment as well as awareness of the memorization process. Robinson gives us his successful "Quiz Games" and internet activities for teaching Shakespeare's language. Shurgot advocates the value of using local stage productions of Shakespeare to make Shakespeare come alive for students. And Osborne asks us to challenge our students' assumptions about the "coherence and continuity" of characterization.

Completing the collection are essays devoted to performance strategies by Joan Mento, Edward L. Rocklin and Sarah Innerst-Peterson, Mary Z. Maher, and Michael J. Collins. Mento approaches diversity from a different angle, that of multiple intelligences, as defined by Howard Gardiner, and suggests ways to reach this diversity when teaching Shakespeare through performance. Rocklin and Innerst-Peterson describe their team-taught course that gave students experience in performing Shakespeare but also in dealing with *Measure for Measure*'s editorial problems. Maher describes her Shakespeare Through Performance course in great detail, enabling us to see the advantage of, and rationale for, such an approach. And lastly, Collins forcefully reminds us and his students that "what we value in *Romeo and Juliet* is [...] our experience of it" and, consequently, bringing the play to life through performance is essential in recognizing the play's "intricate complexity". These latter essays, while appearing to repeat the topics of earlier collections, go beyond the narrow confines of a specific college course to offer approaches within a global environment.

It is somewhat surprising that, given the ongoing scholarly attention to global interpretations of Shakespeare, no such emphasis has been given extensively to pedagogy. Even at the International Shakespeare Association meetings, where such sessions might seem inevitable, sessions on pedagogy have avoided global issues in favor of other topics. What comes to light from the essays gathered here is a series of questions that will engage scholars and teachers in the future. Among these are "How is 'teaching Shakespeare' variously defined? – "How do worldwide appropriations of Shakespeare help determine the instructional practices which teachers employ?" – "What cultural and political constraints impact the teaching of Shakespeare?" – "How is the teaching of Shakespeare appropriated by governments to exercise influence over citizens?" – "Should there be an effort to make the teaching of Shakespeare globally uniform?" "How do global economies effect Shakespeare instruction?" – "What do traditional methods for teaching Shakespeare have to offer in non-traditional settings?" – "What can we learn about worldwide cultures through reports of Shakespeare instruction in those locales?" – "What connections can be made between Shakespeare's Elizabethan England and the cultures of the present day?" and, finally, "How do current events happening throughout the world impact the practice of teaching Shakespeare?" As these and other questions arise, we will begin a dialogue that reaches throughout the world and brings together the voices of those teaching Shakespeare from Los Angeles to Beijing, from London to Rio de Janeiro, from Johannesburg to Tallinn, and from Bozeman to Salzburg. I am glad to be a part of this burgeoning conversation.

TEACHING SHAKESPEARE IN SCHOOLS

Rex Gibson
(University of Cambridge)

A quiet pedagogic revolution occurred in the final two decades of the twentieth century. The teaching of Shakespeare in English schools underwent a sea change, as did the nature of school editions of the plays. Two major influences lay behind the radical transformation of school students' Shakespeare experience. The first was the statutory requirement that Shakespeare should be a compulsory element of the National Curriculum.[1] The second influence was the research and development work of the Shakespeare and Schools project based at the University of Cambridge.[2] This article analyses the principles, methods and practices that now characterise the teaching of Shakespeare in schools in England, and identifies the relationships of school and higher education Shakespeare.

It is a popular misconception that Shakespeare has always been a part of English school students' curriculum experience. In fact, for most English schoolchildren, whether or not they studied Shakespeare was, for most of the twentieth century, a matter of teacher choice. A large number of teachers chose not to introduce their students to the plays. There is not space here to examine the complex reasons which lay behind that negative choice; sufficient to say that the peculiar nature of the English social class structure weighed heavily upon decisions. Throughout much of the twentieth century, many working-class school students went through their school life without becoming acquainted with Shakespeare.

Only with the introduction of the National Curriculum in 1988 did Shakespeare become a required subject of study by all school students. Today, by law, all secondary school students must study at least two Shakespeare plays. At the age of fourteen years, students are assessed on one play by a timed examination. At sixteen they are assessed by coursework. For fourteen year-olds the choice of play is restricted to one of three prescribed by government decree (in

2001: *Macbeth, Twelfth Night, Henry V*). For sixteen year-olds, teachers may choose any play for study, but the range selected is usually limited to a few of those most frequently performed.

This policy of compulsory Shakespeare has coincided with, and been partly influenced by, dramatic changes in the nature of classroom pedagogy. Those changes have largely stemmed from the work of the Cambridge project, which, from the outset, identified three practical implications of "Shakespeare for all": class size, student ability, and motivation. School classes are large, numbering from twenty to thirty or more students. Student ability ranges from skilled, fluent readers to those who can barely read at all. The span of motivation is equally wide. Some students have an eager, positive attitude; others are at best indifferent, at worst, hostile to Shakespeare.

It is cheering to record that, in spite of such practical difficulties, the policy and practice of compulsory school Shakespeare has been largely successful. Even though English teachers at first reacted negatively to compulsion, almost all now strongly support the notion of Shakespeare for every type of student. There is widespread agreement that teachers and students generally embrace their Shakespeare studies with enjoyment and enthusiasm.[3] A major reason for the success of this "Shakespeare for all" lies in the transformation of classroom practice into a pedagogy that adopts active methods which acknowledge the plays as dramas for performance, rather than as primarily literary texts for comprehension. School teachers accept that Shakespeare's language is dramatic language, embodying its own imperative to be acted out in some way. The consequence has been that teachers have increasingly treated Shakespeare as a script to be spoken by their students, and to be explored physically and creatively by them. This acceptance of Shakespeare as a script acknowledges that a play is an allographic work of art[4] requiring completion, or rather re-creation: brought to active life in some kind of performance.

The active methods that constitute classroom practice are based on well-established didactic principles. These recognise that students' motivation and learning are enhanced not just by listening, watching and discussing, but also by speaking and acting out Shakespeare's language. But because school classes are large in size, and contain a wide range of ability and attitudes, the students' 'speaking and acting out' experience differs radically from traditional practice. In that older practice, only a few students (the 'best speakers') were active, reading parts as characters. Now, all students are actively involved in some way. There is, of course, still much reliance on familiar practice. Teacher exposition, watching video performances, discussion, essay writing and theatre visits clearly have a place in any school Shakespeare course. But in the great majority of English classrooms, a substantial fraction of the repertoire of students' Shakespeare study is guided by the social, collaborative and physical principles of a more active pedagogy designed to enable students to take personal possession of Shakespeare's language, characters and stories.

Social and collaborative

Traditionally, most school Shakespeare was an individual activity. Students listened to teacher exposition, then worked on their own on a written task. Today, school Shakespeare in English schools is a cooperative, shared activity. In most lessons, students spend a good deal of time working in pairs or in groups of varying size. Such practice reflects the rehearsal techniques of theatre: a group of actors working together to achieve a performance. Like those actors, students work jointly together on the Shakespeare script, helping each other to understand a scene or episode, and to explore ways of performing it effectively.

But such collaborative activity expands student experience far beyond the purpose of preparing for performance. Whilst it is usual for students to act out short scenes (*Macbeth's* witches scenes are perhaps the most obvious examples), many other forms of collaborative experience are possible. For example, students can share a soliloquy as a kind of internal conversation: a character worrying his or her way through an agonising dilemma, thinking aloud. Because any Shakespeare soliloquy divides up into discrete and meaningful units of thought, two or more students often share the speech between them to bring out the shifts in thought. The most widely used classroom example is Juliet's "How if, when I am laid into the tomb" (4.3.30-58), which moves from one fearful thought to the next.[5] Almost as popular are any of Macbeth's or Hamlet's soliloquies. But many teachers, wishing to give their students a more easily understood speech, use lines from an early play, *Richard III*: Richard's soliloquy as he wakes from his tortured dream before the battle of Bosworth (5.5.131-60). The soliloquy has five or six distinct units of meaning in the first two lines alone:

> Give me another horse! Bind up my wounds!
> Have mercy, Jesu! Soft! I did but dream. (5.5.131-2)

Richard's thirty lines, with over fifty units of meaning, is typically shared in two ways. First, students employ the well-known practice of 'reading up to the punctuation mark'. Here, one student reads to a punctuation mark, then hands on to another student who speaks to the next punctuation mark, and so on. This reading is followed by the students again taking turns to speak, but this time they themselves choose units which seem to make sense, which can be longer or shorter than those dictated by the punctuation. The activity demonstrates how the social nature of the experience helps students' understanding. After the two shared readings, students discuss the units they themselves have chosen. To give only one example, there is always animated argument as to whether "Have mercy, Jesu" represents one thought or two. The value of the discussion is evident as students justify to each other how the choices they have made might be appropriate. The work on this 'easy' soliloquy prepares students to use the same collaborative method on more demanding speeches. With older students, this sharing activity has an additional advantage in that it is often used as an introduction to work on the editorial construction of the plays. Insight into the difficulty (or impossibility) of gaining access to what might have been Shakespeare's own punctuating preferences quickly leads to similarly fraught issues of his language and intentions.[6]

Physical action

The principle of physical action takes very literally Hamlet's advice to the Players: "suit the action to the word, the word to the action" (3.2.15). Because

Shakespeare's language is itself so physical, so full of invitations to accompany the words with movement and expressions, it lends itself powerfully to physical enactment. But school Shakespeare practice differs radically from that of professional actors preparing for performance. In the classroom, every opportunity is taken to show a physical representation of the language, in ways which would be considered at best like the excesses of nineteenth-century melodramatic acting, and at worst, simply embarrassing. Thus, in the example from *Richard III* above, each short phrase would be accompanied with a different action: riding a horse, binding up a wound, pleading and praying, placing a finger on the lips ("Soft!"), sleeping.

The increasing emphasis on literacy in the English curriculum[7] has aided the development of such physical methods. It is today by no means unusual in classes of younger students (up to fourteen years), for the teacher to 'conduct' the whole class through an entire speech in this way. The teacher speaks a short unit and demonstrates an accompanying action; the entire class, whilst remaining seated, repeats the phrase, line or sentence, and imitates the action. There is not room here to give an example of such work with younger students, but readers can easily imagine the appealing opportunities provided by Bottom's Pyramus speech that ends so hilariously with 'Now die, die, die, die, die!' (*A Midsummer Night's Dream*, 5.1.290).

For older students, group work is more usual. Probably the most widely practised activity uses the prologue to *Romeo and Juliet* (Prol.1-14). Here each group of students independently prepares a performance of the fourteen lines, showing each line accompanied by actions. Responses to the first four lines illustrates students' actions:

Two houses both alike in dignity	students portray two groups of proud characters, in a formal, ceremonious entry
In fair Verona where we lay our scene	students show market traders, musicians, jugglers, thieves, gossips, beggars; the bustling life of the city

From ancient grudge break to new mutiny	two groups strike a pose of fierce antagonism
Where civil blood makes civil hands unclean	much appalled wiping of bloodstained hands!

Treating the text as a script, and using physical activity in imaginative, free-ranging social and collaborative work, guides English school teachers in all aspects of their Shakespeare courses. Two of those aspects, language and story, are particularly revealing of the principles in practice.

Shakespeare's language

In the past decade, the study of Shakespeare's language in English schools has increasingly concentrated on five features that distinguish his style: verse, imagery, repetition, antithesis, lists. One surprising outcome of these five focuses of concentration is the finding that English students encounter more difficulties with verse than with the other four components.[8] Whilst students successfully incorporate imagery, repetition, antithesis and lists into their own writing, their success in reproducing Shakespeare's verse form is limited. Sustained mastery of iambic pentameter is rare; most student verse lapses quickly into tetrameter with its familiar four-beat rhythm which characterises the poetry that all English children hear from infancy in nursery rhymes.

    I have addressed this issue elsewhere.[9] Here, it is sufficient to say that the typical Shakespearean metre is not 'natural' to English speakers, nor is it demonstrably acquired through students regularly reading and speaking the lines. Whilst the iamb may be the dominant characteristic of English verse,[10] pentameter with its five-beat rhythm is neither familiar nor much practised. It is generally absent from most examples of modern poetry that all school students encounter. One explanation for the students' lack of success in mastering the metre may lie in their English teachers' distrust what they see as the restrictions of poetic form. Teachers (and students) often feel that such discipline inhibits 'truthful' expression.

English teachers have no such reservations about the other four features of Shakespeare's language: imagery, antithesis, repetition and verse. Imagery is invariably the basis of lessons on metaphor, simile and personification. These go well beyond familiar written activities in which students use imagery as the inspiration for their own writing, or in relating the images to the themes of the play, as for example in Angus' comment on Macbeth as king:

> Now does he feel his title
> Hang loose about him, like a giant's robe
> Upon a dwarfish thief. (5.2.20-2)

or in Queen Margaret's comment in *3King Henry VI* (in a 34 line-long image of sea and ships):

> And what is Edward but a ruthless sea?
> What Clarence but a quicksand of deceit?
> What Richard but a ragged, fatal rock? (5.4.1-34)

In addition to such conventional activities, students undertake physical work, particularly in constructing tableaux of the imagery. Here groups plan and become 'statues' of the language, presenting a visible 'sculpture' that is viewed and commented upon by other students:

> This fell sergeant Death /Is strict in his arrest (*Hamlet*, 5.2.315-16)

> Then should the warlike Harry, like himself,
> Assume the port of Mars, and at his heels,
> Leashed in like hounds, should famine, sword and fire
> Crouch for employment. (*Henry V*, Prol.5-8)

> Look like th'innocent flower, /But be the serpent under't.
> (*Macbeth*, 1.5.63-4)

Similarly, physical activity also accompanies study of the ever-present antithesis, the linguistic correlative of dramatic conflict. Just as Shakespeare's dramas are so richly and variously concerned with conflict, so those antagonisms are embodied in the language as the word is set against the word:

> For night-owls shriek where mounting larks should sing.
> (*Richard II*, 3.3.183)

Such oppositions are emphasised in classrooms in a variety of movements, gestures and body postures. Students turn or sway from side to side, or 'weigh out' the antitheses with their hands, or even work with a fellow student to arm-wrestle their way through a speech to experience the to and fro, oppositional movement. In such active work, and as a basis of written work, Coriolanus' opening tirade, with its multiple antitheses, is an established choice for older students:

> What would you have, you curs,
> That like not peace nor war? The one affrights you,
> The other makes you proud. He that trusts to you,
> Where he should find you lions, finds you hares,
> Where foxes, geese. You are no surer, no,
> Than is the coal of fire upon the ice,
> Or hailstone in the sun. Your virtue is
> To make him worthy whose offence subdues him,
> And curse that justice did it. Who deserves greatness
> Deserves your hate. (1.1.166-75)

Shakespeare's frequent repetitions are also the focus for students' active work. The repetitions take different form: words and phrases; sounds, rhymes and rhythms; actions and events. Once again, conventional work on such topics as alliteration and assonance is supplemented with physical and collaborative work. The Pyramus and Thisbe play in *A Midsummer Night's Dream* is a favoured and congenial introduction for younger and older students alike, especially in the protagonists' final speeches, with Pyramus'

> Now am I dead,
> Now am I fled;
> My soul is in the sky.
> Tongue, lose thy light;
> Moon, take thy flight;
> Now die, die, die, die, die! (5.1.285-90)

and Thisbe's

> Asleep, my love?
> What, dead, my dove?
> O Pyramus, arise.
> Speak, speak! Quite dumb?
> Dead, dead? A tomb
> Must cover thy sweet eyes. (5.1.306-10)

Teachers also often select passages from *Richard III*, because the play contains so many examples of highly patterned repetitions. But the selections are most frequently used not to teach literary terms such as parison and isocolon, but for students to find and express repeated gestures and emphases to match the language repetitions:

> Was ever woman in this humour woo'ed?
> Was ever woman in this humour won? (1.2.215-16)

But of all Shakespeare's techniques of dramatic language, it is his predilection for lists that has afforded most opportunities for active work.[11] Every play yields dozens of lists as Shakespeare piles item upon item in different ways, even managing to pack nine items into a compressed pentameter in the *Romeo and Juliet* First Quarto's version of Capulet's "Day, night, hour, tide, time, work, play, alone, in company" (3.5.176). The most frequently acted-out lists are those of the ingredients of the witches' cauldron in *Macbeth* (4.1.1-38); Jaques' "Seven ages of man" in *As You Like It* (2.7.139-66); and Juliet's list of all the things she would rather do than marry Paris (4.1.77-88). Popularly used lists which describe character include the Lord Chief Justice's description of Falstaff in *Henry IV Part 2*:

> Have you not a moist eye, a dry hand, a yellow cheek, a white beard, a decreasing leg, an increasing belly? Is not your voice broken, your chin double, your wit single, and every part about you blasted with antiquity? (1.2.142-46)

and Malcolm's condemnation of Macbeth as:

> bloody,
> Luxurious, avaricious, false, deceitful,
> Sudden, malicious, smacking of every sin
> That hath a name. (4.3.57-60)

Here, students present a fourteen-item portrayal, showing each of the seven adjectives together with the seven deadly sins of the final two lines. Other lists describe places, again in ways that invite physical enactment, as in Antipholus of Syracuse' lines in *The Comedy of Errors* which create the mysterious and threatening atmosphere of Ephesus:

> They say this town is full of cozenage,
> As nimble jugglers that deceive the eye,
> Dark-working sorcerers that change the mind,
> Soul-killing witches that deform the body,
> Disguised cheaters, prating mountebanks,
> And many suchlike liberties of sin. (1.2.97-102)

Active work on these easily understood lists with their imaginatively expressed but familiar, 'concrete' referents prepare students for more difficult accumulations such as Hamlet's

> For who would bear the whips and scorns of time,
> Th'oppressor's wrong, the proud man's contumely,
> The pangs of disprized love, the law's delay,
> The insolence of office, and the spurns
> That patient merit of th'unworthy takes. (3.1.70-4)

This kind of language work on imagery, antithesis, repetition and lists echoes but revises the method of *imitatio*[12] that Shakespeare himself had experienced as as a schoolboy. In his Stratford classroom he and his fellow pupils were required daily to imitate classical models, writing in the same style as the presented exemplars. The academic demands on the schoolboy Shakespeare were undoubtedly greater than on today's students. For example, Elizabethan schoolboys were expected to learn by heart over one hundred figures of rhetoric and to acquire skill in using them.[13] In contrast, the carefully prescribed objectives of the literacy element of the National Curriculum for England contains fewer than a dozen, and none in their Latin form. Nonetheless, the assumption underlying today's students' literacy studies have their roots in the same 'modelling' procedures: that students learn by imitating preferred examples.[14] But the difference between the Elizabethan and contemporary school experience already illustrated above is even more vividly demonstrated by considering another major aspect of Shakespeare teaching today: story.

Story

Story is at the heart of school Shakespeare. Its appeal is transparent. The unfolding of a story, whether on the page, on stage, or as a listened-to tale, is a familiar and enjoyable experience that has universal appeal. In school Shakespeare, storytelling takes two two forms: the story of the play, and stories in the play. There is of course no such thing as *the* story of a play. Rather, there are different ways of retelling, and all such retellings have their own truth. For younger school students an introduction to the play usually comprises a reading of one of the many 'Stories from Shakespeare' in print. Here, the once popular *Tales from Shakespeare* by Charles and Mary Lamb, still in print after nearly two hundred years[15] have fallen out of favour for reasons concerned with language style, interpretation, and with the curious selectivity of the 'stories'. The Lambs leave out the casket scenes from *The Merchant of Venice*; they tell *Twelfth Night* without Sir Toby Belch, Sir Andrew Aguecheek and Feste, or the gulling of Malvolio; and narrate the story of *A Midsummer Night's Dream* without mentioning Bottom and his fellow mechanicals.

Today the most popularly used collection of Shakespeare stories is that by Leon Garfield.[16] Garfield is also the 'script-writer' of the widely used videos, *The Animated Tales*,[17] which present an animated version of a dozen popular plays, each lasting around 30 minutes of screen time. But as part of an active pedagogy, teachers increasingly prefer their own introductions over these more passive experiences of storytelling. In school classrooms 'storytelling' becomes 'dramatic storytelling'. The student's role changes from passive listening to active participation, creating character, mood and interpretative outcome as they construct meaning from events and language.

In one much-used method of dramatic storytelling, teachers select nine or ten lines which express major events in the play, and teach an introductory lesson in which all students, in pairs or small groups, speak and enact the language. The method gives pupils active opportunities to play major characters and to acquire a sense of the structure of the play from beginning to end.

Using frequent dramatic pauses, the teacher narrates the story and speaks the lines, adding actions and expressions to help the pupils' own speaking and actions. After each line, all the pupils, working in pairs, step into role, repeat the line, and act it out. *The Tempest* provides a frequently enacted practical example (line references are not given to the students; they are provided in note 18)

1 Mercy on us! We split! we split! we split!
2 All hail, great master, grave sir, hail!
3 This island's mine!
4 Wherefore this ghastly looking?
5 I'll kiss thy foot, thou wondrous man.
6 Admired Miranda!
7 Knock a nail into his head.
8 I have made you mad.
9 I do forgive thee.
10 Our revels now are ended.

The teacher commentary that introduces each quotation is brief, but varies widely, usually depending on the age of the students. A sample of one teacher's language with a class of eleven year olds is typical of that used with younger students.

1 Teacher: "Prospero, the Duke of Milan, has been overthrown and exiled to an island by his enemies: his own brother and the King of Naples. Now, after twelve years, his enemies are sailing in a ship near the island. Prospero's servant, Ariel, causes a terrible storm which wrecks his enemies' ship. Everyone leaps overboard. 'Mercy on us! We split! we split! we split!'" As she speaks Shakespeare's words, the teacher enacts them in some way (here, often holding her nose and 'jumping'). The students repeat the words and actions, often clinging together as they 'jump'.

2 Teacher: "Prospero is greeted by his servant Ariel, an airy spirit: 'All hail, great master, grave sir, hail!'" Again the teacher enacts the line, showing a 'greeting' pose for the servant and switching to a 'great master' pose for Prospero. The students in pairs speak and enact the master-servant relationship.

3 Teacher: "Prospero has a slave, Caliban, who hates Prospero because he thinks Prospero has stolen the island from him: 'This island's mine!'" Again, the students speak and enact the master-resentful slave relationship, following the teacher's example.

The activity continues in similar style through moments of treachery, love, drunkenness, murderous scheming and madness, down to Prospero's rejection of

Teaching Shakespeare in Schools

revenge for reconciliation: "I do forgive thee", and the bow and farewell at the end: "Our revels now are ended".

Although such dramatic storytelling introductions raise issues of selection and emphasis, they have proved remarkably successful in giving students a sense of possession of Shakespeare's language and plot line. A similar feeling of confident ownership comes from active work on the many recapitulations of the story which Shakespeare helpfully provides in many plays. With older students the most frequently enacted summary is Friar Lawrence's long summary in *Romeo and Juliet* (5.3.233-264). His recapitulation contains over forty incidents that students act out, from "I married them" (here, students typically show the wedding of Romeo and Juliet), down to "But as it seems did violence on herself". In the same play, as shown above, the fourteen-line Prologue is also frequently acted out in groups, line by line to gain a sense of the story of the play.

A more demanding recapitulation, much used with older students, is Horatio's summary of seven episodes in *Hamlet* (5.2.359-64). This is taught, not as an introductory lesson, but after the students have had some experience of the play. Teachers usually require students to dramatise each 'moment' in Horatio's tale, incorporating lines from earlier in the play to accompany each short portrayal, speaking the lines to which "carnal", "bloody", "unnatural" and other descriptions might refer:

> So shall you hear
> Of carnal, bloody, and unnatural acts
> Of accidental judgements, casual slaughters,
> Of deaths put on by cunning and forced cause
> And in this upshot, purposes mistook
> Fallen on th'inventors' heads.

In *Macbeth*, the sleep-walking scene recapitulates much of the story, as Lady Macbeth feverishly recalls a sequence of events from
"Out damned spot! Out I say!" to "To bed, to bed, to bed" (5.1.30-58). Each small unit of her language enables students to enact Macbeth's fears, the murder of Duncan, the murder of Macduff's family, Macbeth's agonised conscience, her dismissive "a little water clears us of this deed" (2.2.70), Banquo's murder, and

the knocking at the gate.

Classroom Shakespeare in English schools similarly takes advantage of the many 'stories' that are told in every play. These action-filled narratives fulfil various functions, filling in gaps, recounting past or offstage events, creating atmosphere and character, and generally moving the play's action forward. Some of these 'self-contained' tales are selected by the teacher and set as performance tasks for groups of students. The first Act of *The Tempest* is much used by teachers of younger students who act out Ariel's tale of the shipwreck (1.2.196-215), the story of Sycorax (1.2.258-93), and Caliban's narrative of how Prospero's arrival on the island: "When thou cam'st first...." (1.2.333-45). The projected overthrow of Prospero is similarly presented through a selection of the episodes contained in 1.2.66-174. The appeal of such narratives is obvious. All have a recognisable beginning, middle and end, and all lend themselves to a variety of presentation from choral speaking to dramatisation or mime.

For older students, *The Comedy of Errors* yields similarly attractive 'story' opportunities, especially Egeon's long tale of his misfortunes (1.1.36-139) and Antipholus of Ephesus' recounting of all the events in which he has been involved, each of which invites immediate physical enactment, from "This woman locked me out" to "Ran hither to your grace" (5.1.218-52). The Dumb Show in *Hamlet* is also frequently chosen because its explicit stage directions guide students' presentations: *"Enter a King and Queen very lovingly, the Queen embracing him"* to *"The dead body is carried away. The poisoner woos the Queen with gifts. She seems harsh awhile, but in the end accepts his love"* (3.2.120). But for these older students, the most frequently enacted narrative is from *Macbeth* 1.2.1-44: the wounded Captain's account of Macbeth's feats in battle. The episode divides up into over three dozen actable units from "What bloody man is that?" to "Go, get him surgeons".

A quite different method of school student storytelling, common in all English classrooms, arises from Shakespeare's habit of leaving puzzling questions unresolved in each play. The most obvious concerns *Romeo and Juliet*: "Why do the Montagues and Capulets hate each other so much?" That question is the basis of at least one lesson for students of all ages who study the play. Shakespeare's only hint is that the brawls were "bred of an airy word" (1.1.80), but in the classroom groups of students plan and act out the missing scene of the long-ago incident that sparked off the feud. The enactments vary in particular expression, but unfailingly reveal human beings' universal and enduring preoccupations with wealth, territory, sex and honour (or in today's students' terminology 'respect'). This focus on what Stephen Orgel calls Shakespeare's love for "loose ends",[19] finds its most frequent school expression in a few lines in *The Tempest*:

> This damned witch Sycorax,
> For mischiefs manifold, and sorceries terrible
> To enter human hearing, from Algiers
> Thou know'st, was banished. For one thing she did
> They would not take her life. (1.2.263-67)

Here, groups of students work out a presentation of the "one thing" that Sycorax did that saved her from execution by the enraged citizens of Algiers. The results, like the responses to the Montague and Capulet question, also display the underlying structural imperatives of human preoccupations, as students enact Sycorax bringing the King's dead daughter back to life, stilling the storm and earthquake, killing the monster that threatens the city, and so on. Academic Shakespeareans may worry about the relevance of such freewheeling imaginative stories, but English teachers are confident in their belief that such activity is fully consonant with the imaginative spirit of Shakespeare's plays, for example in the redemptive actions that each student group invariably portrays their Sycorax performing.

Even Shakespeare's sonnets can be seen as 'stories', and following the successful practical appeal of the fourteen-line prologue that begins *Romeo and Juliet*, English teachers have increasingly selected sonnets for active work by students. Although the sonnets do not have the dramatic qualities of his plays, a number lend themselves to physical enactment as a small 'story' with its own subject, images, and themes. Groups of students have presented Sonnet 91, "Some glory in their birth", with individual portrayals of pride in "birth", "skill", "wealth", "body's force", etc. The "one general best", of lines 9-14 is sometimes a beloved person, but more often produces unexpected referents: a mobile phone, a CD, a can of drink. In the same way sonnet 29 "When in disgrace with fortune and men's eyes" also produces imaginative portrayals of the "thee" that brings "such wealth". The love triangles of sonnets 42 and 144, with their small "cast list" of Shakespeare, the young man and the Dark Lady have also become favourites for dramatic work In both, deixis turns into physical action as students take roles and 'point out' the many referents. In the latter sonnet students also act out the narrative of temptation ("tempteth my better angel from my side") and doubt ("... suspect I may", etc).

All such active story-tellings recognise that readers actively construct their response to a script, and that Shakespeare is open to multiple interpretations, giving students choice in their responses. The action, as well as the language of a play, yields similar opportunities, and yet another aspect of school Shakespeare might be called 'silent storytelling', a technique that has proved remarkably effective in giving students understanding of a sequence of events. Here, the teacher makes up a list of actions. The list, acted out in mime by groups of students, shows what happens in a particular scene or episode in the play. The following *Macbeth* example has worked successfully in classrooms, with students in groups of six or more (and usually resolving the problem of "eight kings" with considerable panache):

1. Three witches are stirring a cauldron. They drop in foul ingredients.
2. A man enters. He demands to know the future.
3. The witches make a head appear. The head warns the man, then vanishes.
4. The witches make a bloodstained child appear. The child speaks a riddle, then vanishes.
5. The witches make a crowned child appear. The child tells the man to beware of a moving forest. The child vanishes.
6. The man asks about the future again.
7. A line of eight kings appear. The man counts them, horrified. The last king points at him. All the kings vanish.
8. The witches dance, then vanish.
9. A messenger brings the man bad news. The man decides to murder his enemies.

School editions of Shakespeare

I have elsewhere analysed in detail the changes in school editions from the publication of the first school Shakespeare in 1822.[20] Here, a brief account identifies important features of past and present editions. Traditionally, 'unsuitable' passages (usually sexual), were abridged or expurgated; a process known as 'bowdlerisation' after the Reverend Thomas Bowdler, whose edition deleted lines he considered coarse, profane or blasphemous.[21] Up to the 1990s, school editions took scholarly editions as their model, imitating their form and style to convey a veneer of scholarship. Little pedagogic account was taken of the needs, abilities, aptitudes or interests of school students. An explanatory impulse directed the efforts of editors of these school editions. Glosses, notes and scholarly essays combined with a didactic tone (and sometimes a parade of the editor's academic qualifications) to suggest that the implied reader was a passive student whose role was to absorb an authoritative and relatively unambiguous account of plot, character, themes and language A strong impression was created that preferred right answers existed in which students reproduced 'expert' knowledge. The language of the play was treated more as a literary text for appreciation and explication, rather than as a script for active exploration and performance. Even in the 1970s and 1980s little or no acknowledgement was made of the radical developments in Shakespearean scholarship during that period.

The publication of the Cambridge School Shakespeare series[22] dramatically changed the nature of school editions. It recognised that school editions have quite different audiences, aims and functions from scholarly editions, and that the task of a 'school editor' is to directly address matters of pedagogy (an imperative from which the editor of a scholarly edition is free). The Cambridge series is based on the research and development work of the Shakespeare and Schools Project[23] which identified successful methods of teaching Shakespeare in schools and researched features of editions that teachers and students wanted. The research discovered an overwhelming demand for editions of the plays which provided a full 'scholarly' text, but which treated that text as a script by incorporating active methods of teaching and learning.

Cambridge School Shakespeare editions, therefore, use the complete texts established for the New Cambridge series, and employ editorial practices grounded in the realities of school classrooms, the acceptance that Shakespeare's plays were written to be spoken and performed, and a commitment to reader-response theories which acknowledge that readers actively construct interpretation. The 'pedagogy of explanation' of earlier editions is replaced by a pedagogy of performance, or active methods. Here, the play is treated as a play, that is, as a script open to multiple interpretations and performance possibilities, rather than as a literary text. Each edition, therefore, provides a large number of individual, group and whole-class activities which encourage physical and imaginative responses that aid understanding. Throughout the 1990s a similar active pedagogy was adopted by other school editions, and in England an extensive choice of 'active methods' editions is now available.

And what of the link of such pedagogical practice with developments in Shakespeare scholarship over the past two decades? The overwhelming majority of school students is unaware of the nature of current Shakespearean discourse at university level. They have little or no awareness of the theories and abstractions which characterise such discussions of feminism, psychoanalysis, new historicism, cultural materialism, deconstruction, theories of jouissance, marginality or aporia. And, it must be noted in parenthesis, although all English school students study Shakespeare, the great majority do not go on to study his works at university.

Nevertheless, through a battery of active methods that derive from those described above, most school students have access, albeit in untheorised form, to the assumptions and insights of these more recent paradigms of critical or literary theory. The viewpoints of women, the subservient or the oppressed, are expressed in a variety of imaginative approaches as students step into role as major or minor characters, and express their point of view in letters, diary entries, psychiatrist's reports, 'hot-seating' (a student, in role, questioned by others), trials, witness statements. Students may never have heard of new historicism or cultural

Teaching Shakespeare in Schools   23

materialism, but when they express Caliban's thoughts, and give a voice to other low-status characters, servants, soldiers, messengers, they address similar issues to those in scholarly essays: conflict and exploitation, class and gender oppression, tyranny and injustice. As unnamed Montague gang members, female hangers-on to Malcolm's army, or servants at Macbeth's banquet, or one of Lear's hundred, students explore the world of the play in ways which address the same questions as sophisticated theorists. In a more direct mirroring of modern theory, students interpret and enact a scene from a specified standpoint. An example from a recent school edition of *As You Like It*[24] exemplifies the practice:

> Five Directors
>
> Work in groups of five. You are each a director who wants to put on a production of *As You Like It*. But you have very different conceptions of the play! Step into role and argue why 'your' version is the most appropriate.

1 "It's about Nature". You believe that the play is about the goodness of the natural world: how the forest, real animals etc provide moral guidance for human beings. You want to stage the play outdoors, in a real forest.

2 "It's about Art and artifice". You believe that the play is about art and illusion: that Shakespeare is mocking the pastoral tradition in literature and drama. You want to stage the play in a procenium arch theatre using modern technology.

3 "It's about social criticism". You believe that the play is Shakespeare's response to the rebellious protests against land enclosures and food shortages of Elizabethan England. You want to stage the play in a disused factory building.

4 "It's about gender". You believe that the play uses cross-dressing to explores issues of gender and patriarchy. You want to perform the play with either an all-male, or an all-female cast.

5 "It's only a play". You believe that the play is simply an entertainment to make people happy, and that it has no "message" or critical intent.

As students grow older, greater account is taken of Shakespeare's irony, ambiguity and moral complexity, and of how the plays are rooted in the social and political preoccupations of his own time. 'Contextual' studies are now a significant element in Shakespeare examinations for 16-18 year olds in which students are required to acquire and demonstrate knowledge of the literary, social and historical influences which helped shape Shakespeare's dramatic imagination. But such studies, which emphasise that a play is a social and historical construct, are aided by, and are complementary to, the kinds of activities described above. When school students actively and imaginatively inhabit Shakespeare's plays, taking parts, speaking the language, and directly experiencing characters' dilemmas, they develop a motivating sense of ownership. Their empathetic identifications might cause concern to those academics who reject any Bradley-like conception of characters as real persons, but such emotional and intellectual involvement is welcomed by most schoolteachers. For them, an active Shakespeare pedagogy not only develops understanding of language, characters and themes, but also contributes significantly to their students' awareness of moral, social and political issues, and sharpens their insight into the complexity of human relationships.

Notes

1. Department for Education, *The National Curriculum* (London: Department for Education,1995), p. 20.
2. The Shakespeare and Schools Project (1986-1994) was funded by the Leverhulme Trust. Its purpose was to identify successful methods of teaching Shakespeare which increase students' understanding, appreciation and enjoyment of the plays. Project findings are reported in Rex Gibson, *Teaching Shakespeare* (Cambridge: Cambridge UP, 1998), pp. 1-245
3. Peter Thomas, "Shakespeare: Catering for Key Requirements", *Secondary English*, 3:2 (1999), p. 29.
4. Jonathan Miller, *Subsequent Performances* (London: Faber & Faber, 1986), p. 32.
5. References in the text are to the New Cambridge Shakespeare editions (which is that used in all Cambridge School Shakespeare editions).

6 Ann Thompson and Neil Taylor "Editing Shakespeare's Plays", in *Shakespeare: Texts and Contexts*, ed. Kiernan Ryan (London: Macmillan and Open University Press, 2000), pp. 155-65.

7 Qualifications and Curriculum Authority, *Language Learning for Key Stage 3* (London: Qualifications and Curriculum Authority, 2000), pp. 2-3.

8 Fred Sedgwick, *Shakespeare and the Young Writer* (London: Routledge, 1999). Sedgwick's many examples of students' writing, whilst providing ample evidence of their imaginative responses to Shakespeare, also demonstrates their lack of mastery of form.

9 Rex Gibson, "'O, what learning is!' Pedagogy and the afterlife of Romeo and Juliet", *Shakespeare Survey*, 49 (1996), pp. 141-52.

10 Timothy Steele, *All the Fun's in How You Say a Thing; an Explanation of Meter and Versification* (Ohio: Ohio UP, 1999), p. 55.

11 Lists are a surprising omission from Frank Kermode, *Shakespeare's Language*, (London: Allen Lane, Penguin, 2000). Previous academic discussion of the topic seems similarly to have neglected this aspect of Shakespeare's language, which is a central focus of school Shakespeare.

12 Park Honan, *Shakespeare: A Life* (Oxford: Oxford University Press, 1998), p. 53.

13 Brian Vickers, "Shakespeare's Use of Rhetoric", in *A New Companion to Shakespeare Studies*, ed. Kenneth Muir and S. Schoenbaum (Cambridge: Cambridge UP, 1971), p. 86.

14 Department for Education, *Framework for Teaching English Years 7-9* (London: Department for Education, 2000).

15 Charles and Mary Lamb, *Tales from Shakespeare* (1806; repr. London: Penguin, 1995).

16 Leon Garfield, *Shakespeare Stories*, 2 vols (London: Heinemann, 1985, 1994).

17 Leon Garfield, *Shakespeare: The Animated Tales*, 12 vols (London: Heinemann, 1992-4).

18 The Tempest line references are: 1.1.54-5; 1.2.189; 1.2.332; 2.1.302; 2.2.138 and 150; 3.1.38; 3.2.57; 3.3.58; 5.1.78; 4.1.148.

19 Stephen Orgel, "Introduction'", in *Henry V, War Criminal? and Other Shakespeare Puzzles*, ed. John Sutherland and Cedric Watts (Oxford: Oxford UP, 2000) p. ix.

20 Rex Gibson, "Editing Shakespeare for school students", *Editio*, 14 (Tübingen, Max Niemeyer, 1999), pp. 180-99.

21 Thomas Bowdler, ed., *The Family Shakespeare in Ten Volumes, in which Nothing is added, but Words and Expressions are omitted which Cannot, with Propriety, be Read Aloud in a Family* (London, 1820).

22 William Shakespeare, *Cambridge School Shakespeare* 27 vols, ed. Rex Gibson and others (Cambridge: Cambridge UP, 1991-2000).

23 note 2, *ibid.*

24 William Shakespeare, *As You Like It*, ed. Rex Gibson (Cambridge: Cambridge UP, 2000), p. 186.

A 'SEA OF TROUBLES':
TEACHING SHAKESPEARE TO EGYPTIAN STUDENTS

Dalia El-Shayal
(Cairo University)

> It was the best of times, it was the worst of times,
> it was the age of wisdom, it was the age of foolishness,
> it was the epoch of belief, it was the epoch of incredulity,
> it was the season of light, it was the season of darkness,
> it was the spring of hope, it was the winter of despair,
> we had everything before us,...
> (Charles Dickens)

The antithetical fluctuation so cogently expressed in the opening lines of Dickens' *A Tale of Two Cities* mirrors my own feelings as I approached my first teaching experience of Shakespeare's plays. It almost felt like an insurmountable struggle with endless barriers and seesawing reactions. The students always started the course on a remarkably sour note, complaining that they found Shakespeare too difficult and hopelessly complex. Their complaints set a heavy burden on my shoulders trying to find techniques of teaching the course that would not only assist in the understanding of the plays, but would spark their curiosity and encourage them to dig into what they previously assumed was 'too complex'.

In this teaching process, I am primarily concerned, alongside learning, with enjoyment. Therefore, giving the students ample room for expressing their ideas and emotions is an essential first step towards enjoyment. I hasten to add that if eventually students come to hate Shakespeare's work, it is presumably some teacher's fault or some system's rigid entrapment into a threatening or suffocating atmosphere of one exam system or another. This soon leads to the devaluation of their emotions, and thus the lack of enjoyment.

In order to have a more comprehensive idea of the classroom environment I will be referring to, let me first of all introduce and reflect on the background and nature of my students. They are university-level Egyptian students; undergraduates of both sexes who study at the English language and literature department at Cairo University. They have Shakespearean drama courses as a standard part of their syllabus. For many of them, Shakespeare and his works is an untrodden field of study which they approach with great apprehension. My goal in teaching Shakespeare is not all about earlier stages of English or complicated verse structures, nor is it to cover a certain syllabus. It is to teach humanity.

"Shakespeare the genius", "Shakespeare the greatest writer that ever lived", "Shakespeare the unmatched" are repeated clichés that we – the teachers – often use (understandably so) to give Shakespeare his due respect and elevated status among other writers. This, unfortunately, has proven to intimidate students, who often think of him as an 'elitist icon' – the untouchable! In order to humanize the Bard, and abandon lengthy canned lectures on his genius, the students are led to reach this conclusion themselves. They will then have experienced the genius of Shakespeare with no latent fears. Students' involvement is essential in the understanding of this new world – Shakespeare's world. It all reduces the idea that we – the teachers – are the sole custodians of knowledge. They will no longer be recipients of arcane information that already seems to have little relevance to their own twenty-first century lives.

There remains the language barrier, which I may add, is a double barrier. The students, being non-native speakers of English, have huge difficulties comprehending a language that is already a few times more complex than the standard English. One recalls W.B. Yeats' famous lament:

> The fascination with what's difficult
> Has dried up the sap out of my veins, and rent
> Spontaneous joy and natural content
> Out of my heart (Rosenthal, p. 33)

But it is precisely this struggle and difficulty that makes the study of Shakespeare more fascinating and challenging. This becomes " an enabling difficulty [...and that] enjoyment increases with the sense of difficulties overcome" (Gibson, p. 24).

In what follows, I will share my experience of teaching Shakespeare through the years and show the multiple techniques that actually emphasized the students' involvement transforming their attitude from the most resistant to the most enthusiastic. I will do so with particular reference to *Macbeth* and *Hamlet* being (among some others) the most widely taught and enjoyed plays in the English department at Cairo University. The question of how and why Shakespeare's plays remain marvelously attractive and enjoyable to this day has been the concern of many critics and thinkers. My concern here is basically how those plays were the impetus for initiating students' creative responses.

Shakespeare and Egyptian Culture

Dennis Kennedy of Trinity College, Dublin once said that "shifting Shakespeare from one country to another involves cultural displacement". Therefore, he has to be "transmuted into a different creature if he is to make sense and flourish". So in order to dissolve cultural barriers, students were encouraged to constantly try to relate and associate characters, events, themes, etc. with similar or even identical instances present in their own culture. In this case, Egyptian culture. That way the link between Shakespeare's world and their own is established with the purpose of narrowing the gap between the two worlds.

Throughout Shakespeare's life, witches and witchcraft were the object of morbid and fevered fascination, and in *Macbeth* it is obviously an essential part of the making of the play. Superstitious and supernatural elements are credited with directing the events. The witches have diabolical powers and can predict the future, and we hear them clearly say "All Hail Macbeth, that shalt be king hereafter" (1.3.47).

Similarly, and since ancient times, superstitious beliefs have been an integral part of the history and culture of the Egyptian people. For the ancient Egyptians, magic was valuable both in their world and the next, as a way to forestall and control misfortunes. The Moon God, Thoth, who could be shown as a baboon, an ibis, or a man with the head of an ibis, was particularly associated with the secret of knowledge involving magic. Snakes and scorpions embodied the chaotic powers that threatened the ordered world. The human heroes of Egyptian stories are usually not warriors but magicians or priests – men who studied the books of magic kept in ancient Egyptian temples.[1]

With this strong and documented reference to the world of magic and the supernatural, students get to read, absorb and easily relate to the witches' behavior of raising evil spirits or foretelling the future. In Islam,[2] too, the djinn (geni) exists' and can be either benevolent or malevolent. "And we thought that man and djinn would never utter a lie concerning GOD, and that person from any kind used to seek refuge with those among the djinn, but they increased them in folly." (*The Qur'an,* The Djinn, 4 & 5)

One other concept that is inherent in Egyptian culture is that of revenge. 'An eye for an eye and a tooth for a tooth' is an Old Testament maxim with a literal equivalent in Arabic as a *hadeeth shareef*.[3] Revenge is a frequent theme in classical drama and is also a natural instinct. Mostly concentrated in the southern parts of Egypt (ironically called Upper Egypt because of the flow of the River Nile from South to North), and because of serious family feuds, the idea of revenge is quite prevalent. Elizabethan Revenge Tragedy contains the typical formula of a hero and a villain who is to be killed in revenge. Reading about Hamlet's agony and obsession with the idea of revenge soon becomes clear in the students' minds when related to similar existing revenge situations in the South of Egypt.

> And Am I then revenged
> To take him in the purging of his soul,
> When he is fit and seasoned for his passage?
> (*Hamlet*, 3.3, 84-6)

Although revenge is immoral and is seen as a profoundly unsocial act, it still is considered a very human impulse to exact retribution from someone who has done wrong to you or your family. Based on that and on students' knowledge of the still-existing revenge traumas in their own society, they are even able to argue with Francis Bacon, who called revenge "a kind of wild justice". This invariably leads to a broader topic for class discussion.

Many readers of plays tend to overlook stage directions, thinking that they are unnecessary and, sometimes, boring to read. While they are obviously an important part of the stage set-up, they are also essential to a proper and comprehensive reading of any play. This has constantly been an emphatic element in my teaching of Shakespearean plays. Interestingly enough, students were eventually able to find different interpretations and associations to certain types of stage directions.

In *Hamlet* when the "cock crows", it leads my students' minds to compare the function and effect of the crowing cock in *The Arabian Nights* with that in *Hamlet*. In *Hamlet*, the cock crows at a time when the ghost disappears, delaying or aborting the truth about the death of Hamlet's father. Likewise, in the stories of *One Thousand and One Nights*, the cock crows to transport the reader to a new phase where stories of Shehrazad can no longer be related and thus causes delay; awaiting the truth or a pleasure certain to come. This leaves Shehrayar, as well as Hamlet for that matter, with a feeling of nostalgia, a sense of at once fulfillment and loss. This keeps the characters and us – readers and audience – in suspense and brings the action to more of a familiar level of reality.

Egyptian students have had those stories of Shehrazad spun for centuries in family gatherings, public assemblies, and now on radio and television programs. Those stories actually are "interweaving the unusual, the extraordinary, the marvelous and the supernatural into the fabric of everyday life" (Haddawy, p. x). It is the students' ability to acknowledge the significance of such a minor stage direction and also to closely relate it to their own stories that is considered their special achievement. The interesting part of this association is that it could be applicable to other students of other cultures as well. It is not the examination of the Egyptian culture that is the main focus here but how it is used as a tool to testify how association of ideas can be drawn.

Needless to say, also in other Shakespearean plays there is a wealth of references and possible associations with Egypt and the Arab world that could also be used to provoke the students' minds. Take, for example, Lady Macbeth's guilty conscience that screams at the end of the play "all the *perfumes of Arabia* will not sweeten this little hand ". (*Macbeth*, 5.1.43) In *The Tempest*, Sebastian talks about a strange vision that has made him willing to believe any traveler's tale:

> ... Now I will believe
> That there are unicorns; that in *Arabia*
> There is one tree, the phoenix
> Throne, one phoenix
> At this hour reigning there.
> (*The Tempest*, 3.3.26-9)

In his astonishing final speech Othello says of his eyes that they:

> Albeit unused to the melting Mood,
> Drops tears as fast as the *Arabian trees*,
> Their medicinable gum. (*Othello*, 5.2.336-54)

It is also logical to expect such references in *Anthony and Cleopatra*

> I am dying, *Egypt*, dying.
> Give me some wine, and let me
> Speak a little (*Anthony and Cleopatra*, 4.15.40-1)

Anthony calls Cleopatra the "serpent of the Nile" (I.5.24), she fishes in the river, and first presents herself to Anthony on a 'barge' on the water. (I hate to be accused of favoritism but would happily join W.H. Auden in his belief that 'If we had to burn all of Shakespeare's plays but one – luckily we don't – I'd chose *Anthony and Cleopatra*) (Kirsch, 2000, p. 242).

All those obvious references to Arab culture and the students' ability to make certain mental associations between Shakespeare's world and their own help dissolve many barriers.

Shakespeare and the Senses

"One of the joys of dealing with Shakespeare's plays is that nothing is engraved in stone: everything is open to interpretation" (Flachman, 1997, p. 63). Such interpretation need not concern the language nor character traits or themes but could be a different kind of interpretation making use of the senses. Descriptions and images that are mentally photographed are unlikely to be forgotten. With particular emphasis on the visual, I have often used pictures of several paintings by different painters portraying Shakespearean characters or significant events in the plays and asked the students to choose their favorite and write a full analysis of it.[4] This not only provided a vast opportunity for competing interpretations but taught them to appreciate and value another art form that soon became as precious to them as the Shakespearean text itself.

Initially, students tend to mistrust their abilities to do anything other than read, write or study. To break this mind set and to help them gain confidence in their capabilities, I often asked them to draw, for example, all the events of Act Two in *Macbeth* that take place in Macbeth's castle, with different locations in each scene. They may use colors, black and white, pencils and any paper size.(I wish there were room here to exhibit students' impressive recreations of the castle. The amount of enthusiasm at showing their own skills and competing to come up with the best drawings is remarkable. Now whenever there is a mention of Act Two, they only need to remember their own drawings and the events will follow.)

In his interesting article "Making sense of Shakespeare", Charles Frey points out that "... we are all trained, not only as readers, but as citizens in our society, to let sight over-dominate all other sense experiences. " The following lines of Lady Macbeth could be a good material to work with the senses:

> The raven himself is *hoarse,*
> That *croaks* the fatal entrance of Duncan
> Under my battlements. Come, you spirits
> That tend on mortal thought, unsex me here
> And *fill me* from the crown to the toe topfull
> Of direst cruelty; make thick my blood,
> *Stop up* th'access and passage to remorse
> That no compunctious visitings of nature
> *Shake* my fell purpose nor keep peace between
> Th' effect and it. Come to my woman breasts
> And *take my milk of gall,* you murd'ring ministers,
> Wherever in your *sightless* substances
> You wait on nature's mischief. Come thick night,
> And pall thee in the *dunnest smoke of hell,*
> That my *keen knife* see not the wound it makes,
> Nor heaven peep through the blanket of the dark,
> To *cry,* "Hold, Hold". (my emphasis) (*Macbeth*, 1.5.36-52)

Based on the experience of having a sight-impaired student in class (and yet one of the most insightful), I have had to resort to occasional references to the other senses. I used this device to teach the other students to utilize their other senses effectively. In the previous quotation 'hoarse', 'croaks', 'cry' refer to hearing; 'smoke' involves smell; 'fill me', 'make thick my blood', 'stop up', and 'shake' all involve sensations of deep and inner feelings. With this insinuation of the senses into the reading experience, the text is enlivened – enlarged and amplified by the extra values of sensations such as sound and smell.

Personalizing Shakespeare

"I want you to buy a new copybook, keep it at home and think of it as your drama journal". This is among the first things I usually ask the students to do at the very beginning of their drama course. The whole idea of the drama journal is explained and illustrated as we travel through the course. After each class, I give the students an entry to which they have to respond and write about in their journals. The objective of this task is to personalize Shakespeare and his characters. Then the remote world of Shakespeare becomes something they can write about or add to or even emulate. This is designed to build their confidence and encourage their sense of achievement. It is impossible to cover all the entries given to the students but a sample will suffice.

First of all, they are asked to write a full account of their feelings about their first drama class, so at the end of the term they can refer back to it and be able to observe the change (if any). It is a record they can fall back upon; and it could also be a documented reference to their feelings at any particular point of time. When asked whether they have ever performed a soliloquy, students invariably hasten to withhold and severely, almost confidently, shake their heads in denial. When questioned they tend to stretch their imagination and think that soliloquies (those difficult dramatic monologues read only on paper or seen on stage) are or can be part of their daily activity. In fact, they, themselves, are likely to have already performed one or two. I asked them to write a soliloquy in their drama journal – one they have experienced in real life. Students came up with the most powerful and moving monologues, marvelously expressive of their accompanying feelings. For example, one of the students wrote a monologue she performed at a desperate moment when she was lost in the desert. Another wrote a contemplative soliloquy that takes place in her future life foretelling the rich promise of her life to come.

In another entry entitled "The stars will tell you", I instruct the students to think of sun signs that characters in *Macbeth* could belong to. Everyone, it seems, is interested and fascinated with the idea of horoscopes, so the students readily participate in this exercise. Students' choice of words must be associated with a particular sun sign and be derived from the actual events of the play. One of the students chose Gemini to be Macbeth's sign and wrote:

> *Macbeth* (Gemini)
> Your soul is always captured by those you love and you are so much influenced by your soul mate. You are self-determined, loyal and very ambitious. You are ready to do anything to achieve your goals.
> Your color: grey
> Your stone: Onyx
> Stars tell you: Someone you love may lead you to an unpleasant end. Don't let your excessive ambition destroy you. Don't be so happy with any victory you achieve, for it may be followed by a great disaster.
> (Dina Ahmed – second-year student at the English department, Cairo University)

In the opening scene of *Macbeth*, the three witches are gathered to chorus their famous lines "Fair is foul and foul is fair, Hover through the fog and filthy air" (1.1.12-13).They call upon their familiar spirits (demons who helped them with their evil work). The first witch says "I come Graymalkin [grey cat]",the second follows by saying "Paddock [toad] calls", except for the third one who only says "Anon". As a new entry in their journals, I asked the students to create an imaginary spirit for the third witch and write a dialogue that could have possibly taken place between the witch and its demon. Since those spirits are usually animals or birds, students chose rats, snakes, foxes, bats, owls and lizards and came up with the most creative dialogues with the proper stage directions as well. One student took that a step further by burning the edges of the paper on which she wrote the dialogue in her journal to give it a more fiendish effect.

In another entry called "Headlines from the Old Scottish Newspapers" students were asked to write excerpts from the newspapers at the time of Macbeth announcing important events of the year. Some were "A Great Treason in the Royal Court in Scotland", "Macbeth Defeats the Power of Macdonald's Army", "King Duncan Appoints Malcolm as Prince of Cumberland". The challenging part of this activity is the style in which the column had to be written. Students were required to remember that this was not a literary assignment but rather some news written for the press to be read by the public.

In order to humanize or personalize Shakespeare more and more, students are encouraged to celebrate his birthday (23 April). They write and create their own birthday cards for display in class. They come up with some interesting mottos and clichés, mostly borrowed from the plays they have read, and words inspired from our discussions in class. All in all, it turns into a mini festival in celebration of the Bard's birthday after having him leave the pedestal and join them in real life.

Use of Videos

"Shakespeare's plays are designed deliberately to expand the mind – to generate a sense of concentrated vigorous life in emotions and ideas" (Gibbons, p. 36). The production of Shakespearean plays on the screen is no exception. They certainly provide an influx of new material to contemplate and analyze. In coping with modern technologies, we have become quite 'televisually saturated', and we have also come to realize that the relationship between the visual, performing and literary arts is rich and varied. Consequently, a close viewing and analysis of films has proven remarkably effective in examining the written text and its theatrical or cinematic incarnations.

The use of videos in language or literature classes is not a novel technique. Rather it is the order and manipulation of this technique that is my interest here. First of all, the choice of film versions is almost always based on a production that would allow and provide an array of interpretative possibilities and would spare me the trouble of defending its serious imperfections. "Cinematic composition is very similar to theatrical staging. What makes film different are the greater number of compositions and increased possibilities of manipulating the viewer's eye". (David Kranz, p. 355). It is through such techniques as camera work, setting, pace, costumes, blocking, décor and tone that the viewer's eye is captured.

A perfect set-up for my drama course is to view the film almost simultaneously with reading the text. As soon as Act One, for example, is covered in class, a viewing session is held. The students encounter the events on screen while the reading is still fresh in their minds. This close examination of text and image opens the door for multiple interpretations, debates and discussions in class. The film version either meets their expectations or disappoints them. No harm, since it also prepares them for a forthcoming session with its new expectations and disappointments. The success of any production has some criteria on which it is based but sometimes, as Sir Richard Eyre posits "one production [can] soar like a bird of paradise, and others embarked on with just as much optimism and care, fall like dead sparrows from the nest."

The dynamic interaction that follows the viewing always leads to intense class debates. The students observe: how certain lines are spoken, how stage directions are portrayed, how body movements and facial expressions help in emphasizing the meaning, how costumes reinforce the text, and how music heightens certain emotions. Class discussion even ventures as far as lighting i.e. observing that bright light creates a lively and spirited view of the subject while dimmer versions can have contrasting effects.

For my purposes, an excellent example of Shakespeare on film is Franco Zeffirelli's production of *Hamlet*. I prefer this version to the Kenneth Brannagh's (1996), Derek Jacobi's (1980) or that of Laurence Olivier (1948) because of the way it appeals to the young mind. I am by no means ruling out the excellence or the quality of the other productions but I basically use them as alternative versions in order to facilitate debates about differences in their cinematic approaches.

Despite its nightmarish nature and sometimes needlessly bloody scenes, Roman Polanski's production of *Macbeth* also provides ground for abundant discussion and classroom activities. The students enjoy the somewhat *femme fatale* Lady Macbeth in her *petite* form and long hair. The porter scene –

surprisingly too often treated by teachers as insignificant – is, I believe, pivotal. "The language is here not simply providing 'relief' from tragic tension; it offers an alternative to tragic violence".(Andreas, p. 28). Students enjoy the 'speaking up' and 'acting out' along with the pre-eminently aural effect of the actual knocking and the suspense of who is behind closed doors, "Knock, knock, knock, who's there?" (*Macbeth*, 2.3.10).The porter represents the ambivalence that both Macbeth and lady Macbeth characterize. Watching the porter and hearing the knocking on the screen allows the students to not only live the visual/aural moment but in their writing, to take a leap towards maturity – the inevitable consequence of their growing powers of observation. A mention of Akira Kurosawa, *Throne of Blood*, the Japanese version of *Macbeth* with its borrowings from the Noh theater (1956), invariably leads to interesting cross-cultural explorations and interpretations in class.

Still "despite the attractiveness of these resources, there is no substitute for professional or even amateur live performance of Shakespeare's plays" (Beehler, p. 254). The screen performances are best used as substitutes for a live performance which might not be available or accessible. Either way, by the end of the course, having had the simultaneous viewing of the video with the reading of the text, the students will have fully absorbed the aesthetic as well as the scholarly elements of any Shakespearean text.

Teaching through Analogy
The human mind is designed to stretch itself in all directions in search of associated ideas. "Shakespeare offers us hundreds of opportunities to see his characters facing up to the implacable realities of their natures and circumstances ..." (Sedgwick, p. 7) and therefore their minds reflect on human issues in constant occupation of their thoughts. Othello's mind reflects upon jealousy, Macbeth's on ambition, Lear's on misjudgment, Hamlet's on revenge – with a long list to follow. Those human elements represented in the lives of Shakespeare's characters and events give the reader – or viewer – opportunities for comparison and analogy. In

the course of reading any text, I constantly encourage the students' minds to branch out and draw upon their experiences and prior knowledge.

Examples of mental exercises leading to drawing analogies are abundant. In *Hamlet,* Polonious' speech to Laertes before he leaves for Paris entails a lot of fatherly advice on speech, friendship, quarrelling, judgment, money, dress and consistency.

> Polonious: Give thy thoughts no tongue,
> Nor any unproportioned thought his act.
> Be thou familiar, but by no means vulgar [...]
> Beware of entrance to a quarrel, but being in,
> Bear't that th'opposed may beware of thee.
> Give every man thy ear, but few thy voice;
> Take each man's censure, but reserve thy judgment.
> Costly they habit as thy purse can buy,
> But not expressed in fancy: rich not gaudy [...]
> Neither a borrower nor a lender be [...]
> This above all, to thine own self be true ...(*Hamlet,* 1.3.57-80)

Similarly and by means of analogy, Polonious' speech is a distinctive reminder of Rudyard Kipling's famous poem "If" (1910), where the substance of the words is almost identical. The poem deals with human virtue. It examines the ability to master one's dreams and the capacity to take triumphs and losses in stride without complaint. It also offers certain moral values – courage, reticent stoicism and the supreme value of work – as qualities (exact or similar) presented in what Polonious wanted to reflect in his fatherly speech to his son before he goes to encounter the world.

Students get a chance to view both texts and try to compare the tone, the type of advice and how they themselves would react to each sentence of counsel. Additionally, by reading those texts in different ways, they can provide the different tones of either a pompous, bureaucratic, loving, authoritarian or dutiful father. They can also provide mocking or obedient and respectful reactions and then can reconstruct the pieces of advice in order of importance giving reasons for their decisions. On a larger scale, as an extra exercise on drawing analogies, I request the students to find other references that carry the same principle of giving advice. I was truly amazed at the variety and volume of their knowledge and intelligence. One of my students wrote a fantastic analogical analysis of Polonious' speech and Luqman's advice to his son stated in the Qu'ran:

> 13. And when Luqman said to his son, admonishing him: O my son, do not associate others with God, surely polytheism is grievous equity.
> 17. O my son, establish prayer, enjoin good, and forbid evil. And bear with patience whatever befalls you. This is true steadfastness.
> 18. And do not hold your head in haughtiness to people, nor walk in the land conceitedly. God does not love any proud or boastful.
> 19. And be moderate in your walk, and lower your voice ...
> (*Qur'an*, Luqman, 13-19)

Students are never passive receivers of information. They are always constructing knowledge, flying high with their imagination. As Nabokov wrote: "Imagination without knowledge leads no further than the backyard of primitive art" (Meyer). Imagination and knowledge combined can lead to the most creative results from students. In my next choice of an activity of association by analogy, I relied on the students' possible knowledge and potential interests in songs.

The sheer richness of language in Shakespeare's plays intices the imagination to seek other equivalents from everyday life. As an example, Simon and Garfunkel (the greatest American duet) have recorded a sublime version of an anonymous ballad that has become one of the most legendary songs – an aural as well as an intellectual treat. "Scarborough Fair" is a light song that uses a refrain in the second and fourth lines of each stanza that is actually typical of the genre, as is the poignancy of the lyrics

> Are you going to Scarborough Fair?
> Parsley, sage, rosemary and thyme
> Remember me to one who lives here;
> She once was a true love of mine
>
> Tell her to make me a cambric shirt
> Parsley, sage, rosemary and thyme
> Without no seams, nor needle work;
> Then she'll be the true love of mine.

In *Hamlet*, in the heartbreaking scene of Ophelia's madness, she sings recalling the death of her father. She also sings of betrayed love and talks distractedly.

Since sorrows do not come as "single spies /But in Battallions", Ophelia's madness seems to top all previous disasters. And while everyone is appalled by her disorder, she sings again of death and she distributes flowers and herbs

> Ophelia: There's *rosemary*, that's for remembrance, pray you,
> love, remember – and there is *pansies*, that's for thoughts [...]
> There's *fennel* for you, and *columbines.*
> There's *rue* for you, and here is some for me; we may call
> it herb of grace a Sundays. Oh you must wear your rue with a difference.
> There's a *daisy*. I would give you some *violets*, but they withered all
> when my father died. (*Hamlet* 4.5.174-80; emphases mine)

The use of herbs is a common feature in "Scarborough Fair" and in Ophelia's words. I ask the students – using analogy - to think of the symbolic significance of each of the herbs in both texts and to describe what they could possibly represent. Given the very different nature of the texts, their meaning and background, the students were able to give a wide range of imaginary interpretations. Of course, listening to the Simon and Garfunkel song in class was invaluable – an activity that immediately followed the discussion of their renditions.

Continuing with the use of songs, I brought to class another famous song by José Feliciano (a blind Cuban singer and guitar player), entitled "Windmills of Your Mind".[5] The lyrics of this song suggest a journey that might take place in a person's mind. As the title suggests, it is a journey with extreme swinging moods. And like the Windmills of La Mancha, where Don Quixote matched wits against the giants created by his mind, Shakespearean tragic heroes are constructed in a way where their inner thought is constantly moving and swaying. Feliciano's song has those obvious similes (a figure of speech that the students are mostly familiar with and can easily understand)

> Round like a circle in a spiral
> Like a wheel within a wheel
> Never ending or beginning
> On an ever spinning wheel
> Like a snowball down the mountains
> Or a carnival balloon
> Like a carousel that's burning

Teaching Shakespeare to Egyptian Students

> Burning wings around the moon
> Like a clock whose hands are sweeping
> Past the minutes of its face
> And the world is like an Apple
> Whirling silently in space
> Like a circle that you find
> In the windmills of your mind!

While all Shakespearean characters make us reflect on issues related to human life and worries on our own minds, the analogous use of the lyrics of the song provides leeway for the students to start with a general analytical point from which to analyze the specific problems that characters agonize over in the windmills of their own minds.

One last point of analogy, with cross-cultural emphasis, is my personal interest in having the students widen their scope of world knowledge in general, and in this case, with particular reference to world mythology. In Indian mythology, Kali (human head and tiger skin) was known to kill demons. How would that compare with the role and effect of Macbeth's witches'? Similarly, Daghdha's cauldron in one of the Irish mythological stories was filled with milk, swine and animal parts to be boiled and drunk. This draws a perfect comparison with the witches' preparation of their hellish stew to happily chant

> Double, double, toil and trouble
> Fire burn and cauldron bubble   (*Macbeth*, 4.1.35-6)

According to the AfricanYoruba tradition, Eshu and Ifa were Gods who came to earth to tell humans the secrets of medicine and prophecy. In yet another example, the Coyote is among the most popular Native American mythological figures. He plays the role of a crafty sorcerer who eats almost every kind of animal or plant. This would be a wonderfully fertile ground for a full analysis on witchcraft in both *Macbeth* and other mythological references in other cultures. Extensive reading about those figures is required to be able to establish similarities and point out differences, thus the extra knowledge that the students indirectly gain.

Students' Creative Work

After all this involvement, students tend to pour their hearts out and try not only to perfect their assignments but be extremely creative as well. They write their own poems, create imaginary dialogues, draw figures they imagine, take over Shakespeare's language weaving it into their everyday speech and expressions. Imagine my delight on hearing one of my students, as I walked by in the hallway of the department, react to some news given to her by one of her colleagues by saying: "Heaven and earth, must I remember?", to which her friend responded casually "you have a countenance more in sorrow than in anger". Shakespeare's words now, interestingly enough, became an integral part of their daily informal speech.

Another student volunteered a poem reflecting upon Hamlet's complex character and his irreconcilable moral dilemmas. She proudly offered to share it with the class. It reads as follows:

A Soothing Suggestion

'To be or not to be', that is Hamlet's question
To me, 'not to be', is a soothing suggestion
For this world is full of nothing but pain
It seems to be but a world of feign!

Or as Hamlet put it 'tis an unweeded garden'
Sterile, bare ... It's a heavy, heavy burden
That aches this man's heart
And makes him wish his life would depart.

It's a clock that ticks our life away
Every tick brings us near to Doomsday
Thus we wait for death to knock on the door
And soothe our wounded heart that is sore to the core.

No more pain ... enough sorrow
Why should we live in a world so hollow?

(Marwa Gamil – third-year student at the English department
Cairo University- Egypt)

Conclusion

"Shakespeare's plays remain the outward limit of human achievement [...] that which overcomes all demarcations between cultures or within cultures'. (Bloom,

p. x). Indeed for centuries now, Shakespeare's words have had an effect on readers of all ages and colors and cultures. My own students turn into active performers who *learn* as much through their enjoyment and responses as through study and instruction. Teachers should also think of themselves as active learners. Even with their varying degrees of expertise, there is an amazing wealth of knowledge still to be gained from exploring the students' minds. A teacher must have a palpable passion for the task and has to accept – or revive – faith in students' capabilities. The greatest component of teaching is love and faith – love for the subject and faith in the students' incredible abilities.

In their most creative modes, students are able to interact with the texts and "therein see their innermost parts, and the innermost parts of the world they live in, with its grandeur and its squalor, with its palaces and its taverns, with its boudoirs and its brothels" (Sedgwick, p. 19). There lies Shakespeare's genius. It is best felt and valued when the students themselves can reach this conclusion rather than by intimidating them with repeated clichés about the great man's wonders.

"Death, more than birth, is sadly the human measure of time". (Welsh, p. 69) In the four centuries since Shakespeare's death, his hold over our imagination has only multiplied. My Egyptian (non-English speaking) students' involvement with the Bard's work is a living testimony. 'And so stands stricken, so remembering him'.[6]

Notes

1   For more reading on Egyptian mythology see Roy Willis, ed. *World Mythology*, Henry Holt and Company, New York, 1996.

2   Egyptians are 90% Muslims and 10% Coptic Christians, so Islamic culture and references to the Qur'an (the Holy Book) are abundant.

3   *Hadeeth Shareef* is the term used to denote the alleged sayings and traditions of the prophet Muhammed (may peace be upon him). They are divine revelations outside of the Qur'an.

4   Some of the very interesting paintings chosen by the students were Eugene Delacroix "The Death of Ophelia " – Oil on canvas 1853

Alexandre –Marie Colin, "The Three Witches" –1827
Richard Dadd, "The Closet Scene" – Hamlet 1840
Maurice Greiffenhagen, "Laertes and Ophelia " –1885
Madeleine Lemaire, "Ophelia" –1880

For a complete listing of the paintings on Shakespeare's plays and characters check website http://www.emory.edu/ENGLISH/classes/Shakespeare

5   'Windmills of Your Mind' is written by Michel Legrand, and has been performed by many artists like Sting, Neil Diamond, Celine Dion ... etc. It was the Academy Award winning single by Noel Harrison and was in the soundtrack of the movie 'The Thomas Crowne Affair'.

6   Last line in Edna St. Vincent Millay's (1892-1950) poem "Time Does not Bring Relief"

Works Cited

Andreas, James R. "Writing Down, Speaking Up, Acting Out and Clowning Around in the Shakespeare Classroom" in Ronald E. Salomone and James E. Davis, ed. *Teaching Shakespeare Into the Twenty First Century* (Athens: Ohio UP, 1997), pp. 25-32.

Beehler, Sharon. "Making Media Matter in the Shakespeare Classroom" in Ronald E. Salomone and James E.Davis, ed. *Teaching Shakespeare Into the Twenty First Century* (Athens: Ohio UP, 1997), pp. 247-54.

Bloom, Harold. *Shakespeare: The Invention of the Human*. New York: Riverhead Books, 1998.

Eyre, Sir Richard. 'Nothing will come out of Nothing' a lecture given at the Salzburg Seminar 'Shakespeare Around the Globe', 27 Feb. 2000.

Flachman, Michael. "Professional Theater People and English Teachers: Working Together to Teach Shakespeare" in Ronald E. Salomone and James E. Davis, ed. *Teaching Shakespeare Into the Twenty First Century* (Athens: Ohio UP, 1997), pp. 57-64.

Frey, Charles H. "Making Sense of Shakespeare" in Ronald E. Salomone and James E. Davis *Teaching Shakespeare Into the Twenty First Century* (Athens: Ohio UP, 1997), pp. 96-103.

Gibbons, Brian. *Shakespeare and Multiplicity*, Cambridge: Cambridge UP, 1993.

Gibson, Rex. *Shakespeare in Schools*. Cambridge: Cambridge Institute of Education, 1990.

Haddawy, Hussain, transl. *The Arabian Nights,* New York: W.W. Norton & Company, 1995.

Hamlet, Cambridge School Shakespeare. Cambridge UP, 1994.

Kennedy, Dennis. "Shakespeare and the World" to appear in *The Cambridge Companion to Shakespeare Studies,* new edn, ed. Margreta de Grazia and Stanely Wells. Cambridge UP, forthcoming.

Kirsch, Arthur. *W.H. Auden Lectures on Shakespeare*. New Jersey: Princeton UP, 2000.

Kranz, David. "Cinematic Elements in Shakespearean Film: A Glossary" in Milla Cozart Riggio, *Teaching Shakespeare through Performance* (New York: The Modern Language Association of America, 1999), pp. 341-60.

Macbeth, Cambridge School Shakespeare. Cambridge UP, 1993.

Meyer, Priscilla. *Find What the Sailor Has Hidden: Vladimir Nabokov's Pale Fire*, Connecticut: Wesleyan UP, 1988.

Rosenthal, M.L. *W.B. Yeats: Selected Poems and Four Plays*, New York: Scribener Paperback Poetry, 1996.
Sedgwick, Fred. *Shakespeare and the Young Writer*, New York: Routledge, 1999.
Simon, Paul and Art Garfunkel. *Collected Works*, 3-disc set. New York: CBS Record, no. C3K 45322, 1981
The Glorious Qu'ran. Text and translation by Ahmed and Dina Zidan. Islamic Publishing and Distribution, 1996.
Welsh, Alexander. *Hamlet in Modern Guises*. Princeton: Princeton UP, 2001.

* * *

Thanks are due to my students over the years who have been so enthusiastic and interactive. I have constantly admired their hidden (soon exposed) talents and their ability and willingness to explore a world so far from their own realm.

DEALING WITH SHAKESPEARE WITH FOREIGN LANGUAGE STUDENTS: AN EXPERIENCE IN BRAZIL

Daniela Rhinow
(São Paulo)

Drama is a well-known aid in the EFL (English as a foreign language) classroom to foster learners' development in the target language, mainly in terms of vocabulary and pronunciation, through the use of role-play, shadow reading and other techniques. Nevertheless, very rarely the final aim is to promote learning about the play or about theatre in general.

However, using Shakespeare as a teaching tool caters for other needs than that of acquiring language. Surely, a linguistic improvement can be observed, but this is only one of the possibilities to be exploited, because it is undeniable that learning a language implies learning and reflecting about the culture of the people as a whole. In this sense, Shakespeare is recognised as an icon of the idea of English culture, and can enhance the development of cross-cultural studies in terms of literature, society, history, arts and other related issues. No student of English in EFL institutes is unaware of Shakespeare's existence, but very seldom is the access to the original text promoted, even at advanced levels, unless as a curiosity.

The aim of this paper is to report on an experience gathered in dealing with Shakespeare's text with a group of fifteen teenage speakers of Portuguese in São Paulo, Brazil, and the actions taken so that they could understand and profit from staging a play in a foreign language, appropriating the meanings and the speeches through the process. An experience developed not in the classroom itself, but in a drama group of students who multiplied their enthusiasm among other learners.

The Sociedade Brasileira de Cultura Inglesa is an important EFL institute in Brazil, with links to the British Council; its aim is to spread the English language and to promote the cultural interaction between Brazil and Great Britain. In São Paulo state, it has around forty thousand students, most of them teenagers. As part of the cultural calendar, a Drama Festival is held every June to foster integration among the branches and to promote language learning while having fun.

This is the context in which the branch drama groups can flourish. As an extra activity outside the classroom, any student of any linguistic competence can join the group and start rehearsing a play, even without having previous experience in drama, with a clear final aim: to represent the branch in the yearly festival.

The members of the Pinheiros drama group had already been together for a year when one of the actors proposed we should work on "something really difficult". After all, according to this 13-year-old boy, everybody there had plenty of experience already and so we should be more daring. As the director of the group, I thought that was not quite the case, but they seemed so eager to improve that I asked them for suggestions. When the name "Shakespeare" was voiced, there was a general commotion in the room. Their comment was that, though the importance of the author was always mentioned, nobody would ever deal with one of his plays – which are not even read in Brazilian secondary schools, let alone performed. The students had heard many people refusing to work with a Shakespearean text, the most common excuses being: "it's too difficult"; "I don't understand it"; "the language is far too complicated"; "people say it's boring"; "the plays are too long" and "there are too many characters". They did not want any further such excuses. It was impressive to see their enthusiasm, which grew bigger when the idea was mooted: "If we are to stage Shakespeare, we have to deal with *Hamlet*!" Who was I to impede them?

Though *Hamlet* is probably the most well-known Shakespearean text in Brazil, most of the students had never read or seen it, not even in Portuguese. The only glimpse of familiarity was "To be or not to be" (the line, not the soliloquy), and the fact that three of them had seen Mel Gibson playing the role in the cinema. Obviously, staging the whole play was out of the question.

But the actors would not surrender, and so I proposed *The Fifteen-Minute Hamlet*, by Tom Stoppard, a choice immediately accepted even though none of them had read the play. And this is the point where my reflection started: how to work on it? How to make this bunch of totally green teenagers grasp the meanings and perform the thing properly, while enjoying it? How could this be an opportunity to teach Shakespeare?

Of course, to be able to read (or, even worse, to stage) Stoppard's play requires studying and understanding *Hamlet* itself first of all, which was the group's intention. Therefore, I designed a path to introduce these adolescents to the possibilities of the text, which meant a month of diving into the text without aiming to produce anything. First of all, they read and reread a good translation of the play, alone and in groups, and watched the film versions of the story[1]. Next, we discussed the plot and the main ideas involved.

From there, the work focused on the themes of love, revenge, the problem of appearance versus reality, family relations, the fight for power, etc. The actors improvised on such themes in terms of static images and situations in which the themes were the main point. I also chose to bring the themes close to their reality so as to enhance a sense of recognition; therefore, I proposed some improvisation sequences with situations that would sound familiar to them, such as "your boyfriend is behaving strangely towards you; he has got a problem but you don't know whether it is your fault or not; you meet him at school and want to solve the situation." What may sound an oversimplification was in fact a powerful tool to engage the actors. The aim of this activity was to bring the meanings and the situations of the text closer to them, while promoting group integration and physical training.

The next problem was the language. Here, we had to work on two fronts. One, basically linguistic, was to face the original text, comparing it to the translations and trying to make sense of it. Students expanded their vocabulary enormously (most of them were intermediate level), and I called their attention to words and features of Elizabethan English. Then they had to work as detectives and discover where Stoppard had got the lines of his play from. At the same time, pronunciation demanded a lot of attention, and was properly catered for. The other front was leading them to speak a foreign language naturally on stage. For this, they had to improvise scenes in different languages: Russian, Japanese,

An Experience in Brazil

French, Italian. They complained they could not speak any of these languages, and I said: "Well, invent them". By this time, we had been working for some time with verbs of action, so while they said something like "Barishnikov vodka sputnik!" (which was the Russian they came up with) they had to make clear what they meant, for the scene to develop. Again, this may sound weird, but served the purpose of detaching meaning from form, as the poetic language frightened them, and of focusing on meaning itself and dramatic action.

It was only then that they received some information on poetry and rhythm, and the particularities of Shakespearean verse. This discovery was an energy boost to make them work again on the text of the play and start learning their lines. At the same time, they could profit much more from the richness of the play and Shakespeare's language. Little by little, students could come closer to the text smoothly, without fear or extreme reverence, appropriating the meanings and taking part in a game at the same time. It was not an easy task, but the satisfaction accruing was intense.

As any amateur production, the final result of the process had its ups and downs, but we managed to get the prize given by the popular jury, thanks to the effort. But this was not, evidently, the main concern of the group, though everyone was quite happy with it. The most important aspect was the sense of achievement the students had, both as individuals and as a team.

What can we learn from this experience? First, these adolescents had the opportunity to enlarge their views on English culture, literature, poetry, language and drama, and have learned to appreciate Shakespeare immensely. I do not mean to claim they have understood *Hamlet* completely, but the process fostered reading, researching, reflecting, and even going to the theatre, a habit not very much developed in this age group in Brazil. The formation of an audience, essential for the theatre to survive, was influenced by their experience of struggling, and surviving the rehearsals. Moreover, their socialisation and self-esteem profited, in an extension of their capacities.

Many people believe teens are not prepared for this, specially in a language which is not their own and which they do not master. I myself thought it would be too much. Thankfully, my group proved I was wrong. The lesson I learned was that the power of drama, the power of Shakespeare cannot be underestimated. Everyone can find him/herself in Shakespeare, regardless of his/her level of maturity. It is just a matter of letting people get in touch with it and experience it. *That* is the question.

1   The translation used was the one by Anna Amélia Carneiro de Mendonça, published in Rio de Janeiro by Nova Fronteira, 1995. Other translations used are by Millôr Fernandes (Rio de Janeiro: L & PM, 1997) and by Carlos Alberto Nunes (Rio de Janeiro: Ediouro, 1990). The film versions watched were *Hamlet*, UK, 1948, directed by Sir Laurence Olivier; *Hamlet*, USA, 1990, directed by Franco Zeffirelli and *Hamlet*, USA/GB, 1996, directed by Kenneth Branagh.

HOW TO HAVE THE SHAKESPEARE CAKE AND EAT IT TOO

Arthur Kincaid
(Eesti Humanitaarinstituut, Tallinn)

Last year had the look of Shakespeare boom-time in Estonia: two entries each in the Globe 'In the Shoes of Shakespeare' project, three in the Shakespeare Birthplace Trust Millennium Project, the sole university Shakespeare course in the country (mine) received with interest – even the practical aspects – and a conference on teaching early English literature featuring Patrick Spottiswoode, Director of Globe Education. This sense of flourishing was bolstered by the emergence of the new Amateur Drama Association, with its own premises and its own festival, in which some Shakespearean entries appeared: a rather shaky *Tempest* and a very imaginative mainly choreographic *King Lear*, both attempting to convey the general course of the play in about half an hour. It seemed to me the time to try to take hold of this interest, shape it, and take it forward. Last year the British Council organised a very successful English Day, with entries in the categories of debate, performance, essay-writing, and poster-making. Why not, I thought, a Shakespeare Day along similar lines? I suggested this to the British Ambassador, Timothy Craddock, who liked it and felt sure he could get money to support it. He enlisted support from the British Council's English Teaching Consultant, Kevin Beattie, who agreed to promote it in schools. The Ambassador directed that Kevin and I work together in planning the event and bringing it to fruition.

My priority was to site it in suitable premises. Last year's English Day had occurred in a space inimical to performance, and this event could learn from that mistake. Consequently, I obtained quotations for the cost of theatre hire and technical support from the cultural centre whose theatre had proved such a sympathetic environment for the student drama festival. Though two utterly unsatisfactory performance spaces were available free of charge, I persuaded Kevin that money should be spent on suitable premises. When we met to plan the format, Kevin's feeling that an event drew on wider interest if it combined two themes, as well as an impending visit to Tallinn of the Millennium Wheel's designer, led to a focus on Shakespeare's election as "Man of the Millennium". We determined on entries in the areas of performance (including a song or songs set to newly-composed music), debate, essay, translation, drawing, set design, website design, and ultimately submission of The Shakespeare Cake, the last intended to attract entries from the colleges which train in catering.

Before a date was fixed for the event, the cultural centre whose theatre we had intended to hire decided to raise its prices radically, and on top of this, getting wind of the involvement of foreigners, to quote in dollars what they had previously quoted in Estonian crowns (15 crowns = US$1). This led the British Council to oust me from the organising process and accept the free offer of the most notably un-actor-friendly space in the city. The date finally chosen was very early in the coming academic year, and notices were not sent to schools until they reconvened in the autumn. This meant that very little planning or rehearsing could take place before the day. Estonians, who are perfectionists, do not like to turn out rush jobs, and it is probably for this reason that most of the professional schools did not enter and only thirty as opposed to last year's fifty schools participated. There was no time for teachers to lead up to the event, introducing the subject gently and stimulating interest in it, perhaps by having their own Shakespeare days in school with projects, workshops, and videos. Such a lead-in is much more important in the case of a specialised subject than for the more general "English" of the previous year's event. Kevin's term of office ended in the summer, and with his replacement not due for some months the onus of organising fell to British Council administrators not in touch with Shakespeare or Estonian teaching of Shakespeare.

The Shakespeare Day itself began with a debate on the proposition, "Shakespeare is a more appropriate icon for modern Britain than the Millennium Wheel". This activity included a more balanced mix of genders than many of the others did. The winning team and the runners up were both from the English College, a school noted for its excellence in teaching the English language, and the host premises for the Shakespeare Day. Shakespeare won, with four arguments:

- 1. Shakespeare is well known all over the world and so is the best representative for England.
- 2. The Millennium Wheel is not an icon for England because it is a commercial object.
- 3. Shakespeare and his ideas have influenced the world for many centuries and are timeless.
- 4. The Millennium Wheel is folly, not the best way of introducing Britain.

The only argument the opponents could muster was that the Wheel is easily understandable and identifiable.

All submissions in drawing and set design were from girls. Because students from the Art Academy participated, several set models showed imagination and a sense of theatre. The best were not only attractive in themselves but also in touch on a deeper than superficial level with the play they represented. They showed awareness of how a set could be constructed on a reasonable budget and function on a real stage with actors living and moving in it. The winner, for the forest scenes of *A Midsummer Night's Dream*, was by an Art Academy student who had been an amateur actress. Estonians of both Estonians and Russian background have an advantage in being – despite the steady rise in ticket prices – a theatre-going nation, and thus tend to have more theatrical sophistication than is common in other countries, though they lack an academic tradition of dramatic performance.

Website design fared very badly. This was a surprise, since President Lennart Meri's initiative has connected all the schools in Estonia to the internet, and here as elsewhere young people are computer buffs. No prizes were given to any of the five entries. Three showed evidence of massive – sometimes complete – plagiarism, one lifting (very poor) articles wholesale from the 1999 *Microsoft Encyclopedia* without credit, another giving the game away by interspersing material obviously taken from a reference work with its author's own sentences in poor English. Two were inaccessible. Only one showed any flair and initiative. Its author, introducing it in not very good English, explained, "I respect Shakespeare very much, but I wanted to provide some entertainment"[1] (one wonders what he imagines Shakespeare was trying to provide!), and he included a quotation quiz, a survey, and a game ("Kill Hamlet"). Neither the quiz nor the game works, and a rundown of the plot of *Romeo and Juliet*, which intersperses key quotations with pictures, does not credit the pictures' source, leading one to wonder whether quotations had not been compiled by someone else as well. Plagiarism appears to be still a serious (and perhaps unrecognised) problem in Estonia, a legacy from Soviet community of property. The ease with which material is available from the web leads easily to an assumption that it is common property. Teachers seem not to know or care about the problem as yet, and indeed in some institutions of higher education plagiarism and other forms of cheating are normal and rewarded. Though in other areas the country has been quick to catch up with international standards, this is one which seems to lag behind.

The survey portion of this one partly original website was interesting. Though only ten classmates were surveyed, seven girls and three boys, the site designer thinks this reflects general feeling about Shakespeare among highschool students. He observes that Shakespeare is very popular with girls and very unpopular with boys. Though the survey does not support this, the overall gender composition of Shakespeare Day participants would seem worryingly to bear it out. It may be due to the fact that, since men feel pressured to make money quickly to support families, there are far fewer men following arts and humanities subjects than in the years immediately following the end of the soviet era. In the survey itself, positive outweigh negative reactions, with as many positive as negative respondents confessing that they actually have read very little Shakespeare. The gut reactions range from, "I don't care! His compositions bore me to death. I can't believe that this stuff interests someone" to "Ah, ah, Shakespeare!" The student with the best English attributes her negative impression to starting to read at 4 and coming to Shakespeare at 8, when "his plays seemed so dull and strange to me": her early negative impressions still colour her literary preferences.

One boy claiming a positive attitude shows mixed feelings:

... I'm not mad about his plays and I suppose that today they are out-dated because they don't reflect modern reality. Despite this, I still enjoy reading his plays as they tell truthfully about the feelings people experience in various life situations. That's something that will always remain actual because feelings never change.

A girl providing a tissue of unconnected quotations also indicates that Shakespeare's greatness lies in his ability to appeal individually to each generation and person, and to attribute "meaning and value". Others stress the reality of his characters and the power of the human feelings portrayed, particularly in *Romeo and Juliet*.

The website survey responses seem more genuine, perhaps because confided to a classmate, than do many in the essay competition. These entries, written on the spot, appear often to reflect what the students think the judges want to hear. The use of English is generally not of high standard. Insufficient concentration on writing in Estonian schools leads to oral fluency in English far surpassing competence in writing. An interesting observation of the judges was that in many cases the standard of English from students who had not been studying it in school for very long surpassed that of students who had studied it longer. Are the schools not doing their job, and is teaching outside school the key to good English for young people in Estonia? The younger group (ages 13-15/16) were asked to respond to a quotation from *Cymbeline*: "Hath Britain all the sun that shines?" Does the sun shine only in Britain? What do you think?" Most respondents took this as a trick question for which they had to guess the right answer, and identified Shakespeare with the sun: the sun shines on Britain because Shakespeare was a famous writer, who wrote "the poem", "but I like Shakespeare's poems [it is clear from the context that the writer means 'plays'] because they are really (actually) good". Is the student suggesting that this liking survives despite the fact that we are supposed to like them? Another respondent thinks Shakespeare wrote novels as well as poems and plays. The biographical focus noted in my article on Estonian Shakespeare teaching in *Shakespeare and the Classroom* (Fall 1999) surfaces in the biographical rundowns that comprise several of these essays. One shows off wider general knowledge, saying that Great Britain boasts the best writers of the Renaissance, "Thomas Kid, Robert Greene and John Lilly are known everywhere" – news to one who has introduced them to university English majors in many countries, including Britain! One student sees the answer in terms of contemporary fame: "plays such as Romeo and Juliet and Hamlet have brought even more glory and fame to Britain than some famous rock bands to America". The most insightful response goes beyond this: the sun causes growth; literature feeds the mind; other countries and people have their own light and use it in their own ways. None of the respondents sees Shakespeare as international 'property'.

The older competitors (16 and up, including some university students) were given: "'How many goodly creatures are there here! / [...] O brave new world / That has such people in it'. What is the meaning of this quotation for the 21st century?" This gave the older writers an opportunity to respond, through a (distorted) Shakespearean prism, to their own world. With Prospero's comment omitted, they had only one side of the picture, and only one intuited possible irony. In most cases this was taken as a statement, as holy writ, without consideration that it is spoken by a fictional character: *Shakespeare said this*, so it must have been true. According to one response the Renaissance was the best of all possible worlds, in contrast with which ours is full of conflict and self-seeking. Now we have institutions to prevent war, technical progress, and people are starting to become less selfish, but in Shakespeare's time there was no need of these, since people were not selfish and aggressive then. So the quotation no longer obtains because most people are no longer "goodly" but cruel, heartless, egoistical, and self-centred, carelessly destroying the planet. Another view, which shares the assumption that the quotation is a statement of fact, postulates comfortably that "Shakespeare trusted us", and, seeing into the future, was confident that this observation would apply to us.

Others feel the world has changed for the better: Shakespeare writes of "jealousy, silly mistakes, simple-mindedness, wild brave and unpatient men – that is Shakespeare, the contents of his plays [...] In Shakespeare's plays people could kill everyone who offended them", but we no longer live like this. The implication is that we would be wrong to use Shakespearean characters as role-models. Interestingly, another respondent sees a dangerous current trend of using film characters as role-models leading to violence and aggression, while good people are "little" and remain unknown, keeping alive in their obscurity the knowledge that "we can make people do what we want by talking kindly to them". The opportunity is missed to relate this to Shakespeare: the relevance of *King Lear* to this view of society is striking.

One essay distinguishes between inner and outer beauty, arguing that insight into human character reveals its hidden strength, and that this is more apparent in Shakespeare's plays than in everyday life because of the heightened quality of his dramatic situations: characters like Romeo and Juliet, King Lear, Othello, and Hamlet

> enrich our souls in humanity, love and true feelings, [...] give examples of love and respect for each other, being honest and kind-hearted [...] We still have such people and Shakespeare helps these feelings survive among them.

What else can Shakespeare do for us in the 21st century? "We understand our greatance when we see, read, use or touch the greatest creations that are made by us", Shakespeare and other masterpieces of art and technology. "What attracts everyone to Shakespeare still is that he has placed man in the center of everything, him and his search for beauty, truth and wisdom". Ours is a brave new world not only because of technological advances but also because of people, their help and support of each other. Though money and power rule now as they did in Shakespeare's time, Shakespeare reminds us of values. Even those students with the darkest view of their impending inheritance wonder whether it might just be possible "to make the world prosper again so we can say this again".

The on-the-spot translation competition was to render in modern English a passage from *A Midsummer Night's Dream* which the students were given in the standard Estonian or Russian translation. This was the first mechanicals' scene, chosen because, while mostly in prose, it also contained Bottom's "Raging rocks" speech. Most renditions were slavish or combined extreme colloquialism with extreme stiltedness, and the standard of English was not generally high. Only one, by a boy, which won this competition, showed awareness of a need to *speak* the words and produced a fluent and relaxed English style, inventive in its use of colloquial language and in turning the "raging rocks" speech into clever verse.

The performance aspect of the event was undermined from its outset by the British Council's decision to provide it with an unsatisfactory stage and no technical support. My priorities in the intial planning had been: (1) good acoustics, (2) a performer-centred space, (3) competent technical support. The hall in which the event occurred (one of the two I had particularly advised the British Council to avoid because it was unplayable) was high-ceilinged with windows reaching almost from floor to ceiling and no blackout capability. Audience wandered in and out, loudly rattling the chairs as they did so, and chatting instead of watching. Teachers, too, were talking loudly throughout. There was no sense that anyone on the stage deserved attention, and very little was given. To have performed on that stage must have felt like punishment, and those who did so might be forgiven if this experience had inculcated a lifelong hatred if not of Shakespeare at least of performing Shakespeare. The scenes were scheduled back to back over four and a half hours without break, and the scheduling proved chaotic. The organisers attribute the blame for this to Shakespeare and the entering schools. A time limit was given of fifteen minutes. Scheduling fell apart because it lacked contact with reality: many schools chose not to use the whole fifteen minutes, having failed to persuade Mr Shakespeare to write them fifteen-minute scenes. This created gaps in the programme – for which no one had thought even to provide – while whatever group happened to be there at the time another finished was shoved on without adequate preparation. This contributed to the general lack of dignity and respect for performers and performance.

Most of these offerings suffered from the event being scheduled so early in the school year, and it was unfair that they should have been shown to an audience without time for polishing. The lowest ebb came at the start: an entry called "Our Myriad-Minded Shakespeare" began with the triumphal march from *Aida* blasted through speakers, followed by a waltz, then the Alleluiah Chorus, through which assorted quotations were spoken in voices not loud enough to compete with the music. Then Hamlet on a balcony declaimed to Romeo below "To pee or not to pee" and cast down a toilet roll which remained on the floor through the rest of the day. An inexplicably belligerent Hermione's speech was intercut with mad Ophelia wandering in and out. By then we were on Beethoven's 5th Symphony. Either this was postmodernism run to seed or total chaos.

General problems included recitation without interaction. I was saddened to see that a school with which I had done some work two years before – challenged by their tendency to recite and feeling they would derive more interest and benefit from acting – had lapsed back into recitation. Too often there seemed to be little idea of what the play was about, or indeed of what a play was. A Lady Macbeth, who was supposed to be *sleepwalking* (somewhere else) at the time stood and watched the Doctor and Gentlewoman scene before beginning to speak. The citizens responding to a Brutus funeral oration recited dully to the audience rather than interacting with the speaker. A badly cut *Julius Caesar* quarrel scene, with a Brutus who adopted comic poses, and an entirely inaudible Lucius, was inexplicably played around a map of England.

Some entries which used Shakespeare only as a springboard had merit and style. Estonians are more confident here: feeling that Shakespeare is not really theirs, professional directors here often try to make something of their own based on Shakespeare instead of attempting to play his scripts. A choreographed *King Lear* showed an attempt at costume consistency and contained some some strong and impressive episodes (a chorus relentlessly stamping behind Lear's storm speeches crowd in on him). But though some of the moods and situations of the play were stunningly conveyed, this work was not always connected to the play. Though to use a play merely as starting point for a loosely related work is not a bad thing in itself, the entry won a prize in a Shakespeare competition. Another prizewinner, *Othello, Mafia Boss of New York*, translated the bare bones of the plot into (mostly good) modern English and costume, effectively using Shakespeare's lines for moments of emotional heightening. The quality of the acting suggests that these seven people could go on to do the Shakespearean script well.

There were a few imaginative and competent performances of Shakespearean scripts. One – a series of scenes from *Twelfth Night* – suffered, again, from too loud music, though the music was chosen well, conveying mood, encouraging pace, and covering scene changes. The style bordered on musical comedy, and this was the only performance conveying a sense of Shakespeare as entertainer. Sometimes there was more reliance on charm, physical action, and high spirits than on the words. But the cast knew how to connect with an audience, even smiling at them in the curtain lineup, the action was precise, the lines were clearly spoken (as far as they could be heard over the music). A small but very stuffy Malvolio appeared from the outset with yellow garters and women's shiny stockings, which might have undermined his portrayal but did not do so. Feste did not play or sing but mimed to a tape, which would have defeated the point of the role had not the actor been a good mime and very personable. A punk-costumed series of *Midsummer Night's Dream* fairy scenes was stylish, its balletic aspects kept well within the ability range of the company, which included boys. A very tiny Romeo and Juliet (11 and 13), whose love scene – directed by a Russian professional actress – emerged imaginatively from a children's game, was simple, moving, concentrated, and well spoken.

The best performance was by a group of final-year boys from a co-educational Russian school: it erupted down the aisle with energy and shouting. Out of the tumult came an oration by a charismatic, over-confident Brutus, who then stood and watched Antony begin to speak, decided he was not dangerous, and left. Four citizens responded to the speakers, first from the audience area, then from the stage as they made a 'ring' (a semicircle with Antony at its centre), with total commitment and concentration. The whole space was used creatively. The script, retained with limited cutting, was clearly and forcefully spoken. I was so impressed with the Brutus that I regretted he had not been saved for Antony – it seemed impossible the school could have found an equally competent actor for the latter role. I was wrong – the dark, intense Antony was at least as good. This scene, startlingly, did not win a prize or a mention. Yet it is these rare explosions of real quality that make it almost worth sitting through nearly five hours of what sometimes felt like torture.

Was the torture necessary? Poor planning accounted for a lot of it. One has the right to expect that a theatre space, especially for young amateurs, will help and encourage performers, and one trusts the organisation of educational events will show care in selecting an environment which will nurture rather than impede performance. This one was an obstacle to be overcome, and it rarely was overcome: *for almost the whole of the afternoon the words were entirely inaudible.* Professionals originally scheduled to perform as part of the event refused to use this hall – yet schoolchildren, most with no theatrical background and training, were expected to cope with it. On top of that they had a noisy and inattentive audience to contend with. No stage lighting focused attention, and as the sky darkened toward evening, it occurred to no one that there was anything to see in the hall, so the lights were not turned on. The tendency to use very loud music (often incongruous and poorly chosen) further drowned out the words – as if the words were not there to be heard in the first place.

The judging was meaningless. When I conceived this event, my plan for this part of it had been for a carefully selected jury comprising people noted for work in both theatre and education, balanced in linguistic/national background, Estonian, Russian and English, with some specialist knowledge of Shakespeare performance in English. In the event, the jury consisted of Estonian-speaking administrators with far from perfect English and little knowledge of Shakespeare, who admittedly gave prizes to the performances "we liked best". As foreign speakers they went naturally and without exception for performances whose connection with Shakespeare was tangential. In only one case was language privileged, and all three winning groups were rewarded for *getting away* from the Shakespearean script and the English language, not in a single case for direct application to the script. It is worrying that this should have been possible on a 'Shakespeare Day', for the essence of Shakespeare is not his (borrowed) plots. The best overall theatrical performance, the *Julius Caesar* forum scene, was also the one which gave the best rendering of the Shakespearean script, making the language clear, audible (even in that space) and comprehensible, letting it guide the actors to a commitment and concentration such that at no point was a single citizen's attention seen to wander from the Roman forum and the death of Caesar.

The worst general aspect of school Shakespeare performance in Estonia seems to be an attitude of 'ye-olde-ness', of reverence which places Shakespeare in some inaccessible past, in a world no longer ours. Little attempt is made to contact our world in performance. This was shown by the assumption that Shakespeare has to be done in costume, and that so long as it is not twentieth-century the period or periods do not matter, nor do the actual conventions of the period chosen, and periods can be mixed at will. Thus we had in one *Julius Caesar* patricians clothed in tunics, and in another Brutus and the citizens wore Elizabethan while Antony wore eighteenth-century dress, for no apparent reason. The cliché Shakespeare performance in tights is taken for granted as standard here. It is not clear why. The Mafia *Othello* was prefaced by an apology for not wearing tights. The cast wore modern dress confidently, and clearly this lack of awkwardness and embarrassment with costume enhanced their performance. On the other hand, the best *Julius Caesar* scene went a step further and rehearsed sufficiently to wear even the dreaded toga without awkwardness.

The musical entries were a mixed bag. In the case of songs sung to music the students had composed, the words were drowned out and the music either did not support the words or the words were so unclear it was impossible to tell whether they did or not. This was true of what may have been a good composition based on a sonnet, inexplicably given one of the prizes. Piano and violin drowned out voice (due to poor balance of microphones and possibly of scoring as well) in a very long and insufficiently varied work. I was unable to catch enough of the words until it was almost over to determine its Shakespearean basis (Sonnet 66). The standard of playing was very high, and the musicians had good presence – something in which Estonian musicians do not seem generally to be trained. But are these qualities which justify a prize in a *Shakespeare* performance competition? A mixed choir gave an attractive performance of a Vaughan-Williams Shakespearean setting. But this would hardly qualify as "newly-composed music". Finally, a hymn having nothing whatsoever to do with Shakespeare was well performed following an inaudible scene from *As You Like It*.

The prizes chosen did no service in encouraging future study of Shakespeare: dictionaries, games of Scrabble. While still involved in the planning, I had been working on getting business sponsorship to donate copies of recent Shakespeare videos to every participating school – so that the day could serve to help schools build up their usually very limited resources of Shakespeare teaching materials. Individual pupils were to be rewarded in a way which would encourage future interest in Shakespeare as 'user-friendly' – Shakespeare comic books (which include the full text), Shakespeare games and computer programmes. Too much of this event seemed to do just the opposite of encouraging further work in Shakespeare.

What would have made it successful? First, a detailed awareness of how Shakespeare is taught in Estonia, what resources schools lacked, what are their strengths and needs. The event should have grown out of such an awareness and been devised to fill some of these needs. Its vision should have been projected into the future, with a clear sense of what was to be accomplished in the long term. Surely something to be desired for the future is continued contact with Shakespeare, developing a sense that Shakespeare is enjoyable and accessible, not, as it was too often here, torture. If students continue to express rather distant "respect" for Shakespeare, let them at least say next time, "I respect Shakespeare *and so* I wanted to provide some entertainment" instead of "but". An event purporting to stem from a focus on English language teaching might have rewarded the use of that language in the best rendering it has ever known. Prizes should have been related directly to Shakespeare. The quality of judging should have made the students proud to have been thoughtfully considered by experts.

Maris Pähn, a graduate student of mine, compiled a questionnaire for schools which provided some indication of what resources they lack and seek. Among these were videos and workshops on teaching Shakespeare. I pointed out that when workshops had been offered few had attended, but the problem is that in many schools Shakespeare is taught in Estonian or Russian by teachers who do not know English, or teachers who live too far from Tallinn to come: workshops would need to be in their languages and come to them. The biggest obstacle to school Shakespeare was pointed out to me by a teacher of English in a school where I recently performed: schools in Estonia approach everything, including Shakespeare, with deadly seriousness and so resist the more enjoyable educational processes such as games and performance exercises. Perhaps there is an argument for a Shakespeare week, with workshops and games for both teachers and students, and perhaps a performance or performances at the end growing out of these. This could help to encourage a sense of Shakespeare as something to make friends with and play with, not to reverence from, and be kept at a distance. The teachers and students who – despite the insufficient lead time and desperate lack of appropriate facilities – took the time and effort to participate in the event showed initiative which deserves encouragement.

While the Amateur Drama Association (who are giving, as I write this, a Drama in Education seminar) is a very promising sign for the future, it has no state funding, and even if it survives this handicap will take some time to have any effect. School drama teachers are few and far between in Estonia. Performance, if it occurs, needs to be competent enough to justify audience attention and enjoyable enough to encourage future performance. For that more drama instruction and teaching workshops are needed. Funding is required to send at least one Estonian-speaking and one Russian-speaking teacher to the Stratford Summer School in teaching Shakespeare in performance. In the meantime – if there were any financial resources to permit this – some of the Globe's teaching-actors might come to Estonia and give workshops in various regions.

One way in which this event did succeed was in promoting smooth interaction between Estonian- and Russian-speaking students. And there was one element of pure fun: the Shakespeare Cake Competition (which no one from the catering colleges entered). Though many had no evident connection with Shakespeare (except in some cases shape and form), and one claiming to be shepherd's pie turned out to be bread, most were excellent concoctions. The long afternoon ended with the assembled multitude delightedly consuming them. So Shakespeare at least left a good taste in the mouth. Whether it will last depends on future initiatives in giving these participants' effort and initiative the carefully considered encouragement it deserves.[2]

Notes

[1] Quotations from student work are given throughout with spelling and punctuation uncorrected.

[2] Thanks to Katrin Viru, Maris Pähn and the British Council, Tallinn, for providing information.

SHAKESPEARE AMONG SOUTH AFRICAN SCHOOLCHILDREN

André Lemmer
(University of Port Elizabeth, South Africa)

> I walk through the long school room questioning;
> A kind old nun in a white hood replies;
> The children learn to cipher and to sing,
> To study reading books and history,
> To cut and sew, be neat in everything
> In the best modern way – the children's eyes
> In momentary wonder stare upon
> A sixty-year-old smiling public man
> W.B. Yeats "Among School Children"
>
> I walk through the African class room questioning;
> A grade twelve teacher in smart suit replies:
> "My students learn to construe and answer,
> To study Shakespeare plays and poetry,
> To analyse, and parrot everything
> From the study guide" – the students' eyes
> In incomprehension stare upon
> A Shakespeare matric revision man
> (A. Lemmer "Among Matric candidates")

It is in schools that most people in South Africa meet (or at least hear about) Shakespeare. After all, he has maintained a privileged status in South African secondary schools for the past century. In school curricula and syllabuses that have been formulated and followed in South Africa during the past 100 years Shakespeare is generally the only writer mentioned by name. Most learners will have had a Shakespeare encounter at least in their school-leaving (i.e. the grade 12 or 'Matric') year: this is because there is always a question in one of the final external English examination papers on a prescribed play written by Shakespeare.

The nature of that meeting is likely to determine whether there will be any further contact. The fact that many South African school children depart from school determined to have no further truck with the bard indicates that the kinds of engagements with Shakespeare they experience do not always inspire a yen for further acquaintance. "Just mention the word 'Shakespeare' and you can feel the boredom and resignation that dominate the atmosphere", writes Julia Grey, describing recent visits to Gauteng schools.[1]

I can corroborate this: last week I investigated the Shakespeare 'scene' at several 'disadvantaged' Port Elizabeth schools and came away feeling disheartened: in a number of the Black township schools *Macbeth* had been chosen as the (optional) drama for the public school-leaving examination. This was the first and final encounter with a Shakespeare dramatic work for the grade 12's. It many cases it did not seem that the encounter had been a successful one.

The teachers complained about looming external examinations and about unsuitable editions supplied by the Education department. A teacher said: "We have no money to purchase other editions. The pupils encounter difficulties when they have to read the explanatory notes and as a result they have a negative attitude towards Shakespeare books" (more about the role of school editions later). Tellingly, she went on to say, "I do try to change their attitude by explaining certain aspects..." Exam preparation was a big problem: the pupils did not remember the story details; they did not understand figures of speech. Last year, she averred, there had been many detailed content questions and some tricky figures: I flipped through the Eastern Cape 1999 matric paper.

Some extracts had been provided followed by a fusillade of questions: "Explain what happens when Macbeth meets Macdonwald in 3 full sentences" (6 marks, out of 30). Why does the king think Macbeth is noble?(2 marks). Do you think Macbeth is noble? Give 2 reasons (2 marks). Explain whether Macbeth remains brave: refer to examples later in the play (2 marks). Name the 3 titles by which the witches greet Macbeth (3 marks). How do the words of the second apparition create a sense of immortality in Macbeth? (2 marks) How does Birnam wood rise? (3 marks) Macbeth says he 'shall live the lease of nature': what does he mean? (2 marks) Explain how he is proved wrong. (2 marks). Macbeth wants to know if Banquo's descendants will reign. Briefly describe the apparition they show him (2 marks). 'That I may tell pale-hearted fear it lies'. Explain the personification (2 marks)." And so on ...

What is going on here? Easy marking fodder: no doubt of that. A story content focus, yes: the assumption presumably being that narrative is more accessible. An almost compartmentalised focus on the minutiae of some arbitrarily selected extracts – of course: we're 'helping' them by giving them the text. But not all on a plate: let us cut the apparition extract short and see if they can describe the final one; that will catch out those who have not studied the story properly. Throw in a few figures of speech to be explained: this is to jack things up a bit, add some real literary analysis – make it seem like the first language paper.

What, you may well ask, has all of this to do with the purpose of teaching literature, with encouraging students to possess the play, to be moved by character, dazzled by the music of poetry, immersed in an intense dramatic engagement with a blueprint for performance, connected to the issues of power, violence, ambition, corruption that permeate the play and the society they themselves live in?

At a large private school with mainly Black learners I discovered that the same 'unsuitable' edition was in use. The teacher said that the pupils wanted to do *Macbeth* so that they would be able to boast, "I have done Shakespeare". But the reality was that the struggle was too tough. The teacher's self-proclaimed philosophy was: "you haven't arrived until you've done Shakespeare!" (Ironically however, she admitted that she had decided to drop the Shakespeare option in 2001 for the second-language learners!) Her teaching approach? She said she began with an audio-tape, followed by a plot summary and then finally a line-by-line explanation of the text. For the first language group they went "much deeper", with a focus on "figures of speech and themes". Clearly here the bottom-line was examination preparation: the school aimed for high pass rates, and teachers who delivered the goods received a cash bonus.

At a Northern suburbs school (mainly mixed race) I was told that *Macbeth* was selected only by the 'First Language' groups as it was a compulsory set-book at this level. Currently the Grade 10's are studying *Romeo and Juliet,* and the Grade 11's, *Hamlet.* For the so-called second language groups there was no

Shakespeare encounter. Here I was told that the books used were old and in "terrible shape". Various editions were used: 'Longman, Penguins, whatever is available,' the teacher reported. She went on: "The learners mostly don't like Shakespeare – period!"

I asked about teaching approaches used. "It depends on the level", she said: "simplistic at first for grade 10, increasingly in-depth with progress to matric level: we focus on story-line, plot, content, reading, explanations, discussion, some play-acting, tests." "And pupil response?" I asked. "Usually poor", she said. In the more advantaged, ex-white schools, there was a Shakespeare presence in Grade 12 (*Macbeth* has been the only provincial drama prescription now for the past seven years) and usually also in Grade 10 (generally, *Romeo and Juliet* or a comedy). Monique, one of my post-graduate student interns who has recently been out on Teaching Practice in a big comprehensive ex-white school, reports that in many instances pupils are mostly passive in the classroom, with their "only contribution to sometimes read aloud: the whole point seemed to finish the play." The focus in the approaches used, especially with the Grade 12's she said, was mainly the taking of notes on plot, character, themes, figures of speech etc. for examination preparation. The editions being used were the ubiquitous ones I had encountered in the townships and were old and tatty. I had supplied her with copies of a new 'active' edition of *A Midsummer Night's Dream* to take along. "The teachers fell on them like wolves", she says. "The Grade 10 teacher tried out some of the activities which the kids enjoyed."

At another large ex-white (now very multi-racial) English medium school I spoke to the head of the English Department. Currently their learners were studying *A Midsummer Night's Dream* in Grade 10 and *Macbeth* in grade 12. The Grade 10's were looking at *MND* purely as a performance script. Groups were allocated scenes and given an 'outcomes-based' assessment rubric for preparing performances. One criterion on the rubric reads, "How well have the words been conveyed?" Marks have been allocated on this basis for the June reports. There was also a standardized written test with a question asking the learners to imagine they were directors and plan a staging of a scene, with textual justifications for their decisions. The Grade 12's had also been involved in what he called, 'scenario planning' with group presentations of the scenes. One group had presented a 'cross-over' of *Macbeth* and *The Lion King* featuring a song, "I want to be king"?

Another had prepared a 'Macbeth appears on Oprah' presentation. The intention, the teacher said was to build the exam preparation on an initial enjoyment of the play. He also reported that after several years of a 'lit-crit' approach the provincial public examination last year had swung in a performance-based direction which they expected to be sustained this year. He gave an example of this new trend: The following optional 'essay' question had appeared in the 1999 Eastern Cape Prescribed Literature examination paper for 'First Language':

> As the director of a short film on 'Macbeth' you have been told to save money by cutting out some of the scenes of the play. Choose any 6 scenes and explain in an essay why you think they should be included in a film. Your answer should focus on the dramatic impact of the scene as well as what it shows about the main characters.

I asked about editions used: they were still 'stuck' with the old Departmental editions he said, but he had told the pupils to "ignore the left-hand pages" (i.e. the gloss).

I also interviewed an experienced Head of Department at an Afrikaans Secondary School: she was adamant that her Shakespeare classes were a joy and her pupils very positive. She showed me photographs taken earlier this year of herself and her colleagues arriving at school resplendent in Elizabethan costumes. "We do this every year", she said. "On Shakespeare's birthday", we hire costumes and come to school dressed as characters for the plays. "It causes such a vibe."

Her department made use of new active editions; they had a strong drama club in the school, and the classroom approaches used were active and participatory. She thought the key was to approach the plays as performance scripts and to have a lot of visual engagement, including the screening of videos of the plays, after they had been read. The Grade 10 pupils loved acting out scenes and had seen different movie versions of *Romeo and Juliet,* including the recent Baz Luhrman version. This had been linked with film study and a visual literacy programme.

She showed me a recent 'mock' test written by her Std 10 class (grade 12): "You are the director of a production of *Macbeth*:

> Explain how you wish to have the witches portrayed, referring to such aspects as -
> appearance
> costume
> age
> voice type
> special effects (if any)
> Do not forget to include Hecate in your response
> Note, that you have to MOTIVATE your decision FULLY."

A further fillip to some restored faith in the possibilities for Shakespeare among school-children was provided by an interview with an experienced teacher who had worked in Black Township schools for many years. He insisted that of all the literature prescriptions he had taught over the years, the Shakespeare ones worked best. This was because the stories were simple: "Yes, there is initially a language barrier; but after two weeks", he said, "they get into it. Initially we read aloud in class a lot with the minimum of explanations: the sound of the poetry is SO important." His Black students loved doing *Macbeth*. "Particularly the witch scenes", he said. "These were much easier to put across" than in white schools. He claimed that Black children related far more authentically and feelingly ("from the heart" was the expression he used). "The supernatural elements in *Macbeth* especially make a much greater impact", he said. We talked about the centrality of family bonds and relationships in Shakespeare plays, and he said that there too a powerful awareness was evident. He had taught *Romeo and Juliet* and the idea of the clan conflict made a powerful impact. It reminded me of a Cape Town colleague telling me about teaching *King Lear* in a rural Black school and how deeply shocked the children were by Lear's treatment at the hands of his daughters.

While it is true that my bit of 'empirical research' was rather scattered and impressionistic there can be little doubt that there is wide-spread resistance and negativism in our schools, especially where contact with Shakespeare is confined to the Grade 12 school-leavers. This is certainly the case in urban Gauteng, judging from the March issue of *The Teacher*. However, a project has been launched to attempt a rescue of the situation. Ms Grey describes "an experiment" being conducted in 26 Gauteng-based schools as part of a Shakespeare 2000 Festival, in order to

> Find out whether his plays are relics of old (not to mention products from foreign shores) that deserve to be confined to the archives, or 400-year-old artworks that are still meaningful to us today [sic].

Ms Grey extols the work of what she calls a "dramatic hit-squad" of student actors under the leadership of Malcolm Purkey, head of the dramatic arts school at the University of the Witwatersrand: this 'squad' is currently in Township schools in Soweto to see if new life can be breathed into Shakespeare.

We are told how Purkey and his team find they have "a real task on their hands" as they face "a hall full of sceptical matrics at a Johannesburg Secondary School in Mayfair": however, Purkey 'tackles this head-on': "we have a problem", he says (according to Ms Grey): 'We live in Johannesburg, South Africa, it's the new millennium. We have this question: is there a place for Shakespeare in our curriculum and our lives anymore?" With these words, we are told, 'the mood lifts'.

Ms Grey continues: "The youngsters clearly welcome [...] a playful workshop that investigates whether our modern lives and tastes can still accommodate the Bard. And where Purkey really scores", she says, "is when he makes this comparison: 'believe it or not, Shakespeare was the rap artist of his time ...'" We hear how Purkey 'blows the dust off Shakespeare's sonnets,' how he 'gives clues of typical devices and favourite themes', and how he frankly admits "that there are some areas of the works that are destined to remain meaningless to modern scholars ..."

Ms Grey pens an accompanying article entitled: "The great debate: To do or not to do?" where she aims to tackle the issue of why Shakespeare's works "inspire such controversy, taught as they are as school set-work books." On the one hand, she cites what she refers to as the "usual justifications": the works deal with "universal themes", demonstrate a "wizardry of story-telling and characterisation", have "had a massive influence on forms of poetry and plays" and "provide a very powerful lesson on the history of English and how languages change through time." On the other hand, however, she says that she "concedes" that these claims are "not watertight": African artists also deal with "universal themes" and provide "good models"; "shouldn't we be building a canon of home-grown literature that reflects our own history, linguistic expressions and values?" she asks. Her other 'persuasive argument' is that "the value of burdening English second language students with the near-foreign language of Elizabethan English is highly debatable." However, with a quick scramble onto the fence again, we are told: "But there is much to be said about the power of Shakespeare's words, and how they continue to live on even today."

Her ambiguous stance seems to be characteristic of so much of the 'debate' on the place of Shakespeare in schools. Moreover, there are many questionable (and unquestioned) assumptions in the Grey story: there is the either / or assumption (Shakespeare *or* the unnamed 'African poets and playwrights' – no 'and'); there is the (apparent) unquestioning assumption that the 'to do or not to do' great debate about a Shakespeare presence on the curriculum concerns the matric (school-leaving) year only (no mention of Shakespeare for younger learners); there is the suggestion that Shakespeare in schools is a corpse that can be revived Lazarus-like if there are Purkeys enough to provide life-giving breath; there is also the suggestion that there is a relevant 'hit-parade' Bard out there but access requires interventions from Purkeys and their' hit-squads' who can come zapping and rapping in to save the day and rescue those bored, resigned, disaffected kids from an old-fashioned, moribund, irrelevant, inaccessible, traditional kind of Shakespeare.

This is not to say that some of these assumptions are not justified. Interventions from outside – either physically or in the form of materials – can sometimes help to make a difference. I myself have also provided, often with the assistance of my students, back-up and revision 'squads'. I have also attempted to ameliorate the kind of scepticism – and indifference, even animosity – to the Bard encountered by the Purkey squad, with 'playful workshops' (my annual 'Viva Shakespeare' bums off seats, drama workshops have been popular at Grahamstown Foundation Schools' Festivals for some years now) – and through the editing of 'communicative' and 'active' editions.[2]

The 'Viva Shakespeare' workshops that I run at the Grade 11 Grahamstown Foundation Festivals have been very popular over the years. We run 4 X 1 ½ hour sessions (always fully subscribed) with 30 pupils per workshop. The programme includes voice and body 'warm-ups', an activity where the pupils create Shakespearean insults to fling at each other; a 'bums-off-seats' moving to the opening words from *Macbeth* with instructions to experiment with a variety of delivery modes (singing, wailing, laughing, weeping, whispering etc) and emotions (angry, sad, friendly etc.); then groups prepare a choral opening to *Macbeth*, with sound effects (they are provided with various African musical instruments and artefacts, for instance, bongo drums, rain-sticks, 'frogs', rattles, 'owls', African xylophones, jews' harps etc.) The participants are invited to predict what visual effects they would expect for this scene for stage and animated film openings, and then I screen the video openings to an animated version of *Macbeth* (Island World Video) and the RSC Thames Video version directed by Trevor Nunn, and lively discussions follow. Pairs then prepare freeze-frames of 'Two-line scenes', and we end up with groups drawing descriptions of key *Macbeth* scenes from a hat and presenting them in tableaux. Other groups must guess which scenes their fellows have illustrated.

Each year the 100 plus participants complete a quick questionnaire at the end of each workshop: they receive four statements with which they have to 'strongly agree', 'agree', 'disagree' or 'strongly disagree' (1. I enjoyed the V.S. workshop; 2. I enjoy Shakespeare at school; 3. At school we do similar active things when we study plays, eg. by Shakespeare; 4. I wish we could use these active approaches at school). The following table gives some idea of response patterns over the past six years:

Questions/dates
Strongly Agree
Agree
Disagree
Strongly Disagree

Questions/ dates	Strongly Agree	Agree	Disagree	Strongly Disagree
1. (1995)	80 %	20 %		
1. (1999)	72 %	28 %		
1. (2000)	70 %	30 %		
2. (1995)	25 %	45 %	20 %	10 %
2. (1999)	35 %	53 %	11 %	1 %
2. (2000)	33 %	45 %	17 %	5 %
3. (1995)	6 %	12 %	45 %	37 %
3. (1999)	9 %	18 %	60 %	13 %
3. (2000)	7 %	25 %	43 %	24 %
4. (1995)	80 %	20 %		
4. (1999)	69 %	29 %	1 %	1 %
4. (2000)	68 %	30 %	1 %	

CONCLUSION

The statistics indicate that the active approaches we employed are much enjoyed, with a huge majority "strongly agreeing" with the first statement on the questionnaire, i.e. "I enjoyed the *Viva Shakespeare* session." Happily, it appears from the responses to statement two that attitudes to Shakespeare in many of our schools are becoming more positive (It should be remembered though, that participants at schools' Festivals are probably not representative of all senior pupils in our schools: these are the students who by and large are already favourably disposed to the arts).

It is disappointing – but not surprising – that "active approaches" are still relatively rare – even in the kinds of schools that encourage their students to come to Schools' festivals. In 1995 over 80% "disagreed" with the third statement, which suggests that active-type approaches have been experienced at school. However this is changing: more recently this figure has dropped quite significantly.

Possibly the most telling finding is the response to statement four ("I wish we could use active approaches at our school") where there has been overwhelming agreement in each year of the survey.

It is interesting that the most popular activity on the programme is the one that focuses most strongly on the peculiarities of Shakespearian language, that is the "Insults and Curses" item. I would like to acknowledge Susan C. Biondo-Hench's "Insult Sheet" for this wonderful activity.[3] (In fact my students reported that pupils were so taken with it that they were 'insulting' each other courtesy of Susan and Shakespeare long after the workshop was over!)

The "Viva Shakespeare" programme with its emphasis on 'bums off seats' – 'active Shakespeare' gives some indication of at least the kinds of supplementary approaches which might help to rescue Shakespeare pedagogy in the 'New South Africa'. The new 'active' and 'communicative' editions that are now on the market – and which contain many classroom suggestions for active, drama-focussed activities – will, I sincerely hope, provide the life-lines that teachers need for this rescue operation.

Notes

1. *The Teacher*, 5:3, March 2000, pp. 2-5.
2. See the ISEA MacMillan and the Maskew Miller Longman series: e.g. Andre Lemmer and Jane Bursey, ed., *Shakespeare's 'Macbeth'*, Communicative Shakespeare series developed by the ISEA, Rhodes University, Macmillan (1986) and Nigel Bakker et. al., ed, 'Macbeth', Active Shakespeare series, Maskew Miller Longman (1996).
3. Susan C. Biondo-Hench's "Insult Sheet" in Peggy O'Brien, *Shakespeare Set Free* (Folger Press, 1993), p. 125.

ON TEACHING (AND BEING TAUGHT) SHAKESPEARE IN CHINA AND CANADA

Gregory Maillet
(Campion College at the University of Regina)

I. Introduction: "In the shape of two countries at once" (MA 3.2.28-9)[1]

What does one teach when teaching Shakespeare, and how and why should one do so? Should one's answers to these questions remain the same wherever and whenever one teaches, or should they vary according to cultural circumstances? How should the students' culture(s) affect their professor's Shakespearean pedagogy and, conversely, how should a professor's own culture affect what his or her students learn about Shakespeare? Such questions, though infinitely complex, seem central to any attempt to develop a global perspective on how Shakespeare can and should be taught in institutions of higher education. My own perspective on such issues has been shaped in circumstances both foreign and familiar. Just after defending my doctorate, I taught Shakespeare for the 1996-97 year at Peking University,[2] one of the leading arts universities in China, where it is widely known as "Beida". For the following three years, I have been at Campion College, a liberal arts Jesuit college federated with the University of Regina,[3] in my native Canada. Though North Americans usually are interested more in the former experience rather than the latter, I prefer to compare, contrast, and reflect upon teaching both away and at home. The students in both countries are dear to my heart, and considering the two experiences together allows for a much broader account of the cross-cultural exchange inherent in any 'global' pedagogy.

Considering both countries also spurs reflection on the actual nature of cross-cultural exchange, which is so often simplified. To travel and teach, or be taught, about Shakespeare, one must do much more than simply grab the Bard's Collected Works, hop on a plane, and fly halfway around the world. Rather, the old Renaissance conception of the human microcosm becomes valid again, for a teacher must develop both philosophical and practical responses to my initial pedagogical questions if he or she wishes to travel to the unique world of each of one's students, "out where", in the words of Canadian poet Margaret Avison, "theory is challenged by the existence of persons".[4]

II. "The undiscovered country" (*HAM* 3.1.81)

Hamlet was talking about death, of course, but what if life, particularly human culture, is an even greater mystery, with discoveries yet lying far beyond current geographical borders? Both Canada and China are such countries, startlingly different in population and the age of their cultures, but similarly blessed by a vast land, and spirit, from which no traveler, having once truly entered, can ever really return.

China: "How many goodly creatures are there here!" (TEM 5.1.185)

As the Earth's most populous nation, China may well be the country in which to challenge the theoretical concept of culture itself, for its cultural diversity clearly shows the need for an exceptionally broad definition. Rather than the common North American error of 'minority-culturalism', which focuses on visibly distinguishing factors such as skin colour, gender, or class, consideration of China's ninety-one million ethnic minorities[5] (who along with the 'Han' majority speak hundreds of dialects in addition to Mandarin or Cantonese, and hold a wide variety of worldviews) clearly requires a broad definition of culture, such as "the way of life of a people, including their attitudes, values, beliefs, arts, sciences, modes of perception, and habits of thought and activity".[6] However, this definition is so inclusive that only small portions of its wide range of cultural factors could be researched. One must always be on guard against re-presenting a distorted vision of cultures that foreigners have mere surface knowledge of, something to which Said's work on Orientalism has alerted English Studies;[7] yet the inevitability of partial knowledge, it must be stressed, is not simply a problem for those, like myself, who have limited linguistic skills and spent a short period in China. As went a running joke among Beijingers, people who visit China for six weeks write a book, those who stay six months write an article, and those who remain for a year write nothing at all. The deeper problem is that there is such an enormous variety of cultures within China that one can make hardly any significant cultural commentary, on teaching Shakespeare or any other matter, without also being able to cite other aspects of Chinese culture that would contradict one's thesis, or at least force one to admit, "and that's true too" (KL 5.2.12).[8]

During my time in China, it was a wide cross-section of this diversity, holding in common only considerable achievement in the study of English literature, who each morning awoke in me (in classes starting at 7:30 am) something of the wonder at each of their unique, individual worlds. Having taught them for only ten months is perhaps what allows me the foolishness to write about them here, but it might also be taken as a continuation of the exercise in 'negative capability' that Keats, as my Chinese students were fascinated to learn, famously argued was essential for appreciating *King Lear*.[9] Keats is one of the most popular English poets in China, but it was to Hemingway that the Peking University students of English turned to entitle their fine, biannual journal of critical essays and creative writing, which they called *One-Eighth*.[10] This title may be a response to the many foreign teachers who falsely labeled them as shy introverts, or a gesture towards other authorities in their lives, but in teaching them I always kept in mind that their words revealed no more than 'one-eighth' of the collective iceberg that is each of their complex lives.

Canada: "Know'st thou this country?" (*TN* 1.2.19)

The 'one-eighth' image stayed with me when I returned to teach in Regina, a small city sometimes denigrated by Canadians as a place to drive through on the way to the more populous centres of Toronto or Vancouver. Yet anyone aware of Saskatchewan's 'First Nations',[11] 'Metis',[12] or history of global immigration,[13] would not be surprised that among its mere million people are "more than 200 cultures" of ethnic groups who "speak more than 80 languages".[14] Saskatchewan, in fact, is the only Canadian province that does not have a majority from either a

British or French ethnic background, and though the majority of original immigrants were European, these cultures are also too diverse to be labeled, *en masse*, as 'Euro-centric'; as well, for decades now people from other continents have been arriving in ever greater numbers. English dominates the mass media, but geographical isolation, tight-knit communities, and federal Canadian support for multiculturalism have in many ways succeeded in preventing cultural assimilation.

Here too, it is never safe to generalize, but usually my own culture – in ethnic terms, a typically bizarre Canadian mix of Acadien-Scots-Irish-Dutch familial heritage – differs almost as much from that of my Canadian students as from my Chinese, and equally diverse are the cultural differences among the Saskatchewan students themselves. Then, of course, the Elizabethan and Jacobean culture in which Shakespeare wrote also differs at least as much from the cultures of China and Canada as these modern nations differ among and within themselves. One thus begins to appreciate that the *reality* rather than pleasant *myth* of multiculturalism makes difficult even the minimal level of mutual understanding necessary for meaningful cross-cultural exchange. Certainly, it is misleadingly simplistic to isolate a few, often stereotypical 'national' traits, and then select evidence to prove that a nation displays these traits in their approach to Shakespeare. One recent writer, for example, begins a quest, via Shakespeare, for the by now clichéd quest for Canadian identity by asserting:

> The Germans have tended to believe that they are a nation of Hamlets. The Poles have used Shakespeare in a tortuous process of identity-exploration. The Japanese relate very easily to his Elizabethan ideas of honour and revenge.[15]

But how, one wonders, do the Japanese respond to Falstaff's "ideas of honour" (*1HIV* 5.1.129-39), and do *all* or even *most* of today's Japanese youths share traditional notions of honour, despite the numerous changes in their society since World War II? The Chinese are often characterized as Confucian, with deep respect for elderly authority and relatively passive temperaments but, again, does this still apply following Mao's 'cultural Revolution' in the 1960s, which desecrated all things Confucian, or for the 'little emperors' raised under China's 'one-child' policy? For many Chinese intellectuals, I think, the concept of a 'Shakespeare with Chinese characteristics' would sound like a silly parody of one of Deng Xiaoping's major slogans for post-Mao China – 'communism with Chinese characteristics' – and would be useful only for political gain or to humour foreigners, much as I might argue for *Twelfth Night* as *the* Canadian play in the canon, a confused search for identity in which "nothing that is so, is so" (*TN* 4.1.7). Nevertheless, partially aware, at least, of the magnitude of the challenge faced by any 'global', 'cross-cultural' pedagogy, and drawing upon the similarities and differences of two deeply multicultural locales – Beijing and Regina-- we can perhaps avoid a few counterproductive approaches, and then suggest some tentative responses to my opening questions by developing long-and-short term strategies through which peoples of radically different cultures might help each other to study and move towards understanding Shakespeare.

III. "By indirections find directions out" (*HAM* 2.1.65)

In my view, there are at least three 'cross-cultural' approaches to teaching Shakespeare, and literature in general, that are very common but badly flawed, approaches especially problematic in multicultural locales. Within error, though, are always clues to correct that particular problem, and so each is worth reviewing.

"Art Made Tongue-Tied by Authority" (*Son.* LXVI. l.9)

The one most commonly rejected today, in our post-colonial age, is that old, often unnamed pedagogical strategy, authoritarianism, or what Paulo Freire aptly calls, "the 'banking' concept of education" in which "the teacher teaches, and the students are taught; the teacher knows everything and the students know nothing".[16] Though few today publicly espouse it, there seems little doubt that this form of pedagogy is commonly practiced, if only because of the obvious fact that professors do know more about their subjects than most of their students, and they are in a position, for a brief time, to cast an apparently authoritative judgment upon their students' understanding of Shakespeare. Especially while teaching in China, where one's official title is "foreign expert", and one's students have been rigorously trained to show at least outward signs of respect to all authority, it is highly tempting to fall back upon saying, "I have studied and know this to be so; therefore, believe me". The professor may be correct, and substantive knowledge may be passed along, surely a positive result. But we should not underestimate how likely it is that a pedagogy based primarily on regular appeals to personal authority, which many young people in both China and Canada deeply mistrust, will alienate students from the primary object of study, Shakespeare's art.

My Chinese students rarely expressed any rebellious thoughts in public, but privately they left little doubt that they were understandably wary of how not only "art", as Shakespeare said, but artists themselves might be "tongue-tied", or worse, "by authority" (*Son.* 66, 1.9). Many of these students' professors had been victims of herd political violence during the 'cultural revolution', and all remember, though with surprisingly diverse shades of emotion, what they referred to simply as '1989', a metonym in which brevity suggests not "the soul of wit" (*Ham.* 2.2.91) but rather silent tension. Communism in China is a powerful force against foreign cultural authority of any kind, particularly the British, whose crimes during the nineteenth-century Opium wars are still commemorated, for example, as the ruins of the Emperor's old summer palace, and who returned Hong Kong just after my year in China ended. Given this history, Shakespeare can seem an import of questionable value and, despite all displays of outward respect, Shakespearean professors may be even more suspect.

As for Canada, though it is a commonwealth country with strong formal ties to Britain, and though it has not suffered a severe political trauma like that which has shaped the anti-authoritarian ethos of recent generations in many other nations, there is a growing sense of itself as a post-colonial nation. While an undergraduate, it was common for me and my classmates to be much more trusting, for example, of Irish rather than English professors, and before studying him I recall wondering whether Shakespeare was nothing more than a propaganda tool of the old, fading British empire. Certainly, the broadening of English away from the traditional British canon has raised such issues for many Canadian undergraduates today, as has the widespread rejection, at least in academia, of the value of British imperialism. Postcolonial English studies has even alerted undergraduates to the political implications of the proper names that most people in a society grow up taking for granted; to take an obvious local example, Regina was named after Queen Victoria, but the natives had already named it "Wascana", the English transliteration of a Cree term meaning 'pile of bones', a typically comic native tribute to the sacred land of the now nearly extinct Buffalo. In this pedagogical environment, to depend upon Shakespeare's authority as 'high' culture, or upon one's own personal knowledge as the student's singular key to this culture, is to create a serious barrier to any enjoyable engagement with Shakespeare's art, rather than the bridges that an effective education should build. Though it is futile to distort Shakespeare's own politics to make, for example, the 'divine right' of kings more palatable to today's students, professors can be thankful for those elements of Shakespeare's art that do subvert authority, as when Lear says, in a line that draws hearty classroom laughter in both China and Canada, "behold the very image of authority: a dog's obeyed in office" (4.6.153). Once this is said, however, there is no avoiding the students' metaphoric leap to the notion that their professor may also be doing nothing more than barking at them.

"A Mere Hoard of Gold kept by a Devil" (*2HIV* 4.2.103)

A second equally common yet counterproductive cross-cultural pedagogy similarly relies on Shakespeare's self-evident literary greatness and the acceptance of a professor's authority to interpret his significance, but re-presents the latter as humble self-effacement; in this approach, as Gerald Graff has argued in critiquing it, it is alleged that "a good book 'essentially teaches itself".[17] One could interpret this notion positively, to mean that very few students or teachers can fail to learn at least a few valuable things from a great literary text. Also, there is no question that enthusiastic, direct discussion of Shakespeare's plots, characters, and central themes, whether or not this discussion becomes self-conscious of its Aristotelian foundations, will do far more to convey the significance of Shakespeare's works than a dry analysis that dogmatically adapts Shakespeare's thought to that of any independent belief system. Yet even on the most basic level of denotative linguistic meaning, 'good books' such as Shakespeare's texts include such a wide range of references, whether to history, philosophy, religion, science, other literary texts, or the writer's own imagination, that they are in many ways unteachable; their meanings are simply beyond the horizons of any individual scholar, whose life-long labour can only attain an ever greater yet always partial comprehension. Purveyors of Shakespeare Inc., whether commercial or academic, frequently point out that a high percentage of words from his works remain part of the English language. But, especially in multicultural locales far removed from the contexts in which Shakespeare wrote, it is crucial to remember that the absence of any referent for, especially, the subject or verb of a sentence will render the entire sentence incomprehensible. Further, there are the numerous 'false-friend' words in Shakespeare, such as 'maid' or 'weed', whose meanings will likely be comic if interpreted solely within the reader's modern linguistic horizon. Until at least the probable historical meanings of such words are taught, the unlearned reader is bound to be confused and unable to enjoy large portions of even the greatest of texts.

Most defenders of the 'great text teaches itself' mode of pedagogy do, of course, offer their students basic instruction in linguistic and historical matters, but the core of their argument is precisely to limit their instruction to just those facts that literary texts clearly signify, apart from extra-textual realities such as the values of the text's author or audience, especially the values of the interpreting critic himself. Often associated with the New Criticism, in Canada this view became widely influential through the work of Northrop Frye, who continued the nineteenth-century Canadian university appropriation of Matthew Arnold[18] by stressing the need for a 'disinterested critic' who could, paradoxically, teach literature as a means to overcome cultural division and advance towards a classless society.[19] To do so, Frye thought it essential that critics do not study literature "with the object of arriving at value-judgements, because the only possible goal of study is knowledge".[20] For Frye, the knowledge relevant to literary criticism is found only in the first of several familiar Enlightenment binaries – "knowledge and experience, criticism and taste, fact and value"[21] – whose opposition Western philosophy and literary theory has spent much of the last 30 years deconstructing. How the crucial concept of 'knowledge' has then been reconstructed, discarded, or at least italicized, is too complex to summarize here, but most influential, at least in academic circles, has been the legacy of Nietzsche, as seen in the French post-modernists, or the work of American theorist Barbara Herrnstein-Smith, who have followed Nietzche and turned the fact / value opposition on its head, arguing that "value creates value".[22] Canadian students of literature may be unfamiliar with these philosophical debates, but they have felt their impact profoundly in the many new critical movements that have sprung out of the 'revaluation' of Shakespeare, particularly feminism, cultural materialism, new historicism, and post-colonialism. So, too, have students in China, where 'Western Literary Theory' is now a common part of the curriculum for both English and Chinese literature. Pedagogically, the result is that most Shakespeare students, in either country, enter their classrooms profoundly aware, and wary, that their professor's own theoretical biases are likely to influence which 'version' of Shakespeare they are likely to hear; how, then, will be negotiated any differences between this 'version' and their own experience of the 'great text' becomes a question of pressing importance.

If a still surviving Canadian Frygean, and there are some, were to travel to China to teach Shakespeare, he or she would likely hear from at least a few students that the allegedly paradoxical notion that a 'disinterested' critic can help build a classless society is in fact a bourgeois delusion designed to contain the struggle required for a truly communist society to emerge. Marxist political theory classes remain mandatory for all students at Beida, and with the media still largely controlled by the central Party, radical communist politics are voiced among some Beida students. Although its influence today is much diminished, the famous 'little red book' called *Quotations from Chairman Mao Tse-tung*, which still has to be counted as the single most influential book in post-war China, does include within its pages some Marxist literary theory. Though Mao here showed some awareness of the problems caused by a purely utilitarian approach to art, this was always coupled with an insistence on political correctness; thus, he stressed, "we oppose both works of art with a wrong political viewpoint and the tendency towards the 'poster and slogan style' which is correct in political viewpoint but lacking in artistic power".[23] Artistic power must be used in the service of the revolution, for there is "no such thing as art for arts sake"; rather, for Mao, literary works "are, as Lenin said, cogs and wheels in the whole revolutionary machine".[24] Yet it is not the approved work of communist party writers that remain most popular among the people of China, but rather four long prose novels, all written between 1300-1800 A.D., chapters of which are still read on the radio each day during lunch-hour, and widely listened to right before the almost universally practiced afternoon nap. A tradition of art for pleasure's sake is thus very much alive, and certainly most Beida students, aware of the problems caused by radical Marxism during the 'cultural revolution', do not see either themselves or their books as 'cogs' in any 'machine'. The first, and most persistent question that I was directly asked while teaching literature in China was, "are personal experience and objective science both important in literary scholarship?".

I have found a hunger, in both China and Canada, for what we in Catholic educational circles call personalism: for treating each student as a unique individual, for finding forms of education that grant some relevance to each student's own cultural background, and for finding ways to allow one's education not only to understand the world but also, as both the Jesuits and Marx equally stress, to actually change it for the better. Yet the difficulty of the latter task, and the danger of error, means that students in both countries do not want it undertaken too earnestly. For all of these reasons, another favourite Shakespearean speech, in both countries, is Falstaff's famous discourse on Prince Hal's education, in which he argues that learning is "a mere hoard of gold kept by a devil, till sack commences it and sets it in act and use" (*2HIV* 4.2.103-04). The line especially brings smiles when students learn that 'commencement' and 'act' are Renaissance terms for the granting of a university degree,[25] especially if a professor confers such knowledge upon his or her students while raising to their health a tall glass of beer, the national brands of which are, in both Canada and China, quite significant expressions of friendship and patriotic pride.[26]

"Simple Truth Miscalled Simplicity" (*Sonn.* LXVI.11)

Many of today's students no longer smile, however, upon the strategy that many Western academics have consciously or unconsciously used in the past thirty years as a way of acknowledging diverse personal identities and politics in their classrooms, and avoiding the pitfalls of the first two indirections just discussed: relativism. Here again, in diverse forms of Western literary theory, Nietzsche has been the primary influence, particularly the notion that 'knowledge' can never consist of anything more than arbitrary interpretations, driven only by one's own 'will to power' rather than any objective criteria such as 'truth'. Relativism was the consequence, Nietzsche believed, of Kant's fundamentally skeptical epistemology, after which one sees that "there are no facts-in-themselves", for "a sense must always be projected into them before there can be 'facts'".[27] After a genealogy of the history of thought, thinks Nietzsche, "perhaps we shall then recognize that the thing-in-itself is worth a Homeric laugh; that it seemed so much, indeed everything, and is really empty, namely, empty of meaning".[28]

Again, Shakespeare students may not understand the foundations of such philosophy, but through applied criticism they become very familiar with Derridean deconstruction and Foulcaudian historicism that are its most obvious derivatives, or with theorists such as Herrnstein-Smith. On the crucial question of literary value, Nietzschean relativism has often been adopted even by critics with committed moral viewpoints, such as the feminist Annette Kolodney,[29] or the Marxist Terry Eagleton, whose book *Literary Theory* has been widely used as an introductory textbook in both Canada and China. In it, Eagleton tells us that "'Value' is a transitive term; it means whatever is valued by certain people in specific situations, according to particular criteria and in the light of given purposes",[30] and that someday human society might positively evolve, in "a general human enrichment", to a point where "Shakespeare would be no more valuable than much present-day graffiti".[31] Tracing in the past what Eagleton has speculated about in the future, Gary Taylor, co-editor of the prestigious Oxford Shakespeare, has similarly argued, in his *Reinventing Shakespeare*, that for the past four centuries Shakespeare has largely been an effective disguise for the imposition of establishment values, and that his art in itself "cannot claim any unique command of theatrical resources, longevity or reach of reputation, depth or range of style, universality or comprehensiveness".[32]

Such criticism usefully deflates bardolatry and warns against the reinterpretation of Shakespeare as a means to the imposition of authoritarian or colonial values upon unwitting students. But if all criticism of Shakespeare can consist only of similarly arbitrary reinterpretations, then the effect upon students trained in such literary theory, especially in post-colonial, multicultural societies such as China or Canada, can also produce other, less positive results. First, with no authority for the knowledge they teach, professors' professional authority may well be seen as nothing more than an expression of the will to power. This is especially so because the relativistic professor of Shakespeare, who theoretically claims to be equally accepting of all interpretations, usually reverts, in practice to giving higher grades to those that he or she personally prefers. Further, and ultimately more problematic for the entire discipline of literary studies, the cynicism resulting from this classroom experience will cause many students to evade any serious evaluation of Shakespeare's work, since what is needed to do well in the course is simply the regurgitation of the professor's own arbitrary interpretation. The end result, ironically, is that the relativistic approach to teaching Shakespeare produces as much student despair and disgust as does the authoritarian approach.

Yet in my experience teaching Shakespeare in both Canada and China, there have also been many students who instinctively reject the philosophical premises of relativism, and the ensuing pedagogy, to continue their own search for an authentic interpretation and evaluation of Shakespeare. There are many cultural reasons for this, but in both Canada and China there are three key common factors. First, the atheism generally assumed by Nietzschean thought, and by Canadian secular humanism or Chinese communism, is simply rejected by many students in both countries, and its ensuing relativism is recognized as incompatible with the various forms of religion that many of them deeply espouse. Second, the students' common experience of suffering caused by moral error, especially in family life, leads them away from ethical relativism. For such students, for example, it is a "simple truth" (*Son.* 66, 1.11) that both adultery and the false accusation of adultery are seriously wrong.[33] Unsurprisingly, they are not at all sympathetic, then, to Howard Felperin's claim of audience 'aporia' over whether or not Hermione, in *The Winter's Tale*, is truly chaste;[34] rather, they tend to regard such aporias as the critic's own imposition of a relativistic ideology upon Shakespeare's text. Finally, students in both countries, in the age of globalization, have witnessed and been outraged by so many brazen, political abuses of the will to power that rather than cynically accepting such as the 'way of the world' they tend to admire and want to follow the approach of someone like the Czech President, and playwright, Vaclav Havel, willing to risk all on the capacity of the 'will to truth' to speak truth to the powers that be. In China, for example, another of the central slogans used to reject the 'cultural revolution' was "seek truth from facts".[35] Perhaps it is for this reason that, at least in my teaching experience, easily the most popular single Shakespearean character, in both Canada and China, is the Fool in *King Lear*. With him, students recognize that truth can be "a dog" that "must to kennel" (*KL* 1.4.95), but they also foolishly continue to believe that the simple truth of Cordelia, the wisdom of the heart, "is [itself] a dowry" (*KL* 1.1.241) worth committing one's life to. If a professor dogmatically continues to "'miscall'" all "simple truth" as "simplicity" (*Son.* 66, 1.11), such students will regard him or her as, in Lear's angry words, one more "scurvy politician" who "seem[s] to see the things thou dost not" (*Lr.* 4.6.165-6).

IV. *Quo Vadis*: "The map of my microcosm" (*COR* 2.1.56)

A professor, however, cannot play the Fool indefinitely; as Falstaff's young student eventually told him, "How ill white hairs becomes a fool and jester!"

(*2HIV* 5.5.46). What, then, is to be done? Within the preceding analysis of pedagogical error may also be seen, perhaps, three general antidotes. First, the danger of authoritarianism requires what contemporary Jesuits call 'inculturation', the adaptation of teaching to the strengths and weaknesses of any given culture, and the willingness of even the most advanced teacher to learn from the elementary student; this must not be done paternalistically, or as a cynical strategy for subduing opposition, but rather because any human student will have experiences relevant to the understanding of any human subject. Second, because texts do not teach themselves, and everyone's experience is inadequate for the comprehension of great texts, one also needs a personalist but systematic pedagogical method which can aid learners in their quest for understanding. Third, if this method is also to avoid becoming relativistic, one requires a theory of what knowledge is, and how knowledge of both the meaning and value of texts may be attained.

Prerequisite to all three measures, perhaps, is admitting one's own biases or, put more positively, the explanation of one's own inevitably limited response to the final daunting task. My own answers to such questions have largely been formed, perhaps unsurprisingly, by a Canadian Jesuit philosopher and theologian named Bernard J.F. Lonergan. A detailed explanation of his epistemology and resultant pedagogical method is impossible here, but crucial to his response to Nietzsche is a combination of existentialism and phenomenology. Lonergan seeks to develop in all learners an "understanding of understanding", a knowledge of knowledge,[36] by helping each learner notice what is happening within them, what kind of mental operation, during any of the countless but particular, concrete situations in which any human person moves from ignorance to understanding, what happens to them in a "pragmatic engagement in the process of knowing".[37] At the risk of his simple truths being ridiculed as simplicity, fundamentally Lonergan argues that human knowledge is achieved through a "basic pattern of operations" which fall into "four successive, related [as mutually active and interdependent], but qualitatively different levels":

the empirical level on which we sense, perceive, imagine, feel, speak, move... an intellectual level on which we inquire, come to understand, express what we have understood, work out the presuppositions and implications of our expression ... the rational level on which we reflect, marshal the evidence, pass judgement on the truth or falsity, certainty, or probability, of a statement... the responsible level on which we are concerned with ourselves, our own operations, our goals, and so deliberate about possible courses of action, evaluate them, decide, and carry out our decisions.[38]

Lonergan's thought may sound, at first, like common sense, but fully developed it becomes a subtly nuanced response to the broad philosophical tradition. Elements from each level correct the errors, for example, inherent in naïve empiricism, idealism, and Kant or Nietzsche, to produce an epistemology that has variously been called "generalized empirical method" or "critical realism".[39]

The latter, in fact, is the answer I give to that common question of the post-theorized student, usually the second question asked of me even in China: 'what is your critical foundation?'. Again, full explanation is impossible without a separate course; but a short answer is that as a Lonerganian critical realist, I believe that though in this life it will always be incomplete, objectively real knowledge of the meaning and value of Shakespeare can be progressively attained through a pragmatic, methodic engagement, by the human subject, with the subject, Shakespeare's art. Lonergan usefully describes such knowledge as the "fruit of authentic subjectivity".[40] To define this crucial phrase, Lonergan explains that such knowledge comes from a regular commitment to all four levels − "genuine attention, genuine intelligence, genuine reasonableness, genuine responsibility"[41] − but also stresses that being genuine on each level cannot come in isolation, but only in community. The question remains as to whether the Lonerganian approach is general enough to be useful in the multicultural classroom, or merely another case whereby a foreign ideology distorts Shakespeare's art. This question can perhaps be answered only by the students of an authentic Lonerganian, preferably late in their lives; here, however, I can briefly describe the pragmatic, five-part method by which my own pedagogy has sought, and currently seeks, to create a classroom community in which professors and students of diverse cultures mutually move towards an authentic understanding of Shakespeare's meaning and value.

"A Great Feast of Languages" (*LLL* **5.1.34-5**)
The initial step in this process is an invitation to see Shakespeare as a 'great feast of languages', a banquet of delicious linguistic delights that cannot all be sampled at once, and some of which may take time to develop a taste for, but which certainly do have an abundant objective reality. In other words, I invite students to recover a childlike wonder in the discovery of what is in many ways a new language, and many new worlds. In China, Keats' "On First Looking into Chapman's Homer"[42] was very effective for this, but now in Canada my students are also given a quotation from Anika, age 8, who as a student in the class of Lois Burdett, an extraordinary Canadian schoolteacher whose grade two class regularly performs an adapted Shakespeare play each year, made this immortal comment: "Shakespeare is like a big piece of chocolate cake. Once you've started, you wish you could go on and on forever, in a nonstopping dream".[43]

Yet this invitation is also accompanied, continuing the line in *Love's Labour's Lost*, with a warning that students not simply take "the scraps", or subsist on "the alms-basket of words" (*LLL* 5.1.37-9). In case this metaphor is itself foreign to them, I also borrow from one of my old Irish professors, who used to tell us that "reading Shakespeare while looking at the footnotes was like answering the doorbell on your wedding night".[44] Yet students do need some of the information contained in footnotes, as has already been argued, and so for each play taught I have devised scene by scene 'language sheets' that give brief translations of the most difficult Shakespearean words. The principle purpose of these sheets, paradoxically, is to enhance while also overcoming the "defamiliarization"[45] that most students encounter upon reading Shakespeare, particularly in the 'false friend' words mentioned earlier. Both denotation and connotation in Shakespeare are usually polysemous, though, and so 'creative journal' options are also assigned in which word meanings are explored through resources such as Schmidt's *Lexicon*,[46] Onion's *Glossary*,[47] the *Oxford English*

Dictionary, and concordances to other Renaissance English writers. As well as exploring the historical sense, these journals also offer the option of working on the rhetorical sense of Shakespeare's language, so important in his own literary education; in much less detail, some of the complex Renaissance analysis of tropes and schemes can be taught through Sr. Miriam Joseph's classic work on the subject,[48] and through Willard Espy's comical modern adaptation of Henry Peacham's *The Garden of Eloquence*,[49] which both entertains and instructs.

In general, Chinese students, having been through the process of grammatically reconstructing a language completely different from their own, are far superior than Canadian students in the detail with which they approach these exercises, and also in their enthusiasm for them. With Canadian students, who think they should be able to read 'English', after all, the process of 'defamiliarization' must be more direct, without intimidating them. In many ways the next category, performance, serves to do that, but one of its great teachers, John Barton, has also stated perfectly the necessity of detailed attention to Shakespeare's language: "Until we love individual words we cannot love language, and if we don't we won't be able to use it properly".[50]

"The play's the thing." (*HAM.* 2.2.604)

Barton's BBC video series,[51] with accompanying text, is an excellent way to introduce students to the process of acting Shakespeare, gaining credibility not only because of its globally known actors,[52] but moreover because these players are presented as normal people, going through a process of trial and error in trying to authentically portray a challenging dramatic text, not as 'native speakers' of Shakespeare. Barton even dismantles the myth of the 'iambic pentameter" as the constant meter of Shakespearean verse,[53] a dogma fervently believed but barely understood by most Canadian and Chinese students. Videos of actual performances are useful too, of course, but multiple clips of the same scene are highly preferable to the showing of single complete productions, which then tend to become 'the' way to perform a play, in students' minds. Stage history, of course, is an abundant source for teaching the diversity of performance possibilities, especially avant-garde productions such as Peter's Brook's 1969 stage production of *A Midsummer Night's Dream*. In addition, students usually enjoy reading the personal accounts of individual directors and actors, and responding to these in their creative journals.

All of the above, of course, is preparation for the always daunting task of in-class performance. Reviewing the rustics' sparkling performance in Act 5 of *MND* is an effective way to defuse such tension, as are the excellent exercises offered by the Folger Library's online *Performance Recipe-book*,[54] and teachers can also get competitive juices flowing by adapting, for larger groups of students, a recent Shakespeare performance game, *The Play's the Thing*.[55] Inspiring student actors to perform memorized lines may require graded motivation, however, though the option of instead 'reading with feeling' should also be retained. It also helps initially to choose characters that students can easily identify with, such as, in the post-colonial world, Caliban, though of course the many archetypal familial relations in Shakespeare are also of near-universal interest. Scenes with vigorous action, or debate, or even insults (such as those between Hermia and Helena in *MND*) are also quite popular.

Other scenes, such as those between Romeo and Juliet, or the conversion of Shylock, may strike too close to home, but performance is certainly one of the best places for encouraging inculturation. Chinese students, for example, gained confidence from Ruru Li's account of how Macbeth became Ma Pei at one of China's first full Shakespeare festivals, at Shanghai in 1986.[56] Canadian native students, for example, especially those from the Saskatchewan Indian Federated College at the University of Regina where many are studying not only Cree but also other, almost lost native languages, are often quite moved by the moment in *Richard II* when the banished Mowbray laments that his sentence is a "speechless death, / which robs my tongue from breathing native breath" (*RII* 1.3.166-7). On a lighter note, most Canadian students are quite amused to learn of the 1998 production, at Canada's Stratford Festival, which cast one of the "two gentleman of Verona" as a hockey player, and turned the stage into a roller-blading rink.[57] As for their favourite character, rural Canadian students have sometimes transformed the Fool into a kind of plain-speaking lumberjack figure, while in China the Fool became similar to the Monkey character in the classic Chinese novel *Journey to the West*, a prototype of the trickster figure who leads one to wisdom. Whatever scene is chosen, the success of the inculturation may well depend on the sense of fun and creativity with which it is approached, and for that reason my in-class performances are optional. To close again with John Barton, perhaps the most important thing for students to learning about performance is this: "Playing Shakespeare is at bottom to do with playing with words [...] Yes, playing in every sense of playing: playing a game, being zestful, using our wits, spending energy and enjoying oneself. If the actor enjoys the word games, the audience will enjoy them too".[58]

"Well demanded ... My tale provokes that question." (*TEM.* 1.2.139-40)
The first two stages, language and performance, form the basis of my students' experience of Lonergan's initial 'empirical level'. Yet of course they never remain entirely on this level, but rather frequently need also to employ the second, "intellectual level", in which they inquire further, draw connections, and thus experience a crucial moment in Lonergan's epistemology: insight. A central part of a professor's task, however, is to speed this process of inquiry along, and bring to the students' attention interpretative questions asked in other times and places by other similarly engaged, inquiring readers. But in the case of Shakespeare, of course, such a wide variety of questions have been asked that all cannot possibly be presented to the students, who in turn feel that their own questions must be repetitive and insignificant. All Shakespeareans are familiar with this feeling, an angst well expressed by Gary Taylor when he argued that the overabundance of criticism causes Shakespeare's "stellar energies" to be "trapped within the gravity well of his own reputation", allowing critics to "find in Shakespeare only what we bring to him or what others have left behind; he gives us back our own values".[59] If true, this would leave little purpose for cross-cultural dialogue, but in practice, if a professor first insists that students bring their own questions about a play to class, both old and new questions are likely to be found. For example, a number

of male Chinese students, familiar to some degree with oriental military theories, and even more so with the Chinese form of chess that is played all over the sidewalks of Beijing, saw in Hamlet's tactics not indecisive delay, but rather brilliant strategic retreats in preparation for a devastating counter-assault, and their main questions regarded how Claudius could be so easily defeated.

Once students do begin to ask their own intellectual questions, then one can begin to give handouts with the questions of others, drawn from two main categories. First, what might be called the 'perennial questions', those asked about a particular Shakespeare play in almost every age. Why is Iago able to deceive Othello? Is Duke Vincentio in *Measure for Measure* truly benevolent or merely self-serving? Why is Prospero presented as a *magus* in *The Tempest*? Most of these perennial questions are linked to the broad Aristotelian categories of which most forms of dramatic criticism usually employ at least elements: genre, plot, character, theme, diction (or style), spectacle (or performance). Second, one can also introduce the unique questions distinctively associated with particular movements in the history of literary criticism, ranging from neo-classicism, the Romantics, modernism, Marx, Freud, Eliot, and the more recent forms of theory, such as deconstruction, feminism, new historicism, or post-colonialism. Full discussion of these forms of criticism must perhaps be left to more specialized, upper-level courses, but even on introductory levels something of the variety of Shakespearean criticism can be suggested.

Though a long intellectual journey yet awaits any Shakespearean, Lonergan is convinced that the pragmatic process of continually posing questions can break 'the vicious circle' in which contemporary skepticism sees humanity trapped. Insights gained through community dialogue are not incoherent, but rather

> occur within a self-correcting process in which the shortcomings of each insight provoke further questions to yield complementary insights. Moreover, this self-correcting process tends to a limit. We become familiar with concrete situations [...] and we can recognize when [...] that self-correcting process reaches its limit in familiarity with the concrete situation and in easy mastery of it.[60]

'Mastery' may be too lofty a goal for undergraduate education, but at the very least a systematic effort of communal inquiry can achieve a richness of understanding in at least a few areas; or, to return to the metaphor of the banquet, hardy, nourishing interpretations can be shared that provide all with the sustenance needed to continue their individual intellectual journeys towards understanding Shakespeare.

"I and my bosom must debate awhile" (*HV* 4.1.32)

Are any important questions on this journey ever finally answered? Many literary critics today would say no, but Lonergan, whose epistemology is applied even to highly concrete fields of learning such as mathematics and the physical sciences, insists on the necessity of all supposed insights being challenged (as in Karl Popper's concept of 'falsification'[61]) by a third level, that of judgement; in his own words,

> the process of checking [against data] reveals in human knowledge, beyond experience and understanding, a third, constitutive level that is both self-authenticating and decisive [...] once that grasp has occurred, one cannot be reasonable and yet fail to pass judgement.[62]

Lonergan does realize that there are times when a lack of evidence means that "we can only acknowledge our ignorance",[63] and that, unlike cases in which reason may compel us to judge with absolute finality, there may also be cases requiring "probable" or tentative judgements.[64] Yet is either form of judgement necessary, or even relevant, in literary criticism or Shakespeare studies?

It may be helpful here to stress that Lonergan's "process of checking" is dialectical, a comparison of deeply opposed views, as he makes clear when his basic cognitive methods are later transposed into a "method in theology".[65] One can hardly teach some Shakespeare plays, such as *Hamlet* or *Measure for Measure*, without stressing that often Shakespeare's "typical dramatic practice" is, in Harriet Hawkins' memorable metaphor, itself dialectical: "to stack the deck, then shuffle it, to deal the cards, then leave the game, to let his witnesses plead their own cases, and let the evidence speak for itself".[66] Exploring both decks, or, in Gerald Graff's useful phrase, "teaching the conflicts",[67] is undoubtedly an essential part of what one should teach when teaching Shakespeare. Yet this question remains: when teaching the conflicts, should a professor ever express judgement on either side of the debate, or allow, perhaps even encourage, his or her students to do likewise?

Again, Shakespeare's art itself provides a clue. For unlike those plays designed to be almost endlessly dialectical, others seem to make an 'argument' (a common Renaissance term for a play), that works towards more definite conclusions. As Charles Frey argues, speaking of the late tragicomedies or 'romances',

> It has been fashionable for some years to see Shakespeare as the poet of paradox, of multivalence, complementarity, and plurisignation, as if he were a relativist par excellence. But the truth is more nearly that Shakespeare works steadily in his plays toward justifications of service, forgiveness, and familial love.[68]

Certainly one may disagree with Frey, but if neither debater could possibly be wrong, is there an authentic debate going on, or simply a rhetorical game? If the debate is to be genuine, each side must admit that it is possible to misread or misinterpret a text, and that this possibility is one of the principle reasons for bothering to debate at all. As Hawkins again explains,

> so long as we disregard any evidence against our own partial view of Shakespeare's scripts ... nothing is easier than to reinterpret them in terms of whatever ideology we personally, or professionally or politically or theologically, find especially congenial.[69]

Cannot the same be said for the ideology of relativism? Is it not possible to read Shakespeare, or any literary work, and reinterpret its evidence to avoid any definite conclusions? Lonergan's point is that there are times when the evidence may compel us to make judgements that we in conscience must regard as definitive, or at least probable, as Frey does regarding the conclusions of the romances.

Conscience is by nature deeply personal, however, and ultimately the debate, as Henry V tells us, must be between "I and my bosom" (*HV* 4.1.32). This is true not only for the strongest king or the lowliest soldier, but also the most experienced scholar and the unlearned student. It is for this reason that, while a professor must have the right, and may have the duty, to make a public, scholarly judgement, and must grant the same right to his or her students, this judgement must never be forced upon students, or demanded as 'the correct' examination answer. Liberal pedagogical practice of this kind need not slide back into relativism, however, for by the time students are operating on Lonergan's third cognitive level, their interpretations are usually well grounded in Shakespeare's texts, plausible, and coherent, even if one might disagree with their ultimate conclusions. Student response to such practice is impossible to measure quantitatively, but in my own bosom I believe that both Chinese and Canadian students deeply desire and appreciate both the intellectual integrity and interpretative freedom offered by this approach.

"Precious of Itself" (*TC* 2.2.54)

The application to literary study of Lonergan's fourth level, the 'responsible level' of evaluation and action, is perhaps even more controversial. Frye is right to warn that to "subordinate criticism to an externally derived critical attitude is to exaggerate the values in literature that can be related to the external source".[70] Students everywhere are wary of any single, dogmatic system for the reinterpretation or revaluation of Shakespeare, and the last thing my pedagogy hopes to convey is a narrowly 'Lonerganian' or 'Jesuitical' reading of Shakespeare. Yet Herrnstein-Smith is also correct when she describes the issue of the value of literature as the most "venerable, central, theoretically significant, and pragmatically inescapable" issue in literary studies.[71] Simply put, a great many readers and writers of literature have not regarded their texts as the unique, self-contained universes posited by Frye, but rather as ways of exploring and evaluating life itself. Hawkins claims that even the dialectical plays of Shakespeare have this quality, arguing that his plays give us "the very 'books' and 'counter-books' of life itself", which provide "his admirers and detractors alike with countless subjects for further speculation about art and life, and the manifold affinities and discrepancies between the two".[72] Those who view Shakespeare's plays as arguments may take such affinities even more seriously, and affirm even more strongly their desire to evaluate Shakespeare's art in relation to the broadest of moral and metaphysical questions.

Student evaluative criticism must be distinguished from the interpretative effort of the first three levels, and certainly cannot be 'graded' in any way, but to banish it entirely is to make the classroom a lifeless, inhuman place. Cross-cultural classrooms, in particular, will inevitably be sites of strong evaluative differences, but also lively debate. Beyond even the level of interpretative debate, which focuses on what meanings Shakespeare's texts can support, most non-Christian or atheist students, for example, will assign quite different value than do Christian students to crucial dramatic moments in Shakespeare such as Othello's suicide, Lear's prayer for the poor on the heath, or the numerous 'resurrections' in Shakespeare's late plays. On the other hand, since both the Canadian and Chinese political systems differ radically from the monarchies depicted in Shakespeare's plays, my students' evaluation of monarchic political authority is extremely diverse and difficult to predict. To banish such debate, or to demand that students take one side or another in it, would, in Lonergan's view, be an immoral reduction of human freedom. In the very act of debate, students from opposite, or the same, side of an argument are learning to experience what Lonergan calls "apprehensions of value",[73] a necessary prelude to any decisive judgement of value. As with interpretative debates, to deny the possibility of such decision is to impose an ethical relativism that many students will resent.

Lonergan's fourth, 'responsible' level also requires, beyond 'apprehensions' or 'judgements' of value, value-directed action, a familiar element in both Catholic and Marxist education. Beida students, for example, are on occasion required to perform cleaning duties around their university, a seemingly trivial act that does give many of them a sense of pride in their university's profound physical beauty. Though many students might resent such duties, the noted Jesuit educator Walter Burghardt would see them as illustrative of a crucial truth: "I become myself to the extent that I go out of myself".[74] The purpose of education must never be simply self-fulfillment, Burghardt stresses, for "if the normal product of our high schools and colleges is a man or woman simply of enlightened self-interest, these institutions are a peril to the human person".[75] No narrowly materialistic or utilitarian form of action should regularly be imposed upon literature students, but is any kind of organized, ethical group action possible within a university educational setting?

Since coming to Campion, this question has definitively and affirmatively been answered for me by my founding and developing ACTIO, an extracurricular literature performance group that during the past three years, at over twenty different events, has read and performed a wide variety of literary works, including many scenes from Shakespeare, in off-campus settings such as schools, libraries, and coffee shops. The group's name is borrowed from classical rhetoric, to suggest how gesture and tone in performance can expand one's understanding of literature, but its broader ethical meaning was first suggested to me, in fact, at Beida. With few friends and no intelligible entertainment outlets, my wife Jennifer (who was teaching Canadian literature and writing) and I would in our early weeks on campus complain regularly to students of our dull weekends. Soon after, students began to show up at our foreign professors' dormitory, books in hand, and before long we had a regular Friday night reading group of twenty-five to thirty students, sitting on the floor around a small two room apartment, served only tea and biscuits, there for no other reason than the beauty of hearing literature, sometimes Chinese but usually English, read aloud. Certainly the group had many differences in values, as does my current ACTIO group, but one notion that we all shared was the general worth of the literature we read. Its value on those quiet Beijing nights was not contingent, or transitive, but rather "a thing of beauty" that (as Keats said so perfectly as to make a cliché, and as my students have later confirmed in subsequent mails) "is a joy forever"[76] alive in our hearts. It is an objectively real or, in Lonerganian terms, 'authentically subjective' form of value like that which Hector speaks of when warning Troilus not to marry Cressida:

> But value dwells not in particular will
> It holds his estimate and dignity

>   As well wherein 'tis precious of itself
>   As in the prizer. (*TC* 2.2.54-6)

V. Conclusion: "Precious Winners All" (*WT* 5.3.132)

One should not idealize or exaggerate the potential of any literature, including Shakespeare, to unite cultural groups whose potentially dangerous divisions have long festered in human history, divisions which may suddenly be violently exacerbated by social and technological change. Many other forms of social and political *actio* are also needed to reduce such dangers, but meanwhile we should not miss the unique opportunities to which cross-cultural literary dialogue invites us. The post-colonial period has understandably made many sceptical of all universal claims for Shakespeare's value, such as Jonson's famous line that Shakespeare is "not of an age", and historicist criticism has taught us all how valuable it can be to read Shakespeare's plays in relation to his own historical culture. Yet in cross-cultural settings in which many cultural differences are blatantly obvious, the common threads that frequently if not universally unite human beings suddenly seem much stronger.

Jennifer and I vividly recall, for example, one afternoon when Beida hosted a picnic at which Chinese and foreign professors, representing over twenty-five nations and five continents, all brought food beloved by their own nation's taste. Despite the radical differences, and occasionally divergent preferences, all went home happy, nourished, and amazed not only by the delicious variety of food, but even more so at the human capacity to create and peacefully share such cultures with each other. Has not even richer nourishment been shared in my Shakespeare classes, in both China and Canada? In such diverse cultures' intense enjoyment of and engagement with Shakespeare's text, am I not required to see his art as not only 'not of an age', but 'not of a place', either? Often while teaching cross-culturally, I have been reminded of a passage in which the young Thomas Merton, later to be a famous American monk and poet, described why he fell in love with Shakespeare while attending Mark Van Doren's course at Columbia:

> It was the only place where I ever heard anything sensible about any of the things that were really fundamental – life, death, time, love, sorrow, fear, wisdom, suffering, eternity [...] the material of literature and especially of drama is chiefly human acts – that is, free acts, moral acts. And as a matter of fact, literature, drama, poetry, make certain statements about these acts which can be made in no other way.[77]

Merton's favourite topics are not all that Shakespeare writes about, but certainly they are common, important thematic elements of his plays. Students of most human cultures, and certainly of China and Canada, are usually seriously interested in most of these topics, even when they disagree vehemently with the perspectives offered by Shakespeare's vivid, life-like characters. Terry Eagleton may imagine a future in which a "general human enrichment" makes Shakespeare irrelevant,[78] but no matter how successful the scions of science and technology are in crafting a world without pain or suffering, and certainly the positive results over the past century do not overshadow the equally astounding rise in suffering, I am deeply sceptical that the spiritual concerns present throughout Shakespeare's works should ever fail to express key elements of human life shared by otherwise diverse cultures. Even if what today appears to be the most plausible dystopian nightmare, Huxley's *Brave New World*, does come to pass, and we all become very comfortably soma-enriched, we will always need some 'savage' from a less 'developed' culture to remind us that "what [we] need", in fact "is something with tears for a change".[79] Otherwise, no matter what the external progress, we will have lost something internal, the capacity for sorrowful pity, that is crucial to human as opposed to mechanical or animal life.

Certainly my own teaching experiences in both China and Canada leave me very hopeful that, aided by existentially engaged, inquiring, and responsible forms of pedagogy that allow both students and professors to teach each other about Shakespeare's rich value, Huxley's nightmare may never come to pass. Instead, those fortunate enough to study Shakespeare together, to see his art "performed in this wide gap of time since first / We were dissevered" by the pain of human error, and the inevitability of human difference, may yet "leisurely / Each one demand and answer to his part" in the grand drama that is human life (*WT*

5.3.153-56). As in *The Winter's Tale*, which to my mind is Shakespeare's fullest vision of that drama, such questioning and exchange will not occur without misunderstanding, division, or tragic error, but with "patience", "hope", and if we "do awake [our] faith" in each other, finally we will be "precious winners all" (*WT* 5.3.47, 128, 95, 132).

Notes

1. This and all subsequent citations from Shakespeare are to: William Shakespeare, *The Norton Shakespeare (Based on the Oxford Edition)*. Gen. Ed. Stephen Greenblatt. (New York, London: Norton, 1997).
2. In English, the name of this university is often given as "Beijing University", following *pinyin*, the newer, romanized system for transliterating Mandarin. However, in all of the English documents that were given to me during my time teaching in China, the university itself used the spelling, "Peking University".
3. "Federated" here means that Campion College is administratively independent, but its academic curriculum, faculty, and students are fully integrated with the University of Regina.
4. Margaret Avison, "The Jo-Poems", *No Time* (Hantsport, Nova Scotia: Lancelot Press), p. 19.
5. See Ma Zhenling, *Aspects of Chinese Culture* (Nankai UP, 1991).
6. Simon Blackburn, *The Oxford Dictionary of Philosophy* (Oxford UP, 1994), p. 90.
7. Edward W. Said, *Orientalism* (New York: Random House, 1979).
8. All citations from *King Lear* are to the Norton edition's conflated text.
9. John Keats, Letter to George and Thomas Keats (Dec. 21, 27 [?], *The Norton Anthology of English Literature*, ed. M.H. Abrams, 6th edn. (New York: Norton, 1993), p. 830.
10. The allusion is to Hemingway's treatise on bullfighting, *Death In the Afternoon*. 1932. (London: Jonathan Cape, 1958), p. 183. Hemingway writes: "If a writer of prose knows enough about what he is writing about he may omit things that he knows and the reader, if the writer is writing truly enough, will have a feeling of those things as strongly as though the writer had stated them. The dignity of movement of an iceberg is due to only one-eighth of it being above water."
11. This is the term currently used to describe Canada's aboriginal population.
12. The 'Metis' are a distinct cultural group, especially strong in Western Canada, who are descended from both Aboriginal and French ancestry.
13. See John W. Archer, *Saskatchewan: a History* (Saskatoon: Western Producer Prairie Books, 1980).
14. *Why Multiculturalism?* (Regina: Multicultural Council of Saskatchewan, 1999).
15. Keith Garebian, "Bringing Hamlet Home", *The Canadian Forum* (June 2000), p. 16.
16. Paulo Freire, "The 'Banking Concept of Education", from *Pedagogy of the Oppressed*, cited in *Falling into Theory:Conflicting Views on Reading Literature*, ed. David H. Richter (Boston: Bedford-St. Martins Press, 2000), p. 69.
17. Gerald Graff, "Disliking Books at an Early Age", in *Falling into Theory*, p. 45.

Shakespeare in China and Canada 105

18 On this appropriation, see Heather Murray, "Theory and Pedagogy", in the *Encyclopedia of Contemporary Literary Theory*, gen. ed. Irena R. Makaryk (Toronto UP, 1993), pp. 218-19.

19 See Robert D. Denham, *Northrop Frye and Critical Method* (University Park: Pennsylvania State UP,1979), p. 148.

20 Northrop Frye, "On Value-Judgments", in *The Stubborn Structure: Essays on Criticism and Science* (London: Methuen,1970), p. 66.

21 Denham, p. 138.

22 Barbara Herrnstein-Smith, *Contingencies of Value: Alternative Perspectives for Critical Theory* (Cambridge: Harvard UP, 1988), p. 10.

23 Mao Tse-Tung, *Quotations from Chairman Mao Tse-Tung* (Peking: Foreign Languages Press, 1967), p. 569.

24 Mao Tse-Tung, p. 563.

25 See *The Norton Shakespeare*, pp. 103-04.

26 Outstanding Canadian and Chinese examples of which would be, respectively, Molson Canadian and Tsing-dao beer.

27 Friedrich W. Nietzsche, *The Will to Power*, ed. Walter Kaufmann (New York: Random House, 1967), p. 301.

28 Friedrich W. Nietzsche, *Human, all too Human: A Book for Free Spirits*. Transl. Marion Faber (Lincoln, Nebraska: Nebraska UP, 1984), p. 16.

29 Annette Kolodney, "Dancing through the Minefield: Some Observations on the Theory, Practice, and Politics of a Feminist Literary Criticism". *Feminist Studies* 6:1 (1980), pp. 1-25.

30 Terry Eagleton, *Literary Theory: An Introduction* (Oxford: Blackwell, 1983), p. 11.

31 Eagleton, pp. 11-12.

32 Gary Taylor, *Reinventing Shakespeare: A Cultural History from the Restoration to the Present* (London: Hogarth Press, 1990), p. 395.

33 As one female Chinese student told me, "Chou Enlai was a much, much greater man than Mao because he loved only one woman!!".

34 Howard Felperin, "'Tongue-tied, our Queen?': The Deconstruction of Presence in *The Winter's Tale*", in *The Uses of the Canon: Elizabethan Literature and Contemporary Theory* (Oxford: Clarendon Press, 1990), pp. 35-55.

35 See Liu Heung Shing, *China After Mao: 'Seek Truth from Facts'"* (Harmondsworth: Penguin, 1983).

36 Bernard J.F. Lonergan, *Insight: A Study of Human Understanding* (New York: Harper, 1957, repr. 1978), preface.

37 Lonergan, *Insight*, p. 332.

38 Bernard J.F. Lonergan, *Method in Theology* (Minneapolis: Seabury, 1972, repr. 1979), p. 9.

39 Carla Mae Streeter, "Glossary of Lonerganian Terminology", *Communication and Lonergan: Common Ground for Forging the New Age* (Kansas City: Sheed & Ward), p. 327.

40 Lonergan, *Method*, p. 265.

41 Lonergan, *Method*, p. 265.

42 John Keats, "On First Looking Into Chapman's Homer", in *The Norton Anthology*, p. 769.

43 The comment was quoted by Lois Burdett in a paper that she presented to a seminar group called "Playing with the Bard: Shakespeare for Children", which met at the annual Shakespeare Association of America, April 5-8, 2000, in Montreal, Canada. Lois Burdett teaches in Stratford, Ontario, and has also written a number of books that adapt Shakespeare for young children.

44 The professor cited here is Dr. A.J. Black, who brilliantly taught Shakespeare at the University of Calgary, Canada, for over twenty years.

45 This term was popularized within literary criticism by the Russian formalists, of course, but I used it in a less specific way, based on its standard English meaning.

46 Alexander Schmidt, *Shakespeare Lexicon and Quotation Dictionary*, rev. Gregor Sarrazin (New York: Dover, 1902, 3rd edn., 1971).

47 C.T. Onions, *A Shakespeare Glossary*, rev. Robert D. Eagleson (Oxford: Clarendon Press, 1986).

48 Sister Miriam Joseph, *Shakespeare's Use of the Arts of Language* (New York: Columbia UP, 1947).

49 Willard R. Espy, *The Garden of Eloquence: A Rhetorical Bestiary* (New York: Harper, 1983).

50 John Barton, *Playing Shakespeare* (London: Methuen, 1984).

51 *Playing Shakespeare: A Nine-Part Series*, dir. John Barton, with the Royal Shakespeare Company, Films for the Humanities, 1984.

52 For example, Ben Kingsley and Patrick Stewart.

53 Barton, pp. 25-29.

54 The 1995-96 Folger Library Shakespeare Institute; Shakespeare Through Performance Project, ed. Tom Gandy, Jan.-Feb. 2000.

(*http://www.tamut.edu/english/folgerhp/folgerhp.html*)

55 *The Play's the Thing: A Dramatic Introduction to Shakespeare*. Game Creator: Annie Dean. Game Developer: Lorraine Hopping Egan (Ann Arbor, MI: Aristoplay Ltd., 1993, 2nd edn. 1999).

56 Ruru Li, "Macbeth becomes Ma Pei: An Odyssey from Scotland to China", *Theatre Research International*, 20:1 (1995), pp. 42-53.

57 Garebian, p. 18.

58 Barton, p. 117.

59 Taylor, p.411.

60 Lonergan, *Insight*, pp. 286-7.

61 See Karl Popper, *Objective Knowledge: An Evolutionary Approach* (Oxford: Clarendon Press, 1972).

62 Lonergan, *Insight*, p. 340.

63 Lonergan, *Insight*, p. 299.

64 Lonergan, *Insight*, p. 315.

65 See Lonergan, *Method*, pp. 125-48.

66 Harriet Hawkins, *The Devil's Party: Critical Counter-Interpretations of Shakespearean Drama* (Oxford: Clarendon Press, 1985), p. 82.

67 Gerald Graff, *Beyond the Culture Wars: How Teaching the Conflicts Can Revitalize American Education* (New York: Norton, 1992).
68 Charles Frey, *Shakespeare's Vast Romance: A Study of The Winter's Tale* (Columbia, MO: Missouri UP, 1980), p. 47.
69 Harriet Hawkins, *Classics and Trash: Traditions and Taboos in High Literature and Popular Modern Genres* (Toronto UP, 1990), pp. 130-1.
70 Northrop Frye, *Anatomy of Criticism* (Princeton UP, 1957), p. 7.
71 Herrnstein-Smith, p. 17.
72 Hawkins, *Devil's*, p. 63.
73 Lonergan, *Method*, p. 37.
74 Walter Burghardt, *Seasons that Laugh or Weep: Musings on the Human Journey* (New York: Paulist Press, 1983), p. 37.
75 Burghardt, p. 37.
76 John Keats, *Endymion: A Poetic Romance*, in *The Norton Anthology*, p. 772.
77 Thomas Merton, *The Seven Storey Mountain* (New York: Harcourt Brace, 1948), p. 180.
78 Eagleton, p. 12.
79 Aldous Huxley, *Brave New World* (Hammersmith, London: TriadGrafton, 1932, repr.1977), p. 236.

MULTIVALENT SHAKESPEARE: THE SPANISH CONNECTION

Hugh Macrae Richmond
(University of California, Berkeley)

This essay is not about classroom devices for the improvement of teaching. We are hardly short of innovative procedures and technology. It is about states of mind affecting cultural relationships, which are the underlying complicating factors in achieving educational progress under current metropolitan conditions in such cities as London, New York and Los Angeles. For example, California's urban centers have now reached an extreme of multicultural complexity which affects teachers at every level. Thus the largest ethnic group of present students at U.C. Berkeley are of Asian extraction. However, because of their concern to confirm mastery of English expression, I have found that many continue to consider its supreme writer, Shakespeare, to be a necessary part of their undergraduate experience, whether they aim to become engineers, lawyers, doctors, or sociologists. On the other hand, speakers of Spanish will approach a majority in the state as a whole early in this new century, so the Shakespeare Program at U.C.B. is currently developing a project called "Shakespeare, California, and the Spanish Connection" using the continuities of the Spanish and English dramatic traditions as a cultural bridge. In contrast to this largely Catholic tradition, substantial numbers of the professionals in the Bay Area, including university faculty, staff, and students, are Jewish, yet I have been able to lecture successfully on Shakespeare at Jewish community centers and to other sectarian groups from Catholics to Unitarians about religious issues which Shakespeare raises in his presentation of characters such as the Jewish Shylock, the puritan Angelo, and the Catholic Cardinal Wolsey.

However, the multi-ethnic problem is less finite than these readily resolved challenges: typical metropolitan areas such as Los Angeles and Oakland now share with east London (U.K.) the coexistence of over seventy different linguistic and ethnic groups in their schools. The possible permutations of language, national origin, religious affiliation and cultural focus approach the infinite and any educational consensus might appear unlikely either in appropriate methodology or relevant content as far as cultural consistency is concerned. My argument here is that, in literary studies, the contrary is true, as the African ex-slave, Terence, once asserted: "homo sum, et humani nihil alienum a me puto": "I am human, and nothing human is foreign to me." Not for nothing was Shakespeare called "our English Terence" (John Davis, c. 1611, *Shakespeare Allusion Book*, I.219). The degrees of separation may be more limited than one might expect, in cultures as in individuals. If we can integrate and synthesisize these cultures in such a spirit, they can become mutually reinforcing instead of potentially divisive.

In my experience, some modern academics' pessimism about the relevance of the traditional literary canon to the complexities of most modern societies is simply inappropriate. Compatibility can be clearly perceived in the light of the classic tradition as it applies to my own preferred field of "archaic" literary studies, running from the Homeric world as refracted through Greek drama, the diversity of Latin verse, the medieval cosmology of Dante, the syncretic capacity of Chaucer, the comprehensiveness of Shakespeare, and the encyclopedic consolidation achieved by Milton, not to mention the archetypal resonances of the Romantics. For my definition of a classic is not determined by Harold Bloom's *The Anxiety of Influence*, with its Oedipal sense of authors' obsessive rejection of the masters of the past, but by a classic's heroic consolidation of tradition in a way which can be continually redeployed to meet the needs of the present. Each classic text enshrines a distinctive phase of human culture focussed on a formative event in human civilization which is eternally and universally relevant.

If we take my earliest example of Homer, we find that his two epics define the archetypal encounter of proto-European cultures with those of non-European societies, as displayed by the confrontation between the Greek Hellenes and the Trojans, who represent an epitome of Middle Eastern civilizations. However, while we may believe the Greeks provide our supreme cultural precedents, historically the Middle Eastern cultures have their own relevance to Western civilization, as validated by modern archeological study of the trade routes from Phoenicia, to Carthage, thence to Iberia, and finally to the Northern Islands by the western sea-route favored by Shakespeare in *Cymbeline* (as a typical pre-Roman traveler, Imogen sets out westward for the Mediterranean via Milford Haven in Wales, not eastwards via Dover). British mythology claims that the genesis of its culture is owed to the Middle East, as figured in the legends of Aeneas and his grandson Brutus. This imaginative genealogy is sustained by the Elizabethan alternative to the name of the city of London, as seen in Spenser's *Faerie Queene*: Troy Novant, or New Troy. In corroboration, at the opposite end of Great Britain, an Iberian bull-cult (ultimately derived from Crete along similar trade routes) survived near my home in the Scottish Highlands until the nineteenth century. The *Iliad* and the *Aeneid* are thus intimately linked to the definition of European values as contrasted to those of the Middle East, yet the latter are still postulated as radical to the first recognizable British identity formed in the Bronze Age. Indeed, in a recent "New York Times" article, Nicholas Wade has described how modern geneticists have argued that a significant proportion of the modern population of the British Isles display a DNA which confirms this tortuous cultural evolution. Knowing these precedents makes it easier to understand why Shakespeare's *Troilus and Cressida* often seems to favor the gallant Trojans over the cynical Greeks, Hellenising academics notwithstanding.

By insisting on such cultural interconnections, I find it possible to correlate seemingly disconnected ethnic groups, challenging the parochialism of some recent literary approaches which are too narrow-minded and divisive to match the character and needs of a modern multi-cultural society. Teachers need a broader sense of context if a positive assimilation of multicultural experience is to be attained, rather than a fragmented mosaic of each culture's more local, often chauvinistic achievements defined by adversary versions of their relationships. This interpenetration of cultures is deeper and subtler than the recent superficies of technological literary criticism such as the New Criticism can define. This detection of comprehensive continuity can lend plausibility to the relevance of seemingly remote texts and arts. For example, as all encyclopedias record, the Buddhist sculpture of Asia is derived from that of Periclean Athens, via the settlement of Greeks established in Gandhara by Alexander the Great during his incursions into Northwest India. East and west did meet and could understand each other.

This complexity of ethnic interaction might seem to suggest that so explicitly 'English' a poet as Shakespeare can no longer serve as a multi-cultural focus or learning catalyst, but we have already seen his accommodation of my argument in his recension of the Trojan War in *Troilus and Cressida*. Indeed, his coverage of the full chronological and geographical range of most cultures known to Renaissance Europe is remarkably comprehensive (see Appendix). Cultural assimilation can be accelerated by educational uses of Shakespeare along these lines with extremely positive effects for teachers, as we have already discovered in a recent experiment. For the approach has been applied in the multicultural context of the restored Globe Theatre in Southwark, in south-east London, where we have run joint programs for teachers from all over the U.S.A. in company with English instructors teaching in Southwark, themselves exposed to innumerable differing ethnic immigrant groups.

In order to make this process of cultural assimilation fully explicit in such situations, I shall not attempt a generalized account of the many possible correlations, but describe in detail our current specific concern in California to assimilate Shakespeare to the Hispanic tradition in a way urgently relevant to all teachers in modern California, since, in *California in the New Millenium*, Mark Baldassare has demonstrated that in twenty years California will have a population of which 50% are derived from Spanish-speaking backgrounds, and the state will become effectively bilingual. The basic requirement for positive interaction and creative reinforcement will be to establish the coexistence of significant Anglo-Hispanic traditions which are parallel, even identical, and mutually supportive, because they derive from identical roots. A true cultural synthesis can be built on awareness of this complementarity, compatibility, even community of the two traditions.

To validate my assertions about this unexpected cultural complementarity of the Anglo-Hispanic traditions, it is necessary to overthrow the prejudicial dogma about earlier phases in their relationship. The 'patriotic' version of the English relations with Spain from 1500 to 1700 is founded on one phase of these two centuries alone: the piratical adventures of Hawkins, Drake and their ilk, with the consequent Spanish response of the Armada, as seen in Charles Kingsley's *Westward Ho!* However, such adversary aspects of the reign of Elizabeth contrast with the relationship during her sister's marriage to Philip II, not to mention the major period of Queen Katherine of Aragon's marriage to Henry VIII. Moreover, Eamon Dufy has argued in *The Stripping of the Altars* that the English were far less committed to the Reformation than the Anglican tradition would have it, while much of the missionary work in Elizabethan England was carried out by the Spanish Jesuit Order, with whom the Shakespeare family may even have been associated if we are to believe E.A.J. Honigmann's investigation of their recusant potentialities and the theories of Richard Wilson.

Indeed, the more we go back to examine such earlier periods, the more we find congruences between the two national traditions. For example, the Renaissance in both England and Spain followed tardy and incomplete patterns in marked contrast with Italian sophistication and progressiveness. The western European countries both maintained a provincial archaism and pragmatic dubiousness about Italian neoclassical aesthetics as displayed in the constraints of the unities. Leading practitioners in both countries such as Lope de Vega and Shakespeare subordinated the unities to popular taste which favored a highly mixed genre that came to be called tragicomedy, in which sentiment and low humor were realistically comingled. Lope's ironic verse treatise, *L'arte nuevo de hacer comedias en esto tiempo* might well stand as the best contemporary statement of the aesthetic governing Shakespearean drama, providing an implicit refutation of the supercilious code of censure in such academic criticism as Sidney's *Defence of Poetry*. It is not fortuitous that some two hundred English play titles of the period include the word "Spanish".

Multivalent Shakespeare: The Spanish Connection

Shakespeare himself was more significantly interested in Spanish culture than conventional judgment admits. The sources for *The Two Gentlemen of Verona* and the lost *Cardenio* are drawn from the tradition of Montemajor and Cervantes. In *Love's Labour's Lost*, the bravura of Don Armado shares that of the latter author's hero. The plot of *Much Ado* turns on the failure of the two prominent Spanish leaders, the Prince of Aragon, Don Pedro, and his bastard half-brother Don John, to assimilate their Spanish obsession about personal honor to the suppler culture of their Italian subjects in Messina. Indeed, as I have proposed in my essay "Much Ado About Notables", the figure of the Bastard Don John may not be wholly an invention of Shakespeare, since the historical Bastard Don John of Austria (1545-1578) was notorious throughout England for just such bravado and viciousness, as registered in the accounts of Walsingham's secret agents, who described his manic behavior in endless confrontations with his half-brother, Philip II (527-1608) King of Spain, and ruler of Messina as King of Naples and Sicily (he was also brother-in-law to Queen Elizabeth). As in the play, Don John's bastardy denied him the recognition which he felt was his due, particularly in the lack of recognition when he returned to Messina in 1571 after leading the Christian fleets to successful battle at Lepanto with the Turks (in which he was assisted by Cervantes). Don John was widely feared and hated in England as the first instigator of the idea of an Armada against England designed to capture Mary Queen of Scots, whom Don John would marry in order to secure himself on the throne of England. His arrogance and aggressiveness attracted several other artistic incarnations in the period, for he appears in an equally aggressive role in *Love After Death*, a play of Pedro Calderón de la Barca (1600-1681) about Don John's role in the final extermination of Moorish culture in Spain. It is also startling to find that Diego Velázquez (1599-1660), like Shakespeare, portrayed the macabre figure of Don John in the guise of a saturnine clown, in a painting now in the Prado. Neither celebrated the more heroic aspects of this noted general. Moreover, the career of Velázquez at the Spanish court approximates to that of Shakespeare at that of James I, and both artists shared a down-to-earth skepticism about royalty and the aristocracy while cherishing the roles of actors, clowns and buffoons. Velázquez himself even took a female role in one court performance, and his painting, *Las Hilanderas*, reflects an identical socially layered aesthetic to *A Midsummer Night's Dream*, with which it shares a devotion to Ovidian narratives, not to mention the artistic ambitions of professional weavers, shared by Bottom and Arachne (who is the true focus of Velázquez' painting as identified in its original title: *The Story of Arachne*). See Harry Eyres.

The most overt example of Shakespeare's empathy with a Spanish figure must be seen in his climactic female role, in which Sarah Siddons excelled even her famous Lady Macbeth: Queen Katherine of Aragon in *Henry VIII*. She was encouraged to attempt this part because of Samuel Johnson's belief that it constituted the highest ahievement of Shakespeare's art. According to J. D. Mackie's Oxford history of "The Early Tudors" (328), the unfair treatment of the historical Queen Katherine (1485-1536) earned her "much sympathy" from the English, as the responsible counsellor of her spouse which Shakespeare carefully shows her to be in *Henry VIII*. Shakespeare uses his presentation of her divorce to challenge the attack on his 'romances' as "mouldy tales" which Shakespeare encountered from his protégé Ben Jonson in his "Ode to Himself". The very title of *A Winter's Tale* is capped by the original one for *Henry VIII: All Is True*. In no scene is this pretention more apparent than in the trial of the Queen, which not only closely follows the legal proceedings but was also probably staged in the same space as the orginal trial, when the first production had to be switched to the Blackfriar's Theatre after the Globe Theatre burned down. Katherine's insight, dignity, and humility under extreme stress appear heroic in Shakespeare, and illustrative of the highest feminine excellence, as celebrated by her daughter Mary's tutor, the Spanish humanist Juan Vives (1492-1540), in *De institutiones feminae christianae*. Henry's cynical treatment of his Spanish wife was the first tragic step towards the Elizabethan confrontation with Spain, which Shakespeare's sympathetic treatment of Katherine mitigates retrospectively. Significantly the trial scene is similarly recreated by Pedro Calderón de la Barca (1600-1681) in *La Cisma de Inglaterra*.

Multivalent Shakespeare: The Spanish Connection 115

Such local Hispanic allusions may be less significant than the remarkable similarity between the theatrical practices of the Spanish and English theatres of the Renaissance in general, which share more than avoidance of the rigid neoclassicism which caused Sir Philip Sidney to censure contemporary Elizabethan drama. The Spanish *corrales* of the sixteenth century were open-air arenas almost identical in structure and conventions to those of Elizabethan London, with thrust stages, backed by a curtain, and set in a galleried open court, with little scenery. Indeed some of these theatres have survived to illustrate the actual format only approximated to in the reconstructed Globe Theatre in Southwark. Moreover, in the preference for the mixed genre of tragicomedy to the distinct genres of comedy and tragedy, the two traditions anticipate the conventions of modern drama. Like Cinthio in Italy, Lope shared Shakespeare's willingness to accommodate the indiscriminate tastes of his popular audiences rather than accept the fetters of academic theory.

There are long-established obstacles to the modern assimilation of such Hispanic traditions to any existing 'Anglo' norms in California. The first is radical denial of any parity of the two cultures, as George MacMinn's theatrical history of "The Theater of the Golden Era in California" illustrates, ignoring the significance of colonial drama in California by beginning with the Gold Rush period. When I first arrived in Berkeley in 1957, I was told flatly by my Chairman, a leading Americanist, that the history of California as a whole really began with the Gold Rush, as the society of the colonial period was insignificant and irrelevant to modern Californians. However, I soon found that the high Renaissance, baroque, and rococo styles displayed in the art of Milton and his contemporaries were memorably illustrated in the syncretic aesthetics of the restored missions and Presidios of Alta California. Nevertheless, at a major research centre, I was recently still told that pre-1848 California was a "black hole", devoid of culture because there was simply "no-one here" to enjoy it. My earlier attempts to correct such views by encouraging graduate-student research in Anglo-Spanish relations were hindered because graduate students were not even authorized to submit Spanish as a suitable language to satisfy the linguistic skills prequisite to taking the Qualifying Examination for doctoral studies in the English Department. When I started to investigate the Californian theatre tradition, I was told bluntly and repeatedly that there were no early theatres and no manuscripts of plays in the state's regional collections, and no significant continuities with European culture before 1848.

Fortunately, I received other indications to the contrary, demonstrating continuities between Calderón and the Mexican nun Sor Juana who wrote comedies like *The Trials of a Noble House* and *Love Is the Greater Labyrinth*, as well as religious plays such as her *autos sacramentales*, *The Staff of Joseph* and *The True Narcissus*, in the tradition of religious drama running back beyond Calderón to the Middle Ages. Her precedent in turn led me to the Californian scripts of *pastorelas* or Christmas plays in the medieval tradition. This type of performance was diffused throughout California by the culture of the missions, which regularly staged *pastorelas* such as *Los Pastores* of Padre Florencio Ibañez, with its affinities to the English medieval cycles. This play was performed throughout the California chain of missions. Written in 1805, it sustained the tradition of medieval drama which flourished both in England and Spain in celebration of the Festival of Corpus Christi. Indeed, this Californian script closely resembles the celebration of Christmas in the *Second Shepherd's Play*, in theme, concepts, devices, and characterization.

Meanwhile, in the 1840s one of my Scottish compatriots, Jack Swan, followed the pattern of secular performances by the Spanish and Mexican military at the presidios. He opened up the ground floor rooms of a row of houses in Monterey to create a long hall for use as the first commercial theatre in California, well before the Gold Rush (and still in operation). Jack Swan staged swashbuckling melodramas in the Spanish vein, but he also established crucial Shakespearean precedents by staging *The Story of the Gadshill Robbery*, from Shakespeare's Drama of *King Henry IV*, and even *Richard III*. The latter play became a favorite in the Gold-Rush townships along with *Hamlet*, *The Taming of the Shrew*, and *The Merchant of Venice*. The miners flocked to see distinguished Shakespearean actors such as Edwin Booth. The flourishing Californian traditions of Spanish and English drama in the first half of the nineteenth century led to the creation of a distinctively vigorous 'western' style of classical acting in the second half of the century, as practiced by Edwin Booth. This dynamic theatre no doubt explains why one of its representatives, Davis Belasco, was able to dominate the New York theatre later in the century, as described in Craig Timberlake's biography (1954).

So from the early nineteenth century we have two simultaneous and complementary traditions flourishing, one traceable back through the Mexican drama of Sor Juana and the baroque art of Calderón deep into the culture of the Middle Ages which Spain shared with England, while the other referred directly back to the Shakespearean dramas of Renaissance England. Cultural complementarity already existed before the Forty-niners showed up on any horizon. But my crucial point is that this complementarity of Spanish and English theatrical traditions in the Middle Ages, Renaissance and nineteenth century remains current and significant today. I recently attended the Chamizal Festival of Classic Hispanic Drama at El Paso and was delighted to see Juan Ruiz de Alarçon's comedy *The Liar*, as originally staged in Los Angeles by the Antaeus Company, led by Dakin Matthews, with whom I had worked when he was Artistic Director of the Berkeley Shakespeare Festival. The Chamizal Festival is now recognized as the principal celebration of classical Spanish drama worldwide, and it was impressive to see a California production in such distinguished company. More locally, I have been charmed to see the use of Shakespeare providing speech training for mostly Spanish-speaking immigrant children in the full-length productions of Rafe Esquith's Hobart Shakespeareans, based in a Los Angeles primary school whose clientele is largely derived from children with English as their second language. These ten-year olds are actually echoing a nineteenth-century tradition of youthful performers such as the nine-year-old Ellen Bateman, who excelled on California stages in such roles as Richard III, Shylock, Lady Macbeth, and Hamlet. Like my own experience, Rafe Esquith's shows that the perfecting of a Shakespeare performance through repeated rehearsal can also be an excellent way of training equally youthful non-English-speaking students in accurate pronunciation and phrasing of modern English (as we see in the vocal talents of many inheritors of the traditions of British India, such as the ITV presenter Daljit Dhaliwal on ITV/PBS). Similarly in Los Angeles, Jill Holden's Shakespeare Unbound achieves mastery of English among Spanish-speaking students and an appreciation of Spanish language via her bilingual stagings of Shakespeare. These are all part of a interactive pattern of Hispanic and Anglo traditions which are essential if California is to achieve mutual recognition of two of its great cultural traditions.

My final point is therefore that teaching devices and techniques are not the only way to enhance cultural awareness and understanding: there should be a deeper, more positive recognition of shared traditions and their significant interrelation. To enhance this recognition, the Shakespeare Program at U.C. Berkeley has undertaken an outreach to two major multi-cultural communities with strong Hispanic elements: Los Angeles and Oakland. In two two-day programs we begin one evening with examples of the shared dramatic tradition in as series of performances by groups such as the Antaeus Company, the Hobart Shakespeareans, and the Shakespeare Unbound Company. The following day we explore the two complementary traditions authoritatively with the aid of such experts as Professor J. Jay Allen (consultant in the Spanish recovery of Renaissance *corrales*), Professor Susana Hernández Araico (expert on Calderón's bearing on Shakespeare), Director Jean Bruce Poole of the Pueblo de los Angeles State Park (which is restoring the 19th-century Merced Theatre), docent and performer Stephen Harris of the Swan Theatre of Monterey State Park, and other experts in Anglo-Hispanic relations. At very least we hope to enhance mutual awareness and respect, but we also want to demonstrate that dramatic performance is one key to cultural enrichment and even to advances in basic language skills. That Shakespeare anticipated such a role for his work in places like multicultural California is indicated in his own words at the climax of *Julius Caesar*:

> How many ages hence
> Shall this our lofty scene be acted over
> In states unborn and accents yet unknown. (3.1.111-3)

Multivalent Shakespeare: The Spanish Connection

APPENDICES

I. SHAKESPEARE: A CULTURAL CHRONOLOGY

	BRITAIN	EUROPE	ELSEWHERE
PREHISTORY:			
VENUS & ADONIS		Prehistoric Mythology	
M. N. DREAM		Theseus: Legendary Greece	
TWO NOBLE KINSMEN		Theseus: Legendary Greece	
TROILUS & CRESSIDA			2nd Millenium Troy: Middle East
KING LEAR	Legendary Ancient Britain		
CLASSICAL GREECE:			
TIMON OF ATHENS		Classical Athens	
COMEDY OF ERRORS			Pre-Christian Levant
PERICLES PRINCE OF TYRE			
WINTER'S TALE		Magna Graecia: Pre-Christian Sicily	
CLASSICAL ROME:			
RAPE OF LUCRECE		Pre-Republican Rome	
CORIOLANUS		Early Republican Rome	
JULIUS CAESAR		Late Republican Rome	
ANTONY & CLEOPATRA		Early Roman Empire:	Africa, Asia Minor
CYMBELINE	Pre-Roman Britain	Imperial Rome	
TITUS ANDRONICUS		Late Imperial Rome/Goths	Moorish
DARK AGES:			
HAMLET	Danish conquests	Amlethi Saga: 6th C. Scandinavia	
KING LEAR	King Edgar: 9th C. Saxon		
MACBETH	12th C. Scotland		
MIDDLE AGES:			
KING JOHN	13th C. England	13th C. France	
KING RICHARD II	14th C. England		
KING HENRY IV	15th C. England		
KING HENRY V	15th C. England	15th C. France	
KING HENRY VI	15th C. England	15th C. France	
KING RICHARD III	15th C. England		
RENAISSANCE:			
MERRY W. OF WINDSOR	15th/16th C. England		
HAMLET		16th C Reformation: Wittenburg	
SIR THOMAS MORE	16th C. England		
HENRY VIII	16th C. England		
ALL'S WELL		15th/16th C. France: Midi	
AS YOU LIKE IT		15th/16th C. France: Ardennes	
ROMEO & JULIET		14th/15th C. Verona	
TWO GENTLEMEN OF VERONA		15th/16th C. Verona	
TAMING OF THE SHREW		16th C. Padua	
MERCHANT OF VENICE		16th C. Venice	
OTHELLO		16th C. Venice	Cyprus (& N.Africa)
MUCH ADO		16th C. Sicily: Messina	
TWELFTH NIGHT		16th C. Balkans: Illyria	
MEASURE FOR MEASURE		16th C. Reformation Vienna	
[CARDENIO]		[16th C. Spain]	
LOVE'S LABOUR'S LOST		Late 16th C. France: Navarre	
TEMPEST		17th C. Med./ Atlantic (Caliban = Cannibal= Caribal)	

II. Conference Program:
Shakespeare, California, & the Spanish Connection

Two conferences present groups which help advance Anglo-Hispanic cultural interaction, via the relation of Shakespeare to his Spanish contemporaries as a model for multicultural understanding in modern California. The first session will be on 3-4 November 2000 at a Los Angeles District High School; the second, at the Valley Center for the Performing Arts at Holy Names College, Oakland, 23-25 Feb. 2001, as follows: BASIC PROGRAM SCHEDULE FOR LOS ANGELES & OAKLAND Friday evening, 7.30-9.30 p.m.: Pre-Conference Event, Also Free To Saturday Participants: Performances & Discussions of Anglo/Hispanic Culture: 1. Hobart School: "Shakespeare in Multicultural Contexts" 2. Shakespeare Unbound: "Shakespeare & Spanish" 3, Antaeus Company: "Spanish Renaissance Comedy Now" Saturday 9.30 a.m. - 5 p.m. 9.-9.30 a.m. Arrival 9.30-9.50 Welcomes: [October Event: by the Los Angeles Host Institution, the Los Angeles Unified School District] [February Event: President Holy Names College; City of Oakland Representative; H.N.C. Professor Patricia MacMahan] 9.50-10.15 Professor Hugh Richmond (U.C. Berkeley): "Shakespeare and Hispanic Culture in the Renaissance and in California." With video & slide illustrations. 10.25-10.45 Director Louis Fantasia (Shakespeare Globe Centre West): "Shakespeare as a Bridge to other Non-English-Speaking Communities." 10-45-11 Break 11.-12.30 "Shakespeare in Multicultural Contexts" lectures & discussions by Theater Directors Rafe Esquith; Jill Holden; Dakin Matthews; an Oakland leader, with student discussants 12.30-1.30 Lunch 1.30-2. Professor Susana Hernández Araico (Cal. Poly. Pomona):"Spanish Renaissance Drama." Actors present classic texts in English & Spanish, with commentary and audience reactions. 2.-2.30 Professor Velma Bourgeois Richmond: "Shakespeare & the Catholic Tradition in Drama" 3.-3.15 Break 3.15-4.15 Round Table: "Hispanic Theatre: Spain to California" Director Hugh Richmond as Moderator with: Professor Jay Allen (U. Kentucky): "Spanish Stages Then & Now" Director Jean Bruce Poole: "Restoring the Merced Theater at the Pueblo de Los Angeles." Docent Stephen Harris: "Early Monterey and the Swan Theater." With audience questions, comments, and discussion. 4.30-5.15 Jill Holden: "Private Stories, Public Schools"

Bibliography

Baldassare, Mark. *California in the New Millenium: the Changing Social and Political Landscape.* Berkeley: California UP, 2000.

Duffy, Eamon. *The Stripping of the Altars: Traditional Religion in England 1400-1580.* New Haven: Yale UP, 1992.

Eyres, Harry. "Discovering Velázquez." *Daily Telegraph,* 11 June 1999, p. 25.

Honigmann, A.E.J. *Shakespeare: the "Lost Years".* Manchester: Manchester University Press, 1985, rev. edn. 1998.

Ibañez, Padre Florencio. *Los Pastores: An Old California Christmas Play,* transl. Maria Lopéz de Lowther. Hollywood: H.H. Boelter, 1957.

Mackie, J.D. *The Early Tudors, 1485-1558.* Oxford: Clarendon Press, 1972.

MacMinn, George R. *The Theater of the Golden Era in California.* Caldwell, Idaho: Caxton, 1941.

Paz, Ottavio. *Sor Juana.* Cambridge: Harvard UP, 1988.

Richmond, H. M. "Much Ad About Notables", *Shakespeare Studies,* 12 (1979), 49-63.

Rosas, Juan Manuel. *Significado y doctrina del 'Arte nuevo' de Lope de Vega.* Madrid: Sociedad General Española de Libreria, 1976.

Shakespeare Allusion Book: A Collection of Allusions to Shakespeare from 1591 to 1700, ed. C.M. Ingleby et al. London: Gollancz, 1909; repr. Freeport NY: Books for Libraries, 1990.

Timberlake, Craig. *The Bishop of Broadway [:David Belasco].* New York: Library Publishers, 1954.

Wade, Nicholas, "Researchers Trace Roots of the Irish to Spain". *New York Times,* 23 March 2000, A13.

Wilson, Richard, " Shakespeare and the Jesuits", *Times Literary Supplement,* 19 December, 1997, 11-13.

"HERE IS NOT A CREATURE BUT MYSELF": SHAKESPEAREAN RECEPTION IN SOLITARY CONFINEMENT

Laura Raidonis Bates
(Indiana State University)

I have been studying how I may compare
This prison where I live unto the world;
And, for because the world is populous
And here is not a creature but myself,
I cannot do it. Yet I'll hammer it out.
My brain I'll prove the female to my soul,
My soul the father, and these two beget
A generation of still-breeding thoughts,
And these same thoughts people this little world,
In humours like the people of this world;
For no thought is contented. The better sort,
As thoughts of things divine, are intermix'd
With scruples, and do set the word itself
Against the word.
As thus: "Come, little ones"; and then again,
"It is as hard to come as for a camel
To thread the postern of a small needle's eye".
Thoughts tending to ambition, they do plot
Unlikely wonders: how these vain weak nails
May tear a passage through the flinty ribs
Of this hard world, my ragged prison walls;
And for they cannot, die in their own pride.
Thoughts tending to content flatter themselves
That they are not the first of fortune's slaves,
Nor shall be the last – like silly beggars
Who, sitting in the stocks, refuge their shame,
That many have and others must sit there;
And in this thought they find a kind of ease,
Bearing their own misfortunes on the back
Of such as have before indur'd the like.
Thus play I in one person many people,
And none contented. [...]
But whate'er I be,
Nor I, nor any man that but man is,
With nothing shall be pleas'd, till he be eas'd
With being nothing. (*Richard II*, 5.5.1-38)[1]

Scholars and literary critics can interpret this speech from a variety of perspectives: Marxists can celebrate Richard's exposure of religious hypocrisy; psychoanalytic critics can see in it evidence of his schizophrenic personality; while feminists can argue that "any *woman* who but woman is" has the right to feel equally discontented. But on a more literal level, Richard II's final soliloquy – delivered from his isolated prison cell in Pomfret Castle – can be truly appreciated only by those who have experienced solitary imprisonment themselves. To fully comprehend Richard's sense of isolation and aloneness you, too, would have to enter Richard's "little world" – literally.

Today, you would have to pass through the multiple rows of razor-wire fencing that surround the prison compound and enter the "ragged walls" of this "hard world". Abandoning daylight and fresh air, within the super-maximum security division that houses the segregated cells reserved for the most extreme criminal offenders, you would again pass through several sets of iron gates, each patrolled by armed guards who monitor your every movement. Eventually, you would reach a long concrete corridor leading into another world: where prisoners are isolated from human contact and contained within small, bare windowless cages with concrete walls, concrete floors, and concrete beds. You would be sealed inside, behind a door made of institutional green steel peg-board that distorts your vision as you try to peer in – or out.

"There's no way you can know what it's like for us in here", one prisoner is quoted as saying.[2] But did Shakespeare, as further evidence of his universality, in a sense 'know'? To answer this question, you would have to smuggle his text into this harsh environment and examine its reception by "such as have indur'd the like".

And that is what I did.

In previous papers, I have written about other texts I have presented to inmates, arguing the same two-part thesis: The study of Shakespeare has much to offer a prison population – and a prison population has much to offer the study of Shakespeare. In more traditional contexts, I have worked with some of the most prominent Shakespeare scholars in the world – from David Bevington at the University of Chicago to Stanley Wells at the Shakespeare Institute in Stratford-upon-

Avon – but I am also indebted to the gang members who have taught me to appreciate the violent society that shapes Romeo and Juliet's lives, and the murderers who have helped me understand Macbeth's troubled conscience.

Last summer, having acquired access through the educational program for which I teach college-level courses in a number of correctional facilities, I read Richard's soliloquy one-on-one through the metal peg-board doors at the individual cells of more than thirty male inhabitants in four wings of the Segregated Housing Unit [SHU] at the Wabash Valley Correctional Facility.

On my first visit to SHU, an officer escorted me to the upper level of the 'pod', a central control zone that connects four physically separated tiers, each tier containing twelve cells. Gates below are opened by remote control; even officers do not physically enter the tiers – unless a forced 'extraction' is necessary. From this vantage point, there was the sense of an uninhabited place: no sounds could be heard; no movement was visible through the security cameras, which monitor only the empty space at the front of each tier.

Left completely unattended after this brief introduction, I entered the lower level of the pod alone. "Open A, please!" I called out to the guard at the glassed-in control board upstairs, and he pushed the button that released the sliding iron gate. I stepped forward to approach the row of cells, and – as the gate clanged shut again behind me – entered an area out of the range of the security monitors.

The shouts that greeted me were those to be expected of a group of male offenders who have had no regular human (let alone, female) contact for years. They were also a sort of public display intended largely for show – or, I should say, for 'hearing', since the inmates in SHU cannot see into one another's cells (except on their way to the shower at the end of the tier). Women in solitary are especially unwelcome by the authorities, partly due to the stages of undress of the inmates. Because of the stifling heat of the facility and the general inactivity of the inmates' existence, most of my Shakespearean study took place with convicted felons in their underwear. Furthermore, because I arrived 'unannounced', I sometimes stepped up to a cell door to greet an inmate who was in the process of urinating, or masturbating.

Shakespearean Reception in Solitary Confinement 125

I approached the first cell; I could see nothing through the peg-board door because there was no light on inside (many inmates seemed to prefer to sit in darkened cells, turning on their light only when I arrived and then turning it off again as soon as I left). I called out the inmate's name and, with some difficulty, I opened the 'cuff port' – the heavy metal door to the small slot through which food trays are inserted (and through which inmates must place their hands to be cuffed prior to an extraction). I asked Don what kinds of reading he enjoyed and soon learned that the most popular reading material in solitary confinement was 'true crime' stories and novels, followed by the Bible. A few were working independently on their GED – although college students who were sent to solitary (as some of mine have been) automatically lose their educational 'privilege'. I asked Don if he'd be interested in reading a text by Shakespeare. "Shakespeare?" he replied. "Ain't he the one that's quoted all the time? Hey, did he say, 'A lie can make it all the way around the earth before the truth can put on its boots'? I don't remember where I heard it, but I like that one." Another inmate responded equally eagerly because he had heard that Shakespeare wrote the Bible. Whatever their individual reasons, I accepted their enthusiasm.

I took out a copy of my specially prepared text (devoid of footnotes, in easy-to-read twelve-point Helvetica type, and broken into six blocks of text separating the main ideas – but with very few textual alterations) and set the paper on the 'table' of the opened cuff-port ledge. To block out the din of the fans and the shouts of the other inmates, I leaned in close to the peg-board door, which allowed me to see only thirty percent of my fellow reader. My finger scanned the lines of the paper as we read; it was joined by a tattooed hand that emerged from within the cell and followed along – never straying from the text.

With little academic preparation, no previous Shakespeare experience, and all of the mental challenges that solitary imprisonment represents, the fact that they could engage with the text on any level at all is a remarkable testimony both to the readers and the text. In what might be considered a 'close critical reading', inmates examined every word of this speech and, one after another, they validated Shakespeare's vision of solitary confinement: "Here is no creature but myself" rang true for one who emphasized that he had not seen a bird in five years. Another understood Richard's "difficulty in trying to have a rational thought without the mixture of other thoughts" in this mentally challenging environment. And more than one confessed that he, too, had at times plotted the unlikely wonder of "tear[ing] a passage through these flinty ribs".

Other inmates were intrigued by the text but hesitant about reading it with me, so I slid a copy through the tiny crack between the steel door and the concrete wall – in legal terms, this is known as 'trafficking' – and promised to check in with them the following week. When I did, many shared their frustrations; a few admitted to giving up. Kenneth, on the other hand, a black man about thirty years of age who has served nearly a decade in correctional institutions, had dutifully translated the entire soliloquy – into one run-on sentence:

> Saying the world isn't confined as prisoners are, also I'm look upon as an animal and also I can't change the world without their help, when he goes on to say he'll do his best, then he says he's generating his own family in his mind, then there's a generation having every aspect of prison life, because they want us to suffer, then they think it's a joke, then there's religion being interfered with, mix emotions, then there's the children that aren't being taught, then I think he wants so much to provide, then they want to destroy his passion, even though they restrain his physical he can't be restrained or distracted of the pure passion, also for all the pain they've done god will provide an understanding, then they've took shakespeare's pain and felt enjoyment, but their not the last, then they realize the pain shakespeare has endured, they have also shared the same pains, now as I analyze the last paragraph Shakespeare feels he's felt everyone's struggle and there's never any satisfaction, then he goes on to say he won't be or any other man be satisfied until death arrives and ends the pain.

During my first visit to solitary confinement, one long-term resident had laughed when I asked about the opportunity for 'peer work' among GED students in SHU – i.e., the possibility of inmates shouting out study questions instead of obscenities at one another. Marshall insisted that education was one topic that "never gets discussed around here". But the following week, Marshall reported that a heated debate had taken place the evening of my first visit among several inmates regarding the 'correct' interpretation of Richard's soliloquy: One group felt that Shakespeare was describing a figurative prison of the mind, while another contingent insisted that Richard was in a literal prison, like themselves. When I reminded Marshall of his earlier insistence that literary topics would never be discussed here, his smile betrayed a recognition that the impossible – or, at least, the improbable – had occurred. As I turned to leave, he called out after me. "Hey, teacher! Next week, do you think could you bring some *Hamlet?*"

Solitary confinement in the women's facility in which I teach is, in some respects, a less harsh environment than it is in the men's facility – although both are rated levels 3 and 4 (medium-maximum security), with solitary considered level 5 (super-maximum security). While the individual cells in the women's Secured Quarters [SQ] are as small, as isolated, and as cold as those in SHU, they do contain small slits cut into the concrete walls, and even this minimal ray of sunlight can make a big difference. Furthermore, solitary-confinement sentences here are generally shorter, measured out in days or months, not years.

Ironically, on the day I introduced Richard II's soliloquy to my freshman English class at Rockville Women's Correctional Facility, my A+ student was absent – having just been sentenced to a term in SQ. As we studied the soliloquy, the class speculated whether Shannon's soul and brain were "having sex", as Richard's did. One month later, Shannon was released – directly from SQ into my class. Emotionally and physically drained, and presented with an open-book exam for which she was unprepared, she could do little more than face the open book and stare at her blank sheet of paper. She was in tears and verging on hysteria when I gave her a copy of Richard's soliloquy and instructed her – despite her absence during the sessions in which the class had studied the text – to compose an impromptu response paper, incorporating her own experience in SQ. The paper presents a rapid generation of ideas almost out of the author's control – that would seem, structurally, to reflect Richard's "still-breeding thoughts":

> I feel very much alone, a deep sadness rushes through my heart and soul. Sometimes I feel as if the walls are about to close in all around me. I feel my

pulse racing. I'm trying to gasp for air. My mind ventures off to another place ... I, too, have to "people my little world" with my own thoughts. I'm starved for conversation – someone, anyone, to listen so I won't have to repeat the reoccuring images I see when I close my eyes ... I can relate to the feelings of emptiness and loneliness that he experienced....

Anticipating Richard's observation that "I wasted time and now doth time waste me", Shannon wrote:

Time is no concept in solitary confinement. The clock is ticking, but I'm at a standstill.... I feel trapped: nowhere to hide, nowhere to run.... Some days I feel the anxiety growing in my limbs.... I have to get used to the silence. I feel as though life is passing me by – like I had been in a car but the gear shift only goes in reverse.... My emotions are on a roller coaster....

Despite the contention that "there's no way you can know what it's like" for a prisoner in solitary confinement, *did* Shakespeare succeed in accurately representing the physical and emotional conditions of segregated incarceration? In an end-of-semester survey, I asked my Rockville students to assess how 'accurately' Shakespeare portrayed life in the various scenes we had studied (mother-daughter relationships in *Romeo and Juliet;* male dominance/female submissiveness in Richard III's wooing of Anne; love-'hate' relationships in Beatrice and Benedick). Regarding Richard II's soliloquy, they were unanimous in praise for its accurate depiction of isolated imprisonment: Ayanna declared that Richard's thoughts about freedom and his desire to have it were "on point". Beverly felt that his desire to communicate, which could only be performed with his thoughts, was "very real". Telissa thought that the feeling of aloneness portrayed was accurate and "in depth".

Mo, a middle-aged mother of several 'gangster' children, was an avid reader of pop fiction before she enrolled in college and has become a devoted Shakespeare fan during the course of the semester. She has also spent more than one term in SQ during her years of incarceration. On the verisimilitude of Richard's soliloquy, she was emphatic: "*Oh!* Shakespeare did a fantastic job here", she wrote in response to the survey question. "Especially since he had no first-hand knowledge himself – that we know of." And following this wry observation, she drew a smiley face.

"I have been studying how I may compare this prison where I live ...". Through my introduction to solitary confinement, I have come to appreciate the appropriateness of Shakespeare's word choice: This prison where I live. Despite the protests of human rights' organizations, sentences in modern high-tech segregation units are increasing rather than decreasing in length. And contrary to Shannon's experience, "thirty days in the hole" has become an anachronism; today, a one-year sentence – such as the one received by one of my male students who attacked a fellow inmate – is considered 'short term'. On the wall next to each cell in the SHU is a record, much like a medical chart in a hospital, that shows each inmate's arrival and departure date. Many of the inmates I worked with had been in solitary confinement for years – some for decades. Most will remain for years to come, regardless of the common contention among inmates that would make it appear that everyone in prison is innocent – and everyone in solitary is getting out "next week".

Earlier in this article I referred to the segregation unit as the isolated confinement of the "most extreme criminal offenders" – by which you may have thought I meant "most dangerous" or "most violent". While many in solitary have, no doubt, committed murders of various degrees – not only before but also after their initial incarceration – many others are simply habitual offenders, with as many as forty-seven convictions in twenty years. Not heinous enough to merit execution, these chronic repeaters are declared unrehabilitable and condemned to a living death.

Yet, no one is sentenced to *life* in solitary; eventually, all of these caged 'animals' will be released – often, directly onto the streets. And, while many arrive at SHU because of a psychological condition, many more acquire a mental imbalance due to the experience: Human Rights Watch declared that "it is generally acknowledged that all forms of solitary confinement without appropriate mental or physical stimulation are likely, in the long run, to have damaging effects resulting in deterioration of mental faculties and social functions". Shakespeare, clearly, can provide mental stimulation to a population desperately in need.

One day during my third week in SHU, I entered a particularly notorious tier and found it resounding with the intense verbal abuses that two inmates were hurling at one another across the tier. Without hesitation, I stepped into the face of the first of the two hostile inmates and calmly asked, "How's your Shakespeare reading going?" He turned to me, immediately, and with the appropriate modification of his voice level, replied, "I had a couple questions about the middle part. I still don't get what he means by the 'camel' stuff."

Naturally, I can't claim that Shakespeare's humanizing effect is such that every hardened criminal I worked with in solitary confinement exhibited such a dramatic transformation from hostile thug to inquiring 'scholar' – nor even that as many as half of them indicated an interest or basic ability to begin to explore the text I presented. But this experience reaffirmed my conviction that the study of Shakespeare does have much to offer a prison population – even (or, perhaps, especially) those in solitary confinement.

At the same time, a visit to solitary confinement can provide the scholar with a powerful validation of Shakespeare's universality – and a meaningful insight into the isolation that is central to Richard's final soliloquy. Yet, one final challenge remains, one ultimate obstacle to truly understanding Richard's isolation: To gain even a temporary glimpse into the perspective of life inside an isolation cell, you have to enter the cell itself. You have to step up over the metal frame that surrounds the steel door and, immediately upon entering the cell, realize that you are now completely out of sight of any other human being. You have to feel the walls start to close in around you, take a few steps forward, and ... stop. That is all there is – to this "little world".

Notes

1   *Richard II. The Arden Edition.* Ed. Peter Ure. London: Methuen, 1988.
2   *Cold Storage: SuperMaximum Security Confinement in Indiana.* Washington: Human Rights Watch, 1997.

THE 'PLAY' WITHIN THE PLAY: TEACHING SHAKESPEARE TO ENGINEERS

Michelle Ephraim
(Worcester Polytechnic Institute)

At the end of my first day teaching a seminar on "Shakespeare and the Comic Tradition" at Worcester Polytechnic Institute, a private, technical university in central Massachusetts, I asked my students to jot down some of their personal goals for the course. I had already completed teaching two larger lecture-based Shakespeare courses at WPI in the Fall term. With this exercise at the beginning of the Spring term, I had hoped simply to gain some more insight into what was still an unfamiliar teaching situation. This was not only my first year out of graduate school, my first job as an Assistant Professor, but also my first year teaching a class full of technical majors – engineers, computer scientists, and biologists – all of whom would be essentially taking my Shakespeare courses as electives. Later, reading over their comments, I was struck by a predominant sentiment that emerged, expressed most eloquently and pointedly by one biochemistry major: "This being an English course I expect that it will give me some relief from all of the science that I work on most of the day. I hope that it will allow me to make creative output that does not come with the established mechanisms of hard science." Overwhelmingly, they voiced the need for "some relief", a respite from their otherwise restrictive course loads.

Coming from the large state school where I had received my doctorate, I had braced myself for the reluctant, indifferent techie, the kind of student who raises questions about the value of learning Shakespeare in the first place. But instead of resistant non-majors, I encountered at WPI a zealous group of students who had voluntarily signed up for college Shakespeare. My Shakespeare classes were not foundation courses for an English major, as such classes might be for many students at another university; all classes were "introductory" in the sense that they required no prerequisites. My students approached literature not as a discipline but as a brief interlude away from their other classes; instead of problem sets, lab reports, and graphs, they wanted a chance to express themselves creatively. Such enthusiastic students are, of course, every teacher's dream, making for lively and refreshing banter in the classroom. But they were also discouraged by the prospect of the written work I would request of them: they felt intimidated by formal essays, the five-page thesis-driven argument complete with topic sentences and close-readings. And it was hard for me to justify assignments that potentially had no bearing on the rest of their studies. My students would not be required to take a composition class at WPI, and for many who had never had a formal writing class, the "college literature essay" was both a foreign and a potentially demoralizing prospect that threatened an otherwise promising classroom situation. To make matters more complicated, our courses run on seven-week terms. For me, the sheer scarcity of time underscored the importance of getting in as much formal writing practice as possible. But for them, the seven weeks were barely enough time to simply enjoy the literature. In my seminar on Shakespearean comedy, encouraged by the manageable size of the class, I decided to negotiate their need for 'play' with my objective of developing formal writing skills by integrating creative expository exercises into our syllabus. In doing so, I discovered that such assignments enabled many of my students to think about themselves for the first time as 'writers'. As a result, they were noticeably more self-assured when it came to writing traditional essays. Though certainly not mastering formal essay writing at the end of the seven weeks, the students benefited greatly from indulging their creative sensibilities, both from generating the "output" they desired and, in a more formal sense, from building their confidence to write about Shakespeare.

Shakespeare holds an especially revered place at WPI where the curriculum offers an exaggerated version of the heavy Shakespeare privileging that goes on in all types of universities. Required to fulfill a general 'Humanities' credit for their degree, the students had to choose only five courses from a wide selection of offerings in Art History, History, Language, Literature, Music, Philosophy, Religion, and Theater Arts. Though offering no courses devoted exclusively to

Renaissance drama or poetry, our interdisciplinary Humanities department offers no less than four courses on Shakespeare, certainly a number to rival – and perhaps surpass – that of a liberal arts school. But these four classes, filled to capacity almost every time, were an obvious hit with the students – a testimony to both the ambition of WPI students and the mystique that Shakespeare has acquired within this vocation-oriented technical school. The students who had never seen a live Shakespeare production avidly attended Shakespeare adaptations in the cinema and were eager to explore Shakespeare sites on the Internet. The Shakespeare phenomenon at WPI became quite clear to me on the first day of the school year when an engineering graduate student, who had also completed his undergraduate degree at WPI, approached me about sitting in on my Shakespeare course. When I told him that this was fine as long as he did the reading, he seemed surprised, utterly taken aback. He didn't actually have time to do the reading, he explained; what he wanted was to simply "absorb" Shakespeare by listening to our conversations. One of my colleagues would later illuminate what is apparently a pattern among continuing WPI students who did not take literature courses as undergraduates. Suffering from what she coined "Humanities Regret", they wanted a second chance to be enriched by the courses that they had initially chosen to pass up.

For the students who did sign up for my classes, Shakespeare was so symbolically rich a subject on a personal and academic level that it was at times, and almost humorously so, risky to attempt non-Shakespearean material. My seminar students were satisfied with Shakespeare as the sole representative of literary 'culture', but I ventured to add Ben Jonson as the last item on our syllabus. They were at first loathe to waste their Shakespeare time on an unfamiliar author. When we read Jonson's prologue to *Epicoene* in which he promotes the play as appealing to a general public, I noted in class the irony of the situation: "Our wishes, like to those make public feasts,/Are not to please the cook's taste, but the guests." *These* guests sitting in front of me were suspicious of Jonson at first – after all, he was not *Shakespeare*. They gradually accepted him, however – in part encouraged by a fortuitously timed article from the *New York Times Book Review* on Jonson's envy of Shakespeare.[1] I brought it in – indeed, I copied it for every student – so that they could have proof that Jonson was relevant enough to place alongside the Bard himself.

Unlike the graduate student stricken with 'Humanities Regret', my students fully intended to fulfill the course requirements, yet they too had near-magical expectations of Shakespeare. In addition to an unorthodox venture that takes them momentarily out of the practical course of their studies, Shakespeare promises, as he does for all college students, a social cachet and ample ammunition for future cocktail parties. At WPI, he is cathartic fun as well as a mark of advancement to many students, a large number of whom are first-generation college students coming from working-class families.

From a teacher's perspective, such overdeterminedness makes the seven-week course, consisting of four class sessions per week and no exam period, a particularly daunting prospect. Even taking into consideration Gerald M. Berkowitz's daring argument that we are too "driven by a compulsion to be comprehensive" in an undergraduate classroom filled with non-majors, I found that this condensed course system inevitably magnifies all the typical concerns a teacher faces about leaving out 'necessary' material.[2] It became quickly apparent that even with the number of hours allotted to the Shakespeare course in seven weeks, it is unreasonable to expect students to process information as they would during the slower rhythm of a regular semester. The students, reading a couple of acts a night and attending the almost daily lectures, did not have much time to absorb the material and to reflect upon connections between one play and another. The course resembled a language immersion experience, an intensive sprint in which they plow through the material without coming up for air.

But while I could barely catch my breath, the students themselves thrived on this system; for the most part, they voraciously attacked a play a week and made the most of what was for many their only two months of literary study at college.

To paint with a broad brush, technical students have an impressive, unwavering tenacity: they do what you tell them to do, punctually and without resistance. They are mature, voracious learners with the full intention to take as much advantage of their college education as possible. One colleague related to me an anecdote of her first day at WPI when she had dismissed the class early after handing out the syllabus: A student complained that they had paid to get a full hour of class at every meeting. While my unfortunate student stricken with 'Humanities Regret' wanted Shakespeare *sans* Shakespeare, the students who did sign up for the Shakespeare courses came ready to rise to the occasion. Significantly, in the WPI classroom, these budding engineers and scientists have no obstacles such as they would undoubtedly have at a liberal arts school. There are no English majors and no prerequisites keeping them out of the smaller-sized seminars. Instead of being silent in the back row while the students referring to Marlowe and Milton hold court, it is biologists, computer scientists and the like positioned front and center and doing all of the talking.

From the first week of the school year, it was evident to me that Shakespeare provided not only these unique academic benefits but also offered a particular type of emotional freedom. Beyond taking pleasure from the literature itself, the students enjoyed making personal connections with the material in a way that they could not in other classes. They loved debating why Hamlet does not take immediate revenge on Claudius; they fretted extensively over whether Richard III was a sympathetic character. They avidly turned questions into occasions for reader-response. (Thus, for instance, on Othello: "I would never have believed Iago!") The Shakespeare classes provided an 'alternative' environment where outrageous behavior, transgression and rebellion were happily sanctioned. Many students claimed that this was the only course in which they got "to talk", a chance to ask questions not just for the sake of clarification, but for the purpose of a more open-ended, exploratory conversation. One student told me, for example, that she was moved to participate in a discussion of *All's Well that Ends Well* because she too, like Helena, had lost a father. While the majority of their courses equipped them professionally, the Shakespeare course actively reinforced the social skills that they were exercising for the first time in college; they were not only becoming professionals, but also cultured adults with the ability to link literature to their private lives.

While they had endless zest for close reading and analysis in discussion, this was not the case with answering questions in written form. My students at WPI enjoyed their workshop groups, and they carefully studied my copious handouts on close-readings, thesis statements, and counter-arguments. But even bolstered by their peer groups (all required to give written and oral feedback on papers), the students would have difficulty learning and implementing these skills in the frenetic pace of the seven weeks. The fact of my students' lack of background work in analytical writing proved the most challenging aspect of the term. Many did not have these necessary tools, and I consequently felt the comfortable dynamic generated in class conversation wane as we discussed the writing assignments. While normally verbally uninhibited, the students were shy and insecure about asking for help with their papers, overwhelmed by the feeling that they should be mastering skills to which they had only now been introduced.

While it was unrealistic to expect the students to acquire extensive skills of any kind during a single term of the school year, I was convinced that I could build their confidence as writers. In confronting the writing hurdle at WPI, I found precedent in performance exercises, with which I have had great success in each Shakespeare class. Suzanne Burr has voiced a need to "bring our knowledge of stage practice and performance into the college classroom", a call echoed by many Shakespeareans in all types of universities.[3] By discussing the choices made in live performance and in video productions, and, as Miriam Gilbert emphasizes, by acting exercises in the classroom, students are able to recognize and hone their own critical voices. "Performance makes students close readers and exact speakers", Gilbert writes, "and it does so without calling attention to those ends. Aiming at coherence, they usually achieve detail, specificity, even power."[4]

I have found performance to be beneficial in a classroom of technical students in particular. These pedagogical approaches reinforce their own 'power' in a humanities environment: always enthusiastic, my students avidly follow directions and relish any opportunity to participate. During my first year at WPI, I had immediate success with acting techniques in the classroom; the students participated energetically in a wide range of performance-based exercises. They enthusiastically chanted "O" using different voices and tones, an exercise I picked up from Robert B. Pierce that shows students the rich varieties and interpretive possibilities in Shakespeare's language.[5] I invented an activity called the "fifteen second scene" in which the students give a dramatic reading of a section of a play, and then, in fifteen seconds or less, mime the same scene. For example, after leaving the room to plan their interpretive strategies, three students emerged to read excerpts from *Richard II* 1.1, Mowbray and Bolingbroke's vitriolic exchange of accusations and King Richard's failed attempt to mitigate their dispute. After this performance they exited briefly again and returned to silently enact the same scene, playing Mowbray and Bolingbroke pushing each other back and forth, a 'battle' they punctuated with dramatic pauses and menacing looks. Periodically, the student playing Richard would step in and hold the two apart. After both performances, the class discussed the relationship between the 'silent' and 'spoken' interpretations, with much of the commentary focused on how the actors chose to convey the essence of the scene in the brief time limit. Richard II's frantic – and futile – efforts prompted a couple of students to remark on his complete lack of power. Later, they would proudly recall this interpretation as an accurate foreshadowing of Richard's downfall.

I looked for such a student-centered dynamic as I tried to create a functional marriage between writing and Shakespeare, and ultimately I drew upon the theories of Burr, Gilbert and others who have emphasized student interpretation as a way to encourage a more proactive and de-centered classroom. These performance exercises in which the students affirmed their own authority as readers of Shakespeare eventually inspired me to venture into more creative writing assignments that would do the same. Throughout graduate school and during my first year at WPI, I have preferred formal essays to be the backbone of my student's work. But at the risk of shaving off precious time for churning out more traditional essays, I experimented by giving my Spring term seminar students different types of writing assignments that would emphasize their own abilities rather than their inadequacies. Some Shakespeareans have advocated journals and other less structured writing assignments for non-traditional students with little formal writing experience. Nona Fienberg, in what was otherwise a successful seminar on "Shakespeare's Theatre of Power" taught to a group of adult professionals, notes that in "the end, the hardest task of all seemed to be writing about Shakespeare." As a solution, she proposes that in the future with such a group she will "de-center [her own] authority as reader of their writing" by having students write letters to one another in lieu of formal essays.[6] Margaret H. Hartshorn similarly suggests that, at her community college, alternative writing genres such as journal writing are most appropriate for her students.[7]

Because my students are of traditional college age and for the most part not returning adult students, I have insisted on using alternative assignments not as an end in themselves, but with an eye towards the development of their formal writing skills. Marie A. Plasse, responding similarly to her students' difficulty with writing formal essays on Shakespeare, has devised "seed papers", short close-readings, as a way to encourage students to engage more authoritatively with the writing process.[8] While utilizing a different pedagogical strategy, I hoped also to ease my students into formal essay writing through exercises they would find more accessible.

In my seminar on "Shakespeare and the Comic Tradition", I would stick to my main hobbyhorses, close-readings and clear arguments, while providing students with more ways to 'make creative output'. The course, anchored in Shakespeare, was intended as a broader exploration of the comedic genre. We read Plautus and *The Comedy of Errors*, and then moved to problem comedies. At the beginning of the course, I had given them a handout on "critics on comedy" consisting of excerpts ranging from Aristotle ("Comedy is an artistic imitation of men of an inferior moral bent") to George Meredith ("To understand [the work of a comedic writer] and value it, you must have a sober liking of your kind") to the contemporary critic Robert W. Corrigan ("The constant in comedy is the comic view of life or the comic spirit: the sense that no matter how many times man is knocked down he somehow manages to pull himself up and keep on going"). Often I would center discussions on the relationship between these theories and the plays with the purpose of raising questions about the limitations and attributes of the genre.

For the three essays during the term, the students would be able to select one creative option. I supplemented questions such as "Comparing two similar scenes from *The Comedy of Errors* and *The Menaechmi*, discuss how Shakespeare rejects and conforms to Plautine comedy" with more creative options, such as one that asked them to write down their own theory of comedy. Drawing upon their selections of "critics on comedy" for the purpose of developing their own unique arguments, the students scripted their manifestos on the nature of comedy, addressing issues such as the social role of satire and the attributes a comedy must have in order to be successful. They were required to discuss in detail at least one scene of a Shakespeare play, but they were free to incorporate contemporary examples of literature and popular culture into their essays as well.

Instead of fretting that they did not know how to write a thesis statement, or that the extent of their writing knowledge was the highschool five-paragraph essay, they embraced the chance to author their own literature as a way of responding to Shakespeare's characters, language, and narrative techniques. All but one or two students of the fifteen in the course chose the creative options for the first paper. As they proceeded to the inevitable two formal essays that were to follow, they did not become disengaged as I had feared. Rather, after writing creatively, the students were noticeably more forthcoming about discussing their writing, and more active and confident in their responses to my critical comments as well as with one another in their writing groups. Because the assignment required them to play the role of author, the "theory of comedy" project gave them a sense of mastery and personal investment that transferred later to the more unfamiliar essays. For tech students, who are often labeled "non-writers" throughout their high school careers, more accessible – and fun – writing allowed them to prove differently.

Because of my experience with the students at WPI who are so enthusiastic to give their own interpretations of Shakespeare, I was recently struck by a family friend's complaint that his college Shakespeare professor asked too often "What do *you* think?" as opposed to telling the students his own theories about the plays. Having gone to an elite liberal arts school, he attributed to his professors an aspect of celebrity. The Shakespeare class, he implied, was a place to acquire authentic Shakespearean theory as told by an authentic Shakespearean. At WPI, quite differently, where a student once asked me innocently, "What makes you a 'Shakespearean'?", after I was introduced to her as such, the students do not see Shakespeare or the Shakespearean in this light. They are more willing to express their own opinions in class and less likely to consider the Shakespeare professor's thoughts as a commodity to be acquired during the semester.

The process of writing at WPI was most fruitful when I took their desire to forge their own connections to Shakespeare into their writing assignments. Indeed, as I discovered increasingly during my first year, WPI as an institution is grounded in the entrepreneurial spirit of its students; as budding engineers and computer scientists they like to be innovators. In order to graduate, the students must complete three separate independent studies projects, including the "Interactive Qualifying Project" – the "IQP" – a project that marries together the sciences and the humanities.

Broadening my own definitions of what 'counts' as written expression of a student's comprehension of Shakespeare, I came to appreciate the potential fluidity of my role as the Shakespearean in residence at WPI. This was not limited to the classroom in which I integrated creative writing assignments, but extended to the IQP, the university's signature requirement. Planning my first IQP, "Shakespeare on Display", I collaborated with another professor who also serves as the curator of the Higgins armory museum, the only museum devoted exclusively to arms and armor in North America, located only a couple of miles from the WPI campus. Beginning in the Fall term, the three students enrolled for the project will look at incidents of fighting and allusions to armor in Shakespeare's plays in conjunction with research material on arms and armor in the early modern period. Using the artifacts already housed at the museum – and perhaps with the plan to acquire other pieces on loan from other museums in the general region – they will write a proposal discussing their focus for the project as well as their pedagogical goals for the finished project. Once the "humanities" portion of the project is completed, they will actually construct the display case itself, taking care to make the artifacts accessible – both contextually and physically – to their anticipated audience. It is Shakespeare meets shop class.

Once Shakespeare is liberated from formal writing, he is free to show up in some very unlikely places. Suddenly teaching Shakespeare also involves woodworking skill and even a power saw. Such alternative projects are a reminder of how exciting Shakespeare can be when introduced to new clientele: in my case, what now 'counts' as tangible evidence of a student's knowledge of Shakespeare includes not only pen and paper, but wood, glass, nails, and hammers as well. Yet creative projects like "Shakespeare on Display" and the manifestos on comedic theory encourage and allow for 'creative output' while giving students more confidence about their relationship to Shakespeare. Though they are having fun, they are also learning organization, close-reading, and analytical skills that feed directly into their efforts at formal writing.

The end of the academic year at WPI brought with it the revelation that there is a central and wonderful irony to their Shakespeare program. On the one hand, the courses were an aberration, a departure and an exception to their normal course of study at WPI. Yet Shakespeare would become an organic part of the students' lives as they departed upon graduation for their 'real-life' technical jobs. The play was not simply 'play' in the sense of being a departure from their 'real-life' training, but an entry back into the everyday – a way of engaging with everyday life more profoundly and imaginatively.

Although they eventually found interesting the differences between Shakespeare's comedy and Jonson's satire, my students do not study Shakespeare as an entry into the rest of the Western canon; they come to 'play' and to see how Shakespeare speaks to their own experiences. Instead of passively imbibing a professor's authority, they come to understand Shakespeare on their own terms.

My students did not come just to witness a real live Shakespearean, to sit in stunned silence as this figure spoke, but to become authorities themselves.[9]

Notes

[1] Robert Giroux, "The Man Who Knew Shakespeare", *The New York Times Book Review*, 13 Feb. 2000, p. 35.

[2] Gerald M. Berkowitz, "Teaching Shakespeare to Today's College Students – Some Heresies", *Shakespeare Quarterly*, 35 (1984), p. 561.

[3] Suzanne Burr, "Students Write about Shakespeare: The 'Triple Play' in the College Classroom" in *Shakespeare and the Triple Play: From Study to Stage to Classroom*, ed. Sidney Homan (Lewisburg: Bucknell UP, 1988), p. 208.

[4] Miriam Gilbert, "Teaching Shakespeare through Performance", *Shakespeare Quarterly*, 35 (1984), pp. 603-4.

[5] Robert B. Pierce, "Teaching the Sonnets with Performance Techniques", in *Teaching Shakespeare into the Twenty-first Century*, ed. James E. Davis and Ronald E. Salomone (Athens: Ohio UP, 1997), pp. 44-5.

[6] Nona Fienberg, "Shakespeare's Theatre of Power at Millsaps College", *Shakespeare Quarterly*, 41 (1990), pp. 239, 240.

[7] Margaret H. Hartshorn, "Shakespeare for Life: Teaching Shakespeare in General Education Courses to the Non-Traditional Student", in *Ideological Approaches to Shakespeare: The Practice of Theory*, ed. Robert P. Merrix and Nicholas Ranson (Lewiston: The Edwin Mellen Press, 1992), pp. 257-64.

[8] Marie A. Plasse, "An Inquiry-Based Approach", in *Teaching Shakespeare into the Twenty-first Century*, pp. 120-6.

[9] I would like to thank Laura J. Menides and Marc S. Rysman for their helpful comments.

ON TEACHING SHAKESPEARE TO
'THIS DISTRACTED GLOBE'

Chris Hassel
(Vanderbilt University)

To the Gravedigger in *Hamlet*, it is crucial to determine whether Ophelia comes to the water or the water comes to Ophelia. As regards teaching Shakespeare around the world, it is I think less important whether the water of Shakespeare's distracted globe comes to the teacher, or the teacher to the water. Though I have been firmly anchored at Vanderbilt University, in the landlocked heartland of the USA, for thirty years, over the last decade "renowned suitors", students of great multicultural diversity, have come in "from every coast" to study Shakespeare's "fair" if not entirely "speechless messages" with me.[1] Though these unusually good students are often fairly well "Americanized" by the time I meet them, their diverse looks, accents, and attitudes often enrich my classes and challenge my instruction. How would they respond, I wondered, to the questions central to this issue of the *Shakespeare Yearbook*?

To find out, I asked a few of them to write about some of the challenges they have faced in trying to understand a writer so far removed from them in time, place, and perhaps most interesting, cultural background, or on the challenges they have faced (or might face) in trying to represent Shakespeare to their families or culturally diverse friends after attending a class or seeing a Shakespeare film. My hope was that their responses might help teachers here and abroad be more sophisticated about their own presentations of Shakespeare to students around the world. Because of my own insularity as well as a fairly universal tendency to oversimplify the 'other', I naively assumed that this multicultural cast, marked both by their darker skins and their unusual questions and assumptions in class, would respond with great similarity to my request. To my initial surprise and eventual delight, their distinct personalities, backgrounds, and experiences of otherness constantly frustrated my attempts to oversimplify them and complicated my pedagogical considerations. To preserve their individuality and their complexity, I have usually arranged their responses more by person than by topic, though I have sometimes combined these methods of organization for clarity and efficiency.[2]

I will start with Daniel Vo, a Vietnamese-American who is both the most humanistically inclined of these students and the most fully assimilated, and Jennifer Pan, a Chinese student who only moved to the USA and began to study English at the age of ten. Two of the best students, Jennifer and Daniel nevertheless represent almost opposite extremes in confronting one of the most commonly voiced challenges in responding to Shakespeare, the difficulty of his language. To Daniel, understanding and enjoying Shakespeare's language has more to do with Shakespeare's own complex diction and syntax than with the cultural or linguistic difference we are considering in this issue of *Shakespeare Yearbook*. It is the challenge of every good student who has ever tried to read Shakespeare for himself:

> Until my ninth grade year in high school, I had taken on faith that Shakespeare is the world's greatest playwright. That is, until I stumbled across *Romeo and Juliet* or should I say stumbled *through* it. Elizabethan English is daunting and deceptive in that at first glance it seems familiar but the differing definitions and speech patterns can quickly leave one befuddled. Beleaguered by "capons", "cock-a-hoops", and a "pop'rin pear", I depended on footnotes and annotations to unravel dialogues, and my teacher was reduced to a translator, holding my hand from Act I to Act V. In the translation, I got what [Shakespeare] says but missed how well he says it. Unfortunately, a similar pattern developed in subsequent years as I read *Hamlet*, *Macbeth* and *Merchant of Venice*.

But Daniel, as relentless as he is sophisticated, finds opportunity in this difficulty:

> Admittedly, my cultural perspective on Shakespeare is not radically foreign, but the obstacles I encountered and the course I traversed seem reasonably applicable to all Shakespearean neophytes. The first challenge (and the one that probably turns the majority of readers away) is merely comprehending what the author is saying. If translation is cumbersome for English-speaking natives such as myself, one can only imagine the difficulties of deciphering Shakespeare in a foreign tongue. However, comprehension is only a means to the greater goals of appreciation and

interpretation. I was therefore drawn to the college course, Shakespeare on Film, because my high school experience left me with two options: either Shakespeare was overrated or I was an idiot (neither of which I was eager to accept).

To Daniel, "the overwhelming scope and complexity of Shakespeare's material" is a challenge almost as great as the difficulty of his language:

> Shakespeare's breadth forces him to introduce European History, Mythology, Psychology, Visual Arts, Music, Religion, and a plethora of other topics. Frustration mounted as I felt I did not know enough to understand what he was conveying. Whether it be applying Freud to Hamlet, recognizing visual motifs in [the] text, elucidating religious imagery, or catching subtle allusions, Shakespearean scholars scour his work for years, yet I proposed to come away with an "understanding" in a matter of weeks? Strangely enough, I did. Granted, I extracted a more fundamental understanding, but Shakespeare's ability to be appreciated by peasants and professors attests to his skill as a writer.

Like many of his peers, Daniel found the concord of this discord of rich language, complex themes, and broad-ranging context in the serious study of the Shakespeare films:

> When listening to classical music, one can hear a single piece and be done with it or one can listen to that piece recorded by ten different orchestras by ten different conductors at ten different times. Similarly, in my Shakespeare on Film class I encountered Shakespeare on stage or on location. Shakespeare with swords. Shakespeare with guns. Shakespeare in period dress. Shakespeare in no dress. His characters are *dynamic* and subject to changes in motivation, inhibitions, and psychology. When a single character changes, the ramifications are felt throughout the play. This is why plays written hundreds of years ago are still performed. Yes, in the tragedies, everyone still dies in the end and in the comedies, everyone still lives in the end – but how and why the characters get there is a puzzle left to every production. I spend afternoons captivated by Jacobi's psychotic Hamlet, Holmes' deviant Puck, or Olivier's sympathetic Shylock. Films can therefore simultaneously help readers from other cultures overcome the initial barriers of comprehension and appreciation and become a valuable source of new interpretations.

Smart, articulate, and eager to engage his new cultural heritage, Daniel confronts Shakespeare's apparent inaccessibility with his own considerable will and imagination. It may be the hopeless romantic in me, the anachronistic Renaissance humanist, or just the teacher, which may be the same thing, but I find the conflict bracing and the result heartening. Of course it helps that Daniel comes to the task having fully assimilated the language and the culture.

Jennifer Pan, the student who only began to study English at the age of ten, when her family moved to the US from China, has apparently found Shakespeare's language to be an almost insurmountable obstacle; in fact only in the filmed and staged productions of his works can she find an adequate passport into Shakespeare's imaginative world. Indeed, she finds that "the liberties the directors and the producers take with the set, the costumes, and the time period emphasize the idea that Shakespeare's appeal transcends a specific time, place, or culture". Her best example is a production of *Hamlet* at the Alabama Shakespeare Festival:

> Rather than a play set in Denmark centuries ago, the director chose to set the play in World War II Europe. The king wore a general's outfit. The queen and the ladies of the court were dressed in the fashions of the 1940's. Prince Hamlet carried a gun, a weapon appropriate to the times of the period. Although the costumes and the set in the production differ from what Shakespeare had in mind, the play still managed to convey the struggle of Hamlet as he alternates between his desires for revenge and his need to confirm the truth.

To Jennifer, films like the Zeffirelli and the Luhrman *Romeo and Juliets* also help translate Shakespeare's difficult words into images so vivid and moving that she calls them "three-dimensional" in opposition to the "two-dimensional paper" from which they came.[3]

But Jennifer's clear sub-text is that Shakespeare remains for her bound like Prometheus in the text and freed only by production. Even when Jennifer loves a film like Branagh's *Much Ado*, the "physical comedy" of Benedick's and Beatrice's discovery scenes, and its joy, "conveys itself without language". Though the pragmatist teacher in me has long known that even for some "native" afficionados Shakespeare only comes alive in production, the idealist still believes that with my help Shakespeare can leap out of the text just as dramatically as he can live on the screen or stage. I appreciate now much more than I did when I read Jennifer's excellent explications how extraordinary they were. Yet apparently even all that hard and effective work five years ago never brought the text alive for her.

Probably because she lived in another culture for ten years, Jennifer found its parallel stories more useful in approaching Shakespeare than these other students did:

> A parallel to Romeo and Juliet's story exists in Chinese literature. In the classical novel, *Dreams in the Red Chamber*, the two lovers, Jia BaoYu (male) and Lin DiaYu (female), also face obstacles such as their families and the differences in their social positions. In the end, Jia's family forced him to wed someone else, a woman of his equal social status. Lin dies of illness and despair. Jia, after the death of his love, leaves his family and home to search for peace and meaning. *Romeo and Juliet* also depicts a pair of star-crossed lovers whose love triumphs over the hatred of the two families by paradoxically ending in tragedy. By noting these parallels, the bridge between Eastern and Western culture lessens a fraction.

So intent is Jennifer on bridging the gap, even fractionally, that the gap inadvertently becomes a bridge.

The third student, Uzma Hasan, has found both extraordinary gaps and extraordinary connections in her attempts to engage Shakespeare. Even the subtitle of her paragraph on "Shakespeare's Notion of Love", like her interesting later phrase, "Shakespeare love", reveals that Uzma's unique cultural gap is her isolation from Shakespeare's sense of romantic love. However, to Uzma it is not her "Indian-Pakistani background" but her modernity that accounts for this separation:

> It is difficult to convince students that "Shakespeare Love" may still exist and is not simply a romanticized version of "real relationships". Shakespeare's view of love seems quite grand and implies that love ranks above everything else. To Shakespeare, it seems unrequited love would be a catastrophic event in a person's life. However, in today's society, most people do not believe in love at first sight, but rather in the many practical factors involved in love which do not have anything to do with emotions or feelings. Society appears to have become quite disillusioned with love and refuses to believe that a fairy tale ("happily ever after") love story could actually occur in real life. I think this modern view of love is a worldwide sentiment and transcends cultural differences.

As an aging romantic who began his career writing about the blessed madness of romantic love in Shakespeare's romantic comedies, and who still feels deeply moved as well as profoundly amused by Shakespeare's romanticism, even by the romanticism of a film like *Shakespeare in Love*, I am saddened that Uzma ranks "modern reports of love" in the same category as Martian sightings. Not that the attitude is alien in Shakespeare, witness Jaques' actual and Rosalind-Ganymede's pretended skepticism in *As You Like It*.[4] But it seems so absolute in Uzma's world, so universal. I wonder what Uzma or her contemporaries, foreign or domestic, made of my enthusiasm for those plays let alone my romanticized stories in class about my own sometimes ill-fated courtship of my wife Sedley, the love of my life, especially the night I tried ill-fatedly to play Romeo to her Juliet? And is forewarned really forearmed in this case? If Uzma is right, and she may well be, I am apparently the alien here, a hopeless if not a mindless romantic adrift in a sea of astonished disbelief or amused condescension. This makes the romantic and heroic achievements of Branagh's *Henry 5* and *Much Ado* all the more impressive to me, and all the more useful pedagogically, if I want to try to mend this torn cultural fabric.

Interestingly, Uzma also maintains that Shakespeare is sometimes more rather than less accessible to students of other cultures precisely because their inherited value systems are not so 'modern'. For example, even though she has "lived in the US my entire life", she can identify with Shakespeare's depictions of parent-child relationships in terms of her own parents' values:

> [Because] parents in previous eras demanded much more respect from their children, and exerted much more control over them, most internationals, and certainly children in Asian cultures who are traditionally taught to place great importance on parental influence and are accustomed to parents exerting some control in all aspects of their lives may find it easier to relate to Shakespeare's depiction of parent-child relationships than others. Perhaps if the instructor were to constantly point out that such parent-child relationships still occur quite frequently in other countries, it may make the story seem more real.

Uzma's concern here with making Shakespeare more accessible to the American student is apparently genuine, and its repetition in several other statements suggests that giving Shakespeare a "local habitation and a name" is again a much more complicated matter than I had at first assumed.

Arun Goel, Bharath Subramanian, and Derek Williams confirm and complicate these discussions of the challenges of confronting and appreciating Shakespeare's rich diction, his even richer uses of Western context, and the films which sometimes make that complexity more accessible to all of us. Like most of my 'exceptional others', they are all both 'Western' and 'Non-western' at once. English is their first language; the USA is the country in which they were all born and bred. However, all describe themselves as "first-generation Americans". Derek's mother is Chinese, but his father is American. Arun, with two Indian parents, "grew up with the Hindu faith". Bharath describes his parents, also Indian, as "devout Hindus". When one of these bright students writes that he would understand the legend of Jason better if he knew more about the Bible, he illustrates the need for context even as he also reminds me what a tangled web Western civilization, or Eastern, is to the outsider. A thoughtful visit to any exhibit of Chinese art and artifacts, or Japanese, Incan, or Meso-American, reminds me more personally and more painfully of just how little I know about these different cultures, even after sixty interested years of roaming around the globe through museums and *National Geographics*.

Probably because English is their first language, Arun and Bharath agree that "until he can understand the complexity of Shakespeare's language, the reader cannot even begin to appreciate his genius". Plentiful marginal glosses are Arun's first suggested remedy to this problem, close reading in class combined with frequent discussion the second. But because Bharath knows that "translating the work into a different language steals much of the charm and purpose of something like Shakespeare", he proposes focusing first on "simpler works", where the pace should be kept purposely slow and the instructor should take great care to ensure that all are following along". While I have had no experience teaching Shakespeare at this level, it nevertheless strikes me that my own in-class technique early in the semester of explicating vital speeches in close detail, trying to engage all my students in this process of closely reading, reveals an awareness that my native speakers of English also need an early immersion in Shakespeare's words and syntax, though obviously on another level from the mere translation and paraphrase that others than native anglophone speakers, even those as bright as Jennifer, will always need. I never completely leave the close-reading approach, but I often disguise and soften it as the semester progresses. Bharath and Daniel are both keen to perceive that mere translation and paraphrase diminish Shakespeare's greatness; his words are among his greatest glories. Translation and paraphrase are thus essential as starting-places but severely limiting as dwelling-places. The universal themes and stories and characters that these exceptional students often mention in Shakespeare are another useful crutch for them, but like most crutches they are also a poor substitute for their chief vehicle – Shakespeare's extraordinary use of words. It is a remarkable tribute to Shakespeare's greatness that other cultures have found his works extraordinary even when they are deprived of this first and greatest attribute.

Arun and Bharath also reveal the complexity of trying to reconstruct Shakespeare's rich cultural background as part of the process of interpretation. Arun, lamenting his "lack of background knowledge of the Christian religion", the Bible, and the "Classics", knows that he misses allusions and thinks that he misunderstands what he calls "Christian morality" in the plays:

> When Shylock does not give mercy to Antonio, I do not understand why he is held in such contempt. In Hinduism, all agreements are binding and a man lives and dies by his word. In my religion, it would have been insulting for Antonio to *accept* mercy because it would make him less of a man. Because my religion [does not] place as much emphasis on mercy as Christianity, I thought that the Christian characters in the *Merchant of Venice* were being quite unreasonable. If I were Christian, however, I would probably think differently.

Arun does not know it, but some Christians would share his distrust of the Christians in Venice and Belmont, though perhaps they would state it in terms of a troubling discrepancy between precept and practice rather than cultural disjointure. Bharath, whose background is very similar to Arun's, reveals even greater complexity in this matter when he problematizes the Duke's behavior rather than Antonio's: "The importance of Venice as a commercial center explains why the Duke does not assist his friend Antonio in a time of need, which would appear to be the moral thing to do". But in fact, from my own 'Western' and 'Christian' perspective, which I know to be only one of many Western or Christian perspectives, I find Antonio too proud to want much of Shylock's mercy or the Duke's favor. In fact, he seems to me problematically to be looking forward to showing Bassanio and Portia what "a love" he has by laying down his life for his friend.[5] These students, then, are hardly alone in their complex responses to Shakespeare's own great complexity, and the infinite variety of human response that it can sometimes evoke. They just underestimate it sometimes as their own lack of Western 'knowledge' or 'values'.

Arun further complicates my consideration of the pedagogy of reconstructed context when he observes that "however necessary" some religious understanding might be to an interpretation of, say, *The Merchant of Venice*, "it discourages the reader from creating his own conclusions about the text and instead makes him rely on the thoughts of others". Although I know that such a comment might gently criticize a teacher's heavy-handedness with context on a particular day, Arun reminds me of Bharath's similar distress, and Daniel's, that too much translation in a class imposes someone else's interpretation, and therefore deprives the good student of his best chance to respond personally to Shakespeare's work. These problems are complicated by a tradition in many of these cultures of respecting a teacher to the point of never talking in class. Bharath, who seemed to the benefit of our seminar generally to have overcome the stricture, still observed, "when a teacher serves as a moderator, a student would normally be afraid to say anything that could be seen as contradicting him even though there is no right answer". I suspect that some of their difficulties with my lecture/discussion style of reconstructing Shakespeare's rich context and investigating his equally rich language had some connections to these discrepant cultural understandings.

Even when Bharath accepts the usefulness of being taught some of "the religious disputes between Catholics and Protestants or Christians and Jews" while discussing *The Merchant of Venice*, he wonders after learning about such context if the play should be taught at all to students of other ethnic and religious backgrounds: "Even with such information a work such as *The Merchant of Venice* could be seen in other nations as offensive to Jews as well as Christians, and so the local environment must be taken into consideration when choosing what works are to be discussed". Rekha Mody, who is also of Indian descent,[6] disagrees completely:

> I seem to be able to relate the inner Christian battles that many of Shakespeare's characters face with my own confusions, religious and otherwise. This dilemma extends to themes such as the controlling influences of tradition, societal and gender rules, and the parental control evident in many of Shakespeare's works, all of which can be paralleled to my past and current dilemmas. And because I feel very alone at Vanderbilt, lost in the middle of two worlds and not at all sure where I belong, I particularly understand the theme of alienation and the wish for unity or reconciliation that also exists in many of Shakespeare's works.

Rekha persuades me that I should teach *Merchant* or *Othello* to such students precisely because of the relevance of Shakespeare's painful representations of the alien in Western society, but Bharath helps me understand how uncomfortable seminar discussions of relations between 'them' and 'us' might be to someone who is betwixt and between such borders.

Parental authority and romantic love were the context-based issues that surfaced most often in these responses, but again the takes on these issues were also far from uniform. Derek Williams, whose mother was born and raised in Taiwan, was not alone in thinking that such a parent would have trouble believing in a play about "a fourteen-year-old girl falling in love":

> In China, the daughters do what the parents tell them to do. Often, there are also arranged marriages. Therefore, when a young teenage daughter

goes against her parents' wills and marries the enemy of the family, the Chinese cannot relate to the girl's rebellion.

Bharath and Uzma voiced similar concerns. Of course, because all children, even those as complicated as Hamlet, underestimate parental complexity, the dilemmas of Egeus in *A Midsummer Night's Dream*, Capulet in *Romeo and Juliet*, or Brabantio in *Othello* might be more accessible to their parents than Bharath, Uzma, or Derek understand. Of all these students, only Jennifer, who had ten years to absorb Chinese culture, seemed to be aware that it contains literary analogs to such characters and actions.

Bharath and Kofi Dodzie, the Ghanian with whom I will conclude, were the only two students who spoke of the influence of individual sensibility rather than religious, national, or racial background in responses to Shakespeare or any other product and producer of Western culture. Bharath acknowledged himself so analytic, in a social-scientific sort of way, that he tended to apply reductive formulas to complicated artifacts, "approaching a play", for example, "as an equation of sorts", and thus "in a strictly rational manner" "almost looking for an 'answer' as I glean insight about the current work from my past experience". Though Bharath knows that this manner of learning "loses the inherent beauty of the work", his method leads him in one paper to call *Hamlet* "essentially a soap opera", though to give this smart and disciplined student credit he often transcends the limits of his formulaic method in the heat of a classroom discussion, or in response to an instructor's suggestion. Kofi, a black engineering student, also acknowledged that a difference of sensibility separated him from his American counterparts in "most liberal arts courses" that he took at Vanderbilt:

> The engineering training I am under might contribute to a certain lack of analytical creativity due to the emphasis on purely logical analysis. Often my interpretation or lack thereof of what Shakespeare was supposed to be portraying put me in sharp contrast with most of my class. I tend to take prose very literally, and to a large extent, fail to see between the lines. I give writers a lot of credit for meaning what they write and for writing what they mean.

Unlike Bharath, however, Kofi was unwilling or unable to transcend this acknowledged limitation. In fact, a closer look at his complaints about "our" over-reading of the sexual and the modern into Shakespeare reveals that even this statement is more a defense than an apology.

Kofi was born in Oxford, "near Stratford-upon-Avon" as he says, and raised in a Catholic school in Ghana. When he adds that he often heard Shakespeare discussed at home by his Ghanian parents, I begin to wonder if his chafing against our close reading of Shakespeare, which occasionally included Shakespeare's bawdy, had something to do with his idealized memory of a now-distant childhood place and time:

> I find many people to be accusing Shakespeare of trying to conceal many possibly indecent details behind his eloquent arrays of script. I have often found very disturbing, the frequent number of times that he is accused of camouflaged sexual connotation in what could otherwise have been a more lighthearted reference. My problem is that the misinterpretation often robs the work of its beauty, rendering it as some common novel. To me, he is almost a man to be revered, and to break down his work with such brute analysis as one would a sensational newspaper article appears almost insane.

Words like "accusing" and "accused", "misinterpretation", "robs", "brute analysis", and my favorite, his calling me (or most of my students) "almost insane" for sometimes teaching (or discussing) the bawdy bard reveal how unwilling Kofi is to release the Shakespeare he grew up with in his home in Ghana and in his Catholic school.

When Kofi includes Shakespeare among the culturally diverse writings he loved as a child, he also reveals the degree to which each of these stories, even those notorious for their complicating sexual components, were idealized for him:

> My childhood heroes included David (from David and Goliath in the holy Scriptures); Yaa Asantewaa, an Ashanti queen who led her army against the British in 1875; Zorro, the famous Spanish hero, and finally James Bond, alias 007 of His (Her) Majesty's Secret Service. What I enjoyed in all these heroes was their open quest for bravery and honor.

But I am even more interested in Kofi's sense of the effort it takes for any modern young adult to hold on to such an idealized vision, for it confirms my own sense of the importance and the difficulty of helping all my students respond to the extraordinary romanticism and humanism in Shakespeare without ignoring the equally extraordinary naturalism and skepticism. As a modern, Uzma rejects the "fairy tale" of "Shakespeare love". Kofi says that "to really enjoy" such literature, one must take a "blindfolded journey", "allow one's mind to be carried away into the realms of fairytale bliss". To Kofi, the "disparity of intellectual perspective" between him and us results from our "taking the easier route of recreating a modern perspective". Paradoxically, Kofi is enabled by his "blindfolded" perspective to see more of Shakespeare's romanticism than his more modern peers, but less of Shakespeare's complexity.

With Kofi's extraordinary exception, I grew to realize as I assimilated the comments of these students of recent international heritage that their rage to assimilate all things Western often empowered them to engage Shakespeare more effectively than my more traditional American students, who, because they reside within the default setting of cultural comfort, are not only blind-sided by Shakespeare's linguistic and cultural otherness but also ill-equipped to adapt to it. At least these students know that there are gaps to bridge and like their parents, though in different ways, have spent lifetimes going "into the breach". Spoon-fed for a lifetime on the Pablum of popular culture, how many of my "native" students are ready to "carve for themselves" when something really meaty comes their way? They have "cause". Do they also "have will, and strength, and means/ To do't"?[7] For the really important cultural differences in this arena, as Kofi, Daniel, and Rekha all sensed, though in radically different ways, are as much chronological differences as they are racial or national, ethnic or religious. Four hundred years may be even farther from us than four thousand miles when we try to understand Shakespeare's profoundly conflicted and enigmatic responses to such things as Renaissance humanism, the encroaching modernisms of Montaigne, Machiavelli, and Copernicus, or the tensions of the Reformation, though of course mentioning in class our own analogous forms and pressures appropriately diminishes that sense of distance. Though our individual lists would vary, other contextual matters in Shakespeare are even more difficult than these to reconstruct and make relevant. As a result, our Puckish Shakespeare may be able to girdle the globe more readily than he can redeem the time.

The experiences of these exceptional students in trying to understand and appreciate Shakespeare are therefore seldom unique to them, though their otherness can complicate and exaggerate Shakespeare's difficulty. Like all adolescents (and most adults too) they assume themselves to be more disadvantaged and isolated from Shakespeare and from their Western classmates than they really are. The coping mechanisms that have served them so well in becoming assimilated are only imperfectly applied to a writer as complex as Shakespeare, however necessary they might be in attempting to read him as either 'Western' or 'Universal'. Of course, we all oversimplify Shakespeare with reductive and empowering formulas of character, action, theme, and context, not to mention our own pasts, however 'mature' or 'Western' we might be. But these students must deal as well with the complicated over-layering of additional cultural contexts, often skewed by contrasts and sometimes conflicts too between their parents' and their own cultural transplantations. Even this is not completely different from the complexity of the post-modern experience, but it might be more confusing since the complexity of their own personal situation, the complexity of contemporary understandings of literature and culture, and the complexity of the Renaissance must all be part of their attempts at assimilation and understanding. I am therefore deeply impressed by their insights and achievements, and not a little intimidated about teaching Shakespeare to my next set of 'extraordinary others'. Reading their comments has usefully reminded me as well of my own otherness as a sixty-something Southern-American, German-Lutheran, Episcopalian-Agnostical, Anglophilic-Anglophobic, Idealistic-Pragmatic Shakespeare professor who is also still struggling to understand himself, his subject, his students, and his times. I know I will try in subsequent classes to encourage all of my students to grapple together with their common and their not-so-common differences from and similarities to this four-hundred-year-old Shakespeare. If their dialogue also enhances their understanding of one another, so much the better.

Notes

1   *Hamlet*, 1.5.97; 5.1.1-23; *The Merchant of Venice*, 1.1.162-70. This and subsequent references to Shakespeare will cite *The Complete Pelican Shakespeare*, ed. Alfred Harbage (Baltimore: Viking-Penguin, 1977).

2   I take this opportunity to thank my respondents Daniel Vo, Jennifer Pan, Uzma Hasan, Arun Goel, Bharath Subramanian, Derek Williams, Rekha Mody, and Kofi Dodzie, whom I will introduce more fully later in the essay. At least one of their parents and usually both of them come from countries as far afield as Vietnam, China, India, Pakistan, and Africa. In contrast, most of my students at Vanderbilt are white, upper middle-class, and 'all-American' for at least two generations; 80% describe themselves as Christian.

3   On the other hand, Derek Williams, speaking of his mother's Chinese heritage, observes how difficult it can be "for a person of Non-Western European background to understand the mannerisms of actors on film if they are culture-based mannerisms".

4   *As You Like It*, 3.2.240-80, 339-97.

5   *The Merchant of Venice*, 4.1.275.

6   Rekha's parents grew up in East Africa, then lived variously in Canada, India, Texas, Kenya, and Uganda before they finally met and were married in England and then moved to a small town in the Midwestern US, where Rekha was born and raised.

7   *Henry 5*, 3.1.1; *Hamlet*, 1.3.20; 4.4.46-7.

TEACHING A SENSE OF SHAKESPEARE TO HETEROGENEOUS CLASSES

Charles H. Frey
(University of Washington)

When I teach Shakespeare, often celebrated for his cross-cultural appeal, I may hope that cultural diversities of my students will not prevent them from noting Shakespeare's relative universality. If, in this vein, I were to teach that *The Merchant of Venice* stresses a morally evil or inhuman Shylock more than a Jewish or anti-Christian Shylock, I might play down issues of race and religion which could expose my students' diverse values and interpretations. Or I might admit historical, social, and political issues in the play yet still defend a cross-culturally appealing Shakespeare. I might argue, for example, that prejudices against Jews, usury, and even independent women were Elizabethan norms, that Shakespeare would hardly be expected to endanger box office receipts by openly mocking such views, that such views are a small part of the total content of the plays, that of course we know better and can easily discount such views, and so on. In this fashion I could seek to mute cultural prejudices identified by interpreters as embedded in Shakespeare's dialogue. At the same time, I would probably mute some expressions of student diversity currently noted in our classrooms (as now religious debates intensify, immigration heightens ethnic diversity, and men and women studies re-evaluate our ideas of gender). To teach Shakespeare, in this fashion, as being not of one culture but for many cultures, is to teach students that they are significantly thus as well, that what is most important about them is their so-called common, or commonsensical 'humanity'.

Suppose, on the other hand, that I want in my Shakespeare class to focus not less sharply but more sharply upon ethnic, gender-based, or political issues in the plays. In that event, I may find classes puzzled and resentful or even scornfully contemptuous of the resulting Shakespeare whose works seem sometimes to endorse racist, sexist, and politically conservative views (compared, especially, to views of a gentle, congenial, all-embracing 'Will Shakespeare' taught by tradition in many schools). I could try to counterbalance some of the undemocratic content in Shakespeare by emphasizing Shakespeare's skepticism and the anti-authoritarian and anti-patriarchal voices in his plays (reading *The Tempest*, for instance, as partly critical of the slave-owning Prospero), but such moves might seem too little and too late for students who routinely read literature through political lenses. If such students were to conclude, moreover, that Shakespeare's content reflects outmoded attitudes offending diverse groups, then such students might find reasons for dismissing Shakespeare altogether.

Not wanting to throw the baby of literary excellence and ethical instruction out with the bath of troubling politics, I might strive to teach Shakespeare less in terms of political content than of aesthetic form. That technique has been specifically recommended, in fact, by a Professor of English writing in *Harper's* magazine. He argues:

> There is no doubt that many civic and sexual rights remain to be secured in this country; there is no doubt that scandalous inequities persist unattended to. But English professors are not experts on these matters. They are taught how to identify tropes, not how to eliminate racist attitudes. To turn their courses into classes on (say) Post-Colonial Literature with the idea of addressing with some degree of insight the problem of ethnocentrism is to ask someone equipped to catch butterflies to trap an elephant.[1]

Suppose that, following such an argument, I turn in teaching Shakespeare to identifying tropes and other formal, more purely aesthetic concerns. Will I really turn away from problems of racism and of ethnocentrism?

Trope – 'turns' in language – make it, of course, figurative, non-literal. Hamlet traps Claudius "tropically", making Claudius look beneath surface meanings of Hamlet's play to his particular guilt and the threat to him of a murderous nephew. Captain Fluellen says there are figures in all things as he compares Henry V to "Alexander the Pig". Those tropes ask for more, however, than 'identification'. Those tropes ask attentive audiences and readers not only to appreciate aesthetic forms but also to debate specific issues of regicide, of pre-Christian and Christian views of revenge, and of the extent to which out-sized heroes like Henry perhaps hog a stage of history.

If I teach my students not merely to 'identify' Shakespeare's tropes but also to ponder their meaning and function, then I may help my students, furthermore, to *use* Elizabethan and modern English figuratively, trope-ically. To employ tropes in English, however, my students will need to work and play with a wide variety of English language features in historical contexts. In this process, they will study culturally-specific ideas about history, the world, and its peoples that inform the English language and give it part of its character. I doubt whether such work and play with the Englishness of the language can be performed with no trace of assimilative intention or result.

Consider Portia's famous argument:

> The quality of mercy is not strained,
> It droppeth as the gentle rain from heaven ...
> It is an attribute to God himself.[2]

Here, the under-assumptions that a heaven provides rain or that God exists and is a 'he' must be held in mind to appreciate the figure of speech linking mercy and rain. Mercy is given a religious association, very likely a Christian tenor. Even seemingly innocuous words such as 'gentle' are allied at times with the term 'Gentile'. And so on. Weeks of Shakespeare study provide students with innumerable examples of figurative language invoking particular religious assumptions, socio-political views, and other culturally-defined attitudes which cannot always be consciously inspected, detected, and, if desired, rejected by even the most scrupulous readers. We may say an English teacher is asking only that the tropes be 'identified', but actually they are being digested, made familiar and more acceptable in mind. You can hardly use a language figuratively, non-literally, or playfully without having gone inside it and over to it to some degree. And can you go over to a language without accepting, at least provisionally, important parts of the culture which produced it? There are ways that languages look at the world.

Even to learn such a seemingly mechanical matter as Shakespeare's iambic pentameter requires a student to cultivate an ear for a range of English accents, to make Shakespeare's language and culture less foreign, more nearly native or assimilated. Even within Anglo-American culture, moreover, among diverse groups of students who use English as their first language, formal study may favor traditional pronunciation and enunciation, and also choices in speech and staging that invoke class-based attitudes. We English teachers are mired not only in an often ethnocentric language and literature but also in a class-oriented one. Thus, teachers and students who are 'native' speakers of English must decide whether or not to speak Shakespeare by imitating common stage intonations with their received standard British, somewhat upper-class sounds, their elocutionary distinctness so foreign to our everyday speech. Students might shun a Shakespeare spoken in Received British Pronunciation, but the same students must still speak in ways that reflect American speech standards associated with varied social classes. What precision of enunciation and styles of intonation will a teacher ask of self or of students, and with what social or economic class will each decision possibly affiliate the image of Shakespeare as author or the image of students as interpreters? Modern British actors such as John Barton and Lisa Harrow concede that their pronunciation of Shakespeare sounds "much more genteel" than either Elizabethan or much modern American pronunciation generally sounds.[3] Just how genteel do our scansion and other spoken exercises, even in American intonation, leave Shakespeare sounding? And what may be gained or lost in our classrooms by making Shakespeare sound genteel? If, for example, we encourage our students to speak Shakespeare with their own regional and social group inflections, may we in effect turn down the flame under the melting pot and thus perhaps encourage a useless heterogeneity of misplaced accents, failed rhymes, needlessly slurred speech, and cacophonous variety? Or may we celebrate a survival of central significance amid a diversified babble of voices?

Simply teaching 'the words' of Shakespeare thus involves any teacher in issues of domination, assimilation, and pluralism now familiar to academics accustomed to campus debates on multiculturalism, political correctness, and the like. Such debates cannot be dismissed casually. Merely to opine, for example, that Shakespeare offers the diction of common life and that his texts welcome a variety of students' regional, ethnic, class, and education-level inflections will hardly solve the problem of teacher-modeled and teacher-evaluated speaking of Shakespeare. For one thing, many students who hear in their heads Shakespeare being spoken in ways radically different from ways their teacher speaks, will themselves adopt a valuative stance: to yield or to resist. For another thing, some ways of speaking and interpreting Shakespeare are arguably more effective, useful, 'correct', than other ways. Are not most teachers of Shakespeare trying, after all, to *change* ways in which their students speak and understand? I insist that we would make a distinct mistake if we underestimated the extent to which teaching Shakespeare (and most Anglo-American literature) generally appears, and is, incompatible with an extreme pluralism defending such diversities of speech as uncorrected pronunciations, whispered readings, dropped suffixes, misemphasized words and phrases, mistaken meters, fumbled Latinisms, monotones, missed or neglected wordplay, mistaken explications, egregiously biased interpretations, and the like. If some of these linguistic and interpretive practices tend to recur in identifiable subgroups (mispronunciations by ESL users, for example, or total 'bashing' of Petruchio or of Kate by radical separatists of both genders), then teachers of Shakespeare may find themselves attempting to change such practices and concomitant parts of subgroup identity, all in the direction of the teacher's, the institution's, or society's norms of civic culture. Still, by reconciling social diversities in uses of language and interpretation, we teachers soften some sharp edges of pluralist distinction among groups who use language and values differently. May we justify such teaching on the grounds that we are only attacking a useless separatism based on the inadequacies or deficiencies of some groups in speaking or interpreting Shakespeare? I cannot imagine a more delicate issue.

Even a seemingly neutral, philological interest in how Shakespeare's language originally sounded may arouse potentially embarrassing diversities in student standards of propriety. When we pay attention to how Shakespeare's words may have sounded originally, we can hear unedited puns as on 'birthing' and 'burden' or 'keys' and 'case' or 'line' and 'loin' and so on. Class discussion of such puns may not suit the sub-cultural standards of some class members, yet refusing to discuss them may offend the standards of others. Each teacher must decide, in any event, just what proportion of class time to devote to such matters. Shakespeare is traditionally taught as concerned more with religious and political and social morality than with specifically sexual morality. Some of the sexual punning in plays such as *Romeo and Juliet* has long been deleted from high-school editions, and even college editions fail to note a great many sexual references. Lecture and discussion that downplay Shakespeare's sexual language may well seem non-ideological and non-controversial to students; hence their diversities in sense of propriety may seem to be less invoked. Lecture and discussion that direct classroom attention to sexual language in Shakespeare obviously risk raising questions of which diverse standards will be valued or disvalued and in what ways.

What I am suggesting is that sometimes a return to 'basics' of scansion, spelling, pronouncing, and annotating may offer a challenging approach to redefine political categories of classroom diversity. Diversities in gender or class or ethnic background addressed by feminism, cultural materialism, or multiculturalist criticism may not be the only significant diversities to be explored in the Shakespeare class. Occasionally, sheer plodding lexicography may reorganize such diversities. Sometimes the closest reading becomes the most explosive.

The topic of student diversity in the Shakespeare classroom need not be driven, in other words, toward accustomed venues of multicultural and intercultural education. Not all the interesting diversities among people are broadly social and political. Indeed, a new form of closer reading might lead Shakespeare teachers to identify a literally sensational diversity among class members. I am referring now not so much to sensual as to sheerly sensory modes of experiencing Shakespeare.

Consider, for example, the keenly performative nature of Shakespearean dialogue. As part of his dramatizing arsenal, Shakespeare employs literally thousands of exclamations, words that do not denote or name anything but rather express emotion directly, words such as 'ah', 'ha', 'la', 'o', 'ho', 'lo', 'fie', 'foh', 'hum', 'pooh', 'tush', 'tut', and so on. We call such terms, of course, 'ejaculations' or 'interjections'. By sounding emotional tone, they throw feeling from the speaker, and their meaning cannot be apprehended without some sort of tonal registry. An interjection such as 'o', for example, which Shakespeare employs some 2800 times, always looks the same, but it achieves, when vocalized in differing contexts, a remarkable range of intonations. When a student reads Shakespeare aloud and comes upon an 'o' (Shakespeare's un-wooden 'o'), suddenly the student stops naming things, abandons the referential use of language, and enters a realm of tonal expression for feeling, emotion, mood, attitude. I have often noted in my classes both the difficulty and opportunity of such a moment, for the student faces the vulnerability of subjectively enacting the tone of a speech without the busy cover of ordinary, lexical uncoding. And here, individual tones will vary greatly, and individual voice qualities will be heard more precisely as listeners are spared, for an instant, the work of denotative reference.

Students can, to be sure, attempt to speak in monotones, but Shakespeare's invariably emotive dialogue implicitly critiques such a maneuver, and purely tonal interjections, such as 'o', may become glaringly, embarrassingly flat when read perfunctorily. If, moreover, a teacher works to help students create a safe environment for tonal expression, and if gradually intensifying expression is promoted through narrowly incremental steps, then students may note a steadily widening diversity among not only the tones but also the accompanying facial expressions, gestures, postures, and other sensory expressions employed by varied student speakers as they sigh, moan, or angrily shout out Shakespeare's ubiquitous 'o's.

Shakespeare himself accentuates other diverse sensory responses to a single passage of dramatic dialogue. After Hamlet has heard the Player describe Hecuba's grief and after Hamlet dismisses the Players, he says:

> Ay, so, goodbye to you. – Now I am alone.
> O, what a rogue and peasant slave am I!
> Is it not monstrous that this player here,
> But in a fiction, in a dream of passion,
> Could force his soul so to his own conceit
> That from her working all his visage wanned,
> Tears in his eyes, distraction in his aspect,
> A broken voice, and his whole function suiting
> With forms to his conceit?[4]

Teaching Shakespeare to Heterogeneous Classes 165

Thus the conceit or image of merely fictional words can produce a very particular sensory configuration. Listeners, too, are diversified according to internal states of conscience and awareness: the guilty may be maddened, the innocent made pale, and the unknowing struck dumb, all by one and the same utterance. Hamlet expects Claudius physically, palpably to 'blench' or flinch, unlike the other spectators, upon his witnessing precisely the same performance that the others observe more impassively.

Such diversity of enactment and response typifies a Shakespeare class, as well. Students in the class may, for example, hear and speak Claudius's first response to Hamlet's play, "Give me some light", in a range of tones from astonishment and fear to anguish, anger, or even contempt. That range of tones depends not only upon students' diverse beliefs concerning the degree of Claudius's criminality and Hamlet's right to murderous revenge but also upon students' varied intensities and inhibitions of personal response.

The circumstance that Shakespeare's peculiar appeal rests partly upon his intense investment in tonal, voiced, embodied, individuating reaches of language does, it seems to me, open up a wild, literally sensational range of responsive diversity in all readers and spectators, including, of course, students – each of whom variously portrays those embodiments of voice, intonation, gesture, posture, and movement that Hamlet so searchingly identifies. To say that Shakespeare seems, furthermore, an almost uniquely dis-orienting, anti-normalizing author because he expresses so many unconventional and ambiguous yet sensuously-grounded sentiments that resist group assimilation and evaluation is to say that Shakespeare creates a maximum diversity of individual responses. Shakespeare intensifies the diversity of students not only in their ethnic, religious, political, and gender-group affiliations but also in their more private, imagistic, sensory, corporeal, experiential histories, histories which diversify students at more nearly individual levels.

Shakespeare's many images of internal bodily sensation might be cited, furthermore, as invoking somatic diversities among responsive student readers. When Macbeth says that the prospect of murdering King Duncan made Macbeth's seated heart knock at his ribs, each reader apprehends the image through recall of her 'own' experience, if any, of wildly-beating heart. We may assume similarities among readers, but each somatic experience is concrete, physically individuated, and spatially unique in ways we don't generally assume our discursive, shareable thoughts to be concrete, individuated, or unique. In *The Tempest*, the drunken butler, Stephano, says to Trinculo: "Prithee, do not turn me about. My stomach is not constant".[5] Could one know what he meant if one could not consult one's own sensory register of personal bodily experience to which imagination (or 'somagination') of a queasy stomach could be referred? Yet one hesitates to assume that the bodily experience of another is precisely the same as one's own. To say: "I know what you feel" can be as condescending as consoling. To say: "I literally feel in my body what you feel in yours" may push imaginative empathy to absurd extremes. Thus it seems reasonable to assume that a sense of Stephano's inconstant stomach actually varies somewhat from person to person. And hence we may hesitate to say we teach a single sense of Shakespeare to diversified students, even at the most elemental level.

Both body language and bawdy language in Shakespeare provoke diversities of sense. Here is an example. One of my students had taken a Chaucer course before taking my Shakespeare course. In the Chaucer course, the student noted some of Chaucer's bawdy puns on the word 'privy' (meaning 'private'), and on 'privily' and 'privity'. In reading Shakespeare (who of, course, read Chaucer), the student noticed Guildenstern punning with Hamlet that Guildenstern and Rosencrantz are 'privates' in the secret parts of strumpet fortune, about her waist and in the middle of her favors.[6] When the class read *Coriolanus*, the same student decided that Coriolanus treated the Citizens as if they wished to abuse him not only emotionally but also physically, even sexually: the Citizens, for example, speak of putting their tongues into Coriolanus's wounds,[7] and Coriolanus later says to them, perhaps pleadingly, perhaps sarcastically, "I have wounds to show you, which shall be yours in private".[8] I was asked during class discussion whether Coriolanus might reasonably be taken to hint that the Citizens' demand to see his wounded body seemed to him like a sexual invasion. Now, I knew of other instances in Shakespeare (unfamiliar to the student) wherein 'private' could perhaps more easily suggest sexual innuendo (*The Two Gentlemen of Verona* 5.4.71: "The private wound is deepest"; *Pericles* 4.6.91-92: "Come, bring me to some private place. Come, come"; *Twelfth Night* 3.4.91-92: "Let me enjoy my private. Go off"; *Othello* 4.1.1-2: "What, / To kiss in private?"). Was I to take class time enumerating these instances? Was I to mention the view of the lexicographer F. R. Rubinstein that much of *Coriolanus* is suffused with suggestions of sexual seduction and sexual power plays between men?[9] (She cites numerous instances, some of which are more persuasive than others; but she does not cite the student's passage!) I was quite certain that not all the students were equally prepared to judge and attain just those levels of excitement, laughter, disdain, or appreciation that discussion of the student's question or Rubinstein's views might most usefully stimulate. That is, examination of relevant passages for sexual innuendo would inevitably spread the students out along a wide spectrum of psycho-physiological responses and also a wide diversity of views concerning the occasions of Shakespeare's sexual language and its social relevance. Some of the students would almost certainly register shock, disbelief, disgust, or disdain. Others would laugh embarrassedly. Others would consider absorbingly. Others would be over-persuaded. What was I to do?

Luckily, the bell rang, ending the class! At the next class, I gave the students a handout in which I outlined a variety of possible responses and interpretations concerning the remark of Coriolanus, and I gave my own, admittedly fallible, estimate of which views were the more ordinary and which were the more challenging. This example helps to suggest, in any event, how no two people are likely to sense Shakespeare's images in identical ways. Indeed, given the complex data and therefore the likely variety of experiential grounds (including genetic heritage, gender roles, sexual experience, and the like) for imagining Shakespeare's images, action, and character, we might conclude that differences in individual experiences of the 'same' text at basic, sensory levels will constitute a striking form of student diversity in the Shakespeare classroom.

It might be objected that, of course, students of Shakespeare's plays are experientially diverse in their precise sensory imaginings as they read but that such diversity of experience is pedagogically insignificant because the diversity is mostly prediscursive and so unavailable to classroom examination. Or, as Jonathan Culler puts it, "The question is not what actual readers happen to do but what an ideal reader must know implicitly in order to read and interpret works in ways which we consider acceptable in accordance with the institution of literature".[10] I might interpose Stanley Fish's reminder: "the problem is simply that most methods of analysis operate at so high a level of abstraction that the basic data of the meaning experience are slighted and/or obscured".[11] I would add, however, that, for me, yes, some basic data of literary experience may remain prediscursive, unshareable, and, in a sense, therefore asocial, private, subjective, and radically diverse. Still, a significant task of the Shakespeare teacher might be to help students employ more complex registers of such basic data in their own reading or performing. That is, while we most often define our students' experience of Shakespeare in terms of interpretations made diverse by their affiliation to varied social groups, we may also define that experience in ways that respect students' diversities on more personal, sometimes nearly biological levels. Just as one may make love like a missionary or die like a trooper yet still get in touch with one's own particular experience, so also one's students may be taught to discover more than that their interpretations are romantic, sentimental, feminist, or Freudian. They may be taught, I trust, to read more nearly in the present with more particular and precise responses.

Shakespeare's figurative language appeals in its concreteness to the individuating concreteness of personal experience. Imagine a class of students reading Lear's loathsome indictment of female sexuality:

> Down from the waist they're centaurs,
> Though women all above.
> But to the girdle do the gods inherit;
> Beneath is all the fiends'.
> There's hell, there's darkness, there is the sulfurous pit, burning, scalding, stench, consumption.[12]

What any given student imagines, thinks, and feels here depends greatly on just what personal experiences that student may have had and how that student conceives of her or his own body and the bodies of others. Such a passage creates a wide diversity of responses reflecting an equally wide range of attitudes and values gleaned from genetic make-up, body type, configuration of originating family and its shifting experiences and evaluations, partly instinctive responses to odors, hygiene, sensual stimulations, and sex differences, evolving knowledge and opinion of gender roles, sexual morality, and so on. There could hardly be any all-purpose guide to a correct or most appropriate response to such a passage. It speaks to the most intimate portions of our sensory experience and being. It teaches the diversity among us. But then, so does much of Shakespeare and other powerful art. Such art throws us back partly upon the originating cells of our selves. It disorients us, mocking the stock response and undermining group norms. Such art partly drives us back toward our individuating senses, liberating and challenging us to live and feel our very own lives.

Some English teachers may teach students to read tropes or metaphors in ways that expose additional diversities among students. Shakespeare's images, for example, can be apprehended primarily as external, objectified sights or primarily as internal, subjectified feelings. When Macbeth speaks of the "horrid" (literally "bristly") image of Duncan's anticipated murder "unfixing" Macbeth's hair, a reader may perhaps see in imagination Macbeth's hair stand on end.[13] A reader might also remember how such hair-raising experience feels to the nerves in the skin. It is not difficult, moreover, for a clinical psychologist to prove that readers who attend not merely to what an image looks like as a mental picture (the 'stimulus proposition') but even more to what physiological activity the image might appropriately arouse (the 'response proposition'), to prove that such readers themselves experience greater internal physiological activity during imagining than that exhibited by readers who restrict attention to the appearance of the stimulus.[14] By internal activity, I mean changes in heart rate, blood pressure, nerve firings, muscle tension, skin conductance, blinking rates, posture shifts, facial movements, and the like. To illustrate, you could read the following lines so as merely to picture Beatrice and Benedick on stage made to confess their love:

Leonato
 Come cousin, I am sure you love the gentleman.
Claudio
 And I'll be sworn upon 't that he loves her;
 For here's a paper written in his hand,
 A halting sonnet of his own pure brain,
 Fashioned to Beatrice. [*He shows a paper.*]
Hero
        And here's another
 Writ in my cousin's hand, stol'n from her pocket,
 Containing her affection unto Benedick.
 [*She shows another paper.*]
Benedick A miracle! Here's our own hands against our hearts.[15]

You could take the phrase "our own hands against our hearts" as signifying simply 'our writings confess that our affections are guilty as charged'. But then, Shakespeare could have said it that way if he had wished. Instead, the materializing, physical nature of the twin vehicles 'hands' and 'hearts' (and the concomitant spatializing of the preposition 'against') may be taken to encourage an at least momentary addition of sensory, proprioceptive internalization in the reader's or hearer's response. One can imagine and empathically feel not only one's own hand against one's own heart but also against another's heart. Also, 'against' here quietly shifts from suggesting opposition to suggesting convergence, from a hurtful 'against' of contrary disagreement to an intimate 'against' of loving contact. And, as often is the case, Shakespeare has prepared the way earlier in the same play to invite such somaticizing of the images (or somages): "and in her bosom I'll unclasp my heart"; "Then down upon her knees she falls, weeps, sobs, beats her heart, tears her hair, prays, curses: 'O sweet Benedick!'"; "And Benedick, love on; I will requite thee, / Taming my wild heart to thy loving hand".[16] *Much Ado About Nothing* is, it seems, in part a play about hands upon hearts, and readers and audiences will do well not merely to note that but to sense it, to feel it internally.

 This second style of reading is almost certain to produce more than customary feeling and emotion in most senses of those terms – somato-visceral, cerebral, commonsensical. Yet the contexts of study and discussion traditionally provided for students of Shakespeare (and other artists) rarely encourage such a style of reading and response. It is not improbable, in fact, that many students who read those lines of Benedick's do not bother even to 'see' hands or hearts but merely note a confession of love, thus converting Shakespeare's sensuously-evocative image to a relational observation and abstract proposition.

A Shakespeare teacher who teaches students how to convert sight images to internal response propositions (and their accompanying somatic sensations resulting in enhanced physiological activity) obviously directs class attention to the corporeal diversity of the students. Attention is thus paid to those most palpable and individuating differences among the students, differences of the space their bodies occupy and the unfathomable complexity and particularity of their interior experiences.

Having reached this stage in the argument, I wish to concede immediately that I have raised, so far, many more problems than I have solved. I have suggested few means, for example, through which to negotiate between the broadly social understanding of Shakespeare and the more private and diverse perceptions I adduce (perceptions perhaps in turn shaped partly by social promptings). I also suppose that our very attempts to articulate differences among our diversely private experiences of Shakespeare do much themselves to socialize and normalize what once seemed internal, bodily, prediscursive. What sort of politics may covertly be recommended, furthermore, by a program for trying to read ever more nearly in the present, ever closer to seemingly a-social and improvisatory experience, assuming such a thing were possible?

Without attempting finally to answer such a question, I would still surmise that my interest in authenticating diverse but acceptable experiences among individual students as readers could promote an argument for reconceiving the nature of close reading, for reviving or revising topics of sensation, perception, and feeling in the English classroom, and for broadening some views of how identities, attitudes, and values are constructed. My view is that art, at least Shakespeare's art, can both reinforce and contest cultural norms. Shakespeare wrote the same plays to be played before the monarch and in the red-light district. There are diverse appeals within single documents. There is much in the plays that is racist, sexist, and authoritarian. There is much that is anti-racist, anti-sexist, and anti-authoritarian. Concreteness of language nonetheless militates against overly abstract or categorical interpretation. At a level that is not so clearly political but is not merely aesthetic, Shakespeare employs his materializing imagination to help us, in Gloucester's terms, "see feelingly" so as not merely to recognize but care for the otherness we continually confront. In so doing, we perceive both an outer and an inner diversity, equally ours to acknowledge. As we struggle to acknowledge things of bodily darkness and death beneath our seemingly non-physical ideas, Shakespeare can help us to face such bodily workings of our beating minds (to employ Prospero's phrase), beating minds which are sometimes best stilled by a turn or two of contemplative walking or by thinking through the rhythms of our breath.

The teaching and study of Shakespeare can encourage valuing diversities in both social and individual dimensions. Such individually-celebrated diversity need not reinstitute an outworn, essentialist individualism or a destructive reverence for the autopoetic subject. I speculate that every culture needs and might employ art such as Shakespeare's to bring us to our senses (as I argue in *Making Sense of Shakespeare* to which this piece is indebted).[17] Such teaching of Shakespeare can help to dissipate an often-threatening dominance of social authority among particular lives, to legitimate personal and emotional and social intelligence as well as rational and abstract intelligence, to resurrect the body and the galactic yet engaging distances between our truly personal, somatic experiences, to re-establish the responsibility of each person to fear her own, unique death so as to feel her own, unique life. Shakespeare's relentlessly concretizing imagination points us downward to the material, feeling concomitants of abstract ideas and moral states. What is the feeling part of being guilty? It is when 'Amen' sticks in your throat and you cannot rub bloody spots off your hands. What is the relation of mental hate to bodily pleasure? It is when a man mistakenly makes love in the dark to a woman he thinks he despises: as Helena says, just after such intercourse, "O strange men! /

That can such sweet use make of what they hate".[18] Horatio will not feel abstractly 'sad' when he relates Hamlet's story; no, Horatio will draw his "breath in pain".[19] Cordelia complains not of her sisters' wickedness *per se* but of the way they are using their eyes and tongues; Cordelia leaves them not 'sorrowfully' but with "washed eyes,"[20] and she continues weeping until her death. Is the material sign emblematic of an immaterial reality? Or is the material sign, the somatic expression, the use of this fleshly life, partly its own significance and value? Lear at the last looks on the still body of Cordelia and cries out that what he wants is her life, her breath, the elemental life owned by "a dog, a horse, a rat [...] Thou'lt come no more".[21] We're either here, in the breath and feeling of the present, or else gone apart into an abstract non-life.

Beneath or within formalism lies informalism. We can seek external confirmation of our perceptions of the art object, and we can create a consensus reality concerning its properties amenable to discourse. That is, I take it, a traditional aim of formalist study. We can also concede, however, that what such formalism tends to label ambiguity objectively present in the words of the literary text often can be more accurately labeled an unsettled diversity of responses among and within ourselves as readers.

A final comment. It is often said that Shakespeare wrote for the theater and not for readers, so that his plays should be studied in performance. While much may be learned about Shakespeare by studying films and live performances and even more may be learned, I think, by student performance itself, still such study may tend to reduce creative diversity of responses to Shakespeare. Theater productions interpret the texts, revealing some possibilities, but obscuring many more, and the decorous conditions of reception among most theater and film audiences tend to restrict diversity of response. Strange to say, moreover, but still true, actors often reveal limited connection to their voices, bodies, and feelings, and their individual performances frequently suffer from overstylized, stereotypical readings. Student readers, on the other hand, can be encouraged to read experimentally, somatically, and individually according to their diverse capacities.

They can work flexibly back and forth between guided and self-led responses. Such readers may well have been desired by Shakespeare. Certainly, after his death, his friends put themselves to much trouble and expense to publish for readers the first collected edition of his works, and, in their Preface to the *First Folio* addressed "To the great Variety of Readers", they wrote:

> it is not our prounice, who onely gather his works, and giue them you, to praise him. It is yours that reade him. And there we hope, to your *diuers capacities*, you will finde enough, both to draw, and hold you: for his wit can no more lie hid, then it could be lost. Reade him, therefore; and againe, and againe: And if then you doe not like him, surely you are in some manifest danger, not to vnderstand him. And so we leaue you to other of his Friends, whom if you need, can bee your guides: if you neede them not, you can leade your selues, and others. And such Readers we wish him.[22]

And such readers, readers learning to lead themselves through their diverse capacities, I wish my students. May Shakespeare draw and hold them, to see more feelingly, to sense the pain or bracingness of each particular breath, and to go forward accepting the tragic and comic mystery of how diverse we are.

Notes

1. Louis Menand, "What are Universities For?", *Harper's* (December 1991), pp. 55-6.
2. *The Merchant of Venice* 4.1.182-93. Quotations of Shakespeare follow *The Complete Works of Shakespeare*, ed. David Bevington (rev. 4th edn; New York: Longman, 1994).
3. John Barton, *Playing Shakespeare* (London and New York: Methuen, 1984), p. 52.
4. *Hamlet* 2.2.549-57.
5. *The Tempest* 2.2.114-15.
6. *Ham.* 2.2.222-36.
7. *Coriolanus* 2.3.7.
8. *Cor.* 2.3.76-8.
9. Frankie Rubinstein, *A Dictionary of Shakespeare's Sexual Puns and their Significance* (London: Macmillan, 1984), pp. 322-3.
10. Jonathan Culler, "Literary Competence", in *Reader-Response Criticism: From Formalism to Post-Structuralism*, ed. Jane P. Tompkins (Baltimore and London: The Johns Hopkins University Press, 1980), p. 111.
11. Stanley E. Fish, "Literature in the Reader: Affective Sytlistics", in *Reader-Response Criticism*, p. 76.
12. *Lr.* 4.6.124-9.

13 *Mac.* 1.3.136.

14 See Peter J. Lang, "Language, Image, and Emotion", in *Perception of Emotion in Self and Others*, ed. Patricia Pliner, et al. (New York and London: Plenum Press, 1979), p. 113; and Gregory A. Miller, et al., "Individual Differences in Imagery and the Psychophysiology of Emotion", *Cognition and Emotion* 1:4 (1987), pp. 387-8.

15 *Ado.* 5.4.83-91.

16 *Ado.* 1.1.311; 2.3.150-2; 3.1.112-3.

17 Charles H. Frey, *Making Sense of Shakespeare* (Madison, NJ: Fairleigh Dickinson University Press, 1999).

18 *All's Well that Ends Well* 4.4.21-2.

19 *Ham.* 5.2.350.

20 *Lr.* 1.1.272.

21 *Lr.* 5.3.312-3.

22 *The Norton Facsimile First Folio of Shakespeare*, ed. Charlton Hinman (New York: Norton, 1968), p. 7.

TEACHING SHAKESPEARE IN THE MULTI-CULTURAL CLASSROOM

Edna Z. Boris
(LaGuardia Community College, City University of New York)

The college at which I teach, LaGuardia Community College of the City University of New York, has one of the most diverse student bodies in the country. At the last count of which I am aware, though the number has probably already changed, 129 countries were represented. If there are 30 students in a class, they are likely to come from 25 countries. Such a classroom can provide a microcosm of the worldwide interest in Shakespeare.

In each class there are some students with virtually no knowledge of Shakespeare and others who have read and seen several plays. Similarly diverse are the students' learned classroom behaviors: some come from cultures where even asking a question is inappropriate while others have the intellectual and personal maturity of doctoral candidates. In this context, developing assignments, techniques, and approaches that will encourage active learning and exchanges of ideas is essential. Described below are several activities for individual students, for small groups, for the whole class, and for the instructor.

While the exercises and techniques as I use them are designed to meet specific needs of a particular student population, others may find useful ideas that can be tailored for their students and purposes. The techniques can be adapted for introductory level courses where Shakespeare is just one element and for courses devoted entirely to his works; many of the techniques can be used in other courses as well. Although I would not use all of these techniques in any individual course, the order of presentation roughly follows the likely timing in a semester for introducing each technique.

Getting started with ice-breaking circle games and visual aids – Some students seriously fear reading a Shakespeare play because of the poetry, 400 year-old English, and what they perceive as the solemnity of his canonical position. To help overcome these fears and to prepare them for the broad range of experiences that study of Shakespeare can offer, I usually do some of the following early in the semester.

We arrange the seats in a circle. Everyone receives a several-page, stapled handout containing a "You Are Quoting Shakespeare" exercise, a Shakespearean Insult exercise, and a Shakespearean Compliment exercise. In the Quote exercise, varying numbers (2 to 5 or 6) of famous brief quotations are clustered and followed by the statement in boldface, "You are Quoting Shakespeare". One by one each of us in the circle reads a single quote; in unison we all read the boldface refrain. After we have completed that exercise we use the Insult exercise which contains two columns of adjectives and a final column of nouns. Each person selects an adjective from column A, another from column B, and a noun from column C to direct an 'insult' at one other person in the circle; that person then selects someone who has not been 'insulted' and directs a new insult at a new individual, and so on. This prevents any one person from receiving all the insults; there is always one student who has the courage to direct an insult at me, to everyone's amusement. We end on a more positive note by directing a few compliments towards each other. Allison Miller and Annette Dailey of Blue Springs South High School in Blue Springs, Missouri, distributed these materials at the 1996 National Council of Teachers of English (NCTE) Teaching Shakespeare conference held in Louisville, Kentucky. Jerry Maguire of Center Grove High School in Indiana developed the Shakspearean Insult and Compliments three-column sheets. The insults first appeared in Peggy O'Brien's *Shakespeare Set Free* (125); the compliments were printed in the first issue of *Shakespeare Magazine* (www.shakespearemag.com). Many web-sites have since appeared using the insults idea. Students at all levels (as do colleagues) enjoy these games.

If there is time that same day or soon thereafter, I will distribute for examination many photographs, pamphlets, and materials about Shakespeare and Stratford-upon-Avon. To continue a tradition begun for me by my own undergraduate Shakespeare professor, Leonard Lief at Hunter College, I also show a copy of Eric Partridge's *Shakespeare's Bawdy* in the 1960 paperback with a charming cover to alert students that they need to watch for many layers of meaning in the texts they will be reading.

One other visual aid that I almost always use is a transparency of an illustration of the original Globe's interior that Patrick Spottiswoode (Director, Globe Education) distributed during the National Endowment for Humanities 1995 summer institute, the Center for Renaissance and Shakespearean Staging ("CRASS"). For a few minutes during which time each student must jot down an observation, I show the image as large as possible on a classroom wall; then I turn off the projector. We hear what everyone observed (there is usually little duplication) such as the crowding, the hats, the few women, the sky, the sports-arena-like sightlines and atmosphere. After everyone's observation has been mentioned, we again look at the image and discuss what it might generally have felt like to be present in that audience or performing on that stage.

Student advance preparation – For each Shakespeare play that an introductory class reads I distribute **Reading Guide Questions** at least a week before we will begin discussing the play. These are arranged chronologically and are designed to help students understand the plot. At the top of the first page is a statement like the following:

> These questions will help you understand the most important actions/events in the play. As you read and answer them, make note of the following: (1) any passages that you want to discuss in class (2) any passages you find truthful, or interesting, or puzzling. For **every** class, you should **decide ahead of time what selection you would like the class to discuss** (be prepared when I call on you).

When I first distribute the guide questions, we spend class time discussing how to use them. I suggest that students jot answers on the pages as a way to have the facts of the play ready to hand. If there will be an open book quiz or test during the term, I will allow students to use their answers on these sheets and any other notes they may have.

We then spend several minutes discussing the second part of the instructions. For each play that we read, every student must have selected for all sessions at least three passages that he or she would like the class to examine (three so that if other students by chance select the same passages, everyone is still likely to have something to request). First I will ask for volunteers one by one to direct our attention to their selected place and ask each selecting student to read a bit of the passage and explain why it was chosen. The whole class will then discuss the passage for whatever time seems appropriate. Sometimes the answer is a quick factual one, what something means; sometimes there is no ready answer because the passage is ambiguous (exploration of ambiguity is usually rich, with many students contributing); sometimes we may need to do some research or thinking and will have to come back to the answer on another day. Whatever the situation, the student selection is always of value and interesting (even if only to indicate that a student is spending time on something so obscure as to not merit attention).

The student tells us the act, scene, lines, and who is speaking; in a more advanced class I may ask the student to also give us a bit of context; otherwise I will supply that (after a quick glance, if it is not a passage that I immediately recognize). In some classes we may have time for several student requests; in some classes I do not allot any time to this activity, but the student obligation to be prepared with a request is always in effect. After a few occasions of asking volunteers to make the selections, I call on students. If any are not prepared, I will make a big deal of that, especially early in the term, by asking them to speak with me privately or by saying, "I'm making a note of your lack of preparation today." This student obligation to make selections leads to mutual exploration and discovery.

Keeping Daily Classroom Minutes – Both for students whose classroom skills need improving and for sophisticated students, keeping records in the form of classroom minutes of each class meeting can be an enormously useful technique.

The opportunity to prepare and then read minutes of a class meeting helps sophisticated students to polish skills they will possibly need in their professional careers. Knowing that there is an official record of what each class covered can be a comfort for a student who may have to miss several classes. For an upper-level class, I just announce firmly that everyone in the class will have at least one chance to do this, ask for a volunteer the first day, and hand the person a special set of paper that will write through to make two copies; then at the end of class I collect one of the sets and the volunteer takes the other home to look over. We begin the following class by hearing the minutes read aloud and inviting additions or corrections. If the student is absent, I read from my copy. If the student is present, the student has the option of handing in at a later date a corrected written version for a grade. Otherwise, the student just receives a check mark for having done the minutes.

For less sophisticated students the exercise can be a help to improve their note-taking and classroom speaking skills. In this case I will begin by having the entire class keep minutes for one class and hand them in. Then I select the examples that are well done to read aloud as models for students to follow. After that each student must take at least one turn doing minutes, following the same procedure (special paper to make two copies, reading aloud, optional rewrite). The most difficult aspect to master is the degree of specificity needed – just topic headings is inadequate; too much detail takes too much time. One guideline that I offer student minutes-keepers is to ask themselves, "What would someone who is not here today need to know?"

As minutes are read, I can tell by watching student faces what needs to be discussed again because not enough students understood. Particularly when teaching more than one section of the same course at the same time I find that having students keep classroom minutes helps me keep track of what different sections have covered on particular days. Of greatest value to everyone, students and teacher alike, is how quickly hearing the minutes of the previous class can bring us all to the same place at the same time, especially after a long weekend or vacation. This technique is discussed in "Classroom Minutes: A Valuable Teaching Device", which was published in 1983 and reprinted in 1984.

A Student Role in Syllabus Planning – A technique that would work in upper-level, advanced (even graduate) Shakespeare courses is to invite student requests/suggestions that the instructor will take into account in planning the syllabus. I have used this technique in introductory survey literature courses and in drama courses, but it could add some interest to an upper-level Shakespeare course.

What is essential is for the instructor to limit student choices to a range that is acceptable to the instructor. For example, if a class is going to be working with the Sonnets, spending class time on each is probably not possible. Which sonnets should be given particular attention? The instructor may sometimes wish to fully control the choice and at other times may not; at those other times, the instructor can do something like the following:

Begin by requiring written statements (I usually specify 500 words) from students in which they argue that a particular poem be discussed. I tell the students to think of themselves as the lawyer representing that poem before me, the judge. In an upper-level class where students have considerable familiarity with Shakespeare's plays a similar challenge can be given students to help influence which plays are given top priority in class – among the comedies, histories, tragedies, romances, which plays to read, which to spend most class time discussing.

After receiving the requests (which I frequently use to diagnose their writing skills early in the term), I proceed in one of two ways. In one process, I make the syllabus decisions entirely myself, keeping in mind what students asked for, and announce the results in the form of a printed syllabus. In the second process, I make some choices and then allow class presentations and votes to determine the remaining choices. To do this, I will list on the board the candidate works and who requested (sponsored) them. Before the next class, everyone is to look over the candidate works, and the sponsor(s) is (are) to plan a brief oral presentation. The class hears all the sponsor presentations and then votes. Knowing that a semester will end before we accomplish everything we want to accomplish, we will rank the selections by the numbers – the one receiving the highest vote count we turn to first and so on. This can all be done quickly; the student involvement in decision-making helps them feel responsible for the success of the class and has positive spill-over effects. An article on this technique appeared in 1994 in *Exercise Exchange*.

Character Teams – The number of students in a class and the number of characters in a play can determine whether I will set up teams of students to discuss just major characters or major characters and some minor characters. A maximum of 5 or 6 students per group seems to work best.

A character-related task that works well as an entirely in-class group activity is for members of each group to decide what first impression they would want the character to make if they were staging the play and what evidence supports that first impression. A good follow-up activity is for members of each group to decide before the next class when (if ever) that first impression changes and what the supporting evidence for change is; the groups can then reconvene during another class for discussion of changes. Whether the groups report just on first impressions then later report on changes, or whether the groups report on both at the same time can be decided on a case-by-case basis.

Should the class subsequently have an opportunity to view a performance involving the characters, the character teams can be invited to critique the performance. Students from other character teams can of course comment on any character. At different times in the term I will set up random groups (counting off), allow students to select their own groups, or set up groups according to where students are sitting.

Facilitating Student Interaction – Even classes in which students work in groups are all too often more teacher-centered than necessary. Many teachers (myself included) respond immediately to individual or group student contributions. Instead we instructors should encourage individual students and student groups to respond to each other's ideas before we do. When seats can be arranged in a semi-circle or full circle rather than in rows facing a front podium, students can see each other as well as the teacher. But whatever the seating arrangements, when students direct their comments to me, I encourage them to face and address each other by assuring them that I will hear them. Sometimes I refuse to look at a student who insists on directing comments only to me – I will walk behind that student's section of the room or off to the side. Eventually, students understand my quick wave towards the class and will address their remarks to their fellow students. Gradually such a process encourages students to listen actively to each other and to contribute to the discussion.

Performance Groups – Two ways that I have used performance groups are to kick off and to finish a semester. At a commuter college with a student body that has work and family in addition to school obligations, LaGuardia's students cannot meet outside of class, so any rehearsing must be done during class; this restricts the amount of time we can devote to student performance.

To kick off a semester, I have used the opening 58 lines of *Hamlet*, an exercise that Patrick Spottiswood had introduced at CRASS. Frances L. Helphinstine also uses this scene, as discussed in "Using Playgrounding to Teach *Hamlet*." Providing no information about the play and saying only that the students are to stage the scene (without memorizing the lines), I count them off to form random groups of 4 to 6 people (the Ghost and Francisco can double if necessary; an extra person can serve as understudy/director); each student receives a one-page photocopy of the lines. We will then spend part (generally 30 minutes or less of our 60-minute periods) of the next two or three classes breaking up for student rehearsals aimed at a designated performance day. Students will find near-by places to work in privacy; I check on each group to answer questions as needed. We will begin subsequent classes by discussing general questions that have come up during rehearsals and making decisions about the performance day such as how to handle classroom lighting, whether to have a thrust or proscenium stage, what part of our room should be the wings, etc. So far no student group has staged the opening lines with the emphasis on Francisco's "Nay" and on "me" ("*Nay*, answer *me*"), to assert his authority as the one on duty and to emphasize that the wrong person asks the opening question of this play. Only one group has said that they understood but did not know how to convey this wrong-person opener.

Students usually form strong bonds through the experience, making friends who encourage each other to continue even as the course becomes more difficult and challenging; they are fascinated to see how other groups solve problems that they have wrestled with; even shy students have managed with group support to perform their lines and actions. When I have asked for subsequent written comments as to whether they thought the activity brought enough benefits to merit the time invested, student response has been universally favorable. That experience becomes a base on which to build later in the term. For example, when we discuss the concept of 'embedded directions', students will remember Bernardo's "Well, sit we down", which invariably some groups had enacted by sitting and some had not.

Sometimes the student bonding in the random first groups is so strong that getting students to agree to work in other group combinations can take an effort, but one that I will insist on at times. Eventually, depending on the task at hand, I allow students to self-select groups.

As a final group activity, I have frequently used scenes from *Twelfth Night* and devoted part of many class periods for rehearsal. The scenes that we decide to do have varying numbers of actors, so students can choose their preferred scene and preferred number to work with. Generally I will describe several candidate scenes and let the class decide which ones we will do so that every student has a role. Among the scenes that I have used, several involve Malvolio: his finding the letter, wearing yellow stockings, and being imprisoned; a scene that I always use is the Cesario/Aguecheek duel; sometimes I use the final scene; sometimes I use the "patience on a monument" scene, which I refer to as "two men in love"; for the two students who do that scene, I usually require that they play it twice, reversing roles each time.

Whether as a kick-off or late-semester activity, I record participation, perhaps with a plus or minus to indicate effort, but no grade. The experience itself is what matters.

Performance Evaluation Comment Sheets – whenever students observe student performances, I require that they make written evaluations of what they have seen and that those evaluations be given to the performers. Students help decide what should be evaluated. The most recent application of this process used the following:

Give examples wherever possible in responding.

Observer's Name:_____ Group:_____

How well did the group work out entrances, exits, positions (i.e., blocking)?

Were the lines well delivered, with emotion?

Were actions suited to the words?

What special efforts has the group made?

Miscellaneous comments?

For however many groups we will be observing, all of us will have a stack of half-sheets of paper printed with these instructions. After each group performs, we spend a few minutes writing our reactions while they are fresh; then the next group gets ready to perform. I collect all the comment sheets, look them over, then return them to each group at the following class. When used to evaluate the kick-off performances, the comments show students the difference between specific and general observations. When used to evaluate end-of-term performances, the comments usually reveal considerable sophistication in student critiques.

Student Awareness of Editing/Textual Decisions – Having all students use the same edition of a play or sonnet under discussion is convenient in rapidly getting everyone to the same page. When several different editions are available in the room, however, students quickly begin to become aware of how unstable the 'text' actually is, become aware of editors' hands. Any time we examine lines and stage directions, students read aloud variations they may have in their editions; the class will, when appropriate, discuss the merits of the various editing choices. When everyone has the same edition so that such discoveries do not emerge during the term, devoting at least one class to this topic is a good idea. The instructor can bring in photocopies of one speech or moment as handled in a variety of editions over whatever period of time (several centuries are available, but several current editions can serve to make this topic's importance readily evident). Two excellent articles for students to read in conjunction with this exercise are Sandy Feinstein's "Crossbows, Lutes, and Coitus, or, What Does Editing Lady Macbeth Mean?" and Steven Urkowitz's "'Well-sayd olde Mole' – Burying Three *Hamlets* in Modern Editions".

Translations – Since so many of my students are immigrants for whom English is not their native language, the question of translations is one that I often address early in the term. Students are responsible for working with the text in English, using whatever will help them. Having a translation in their native language alongside the English text is fine with me. Over the years I have learned that students whose native languages are Indo-European will sometimes have an easier time with Shakespeare's English than will students who know only American

English; when they hear that, many students become more confident in their abilities to succeed in the course.

As one kind of independent project, I invite a student or several students to perform a speech or scene in their native language so that the class can hear what Shakespeare's words would sound like in another language. For fun, this can be done with the class not knowing what speech or scene and having to guess (an idea suggested by Professor Barbara Bowen of Queens College at a CUNY Shakespeare forum several years ago). As another kind of independent project, I have encouraged students to compare two or three translations by analyzing how one speech is handled. This project was inspired by Werner Habicht's paper, "There's the Rub: Translating Hamlet's Thought Process", which I saw in draft form. So far several students have expressed interest in doing such a project, but no one has yet actually done it.

Independent Projects – In an upper-level Shakespeare course I require that each student complete an independent project, which can be (1) a traditional research paper or (2) a research and design or research and performance project. Students who choose the second option I caution that this is double work, but for those who accept the challenge their experience can be memorable for them and for the class. Since these projects are done not in a theater or art class but in a literature course, I stress that the written component will largely determine the grade; realistically, however, a breathtaking performance or design will affect the grade too. One advantage of our New York City location is the availability of the circulating and reference materials of the New York Public Library's specialized Performing Arts Library, normally located at Lincoln Center, which I make sure that students know about. In addition, the ever-evolving electronic databases and internet resources available for research have led me to arrange for a librarian to provide a special Shakespeare research orientation session conducted in the library's instruction room where students have computer work stations and overhead projection screens to observe and use in becoming familiar with computer-assisted searches.

So far the best performance projects were as follows. One was a staging of the Hal/Hotspur combat in *1 Henry 4*, with each student researching and choreographing appropriate actions, supported by each one's separate written analysis and justifications. Another was one student's performing Hamlet's first and last soliloquies to convey her sense of his development in the play, again as supported by her written analysis. One option I have not yet tried is for students to produce a video of their performance and show the tape rather than do a live performance before the class.

The two best design projects so far have been as follows. One involved sketches of all the costumes for Hamlet and Ophelia as if for a production set in America in the 1950's and based on McCarthyism, to emphasize the theme of spying in *Hamlet*. The second involved gorgeously colored drawings of all the costumes for Viola, Olivia, and Orsino as inspired by the ancient Persian tales narrated by Scheherazade and known as *Arabian Nights' Entertainment* or *A Thousand and One Nights*, to emphasize the theme of a woman's surviving by her wits in *Twelfth Night*.

Early in the semester I will bring in examples of projects (including traditional research papers) to show the class and will distribute an information sheet like the following one.

Suggestions for Independent Shakespeare Projects   Professor Edna Boris

Your project should be based on one or more of the plays we are reading for this course, but you may use an additional play in combination with one of the plays that we are working with. Speak with me ahead of time about whatever you wish to work on and make sure you have my approval. A traditional research project should result in an essay that is approximately five pages, double spaced, in length. A performance or design project should be accompanied by an appropriate written explanation with documentation of supporting research (no pre-set number of pages). You should choose something that interests you so that you enjoy doing the project as much as possible.

1. **Performance Project** – can be done individually or collaboratively. If individually, select two major speeches, either by the same character or different characters. If collaboratively, select a significant scene with meaningful roles for however many people work together. In deciding how the speeches or scene should be performed, you should consult not only literary criticism of the play(s) but also performance history, where available, including tape and film. Confer with me about scheduling a performance date. The written explanation and documentation should be submitted at the due dates below. In addition to providing a written explanation and documentation for the decisions made in shaping the performance, those who work collaboratively should give an account of each person's contribution to the project.

2. **Design Project** –

A. Costumes – choose at least two characters from one play and decide how they would be dressed throughout the play. How many changes in clothing? What kinds of changes? Provide drawings that are as detailed as possible, showing the changes. In deciding how the characters should look, you should consult not only literary criticism of the play(s) but also performance history, where available, including tape and film. Since costumes would have to be **part of a complete approach to the play,** the explanation of the costumes should include an indication of the whole project: what theater, what audience, when, what period dress, etc. as well as documentation of the sources that influenced the design decisions.

B. Scenery/Props – make drawings and/or a model for all the scenery for one play – indicating all changes of scenery and props. Explain and document the decisions you make.

3. **Traditional research paper** –

A. Choose an idea or theme such as disguise, revenge, spying, or self-deception, for instance, and discuss how it is used in one or two plays.

B. Compare two or three translations into your native language of key speeches in one of Shakespeare's plays. The translations can be from different periods of time or contemporary to each other. What do you learn about how Shakespeare is treated in your native language and perhaps in your native country?

C. A topic of your own devising – speak with me about whatever you're thinking of doing.

Key dates (hand in a statement or the page or the whole project, as appropriate):
Thursday, April 22, tentative topic
Thursday, April 29 working bibliography
Thursday, May 6, thesis statement and essay map
Thursday, May 20, project due
Thursday, June 3, optional revisions of project due – *only projects handed in on-time may be revised for a higher grade*

This approach to independent student projects was discussed both in the *Shakespeare Newsletter* and in *Shakespeare and the Classroom*.

Structured Viewing – Following a tip from Bernice Kliman (offered at CRASS), that one should never just show a film but should always assign people specific things to look for while they are watching, I have so far tried assigning the following to students when we were viewing selected moments in Olivier's and Branagh's *Henry V*. The quality of observations, insights, and discussion that resulted from this exercise was much higher than had previously been the case (students pointed out, for instance, that in the Olivier film the costumes were always immaculate, which was certainly not the case in the Branagh version).

1. number of seconds for each shot
2. sequence of shots (close, mid, far, zoom in/out)
3. costumes – details, changes
4. lighting – changes
5. music – when, what kind
6. sound – what effects and how used
7. setting – details, changes
8. pacing of lines & to whom addressed

At different times in the semester one can use different assigned tasks depending on the class. Sharon A. Beehler's "Making Media Matter in the Shakespeare Classroom" offers lists of filmic devices, questions for film and videotape versions, and a recommended classroom procedure for using films/videos. At the 1999 Shakespeare Association of America seminar "*Exit Pursued by a SD]: Hamlet* and the Staging of Stage Directions" John Meagher (Toronto) provided a hierarchy for student focus on text, the responsibility to evaluate "what the text requires, invites, tolerates, discourages, forbids". Setting these out to challenge students as they watch productions and then read - or read and then watch - can get them to examine the text closely.

Oral Reports on Criticism – That there exists a more than 400-year-long continuous body of commentary on Shakespeare's work offers both a challenge and an opportunity for teachers and students. The oral report exercise described here can be designed for varying levels of student preparation and sophistication, from the most basic to the most advanced. I use the exercise at the freshman level to help students gain some perspective on the play that they are reading and to reinforce basic researching, citing, and speaking skills.

For one of the plays on which we shall spend several weeks, usually *Hamlet* or *Othello*, I announce that each student will make a brief oral report, approximately five minutes in length, summarizing what three critics have had to say about one character in the play. The students must identify the critic, the date and place of original publication, and where they found the criticism if that was not in the original publication. I give them approximately two weeks' lead time before the reports are due. The reports may take one or more class periods, with students speaking one after another until everyone has had a turn, or a few students report at the beginning or end of several classes, or both may be done – one designated report day and chances for make-up in subsequent class sessions.

In recent years our English Department has adopted a requirement that students attach photocopies or printouts of all sources that they use in a paper, at least of the pages cited and of the pages that identify the source. For this oral report exercise I now require that students have the photocopies or printouts with them so that if any questions arise we have the information to provide answers on the spot.

This oral exercise is thus designed to help provide a structured situation that gives each student practice speaking informally before a group. To make the exercise as non-threatening as possible, I announce that it will not be graded but done for credit, and I use a system of checks with plusses and minuses to record the degree of effort each student puts into the project. Although I acknowledge that this is not a public speaking class and that students will not be graded on their 'performance', I encourage students to establish eye contact with their audience and to speak loudly and clearly enough to be heard easily. When the class is listening to the reports, students themselves encourage the reporting student to speak in a way to make the report as comprehensible as possible.

The course in which I most frequently use this exercise is called *Writing Through Literature* and is the upper level composition course (ENG 102), for most students the last writing course they will take (for many it is also the only literature course). In the lower level composition course (ENG 101), students should have written research papers, but if a long time has elapsed between the two courses students may have forgotten (or not well learned in the first place) how to do college-level research. This oral report exercise thus sharpens those skills before students have to write a research paper for the course. We briefly discuss what sources are and are not appropriate at college level, an element of this exercise that has become increasingly important with the advent of internet research.

Generally I let students choose whatever character they wish, even if this means that some characters are reported on by many students and some are not reported on at all, but it would be easy to ask students to specify ahead of time by having students sign up for characters or state in class ahead of time which character they wish to report on and then encouraging students to choose under-selected characters.

In each class as we hear the reports, students show a wide range of enterprise, a function of how much time and interest each brings to the assignment. Several will choose the most prominent character, Hamlet or Othello, rely just on one volume of *Shakespearean Criticism* for excerpts, and choose the first three critics that they come across such as Samuel Johnson, William Hazlitt, and Samuel Coleridge. Others will choose a character harder to research, such as Horatio or Roderigo, and travel to other libraries to find articles in little known publications. In a recent class both the riches and dangers of internet research became apparent when one student found an 1880 letter from a prominent actress about her preparation for and experience in the role of Ophelia, while another gave us excerpts from what turned out to be a draft paper by a high-school student. When we are listening to the reports, I encourage the class to sit in a circle and allow the students to speak from their seats as a way of making the exercise less intimidating. Occasionally a student will prefer to stand at the front of the room.

Even when several students choose the same character and the same critic to summarize, what the students say and how they say it is sufficiently distinctive that whatever repetition occurs is not a problem. We usually hear diverse and interesting ideas about many characters. But the perhaps most valuable aspect of this exercise occurs after we have heard approximately ten student reports, which means we have heard what thirty critics have had to say at various dates, since students must identify the date of each critic's comments. Just from hearing the date of the criticism, the critic's gender, and the character's name, students begin to be able to predict what a critic will say. They thus gain valuable insight into the passing fashions in intellectual history, a lesson that the long time-span of Shakespearean commentary facilitates.

The broad range of information that we hear greatly enriches everyone's understanding of the characters, of the play, and of the many approaches that have developed historically and continue to develop. Students are often inspired by something another student has uncovered and will pursue that idea in a paper of their own. Thus a researcher's being able to 'mark the trail' by providing all necessary citation information so that someone else can retrace her or his steps becomes a meaningful responsibility. For those few students who have trouble mastering what I call 'double citation', which reports on both the original location and where the criticism was actually found, repeatedly drawing class attention to these facts should make the required procedure clear. Not just the Gale compilations but any collection of essays necessitates that awareness of the researcher's responsibility to know both the original publication information and the information about the compilation, if they differ.

An observation that I have not yet made known to students after this exercise is that the character and criticism that each selects reveals something not only about the time in which each critic wrote but also suggests insights into the student at that moment in her or his life. A slightly longer version of this Oral Report section will appear in the forthcoming Modern Language Association's *Approaches to Teaching Hamlet*, edited by Bernice Kliman.

Collaborative Groups to Master Bibliographic Form – To introduce or review bibliographic citation (MLA style), I sometimes have groups of students work together to produce a brief Works Cited or Sources 'page' that they put on a section of chalkboard. Each student contributes one item, and the whole group is responsible for 'its' board. The class as a whole reviews each board directing me to make any needed changes (usually in different color chalk to emphasize the corrections).

Such basic concepts as alphabetical order (and how to decide what name or word determines placement), hanging indentation, categories of information as well as their order and their punctuation tend to stick better with more students (not all) after they have participated in this activity. Otherwise, many do not perceive the essential elements in the handbook models. This technique is more fully discussed in a *Collaborative Learning Sourcebook*, which was published in 1994 by the National Center on Postsecondary Teaching, Learning, and Assessment.

Student Daily Feedback and Input into Final Grades – On occasion at the end of an individual class I invite or require that students write brief questions or reactions to whatever we have done in class. These are jotted (anonymously or signed, as each student prefers) on small slips of paper that students hand to me as they leave the room (I may stand at the door to collect them as an exit ticket). This enables shy students or students who wish to raise a difficult subject to make their views known at minimal risk. Depending on what is asked or said, I will respond privately or in class but not identify who raised the topic or issue.

At the end of some courses I will require students to write a self-assessment and justification for the final grade each believes she or he should receive. On the whole, students are remarkably honest in such documents; their assessment usually matches my own. At some point in their professional careers students may be called upon to do this, so the exercise can be career preparation as well as an academic exercise. This technique is discussed in "A Final Memo", an article I wrote in 1979 for *ABCA Bulletin*.

In no one course would I use all of the above techniques. The level of a course and the combination of students in a particular section will affect which approaches I will select or emphasize. My goals are usually to sharpen the students' sense of responsibility for their own learning and to enhance their analytical, researching, citing, and public speaking skills at the same time as they gain a broad perspective on Shakespeare. In giving students a chance to control some of what takes place in a course both in and outside of the classroom, I try to develop techniques that facilitate creating an atmosphere of shared inquiry and learning that benefits students and instructor alike.

Works Cited

Beehler, Sharon A. "Making Media Matter in the Shakespeare Classroom." In Salomone, pp. 247-54.
Boris, Edna Zwick. "Classroom Minutes: A Valuable Teaching Device", *Improving College & University Teaching*, 31 (Spring 1983), 70-73. Repr. in *Innovation Abstracts*, Vol. VI No. 5 publ. by the National Institute for Staff and Organizational Development, Austin, 1984.
---. "A Final Memo", *ABCA Bulletin*, 42 (American Business Communications Association; March 1979), pp. 41-2.
---. "Mastering Bibliographic Form through Collaborative Learning", *Collaborative Learning: A Sourcebook for Higher Education*, Vol. 2, National Center on Postsecondary Teaching, Learning, and Asessment (NCTLA), University Park, Pennsylvania, 1994.
---. "Oral Reports on Criticism." In Kliman.
---. "A Student Role in Syllabus Planning," *Exercise Exchange*, 39, Spring 1994, pp. 10-11.
---. "Teaching Shakespeare: Non-Traditional Research Topics", *The Shakespeare Newsletter*, Fall 1992, p. 41; discussed in *Shakespeare and the Classroom*, I (Spring 1993), p. 15.
Feinstein, Sandy. "Crossbows, Lutes, and Coitus, or, What Does Editing Lady Macbeth Mean?" *Exemplaria* 9:1 (1997), pp. 165-87.

"Oral Reports on Criticism." Kliman, Bernice, ed. *Approaches to Teaching Hamlet*. New York: Modern Language Association, [expected publication date 2001].

Habicht, Werner. "There's the Rub: Translating Hamlet's Thought Process." Seminar (chaired by J.-M. Deprats) paper presented at the International Shakespeare Conference in Stratford-upon-Avon. 1998.

Helphinstine, Frances L. "Using Playgrounding to Teach *Hamlet*." In Salomone, pp. 50-6.

O'Brien, Peggy. *Shakespeare Set Free: Teaching 'Romeo and Juliet', 'Macbeth', 'A Midsummer Night's Dream'*. New York: Washington Square Press, 1993.

Partridge, Erik. *Shakespeare's Bawdy*. London: Routledge & Kegan Paul, 1947; repr.: New York: E.P. Dutton & Co., 1960.

Salomone, Ronald E. and James E. Davis, ed. *Teaching Shakespeare into the Twenty-First Century*. Athens: Ohio UP, 1997.

Urkowitz, Steven. "'Well-sayd olde Mole' – Burying Three *Hamlets* in Modern Editions." In *Shakespeare Study Today*, ed. Georgianna Ziegler (New York: AMS Press, 1986), pp. 37-70.

TEMPO/TEMPEST: THE TIMELINESS OF SHAKESPEARE IN THE DIVERSE CLASSROOM

Lloyd Edward Kermode
(California State University, Long Beach)

This essay proposes a rigorous, responsible, and highly engaging method of presenting Shakespeare to a diverse student body. Through an interrogation of the concepts of the 'foreign' and the 'alien' in early modern English life and literature, the students find that Shakespeare speaks to our time in complicated yet accessible ways. This is largely because such early modern concerns might be closely related to our own places in a modern culture full of alienating practices. Although I concentrate on *The Tempest* for the purpose of this paper, a similar plan could be brought together for other plays that deal with (inter)national and cross-cultural encounters: *The Comedy of Errors, The Merchant of Venice, Measure for Measure, Richard II, Henry V, Titus Andronicus, Othello*, and others.[1]

Various approaches – including some performance-based role-playing, status games, modernized psychodrama and improvised play – seem to leave Shakespeare in the dust in an attempt to get students actively engaged. The continuing preferences for using such methods to teach students 'values' through literature and for getting them 'in touch with themselves' are, although well-intentioned, in danger of writing Shakespearean texts and contexts out of courses that bear his name. The textual readings and practical approach I outline here show how we can remain with early modern Shakespeare and still speak to the modern classroom in various parts of the world. The methods I suggest can be applied with variation to general education, survey, lower- and upper-level Shakespeare courses, and graduate classes.

I.

In my class, I begin the contextual segment of this approach to teaching *The Tempest* by mentioning the growing level of contact between foreigners and English in the sixteenth and early seventeenth centuries. I show an overhead[2] of a paragraph from John Deacon's *Tobacco Tortured* (1616).[3] Published just a few years after *The Tempest* was written, it comically and perhaps ironically comments on a problem that had been plaguing the English throughout the previous century: the perception of 'infection' of the English by foreign vices. In 1616 Deacon could include the New World vice of smoking to European follies affecting the English(man). It is easy to bring out the angry pleasure with which Deacon writes this highly alliterative passage.[4] He concludes, "From whence (I pray thee) do all these, and sundry such other prodigious pollutions of mind and bodie proceede, but from an inconsiderate conversing with the contagious corruptions, and customes of those the forenamed countries?"[5] Since I present English contextual documents to reveal early modern native attitudes to aliens, I keep reminding the students that the 'natives' in many of these plays – mostly Catholic Italians and ancient Romans – were of course foreign to the Shakespearean audience. The contemporary English audience's own relationship to the stage alien, then, is nearly always at an additional remove from the 'native'/'alien' encounter depicted in the plays.

I like to make sure that no single aspect of a presentation in class is taken for the truth by the students, so I continue by asking them to balance Deacon's antagonistic stance with the question of what the fruits of foreign travel should be, both for the Renaissance traveler and for us.[6] The students and I talk about hearing and speaking other languages, observing different cultures,[7] purchasing foreign products, noting what is similar as well as different in other parts of the world. Also, I counter an impression the students may be getting through the opening presentation and discussion that the Elizabethans and Jacobeans were great travelers and tourists. To the contrary, foreign visitors to England noted that the English did not like foreigners, hardly associated with them, and chose to experience at their playhouses what people from other countries experienced by going abroad, including hearing Dutch, French, Italian, Latin, and Spanish speech.[8]

As the students start to feel more confident that they know a lot about their world compared to the early moderns, I confirm that they may be right. However, I redress that view by showing them a twentieth-century newspaper advertisement I found reproduced in a book on American attitudes toward Africa.[9] This AT&T advertisement introduces the paradoxical way in which the 'global village' is presented to the Western public as highly accessible, yet something about which we need know little in depth. In this document, the text highlights low rates and easy connectivity "from Peoria to Pretoria". An accompanying diptych purports to illustrate the claim by showing a couple of American kids with cows and a group of nomadic shepherds in savanna land with their herd. The implication is clear: AT&T connects those living in the middle of nowhere. However, Pretoria is a major urban area, four times the size of Peoria; yet the social structure is such that working children would not have access to telephone lines. That town somewhere in Illinois, too, is chosen for a similar reason: to AT&T's target audience, it is just as foreign – some country place with cows everywhere. Of course, Peoria is another major urban conurbation, chosen because of its alliterative link to the South African city. This advertisement's easy images of the 'foreign' falsely comfort us with the assumption that we need not investigate matters of difference further. I align the modern ability to learn about other cultures and places in our armchairs through the world wide web and other media with what would have been familiar to Elizabethans – their ability to learn (and mislearn) about the foreign not by going abroad, but by using another popular information highway: the theater. Both on the stage and in prose tracts, the English rehearsed an already-received idea of what the 'foreign' was.

This simple one-to-one early modern/modern connection needs further grounding. The AT&T advertisement assumes that locations in our own country remain foreign to us, and this would have been a very familiar notion to the English men and women of the sixteenth and seventeenth centuries. They tended to use the word 'alien' to mean a person from overseas and the word 'foreigner' more generally to mean any person who was not originally from the town in which they now resided. Such persons usually came to town from the English countryside or other towns. English 'foreigners' and 'outlandish' 'aliens' increasingly surrounded urban residents of England, and in London one could pick up a wide variety of imported goods in the marketplace. These varied from vain trinkets to the fine new textiles of Dutch immigrants, who, along with the French, had been settling in significant numbers since the 1560s, streaming into England to escape Catholic persecution on the Continent.[10]

There was the (to us, familiar) conflict among the English between appreciating the new skills of the aliens, yet resenting the places they took in the domestic market. And there was, of course, the strangeness of the aliens – their lifestyle and their religious practice. Writers lamented the un-Englishness of the City of London and the increasingly strange behavior of the English people who lived there, clearly influenced in bizarre manners and fashion by aliens, making the native more and more 'alien'-like.[11] The strangeness of influential 'aliens' became particularly stark later in the sixteenth century and in the early seventeenth century as Londoners witnessed black servants, 'New Christian' Jews, and images and even living examples of the New World 'savage'. At this point, the students might usefully consider the notion of the self, the familiar, or the native as foreign. Especially in a culture like southwest coastal America, where I now teach, we should seriously question the place of each person as an example of diversity in a large, single country. The students begin to ask questions of identity and cultural imposition that are currently under debate by political and cultural critics, without us having to impose actual examples of this difficult criticism on them.[12]

I try to alternate between student inquiry/open forum, and lecture/information sessions during each class. Having lectured here, then, and opened up the floor for modern-day reflection, I turn to a set of images aimed at illustrating the levels of such English and European contact with, and response to the 'alien'. I have varied my choices of pictures to talk about, but a set of examples might begin with the 1600 portrait of the Moorish ambassador to Queen

Elizabeth. This man is depicted as fair (or "tawny", Shakespeare might say), well-dressed with a well-shorn beard. His eyes look intelligent and serious but not severe. He wears a sword and his right hand is placed on his breast. Students note the hand 'over the heart', the elaborate dress weapon, and the subdued austerity of the portrait (he is not on a rampant horse, for instance). We might move then to a depiction of a less-favored man, and a good Shakespearean example would be the Jew. I have used the title page and woodcut to a German song about a Jew who sacrifices a Christian child. I mention the line in Marlowe's *The Jew of Malta*, where Friar Jacomo responds to Friar Bernadine's announcement that the Jew has done something terrible with the guess, "What, has he crucified a child?" (3.6.49). The Friar's question suggests that this would have been a familiar mythical image and joke to an early modern audience. (Nashe's *Unfortunate Traveler* might also be cited here for the diabolical and ridiculous depiction of the threatening Jews Zadoch and Zachary.) The woodcut image has a Jewish male wielding a knife over a bowl, presumably to catch blood. A Christian boy is tied to a post, covered in cuts and with his head fallen to one side. In this second image, the sense of the 'alien' shifts to the mythical, the 'making monstrous' of men.

The third image I show takes us from the realm of monstrous men to actual man-monsters. The first and third of these images have now been collected in the Arden introduction to *Othello*, making them easily accessible. The German woodcut is reproduced in R. Po-Chia Hsia's excellent book, *The Myth of Ritual Murder*.[13] This third image, from Sebastian Munster's *Cosmographia* (1572), shows the students that for some time before *The Tempest*, images of utterly alien beings were available in England. In fact, I tell the students early on that most drama tends to arrive late on the critical scene of controversy. Hence (often medieval) anti-Semitic stories re-circulated throughout the sixteenth century long before *The Merchant of Venice* played in London, and travelers' tales were old enough to be ironized by the time of *The Tempest*. Included in the Munster woodcut are the anthropophagus, the wolf-man, Siamese twins, a Cyclops, and a uniped ("Oh my God, he's shading himself!" shouted one of my students when he realized why this being had one big foot raised above him while lying on his back). They laugh at these, of course, after being a little disturbed by the Jewish portrait. I ask them how they think the early modern English could be so gullible as to believe in these animals, and they generally think such credulity ridiculous. So I draw an elephant on the board and compare its ridiculous nose to the uniped's foot; elephants do not have feet or hooves – their legs just stop with nails. Then I draw a giraffe and compare that neck to the anthropophagus without a neck. Suddenly the creatures do not seem so implausible. I sometimes do the same with native apples and berries versus foreign and alarming pineapples and bananas. Now the senses of 'strangeness', 'weirdness', and credibility are beginning to combine in a complicated matrix of cultural myth, story, observation, and intuition. This unsettling of first impressions and assumptions about the early modern view of the world prepares students to talk more freely about what audiences might have made of *The Tempest*. The sense of 'normal' animals and plants would of course vary globally and it would make an interesting study to see how (or whether) such a cultural and geographical factor affects student reading of the 'strange' in the play.

During the relatively short period in which Shakespeare was working in London (a little longer than the two decades following 1590), travel outside of England was limited to a very few Englishmen and women. Foreign trading companies such as the Venice company and Turkey company were formed in the 1570s and 1580s, several ships left for America, and officially-sanctioned piracy in the Atlantic continued through the last couple of decades of Elizabeth's reign. However, the experience of the foreign remained for the great majority of English in books, ballads, broadsheets, and plays. If I have not already done so in the course, I make sure by this time that the students have a sense of the burgeoning of the public theaters in and around London. I also mention the context for Shakespeare by citing a few other plays that discuss the 'alien' in various ways. In the context of these theaters, I suggest to the class that the two main ways of getting to the theaters – crossing the Thames river to the South Bank, or trudging across fields to the northern suburbs – may be seen as microcosmic journeys across water or land. Playgoers left the City proper, a district under the direct control of the anti-theatrical Lord Mayor, and crossed into new, foreign territory, that of the Liberties and suburbs, where the Queen's (and after 1603, King's) Privy Council held sway and the more lenient Justices of each suburb put law into effect. And in those locations were theaters that pretended to be worlds unto themselves, full of 'alien' matter. When at the beginning of *Henry V*, then, the Chorus in the Globe theater asks whether "this unworthy scaffold", "this cockpit", "this wooden 'o'" can "hold / The vasty fields of France" (Pro. 10-12) and asks us before Act 2 to suffer "the playhouse" to be "transported" "to France" (2.0.34-8) and back again, he has a cooperative, captive audience that has come here for exactly such a transporting experience. Such a shifting theater also represents a complex *theatrum mundi*.

The students (and all of us to some point) want to get a sense of a singular 'early modern' attitude to travel, strangeness, and the self. To illustrate the impossibility of easy answers in a politically volatile period, I simply present in another overhead a timeline table of Shakespeare's 'alien' plays next to a parallel list of political and social events, including the first Spanish Armada, events in Ireland, anti-alien riots, visitations of the plague, proclamations against moors and playing, relations with France and Spain, and so on. Changes over short periods of time can radically alter audience perception and reader reception.[14] We have to keep impressing upon our students the fact that time as well as place alienates us, and that our Shakespearean guidebook raises as many questions as it answers. This selective list of social and political events that affected the lives of the English in profound ways begins to reveal how mistaken we are if we think of a singular concept of the Renaissance 'mind' or 'experience'. While we teach our courses in Shakespeare (and Renaissance literature in general), we have the opportunity to inform our students fully of the complexity of the world in which they live, despite the insistence of various media that the world is an easy place to navigate. And concomitant with that, we must remind them that any cultural location or period similarly experienced complexity in its own discoveries of self and other; such complexity means that we cannot say "in the Renaissance, *they* thought ..." without taking into account the various identity markers of the "they".

What was their class, gender, ethnicity, religion, geographical location, parentage, job, family size?

In the classroom, and in particular the Shakespeare class, the text of the play (with all the added difficulties of textual transmission) reveals these complexities of identity. As a reader, writer, and educator about the early modern period in a diverse classroom, it seems to me that a primary pedagogical responsibility lies in conveying the density both of the texts we look at and of the connections between the early moderns' and our own experiences of investigating difference. This is not to shift easily between the sixteenth, seventeenth, and twentieth centuries, but to provide windows of recognition or familiarity for further observation and investigation of strangeness and difference. Effective pedagogical parallels should be imperatives, instructions to reevaluate what we think a subject's place in any specific culture is compared with the way that subject's place in the culture is represented by others. The students may get a familiar understanding of such a problematic if they try to categorize themselves, friends, and family members within popular culture's groups: for instance, the terms 'Generation X', and 'post grunge' denote groups of thirty-somethings with which today's students will largely not want to be associated and they will probably provide you with more up-to-date terminology being applied to their age-group. Popular culture time moves so rapidly, however, that those who attempt social categorization fall behind fashion in the process of doing so. This exercise amusingly exposes the students' self-awareness (and self-consciousness) of their subject position, while teaching them that (often judgmental or prejudicial) ideas about groups of persons, both familiar and alien, are constantly shifting and usually inadequate.

II.

I shall now provide specific examples of passages I close-read with my students. After a couple of introductory remarks, I annotate a number of passages from *The Tempest* to highlight the lines' importance in the discussion of the place of the foreign or the strange, and their significance to a discussion of diversity and global Shakespeare. We close-read in Acts 1 and 2 especially, plus 3.3 and 5.1, and the scenes reveal tensions between what the politic characters say and what they believe. Sometimes other characters call them to task for these inconsistencies, and students spot this. Students also recognize from their own worlds the familiarity and pitfalls of professing an extreme politics of either idealism or tyranny. Having investigated in this manner, a diverse class may find itself in agreement on large issues of cultural behavior and assumption. This can lead back into a brief sideline discussion of how modern peoples from Europe, Africa, North and South America, Australasia, and Asia can be in such accord; the issue of cultural assimilation (and, in my classes, 'Americanization') comes into play. Such a sideline should be well mediated by the instructor, for it can very easily fall away into fluffy opinion; but it can also crucially fold us back into the issues of whichever play we are studying: Miranda's 'education', or Othello's 'assimilation' for better or for worse, or Shylock's own use of the Venetian system of prejudice. To reiterate a point, class discussion of modern socio-cultural politics should not be directed toward teaching 'correct' ethics and values as an end in itself (for this burgeons out of good literature anyway). Rather, it should be designed to return us to the text of study. This does two things at once: it teaches modern notions of selfhood by analyzing our individual places in multi-ethnic and hierarchical societies, and it answers in practical terms the perennial question, "why is Shakespeare relevant?" by showing that the modern to some extent relies on (and is certainly illuminated by) the early modern, to which it continually refers.

I make my way into *The Tempest*, beginning with the familiar general question, "Where is the island in the play?" A class finds out that the unnamed Mediterranean island could also be (with varying plausibility) America, Ireland, Britain, or, like Utopia, all of these and none of them. These geographical and psychological locations can be investigated in as much depth as seems appropriate for the class. Such conceptual analyses rely on each student's ability to think about and interrogate relationships in general as well as the way they are depicted in the text. As such, this can be an interesting and useful area of concentration for a class in which the instructor wants to de-emphasize the difficulty of the language. Even though *The Tempest* is a very 'historical' text, I avoid a long, initial lecture on history because many of the students will simply write down what I say and forget it. Instead, I continue the method of interspersing presentation and discussion by selecting a couple of moments in each Act where the text indicates Shakespeare's use of contemporary documents or events. When we get there, I present a brief historical detour, explaining that history is not just a parallel discipline but an informative one that opens up questions about *who* says *what* in the text, *when*, and *why*. Thus we can involve students in responsible new-historical thinking without confusing them. They learn that sometimes an historical event forces a text to engage with it, and sometimes a text enters a dialogue about historical circumstances such that history itself has to be re-read in light of the existence and tone of the literary text. By this means, students gradually absorb a network of critical and social thinking to bring to their reading, and as we go along we can concentrate progressively more closely on the intricacies of the text as dramatic script and literary artifact.[15]

I stick with the early modern experience in discussing relations between these possible island locations, but some better-informed instructors could perhaps profitably incorporate other colonial engagements and conflicts to complement and illuminate those suggested in the play – Mexican-American, Arab-Israeli, Serb-Croat, Zimbabwe blacks and white farmers. This may also prove useful in drawing non-native speakers into the relevance of the play to their experience or realm of knowledge. The location of the island in *The Tempest* seems to spread out as the play goes on, at first more familiar and then more alien, in the process becoming almost surreal. It is at first in the Mediterranean. Prospero's tale to Miranda that they were borne "some leagues out to sea" (one league = 3 miles), that their boat was "rotten" and "not rigged", and that the rats have "quit it" (1.2.145-8) all suggest that they cannot have floated far before reaching the island. The tempest itself seems to happen "upon the Mediterranean float" (1.2.235).

Images and film stills of actors playing Caliban can bring the active island to life and stretch the students' ideas of what he might look like. Prospero talks of him as "A freckled whelp, hag-born" (1.2.285), and such an image can be compared with Richard II's reference to the Irish as the "rough rug-headed kerns" (*Richard II* 2.1.157) or to the animalistic Irish and Picts, tamed and hunted down by Cromwell in Marvell's "Horatian Ode" (lines 73-4, 105-12). In both these comparative cases, the very alien categorizations denote geographical neighbors. The students might want to talk about whether human beings tend to be harsher in representing difference when it exists in close proximity rather than at a distance – again, other familiar civil conflicts may be usefully referred to.

Gonzalo's much-studied wish for "plantation of this isle" (2.1.143) is rightly linked to its major source, Montaigne's essay "Of the Cannibals", in John Florio's 1603 translation. What is less noted, and important for the students to take into account, is that Montaigne's (and Shakespeare's) enlightened opinions come from armchair travel. John Hariot's report from Virginia is a tract often presented to students side-by-side with Montaigne as directly comparable. Hariot's text, however, frequently damned for its colonial views, comes out of experience. When the texts are presented honestly, the students have much to offer in the discussion of how a removed practitioner of liberal theory differs from the harsher tones of a reporter with first-hand experience. Now, to read Gonzalo's speech alongside Montaigne uncritically is to assume a New World connection at this point.[16] It may be there, but the New World was hardly considered an 'isle'. Britain, however, is an island, and it is useful to suggest to the students early on in the reading of the play that references to the foreign should always be read as possible double-speak – they may be discussing the other or providing an allegory of native traits. Short extracts from *Utopia* (along with a biographical sketch of Thomas More's place in Henry VIII's England and government) can be useful to illustrate the point. At the same time as the students realize that Shakespeare may be talking with such a double intention, then, they also learn that he is open to mistakes in representing the other, for his learning comes from reading at home, not observing abroad. This leaves a doorway open for them to disagree with Shakespeare's representation of the alien, and helps in the process of getting them to engage with the text on critical and creative levels above that of general comprehension.

The island drifts into the mists between a real and a conceptual place as we read through Act 1, Scene 2. Antonio laments the loss of Claribel, daughter of Alonso, King of Naples, because she has married an African King. He talks of:

> She that is Queen of Tunis; she that dwells
> Ten leagues beyond man's life; she that from Naples
> Can have no note – unless the sun were post –
> The man I' th' moon's too slow – till new-born chins
> Be rough and razorable[.] (2.1.242-6)

Antonio's lines seem to reveal an affected hyperbolic response to the loss of Claribel. However, in a play in which words call matter into being and illusions fool the most sober men, this (mis)statement surely makes us consider seriously its truth value as an indication of Antonio's (and for that matter Alonso's) psychology. He talks of Tunis as a distance (presumably from Naples) "Ten leagues" *further* than a man's life*time* – presumably seventy years or so (of travel). The trip is actually a middle-distance sail across and along the Mediterranean. Apparently a message in Antonio's altered world takes a relatively short fifteen to eighteen years to get between the two points. The hyperbolic representation of space and time moors the island and makes it unlocatable; we clearly cannot rely on such characters to give us accurate geographical information. We could argue that these imaginary distances relocate Tunis and Naples in other places, conceptually further apart than two places could ever be on earth. They are therefore psychologically nowhere (certainly nowhere dangerous for the plot Antonio hatches with Sebastian). With this in mind, the students might go back to the Gonzalo speech and reconsider the impossibility of locating his 'isle'. The longevity of the trope of the ideal as existing nowhere might be illustrated in class by mention of Samuel Butler's 1872 utopian book, *Erewhon* (almost 'nowhere' backwards).

We can return to *Richard II* for comparison of this kind of hyperbole: we hear of Richard "wand'ring with the Antipodes" (3.2.43-7). Richard is referring to his time in Ireland. Ireland is hardly the other side of the world geographically, but it is politically useful to portray the neighboring enemy as so alien. This idea adds to some of the notions we have come across throughout these lectures and discussions on *The Tempest*. If the class reflects back on the exercise of attempting to categorize themselves within popular culture, it is possible to see here that if for any reason a writer misplaces a subject (be it a person, a people, or a location), it leaves that subject open to invention, distortion, and re-creation on the writer's terms. The students should work here toward an understanding about the nature of rhetorical strategies that deliberately set up subjects to be misrepresented. Rather than simply airing their disagreement with a moment in the text, then, they will be able to backtrack and point out where they, as readers or audience members, were misled. This is of course a basic introduction to careful critical reading for any type of persuasive text, and in an advanced or graduate class it should be applied as reading methodology to critical essays.

Trinculo's joke at 2.2.26-9 on Caliban the 'fish' has been talked about often, so I do not want to rehearse those points here. As well as the double-edged play on the phrase "There would this monster make a man", it is important to have the class note the tactic Shakespeare uses of connecting this all to England. Trinculo claims to have been in England, and therefore knows what the English are like. There is nothing 'English' about the content of the play, other than its genre, up to this point, and this moment clearly provides an imaginary connection of comprehension between two cultures. The suggestion is that this must be a mutual connection: since Trinculo can joke about the 'nature' of the English, the audience is surely privileged to pass judgment on these Italians.

The first half of the play builds up such strong images and arguments for the existence of the island and its residents, whether in physical (if mysterious) fact or in the reasonable mind, that it is alarming to see Shakespeare allow his characters to undercut some of this creation. Gonzalo's apparent support for travelers' tales at 3.3.43-7:

> When we were boys,
> Who would believe that there were mountaineers

> Dewlapped like bulls, whose throats had hanging at 'em
> Wallets of flesh? Or that there were such men
> Whose heads stood in their breasts?

is undercut on two levels. First, can this really be the Africa or New World of such texts as Munster's *Cosmographia*, which the students saw earlier? After all, what Gonzalo sees are spirits, not the actual beings. On the other hand, perhaps this *is* what such travelers' tales consist of, air and imagination, just like Prospero's masque. The issue can be illuminated and investigated by screening scenes from Peter Greenaway's film, *Prospero's Books*. Its length, slow pace, and perhaps its 'artiness' deter many teachers from using it. However, it is a very intelligent, beautifully constructed, and important work of art, which brings books of travelers' tales to life and valorizes the text (even through its rich filmic quality). It provocatively suggests a thesis that the whole tempest, island, and story may be events going on inside Prospero's head (or in his books, which is to say largely the same thing in the realm of the film). Some students are already tasting this possibility by the time we are into Act 3 of the play. However, the realization that all of our concrete socio-political argumentation might be undercut because this whole play is simply the dream vision of an old man remains a bitter pill to swallow. They (quite rightly) resist such a reading, because so much of such complexity has happened and affected too many people for us to think in such a 'blanket' way about the 'production' of the play-text.

There are two final undercuttings. Miranda's famous exclamation, "O brave new world / That has such people in't!" (5.1.186-7) is of course a reference all at once to people of the old world, yet to a location in which old worlders are traveling – hence a new world – and thirdly to a place in which conflict and resolution is being worked out between old residents and new residents, which for the Jacobeans might have suggested the long-standing situation in Ireland. Such a loaded statement almost 'brings home' the island. It remains an unplaceable, confusing location, but at least it turns toward 'home' (i.e. as a combination of Italy and the 'British Isles') by making its place references recognizable, unlike Gonzalo's impossible isle and Antonio's impossible geography.

The Timeliness of Shakespeare

After all the possibilities of these passages, each of which opens up various questions of cultural and rhetorical exchange, Prospero stands in the Epilogue and appeals to the audience: "Let me not / ... dwell ... / In this bare island" (5, 7-8). Where is he? Of course, he is on the bare theater stage in need of applause to waft him home. But as he stands on the cusp of theatrical reality and dramatic fiction, a question not often asked is whether he really *is* trying to get home; or have we recognized the familiarity of his strange location through its serious and comic class and ethnic conflict? If this bare island represents a 'Britain' that pleases Shakespeare no longer, or a stage to which he has no more to offer, then Prospero (like all epilogue speakers, only more profoundly) is leaving as well as coming home. Is he asking to get away from civic responsibility at home to seek out Gonzalo's utopia? This would almost be a death-drive, searching for the impossible. Does such a plea to escape innocently precede discovery and education; or (since Prospero has abjured his magic) does the request implicate the text in the European colonial endeavor – ordinary men 'brave-ing' the New World?

Having investigated the plays in this involved manner, 'the Renaissance' should no longer be a singular idea for students; 'the theater' should no longer be thought of as a simple single entity, but as it was: multiple locations serving different audiences; and the text should no longer be expected to yield single answers to any single questions. Instead, they produce multiplicity, and within themselves provide us with the tools for critical investigation of fiction and history in the Renaissance, tools that happen to fit various nuts and bolts of our modern lives. Through a number of quite involved critical approaches – formalist, new historicist, post-colonial, feminist, semiotic – we can reveal to students a world at once remarkably isolated from, and remarkably hungry for knowledge of the other. It is a world full of prejudice, and one in which people are fighting to overcome their conflicts. It is also a world in which little men fight authority, and where family and governmental units of control are compared and contrasted. It is, of course, the students' own worlds. But it is not so because Shakespeare's plays speak to us in some romantic, grand way, in which the 'human' is invented before our eyes and universal experience revealed. Rather, Shakespeare speaks to us – and I think especially to various bodies of English- and foreign-language students – because his reading and writing were in constant engagement, negotiation, and conflict with the increasingly mixed urban culture in which he worked and lived.

Notes

1. My quotations from the plays are taken from the Norton Shakespeare, ed. Stephen Greenblatt, et al. (New York: Norton, 1997). The editors' new-historical approaches produce pithy and relevant introductions to the plays, some good illustrations, and less un-Renaissance coyness about footnoting bawdry than the other major editions. Hopefully, a second edition will correct, adjust, and clarify some infelicities and inadequacies in the footnotes, and reduce or cut the interpretive notes. It might also consider adding some further contemporary documents to the appendix and some color images if the price can be kept down.
2. I would like to replace the overheads with a powerpoint presentation where possible in the future. The students ask to see the earlier images, and it can be very useful to place the textual extracts on one side of the screen alongside the images they have been looking at – something that is cumbersome with transparencies.
3. This text is available as a Da Capo press reprint (Amsterdam: Da Capo Press, 1968), p. 10 (sig. Cv).
4. I quote documents and suggest extra readings and materials in the footnotes so as to keep the body of the essay as much a practicum for teaching as possible, with an eye primarily to classes of diverse knowledges and abilities. Deacon's paragraph notes that, because of "Our carelesse entercourse of trafficking with the contagious corruptions, and customes of forraine nations [...] so many of our English-mens minds are thus terribly Turkished with Mahometan trumperies; thus ruefully Romanized with superstitious relickes; thus treacherously Italianized with sundry antichristian toyes; thus spitefully Spanished with superfluous pride; thus fearfully Frenchized with filthy prostitutions; thus fantastically Flanderized with flaring net-works to catch English fooles; thus huffingly Hollandized with ruffian-like loome-workes, and other ladified fooleries; thus greedily Germandized with a most gluttonous manner of gormandizing; thus desperately Danished with a swine-like swilling and quaffing; thus skulkingly Scotized with Machiavillan projects; thus inconstantly Englished with every new fantasticall foolerie; thus industriously Indianized with the intoxicating filthie fumes of Tobacco, and what not besides?"
5. In a special topics or graduate class, the idea of 'contagion' could be related back to earlier Tudor drama, such as *The Tide Tarrieth No Man*, with the dangers of religious infection, or to contemporary pathologies of disease.
6. In a class in which the plethora of information and back-and-forth argumentation might get confusing for students, we might suggest a columnar method of note-taking to them (which will probably only work for those with a well-organized mind). After all, so much of this approach relies on comparison and argument between contrasting readings. They might head their columns "early modern" and "modern" or "insular/prejudicial" versus "outgoing/aware". We might also simply use such a method on the board and build up the columns with information as each class goes on.

7   Bacon writes accessibly about one early seventeenth-century man's opinion in his short essay "On Travel". Here he advocates travel, with necessary precautions, and encourages bringing home the flowers of foreign experience for appreciation, while taking care not to plant a foreign root in England.

8   Walter Rye has collected contemporary documents of the relationship between the English and foreigners. Some are amusing and useful for quotation in class. See *England as Seen by Foreigners* (London: John Russell Smith, 1865).

9   Curtis A. Keim, *Mistaking Africa: Curiosities and Inventions of the American Mind* (Boulder: Westview Press, 1999).

10 By the 1580s, Norwich's population was one-third Dutch and French. For an extended account of immigration and foreign-English relations in the sixteenth century, see Laura Yungblut Hunt, *Strangers Settled Here Amongst us: Policies, Perception and the Presence of Aliens in Elizabethan England* (London and New York: Routledge, 1996). For the sixteenth-century obsession with new fashion, see Sara Warneke, "A Taste for Newfangleness: The Destructive Potential of Novelty in Early Modern England", *Sixteenth Century Journal* 26 (1995), pp. 881-96.

11 Examples from the sixteenth and seventeenth centuries are cited in Hunt, *Strangers settled here amongst us*. See also Anon., *The Lamentation of England* (1556-7), with many statements about the literal problem of aliens under Marian rule; for instance, "Oh what a plage is it to see strangers rule in this noble rea[l]me violently, wher befor time tr[e]we harted Englishmen haue gouernid quietly" (sig. A3v, p. 5); also the usury tracts, among them Thomas Wilson, *A Discourse upon Usury*, R. H. Tawney, ed. (1572; London: G. Bell & Sons, 1925). On p. 232 Wilson calls modern English usurers "worse than Jewes", since they have taken over that un-English trade from the Jews who were expelled in 1290; W. R., *The English Ape, the Italian imitation, the foote steppes of France* (1588) for the English "ape-ing" foreigners; Anon., *The Minte of Deformities* (1600), which laments the importation of foreignness among the fickle English: "To day like a French garboile, round and flat, / to morrow like a Spaniard, naught but britch, / Then in the strange Italian natiue plat, / then in the whotte Barbarians swelting pitch, / that I doe wonder that in London trades, / like Kitchinstuffe (what fashio[n]s haue you maides.[)]" (sig. B); Henry Peacham, *The Compleat Gentleman* (1622): "Within these fiftie or threescore yeares it was a rare thing with us in England to see a *drunken man*, our nation carrying the name of the most sober and temperate of any other in the world. But since we had to doe in the quarrell of the Netherlands, about the time of Sir John Norrice his first being there, the custome of drinking and pledging healthes was brought over into England: wherein let the Dutch bee their owne judges, if we equall them not; yea I think rather excell them" (Quoted in Rye, *England as Seen by Foreigners*, p. 194 n. 20).

12 Having said that, in upper-level courses I do use this criticism to delve further into this area. For examples, Paul Brown, "This thing of darkness I acknowledge mine: *The Tempest* and the discourse of colonialism" in *Political Shakespeare: New Essays in Cultural Materialism*, ed. Jonathan Dollimore and Alan Sinfield (Ithaca: Cornell UP, 1985), pp. 48-71; Francis Barker and Peter Hulme, "Nymphs and reapers heavily vanish: the discursive con-texts of *The Tempest*" in *Alternative Shakespeares*, ed. John Drakakis (London and New York: Methuen, 1985), pp. 191-205, 235-7. These and other important cultural/political essays have been collected in a new edition of the play, edited by Gerald Graff and James Phelan (Boston and New York: Bedford/St. Martin's, 2000).

13 Hsia, *The Myth of Ritual Murder: Jews and Magic in Reformation Germany* (New Haven: Yale UP, 1988).

14 In an advanced course, the performances of *The Jew of Malta* in 1592 and 1594 (before and immediately after the execution of Rodrigo Lopez) could be cited as an example of dramatic political alteration of a text within a short space of time.

15 I point this out in some detail in response to multiple student evaluations that cited this method of involving history as one of the most revealing and useful aspects of the course.

16 See Charles H Frey, "'The Tempest' and the New World" in *Experiencing Shakespeare: Essays on Text, Classroom and Performance* (Columbia: Missouri UP, 1988), pp. 48-62. In this essay, Frey provides further texts to support a New World reading of the play. He argues for using not only travel texts that are strict sources (i.e. texts that Shakespeare probably knew), but also unfamiliar texts as useful information for assessing the general cultural climate in which *The Tempest* was played (see esp. pp. 53-4).

REWRITING RACE THROUGH LITERATURE: TEACHING SHAKESPEARE'S AFRICAN PLAYS

James R. Andreas
(Florida International University)

As we enter the new millennium, most teachers might probably agree with W. E. B. Dubois' prediction that race, or what he called "the color line", was the major problem plaguing the twentieth century. We understand that race is a sensitive topic, one that most of our students, and even more of their parents, would like us to ignore. Discussion of racial topics invites embarrassment for the teacher, uneasy silence from our classes, and occasional sniggers from the uninformed. One of the major planks of President Clinton's platform for a second term was the initiation of a national dialog on race which never materialized in terms of money or mandates for curriculum changes or grant initiatives from FIPSE, NEH, or state humanities councils. And yet 1) periodic 'race' riots still erupt, as witnessed, fairly recently, over the trial of the police who beat Rodney King; 2) the nation is still divided along racial lines, as was illustrated by its obsession with the O.J. Simpson case; 3) over forty per cent of South Carolinians voted to retain the anti-miscegenation statutes in the state constitution in the last state election; and 4) hate crimes like the beating and dragging of James Byrd in Texas still outrage communities of both races. Cannot something be done? Can teachers address race without giving up time devoted to preparing our students to excel in the various disciplines they are required to know by state mandate in the schools and by moral mandate in the universities and colleges of the country? Finally, do the plays of William Shakespeare, long held up by the English-speaking west as the the icon of elitist, colonial culture, have anything to teach about the sensitive topic of race and life in a postcolonial world?

In our English classes, the answer is clearly yes. In this article I want to propose a controversial but relatively painless Shakespeare curriculum for our high school and college classes where racial issues might be addressed straightforwardly, if not redressed along partisan political lines. I find students are fascinated by the anticipation Shakespeare provides for racial attitudes, behaviors, and stereotypes that they might have considered wholly contemporary rather than Early Modern. However, the playwright lived at a pivotal moment in the history of Western expansion and colonialism. He witnessed and recorded the construction of racial identities – Irish, Jewish, and African – when the English national identity and the notion of Western 'whiteness' were being forged and the enterprise of slavery was just getting underway in England.

No one would contest the fact that Shakespeare was intrigued by the Jewish question, and yet he only wrote four acts of a single play, *The Merchant of Venice*, about a Jew and his fate in the Western world. And yet Shakespeare wrote no less than five plays that interrogate the relative merits of the classical and the emerging Early Modern views of Africans: *Titus Andronicus, The Merchant of Venice, Othello, Antony and Cleopatra,* and *The Tempest.* These plays, produced, edited, and explicated for centuries as if their racial themes were invisible, i.e. non-existent or at best irrelevant, reveal that Shakespeare was in a unique position to understand the forging of the concept of race in the late sixteenth and early seventeenth centuries and to register a decisive reaction to the rise of European and American slavery.[1] The playwright was reacting not simply to literary sources that dealt with Africa but with contemporary African personalities and issues. Each play introduces an 'Ethiope', as Africans outside of Egypt were generally known in the period, who occupies a pivotal position in his or her respective play: Aaron, Morocco, and Othello, all Moors, Cleopatra, an African queen, and Caliban, whose mother, Sycorax, is from 'Argiers', in other words Algeria. That these characters are widely diverse, representing a full spectrum of human possibility and achievement, suggests that Shakespeare was not nearly so fixed in his opinions of Africans as we might assume, or his literary successors certainly became. In Aaron we have a villain nearly as interesting as Iago but one with whom we come finally to sympathize as he responds tenderly to the birth of his mixed-race son whose very life is threatened by a racist empire. Morocco is perhaps the worthiest of Portia's suitors, Bassanio notwithstanding, but is unabashedly rejected in Belmont because of his 'complexion'. Othello is a great Venetian general who reacts to Iago's hateful prompts by committing the very crime the terror of miscegenation conjures up in the mind of the racist: he murders the white wife he loves. Cleopatra, both a Ptolemaic and an African queen, paints a picture of Africa as a continent offering rich alternatives to the cold imperial ambitions of Octavian Rome. And finally, at the end of his dramatic career, Shakespeare gives us Caliban, representing the slave who was indeed about to be sold on the auction block in South Carolina in 1619, but a slave who is shown to have been unfairly stripped of his land, his language, his customs, and his liberty by Prospero.

There has been a positive fury of scholarly papers and books of late devoted to recovering the emergence of racist ideologies in the travel literature of the early modern period subsidized and designed to implement the slave trade during Shakespeare's time.[2] What has been overlooked in most of these studies, however, is the astonishingly positive view of Africa bequeathed to the early modern period by the ancient world that is easily available and accessible to students.[3] I provide my students with the following information by lecture and handouts. In ancient Greek and Roman literary and historical discourse, Africans, known to the Greeks as either Libyans or Ethiopians, were revered as the friends and darlings of the gods and as originators of dignified, solemn religious traditions. Herodotus compares the religious mythologies and observances of the Africans and the Greeks throughout the *History*. He tells us the Auses in western Africa held an annual festival in honor of Athena at which girls were paired off into two teams which fought one another with sticks and stones: "they say this rite had come down to them from time immemorial, and by its performance they pay honour to their native deity – which is the same as our Greek Athene" (4.181). Herodotus also credits the Auses with parallel deities, just as he compares the Egyptian deity Osiris with the Greek Dionysus, knowing quite well, he claims, that Dionysus himself was descended from African deities.[4] The religious rituals of Africans were thought actually to have been initiated by the gods themselves. Homer, as the fount of ancient wisdom, spread the reputation of Africans far and wide when he referred in the *Iliad* to the "blameless Ethiopians" living piously in a land which so pleased the gods that Zeus once feasted there for twelve days with the entire Olympian court in tow (*Iliad* 1.423-24). At the very outset of the *Odyssey* a god of real Olympian status, Poseidon, visits African peoples deep in the continent to share their feast:

> But it happened that Poseidon went for a visit a long way off, to the Ethiopians, who live at the ends of the earth, some near the sunrise, some near the sunset. There he expected a fine sacrifice of bulls and goats, and there he was, feasting and enjoying himself mightily (I. 22-26).[5]

These sentiments were echoed throughout antiquity. Diodorus of Sicily reaffirms the dignity and religious insight of Africans in the ancient world. "And they [historians] say that they [Ethiopians] were the first to be taught to honour the gods and to hold sacrifices and processions and festivals and the other rites by which men honour the deity; and that in consequence their piety has been published abroad among all men, and it is generally held that the sacrifices practiced among the Ethiopians are those which are the most pleasing to heaven."[6] Ethiopians were, moreover, declared to be the first human beings on earth and the inventors of writing. Diodorus, blending the historical with the theological, claims that the Egyptians were "colonists sent out by the Ethiopians, Osiris having been the leader of the colony". Most of the practices we associate to this day with Egypt are identified as Ethiopian in origin: "the belief that their kings are gods, the very special attention which they pay to their burials, and many other matters of a similar nature are Ethiopian practices". Colossal Egyptian statuary and the clean-shaven appearance and symbolic dress of Egyptian priests are also said to be Ethiopian in origin (3.2.4-5). The Ethiopian art of writing, hieroglyphics, was thought to have been passed on to Egypt which was considered by many ancient geographers and historians to be a colony of Ethiopia. Diodorus discusses "the Ethiopian writing which is called hieroglyphic among the Egyptians" at length, providing a very sophisticated analysis of its difference from the Greek alphabet and writing. Sacred Egyptian writing known only to priests was learned "from their [Ethiopian] fathers as one of the things which are not divulged, but among the Ethiopians everyone uses these forms of letters" (3.2.5-6). In marked contrast to later notions that aboriginal white skin was burned black by the sun or by some transgression of native peoples, white was thought to denote the *absence* of pigment, suggesting that black was the original color of human beings. In an account that sounds very contemporary, Diodorus explains that as dark-skinned people Ethiopians were the "first of all men", not the latest variety of the human species, as Renaissance travelers, geographers, and historians tended to believe, because:

> Those who dwell beneath the noon-day sun were, in all likelihood, the first to be generated by the earth, is clear to all; since, inasmuch as it was the warmth of the sun which, at the generation of the universe, dried up the earth when it was still wet and impregnated it with life, it is reasonable to suppose that the region which was nearest the sun was the first to bring forth living creatures (3.2.1-2).

There was a view in classical literature of the 'other' Ethiopians to be sure – wild and savage creatures living deep in the unexplored interior of the continent – but those tribes were considered to be the aberration from the rule of civility in the dominant cultures of Africa.[7]

Shakespeare's plays are positively – and negatively – studded with references to Ethiopians, African lore, and black characters that ultimately reflect ancient Greek and Roman views of Africa. The colonial view of Africa which emerged in the early modern period, however, as Peter Erickson, Kim Hall, Joyce MacDonald, Alden and Virginia Vaughan and others have shown, is fully refracted through the concoctions of the travel literature collected by Richard Hakluyt, Samuel Purchas, and Leo Africanus, among others. Hakluyt's writings are available in a comprehensive Penguin anthology. These travelogues, a blend of the imaginative and historical, were commissioned by early modern governments to destabilize the ancient view of Africa and support the emerging racist ideology which justified the commodification and exploitation of human beings we now know as the 'peculiar institution' of slavery. After having employed black entertainers in her own court, Elizabeth authorized a series of deportation edicts from 1596 to 1601 designed to promulgate the image of a race ripe for economic exploitation in the new world. "[S]he promoted England's involvement in the slave trade through her support of the slaving ventures in the 1560s of John Hawkins, whose father William had made the first English voyage to West Africa in 1530."[8] A few passages from Hakluyt should demonstrate to students that by Shakespeare's time, the classical view of Africans was in contention with the entrepreneurial drive to commodify the 'negro' for profit. Miles Philips, for instance, writes of a voyage by John Hakwkins to the West Indies via Africa in 1568:

> Upon the coast of Guinea, we obtained 150 negroes [...] so that thereby our general assaulted, and set fire upon a town in which there was at least the number of eight or ten thousand negroes, and they perceiving that they were not able to make any resistance sought by flight to save themselves, in which their flight there were taken prisoners to the number of eight or nine hundred, which our general ought to have had for his share. . . but our general notwithstanding finding himself to have now very near the number of 500 negroes thought it best to depart with them, and such merchandise as he had from the coast of Africa, towards the West Indies. (Hakluyt, 132-3)

Africans, now denoted simply by the color of their skin as 'negroes', are slaughtered by the thousands and survivors are enumerated as cargo to be shipped to the New World in exchange for rum and sugar. Students, in short, can be shown precisely how the extreme views of Africa that obtained in the sixteenth and seventeenth centuries, influenced by the rise of the slave trade, complicated texts in praise of the African heritage in the classical tradition.

The entrances of Shakespeare's Africans onstage are designed to arouse and sustain dramatic curiosity about characters who are being progressively marginalized during the emergence of European colonialism. His Africans are characters who are "reduced to a negative sign" and manipulated to play the crucial role in "a ritual of exorcism", as Ralph Ellison says. They are constructed to expose, actually to predispose, a national audience to the official ideas of Africans espoused in the travel literature which is subsequently deconstructed in the remainder of the Shakespearean play by reaffirming ancient, more humane views of the African subject. As Ellison articulated the process for African American literature some time ago, in his African plays Shakespeare often "start[s] with the stereotype, accept[s] it as true, and then seek[s] out the human truth which it hides".[9] To put this hypothesis in Shakespeare's own words, his African plays are all about 'reputation', for it is reputation that can manipulate impression, fixing outcomes in the relationship between races, classes, age groups, or genders. No one knows this better than Iago, because he proves himself a master manipulator of the appearances and illusions that condition expectations in his game of the handkerchief, preying on the weakness of the 'perjur'd eye' with its tendency to mistake visual observation for real knowledge. Iago confides to his victim, Othello,

> Good name in man and woman, dear my lord,
> Is the immediate jewel of their souls:
> Who steals my purse steals trash; 'tis something, nothing ;
> 'Twas mine, 'tis his, and has been slave to thousands:
> But he that filches from me my good name
> Robs me of that which not enriches him
> And makes me poor indeed. (*Othello*, 3.3.155-61)[10]

Racism is predicated on the imputation of good or evil to a targeted member of a cultural community as a self-fulfilling prophecy. Reputation conditions real impressions and conditions and fixes behavioral outcomes.

Students are impressed when shown the first appearance of an African on the Shakespearean stage. They are equally startled by the only woodcut which depicts an Elizabethan performance of a play by Shakespeare: the pen-and-ink sketch attributed to Henry Peacham which shows Aaron the Moor in *Titus Andronicus* on the far right in bold and black relief, larger than his dramatic companions onstage, with sword unsheathed as if to protect Tamora's two sons from execution by Titus. Aaron's is the only appearance on a Shakespearean stage by an African which is not prefaced by dialogue designed to prejudice the viewer or reader against him.

Peacham's drawing provides the violent context lacking in Shakespeare's rendering of the scene where Aaron is simply listed in the procession of enemies conducted into Rome by Titus Andronicus behind the coffin of Titus' son, who has been killed in action. The subsequent action of Aaron in the play is, of course, despicable, but not irredeemable. Anticipating the villainies of Iago as an evil stage-manager, Aaron incites the sons of Tamora, Demetrius and Chiron, to rape and mutilate Lavinia but does not join in that rape. He also frames Titus' sons Martius and Quintus with the murder of Bassanius, who was also murdered by Tamora's sons. Finally, he conspires to get Titus to cut off his hand by convincing him that the lives of his sons will be spared by his sacrifice.

However, in this play Aaron is something of an amateur as an aggressor. He watches Romans and Goths systematically murder, mutilate, rape, and even devour one another – who's the cannibal in this play? – while manipulating European violence to his own advantage. And far from being motiveless, as Ruth Cowhig suggests, Aaron's enemy is the Roman empire who holds him captive and brands him inferior as a Moor and a black man.[11] Geraldo de Sousa has recently argued, "Perhaps realizing that the Roman empire is simply too powerful for him to bring down on his own, Aaron focuses on representative Romans, especially Lavinia and Titus, whose bodies he wants to ravage, rape, pillage, mutilate, and above all inscribe as emblems of Roman racial prejudice and violence."[12]

If *Titus Andronicus* critiques the brutal sacrifice of children in support of the Roman concept of *pater familias,* then Aaron qualifies as the 'hero-villain' of the action, as Cowhig calls him. He is the father in the play who defends his child with his life rather than sacrifice him for the good of the state. As the product of a miscegenistic union with Tamora, his baby is at risk. In a famous passage from the play, Aaron's defends the very life of his infant son who is endangered by his mixed-race complexion. To Chiron and Demetrius, who would murder their own brother in cold blood because of his "hue", Aaron defends the baby's blackness in a speech that anticipates Shylock's defense of Jewishness, or Emilia's defense of being female:

>   ... is black so base a hue?
> Sweet blowse, you are a beauteous blossom, sure. [...]
> [*Takes the Child from the Nurse, and draws.*]
> Stay, murderous villains! will you kill your brother? [...]
> What, what, ye sanguine, shallow-hearted boys!
> Ye white-limed walls! ye alehouse painted signs!
> Coal-black is better than another hue,
> In that it scorns to bear another hue;
> For all the water in the ocean
> Can never turn the swan's black legs to white,
> Although she lave them hourly in the flood.
> Tell the empress from me, I am of age
> To keep mine own, excuse it how she can. (4.2.71-2; 88-105)

Aaron here defends his child and his "hue" against a culture that threatens him simply for being born black, and in so doing reaffirms his humanity, loyalty, honor, and bravery, all qualities attributed to the African character by ancient writers.

The reputations of the remaining African characters we will discuss all precede them, and these reputations are tarnished, or rather "burnished". Venice is obviously the 'liminal zone' Shakespeare reserves for his most extreme multicultural experiments, because, as Walter Cohen and others have shown, it is *the* early modern city where capitalistic exchange necessitated the clash of cultures, not to mention the cross-roads of Western, near-Eastern, and African civilizations.[13] Profit trumps even race and cultural difference in Venice, at least in the short run. The play, in particular the casket "lottery", as Nerissa calls it, is about the fatal error of mistaking outward show for inward substance, the error to which most capitalistic enterprise is prone even within a Christian context. Although Bassanio wins the lottery, after coaching (i.e. cheating) by Portia through the lyric she chooses to direct him to the casket of lead, other candidates for Portia's hand are reviewed in advance of their appearance on-stage. Portia confides:

> I pray thee, over-name them; and as thou namest them, I will describe them; and, according to my description, level at my affection. (1.2.36-8)

Affections are preconditioned in the 'descriptions', actually the prescriptions delivered in advance of the appearance of the character on-stage. The Neapolitan is dismissed, "for he doth nothing but talk of his horse" and is judged a very "colt" whose mother must have dallied with a "smith", a horse-shoer (40-44). The County Palatine is thought to be so full of unmannerly sadness in his youth that he is well on his way to becoming a "weeping philosopher" in his dotage (46-53). A series of suitors are then dismissed according to national stereotypes, a bit Shakespeare had already perfected in Dromio's routine about global Nell, the kitchen wench, in *The Comedy of Errors*. Monsieur le Bon is the effeminate Frenchman who "falls straight a-capering" when he hears "a throstle sing", and fences "with his own shadow" (56-65). Baron Falconbridge is the stupid 'Brit', "dumb" in that he speaks no Italian or Latin, only his native English, and gaudily dressed according to whatever European fashion is in vogue (68-76). The Scot is feisty, always quarreling with the Englishman, and the German is, of course, a drunk. The Europeans are all judged by their behavior, albeit a behavior that is assumed to correspond to the national stereotype circulating about their respective cultures. Only Morocco is prejudged by his appearance, his "complexion" or "hue" alone. He is expelled unceremoniously from the court of Belmont not because of a failure in virtue, achievement, courage, or even national origin, but because of the color of his skin, the visual marker of otherness and inferiority. When it is announced that the Prince of Morocco is arriving unexpectedly, Portia confides in a cynical, saucy manner worthy of an Iago:

> ... I should be glad of his approach: if he have the condition of a saint and
> the complexion of a devil, I had rather he should shrive me than wive me.
> (1.2.129-31)

Portia opts for the superficial once again, the very flaw to be excoriated in the lottery of the caskets and in her legal diatribe against Shylock. Unlike Desdemona, she cannot love a man who might be a saint if his complexion is black. Morocco is aware that his condemnation-by-complexion precedes him. His first words confirm the suspicions students will see displayed in the travel literature where blackness is considered an aberration from aboriginal whiteness.[14] The Prince of Morocco is disliked for his color, or rather his discoloration. But he, like Aaron, remains resolutely loyal to his "hue".

> Mislike me not for my complexion,
> The shadow'd livery of the burnish'd sun,
> To whom I am a neighbor and near bred. (2.1.1-3)

He is chidden for his choice of the golden casket, because "All that glisters is not gold" (2.7.65). His eye is "perjur'd" by superficial appearances, as Joel Fineman suggests.[15] And yet Portia herself dismisses the Prince for his 'hue', his skin color, in a flippant aside worthy of Iago. "A gentle riddance. Draw the curtains, go. Let all of his complexion choose me so"(79-80). Surely there is an irony here. All in all, Morocco does not do too badly in the spousal sweepstakes for Portia. He seems the best of the lot, socially superior to Bassanio and personally superior to Aragon, who opens the silver casket only to find "the portrait of a blinking idiot" staring back at him. There is, in other words, more than a touch of the ancient's view of the noble African in Morocco, who is summarily dismissed by Portia in a lottery designed by her father to teach her not to judge a book by its cover or, presumably, a man by his color.

I have argued for a revised curriculum in Shakespeare elsewhere and will not repeat those arguments here.[16] Suffice it to say that *Othello* is a tragedy undeniably suitable for the classroom if students are to be fed a steady diet of tragedy. Up through the nineteenth century, it was the favorite and most frequently performed Shakespearean tragedy. The play is as tightly constructed and focused as *Macbeth*, as elevated in its language as *Hamlet*, as politically trenchant and topical as *Julius Caesar*, and as erotically riveting as *Romeo and Juliet*. Indeed, of the four standard tragedies, it perhaps most resembles *Romeo and Juliet* as an extraordinary love story. I like to tell students that the conclusion of *Romeo and Juliet* posed a dramatic challenge to Shakespeare. What if he told the story of two lovers who faced similar difficulties from their respective cultures, both Italian and contemporary as a matter of fact, but in the second story, we are led to believe that

Romeo himself, not fate, or the Capulets, or the Montagues, kills Juliet? What sort of twisted logic could possibly lead such a Romeo to so horrid a crime that would contradict everything we had come to know of his love for Juliet? Such is the dramatic challenge Shakespeare posed for himself in *Othello*. The catalyst for that challenge is, of course, Iago, who uses racism as his instrument to undermine faith in the relationship of Desdemona and Othello and the credibility of Othello even in his own eyes.

No character in Shakespeare is more dramatically *preconceived* before his entrance onstage than Othello. By the time of *Othello*, Shakespeare had mastered the dramatic representation of the Western racist paradigm. Iago is such an engaging villain because he plays the familiar bigot's game of appealing, however subconsciously, to the deeply instilled fears Early Modern European culture has concocted about the racial 'other'. He does not simply address the audience throughout the play, he confides in it, projecting and reflecting its xenophobia onto Othello before we get our first glimpse and direct impression of this celebrated general. Iago manipulates the essential strategy of racism: he poisons the mind with preconceptions about the 'other' before the person of that 'category' is ever encountered in the flesh, person to person. As John Wideman has written, "Race is not a set of qualities inhering in some 'other', it's the license to ascribe such qualities allied with the power to make them stick."[17]

The theme of jealousy in the play is rooted in erotic fantasies about the professional and sexual prowess of the 'other'. Iago is often characterized as driven by "motiveless malignity",[18] but he confides to us that he is jealous of the Moor not only professionally – for he has been passed over for promotion by both Othello and Cassio – but also sexually. He confesses that "I hate the Moor, / And it is thought abroad, that 'twixt my sheets / He (Othello) has done my office" (1.3.386-8). What students find most fascinating about the opening scene is that during Iago's conversation with Roderigo, the plot of the play is hatched spontaneously and fully blown in response to a single racist cue. After Iago fully identifies himself as an anti-god with the power to re-create human beings in his own nasty image – "I am not what I am (1.1.65)" – Roderigo offhandedly delivers the first racist epithet in the play, "What a full fortune does the thicklips owe / If he can carry't thus!" Iago replies, slowly and deliberately, "Call up her father". By constructing the racist composite of Brabantio's new son-in-law, he will "poison his [Brabantio's] delight" (69). Drawing on the visual terminology of racism once again, Iago claims Brabantio's joy "may lose some colour" (73).

Brabantio is "roused" – both raised from bed and aroused with racist fury – by the 'reputation' of Othello that is reconstructed for him in the dark of night by the riotous Roderigo and Iago. Othello is first of all branded a thief, not only for "stealing" Brabantio's daughter, but his "bags" (80) which carries the double suggestion of castration that we hear in Shylock's loss of his daughter and his "stones" in *The Merchant of Venice*. "Even now, now, very now, an old black ram / Is tupping your white ewe" (88-89). Othello's love for Desdemona is expressed in terms of animal savagery, sexual rapine, and stolen property, all projected on a character that has yet to appear before the audience. "The devil will make a grandsire of you" (91). Because Othello is black, he is a thief, a rapist, a savage, an animal, a devil. As Iago says later in the play, he will "set down the pegs that make this music" (2.1.200). He has sent us spinning down the Great Chain of Being, here. The image of the African is devolving. Like a musician, Iago rings changes upon the principal building blocks in the construction of the racist paradigm designed not only for Blacks, but for the Irish, the Jews, and any other racial 'other' that will one day find itself useful in fueling the ambitions of empire. In full swing, and having the ear of Brabantio, he hammers away:

> you'll have your daughter covered with a Barbary horse; you'll have your nephews neigh to you; you'll have coursers for cousins and gennets for germans. [...] your daughter and the Moor are now making the beast with two backs. (1.1.111-17)

Roderigo, slow-witted as he is, has now tuned in on the game. He adds, "your fair daughter" has been transported by a "knave", a "gondolier" to "the gross clasps of a lascivious Moor" (125-6). In "gross revolt" against her family and her race, Desdemona has given herself to "an extravagant and wheeling stranger / Of here and every where" (134-7). Roderigo's words are well chosen here, for Leslie Fiedler's notion of the Shakespearean 'stranger', is so serviceable precisely because as a mental figment, or what I like to call a 'pigment' of the imagination, the paradigm of the thieving, super-masculine, oversexed, demonic black man is fully established as "here and every where".[19] All such a paradigm needs is the vague visual marker of a 'black' person to release its poison. Iago has fully mastered the most important of the new imperial paradigms – the visual marker of color. As Brabantio responds, the dream, the nightmare of racism has now been fully installed in his consciousness. "This accident is not unlike my dream", the beleaguered father mutters, "Belief of it oppresses me already" (143).

Iago continues to prey upon the vulnerability of all the players to sneaking suspicions about the behavior of the racial alien – even Desdemona, but most of all Othello himself. "Rude as I am in speech, and little blessed with the soft phrase of peace", Othello declares while suing for Brabantio's daughter in marriage, belatedly, of course. As alien, Othello doubts his capacities for speech – and for peace (1.3.81-2). "Haply, for I am black, / And have not those soft parts of conversation / That chamberers have" (3.3.264-5). Brabantio, for one, is simply aghast that Desdemona has chosen 'to marry one'. Would his daughter "... t'incur a general mock, / Run from her guardage to the sooty bosom / Of such a thing as thou – to fear, not to delight" (1.2.69-71)! The disturbed father feels certain that Othello has influenced his daughter's foul choice with powerful drugs (1.2.73-5). Iago plies Othello with blatant racist arguments.

> Ay, there's the point; as (to be bold with you)
> Not to affect many proposèd matches
> Of her own clime, complexion, and degree,
> Whereto we see in all things nature tends –
> Foh, one may smell in such, a will most rank,
> Foul disproportions, thoughts unnatural. (3.3.228-33)

Iago suggests throughout the play that Desdemona is not to be trusted because she has already committed the unpardonable sin against her 'kind': the sexual choice of an alien. Even Othello is buying the argument, as is indicated by his admission that Desdemona's name and virtue has been blackened and fouled by her relationship with him: "Her name, that was as fresh / As Dian's visage, is now begrim'd and black / As mine own face" (3.3.386-7). Of course, Othello is driven by such manipulation to kill the thing he loves, but only after he has commanded the sympathy of the audience for all the solid virtues attributed to Africans in the ancient world – courage, military accomplishment, honor, and deeply religious convictions. And in his final speeches and suicide it is generally acknowledged that he redeems himself.

With Cleopatra Shakespeare enters new and controversial African territory. She is not the only black female in Shakespeare's plays, black by her own admission – "Think on me, / That am with Phœbus' amorous pinches black" (1.5.27-8). In *The Merchant of Venice* Launcelot Gobbo has gotten a "Negro" – Shakespeare's only use of that relatively new word pejoratively designating the race of Africans in the Renaissance by their color – a "Moor" pregnant, and he exchanges barbs with Lorenzo on the subjects of mixed marriages and miscegenation. To Gobbo's cracks about Lorenzo, a Christian, marrying Jessica, a Jew, Lorenzo responds:

> I shall answer that better to the commonwealth than you can the getting up of the Negro's belly; the Moor is with child by you, Launcelot. *Launcelot.* It is much that the Moor should be more than reason; but if she be less than an honest woman, she is indeed more than I took her for. (3.5.37-42)

In both his Venetian plays, Shakespeare is dealing with issues of interracial and inter-religious marriages. The "Negro", off-stage and pregnant though she may be, here tarnishes the reputation of Launcelot, the familiar figure for betrayal in the Middle Ages and Renaissance, though his "treason of the blood".

Cleopatra represents, of course, the other end of the African social spectrum for the Europeans with whom she relates – a queen in most productions but a pharaoh in her own mind and in the annals of history. The last, in fact, and most notorious of four millennia of Egyptian pharaohs, Cleopatra epitomizes the exotic characteristics attributed to Africans in antiquity. She combines both the allure and seduction of the continent with the courage, indomitability, ingenuity, and deep sensuality of its people. She is a Queen, outranking even the Prince of Morocco and the general, Othello, in social status. To Octavius she is not a pharaoh or even an African, but a descendent of Greek kings, a "Ptolemy", as many Western commentators considered her. Antony has been feminized by a descendant of the Ptolemies; she wears the pants in the relationship: "Antony is not more man-like / Than Cleopatra; nor the queen of Ptolemy / More womanly than he" (1.4.5-7). Octavius snidely refers to Cleopatra as a Ptolemy twice more and desires to lead her ultimately back to Rome in the chains appropriate to the slave. To the future emperor of Rome, she is already a "slave" and a "knave" who would enchant Antony, as Othello was supposed to have done with Desdemona:

> ... Let us grant, it is not
> Amiss to tumble on the bed of Ptolemy;
> To give a kingdom for a mirth; to sit
> And keep the turn of tippling with a slave;
> To reel the streets at noon, and stand the buffet
> With knaves that smell of sweat. (1.4.16-21)

In the West, Cleopatra remains a Ptolemy as well, lilly white, or maybe only as dark as an Elizabeth Taylor. In production she is invariably white, usually accompanied by a black Iras or Charmian, although she refers to herself, eerily echoing Othello, as clearly black and old in the play.

Moreover, Cleopatra, is introduced to us before her first appearance onstage by Demetrius and Philo. Like her fellow Africans, her reputation precedes her. She is the "tawny front" who has beguiled Antony, that "plated Mars" and "triple pillar of the world" now transformed "into a strumpet's fool" and "the fan / To cool a gypsy lust." (1.1.6-13). Pharaoh she might be, and unquestionably Shakespeare's greatest tragic heroine, in Roman eyes Cleopatra is a strumpet and a gypsy, in other words, black. Unlike Aaron, Othello, and Caliban, however, Cleopatra never becomes so disconsolate, so demoralized by European presuppositions about her that she allows herself to devolve into a confirmation of the stereotype. She is content to remain Antony's "serpent of old Nile" (1.5.25) without ever succumbing to the hatred and suspicion she inspires in the interlopers who people and would control her court, as Aaron, Othello, and Caliban certainly are driven to do.

Students find it incredible that Shakespeare provides us with one of literature's earliest depictions of an African slave on an island plantation within ten years of the sale of the first black man in America. Caliban comes onstage just after Ariel, the 'house Negro' in Aimé Cesaire's revision of the play, has asked Prospero for his "liberty" and reminds his master of their contract. If *Othello* is about reputation, *The Tempest* is about servitude – voluntary servitude inspired by love, and forced labor, inspired by fear. What looks like an affectionate relationship between master and servant quickly degenerates into a coercive, threatening domination. When Ariel balks at his servitude, Prospero barks,

> Thou liest, malignant thing! Hast thou forgot
> The foul witch Sycorax, who with age and envy
> Was grown into a hoop? Hast thou forgot her? (1.2.256-8)

reminding Ariel that he was slave to the "damn'd witch" Sycorax. Sycorax, the mother of Caliban, was from "Argiers", Africa. Africans, of course, sold fellow Africans into slavery to European traders. Prospero, like his contemporaries who profited from the trade of slaves, conceives of himself as a liberator, rescuing victims of the European sale of flesh for his own, grander enterprise. Sycorax is a wizard of sorts who is banished for her sorcery to the island plantation where she delivers "a freckled whelp hag-born – not honour'd with / A human shape" (82-3). Both Ariel and Caliban are referred to as "slaves", but Caliban is "monstrous". The entrance of Caliban is anticipated as visually offensive. Miranda considers him a "villain [...] I do not love to look on" (309). Prospero counters mysteriously that his appearance, which includes his shape, size, and 'hue', marks him visually as the slave designated to do the hard labor of the island:

> But, as 'tis,
> We cannot miss him: he does make our fire,
> Fetch in our wood and serves in offices
> That profit us. What, ho! slave! Caliban! (310-13)

Students will recognize the 'optical proof' for slavery once again. There is a double entendre in the word "miss", of course – to do without and to see, but clearly Caliban as a slave is visually marked for "offices / That profit us." The physical monstrosities of the black alien anticipated as metaphors in *Titus* and *Othello* are here reified in the misshapen, fishlike, inhuman appearance, smell, and shape attributed to Caliban, who becomes the heir to all modern monsters from Frankenstein to Quasimodo and to all monstrous depictions of racist 'others' we have seen deployed as lately as the case of the supposed abduction of the children of Susan Smith by a menacing-looking black man in South Carolina. And yet, as in the case of Caliban's African brothers, there is a certain dignity attributed to him by play's end as the knowledgeable aboriginal of the island. He knows the terrain and the music of the isle intimately and affectionately.

We have come full circle here. Shakespeare begins his story of the African in the ancient world, in *Titus Andronicus* and *Antony and Cleopatra*, then establishes the 'reputation' of what he calls the 'Negro' in the 'Merchant' and the 'Moor' of contemporary Venice, and takes us finally into the dismal European future of slavery on the "still-vex'd" island akin to "Bermoothes" (1.2.229) in *The Tempest*. By career's end Shakespeare had perceived the transmutation of the racial paradigm of the black African as ripe for colonial and capitalistic exploitation. During his creator's lifetime, Othello, in a sense, had been sold back and Cleopatra was taken into slavery. The pre-colonial view of Africa was complicated, and certainly not as pejorative as it became during Shakespeare's time and as it remains in our own. The dignity that the plays ascribe to Morocco, Othello, Cleopatra, and even at times to Aaron and Caliban, is not nearly so extraordinary as it might seem at first glance.

Shakespeare's more controversial plays, *The Taming of the Shrew*, *The Merchant of Venice*, *Othello*, and *The Tempest* seem to reel off rituals of exclusion and conformity that represent the core values of European patriarchy and dominion. The domestication of an unruly female, the conversion of a troublesome Jew, the disastrous effects of a biracial marriage, the resistance of a slave overcome: everything seems to be in perfect order from the Western, patriarchal perspective. But while Shakespeare presents what appears to be sacrosanct and inviolate in the Western experience, he leaves his audience uneasy about what might have been, could be, or might actually be in the European world. He deliberately draws on the 'master plots' of the Western canon which are then retold while they are untold, exposed, revealed for what they may well be – deceptions used to prop up untenable, unproductive propositions about human experience. Ultimately, Shakespeare's African characters leave us thinking deeply about the great problems to come in the western experience, what DuBois called the 'problem of color' which has plagued the culture for centuries.

Jacques Derrida writes, "There's no racism without a language."[20] Students, it follows therefore, can be shown that racism – and all the violence that is historically associated with it – is generated by language. Racial difference is not genetically 'real', nor is it grounded in real experience but is a product of verbal conditioning. Racism cannot long survive without the verbal and symbolic apparatus that generates and sustains it: the names, the jokes, the plays, the speeches, the casual exchanges, the novels. In short, racism is a cultural virus that is verbally transmitted and its antidote must therefore be verbally administered as well. Shakespeare adapted his source for *Othello*, Giraldi's Cinthio's *novella* of Othello, Iago, and Desdemona in his *Hecatommithi*, by adding the compelling motif of race reflected in the rise of the morally questionable slave trade in sixteenth-century Europe. Shakespeare in turn offers *Othello* and its companion plays about Africans, as opportunities for his audience and our students to consider the behaviors and the consequences of the new form of xenophobia that continues to plague Europe and America up to our own day. These plays offer teachers and students a quiet, legitimate opportunity to discuss the controversial subject of racism in one of the last places where free and open debate is allowed to thrive – the American classroom.

Notes

1. As Edward Berry explains, "Critics have tended to ignore or underplay the issue of Othello's race. The topic of race has always been explosive, particularly when it involves miscegenation". Until late in the twentieth century, under the influence of literary modernism, critics like F. R. Leavis and T. S. Eliot do not, according to Berry "even allude to such matters; both treat Othello's moral flaws as universals. The weight of critical tradition, then, presents a Shakespeare who finds racial and cultural difference insignificant and who assimilates his Moor into the 'human' condition". "Othello's Alienation", *Studies in English Literature: 1500-1900*, 30 (1990), p. 315.

2. The growing bibliography of such studies includes Emily Bartels, "Making More of the Moor: Aaron, Othello, and Renaissance Refashionings of Race", *Shakespeare Quarterly*, 41 (1990), pp. 433-54; Anthony Barthelemy, *Black Face Maligned Race: The Representation of Blacks in English Drama from Shakespeare to Southerne* (Baton Rouge: Louisiana State UP, 1987); Ruth Cowhig, "Actors Black and Tawny in the Role of Othello – and Their Critics", *Theatre Research International*, 4 (1979), pp. 133-46 and "Blacks in English Renaissance Drama", in *The Black Presence in English Literature*, ed. David Dabydeen (Manchester: Manchester UP, 1985), pp. 1-26; David Dabydeen, *The Black Presence in English Literature* (Manchester: Manchester UP, 1985); Jack D'Amico, *The Moor in English Renaissance Drama* (Tampa: South Florida UP, 1991); Peter Erickson, "Representations of Blacks and Blackness in the Renaissance", *Criticism*, 35 (1993), pp. 499-527; Henry Louis Gates, "Writing, 'Race,' and the Difference It Makes", in *Loose Canons: Notes on the Culture Wars* (New York: Oxford UP, 1992); Kim Hall, "Refashionings of Race", *Shakespeare Quarterly*, 41 (1990), pp. 433-54, *Things of Darkness: Economies of Race and Gender in Early Modern England* (Ithaca and London: Cornell UP, 1995), "'Troubling Doubles': Apes, Africans and Blackface in Mr. Moore's Revels", in *Race, Ethnicity and Power in the Renaissance*, ed. Joyce Green MacDonald (Totowa, NJ: Fairleigh Dickinson UP, 1997), "Beauty and the 'Beast' of Whiteness: Teaching Race and Gender", *Shakespeare Quarterly*, 47 (1996), pp. 461-75, and "Culinary Spices, Colonial Spaces: The Gendering of Sugar in the Seventeenth Century", in *Feminist Readings of Early Modern Culture: Emerging Subjects and Subjectivities*, ed. Lindsay Kaplan, Valerie Traub, and Dympna Callaghan (Cambridge: Cambridge UP, 1996), pp. 168-90; Eldred Jones, *The Elizabethan Image of African* (Charlottesville: Virginia UP, 1971) and *Othello's Countrymen: The African in English Renaissance Drama* (London: Oxford UP, 1965); Ania Loomba, *Gender, Race, Renaissance Drama* (Manchester: Manchester UP, 1989); Karen Newman, "'And wash the Ethiop white': Femininity and the Monstrous in *Othello*", in *Shakespeare Reproduced: The Text in History and Ideology*, ed. Jean E. Howard and Marion F. O'Connor (New York and London: Methuen, 1987), pp. 143-63; Elliot Tokson, *The Popular Image of the Black Man in English Drama, 1550-1688* (Boston: G. K. Hall, 1982).

3. For an exhaustive presentation of this generally positive view, see Frank Snowden, *Blacks in Antiquity: Ethiopians in the Graeco-Roman Experience* (Cambridge, MA: Harvard UP, 1970). See Snowden's update on the subject in "Ethiopians and the Graeco-Roman World",

in *The African Diaspora: Interpretive Essays,* ed. Martin L. Kilson and Robert I. Rotberg (Cambridge, MA: Harvard UP, 1976), pp. 11-36.

4   Herodotus, *The Histories,* transl. Aubrey de Sélincourt (New York: Penguin Books, 1954). This *Famous Hystory of Herodotus* was translated for Elizabethan readers by Barnaby Rich (London, 1584; reprint, New York, 1924). On the depiction of the 'other' in Herodotus, see François Hartog, *The Mirror of Herodotus: The Representation of the Other in the Writing of History,* transl. Janet Lloyd (Berkeley: California UP, 1988).

5   *The Iliad,* transl. Andrew Lang, Walter Leaf, and Ernest Myers (New York: The Modern Library, 1968).

6   *Diodorus of Sicily,* trans. C. H. Oldfather, 12 vols. (Cambridge, MA: Harvard UP, 1961), vol. II, 3.2.2-3.

7   On the circulation of the pejorative view of Sub-Saharan Africans in Elizabethan travel literature, see "Before *Othello:* Elizabethan Representations of Sub-Saharan Africans", *The William and Mary Quarterly,* 54 (1997), pp. 19-44.

8   Peter Erickson, "Representations of Blacks and Blackness in the Renaissance", *Criticism,* 35 (1993), p. 503.

9   "Change the Joke and Slip the Yoke", in *The Collected Essays of Ralph Ellison,* ed. John F. Callahan (New York: The Modern Library, 1995), p. 103.

10 All quotations are taken from *The Riverside Shakespeare,* ed. G. Blakemore Evans (Boston: Houghton Mifflin, 1974).

11 Although Cowhig celebrates Aaron, who "belongs to the tradition of the villain-hero", she claims "Aaron's actions have no adequate motive". See "Blacks in English Renaissance Drama", in *The Black Presence in English Literature,* ed. David Dabydeen (Manchester: Manchester UP, 1985), p. 3.

12 "Race, Text, and Memory in *Titus Andronicus*", paper delivered in the "Renaissance Aliens" special session at the 1996 meeting of the South Atlantic Modern Language Association, p. 13.

13 "*The Merchant of Venice* and the Possibilities of Historical Criticism", in *Materialist Shakespeare: A History,* ed. Ivo Camps (London: Verso, 1995), pp. 71-92. See also "The Rhetoric of Exclusion: Jew, Moor, and the Boundaries of Discourse in *The Merchant of Venice*", in *Race, Ethnicity, and Power in the Renaissance,* ed. Joyce Green MacDonald (Totowa, NJ: Fairleigh Dickinson UP, 1997), pp. 19-35.

14 One Andrew Thevet, according to Virginia and Alden Vaughan, argued that "very black skin, [...] 'commeth of a superficial action': extreme heat draws warmth from the heart and other interior parts to the surface, leaving the dark Africans with scorched skin but inwardly cold" (p. 22).

15 See "Shakespeare's 'Perjur'd Eye', in *The Subjectivity Effect in Western Literary Tradition* (Cambridge, MA: MIT Press, 1991), pp. 91-119.

16 See James R. Andreas, "Neutering *Romeo and Juliet*", in *Ideological Approaches to Shakespeare: The Practice of Theory,* ed. Robert Merrix, Nicholas Ranson (Lewiston, NY: Edwin Mellon Press, 1992), pp. 229-42 and "Silencing the Vulgar and Voicing the Other Shakespeare", *Nebraska English Journal,* 35 (1990), pp. 74-88.

17 *Fatheralong* (New York: Vintage Books, 1994), p. xv.

18 The famous pronouncement of Samuel Taylor Coleridge. *Coleridge's Writings on Shakespeare* (New York: Capricorn Books, 1959), p. 171.

19 *The Stranger in Shakespeare* (New York: Stein & Day, 1973).

20 Jacques Derrida, "Racism's Last Word", in *"Race", Writing, and Difference*, ed. Henry Louis Gates, Jr. (Chicago and London: Chicago UP, 1985). "The point is not that acts of racial violence are only words, but rather that they have to have a word. [Racism] institutes, declares, writes, inscribes, prescribes" (Derrida, p. 331).

"AND THAT'S TRUE TOO": TEACHING THE CONFLICTS IN SHAKESPEARE'S WORKS

Jane Carducci
(Winona State University)

I

In our contemporary global society, it is imperative that we discard our western ethnocentrism and put on the robes of sartorial internationalism. Betty Jean Craige goes so far as to say, "More than ever before, cooperation among the earth's diverse inhabitants is necessary if the human race is to survive through the next few centuries" (395). She goes on to argue that "we are all hybrids, impure and intermingled. The challenge is to intermingle peacefully" (400). One way to send our students out into the world dressed for peaceful intercultural mingling is to expose them to diverse texts and critical analyses – to teach the conflicts. I have found that students' exposure to the conflicts surrounding Shakespeare's work – politicized or not – leads to interesting discussions of the primary text, and reading critical debates helps students inhabit Shakespeare's works, engaging "more deeply in [the work's] themes, language, and structure" (Graff and Phelan, 103).

Not all educators agree with this idea: some feel that having students study critical arguments is counterproductive: not only are students diverted from the primary text, but they are also prone to replace their own responses with those of the critics. But Gerald Graff and James Phelan argue that "all responses are mediated" (102) and the "choice is not between direct and mediated reading but between different kinds of mediation" (103). Some people also lament the imposition of politics on the literature of canonical status, and George Will specifically protests that politics "represents the disguised or unexamined assumptions and interests of a dominant class, sex, race" (72). Will argues further that supplanting esthetic with political responses to literature "makes literature primarily interesting as a mere index of who had power and whom the powerful victimized" (72).

It seems clear that if we expect our students to think critically, they need to have literary critics as role models, exemplary scholars who present well-developed diverse opinions in logical, reasoned essays. Graff and Phelan note that it seems contradictory, in fact, for teachers to expect students to produce effective literary criticism without offering examples of such criticism (103).

Teaching the conflicts in Shakespeare's works is also an important step in the students' cognitive development. In William Perry's study about intellectual development in college, he finds that students often move cognitively from dualism (what is known, certain) to multiplicity (recognizing different perspectives, all of which are valid) to relativism (critical thinking) and, finally, to commitment (a contextually appropriate truth). It is likely that Perry would see students exploring various and contradictory points of view as a sensible and challenging task prompting students to understand the differences among multiple perspectives. From there, students can take a firm stand on the alternatives, opening up new intellectual horizons and in-depth scholarship. Further, students can relate these learning processes to personal values, taking a firm stand and supporting it.

This invitation to critical debates also allows students to participate as guests in Kenneth Burke's parlor of critical discourse. Students find that when they enter the parlor, others proceeding them have engaged in a heated discussion, "a discussion too heated for them to pause and tell you exactly what it is about" (qtd. in Klooster and Bloem, 37). Students listen for a while and then offer their opinion. As Burke describes:

> Someone answers; you answer him; another comes to your defense; another aligns himself against you to either the embarrassment or the gratification of your opponent, dependent on the quality of your ally's assistance. However, the discussion is interminable. The hour grows late, you must depart. And you do depart, with the discussion still vigorously in progress. (37)

With this paradigm, students gain background knowledge about the conflicts in literature and realize that people take these different approaches seriously. They see it is possible to approach a text in more than one way and that often critical readership is informed by ideological positions and cultural values. They discover that to gain validity, one's perspective must be grounded in, and authorized by, textual, cultural, and knowledge-based support. They can even begin to trust that their opinions are well grounded and valuable persuading "others to accept [their judgments], and to listen to their arguments in turn" (Graff and Phelan, 106). Students can then exit at the end of the semester knowing the debate will continue.

Finally, the reason for introducing students to critical conflicts is to help them recognize nonsense and excel in the kind of analysis and reasoned argument that will make them effective citizens in a global society. Graff and Phelan would agree:

> Simply to opt out of the debate is to surrender one of the most important forms of action available to a citizen of a democracy. In short, value judgments and debates are both inescapable and important. (106)

In making sense of their world by reading and reacting to the conflicts, students become contextually solid, can take the best of what is offered, and can model rigor and a tolerance of diversity.

II

Reading and reacting to conflicts is exactly what we do in my non-traditional, feminist approach to Shakespeare. Like Torri Thompson I introduce students to the feminist viewpoint and "the idea that we all have to take a perspective, make a choice that we know is inherently incomplete and exclusionary" (69). By reading the conflicts we can eventually claim responsibility for our perspective as a trustworthy position, one to which we can commit. To this end, we spend the semester discussing Shakespearean texts along with a variety of critical, social/cultural, and philosophical discursive traditions. These works compose the intertextual constellation for the class. Thompson defines this constellation as "a grouping of more or less equal texts which together form a 'picture', as opposed to the 'literary' text functioning as a star around which all the other textual planets revolve" (70). In this context, the Shakespearean poem or play becomes another cultural artifact. Students interrogate, for example, the construction of gender in Renaissance culture, and analyze the connection between gender and genre as socially constructed and politically motivated categories. By doing this, we can "present the most traditional texts from multiple perspectives which suggest the inconsistencies, contradictions, and complexities that shaped the gendered female body in early Modern England" (Thompson, 67).

We begin by demystifying Shakespeare himself. For example, we know that Shakespeare was baptized on April 26, 1564, and that usually this ceremony was performed three days after birth. We have to infer, from this information, that Shakespeare's birthday was April 23. We have no historical records to verify this. So we are already on slippery ground. *Traditionally*, then, we set Shakespeare's birthday on April 23 (underscored by the convenience that he also died on April 23 and that this is St. George's Day, celebrating the patron saint of England). Students are also surprised to discover that we're not even certain about Shakespeare's appearance. We have only two reliable sources for his image: The one above his grave in Holy Trinity Church at Stratford was sculpted by a Dutch stoneman, Gheerhart Janssen. The other portrait, which appears on the title page of the First Folio, was engraved by Flemish artist Martin Droeshout. Furthermore, we do not have a consistent spelling of Shakespeare's name found on many documents; orthography ranges from *Shackspere, Shaxper, Shagspere,* to *Shaxberd*.

We continue to explore some issues of biography with a discussion of authorship. Little is known about Shakespeare's life and, in fact, the anti-Stratfordians argue that someone else wrote the plays. The debate about who wrote the plays dates back to 1780 when James Wilmot traveled to Warwickshire where Shakespeare lived. Finding no physical evidence to support that fact that Shakespeare was indeed the author, Wilmot burned his notes and later revealed that he thought Shakespeare's works were written by someone else. Over the years candidates have included Sir Francis Bacon, Christopher Marlowe, and even Queen Elizabeth; the majority of anti-Stratfordians today support Edward De Vere (1550-1604), 17th Earl of Oxford. To emphasize the social significance of this issue we read the article "Looking for Shakespeare" in *The Atlantic Monthly* (1991). Tom Bethel presents the basic arguments against Shakespeare and for Edward De Vere; the case for Shakespeare is offered in a rebuttal by Irvin Matus. I accompany this assignment with a PBS film *The Shakespeare Mystery*, a helpful – if somewhat embarrassing – 55-minute look at the authorship question. I also take my *Shakespeare Newsletters* to class. When Louis Marder was the editor, the anti-Stratfordians got lots of press. They bought advertising; Marder apologized, but their money helped sustain the *Newsletter*.

We see that the authorship question goes beyond academia and spills over into our popular culture. The ubiquitous Shakespeare appears in strange and unexpected places: cartoons, a Joe Bazooka bubble gum wrapper, and a newspaper article about Shakespeare being baptized by the Mormons. I ask students for other examples of common cultural references to Shakespeare, and they have offered various samplings: Shakespeare still sells with popular movies like DeCaprio's *Romeo and Juliet*, and Kenneth Branagh is making a living with his productions of Shakespeare's plays. One student even referred to a memorial reconstruction from *Julius Caesar* in *The Guns of the Magnificent Seven* (1970). (Chris: "Los cobardes muerten muchas tiempas; el valiente, mas uno." Chico then translates this, "The coward dies many times; the brave man [pause] only once.")

Even though we are culturally inundated with Shakespeare, students are surprised that critical reception to his works has been uneven. For example, early on William Drummond complained that "Shakespeare wanted art" (127). Ben Jonson even noted that "Shakespeare had an excellent phantasy, brave notions, and gentle expressions: wherein [...] he should be stopped" (118). By 1921, however, the Newbolt Report confirmed Shakespeare as the cornerstone of English education: "Shakespeare is an inevitable and necessary part of school activity because he is our greatest English writer." We assumed that teaching Shakespeare was teaching the truth; he valorized all that is valuable in our culture. Shakespeare became his work, a kind of secular scripture, dogma.

This traditional approach to Shakespeare's works has changed since the 1970s. There are now many approaches to Shakespeare: Psychoanalytic, New

Historicist, Marxist, Reader Response, Cultural Materialist, and Feminist. In "Reconstructing Shakespeare", David Bevington offers a solid introduction to the issues. He says, "If we've learned anything in the last twenty years, it's that criticism enjoys an intrinsic life of its own in which the literary work changes and grows as we ask new questions of it" (22). Representing the traditionalists is Richard Bernstein in his review of a book by Richard Levin, who attacks feminist perspectives on Shakespeare. Levin "describes himself as a supporter of feminist goals and says he is a member of the National Organization of Women. But in his scholarly life he nonetheless supports the more traditional fashion of Shakespeare criticism" (C18). What we learn, of course, is that there is no definitive text in Shakespeare's canon.

And traditionally we often talk about the 'universality' of Shakespeare. But in Charles Larson's essay "Heroic Ethnocentrism: The Idea of Universality in Literature", Larson argues that "our concept of universality rarely takes into consideration the experiential aspects of a culture that may, indeed, shape our interpretations of a piece of literature" (463). In other words, our notion of the 'universal' is our cultural response shaped by Western tradition; "what is 'natural' in one society is not natural at all, but *learned*" (emphasis Larson's, 464). Larson's idea is manifested in a social construction of *Hamlet*: "Shakespeare in the Bush", an anthropological study by Laura Bohannan. Bohannan shows the difficulty of translating the meaning of *Hamlet* to the Tiv in West Africa. We feel the cross-cultural confusion and frustration when Bohannon is offered a whole new interpretation of *Hamlet* by the Tiv elders. Culturally constructed, these different meanings can lead students to discover that ethnocentrism is not unique to Westerners: After listening to Bohannan's tale of *Hamlet*, one Tiv elder admits that she "told it with very few mistakes" and concludes, "You must tell us some more stories of your country. We, who are elders, will instruct you in their true meaning, so that when you return to your own land your elders will see that you have not been sitting in the bush, but among those who know things and who have taught you wisdom" (6).[1] Students are beginning to see that there are many different ways to approach Shakespeare, and, as Leah Marcus reminds us in

Puzzling Shakespeare, we cannot, nor should attempt to come up with definitive readings of any cultural construct: "The Shakespeare we want is not a man [...], but an 'ongoing cultural activity'" (219).

After destabilizing Shakespeare himself and looking at various social constructions of his works, we are left with his texts. Students are puzzled by the instability of the text "because of our society's privileging of print culture" and its permanent and objective verifiable reality (Thompson, 68). But now students begin to wonder: How reliable are Shakespeare's texts after all? What authorizes them? What influences do we bring to help make meaning? Are the plays no longer repositories of universal truths?

Shakespeare produced his plays in complex and often ambiguous conditions; the materials that form Shakespeare's context are interconnected and interdependent. The Sonnets are a good place to start with the problems in textual history. We nod at Wyatt, Surrey, Sidney, Spenser, Barnfield, and Wroth, recognizing these poets and their works as an offshoot of the Petrarchan tradition in which Shakespeare is participating. Secure with this background information, we move on to various poems in Shakespeare's sequence. We are then confronted with the problem of chronology (when were these sonnets actually written? rewritten?) and the ordering of the sonnets. If we accept Thomas Thorpe's ordering (1609) we find a disjointed narrative involving a stormy *menage à trois*. Traditionally we discuss the first 126 sonnets as addressed to a Young Man, the remainder to the Dark Lady – on the whole, a dark, unredeemable vision. (*A Lover's Complaint* adds a misogynistic complement to the sonnets themselves.) But we are standing on shaky ground again, since the sequence has an unstable authorization. Then we add the debate about the poet: Can we infer from the text that Shakespeare himself had homoerotic concerns? Students are often surprised at the exploration of passion and lust that these poems contain.[2]

After the sonnets, *Twelfth Night* offers a smooth transition, a play concerned with relevant gender issues. In fact, students are intrigued with the fact that a boy actor would have been playing Viola, who then disguises herself as a boy. David Bevington has noted, "The motifs of Olivia's attraction for another woman (both actors would have been boys) and of Orsinio's deep fondness for a seeming young man ('Cesario'), which mature into sexual love, raise delicate suggestions of love between members of the same sex" (328). Students like discussing these issues of gender complication, homosexuality, and cross-dressing in this play, an excellent example of 'transvestite theater'.

Students learn that how we dress is important; Marjorie Garber has argued that "clothing constructs (and deconstructs) gender and gender differences" (3). My students decided to experiment with this notion: a few men in the class volunteered to walk around campus for a day dressed as women.[3] Students reported on their experience the next class period. Reactions varied: Some students were actually threatened, most were treated with contempt. Others were deemed curiosities, while a few experienced acceptance. One student commented that he often felt himself to be the outsider, the 'other' who did not fit into a comfortable, neat category and so was ostracized. Another student (a drama major) was surprised to learn that his peers were indifferent to his cross dressing; evidently other students thought there was nothing strange in his fashion choice for the day. This experiment generated a lively class (and university-wide) discussion. Students could see that by cross-dressing, by creating a 'third sex', they were creating the conflict we were discussing by challenging the "easy notions of binarity, putting into question the categories of 'female' and 'male'" (Garber, 10). Transgressing these sexual borders clearly caused anxiety; these students, as cross-dressers, threatened the established social order, just as in Shakespeare's time.

In Shakespeare's time, the sumptuary laws in England regulated dress: "cross-dressing, as fact and as idea, threatened a normative social order based on strict principles of hierarchy [...] of which women's subordination to men was a chief instance" (Howard, 418). The point of these laws, established by Queen Elizabeth in 1597, was to make certain a person's social role could be read without ambiguity or uncertainty; a subset of this law had to do with gender – to keep a woman in her place.

Garber adds that transvestitism produced "anxieties about the possibility that identity was not fixed, that there was no underlying 'self' at all, and that therefore identities had to be zealously and jealously safeguarded" (32). *Twelfth Night* turns on identity. The title of the play refers to the twelfth day after Christmas, the Feast of Epiphany when Christ revealed himself – his identity – to the wise men. The title enhances the fact that in the play each character is revealed, seen for what she/he is. The characters' identities are also revealed to themselves. Viola, the most complete character in the play, valorizes the Jungian notion of wholeness, coupling the strong opposites of masculine and feminine in her disguise. (Her twin brother, Sebastian, underscores this notion of opposites.) Even in disguise, she does not deceive herself and maintains her integrity.

If the play turns on identification, it also warns against misidentification. Gerald Else has translated *hamartia* as "misidentification" (378-92), and it may indeed be Antonio's tragic flaw that he misidentifies his relationship with Sebastian and becomes the disappointed lover. Students realize that the issue of identity is a complicated one – often culturally prompted rather than innate. The familiar categories of masculine and feminine blend together, and students see, as Judith Butler has argued, that gender roles and identity are all performance (14), that there are cultural imperatives of gender behavior. By looking at these complicated issues in *Twelfth Night*, students are forced out of the comfortable dualities of our western culture to face the conflicts of identity categories, categories that Butler promotes "as sites of necessary trouble" (14).

A comfortable – or uncomfortable – closure for the course is *The Tempest*. We tap into the issue of rape and get a brief glimpse of the 'stranger' in Shakespeare. As Meredith Anne Skura notes, Caliban (the stranger) resembles the "demonized women, Moors, and Jews in the canon" (289). The book I use for this class is edited by Graff and Phelan. Besides offering sources and contexts, the editors present some classic essays about power and the postcolonial paradigm. For this class we look at Skura's essay, "Discourse and the Individual: The Case of Colonialism in *The Tempest*", followed by an excerpt from Ania Loomba's *Gender, Race, Renaissance Drama* and the essay "Miranda, Where's Your Sister?: Reading Shakespeare's *The Tempest*".

In closing the course, Miranda's plight in a patriarchal society may represent what many of the women experience in Shakespeare's plays – and during Shakespeare's time. Prospero may render up his borrowed power to Caliban and Ariel, but he never emancipates Miranda. She is victimized (in this case caught up in the politics of colonialism), and traded for her father's ambitious gain. She is innocent, trusting, and suggestible, and Jean Howard notes that Prospero, capitalizing upon her receptivity, "could easily control her every response" (147). Could? in fact, he does. Not only does he berate her and control her, he devalues her and possesses her; she is the scapegoat for his anger and must suffer through his moments of insecurity, paranoia, self-discovery, and confessions of guilt. Even the base Caliban has tried to use Miranda, and the divine Ferdinand may prove an unworthy choice. No wonder, in this male-dominated and abusive world, Miranda's only memory of her former life is of her serving women – women who probably treated her kindly and fairly. Finally, in her exile, she has, in Rosalind's words about Celia, become a "young maid with travel much oppressed" (*AYL* 2.4.74). In fact, Miranda's voyage to the island as a child and her subsequent journey into adulthood offer her, like many other of Shakespeare's women, no more than a subaltern space.

III

By the end of the semester, our readings have included samples of Renaissance conduct literature, Shakespeare's works, and critical theories. Students have read the debates and questioned the texts, looking at Shakespeare and his works in new ways. More specifically, with this feminist approach, we have interrogated what Joan Walsh Scott calls the "often silent and hidden operation of gender" (17) which reflects the Renaissance patriarchal desire to control and dominate women.

More broadly, reading the conflicts expands my students' vision, and they seem convinced that studying these debates is important. In fact, one student commented, "It seems to me the problems arise when we insist on one preferred and orthodox reading." Graff and Phelan would agree: "Controversy for us is not the opposite of reaching resolution but a precondition of doing so" (101). Karen

Newman argues, in fact, that it is important for students to have "a promiscuous conversation [with] many texts" (xiii). Students realize that to gain validity, their perspectives must be grounded in and authorized by textual, cultural, knowledge-based support. Teaching the conflicts is one way to acquire this support. As Stephen Greenblatt notes, "The art that matters is not cement. It is mobile, complex, elusive, disturbing" (B1).

Notes

1. Other cultural constructions are also instructive. Students might take a look at a short play by Richard Curtis, *The Skinhead Hamlet*, which is translated into modern English "to achieve something like the effect of the New English Bible", or Tom Stoppard's film, *The Fifteen-Minute Hamlet*, or Shel Silverstein's "*Hamlet* as Told on the Street" in *Playboy*, January 1998. Students might also be interested in a recent production at the Brooklyn Academy of Music in New York: *Máquina Hamlet*. The spoken lines are in Spanish with English subtitles. This adaptation of Shakespeare's *Hamlet* is "a mere eight pages contrived from disjointed literary citations and harshly poetic declamations [...] a play about intellectuals whose introspection leaves them helpless" (Weber, 1).

2. The movie *Shakespeare in Love* poses an interesting crux based on the sonnets. Thinking he is sending his love-message to a young woman, the young 'Shakespeare' reads Sonnet 18, "Shall I compare thee to a summer's day", to Thomas Kent, a woman who is dressed as a man. The gender issues here become more complicated when we note that originally this sonnet was written to a young man. Certainly there is tension created through dramatic irony when, in the movie, 'Shakespeare' kisses the young man passionately; we know the man is really a woman, but 'Shakespeare' does not. *Measure for Measure* would be a relevant transition play; like the sonnet sequence, this play offers a dark vision of lust and the plight of women in England during this time. *Romeo and Juliet* is also concerned with the idea of forced marriage and the lack of options for women in a patriarchal society.

3. We live in a small, rural midwestern town in the United States where we receive farm reports on the radio; the university maintains about 7,000 students many of whom come from local and regional high schools.

Appendix

Depending on our time in the semester, we look at the following other works by Shakespeare: *The Taming of the Shrew, Macbeth, The Rape of Lucrece* and *Titus Andronicus*. In Frances Dolan's edition of *The Taming of the Shrew*, the editor offers solid background information about the play. Dolan has gathered together the popular sixteenth- and seventeenth- century debates about marriage, women, and domesticity. We look at *A Homily of the State of Matrimony*, excerpts from Robert Snawsel's *A Looking Glass for Married Folks* and T.E.'s *The Law's*

Resolutions of Women's Rights. We also read sections on the household and women's work. Students are shocked at the wife-beating excerpts from William Whately's *A Bride-Bush* and William Gouge's *Of Domestical Duties: Eight Treatises*. We also look at a ballad which may have been a source of Shakespeare's play: *A Merry Jest of a Shrewd and Curst Wife Lapped in Morrel's Skin, for Her Good Behavior* (c. 1550). This tale "depicts domestic disorder as caused by a woman who refuses to feed her servants and fights" as if she were a man (255). Shakespeare changes the physical abuse to psychological maneuvering, using the methods of falconry and witch watching. Discussions about this play are often very productive: Is Shakespeare's Petruchio actually more humane in his psychological abuse of Kate than his predecessors? Besides *A Merry Jest*, Dolan offers analogues about falconry and witches. I add Hugh Latimer's *Sermon for Edward VI*, Linda Boose's "Scolding Brides and Bridling Scolds: Taming the Woman's Unruly Member", and Karen Newman's "Renaissance Family Politics and Shakespeare's *Taming of the Shrew*"; we also look at *Two Horrible Murders* about two husbands who kill their wives.

After the *Shrew*, we move on to *Macbeth*, edited by William Carroll. This edition offers some cultural constructions of *Macbeth* under the title, "The Cultural Afterlife of Shakespeare's *Macbeth*". Besides contemporary discourse on sovereignty, treason and resistance, and a section on the cultural construction of Scotland, Carroll devotes a whole section on witchcraft and prophecy and discourses of the feminine. Besides the essays in Carroll's edition, we also read three essays from Susanne Wofford's *Shakespeare's Late Tragedies* (New Jersey: Prentice-Hall, 1996): Marjorie Garber's "Macbeth: The Male Medusa", Peter Stallybrass's "Macbeth and Witchcraft", and Rutter and Cusack's, "Lady Macbeth's Barren Sceptre". Susan Snyder's essay, "Macbeth: a Modern Perspective" (pp. 197-207 in *The New Folger Library Shakespeare* edited by Barbara A. Mowat and Papul Werstine) is also a wonderful introduction to the women's plight in the play.

Shakespeare's narrative poem *The Rape of Lucrece* and his play *Titus Andronicus* contain valuable information about gender concerns. Specifically, we focus on the issues of rape and honor as they concern the characters of Lucrece and Lavinia. For example, the notion of honor in Early Modern Europe was different from ours; if a woman was raped, she became dishonored – so much so that she might take the man to court and charge him with rape to retrieve her own honorable reputation rather than to punish him. "For this reason sometimes [women] requested that the judge force their rapists to marry them [...] it was often the easiest way for a woman who was no longer a virgin to establish an honorable social identity as a married woman" (Wiesner 51). Susan Brownmiller's book, *Against Our Will: Men, Women and Rape* (1975) is the classic, but articles such as "The Swallowing Womb" by Marion Wynne-Davis, "'Rape, I fear was root of thy annoy': The Politics of Consent in *Titus Andronicus*" by Sid Ray, and an unpublished article "'Thou map of woe, that thus does talk in signs!': Lavinia, Blood, and Language" by Evelyn Gajowski are helpful.

Works Cited

Bernstein, Richard. "A Traditionalist Takes On Feminists Over Shakespeare". The New York Times (March 1, 1990), pp. C17-C18.
Bethel, Tom. "The Case for Oxford". *Atlantic Monthly* 268:4 (October 1991), pp. 45-61.
Bevington, David, ed. *The Complete Works of Shakespeare*. 4th ed. New York: Longman, 1997.
_____. "Reconstructing Shakespeare". *University of Chicago Magazine* (Spring 1990), pp. 21-5.
Bohannan, Laura. "Shakespeare in the Bush". *Natural History* 75:7 (1966), pp. 28-33.
Boose, Linda. "Scolding Brides and Bridling Scolds: Taming the Woman's Unruly Member". *Shakespeare Quarterly* 41:2 (Summer 1991), pp. 179-213.
Brownmiller, Susan. *Against Our Will: Men, Women, and Rape*. New York: Simon & Schuster, 1975.
Butler, Judith. "Imitation and Gender Subordination". *Inside/Out: Lesbian Theories, Gay Theories,* ed. Dianna Foss (New York: Routledge, 1991), pp. 13-31.
Carroll, William, ed. *Macbeth Texts and Contexts*. Boston: Boston UP, 1999.
Craige, Betty Jean. "Literature in a Global Society". *PMLA* 106:3 (May 1991), pp. 395-401.
Dolan, Frances, ed. *The Taming of the Shrew Texts and Contexts*. New York: St. Martin's Press, 1996.
Drummond, William. "Ben Jonson's Conversations with Drummond of

Hawthornden". In *Seventeenth-Century Prose and Poetry.* 2nd edn, eds. Alexander Witherspoon and Frank J. Warnke (New York: Harcourt Brace, 1963), pp. 127-130.
Duncan-Jones, Katherine, ed. *Shakespeare's Sonnets.* London: Arden, 1998.
Else, Gerald. *Aristotle's Poetics: The Argument.* Cambridge, MA: Harvard UP, 1963.
Fitz, Linda. "'What Says the Married Woman?': Marriage Theory and Feminism in the English Renaissance". *Mosaic* XIII: 2 (Winter 1980), pp. 1-22.
Gajowski, Evelyn. "'Thou map of woe, that thus does talk in signs': Lavinia, Blood, and Language". Presented at the English Renaissance Literature Session. Rocky Mountain Modern Language Association, Oct. 26, 1996.
Garber, Marjorie. *Vested Interests.* New York: Routledge, 1997.
Graff, Gerald and James Phelan. *The Tempest: A Case Study in Critical Controversy.* New York: St. Martin's Press, 2000.
Greenblatt, Stephen. "The Best Way to Kill Our Literary Inheritance Is To Turn It into a Decorous Celebration of the New World Order". *Chronicle of Higher Education* 37:39 (June 12, 1991), p. B1.
Howard, Jean. "Crossdressing, the Theatre, and Gender Struggle in Early Modern England". *Shakespeare Quarterly* 39:4 (Winter 1988), pp. 418-40.
Jonson, Ben. "Timber: Or Discoveries Made Upon Men and Matter". *Seventeenth Century Prose and Poetry.* 2nd edn, eds. Alexander Witherspoon and Frank J. Warnke (New York: Harcourt, Brace, 1963), pp. 118-126.
Klooster, David and Patricia Bloem. *The Writer's Community.* New York: St. Martin's Press, 1995.
Larson, Charles. "Heroic Ethnocentrism: The Idea of Universality in Literature". *The American Scholar* 42 (Summer 1973), pp. 463-75.
Latimer, Hugh. "Sermon for Edward VI". *Sermons by Hugh Latimer,* ed. George Elwes Corrie. Cambridge: Cambridge UP, 1944.
Loomba, Ania. "Gender, race, Renaissance Drama". *The Tempest: A Case Study In Critical Controversy,* eds. Gerald Graff and James Phelan (New York: St. Martin's Press, 2000), pp. 324-36.
Maclean, Ian. *The Renaissance Notion of Woman.* London: Cambridge UP, 1980.
Marcus, Leah. *Puzzling Shakespeare: Local Reading and Its Discontents.* Berkeley: California UP, 1988.
Matis, Irvin. "The Case for Shakespeare". *Atlantic Monthly* 268:4 (October 1991), pp. 64-82.
Newman, Karen. *Fashioning Femininity and English Renaissance Drama.* Chicago: Chicago UP, 1991.
Perry, William. *Forms of Intellectual and Ethical Development in the College Years: A Scheme.* Cambridge, MA.: Bureau of Study Counsel, Harvard University, 1968.
Ray, Sid. "'Rape, I fear, was the root of thy annoy': The Politics of Consent in Titus Andronicus". *Shakespeare Quarterly* 49:1 (Spring 1998), pp. 22-39.
Scott, Joan Wallach. *Gender and the Politics of History.* New York: Columbia UP, 1988.
Skura, Meredith Anne. "Discourse and the Individual: The Case of Colonialism in

The Tempest". *The Tempest: A Case Study in Critical Controversy*, ed. Gerald Graff and James Phelan (New York: St. Martin's Press, 2000), pp. 286-322.

Snyder, Susan. "Macbeth: A Modern Perspective". In *The New Folger Library Shakespeare*, ed. Barbara Mowat and Paul Werstine (New York: Washington Square, 1992), pp. 197-207.

Thompson, Torri. "Studies in Shakespeare: Strategies for a Feminist Pedagogy". *Feminist Teacher* 8:2 (1992), pp. 67-74.

"Two horrible and inhumane murders". In *Reprints of English Books, 1475-4*. Ed. Joseph Foster. England: Claremont, pp. 1-25.

Weber, Bruce. "'*Maquina Hamlet*': To Be, or Not to Be, or Something". *Theater Review*. New York Times (October 20, 2000), p. C1.

W.H. *An Apologie for Women*. Oxford: Joseph Barnes, 1609.

Wieser, Merry. *Women and Gender in Early Modern Europe*. Cambridge: Cambridge UP, 1994.

Will, George. "Literary Politics". *Newsweek* 117:16 (April 22, 1991), p. 72.

Wofford, Susanne, ed. *Shakespeare's Late Tragedies*. NJ: Prentice-Hall, 1996.

Wynne-Davis, Marion. "'The Swallowing Womb': Consumed and Consuming Women in Titus Andronicus". In *The Matter of Difference: Materialist Feminist Criticism of Shakespeare*, ed. Valerie Wayne (Ithaca: Cornell UP, 1991), pp. 129-51.

READING AND TEACHING SHAKESPEARE'S PLAYS

C.W. Griffin
(Virginia Commonwealth University)

In a survey of the members of the Shakespeare Association of America, which I conducted in 1995, almost all respondents agreed that the goal of their undergraduate Shakespeare courses, was, as one emphatically put it, to help students "learn, finally, to READ". Another put it this way: "My first goal is to teach them the pleasures and rigor of reading well – to infect them with the stuff". Respondents further agreed that reading a Shakespeare play meant more than simply decoding its words and sentences. "Close reading" was the term used by one to describe the process. Others were more explicit: One spoke of leading students to "understand that there is a difference between semantic meaning and critical meaning", while another described herself as teaching students to "read between the lines of dialogue" and as preparing them for a text that was "unstable: not only will words contain multiple meanings, but the text will betray the extent to which it was composed with an amazing potential for evolution and change".

As I reflected on my Shakespeare colleagues' goal of teaching students to read and interpret the plays, I began to realize just how little we actually know about how our students go about reading the plays. Do they read fast, the way most read fiction, or slowly, the way we teach them to read poetry? Do they pause to reread difficult passages, or do they just skip over them? For that matter, how much of the play's language do they understand as they read? And do they think interpretively as they read.

To answer such questions, I have conducted two observational studies of students engaged in the actual process of reading a Shakespeare play. The first focused on exceptional readers, those students whose ability to understand and interpret the plays sets them apart from the rest of the students in advanced and graduate Shakespeare classes. The second was of a broader range of students, drawn mostly from general education classes, whose majors ranged from English to sociology and psychology, from criminal justice to environmental science, and from accounting and math to crafts and sculpture. (My public urban institution, I should mention, accepts a relatively broad range of students: Last fall, for example, the average SAT of entering freshmen was 1026 and the average high school GPA was 3.01.) In this article I want to describe the results of this research and reflect on the implications it may have for our teaching.

Adapting a research procedure from composition and reading studies, we (in the second study I had the help of a graduate assistant) interviewed students as they actually read a play, in most cases *Antony and Cleopatra*, interrupting them at certain points to identify what had been in their awareness as they read. Our instructions were simple: "Read as if you were at home preparing yourself for a class discussion". In order to find out how readers went about beginning to read a play, we first interrupted them after just four minutes; subsequently, we interrupted them after reading periods of eight minutes. How much students were able to read during the interviews, which lasted an hour or so, depended on how much they had to tell us after each interruption and on how much discussion ensued. Most students finished at least the first two scenes, 244 lines. The question that gave us the best glimpse of how readers processed a Shakespeare playtext was simply: "What has been going through your mind for the last few minutes?" For our second study of the broader range of readers, we also asked questions that helped us determine how well they read and the problems they encountered.[1]

From these two studies have emerged three kinds of readers, distinguished from each other by the extent to which they comprehend and are therefore able interpret a Shakespeare play. (Comprehension, as David Bordwell defines it, "is concerned with apparent, manifest, or direct meanings, while interpretation is concerned with revealing hidden, nonobvious meanings".[2] After revising my terminology several times, I have now come to identify these readers as unskilled, intermediate, and skilled readers. In the rest of this paper, I want to describe how each of these types of readers goes about reading a play and then explore what their reading practices might imply for our teaching.

UNSKILLED READERS

Language: Since Shakespeare's language creates some degree of difficulty for most of his readers, it is not surprising that the ten unskilled readers interviewed in the second study (three of whom had never read a Shakespeare play in their lives, while four had read only one) hardly knew what the characters were talking about. What was startling, though, was the degree of estrangement from the language that some of these readers felt. One, a highly disciplined, older student, said that "it was like reading Greek at first". "My first impression was man, who reads this and understands it", he continued. Another, also mature and conscientious, said: "Well, to be honest with you, when I read through this, some of the words that I'm reading kind of sound like the Old Testament to the Bible, the thou's and the thee's". A little later, he said in frustration: ". . . I don't understand why I can't understand it. I mean they're English words, it's just that they're put in a context that I'm not certain of to be honest with you".

Situational Knowledge: Reading any text involves a good deal more than mechanically decoding words and sentences. It is rather, as recent theorists have shown, a dynamic process wherein we draw on bottom-up information provided by the text, including graphophonemic, orthographic, and morphemic features and top-down information provided by our knowledge of semantics, syntax, pragmatics, as well as our knowledge of text conventions and the world in order to develop an explanation that accounts for the details of the text. Texts are often not self-explanatory; thus, if we fail to bring to our reading prior knowledge of the situation they represent, we will fail to understand them.

Unskilled readers frequently lack such situational knowledge. Only one of the ten unskilled readers we interviewed, for example, seemed to know anything about the historical context of *Antony and* Cleopatra. Thus, most had no way of understanding the opening speech of the play, where Philo expresses his contempt for a general whose "captain's heart" has "become the bellows and the fan/ To cool a gypsy's lust" (1.1.6-10). Failing to follow this speech, they missed its allusion to Antony's central conflict between duty and desire. In addition to not knowing the play's background, these students lacked other kinds of knowledge that would have facilitated their understanding of the play. Seven, for instance, did not know what a soothsayer was; thus, they had no hope of understanding the action in scene two nor what the presence of a soothsayer might foreshadow about the play's outcome.

Reading Processes: But behind these readers' problems in language and knowledge lies a deeper problem: Most simply do not know how to read a poetic, dramatic text, especially one that is as formally complex and culturally removed as a Shakespearean play. A number, for example, read it too quickly to notice much of anything important. In the four minutes allotted for reading the beginning of the first scene one read the whole of the first scene and part of the second, about eighty lines, while three others openly admitted that they were reading too fast. One of the questions we asked at the end of each interview was whether students had become aware of anything about the way they read that they didn't know before. One student answered as follows:

> I need to be a little more observant. I mean not that I just sort of breeze through it, but I sort of just like, I guess when you're assigned 100 pages to read, you're sort of like, okay, I don't care I'm going to read this and like I'll remember a little bit of it, enough to go in and raise my hand and talk for two seconds to make the teacher think that I'm a good student. . .

The edition used in these studies, the Norton, contains marginal glosses and contextual footnotes. While most unskilled readers tried to make use of the glosses, two had to be shown what they were for. A few ignored them: When asked whether he used the glosses, one young man said: "Nah, I just keep going". And although most students felt that the marginal glosses were accessible because they occurred right beside the word they didn't understand, they were bothered by the explanatory footnotes, both because they had to interrupt their reading to go to the bottom of the page to consult a note and because they felt that some notes overwhelmed them with too much information. One reader said that one footnote was so long that she just decided to stop reading "because that was just ridiculous".

To the unskilled readers I have been describing, reading a Shakespeare play must, at least in the beginning, seem like a very strange and unusual process, somewhat like overhearing a conversation in a strange dialect when they don't know the identities of the speakers, have no idea where they are, and, of course, don't understand what they are talking about. At institutions that are relatively selective, teachers of Shakespeare may never, or only rarely, encounter such unskilled readers. It is likely, though, that teachers at less selective institutions, whether two- or four-year, will be faced with at least a few unskilled readers in their classes.

SKILLED READERS

At the other end of the spectrum from the unskilled readers in my two studies were skilled readers, whose reading abilities and practices resulted in their understanding so much of what they had read that they were free to interpret it. Many of these skilled readers had been extensive readers for many years: One said that she couldn't watch TV or even eat without reading; another said that he'd "rather read than eat or sleep". And in contrast to the unskilled readers I discussed earlier, some had read a number of Shakespeare's plays. Two had read three plays, one six plays in high school, and another, when asked how many plays she had read, said simply: "A lot". One, an accounting major who had "loved reading in high school" and who owned the complete works, had tried reading plays on her own; she also mentioned having read "a lot of poetry". Another responded to our question about her reading experience with, "I mean it's Shakespeare, it's great. I love it. It's poetry".

Knowledge: Because they were all aware of at least the bare outlines of the historical background for the play, these skilled readers were much better prepared than the unskilled ones to follow the play's first scene. One, for example, who knew about the Roman triumvirate and Antony's infatuation with Cleopatra, said that knowing the background "really helped a lot". Another, who had known the story "for a long time," said that without this knowledge, reading the play would be "more difficult for sure". And unlike many of the beginning readers, all these readers knew what a soothsayer was, while a number even reflected on the significance of that character's presence.

Reading Processes: It is the way they went about the act of reading itself that distinguished these skilled readers most sharply from the unskilled ones. In fact, they approached their task so differently that their activity might more accurately be described as studying or examining the play rather than simply reading it. When working at their best, these readers are usually first-time rereaders (i.e., they intend to get all they can from the text during their first reading rather than reading, say once for plot and later for meaning), who read slowly and carefully, taking the time to check the glossary and footnotes, and in a number of cases, to mark up their own texts copiously. Reading for them is a process of thoughtful engagement, primarily with the world created by the play's language and secondarily with that language itself. The best can hardly read a speech (sometimes not even a line) without thinking about it, inferring characters' thoughts and feelings, speculating on the hidden dynamics of their relationships, raising questions about word meanings and patterns, and feeling their way toward larger issues and themes.

Interpretation versus Comprehension: While their unskilled counterparts are struggling mightily to comprehend what is being said and done in a play, these more skilled readers, because of the intensity with which they read, can comprehend so well that they can devote the bulk of their time to interpretation, most often of what characters are thinking and feeling. For instance, almost all sensed the depth of Antony's infatuation with Cleopatra, and all discerned how much Antony's Roman comrades scorned him. Most saw that Cleopatra so mistrusted her position with Antony that she needed to manipulate and control him, and a number picked up on the comic undertones of the second scene. Just to illustrate the range of these readers' interpretative abilities, here are interpretative comments from our interview with one student:

> ... Antony and Cleopatra's relationship right now is the big problem now among his soldiers [...] Cleopatra's problem is that she doesn't really believe that Antony's going to stick by her because he doesn't love his wife in the first place [...] She seems very sarcastic with him and I just wanted to know if she was flirting with him or she was generally a little bit upset with him [...] I was trying to figure out how truthful Antony was being and what he was saying [...] understanding how Antony is here with Cleopatra and not paying attention to what's going on. He hasn't been protecting his provinces like he's supposed to be and they've been attacked and his wife has joined forces with his brother and they lost against Caesar and his wife has just died [...] I like the scene [scene 2] between, right after that very serious scene with Antony and Cleopatra, with the ladies and gentlemen and how they are joking with one another. Their joking has a sick sarcasm to it about Cleopatra being in command and all that stuff. It's strange that Cleopatra keeps looking for him and then when she finds him she like walks away.

As I listened to these skilled readers talk about their interpretative impressions (and later as I studied the transcriptions of their interviews), I felt privy to a rich flow of consciousness as they constructed from the play's dialogue what characters were thinking and feeling. Rather than needing a teacher's help in comprehending the obvious meanings of the dialogue, these readers were prepared for a class discussion in which they might pool their interpretations of characters' subtexts and then help each other toward a more global discussion of thematic and cultural patterns.

INTERMEDIATE READERS

It is a shock to go from an analysis of the transcriptions of skilled readers to those of their intermediate peers, for as with unskilled readers, once again one encounters students who have major difficulties comprehending the play. Although few of these readers felt as estranged from the language as the unskilled ones did, most had serious decoding difficulties, both with semantics and syntax. Some did not know the meanings of 'dotage', and 'gypsy', which were glossed, and 'twain' and 'presages', which were not. One did not even know the meaning of one of the glosses itself, the word 'lascivious', while a number, like the unskilled readers, did not know what soothsayer was.

These intermediate readers had an equal amount of trouble with the length and syntax of some of the play's sentences: One described himself as bothered by the way the words "are placed in the sentence", another by the "fragmented language", and still another by passages of "long dialogue", One reader, who wished for a modern English version of Shakespeare, summarized the problems of a number of readers in this group when he said: If the sentences "get real long and lengthy and there's a lot of words I don't understand, it makes it harder to read".

Reading Processes

While it is no doubt true that some of these intermediate readers' problems can be attributed to the level of their general reading skills, most arise, I think, from the way they go about reading a play. Unlike most skilled readers, for example, who progress very slowly through the play (a number actually apologized for reading so slowly) because they are studying and scrutinizing it so minutely, not one of the twenty-three intermediate readers we studied apologized for reading too slowly. Over half, in fact, read much too fast, often reading about twice as much in the same period of time as their more skilled counterparts.

An even more stark contrast between the two groups lay in their attitude toward reading the play, for while almost all the skilled readers we interviewed were first-time, final readers (determined to glean as much meaning as they could from the play on first reading), many of these intermediate readers were first-time, second-time readers, who are satisfied to read the first time, according to two, "just trying to get a feel for what's going on", or trying to "get an overall sense of what's going on in the play". One pretty bright, mature student, who had the historical and philosophical background to frame his comments during class discussion in very impressive (if somewhat glib) generalizations, described his reading process in this way:

> Typically, what I do when I read something, especially something that's a little bit difficult, at first, is I read through it without looking at too many of the notes and too many of the words, just enough to get through it, and then I go back after I've read the first act and read it again with the notes and everything to fill in the part that I don't [...] that I've missed on first reading; the first time through I don't try to pay too much attention to detail; often what I'll do is read two or three acts or three scenes and then just go back and start again.

Although they may be well-intentioned, will most undergraduate students, particularly English majors with their typically heavy reading loads, find the time to reread a play that they have previously just skimmed? Or will they read more often like this student, whose comment reveals that he rereads a play only when forced to:

> Um, normally what I would do with a play like this is go through it, go through the entire act or play or whatever and get a basis, general idea of what's going on and then if I had to go back for deeper reading or for writing on it I would go out and reread it you know sometime later. . . .

Since any reader of a play must infer what is happening from his or her understanding of the dialogue, just how much of a "general idea of what's going on" can be gleaned on first reading? It seems likely to me that these readers are mistakenly applying techniques for reading prose fiction, where one can skim through narrative description and thereby get a general idea of what is happening, to the reading of a very different genre.

The result of intermediate readers' limitations – their problems with Shakespeare's language, their speed in reading, and their misguided reading goals – is that they comprehend so little that they hardly engage in interpretation at all, while their skilled counterparts comprehend so much that they work continually in the interpretative mode. Typically, when these intermediate readers are asked, "What has been going through your mind as you have been reading for the last few minutes", their answers focus on their confusion, on what they didn't understand; while skilled readers respond to the same question with a flood of speculations and questions about characters and their interactions:

IMPLICATIONS FOR TEACHING

This research has made me realize just how elastic the term 'reading' is, stretching as it does, in David Bordwell's terms, from comprehension to interpretation or in Robert Scholes' terms from reading (decoding the language of the text) through interpretation (discerning its themes) to criticism (critiquing the text or its strategies). If a Shakespeare classroom is to be the site (as most Shakespearean's seem to think it should be) of continuous reading and rereading, then it may, at least in certain instances, have to stretch itself enough to teach less skilled readers to decode the text while sharpening the interpretive skills of those more highly skilled. Each Shakespeare teacher will have his or her own way of accomplishing this task. Here are a few strategies that occur to me:

Shakespeare's Language: Both unskilled and intermediate readers struggle to understand Shakespeare's language. To unskilled readers, as I have shown earlier, it often seems like a foreign language. Those of us who face such readers in general education or introductory Shakespeare courses may have to find ways to demystify the language for them. One strategy might be to begin the semester by describing the kinds of reading problems students will encounter as they read the plays. An exercise "Shakespeare's Language: A Computer-Based Tutorial for the Macintosh Computer" (unfortunately only available to Macintosh computer users but easily adapted for classroom use) created by Randall Robinson, in collaboration with Peter Holben Wehr, might be particularly helpful for unskilled readers. In it, students are given a fairly lengthy passage from a play, asked to identify words or phrases that are troublesome, and then directed to place these elements into one of nine categories: familiar word with unexpected meaning, obsolete word, unusual suffix, unusual verb or verbal, unusual pronoun, metaphor or personification, omission of syllable, unfamiliar arrangement, or omission of word. Individual instructors will revise this list as they see fit.[3]

While it may be possible, in a lesson or two, to assure unskilled readers that Shakespeare's language is not as strange or impenetrable as they thought, teaching intermediate readers, those familiar with the language but who still comprehend so little that they are not prepared to engaged in serious interpretive work, is a more daunting task. The most practical approach I have found for teaching such students is that developed by Professor Randal Robinson, whose work I alluded to in the last paragraph. In his invaluable ERIC publication, *Unlocking Shakespeare's Language: Help for the Teacher and Student* (available from NCTE for $10.95.), Robinson describes the results of his four-year effort to identify the principal language problems that both high school and college students encounter as they read Shakespeare's plays. He found that "unexpected arrangements of words, familiar words used with unexpected meanings, and omissions of syllables, parts of syllables, and words cause particularly significant difficulties for readers of Shakespeare". In addition, he discovered that student readers of Shakespeare will have difficulty with Shakespeare's use of second person pronouns; emphases produced by repetitions; associations of metaphor and personification; wordplay, especially when bawdy; unexpected meanings of familiar affixes; pronouns with no specific or nearby antecedents; and unusual uses of infinitives, objects, reflexive pronouns, and auxiliary verbs.[4]

Most of Robinson's book is devoted to a series of exercises that give students practice in decoding the kinds of unusual syntactic arrangements and omissions that occur in Shakespearean sentences; in addition, by the way, his book contains a dictionary of 112 words whose meanings have shifted since Shakespeare used them. Basing his exercises on the premises that (1) we must learn the conventions of our own discourse in order to understand unfamiliar texts and that (2) we always acquire new knowledge by relating it to old, Robinson's exercises move students from their intuitive knowledge that a modern English sentence contains a subject, a predicate, and a complement to a familiarity with Shakespearean patterns that alter, interrupt, or delay this sequence. In the process, students practice rewriting Shakespearean sentences that begin with complements and predicates; or those containing clauses that delay the appearance of subject-verb or phrases that separate related parts. A typical example from Robinson is this passage, drawn from Iago's second soliloquy:

> Three lads of Cyprus – noble swelling spirits,
> That hold their honors in a wary distance,
> The very elements of this warlike isle –
> Have I to-night flustered with flowing cups.
> And they watch too. (2.3.51-5)

From practice with such passages, students will develop the ability to discern the three major parts of any Shakespearean sentence, no matter how complicated, and to rewrite (first on paper and then mentally) the sentence around these elements.

Students' Reading Processes: As I've shown in the previous section, the major reason why unskilled and intermediate readers have so much difficulty comprehending Shakespeare's language is that they, in contrast to skilled readers, read too fast, often skipping over words and phrases they do not understand and often ignoring helpful textual apparatus. In addition to some elementary work on how to make use of textual apparatus (dramatis personae, stage directions, scene designations, glosses, and footnotes), how else can we lead students to read the text with some of the same care and thought as skilled readers? Perhaps my interviews with student readers holds a partial answer.

One of the benefits of the interviews for students who participated was that all became more conscious of the way they read a play and some of the fact that they missed a lot by reading so fast. Two students expressed what they had learned as follows:

> It actually helped knowing that I should go back and go back, because usually I just skim through something and I'm like, you know, I read it and why didn't I get it and it's because I need to spend more time on it.
>
> I'm been trying to read more into it so I think it has kind of changed a little bit. Instead of just kind of reading it and kind of taking in a little bit, I've been trying to read it really carefully and pay a lot of attention to it which would certainly help me out a lot for other classes.

Having students conduct reading research in the classroom might be a way of bringing other intermediate readers to similar realizations. One might have students do a bit of research on themselves by reading an exchange between two characters (say the opening exchange between Theseus and Hippolyta in *A Midsummer*

Night's Dream or that between Gloucester and Kent in *King Lear*), paraphrase (translate might be a better tactic) what the speakers had said, and then describe what they had to do in order to translate accurately (check the meaning of a word in the glossary or a dictionary, rearrange unusually worded sentences, unpack figures of speech, etc.). A second step might be to have students continue their research, this time on each other: For example, a pair of students might each read a passage silently, then compare their paraphrases of the passage, and finally discuss how they went about comprehending the passage. During ensuing class discussions, one would hope that less skilled readers would learn how carefully their more skilled counterparts went about reading a play.

Backgrounds and Summaries: In order to determine how useful to student readers summaries and background descriptions might be, near the end of our interviews we gave students a description of the historical background of the play (which described the formation of the triumvirate and the reason for Antony's trip to Egypt) along with about a 200-word summary of scene 1. After they had read these materials, we asked students to read scene 1 again. When they had finished, we asked whether the materials had been helpful or not.

Not surprisingly, all the unskilled and intermediate readers agreed that the summary, but more especially for a number of readers, the background sketch, was very helpful. One unskilled reader said, "Before it was just a bunch of fancy words and now it actually makes sense", while an intermediate reader said, ". . . it's a lot easier to understand and a lot easier to figure out, like why things are happening the way they are and what's going on exactly". Two other intermediate readers agreed that the materials freed them to spend more time interpreting what they had read: One said, for example, that with the materials "you can generalize it more", while the other said that you can "start getting into deeper meaning".

We also asked students whether having a summary and background sketch would make the play boring to read. A number said that having such materials would have just the opposite effect: One was "excited" because he understood the scene more, another said that "you kinda get more interested", while a third said "it's giving me enough to make me want to read it, and enough to make me, like, understand what I'm gonna read". Two students did suggest that teachers might actually introduce them to the play's background, major characters, and major incidents when the play was first assigned.[5]

Interpretive Skills: No matter how much time we are willing to spend helping students learn to comprehend, our ultimate goal is to teach them how to interpret. In his study of the cognitive and rhetorical processes involved in film interpretation, Bordwell posits that "in interpretation, meaning is arrived at through an interplay of conceptual schemes and perceived cues" (129). The processes that govern this interplay have been called by literary theorists interpretative strategies (Stanley Fish), interpretive operations (Jonathan Culler), or interpretive conventions (Steven Mailloux).[6] In his study of six advanced graduate students' cognitive processes as they interpreted three poems, Eugene R. Kintgen identifies such interpretative strategies as reading the text and then selecting a portion to concentrate on; reflecting on phonological features, word meanings, syntax, or tone; paraphrasing, arriving at deductions, and making connections; and generalizing, testing, justifying, and qualifying.[7] Since readers in my studies were limited in their reading to a few scenes in the hour or so we had for reading and discussion, I cannot offer anywhere near a complete description of the interpretive strategies on which they relied. I can, though, describe some of the more formal interpretive rules they followed as they read, rules that might aid other students in their efforts to interpret plays.

Although he draws his rules from the reading of prose fiction rather than drama, Peter Rabinowitz's classification of rules of notice, significance, configuration, and coherence will enable me to describe some of the implicit rules followed by the skilled readers I studied. (Because Rabinowitz's scheme is not intended, in his own words, as "an absolute and exhaustive classification" some of the following rules can fall into more than one category).[8]

Rules of Notice: According to Rabinowitz, rules of notice assign priority to certain textual details, telling us which features could serve as the basis for an interpretation. One of the first elements skilled readers tend to notice when reading a play is how the characters are aligned. Readers will say they are trying "to sort everybody out", "to get a sense of who the characters are" or "to get the characters straight". In addition to character alignments, some skilled readers also noticed graphic images, especially repeated ones, as well as sexual allusions and *sententiae*. In our discussions, several of these readers actually pointed out that they look for important images as they read: One said that she needs "a string, image, something recurring to hang everything on", while another said she was "always trying to figure out what's going with images". One reader wondered about the "innuendo of the image of the crocodile and the serpent", another noticed Antony's image of "letting Rome in Tiber melt", another noted his reference to "strong Egyptian fetters", while a number of readers, about a third, noted the repeated images alluding to fertility and sexuality. Surprisingly to me, at least, was the fact that five readers noticed *sententiae*, including Antony's comment that "there's beggary in the love that can be reckoned", and Caesar's pronouncement that the common people follow the "varying tide" whichever way it goes.

One subcategory of rules of notice is what Rabinowitz calls rules of rupture, those textual features that "stand out because they disrupt the continuity of a text or when they deviate from the extratextual norms against which they are read" (65). The stylistic shifts that some readers noticed were that shift from Antony's poetic exchange with the messenger in 1.2 to his prose dialogue with Enobarbus immediately following and from the personal, more intimate style of discourse in Egypt to the colder, more business-like style of the Romans in 1.4. Rupture rules also lead us to note the inappropriate in a text. Thus, four readers noticed that when Cleopatra enters in 1.2, Enobarbus says, "Hush, here comes Antony". One of these speculated that this mistake played into a theme of illusion that he had noticed before, while another felt that Enobarbus was implying that Antony was not much of a man.

Rules of Signification: If rules of notice guide us to important textual details, these rules tell us how to draw significance from these details; how to arrive at acceptable interpretative inferences from them. Some readers who noticed important images, for example, went on to speculate about their significance, one noting that the image of game suggests "the Roman competitive spirit", while another felt that Cleopatra's image of reeling in fish and thinking "every one an Antony" created an image of her being in a game with Antony. Readers also attached particular significance to functional characters such as the soothsayer and messengers. Fully two-thirds of these skilled readers wondered about the significance of the soothsayer's telling Cleopatra's attendants' fortunes in 1.2, most speculating that his presence was, in the words of one, "some form of foreshadowing". Some readers also found the presence of messengers in the play significant, one noting perceptively that you can judge characters by the way they treat messengers in certain situations. For Rabinowitz, one set of these signification rules are those that "permit us to assume that characters have psychologies and to draw conclusions about those psychologies from their actions" (44). In this regard, I have already described the extent to which many of our readers were preoccupied with characters in the play, particularly with their motivations, attitudes, and relationships to each other.

Rules of Configuration: According to Rabinowitz, these rules are basically predictive, permitting us to make guesses about what will happen in the later parts of the text. One important rule of configuration for these readers is that a tragedy such as *Antony and Cleopatra* will begin by setting up a problem to be dealt with later in the play. One reader said that the beginning "immediately sets up the tragedy, encapsulates the tragedy", another said that "there's a problem already at the beginning", another that "Philo delineates the problem", while another put it this way: "Shakespeare always seems to have two people come on and start talking about the problem and then have the problem proceed on the stage". Related to the problem at the beginning rule is the more general rule that what happens in a play is often foreshadowed in various ways; in this regard, I have already mentioned that a number of readers saw the presence of the soothsayer as boding ill. Readers also noticed other foreshadowings: One said that the "relationship between Antony and Cleopatra is flawed and will probably turn out badly" another found foreshadowing in Cleopatra's line about the "serpent's poison", and another wondered whether Charmian's joke in 1.2 about Alexas marrying a woman who would die was foreshadowing.

Rules of Coherence: The fundamental rule of coherence, says Rabinowitz, is the assumption that the work *is* coherent and that apparent flaws in its construction are intentional and meaning bearing. We invoke rules of coherence when a text appears to resist such an assumption. Examples of such rules are rules of surplus, which lead us to "assume that surplus is intentional and that we are supposed to interpret it in one way or another ..." (154). Following a rule of surplus, a number of readers paused over Enobarbus's cynically joking responses at the end of 1.2, first to Antony's desire to leave Egypt and then to his news that Fulvia is dead. Helped by a footnote that identified the bawdy resonance of Enobarbus's words "kill" "death" and "dying", they wondered about the function of his sexual allusions.

In his first chapter, Rabinowitz makes the point that literary parallelism can be treated in any of the four categories of rules, for it involves attention (rule of notice) to parallel elements, reflection on their import (rule of significance), recognition that one element may be followed by a parallel to it (rule of configuration), or a later realization that one element does parallel another (rule of coherence). Whatever specific rules were involved in their recognition and interpretation, more readers focused on correspondences and oppositions, especially on oppositions, than on any other textual element I have mentioned. Two, in fact, noted that they approach a text looking for dualities and oppositions, while another, more specifically, wondered what the second scene involving the soothsayer and Cleopatra's attendants mirrored. No matter how they described them – as conflicts, contrasts, oppositions, contradictions, juxtapositions, etc. – a number of readers saw oppositions between characters (Cleopatra versus Antony), between metaphorical associations (Antony with Mars, Cleopatra with Isis), between settings (Egypt versus Rome), between values (one reader noted that "Cleopatra becomes synonymous with Egypt, while Caesar is the epitome of the Roman ideal"), between atmospheres (one felt that the Egyptian scenes were "more organic, more complex and emotional" than the Roman ones), and between themes (duty versus love, pleasure versus responsibility, public versus private, puppet versus master, and spiritual versus superficial).

While I have not discussed all the textual elements that these skilled readers noticed and speculated about, I have, I think, covered the major categories. Most readers will, I am sure, be struck by the variety of elements noticed by these skilled readers, as a group. But I must add that no two readers noticed anywhere near the same group of elements. In fact, with the exception of aspects of character/relationships and, to a much lesser extent, that of parallels and oppositions, one is also struck by the lack of consensus among these readers about which textual features to notice.

Why were these skilled readers, most of whom had taken at least one Shakespeare course, not more agreed on which textual features might be useful to an interpretation? Is it because they had not been taught what features of a play are most likely to serve, to broaden one of Rabinowitz's words, as "scaffolding" (53) for an interpretation? Or is it because we teachers of Shakespeare tend to focus on the interpretative features that are most salient to the particular play under discussion, with the assumption that our students will extrapolate from a discussion of image patterns in *A Midsummer Night's Dream* or *Macbeth*, from Othello's style of speaking as opposed to Iago's, or from the function of parallel plots in *Henry Four, Part 1* or the green/golden world pattern in the romantic comedies, etc., to the significance of image patterns, stylistic decorum, and contrasting plot structures in other plays. And if this approach to teaching such interpretive strategies is not successful, what approach would be?

Perhaps we might teach certain play-reading rules more explicitly than most of us do now; a good place to begin might be with the rules followed by the skilled readers I studied. Perhaps also we could work indirectly, attempting to heighten our students' awareness of such rules by encouraging them to discuss rules they have found important in interpreting a particular play? One wonders also whether there might be a fairly simple schematic way to present important interpretation rules to students; Rabinowitz's scheme may be little too complex and overlapping for undergraduate students to master. Is there some other scheme, perhaps a very general one that taught students to look for repetitions (of key words, images, scenes), contrasts (between characters, scenes, speech styles), shifts (from one verse form to another, from verse to prose), key moments (openings, soliloquies, asides, crises), allusions (to classical figures, to the Bible), etc.? However we do it, and whatever we call them – semiotic codes, interpretative strategies, literary conventions, or reading rules – my studies of skilled readers suggest to me that all our students could benefit from a more detailed and complete knowledge of those textual features in a play that skilled readers typically recognize as having interpretative significance.

CONCLUSION

In this conclusion, I want to turn away from what we might teach students about reading Shakespeare to something these students have taught me. It has seemed to me that if we teachers of Shakespeare could articulate precisely what makes plays different from the other genres we teach, we could do a better job of teaching them. Does the difference lie in the fact that, unlike an a lyric, epic poem, or novel, which are completed authorial performances, a play is a script, a blueprint, a set of directions for performance? Partly. Or does the difference inhere more in the very etymology of the word 'drama', associating, as it does, the genre with action, both verbal and physical? Partly. Closer to the mark, it seems to me, is the fact that plays like those of Shakespeare are marked by the absence of an authorial or narratorial voice, whose absence creates extensive blanks or gaps that the reader must fill in order to create the imaginative world of the play. In this regard, it is interesting that Wolfgang Iser, who posits that the gaps created by narrative texts are what involve readers in the act of creating meaning, uses as an example of gaps a comment of Virginia Woolf on character and dialogue in the novels of Jane Austen:

> Jane Austen is thus a mistress of much deeper emotion than appears upon the surface. She stimulates us to supply what is not there. [...] The turns and twists of the dialogue keep us on the tenterhooks of suspense. ...

Iser comments: "What is missing from the apparently trivial scenes, the gaps arising out of the dialogue – this is what stimulates the reader into filling the blanks with projections".[9]

I never realized the full import of Iser's comment until I had observed student readers, especially highly skilled ones, reading and rereading a Shakespeare play. As I mentioned earlier, the skilled readers in my study focused, for the most part, on the relational dynamics of characters in the plays (their alignments, motivations, and responses to each other). Partly this was so because they were working with the first part of a play, where readers have to establish the nature of characters and their relationships. But partly it is because of the very nature of drama itself: What is a play if it's not a set of speech acts, acts that have, according to speech act theorists, locutionary, illocutionary, and perlocutionary force. A locutionary act is the actual utterance of a sentence with a certain sense and reference (equivalent to meaning in the traditional sense); an illocutionary act is what the speaker actually performs or intends to perform in the utterance (whether it be a promise, statement of fact, question, command, curse, etc.), while the perlocutionary act is the consequence of the illocution (the effect that is actually created).[10]

According to John Searle, while the author of fictional discourse is not performing an illocutionary act but only pretending to, the author of dramatic discourse is creating a kind of recipe, a set of instructions, for how performers are to perform speech acts. A performed play, says Searle, is not a pretended representation of a state of affairs but the pretended state of affairs itself, in that the actors pretend to be the characters.[11] Thus, if in reading or seeing a play, we are to enter into the world of the play, we must perforce be vitally interested in the meaning of what characters say, in what they intend to mean, and in the effect they have on others; i.e., we must be interested in what I have been calling the relational dynamics of the characters in a play.

To assert that the nature of characters in a play is usually so obvious as to render such analysis unnecessary is to underestimate what the skilled readers in these studies are trying to do: They are not simply attempting to label characters; they are trying to understand their relationships by comprehending and interpreting the implications and effects of what they say. And to assert, as some poststructural theorists do, that characters in a play are not real, but rather simply collocations of words that are then constructed as characters by readers and audiences, is to beg the question of how we are to think about characters, for if we are to enter the represented world of the play (and, at least some of the time, readers and audiences wish to do this), then we must treat characters, their words and their actions, as an important feature of that world.

Let me give one example from *Antony and Cleopatra* of how important an awareness of the implications of a speech act can be: In act 2, scene 2, there is a famous moment when Cleopatra is described as she approached in her barge along the river Cydnus to meet Antony for the first time. As Plutarch, Shakespeare's primary source (in North's translation),[12] puts it, Cleopatra, rather than being intimidated by Antony, but proud of her own royal lineage and rich country,

> disdained to set forward otherwise, but to take her barge in the river of Cydnus, the poope whereof was of gold, the sailes of purple, and the owers of silver, which kept stroke in rowing after the sounde of the musicke of flutes, howboyes, citherns, violls, and such other instruments as they played upon in the barge. . . .

Plutarch continues, describing Cleopatra lying under a pavilion covered by gold tissue, attired like Venus, fanned by pretty boys, accompanied by gentlewomen who appeared like the Nereides, etc. Leaning heavily on Plutarch, Shakespeare's passage, while transformed into poetic language, describes Cleopatra's approach in an almost identical fashion:

> The barge she sat in, like a burnish'd throne,
> Burned on the water: the poop was beaten gold;
> Purple the sails, and so perfumed that
> The winds were love-sick with them; the oars were silver,
> Which to the tune of flutes kept stroke, and made
> The water which they beat to follow faster,
> As amorous of their strokes. (2.2.201-7)

Using Plutarch's prose as a basis of comparison, Shakespeare teachers are able to give their students a glimpse of how his poetry – with its diction, rhythms, parallels, and figures – works.

But however similar the two passages are linguistically, their literary functions are very different. Occurring in his narrative just before Antony and Cleopatra meet, Plutarch's lavish description helps his readers understand just why Antony was, in his words, so quickly "ravished with the love of Cleopatra. ..." In Shakespeare, however, the passage works differently, for it occurs in 2.2, long after the play's audience and its readers have seen, through Antony's words and actions, just how infatuated he is with Cleopatra. Thus, although likely captivated by the lavish rhetoric of the passage, a close reader also has to wonder about its function as a speech act – what is the speaker's intention and what is the impact of his words on others in the scene? Since the speaker is Enobarbus, Antony's cynical soldier companion who had earlier made such fun of Cleopatra and her passion for Antony, the reader wonders why he should seem so entirely taken with her here. Is he attempting to impress his listeners, Caesar's soldiers Agrippa and Maecenas, with the beauty of his general's mistress? Or has even he been captivated by Cleopatra's beauty? Or is he speaking wryly and ironically, perhaps making fun of Cleopatra and his general's infatuation in front of his soldier companions? Whatever an individual reader's response is, it is shaped by his or her knowledge that the speaker is not a narrator, but a character in the play, whose words grow out of some motivation and have some impact on the people to whom he is speaking.

To ignore the importance of a character's speech acts in our teaching by focusing solely on the play's larger issues, themes, and cultural patterns is not just to deny the felt life of the play; it is to deny the very phenomenological feature that constitutes the play's existence.

Notes

1. For a complete description of the study of exceptional readers, see my article "Students Studying Shakespeare" forthcoming in *The Upstart Crow;* for the details of the second study, see *Shakespeare and the Classroom,* 8:2 (Fall 1999), pp. 35-9.

2. David Bordwell, *Making Meaning: Inference and Rhetoric in the Interpretation of Cinema* (Cambridge and London: Harvard UP, 1989), p. 2. Robert Scholes makes a similar distinction between reading, criticism, and evaluation in his *Textual Power: Literary Theory and the Teaching of English* (New Haven and London: Yale UP, 1985), pp. 21-4.

3. One hopeful note about teaching unskilled readers: Even those readers who seemed the most puzzled by Shakespeare's strange language did, as they progressed through the first part of *Antony and Cleopatra,* become more comfortable with the language. Just the act of talking with someone about their difficulties seemed to relieve some of their anxieties.

4. Randal Robinson, *Unlocking Shakespeare's Language: Help for the Teacher and Student* (Urbana, Illinois: ERIC Clearinghouse on Reading and Communication Skills and NCTE, 1988), pp. 3-5.

5. Since most readers seemed to understand the play's action and its language better as they read, they may not need as detailed a summary of the last part of a play as they do of the first act or so.

6. Stanley Fish, *Is There a Text in this Class: The Authority of Interpretive Communities* (Cambridge and London: Harvard UP, 1980), p. 168; Jonathan Culler, *Structuralist Poetics: Structuralism, Linguistics, and the Study of Literature* (Ithaca, NY: Cornell UP, 1975), p. 162; Steven Mailloux, *Interpretive Conventions: The Reader in the Study of American Fiction* (Ithaca, NY: Cornell UP, 1982), pp. 126-58.

7. Eugene R. Kintgen, *The Perception of Poetry* (Bloomington: Indiana UP, 1983), pp. 29-37.

8. Peter Rabinowitz, *Before Reading: Narrative Conventions and the Politics of Interpretation* (Ithaca and London: Cornell UP, 1987), pp. 42-6.

9. Wolfgang Iser, *The Act of Reading: A Theory of Aesthetic Response* (Baltimore and London: Johns Hopkins UP, 1978), p. 168.

10. Sandy Petrey, *Speech Acts and Literary Theory* (New York and London: Routledge, 1990), pp. 12-16.

11. John R. Searle, "The Logical Status of Fictional Discourse", *New Literary History,* 6 (1975), pp. 319-32.

12. *Plutarch's Lives of the Noble Grecians and Romans Englished by Sir Thomas North Anno 1579* (New York: AMS Press, 1967), vol. 6, p. 25.

REMEMBERING THE WAY INTO SHAKESPEARE

Joyce Sutphen
(Gustavus Adolphus College, Saint Peter, MN)

In the last years of the millennium, movie and video screens were filled with images of sixteenth-century thugs who delight in torturing bankrupt theater managers, witty royal personages who almost save the day, and young lovers who must part. The world loved *Shakespeare in Love*; it was a solid hit for the bard at the end of a string of hits, including the Mel Gibson *Hamlet* – as my students call it, Branagh's sun-drenched *Much Ado About Nothing*, and the Branagh *Hamlet*, featuring Blenheim Palace and a whole courtyard full of Hollywood stars. Shakespeare it seems, was still popular after more than 400 years.

Popularity is something. It will draw students to a Shakespeare class, but it often leaves them at the door without a key or a clue. The students who laugh when Michael Keaton gallops his imaginary hobbyhorse into a clearing, understand that Dogberry is a pretentious dolt, but when they read "but truly, for mine own part, if I were as tedious as a king, I could find in my heart to bestow it all of your worship" (*Much Ado* 3.5.20-2), they might not see the humor in it. Words have a different subtlety than moving pictures; they often do not divulge themselves until a voice gets inside of them, preferably a voice that "gets" what the words are saying. This is why I insist that much time in my classroom is spent reading Shakespeare out aloud, and this is also why I insist that time outside of the classroom is spent preparing to recite Shakespeare's language, from memory.

Yes, I make my students memorize Shakespeare. I insist on what seems to many an old-fashioned practice. From the first day of class, they know they will read a selection of Shakespeare's plays, that they will write papers, give group presentations, and that they will memorize *at least* twenty-five lines of Shakespeare. I ask the students to memorize the lines carefully; I want every word exactly in place. Close isn't good enough. I also ask that they think about why they chose the lines they did, what they learned about the speech itself, what they noticed about the speech in context, and finally that they reflect on how easy or difficult it was for them to memorize the lines and how they actually put the lines into their memories. All of this requires a certain amount of self-conscious observation and makes for good journal assignments.

The benefits of requiring this memorization are myriad: First of all, there is the group's reaction to the assignment: *Memorize* Shakespeare? I hear a collective gasp, the flutter of something – surprise? dismay? – going around the room. This gives me a chance to talk about memory. I ask them to discuss the connotations of 'memorize' and 'memorization'. We soon agree that memorization is held in low esteem in our times, that it is often referred to as 'rote', a kind of mind-work on the level of simple repetition, far below those higher cognitive procedures that involve application, synthesis, and evaluation. Memorizing dates, theorems, or poems – what good is that? Any information one needs is available just over there in a book or (much more quickly!) on the internet. There seems to be no point in storing information in one's head – unless, for some odd reason, it might come in handy on a desert island.

Students are usually right to be suspicious of memorization – especially the sort of memorization they have experienced. Most of the dates and formulas they crammed into their heads in high school have disappeared; in fact, cognitive psychologists say that only twenty percent of passive learning sticks with us, but active has four times the staying power. We talk then about the differences between active and passive learning so that they establish what sorts of things seem to enhance memory: emotional involvement (ranging from pleasure to pain), visual connections, systematic divisions, rhymes, odd associative keys, and catchy ways of ordering material. Without going into a disquisition on the subject, I suggest that we moderns have a very watered-down, wearisome way of memorizing, and I briefly describe a few of the old systems of places and images that helped accomplish prodigious feats of memory, not neglecting to bring illustrations of some of the exotic and violent images used by even the most pious scholars. I maintain that it was not the printing press that did away with memory culture, but the combination of the Puritan dislike of extravagant images and the scientific method's practice of observation, which bankrupted the idea that knowledge came down from the ages. Most importantly, I declare that memorization should involve active learning, that they will memorize more quickly and retain the passage much longer (as long as they like) if they take a creative approach to memorizing.

This is a useful discussion at the beginning of any term, since it sets things out on the table. I begin by admitting that I spent most of my student life in passive learning situations. I sat in large auditoriums with hundreds of other students and took copious and careful notes; weeks later I reviewed the notes and took a test. I always did very well and almost always got an A, but all I remember now from Cultural Anthropology is what a boy I loved scribbled in the margin of my notebook and the titles of papers I wrote. Everything else has vanished into thin air.

I confess how much I disliked having what I read flow through my consciousness like a stream – never the same stream twice. Eventually I grew tired of having knowledge flit through me, of knowing many things only vaguely. I wanted to be able to keep some things in my head, to store – as the speaker in *The Wasteland* says – some fragments against my ruin. The thing that absolutely convinced me was something that happened at a graduate school meeting. A roomful of us awaited the arrival of a speaker, and one of the professors suggested we pass the time by saying poems that we knew. None of us knew any poems by heart. Not one person in the room – all of us literature people, many of us poets and writers – could say a poem, except, of course, the man who'd suggested it, and he was embarrassed to have revealed our deficiency. I was embarrassed for the rest of us, however, and decided at that moment that I would memorize poetry.

Students like hearing some of the educational history of their teachers, just as they like looking at the books on the office shelf. These sorts of things make them more aware of their own learning processes, which I think, is always a good thing. They also like enthusiasm and conviction, even if they do not share it, and most of all, they enjoy eccentricity. "Professor Sutphen", they say, "is *wild* about Shakespeare's sonnets. She memorizes them when she drives her car, when she walks across campus, and when she waits in line – she knows dozens of them".

I certainly don't claim to be the only teacher in America asking students to memorize poetry; in fact, it seems that memorizing is coming back into fashion: in the bookstores, there are new collections of the "best poems to memorize", and books and articles that re-examine the role memory plays in human intellectual life. The former Poet Laureate of the United States, Robert Pinsky says,

> It may be that our education in poetry has devoted too much energy to poems as objects for saying clever things about, and not enough to the apprehension of poems through the basic processes of reading aloud, memorizing, even writing out longhand or typing personal copies. The pleasures of having a poem by heart, if not necessarily always greater than those of analysis, are more fundamental. (16)

For students of Shakespeare, the pleasures and rewards of having lines by heart are especially "fundamental", since there is so much to notice at once in Shakespeare's language, so much that asks for careful study. Memorization demands this sort of attention to detail, so that every word will appear in its place. Shakespeare is best understood when the multiple suggestions and interconnections are taken into account, but students are not used to reading in a way that accommodates these aspects of the work. They read for plot; they move forward in the text as if it were on a video tape. If anything, they are prone to fast-forward over language they do not get, especially if the section in question does not seem to relate the action. In this way, speeches such as Benedict's "This can be no trick; the conference was sadly borne [...] Here comes Beatrice. By this day, she's a fair lady. I do spy some marks of love in her" (*Much Ado* 2.3.216-40), Helena's "How happy some o'er other some can be!" (*A Midsummer Night's Dream* 1.1.226-61), and even Hamlet's "To be or not to be" (3.1.56-90) are skimmed over, especially by readers new to Shakespeare. They want to get through the play, understanding the plot and remembering the characters – an initial goal to be sure.

Of course there are ways to get students to go deeper, to linger in the language. Reading a passage out loud, pointing out notable features, commenting on possible implications of various words is worth its weight in gold. I used to avoid this, shying away from explaining what seemed obvious, but I have learned that it never hurts to dwell on a line or two. For example, just before Hamlet's speech in Act 2.2, which begins: "Ay, so, God bye to you. – Now I am alone. / O, what a rogue and peasant slave am I!" (2.2.559-60), Rosencrantz says "Good my lord" as he exits. Why "Good"? Is Rosencrantz agreeing (as in "Good, we'll do it") to Hamlet's "Follow him, friends. We'll hear a play tomorrow" (546), or to his later "friends" statement, one that seems, after the private conversation regarding *The Murder of Gonzago*, directed at everyone: "My good friends, I'll leave you till night. You are welcome to Elsinore" (556-7). Is Rosencrantz saying "Good – we'll have a play?" or "Good – we are welcome to Elsinore?" or "Good – you'll leave us till night *and* we welcome to Elsinore"? Since Hamlet adds "good" to "friends" the second time, might that be Rosencrantz's emphasis in his last three words? Are we your "good" friends?

Probably not, given Hamlet's "Ay, so, God by to you". Hamlet's response could indicate that he hears Rosencrantz's "Good" as a clipped "Good-bye". It might be a sort of Wittenborgian slang, just as we today often say "Bye". This would explain Hamlet's "God by to *you*"; Rosencrantz alters the normal "good-bye" – either on purpose or accidentally – and Hamlet, picking up the alterations, alters it again, but what does he want to imply by "God by to you"? Is it said with sarcasm? or weariness? And are Rosencrantz and Guildenstern meant to hear this first part of Hamlet's speech? No, clearly not, because they *exeunt* according to the stage directions. Perhaps someone lingers; most likely it is only words hanging in the air, but there seems to be a pause, a pivot, and then: "Now I am alone".

This kind of interrogation can be very helpful, as a way into the text, but it is pure explication in, I suppose, the manner of George Lyman Kittredge, a man who taught at Harvard one hundred years ago. "In his principal Shakespeare course, he explicated the text line by line and rarely completed six plays a year"

(Frey 548). This approach proved daunting and limited; the reaction to its "word-by-word method sent teachers of Shakespeare towards broad interpretive concerns: "the Kittredge school gave way to a different system of linguistic analysis focusing on word patterns, images, metaphors, ironies" (549). These mainly 'close reading' methods and activities, though they seemed objective, were often connected with words such as 'timeless' and 'universal'; eventually teachers and students began to detect problems in these sorts of presentations – thus the emergence of Feminist, Marxist, and New Historicist responses to Shakespeare.

I make this quick survey of the some of the historical phases in Shakespeare studies (thanks to Charles Frey's "Teaching Shakespeare in America") because I happen to think each one of these approaches is valuable in the evolution of understanding. Having students memorize a passage invites them to experience aspects of each phase; it's ontogeny recapitulating phylogeny in action: first they concentrate on words, individual words: "Let me not to the marriage of ... [what? what kind of minds? ah, *true*] true minds / [what? permit? no ... *admit*!] Admit impediments [*Impediments*?? What does that mean? What is it to "admit" one?]" (Sonnet 116. 1-2). As they are memorizing, they meet words in a new way. They can't blur out the word 'impediment' the way that they do when they are reading; they have to think it, grasp it, figure it out so that it stays in mind, fits into the thing they are learning to say.

The difference between my students and Helen Vendler is legion, but even though she is one of the most accomplished of literary critics, and even though she has been reading Shakespeare for decades, she says:

> To arrive at the understandings proposed in my commentary, I found it necessary to learn the *Sonnets* by heart. I would often think I 'knew' a sonnet; but then, scanning it in memory, I would find lacunae. Those gaps made me realize that some pieces of the whole must not yet have been integrated into my understanding of the intent of the work, since I was able to forget them. The recovery of the missing pieces always brought with it a further understanding of the design of that sonnet, and made me aware of what I had not initially perceived about the function of those words. No pianist or violinist would omit to learn a sonata by heart before interpreting it in public performance, but the equal habit of knowing poetry by heart before interpreting it has been lost. (11-12)

While it most likely that Helen Vendler's desire (and desire has much to do with remembering!) to 'know' a sonnet is greater than that of most people, I would say that the phenomena she describes are experienced by anyone who memorizes a poem. My students may not have the same intrinsic desire to understand the passage, but they do want to be 'perfect', for two reasons: their grade and their peers, both of which will register how successful they are in speaking the passage from memory. I explain that 'perfect' is a very Shakespearean way to put having every word in place and that the opposite, in Shakespeare's own words, is 'imperfect' as evidenced in Sonnet 23:

> As an unperfect actor on the stage,
> Who with his fear is put besides his part,
> [...]
> So I for fear of trust forget to say
> The perfect ceremony of love's rite. (1-2, 5-6)

To demonstrate how to understand a word in its context, I read Stephen Booth's commentary on this sonnet, which paraphrases the first line in this way:

> like an actor who has not properly learned his part (Shakespeare sometimes uses 'perfect' to mean 'word-perfect'; see line 6 [above] and *MND* 1.2.95-6: 'There we may rehearse. [...] Take pains; be perfect'). (171)

After that we look up the word 'perfect' in the *OED*, where we find that one of its meanings is "Thoroughly learned or acquired, got by heart or by rote," "at one's fingers' ends'". I do these searches casually, but deliberately: I encourage them to go to the notes, to the *OED* as they learn their passages, and I continually demonstrate this sort of accumulative understanding.

Along with this word-by-word emphasis, memorization encourages students to notice large and small patterns in the passages they choose. In order to speak the speech so that it makes sense to a listener, the speaker has to understand it herself. She must know who is speaking, who is listening to the speech, what circumstances surround the speech, and most of all what the speaker is trying to accomplish with these particular words. I encourage the students to ask these sorts of questions as they begin to memorize the speech, much in the way that a director would encourage an actor to explore a speech. Indeed, this memorization project shares many of the challenges and rewards of performance in the classroom, with one clear advantage: each student can be whoever he or she wants. They do all of their own casting and directing; there can be an eyrie of Hamlets, and enough Beatrices to make the world merry with wit.

This performance focus (what is happening in this speech? what does the speaker want? what is the speaker feeling and thinking?) requires attention be paid to logical constructions, emotional cues, and images – the very things that close reading and interpretation requires. I ask students to help the class listen to their memorized passage by explaining the situation that produced the speech, telling us about the motivations of the speaker, and explaining images that might seem puzzling on first hearing, and I suggest they give us this information before they give us the speech. This would be a lot to require on the spot, but by the time the students give their memorizations (towards the end of the semester) we have discussed passages in this manner in class, and I have also had them consider these sorts of things about their passages in their reading journals.

After they have said their lines, I ask them to talk about the challenges they faced as they memorized the passage. What words were the ones that kept hiding from them, which were the ones they stumbled over? Is the meaning, the main trajectory of the speech, quite clear – or are there problems, things that could be said in more than one way? Does anything in the speech make them cringe? Is Shakespeare presenting a way of thinking that is limited in a certain way? What new perspective on love or death or time did they discover? And why, oh why, did they choose these lines to memorize? What was it that made them want to put this particular passage into their memories?

I like to dwell on that last question, to emphasize that in the final analysis it will be the things that they cared about that they will remember from their studies. It is clear to me that they care about how well they say their lines in front of their peers; even though my manner is encouraging and relaxed, the days set aside for saying passages are charged with nervousness, excitement, and much pleasure. Sometimes I think they are the best days of the course, and I know that what happens when a student steps up to say Helena's "How happy some o'er other some can be!" speech (*A Midsummer Night's Dream* 1.226-51), Richard's "Let's talk of graves, of worms, and epitaphs" (*Richard II*, 3.2.145-77), the Duke's "Be absolute for death; either death or life / Shall thereby be the sweeter" (*Measure for Measure* 3.1.5-41) or Prospero's "Ye elves of hills, brooks, standing lakes, and groves" (*The Tempest* 5.1.33-57) it is the culminating event of a process that attempts to get them into the text, speaking it from the inside out.

There is one more thing about the memorization project and it is something that I cannot require: I tell them that a memorized passage is like a newly planted tree. At first it requires watering and some special care (little stakes and strings, protection from critters eating at its bark). A newly memorized passage needs to be repeated every couple of days, even after it is completely in the memory. Then, perhaps it can survive for a week or two before they check to see if all of the words are there, all of the rhymes in perfect order – and so on. If they give their memorized passage some maintenance care after they have triumphed in the classroom, it will occupy a secure place, the way a tree is relatively carefree once it is established. And then, who knows? Sometime in the new millennium, they may find themselves on a desert island and glad of Shakespeare's company.

Works Cited

Booth, Stephen, ed. *Shakespeare's Sonnets*. New Haven: Yale UP, 1977.

Frey, Charles. "Teaching Shakespeare in America". *Shakespeare Quarterly,* 35:5 (1984), pp. 541-59.

Pinsky, Robert. "A Man goes Into a Bar, See, and Recites: 'The Quality of Mercy Is Not Strained'". *The New York Times Book Review* [date needed], pp. 15-16.

The Riverside Shakespeare. ed. G. Blakemore Evans et al. Boston: Houghton Mifflin, 1974.

Vendler, Helen. *The Art of Shakespeare's Sonnets*. Cambridge, MA: Harvard UP, 1997.

SHAKESPEARE'S LANGUAGE AND THE GOALS OF TEACHING

Randal Robinson
(Michigan State University)

The partition behind Sarah Kasabowski's head made this half an office. When Sarah stood up, above my green Steelcase Michigander chair, her intensity overtook me. "Nobody wants to misread Shakespeare", she said. "You really ought to understand, Randal." Squinting, she looked through the eight-foot window toward Rulin Health Center, known for foolish diagnoses. "It makes me feel ugly", she said, and moved toward the door. Her ski jacket had the sun and its rays stitched on the back of it. "I want to feel like I'm worth keeping", she said. Then she was gone, to make the seven turns that would free her of Morrill Hall. That was the day, twenty-eight years ago, when I learned I was not teaching Shakespeare but self.

> *For more than a hundred years we have made Shakespeare's plays the chief texts for teaching excellence in readership in English. But, more often than not, we have thrown students into Shakespeare's language without benefits of methodical, research-based guidance. Leaving students alone to fail as readers, we have failed as teachers – even in the most basic requirement: to tell students what to expect in the language we have provided.*[1]

Wising Up

It's the first day of class. Shakespeare. I'm being looked at by forty-five strangers. Secretly they're asking, "Is this guy a teacher or a professor?" It's a fair question. "Does he want to guide me or talk at me?"

Near the end of the period, after meandering through the syllabus, hanging drawings of Shakespeare's stages, and swearing several times that I will not expect genius in the acting groups, I hand out a sheet containing the conversation of Florizel and Perdita that opens Act 4, scene 4 of *The Winter's Tale* (lines 1-54).

Shakespeare's Language and the Goals of Teaching

A little summary at the top of the handout puts the dialogue in context. My instructions say, "Mark every word, phrase, or segment with which you want assistance. Mark specific words, phrases, and segments. Do not mark large blocks of text." I leave the students fifteen minutes to read and mark the passage. I tell them, this is an exercise in self-monitoring, in metacognitive awareness. A few education majors look on me gravely. The rest laugh at my phrasing. Few give the passage more than eight minutes before they deposit the sheets with me, little concerned that come Wednesday, they will have to reconsider themselves.

Wednesday arrives, the students return, and we do the gong show.[2] "I'll read through the passage sentence by sentence", I tell them, returning their marked sheets, starting to learn names. "Whenever I read a word, phrase, or segment with which you want assistance, say 'gong'. If you don't gong me, I'll assume you understand the sentence fully, and I'll ask you any question I want to ask." I try to be emphatic. "Any question I want to ask. You're safer if you show real ignorance." They don't believe me. This is a classroom. Showing ignorance is never prudent.

I read Florizel's opening sentence.

These your unusual weeds to each part of you
Does give a life; no shepherdess, but Flora
Peering in April's front.[3]

Nothing. I twist my mouth. I huff. I whimper. I read it again. Still nothing. "Okay", I say, "I can ask you anything." Laurie says, "weeds". "Good. What do you think it means?" George knows. It means 'clothes'. He's had Matheson's Chaucer class. So we're off and running in Agriculture Hall.

We deal with 'life', 'part', 'Flora', 'Does', and 'Peering in April's front'. Noah chooses this last one, and I make my customary demand: "Choose the one word you most need help with. Focus." "All of it", says Noah, his eyebrows twisting against his sock cap. "Okay, I'll give you help with 'April' then. 'April' is the ...". "I know what 'April' is", he says, confident that he could crush me in a fair fight – 'front!'" "Good. What do you think it means." "Opening". "Brilliant". "What about 'Peering'?" he asks. "Does that mean 'appearing'?" "Yes, probably. Good. Maybe coming out in a peeping kind of way. Appearing by peeping out. Good." Noah smiles. "Consider yourself gonged", he says. Everybody laughs.

We continue in this fashion. The students gong various familiar words with unfamiliar meanings: 'petty', 'on', 'extremes', 'mark', 'mess', 'glass'. Some they don't gong, and I challenge. "What about the 'But' in 'But that our feasts / In every mess have folly'? What does that mean?" And: "What about the 'used' in 'your greatness / Hath not been used to fear'?" To their surprise, the students find only one archaic word that troubles them ('swain's'). They're used to thinking, "If I can just find all the strange words and translate them, I'll have Shakespeare whipped."

"How many of all these elements that you're gonging today", I ask, "did you mark last time?" "'Bout two", says Linda. Everybody laughs.

> *Students need to locate themselves within a community of readers, to avoid shame. Usually they come to an undergraduate Shakespeare class with a six-year history of frustration. Ninth grade told them, "Just read for the sense of the passage", and having taken that as an invitation to read in bits and pieces (what else can it be?), they have missed the meaning more often than they've found it. Then, humiliated, frustrated, they've turned against themselves. "I'm too stupid ever to read Shakespeare well." Discovering why they've failed, in a room with others who have also failed, makes laughter possible, and recovery.*

Delighted by their alacrity in finding deceptive familiar words, the students have more trouble with twists of syntax. I read aloud:

> Your high self,
> The gracious mark o' the land, you have obscured
> With a swain's wearing, and me, poor lowly maid,
> Most goddesslike pranked up.

I say: "Rearrange the words of this sentence. Put them in an ordinary, colloquial order. Don't add a word, omit a word, or translate a word. Just rearrange." The room is quiet. Then several odd combinations appear, even, "You, your high self, the gracious mark of the land have obscured a swain's wearing and obscured me, poor lowly maid, most goddess-like pranked up." "What happened to the 'with' that Perdita had – in 'With a swain's wearing'?" I ask. "I left it out", says Greg. "Didn't need it." Jean saves us. "You have obscured your high self, the gracious mark of the land, with a swain's wearing, and you have pranked up me, poor lowly maid, most goddesslike." "Excellent", I say.

Then I add: "Did you notice that Jean augmented an elliptical construction?" "I did what?" asks Jean. "You filled in an elliptical construction." "I didn't mean to. Is that good or bad." "It's good." I read:

> *Florizel.*   I bless the time
>   When my good falcon made her flight across
>   Thy father's ground.
> *Perdita.*   Now Jove afford you cause!

"Here's an elliptical construction", I say. "Perdita expects Florizel to add some words mentally to make sense of her statement. She leaves words just implied – the way you do when you say, 'If you see Gayle, I'm at the library, and don't laugh when you say it.'" I pause, say the sentence again, and wait for looks of comprehension. Then I ask, "What word or words does Perdita leave implied?" Silence. I ask, "Cause for what?" Silence. "Cause for what?" Finally, "Cause for blessing the time."

> *The most significant causes of difficulty in Shakespeare's language are familiar words with unfamiliar meanings (because they're deceptive); elliptical constructions (because students don't feel they have the right to add words to Shakespeare the way they add words mentally in conversations); and constructions with words oddly arranged. Peculiar arrangements can be especially nettlesome to students for whom English is not the primary language. "I've spent so much time adapting to the syntax of Modern English", said a woman from Costa Rica, "that I don't want to adapt to the syntax of Shakespeare's English – I'm fighting it."*

By the last part of the class meeting, the students are finding Shakespeare's language more predictable. I divide the troublesome elements into two categories. "First, stuff you can flatly misread – like 'used' and 'mark' and 'piece of beauty rarer.' And second, stuff you can *under*-read. Like 'Thy' and 'In every mess have folly' and 'Humbling their deities to love.'" Misread and under-read. Simple. The bad part of the mystery is fading.

> *Only a predictable language can give a reader pleasure.*[4] *When language welcomes you and then hides from you, it becomes the malicious trickster, the bad cue-giver, the shape-shifter in the kitchen*

armed with knives. Each time readers confront such a language, reluctance to confront it ever again increases. Sooner or later, readers take revenge by calling the language 'dead to me'.

Three minutes left and I have too much to say. "Your goal in this class should be to change your reading habits slowly. You won't have time to read any whole play well. You just won't. But you can read some characters well. The character you'll do in the acting group", I say, "and two or three others. Think of yourself as Perdita, for example. You're doing her on stage. For $10,000. What do you communicate with your language? Every little piece of it. What does Perdita's language reveal about her. What does it make you become?" I'm saying too much. Getting too close to lecturette. They're drifting. "I have a booklet for you. It follows up the gong show. It's a survey of main difficulties in Shakespeare's language. It tells you more what to look for." They take the handouts and zip up for walks across the river, to classrooms in Wonders, McDonel, and Wells. "This was fun", says Greg, as he leaves. "Do it again sometime", says Linda. "I enjoyed it." "So did I."

After the class I turn my head toward the dark inside of my Kelty backpack. "It makes me feel ugly", Sarah said, about misreading Shakespeare's language. I tried to understand: ugly ... weak ... not in control ... laughable ... I couldn't make it work for me – that language ... I was no good. "You really ought to understand, Randal" ... help me be grown. Yes, I really ought to understand.

The twenty-page booklet I give the students starts with a three-page introduction.[5] *The booklet, I say, gives descriptions of challenging elements all modern readers of English are inclined to handle poorly. Responding to these elements, we're inclined to misread or under-read. In this introduction I cite passages that give difficulties of both kinds, and I summarize the processes of misreading and under-reading those difficulties often provoke.*

Then come the descriptions of challenging elements. Group A presents: "Difficulties Associated Mainly with Misreading". It includes: familiar words with unfamiliar meanings; obsolete words; words that contain familiar suffixes with unfamiliar meanings; troublesome verbs and verbals; words arranged in unusual ways; segments with words merely implied; words with syllables and parts of syllables merely implied; and troublesome pronouns of four kinds (unexpected reflexive pronouns,

pronouns without expected prepositions, pronouns without clear antecedents, and royal plural pronouns).

Group B presents: "*Difficulties Associated Mainly with Under-reading*". It includes: *familiar pronouns; metaphors and personifications; idiosyncratic syntactical patterns; couplet rhymes, stanzaic forms, metrical irregularities; and word play.*

Noting and Asking, and More

A week later in the semester, students are practicing their interchanges with Shakespeare's language. Their coming-of-age text is *Romeo and Juliet*. I'm assisting through a course pack called "Quiz Games with Shakespeare's Language: *Romeo and Juliet*". In "Quiz Games", I present more than five hundred questions on the language of *Romeo and Juliet* and commentaries to accompany the questions.

Each question appears with a choice of answers. Because students know the multiple-choice format well, I can avoid giving them alienating instructions about fundamental activities. Here are fifteen of the thirty questions on the language of the masque scene (Act 1, scene 5).

1. By the end of the scene, Juliet has become:

    a) giddy; b) relieved; c) fearful; d) lethargic

2. Capulet says he has seen the day when he could "tell / A whispering tale". Capulet's 'whispering' is a familiar word with an unfamiliar meaning. The part of 'whispering' that especially needs translation is:

    a) 'whisper-'; b) '-ing"

3. Romeo says of Juliet:

    The measure done, I'll watch her place of stand
    And, touching hers, make blessed my rude hand.

    You can clarify these lines by rearranging the words. In rearranging, you would move:

    a) 'my rude hand'; b) 'touching hers'; c) 'The measure done'

4. Capulet says of Romeo: "'A bears him like a portly gentleman...." The best description of Capulet's word 'portly' is:

a) a familiar word with an unfamiliar meaning; b) a word that means 'fat' but suggests also 'good natured'; c) a word with a syllable missing

5. Capulet says that "Verona brags" of Romeo. Capulet here personifies Verona, indicating that it can brag. Why does he personify Verona? (Consider the context carefully before you choose an explanation.)

a) he wants to resemble a clever schoolboy; b) he wants to subdue Tybalt by invoking the authority of the whole city; c) he is being sarcastic in his praise because Romeo is the son of his enemy

6. Chastising Tybalt, Capulet says to him: "This trick may chance to scathe you." The appropriate classification for Capulet's word 'trick' is:

a) familiar word with an unfamiliar meaning; b) metaphor; c) word that needs another, implied word to make its meaning clear

7. Tybalt says:

Patience perforce with willful choler meeting
Makes my flesh tremble in their different greeting.

When he refers to 'Patience' and 'choler' meeting, Tybalt is talking about:

a) an event he sees occurring at the party; b) a process he feels occurring inside him; c) an event he fears will occur in the near future

8. In the first five speeches Juliet speaks to Romeo, what pronoun or pronouns does Juliet use toward Romeo?

a) only the familiar pronoun 'thou'; b) only the formal pronoun 'you'; c) both the familiar pronoun 'thou' and the formal pronoun 'you.'

9. In the first eighteen lines of dialogue they speak with one another, Romeo and Juliet become collaborators. Which one of the following do they *not* create together?

a) rhymes; b) a line of verse; c) a series of metaphors in which they turn religious words to new uses; d) a plot; e) kisses

10. Juliet says: "Saints do not move, though grant for prayers' sake." In this statement, Juliet leaves two or three words merely implicit. The words that Juliet expects Romeo to add mentally after 'though' are:

a) saints do; b) saints do not; c) saints moving

11. Romeo says: "Thus from my lips, by thine, my sin is purged." To make this line clearer you could:

a) rearrange words; b) comment on a simile; c) translate one or more than one familiar word with an unfamiliar meaning

Shakespeare's Language and the Goals of Teaching 291

12. Thinking of Juliet, Romeo says: "Is she a Capulet? / O dear account! My life is my foe's debt". An appropriate paraphrase for 'My life is my foe's debt' is:

a) my life is my enemy's to claim; b) my life must be paid to me by my enemy; c) my life will be cancelled out by my enemy

13. Thinking of Romeo, Juliet says:

Go ask his name. If he be married,
My grave is like to be my wedding bed.

The paraphrase that best reveals the most certain meaning of Juliet's statement is:

a) If he's married, and I can't have him, I'll probably never get married – I'll die first, and I'll marry death in the grave. b) If he's married, I'll marry someone else and feel dead. c) If he's married, I'll kill myself.

14. In presenting "If he be married," how many syllables should a performer give to 'married'?

a) one; b) two; c) three

15. Juliet says:

My only love sprung from my only hate!
Too early seen unknown, and known too late!

Select the statement that best gives the sense of Juliet's second line, "Too early seen unknown, and known too late!"

a) A man who, now that I know who he is, I wish I'd never seen him; b) A man seen by me and fallen in love with by me before I knew who he was, and a man known to me too late; c) A man who saw me before he knew who I was and a man who, now that he knows who I am, he'll reject me.

Through such questions I model an attitude. I'm the reader as Costard the intrusive swain. I let pass without interest no communication of any kind – whether by meter, rhyme, syntax, metaphor, personification, mood of verb, suffix, patterns of sound, or any similar means. Whatever a character can state, imply, or suggest, I can notice, and speeches I cannot fully understand, I can undertake to understand, like a relentless child, scene after scene. This is my first role in "Quiz Games." I note and ask, note and ask, over and over and over again.

> *Nobody gets anywhere with a language without repetition in listening and repetition of asking. Consider Mary, who's one year old. Standing at the stove, Mary hears her mother, Nuala, say: "The cookies are burned." "Burned?" answers Mary, wondering if she know the meaning of her mother's "burned." "Burned", Nuala says, as she gives Mary a cookie top to smell. Yes, Mary knew her mother's meaning of "burned." "Look", Mary says, "cookie burned". "Throw it away", says Nuala and hands Mary the cookie. "Bozzie", says Mary, testing her mother's 'away' to see if it can mean 'to Bozzie the dog.' "No", says Nuala. "Throw it all the way away. Bozzie won't like it." Nuala holds out the waste basket. Mary hurls the darkened cookie into the blue plastic with authority. "Away!" Mary says, and smiles. "Away!" Mary is pleased. Over and over she works on her English, noting and asking, reading the texts of her mother world.*

Noting and asking is not all I do in "Quiz Games". I also play the knowing professor. For each of the five-hundred odd questions, I provide a commentary. A commentary tells the right answer. A commentary also gives information on language, and a commentary may, in addition, provide information on character or culture. Here are the fifteen commentaries that accompany the fifteen questions quoted above, on lines in the masque scene of *Romeo and Juliet*.

> 1. **Juliet's Final Mood.** By the end of the scene, Juliet has become fearful. As she shows in her last two speeches, she expects a difficult future, now that she has fallen in love with the only son of Montague. "Prodigious birth of love it is to me", she says, "That I must love a loathed enemy."
>
> 2. **"whispering tale."** The correct answer is: '-ing'. In the 'whispering' of Capulet's phrase 'tell / A whispering tale', the suffix, '-ing', is the troublesome part. Capulet's 'whispering tale' means 'whispered tale'.
>
> 3. **"The measure done, I'll watch her place of stand / And, touching hers, make blessed my rude hand."** The correct answer is: 'touching hers.' To make Romeo's lines clearer, move that phrase. Say: "The measure done, I'll watch her place of stand and make blessed my rude hand, touching hers." You might clarify further by adding the implied contraction, 'I'll': "The measure done, I'll watch her place of stand and I'll make blessed my rude hand, touching hers."
>
> 4. **"'A bears him like a portly gentleman."** Capulet's 'portly' is a familiar word with an unfamiliar meaning. Capulet's 'portly' is related to the word 'deportment'. It means 'of good deportment', 'well-behaved'.
>
> 5. **"Verona brags ...."** The correct answer is: He wants to subdue Tybalt by invoking the authority of the whole city. When Capulet personifies Verona and tells Tybalt that "Verona brags" of Romeo, he is

urging Tybalt to put himself in harmony with the community and show respect for Romeo.

6. **"This trick may chance to scathe you."** In Capulet's statement, 'trick' is a familiar word with an unfamiliar meaning. Capulet's 'trick' means 'foolish action' or 'trait of character.' So Capulet is saying: "This foolish action (or this trait of character) may injure you ('scathe you')."

7. **"Patience perforce with willful choler meeting ..."** When Tybalt speaks of 'Patience' and 'choler' meeting, he is speaking of a process he feels occurring inside himself. Tybalt is experiencing an inner conflict. He wants to show a manly strength in 'Patience' as he controls his anger ('choler'), but he also wants to show his anger openly and aggressively, in a manly fashion.

Additional Comment. In sixteenth-century texts, the word 'patience' may refer to strength in suffering. When a person endures pain with self-control, maintaining mental stability while suffering, that person shows 'patience'.

8. **Juliet's Pronouns.** In her first meeting with Romeo, Juliet uses only the formal pronoun 'you'. Juliet is behaving in the way others in her culture would expect a young woman of her position to behave. She is less overt than Romeo in expressing her desire to become intimate with another person.

Additional Comment. Juliet will behave differently in the orchard scene (Act 2, Scene 2) when she believes herself to be alone. Compare the pronouns she uses in the orchard scene to refer to Romeo with the pronoun she uses here.

9. **Creations of Juliet and Romeo in the First Eighteen Lines.** The correct answer is: a plot. Romeo and Juliet do not create a plot together in their first eighteen lines of dialogue. But they do create much else. First, they create rhymes: enough to make a sonnet plus a quatrain. Their rhyming words for the sonnet are 'hand', 'this', 'stand', 'kiss'; 'much', 'this', 'touch', 'kiss'; 'too', 'prayer', 'do', 'despair'; 'sake', 'take'. Their rhyming words for the quatrain are 'purged', 'took', 'urged', 'book'. Romeo and Juliet also create a line of verse together: "Give me my sin again. You kiss by th' book." In addition, Romeo and Juliet create two kisses together (they probably kiss after the sonnet, then again after the quatrain). Finally, Romeo and Juliet create a series of metaphors together. Romeo imagines Juliet to be a holy saint to whom he will show devotion by giving kisses to her hands and lips. Juliet imagines Romeo to be a devout pilgrim whose prayers she is granting.

Additional comment. The religious references suggest that Romeo and Juliet are looking for salvation, not in heaven but on earth, in the experience of love, and that they are deciding to seek that salvation through one another.

10. **"Saints do not move, though grant for prayers' sake."** Juliet expects Romeo to add mentally the words 'saints do' after 'though'. Juliet means: "Saints do not move, though saints do grant for prayers' sake."

11. **"Thus from my lips, by thine, my sin is purged."** You can readily clarify Romeo's line by rearranging the words. Here's a rearrangement: "Thus my sin is purged from my lips by thine." Neither of the other two answers can be appropriate: in this line Romeo does not use either a simile or a familiar word with an unfamiliar meaning.

12. **"My life is my foe's debt."** The appropriate paraphrase is: My life is my enemy's to claim. Romeo means, in falling in love with Juliet, he has lost rights to his life. His life is now something he owes to his enemy – a debt he owes – something to be claimed by another.

13. **"Go ask his name. If he be married, / My grave is like to be my wedding bed."** The correct answer is: If he's married, and I can't have him, I'll probably never get married – I'll die first, and I'll marry death in the grave. This paraphrase presents the most certain meaning of Juliet's statement.

14. **"married".** A performer should pronounce 'married' with three syllables, as 'mar-ri-ed'. Giving three syllables to 'married', a performer makes the appropriate rhyme of 'bed' and '-ed'. Also, the performer gives the line the ten syllables expected in an iambic pentameter line: go, ask, his, name, if, he, be, mar, ri, ed.

15. **"Too early seen unknown, and known too late!"** The best of the three paraphrases is the second one: A man seen by me and fallen in love with by me before I knew who he was ["Too early seen unknown"], and a man known to me too late ["and known too late"].

I claim virtues for these commentaries. They arise from the text and serve the text directly. They keep me brief, modest, and subordinate. Also, they are postponeable. Because the commentaries appear on the left-hand pages of a spiral bound course pack, students can simply turn the commentaries under until they choose to be informed. I, in the commentaries, am the attending intermediary – waiting to be heard.

And Meanwhile, The Wide World Web

I have packed up my "Quiz Games" and gone with anxious gall bladder to the Virtual University and the Faculty Facility for Creative Computing. Adobe GoLive protrudes from my Kelty. I feel comic and old.

The University, I discover, has Widgets. I fight my impulse to see diseases of the skin. One of the Widgets is Query. Using Query, I can adapt "Quiz Games" for the Internet. Students can practice as readers on line. The process is easy to picture.

I imagine myself a student. I am facing the Internet version of "Quiz Games".[6] A scene from *Romeo and Juliet* sits partly visible in a window to the right. I can make the text scroll up and down within the window. My set of multiple-choice questions on the scene sits in a window to the left. I can make the questions scroll inside their window, too. I read the text patiently. Then I turn to the multiple-choice questions and I choose answers by clicking on radio buttons. Beside most of the questions are line numbers. When I click on the line numbers next to a question in the left window, I make related lines of text show in the right window. Slick.

After I choose all my answers, I send them to the Server – something, as I picture it, with lizard's tail and nostrils of a boar. The Server responds. It has received my submission, and if I want it to, the Server will show the multiple-choice questions again, will give me the commentaries on them, and will tell me which of my answers were right, which were wrong. I click a button to say yes, provide for me. Suddenly the contents of the left window change. Now, ready to scroll inside the window are all my multiple-choice questions, the commentaries, and my responses, judged. I look at my score. The Server tells me, if I want, I may consider the questions again and submit a different set of answers. For a lizardly boar, the Server is nice. It holds me out a second turn.

Does this medium appeal to me? Not really. I like paper. "So what?" says my wife, with the authority of a Myers-Briggs type indicator provider.[7] I know, I'm very odd. I'm an INFJ in personality type, part of a group that comprises only 1 % of the citizens of the United States. "You should generalize from yourself to almost nobody", she says, and gives me a book to read. The title alone suffuses me. "*Growing Up Digital*", it reads, "*The Rise of the Net Generation*".[8] That's two generations away from mine. I grew up on radio. I'm overwhelmed with information. I come away with one main thought. Cyberspace can be attractive to

N-Gen readers. For them, cyberspace is where, when you go there, you're never alone.

> *Nobody wants to learn to read solo. All too routinely, teachers of mature students who are still learning to read, and of younger students who believe they ought to be mature (at least in reading), have failed to give assurances that the students are ordinary, not abnormal – have failed to say: "No reason to learn to read in hiding, however old you are." The teacher in cyberspace reassures by the subtext of cyberspace itself: its sheer electrical presence, its colors, movements, and lights. "Learn to read and I'll be with you. Not as well as your father, who sat with you on the sofa sharing* Are You My Mother?, *but with you. Through the Server. Through my plans. In cybercode. And since I am with you, I must think your learning to read is good."*

This is a start, I think, the "Quiz Games" in cyberspace. I'll settle for it. It's just part of a whole anyway: with *Unlocking Shakespeare's Language*, the gong show, the "Quiz Games" as course pack, and my weird Spolinesque improvisations with language.[9] They all serve a single conviction: that learning to read Shakespeare's language is a glory for the self.

They're all part of a drift, too, toward the future, where the possessors of my land-grant academy will change. Sarah Kasabowski has long since made her seven turns through Morrill Hall, and left me looking always for another second chance. I imagine it where the drift rises, and Sarah Kasabowski's granddaughter is arriving, in the class of '25. For a teacher, no time is too far away.

Notes

1   Homer Swander discusses the history of Shakespeare's plays as classroom texts in "Teaching Shakespeare: Tradition and the Future", in *William Shakespeare: His World, His Work, His Influence*, ed. John F. Andrews (New York: Scribner's, 1985), vol. 3, pp. 873-87. Although in general teachers have not provided adequate assistance with Shakespeare's language, the last fifteen years have brought promising developments. The Folger Shakespeare Library and the National Council of Teachers of English have sponsored workshops and seminars on the teaching of Shakespeare's language, and teachers have shared insights through various publications. My *Unlocking Shakespeare's Language: Help for the Teacher and Student* (Urbana: NCTE) appeared in 1988, and since the early 1990s, numerous teachers have described exercises intended to help students become more comfortable with Shakespeare's language. Especially prominent are essays that emphasize uses of performance, performance-related activities, and a whole language approach. For example, *Teaching Shakespeare Today*, edited by Ronald E. Salomone and James E. Davis (Urbana: NCTE, 1993) includes Sharon Beehler's "Teaching Shakespeare's Dramatic Dialogue" (pp. 14-23), Elizabeth Oakes'

"Enacting Shakespeare's Language in *Macbeth* and *Romeo and Juliet*" (pp. 85-89), and John Wilson Swope's "A Whole Language Approach to *Romeo and Juliet*" (pp. 218-30). The three volumes in the Shakespeare Set Free series, published by the Folger Shakespeare Library from 1993 through 1995, present similar essays. For example, the section on *Romeo and Juliet* in volume one provides information on class meetings devoted to "A Choral Reading of the Act 1 Prologue", "A Performance of 1.5", "Praiseworthy Promptbooks", "Language Tricks", and "Subtext, Stress, and Inflection" (*Shakespeare Set Free: Teaching "Romeo and Juliet", "Macbeth", "A Midsummer Night's Dream"*, ed. Peggy O'Brien, et al. [New York: Washington Square Press, 1993], pp. 117-99). Essays in the more recent *Teaching Shakespeare Into the Twenty-first Century*, also edited by Ronald E. Salomone and James E. Davis (Athens: Ohio UP, 1997) introduce still other exercises for teaching Shakespeare's language. For example, in "Paraphrasing Shakespeare" (pp. 11-17), William T. Liston, observing that most students need encouragements to slow themselves as readers, so that they can isolate in passages elements that cry out for close attention, recommends the "daily paraphrase". And in "Making Sense of Shakespeare: A Reader-Based Response" (pp. 96-103), Charles H. Frey recommends activities that can help students engage emotionally with Shakespeare's language.

2   The Gong Show was a television program popular in the United States several years ago. In the Gong Show amateurs gave performances of various kinds and a panel of judges observed. A judge could at any time bring a performer's act to a halt by striking a large gong. By associating students with the judges on that television show, I suggest that students are exercising power, not showing weakness, when they gong parts of a reading to ask for help.

3   My texts for *The Winter's Tale* and *Romeo and Juliet* appear in *The Complete Works of Shakespeare*, 4th edn., ed. David Bevington (New York: Longman, 1997). Bevington became the editor for this collection with the second edition, which was a revision of the edition by Hardin Craig. The second edition, published by Scott, Foresman, appeared in 1973.

4   For a discussion of the processes readers use to sample, infer, and predict, and for information on the importance of predicting in reading, see "Reading and Reading Strategies: The Making of Meaning", in Yetta M. Goodman, Dorothy J. Watson, and Carolyn L. Burke, *Reading Strategies: Focus on Comprehension*, 2nd edn. (Katonah, NY: Richard C. Owen, 1996), pp. 3-14. (The first edition, published by Holt, Rinehart, and Winston, appeared in 1980.)

5   The booklet is available on the Internet at: http://www.msu.edu/user/robins29/shakeslang.

6   Act 1, scene 5 of the Internet version of "Quiz Games with Shakespeare's Language: *Romeo and Juliet*" is available on the Internet at: http://www.msu.edu/user/robins29/shakeslang. When asked for a user identification, enter "puck". When asked for a password, enter "1595".

7   The Myers-Briggs Type Indicator is an instrument widely used in educational and vocational settings, businesses, and non-profit organizations. The Myers-Briggs Type Indicator provides information on a person's preferences for interacting with the world, taking in information, and making decisions.

8   Don Tapscott, *Growing Up Digital: The Rise of the Net Generation* (New York: McGraw-Hill, 1998).

9   I describe such exercises in "Improvisation and the Language of Shakespeare's Plays", *Nebraska English Journal*, 35, nos. 3 and 4 (1990), pp. 54-64. My term "Spolinesque" alludes to the works of Viola Spolin. Especially valuable is Spolin's *Improvisation for the Theater* (Evanston: Northwestern UP, 1983).

LIVE FROM THE COAST:
IT'S SHAKESPEARE TONIGHT!

Michael W. Shurgot
(South Puget Sound Community College)

In his "Foreword" to *Walking Shadows*, a listing of Shakespeare's plays on film and television in Britain's National Film and Television Archive, Kenneth Branagh writes:

> I am very pleased to be able to recommend this book to lovers of Shakespeare and the screen alike. As the reader will discover, film has served not only as a means to preserve the performances and productions of the past, but has expanded our understanding of how Shakespeare may be presented. Shakespeare's plays were written for the stage, but they will become nothing if they do not remain popular. Through the media of film and television millions have learnt [sic] to appreciate the poetry, the drama and the sheer entertainment value of the greatest plays ever written.[1]

Branagh is certainly right about the historical and hence pedagogical benefits of preserving productions of Shakespeare's plays on film. The superb work of numerous actors and directors who have interpreted Shakespeare's plays can now be 're-viewed' not only at movie houses during Shakespeare film festivals throughout the world, but also more immediately in virtually any classroom worldwide, as video and other media technologies allow instructors, regardless of where they teach, to include historically significant and contemporary film and television versions of the plays in their teaching.[2] Consider, for example, the significant pedagogical value of being able to show students clips from two of the finest recent productions of *Othello*: Trevor Nunn's 1990 production with Ian McKellen as Iago, Willard White as Othello, and Imogen Stubbs as Desdemona; and Janet Suzman's 1988 South African production starring John Kari as Othello, with Richard Haddon Haines as Iago and Joanna Weinberg as Desdemona. Being able to contrast the production choices of these two superb versions of *Othello* allows one's students to appreciate readily the 'openness' of a Shakespearean script and the various imaginative ways that actors connect Shakespeare's language to his characters.[3]

Branagh's recommending *Walking Shadows* to "lovers of Shakespeare and the screen alike" also addresses the increasingly sophisticated body of critical studies of Shakespeare on film and television. Beginning with books such as Roger Manvell's *Shakespeare and the Film* (1971) and Jack J. Jorgens's influential *Shakespeare on Film* (1977), scholarly study of Shakespeare on film and television has become a major critical genre. Every meeting of the Shakespeare Association of America now includes seminars and papers devoted to film and television criticism; most anthologies of Shakespeare scholarship, especially those devoted to teaching, now include several essays on recent film and television productions of the plays; *Shakespeare Bulletin* now incorporates the newsletter "Shakespeare on Film", and film essays often appear in *Shakespeare and the Classroom*; and several collections of essays and scholarly books have been devoted to critical and historical studies of film and television versions of the plays.[4]

Given the wide availability, and hence the increasing use, of so many film and television versions of Shakespeare's plays, especially the BBC series,[5] in easily accessible video formats for the classroom, and the international proliferation of Shakespearean film and television criticism, Shakespeare students around the world are increasingly likely to see the same versions of the plays in their courses and read the same criticism. I suspect, for example, that both Nunn's and Suzman's productions of *Othello*, which even my small community college library owns, have been seen by students in high schools, colleges, and universities on every continent where Shakespeare is studied. While some might argue that the world-wide distribution of American and especially British productions is yet another form of western cultural imperialism, nonetheless one cannot deny the pedagogical value of being able to show one's students McKellen's Iago, Kari's Othello, Stubbs's Desdemona, or the American Kevin Klein's Hamlet in the New York Shakespeare Festival production. Film and video versions of the most popular of Shakespeare's plays have indeed made all the world a stage for their viewing.

All of the above seems pedagogically fine. I too use videos in my Shakespeare classes, and sometimes (usually near the end of the term) commit what some of my colleagues consider the heresy of showing an entire film version of one play after only minimal classroom study in order to give students the opportunity to experience a play as they would in a theatre: fresh, with little professorial backgrounding and preparation, lest their critical opinion of what they will experience be decided beforehand and they 'see' the production, and hence the play, only as they believe their instructor wants them to.[6] However, in every Shakespeare class I also insist that my students experience at least one play as it was originally intended to be experienced: in a live theatre. Branagh's "Foreword" to *Walking Shadows*, while praising film versions because they will help the plays "remain popular", recognizes that Shakespeare's plays were "written for the stage" yet suggests that they will "become nothing" if they are not kept "popular" in film and television versions. Coming from a distinguished stage actor, this remark is quite surprising, despite the success of his many film versions of the plays, and suggests that live theatre productions cannot sufficiently keep the plays popular. I would argue also that Branagh's remark poses two serious pedagogical dangers: one, that extensive reliance on film and television versions of the plays may homogenize the teaching of them, because students everywhere will probably see the same widely-distributed film or television versions that their instructors eagerly introduce; and secondly, that having seen only film or television versions students will have experienced little of the actual theatricality of a Shakespearean play and may accept the video versions as definitive.

In the remainder of this essay I describe the exigencies, joys, frustrations, and ultimately the benefits of taking my students to see live productions of Shakespeare's plays in three west-coast American cities: Seattle, Wa., and Portland, Or., each with about 400,000 inhabitants and several successful theatre companies; and Olympia, Wa., a smaller city of about 40,000 inhabitants, the home of my college and of one semi-professional theatre company, Harlequin

Productions. While turning the video equipment on and the classroom lights off for a fifty-minute viewing of scenes from different versions of *Hamlet* is much easier than organizing a weekend trip for about twenty-five students (and their spouses, siblings, partners, etc.) to see one live production of the play, I would argue that the educational benefits of these excursions far outweigh their difficulties, and that local and regional productions can often stimulate students in surprisingly effective ways. Certainly live performances, especially in the kinds of companies and theatres I discuss below,[7] can never compete visually with large-scale, well financed film and television versions of the plays (what theatre company in the world could match the visual excitement of Branagh's film *Henry V* or McKellen's *Richard III*?). Nonetheless, only living, breathing, sweating actors just a few feet away can convey the immediacy and spontaneity of the medium for which Shakespeare wrote. I shall argue that seeing live performances as a group enriches students' appreciation of Shakespeare's plays as plays and encourages students' communal exploration of a Shakespearean play in ways that film viewing cannot.

I generally teach Shakespeare in either the fall or spring quarter, and in every class I make attending a live performance a requirement, not an option. In fact, I design my class syllabus around the scheduled Shakespeare productions in the region, *not* around the video versions available in the college library or what I feel like teaching that term. This approach means extra work for me, including checking the area companies' schedules well in advance; securing (and initially paying for!) about 20-25 tickets, often miles away in either Seattle (65) or Portland (120); organizing transportation, including driving one of the college's buses; providing directions to the theatre if we are going to Seattle or Portland; and making sure that all the students and their guests actually have a ride. Once at the theatre, I then have to make sure that all are in their seats at curtain time. While most of this work will be obvious to anyone who has organized field trips for his/her students, and may seem out of place in an essay about teaching college-level Shakespeare classes, I mention the obvious only to emphasize how much more work all this is than flipping a few switches on a video machine and then sending the tape(s) back to the library 50 minutes later.

The following pages highlight a few scenes from four productions to which I have taken students: two of the *Taming of the Shrew,* one in Portland and one in Seattle; one of *The Merchant of Venice* in Portland; and finally one of *Twelfth Night* in Olympia. While the productions varied widely, each proved theatrically and pedagogically valuable in ways that a video version shown on a screen could not be.

Tygres Heart Shakespeare Company in Portland generally features young actors in inventive, often startling stagings. Its *Shrew,* in fall, 1999, continued this tradition. The set for the production was a huge, three-tiered scaffolding upstage, a kind of steel 'tiring-room', that was clearly visible to the audience. Here the actors changed clothes, stored all their personal stuff, such as suitcases, clothes, props, radios, make-up kits, etc., as traveling actors must, and here they also carried on among themselves several 'real-life' relationships which hilariously carried over into their 'stage lives'. Among these were Bianca's flirting with the actors playing both Petruchio and Hortensio, which infuriated Spencer Conway as Lucentio every time he was on stage as he watched 'Bianca' sexually arouse 'off-stage' two other actors in the company. Also fascinating theatrically was the professional anger of the actress playing Kate, who complained from the scaffolding before the play opened that since she had studied acting at the Juilliard School she resented having to 'play with' the actor playing Petruchio, who had attended some nameless public university in the vast Canadian wilderness. In fact, Luisa Sermol (Kate) really did attend Juilliard, and Timothy Hyland (Petruchio) really did study at the University of British Columbia in Vancouver, B.C., hardly (by the way) a wilderness. Thus the students saw a marvelous demonstration of the blending of 'real' and 'theatrical' reality, as the 'playing' of the scenes between Bianca, Hortensio, and Lucentio, and then between Kate and Petruchio, echoed the supposed sexual jealousies and professional rivalries of the actors as they 'played' the 'real lives' of a band of itinerant actors.

The initial encounter between Kate and Petruchio was sexually the most explicit I have ever seen, and proved both shocking and thrilling to my students. When Sermol encountered Petruchio in 2.1, she was not only an infuriated Kate sent out to see a supposed wooer, but also an angry actor wishing to prove her mettle against the supposedly untalented Canadian woodsman. Accompanied by Dave Brubeck's *Take Five*, Sermol, in a low-cut bodice, high skirt, tossed hair, and leather boots, sauntered in and stood atop a small pedestal center stage. Their initial dialogue unfolded as Petruchio walked around the pedestal, each eyeing the other and showing obvious sexual interest even as they obviously 'competed' for the most clever words and gestures, thus combining brilliantly the professional rivalry of the actors with the developing interest in each other that Shakespeare has built into this initial clash between Kate and Petruchio.

By "Come, come, you wasp, in faith you are too angry" (2.1.209), they were belly to belly, Petruchio stroking Kate's thighs and buttocks as she churned against him, each trying to 'out-act' the other in lasciviousness. Surprised by Petruchio's "tongue in your tail" quip, Kate slapped him twice, but on the third try he grabbed her arm and held her rigidly. Kate's jokes about "crest", "coxcomb", and "combless cock" led Petruchio to unbutton his pants, and, as I deduced from the roaring of spectators opposite me, to reveal his privates. When Kate insisted that she saw a crab, Petruchio's "Then show it to me" proved his hysterical undoing. Kate pointed directly at his genitals and shouted "Had I a glass I would", thus brilliantly belittling his sexuality and showing him the far less adroit 'actor'. Kate's bawdy prompted Petruchio to tackle Kate and hold her on the pedestal as he moved vigorously over her, in obvious imitation of sexual intercourse, while ironically praising her "pleasant", "gamesome", and "courteous" character.

The ease with which the actors moved between their 'real' and 'stage' lives transformed Shakespeare's unfamiliar Induction into a modern equivalent in which the actors were clearly performing a 'play-within-a-play' that was perfectly comprehensible to my students. Although admittedly some students were embarrassed, nonetheless they were able to appreciate the obvious sexual energy in Shakespeare's script and to sense the spontaneity of human sexual attraction.

Students saw actors as people like themselves with similar human needs and complications "acting out" our common humanity both "off stage" and "on stage" in production choices which not only clarified the dramatic value of Shakespeare's Induction but also emphasized how drama mirrors all our lives, actors, instructors, and students alike.

Two scenes from the Intiman Theatre's contemporary setting of *Shrew*, in spring 1997, were equally valuable pedagogically. After the Petruchio-Kate encounter in 2.1, Laurence Ballard as Baptista hosted an outrageous bidding game for Bianca. Gremio and the disguised Tranio projected onto a large screen upstage images of their possessions, including huge houses in Bellevue, Wa., the home of Microsoft and its many millionaires; jet planes, courtesy of Boeing; and ski chalets in the Olympic and Cascade mountains, to the east and west of Seattle. Between them Baptista furiously operated an adding machine, adding up the 'value' of his younger daughter. After the stirring clash between Kate and Petruchio in 2.1, spectators understood exactly why Kate would be angry at her father and the society he represented, and thus initially see Petruchio as a way out of this repressive, greedy family. In fact, after their farcical wedding, Kate happily jumped on Petruchio's Harley-Davidson as they sped out of town.

The final, poignant scene provoked heated debate in my class the following Monday. Bianca's wedding was lavish; Baptista had obviously done well earlier in the bidding war. The bet Petruchio makes on Kate, which Kate used as a pretext to stage a well-played attack against her sister and the Widow, produced piles of coins for the couple which they initially scooped up as they danced around the stage. Then, just before they exited, they suddenly looked at each other, paused, and then threw the coins into the air and headed for the nearest bedroom. They thus showed their contempt for the society in which the others were obviously still trapped. The Widow suddenly slapped Hortensio, and then left the stage, leaving him bewildered. Bianca, wealthy now beyond imagining, left Lucentio, walked to the front of the table, sat down, and tearfully began swigging a full whiskey bottle. Spectators rejoiced in Kate's and Petruchio's having abandoned this society and its obsessive pursuit of wealth.

This conclusion raised several questions which my students debated vigorously. Was the final scene too emphatic, creating an obvious reason for Kate to accept Petruchio? Was the admittedly farcical violence Kate experienced at Petruchio's estate minimized when compared to her father's repressive money-grubbing? Was Bianca initially too cardboard and passive a figure for the audience to accept her sudden, angry, and depressing boozing at the end? Whatever students' reaction to these scenes, especially the conclusion, the intensity of the stage performances and, as with the Tygres Heart production, the staging and characterization galvanized considerable debate about the relation between the performance and Shakespeare's script. Further, since each production cast *Shrew* in a modern setting, students were able to connect readily Shakespeare's script with their own lives, recognizing both the prevalence of human passion and the potentially corrupting influence of wealth.

Two moments in the Tygres Heart's production of *The Merchant of Venice* in spring 1998, bluntly dramatized the play's anti-Semitism. A brief dumb show preceding the play featured a Jewish family, including a small boy carrying a model trading ship, walking toward center stage. Salerio and Solanio, who had been standing upstage left watching the family, suddenly accosted them, pushed the parents away, and stole the boy's ship. When the father tried to retrieve his son's toy, Salerio suddenly drew a knife with which he threatened both the father and his son. Then, as the trembling Jews hurried off stage, Salerio and Solanio laughed at them and Salerio threw the toy ship into the air: a prize stolen from the despised Jews.[8]

The second moment occurred at the end of 4.1. As the stage cleared, a spotlight shone upstage left, Shylock's and Jessica's home for this production. Suddenly, spectators saw the silhouette of a man – Shylock – hanging himself. After the performance, during a scheduled talk-back with the actors which was immensely beneficial to my students and which obviously cannot happen after watching a film, Keith Scales, who played Shylock, explained that suicide was Shylock's final revenge. According to Scales, in this conception of the play anti-Semitism was so powerful that only in death could Shylock retain his Jewish identity. His explanation for this production decision, which he said was his, not the director's, recalled the opening dumb show, and brought full circle the relentless highlighting in this performance of the play's anti-Semitism. Rather than live dishonestly and fearfully in a society where 'Christian' jesters steal from children and then threaten them and their parents with knives, Shylock chose death so that, ironically, his Jewish identity might live. Several of my students engaged Scales on this point, asking whether he thought that anti-Semitism was overdone in this production. Scales said he did not agree with that point, explaining that several characters, including Antonio, Launcelot Gobbo, and especially Gratiano express vehement anti-Semitism in the play, and that Shylock's suicide made perfect sense when considered against such prevalent bigotry. Scales also argued, in response to another of my student's questions, that he did not believe that the entire play was anti-Semitic, but rather that it contained several bigoted characters, and he emphasized that the Christian community simply fails to recognize its own prejudice. This "talk-back" thus addressed some critical questions about the play, and hearing an actor address the same questions I had raised in class with excerpts from scholarly essays emphasized that instructors do raise questions in class that are pertinent to performance.

The Harlequin Production's "rock 'n roll" *Twelfth Night* in late spring, 1997 (my spring 1997 class saw two live performances) created a totally different theatrical experience. In director Scot Whitney's time-warped production, Orsino/Elvis met Olivia/Madonna in the Material Girl's heavy-metal disco palace. Whitney's notes explained that Viola and Sebastian, the only characters in Elizabethan dress, were shipwrecked in "Dyleria". A five-piece band, playing "above" as in an Elizabethan theatre and resembling the Beatles' on the cover of *Sergeant Pepper's Lonely Heart's Club Band*, played tunes from Little Richard to Fats Domino to The Beatles and The Rolling Stones, while two scantily dressed young women with 'big hair' belted out the lyrics from on-high stage left. In Whitney's concept, Orsino's opening line, "If music be the food of love, play on", animated the entire show, and thus virtually every scene included characters momentarily 'stepping out' of their role to sing a rock 'n roll song appropriate to their dramatic situation, as if they were auditioning for a regular gig at Olivia's/Madonna's disco. Thus, Toby was a chubby "Blues Brothers" John Belushi; Fabian, in dark suit and simple black tie, Buddy Holly returned from the grave to sing of Peggy Sue; Maria a 60's Grateful Dead hippie in bell-bottom pants and tie-dyed shirt; Sir Andrew Aguecheek a David Bowie look-alike in a corduroy bell-bottom suit and white leather platform shoes; Antonio a 90's punk-rocker in torn red-plaid pants, motorcycle jacket, and spiked red hair; and Feste, a.k.a. John Lennon, sang with a melancholy longing for the simplicity of *All We Need is Love*.

While Whitney's concept seemed clever to my students, they also grasped that this time-warped production also obscured much of the poetry of the play, as well as the emotional tenderness and complexity of many of its scenes, especially between Orsino and Cesario and then Olivia and Cesario. The Viola-Sebastian reunion in act five was also accompanied by song and thus not allowed to stand alone as the "most wonderful" dramatic moment it is in the play. By mid-point of the production, spectators knew that regardless of the scene being played before them, a very loud version of either a rock-'n-roll standard or a song written just for this production was imminent, and my students sensed what can happen when a director's concept simply overwhelms a received script. Because virtually all the moments in this production became occasions for a very loud audition at Madonna's disco, the many different moods of this most complex comedy seemed flattened.

Notwithstanding the above criticism, one feature of Whitney's concept worked superbly, and was greatly appreciated by my students. Malvolio initially appeared in a business suit, white shirt, and classy silk tie, clearly out of place at the disco. After the letter scene, he sang, what else, The Box Tops' *The Letter*, accompanied by Toby, Fabian, and Andrew. Then, once convinced that Olivia loved him, he reappeared as a screaming Alice Cooper freak [9] with a yellow guitar that he pointed sexually at Olivia as he sang a raunchy song called *The Volume of My Love*. Malvolio as Alice Cooper was oh so obviously 'auditioning' at this disco in as radical a transformation as love has ever wrought. Yet in the interrogation scene, this transformation became quite sad; Malvolio's prison was the inside of a huge hollow speaker, with the word "Malvoliater" scrawled across the top. As I noted in my review, the 'volume' of Malvolio's mad love was insufficient to attract the attention of the Material Girl he thought he loved.

Malvolio's final appearance in act five was both funny and startling, and pedagogically quite valuable. Malvolio came onstage physically disheveled and mentally deranged – Alice Cooper after a bad trip – but he knew where he was. He expressed his rage in a mad, violent guitar solo that ended with his biting the strings (ala Jimi Hendrix smashing his guitar) causing an electrical shock and thus his symbolic death. This 'death' ended violently both his mad love and his hopeless ambition, and suggested to my students how a 'concept', in this case for a particular character, can be carried through with some theatrical logic (the failed rock musician/lover driven to disco-madness by his ambition and narcissism) even as the larger concept has seemed to obscure, if not obliterate, much of the dramatic and poetic complexity of Shakespeare's script. My students thus experienced simultaneously in the Harlequin production a brash theatrical approach to one of Shakespeare's most complex plays, some sense of how a concept can overwhelm a play's most subtle features, and also how a concept for one character can 'work' if it is thought through within the director's approach, even if that approach does not necessarily succeed as well with the entire play.

These four productions were unique, and certainly varied in approach and quality, and in these features lies their principal usefulness as teaching aids. These productions were not filmed and thus could never be repeated; my students had to be attentive every moment they were in the theatre, for they could not review the productions again later in the library. While the inability to review particular moments from a live performance prevents one from studying a certain performance choice (i.e, blocking, facial expressions, gestures, etc.), nonetheless students who are exposed to live theatre do experience a play as Shakespeare meant it to be experienced, and the more live theatre students see the better they will appreciate the spontaneity and immediacy of the actor's performance. Further, as I noted above, the exigencies of taking 25-30 students to see a

Merchant of Venice or a *Taming of the Shrew*, as I do for every Shakespeare class, impresses upon my students (and upon me; I keep thinking to myself "This production damn well better be good!") the value of live theatre as a communal cultural experience. I have also noted that at the end of each class, students often write on their evaluations that the trip to Seattle or Portland or even to downtown Olympia was among the most educational and enjoyable experiences of the class, for they generally recognize the connection between the effort involved and the resulting rewards. Such trips also often create a surprising camaraderie among the students, which is nearly impossible in most American community college classes where students' significant age and life-style differences preclude any bonding once the class hour ends.

The four performances I have described above were not nor will ever be known as 'world class' interpretations of Shakespeare's plays. Beyond reviews of them in journals such as *Shakespeare Bulletin*, they have no after-life: they will never be seen again via video versions in classrooms in New York, London, Berlin, Sydney, Istanbul, Mexico City, New Delhi, or Helena, Montana; and the actors my students saw will never have the fame or exposure that the stars of the BBC series or of Trevor Nunn's film versions have. Yet each of these productions, because of their immediacy as live theatre and because of the effort required simply to get to them, taught my students more about Shakespeare as a playwright and about his chosen venue than all the technological gadgetry of the modern classroom could ever do. And while obviously these productions can never benefit students around the world, as John Kari's Othello or Ian McKellen's Macbeth can again and again, I urge my colleagues everywhere to make the kind of effort I describe here to take one's students to live local or regional productions of Shakespeare's plays. The fine moments that one's students often discover in such productions will, I wager, live longer in their memories – and yours – than any computer-assisted combination of wires, buttons, and video cassettes could ever produce.

Notes

1. Kenneth Branagh, "Foreword" to *Walking Shadows*, ed. Luke McKernan and Olwen Terris (London: British Film Institute, 1994), n.p.

2. Two essays that address directly and creatively the use of various media in the Shakespeare classroom are: H. R. Coursen, "Uses of Media in Teaching Shakespeare", in *Teaching Shakespeare into the Twenty-First Century*, ed. Ronald E. Salomone and James E. Davis (Athens: Ohio University Press, 1997), pp. 193-200; and Sharon A. Beehler, " Making Media Matter in the Shakespeare Classroom", pp. 247-54 in the same book.

3. The importance of students' recognizing the 'openness' of a Shakespearean script is clearly articulated by Miriam Gilbert, "Teaching Shakespeare through Performance", *Shakespeare Quarterly*, 35 (Summer, 1984), pp. 602-8.

4. A representative, although not exhaustive, list of books devoted to Shakespeare on film and television includes the following: Roger Manvell, *Shakespeare and the Film* (London: J.M. Dent & Sons, 1971); Jack J. Jorgens, *Shakespeare on Film* (Bloomington, London: Indiana UP, 1977); Stanley Wells, ed., *Shakespeare Survey*, Vol. 39: Shakespeare on Film and Television (Cambridge: Cambridge UP, 1987); J. C. Bulman and H. R. Coursen, ed., *Shakespeare on Television: An Anthology of Essays and Reviews* (Hanover and London: New England UP, 1988); Anthony Davies, *Filming Shakespeare's Plays* (Cambridge: Cambridge UP, 1988); Samuel Crowl, *Shakespeare Observed: Studies in Performance on Stage and Screen* (Athens: Ohio UP, 1992); H. R. Coursen, *Watching Shakespeare on Television* (Rutherford: Fairleigh Dickinson UP, 1993); Anthony Davies and Stanley Wells, ed., *Shakespeare and the Moving Image* (Cambridge: Cambridge UP, 1994); Lynda E. Boose and Richard Burt, ed., *Shakespeare, The Movie* (London & New York: Routledge, 1997); Robert Shaughnessy, ed., *Shakespeare on Film* (New York: St. Martin's Press, 1998).

   Individual essays on teaching film and television versions may also be found in *Teaching Shakespeare into the 21st Century*. There are also informative essays on using film and television performances in the special summer teaching issues of *Shakespeare Quarterly* in 1984, 1990, and 1995. Two books by H. R. Coursen, *Shakespearean Performance as Interpretation* (Newark: Delaware UP, 1992), and *Shakespeare: The Two Traditions* (Madison: Fairleigh Dickinson UP, 1999), examine, like Crowl's *Shakespeare Observed*, both stage and screen productions of the plays. In another recent book, *Reading Shakespeare on Stage* (Newark: Delaware UP, 1995), Coursen includes a superb essay, "Television and Live Performance", in which he strongly argues that television impedes our ability to respond to live performances. Coursen writes: "What television cannot achieve is a sense of 'metadrama', that is, the invitation from the world of the play to enter it and participate in the creation of illusions that becomes powerfully real in the emotional and imaginative sense" (pp. 29-30).

5. I mention the *BBC Shakespeare* simply because that series is everywhere, and everywhere advertised; I still receive flyers in the mail offering 40% discounts if I buy four or more of the plays, and one free if I buy at least six. Those productions, for better or worse, are arguably the most watched of Shakespeare's plays in history, may be the only versions which many students ever see, and thus may become the 'standard' interpretation for thousands of students world wide.

6. In "Teaching Shakespeare in America", *Shakespeare Quarterly*, 35:5 (1984), pp. 541-59, Charles Frey argues elegantly against an approach to teaching Shakespeare in which the instructor seeks "authority and ownership" of the text. Frye describes such an approach as inappropriate to "student-centered teaching" (553). In "'So Quick Bright Things Come to Confusion': Teaching Shakespeare in the Heterogeneous Classroom", in Salomone and Davis, pp. 139-47, I attempt to extend Frye's idea of the "student-centered classroom" to teaching Shakespeare in a multi-cultural, highly varied community college classroom with students ranging in age from 18 to 60. Using a film version of a play which one has seen and

It's Shakespeare Tonight! 311

evaluated before gives the instructor considerable power to influence how students will 'see' that film version, even if one is using a film version because one wants students to experience a production fresh. Stephen M. Buhler, in "Text, Eyes, and Videotape: Screening Shakespeare Scripts", *Shakespeare Quarterly*, 46 (Summer, 1995), pp. 236-44, explains convincingly the pedagogical advantages of comparing different film versions of a Shakespearean play (*Henry V*), yet cautions that "a little learning about a given production can be a limiting thing, since we may ascribe to the production a controlling theme that becomes our own 'definitive' reading of this particular interpretation" (p. 237). When one takes one's students to a live performance that neither instructor nor students have seen before, authoritative interpretations are foreclosed. The Shakespearean script becomes completely 'open' for both instructor and students because the 'playing field' (i.e., the stage) is level for all.

7   The productions discussed, and the dates of my reviews of them, are as follows:

The Taming of the Shrew, Tygres Heart Shakespeare Company, Portland. September 30-November 7, 1999. Reviewed in *Shakespeare Bulletin*, 17:4 (1999), pp. 37-8.

The Taming of the Shrew, Intiman Theatre Company, Seattle. May 21-June 15, 1997. Reviewed in *Shakespeare Bulletin*, 15:3 (1997), pp. 25-6.

The Merchant of Venice, Tygres Heart Shakespeare Company, Portland. April 15-May 24, 1998. Reviewed in *Shakespeare Bulletin*, 16:3 (1998), pp. 22-3.

Twelfth Night, Harlequin Productions, Olympia. June 5-July 5, 1997. Reviewed in *Shakespeare Bulletin*, 15:3 (1997), pp. 27-8.

8   As I wrote in my review, "This initial theft not only anticipated the later theft of Shylock's daughter and his ducats, but also signaled the relentless contempt with which the Christians treated the Jews." *Shakespeare Bulletin* 16:3, p. 22.

9   Malvolio appeared with "long tangled hair, huge eyelashes, flaming yellow spandex pants and shirt covered with yellow streamers and sequins, a red and yellow cape, [and] pointed yellow shoes". *Shakespeare Bulletin* 15:3, p. 28.

SHAKESPEARE AND THE CONSTRUCTION OF CHARACTER

Laurie Osborne
(Colby College, Waterville)

I cannot think it a good use of time to put pupils to the study of Shakespeare at all, until they have got strength and ripeness of mind enough to enter, at least in some fair measure, into the transpirations of character in his persons. For this is indeed the Shakespeare of Shakespeare. And the process is as far as you can think from being a mere formal or mechanical or routine handling of words and phrases and figures of speech: it is nothing less than to hear and to see the hearts and souls of the persons in what they say and do; to feel, as it were, the very pulse-throbs of their inner life. Herein it is that Shakespeare's unapproached and unaproachable [sic] mastery of human nature lies.[1]

In the late nineteenth century, Henry Hudson lays out the importance of character as part of the "eminent" learning of Shakespeare which he seeks to advocate above the rote memorization in place at that time. Hudson is reacting against the kind of pedagogy reflected in the editing of Victorian school editions which present Shakespeare's plays as "a quarry for information, as a repository of brain-teasing points of grammar and philology, and so as the basis for exercises in deduction".[2]

Condemning such excavation as "a continual process of alternate crammings and disgorgings" (p. xxii), Hudson envisions gender-specific disaster as a result: "if the thing is not spoiling the boys, it is at all events killing the girls" (p. xxiii). Like Mary and Charles Lamb earlier in the century, Hudson envisions the female reader as particularly in need of a careful, long-term introduction to Shakespeare.[3] According to Hudson, although the practices current in his time seem to make girls "preternaturally bright and interesting for a while", such blossoming is premature, "so, when the proper time arrives for them to be in the full bloom of womanhood, leaf, blossom and all are gone, leaving them faded and withered and joyless; and chronic ill health, premature old age, untimely death are their lot and portion" (p. xxiii). This litany of ills culminates in his prediction that Massachusetts "will in no very long time come to be almost one continuous hospital of lunatics" (p. xxiv).

Coded into this dissection of nineteenth-century pedagogical practice alongside its assumptions about gender is the argument that teaching Shakespeare through absorption and testing is designed to train students as Shakespeare scholars; this goal is folly since "of the students in our colleges not one in a thousand, of the pupils in our high schools not one in a hundred thousand, can think, or ought to think, of becoming Shakespearians" (p. viii). There is more going on here than a protection of academic monopoly in his plea that "teaching should be shaped to the end, not of making the pupils Shakespearians, but only of doing somewhat – it cannot be much – towards making them wiser, better, happier men and women"(p. viii). Hudson asserts that "the most and the best that we can hope to do is to plant in the pupils, and to nurse up as far as may be, a genuine taste and love for Shakespeare's poetry"(p. ix). Although Hudson envisions this taste as "a prolific germ of wholesome and improving study" which "will naturally proceed till, in time it comes to act as a strong elective instinct, causing the mind to gravitate toward what is good, and to recoil from what is bad" (p. ix), it cannot be acquired through the existing methods of teaching but can only derive from learning in "the eminent sense" which requires an investment in Shakespeare's poetry which in turn (as my opening quotation suggests) depends upon the student's "entrance" into Shakespearean character.

Hudson's vision of character as "the hearts and souls of the persons in what they say and do" combined with the organic metaphor of slow-growing, utterly internalized knowledge positions Shakespeare and his characters as the internal regulators of what is good and what is bad as well as the subliminal key to wisdom, virtue, and happiness. The naturalizing language of "planting", "germ" and "blossoming/withering" matches the "ripeness" of the young minds dealing with Shakespeare's characters and the "pulse-throbs" which those characters are envisioned as possessing. So insistent and so opposed to the "mechanical" rote memorization, this language embeds the repressive ideologies of gender and class hierarchies "naturally" within both the "ripe" students and the "throbbing" characters.

Even a cursory reading of Hudson's pedagogical analysis reveals its ideological imperatives, as no doubt our discussions reveal ours. Certainly we face some of the same issues: students who are not and will not become Shakespeareans, concerns about the methods and usefulness of evaluation, and, most important, the large question of what purpose learning about Shakespeare's plays will serve for our students. "Why teach Shakespeare now?" seems the most important question with "how?" running a close second. I cannot answer either as fully as I would like, but I teach his plays because I find it pleasurable to struggle with them and hope to share the struggle as well as the pleasure with my students. However, unlike Hudson, I am very suspicious of any claim that enjoying Shakespeare can function as an internal moral regulator of good and evil. I am even less certain that his texts can or should be internalized in the ways Hudson describes. What Shakespeare's plays allow, under a culturally sanctioned brand name, is an interrogation of the history of already internalized categories, an examination of what literature can do over time. And so, to paraphrase Foucault, I teach Shakespeare in some courses to ask a question: what is a character?[4]

> "In fact, 'character' is the servant of a certain order that parades itself across the theater of writing."[5]

Helene Cixous's comment clearly applies to Henry Hudson's "theater of writing". When she interrogated the term 'character' twenty years ago, Cixous suggested that character had been endowed with the psychic energies and projections of its receivers. As Cixous notes, literary characters are not, in their purely linguistic existence, full, complete, psychologized persons. They cannot have depth; their shape, their vitality, derives from an historical moment which gives them context and from the energies of readers who project their own imaginary fullness onto a linguistic trick. Even though Shakespearean characters self-evidently have a life which is not purely language during performances, critiques like Cixous's reached rapidly into Shakespearean studies. Since the seventies, critical strategies based in Jacques Lacan and Louis Althusser have led inexorably to the identification of character as the pale and insubstantial sister of subjectivity, which is itself vastly more important yet almost equally fictional in our so-called lives.

Thus Shakespearean character, like God and the author, died. As Joseph Porter points out, the term all but disappears from the *Shakespeare Quarterly* bibliography in the eighties and nineties even while individual personages from the plays maintain their position in the critical line-up.[6] His analysis ultimately suggests that discussing Shakespearean character is irreducibly political. This position is born out by the new character critics, though sometimes in very different ways. On the one hand, Alan Sinfield somewhat grudgingly concedes that "some Shakespearean *dramatis personae* are written so as to suggest, not just an intermittent, gestural, and problematic subjectivity [sic], but a continuous or developing interiority or consciousness; and we should seek a way of talking about this that does not slide back into character criticism or essentialist humanism".[7] His method of resisting the "slide back" into character criticism is to require that we read Shakespearean character as "situated at the intersection of discourses and historical forces that are competing, we might say, to fill up [their] subjectivity" (p. 63). In taking into account such Early Modern discourses, Katharine Eisaman Maus argues that the sheer persistence of the trope of interiority in those discourses means that we must rethink our ban on character's interior selves.[8] To put in another way, we should allow Shakespearean character "that within which passes show" as a construct which recurs throughout Early Modern texts.

All three critics – Porter, Sinfield, and Maus – offer fuller accounts of the history and current controversies about character in Shakespeare studies than I intend to explore here. My principal concern is how to teach Shakespearean character. In my experience, doing so can become a headlong collision between the nineteenth-century and the twentieth-century, between the fervent acceptance of Shakespeare's genius, particularly in rendering his characters as character-building for the reader, and skeptically resistant readings of the politics of producing both Shakespearean and student characters. It often seems to me that students embrace the nineteenth century while I try to introduce the twentieth. For example, even when I explicitly point out how Thomas Whateley is using his comparison of Richard III and Macbeth as much in order to evade criticisms of Shakespeare's plot structures as to validate character, some students inevitably get caught on the advancement of Shakespeare's "peculiar genius" for creating character and write essays which hail the perfection of this or that character.[9] On the surface, this kind of encounter seems to establish me comfortably in the current, better informed, and progressive position, bringing ideological light to the masses. However, the situation is immeasurably complicated because I see both positions, nineteenth and twentieth-century, as comparably valid and potentially connected. Only the historical context and nature of the ideological imperatives have shifted. We continue, as nineteenth-century critics did, claiming to write about character in Shakespeare when we are actually writing our version of identity. Our ideas about character are just as constituted and fragmented by the competing current discourses and ideologies that allow us to make sense of our selves for ourselves.

We can now readily perceive how nineteenth-century ideologies inform and enforce Victorian readings of Shakespeare's female characters, prehistories of characters and revealing comparisons between them. And, of course, discussions of teaching like Henry Hudson's are particularly transparent. However, such agendas accompanied and even motivated the incorporation of Shakespeare into the curriculum. From the model for regularized grammar and memorization skills to the inspiration which can build students' characters, Shakespeare's plays have become part of educational as well as theatrical performance. Moreover, just because we now see earlier partisan uses of Shakespeare as embarrassingly blatant does not mean that we sufficiently perceive our own. Assumptions about character in the moral sense continue to motivate teaching, especially in explorations of historical differences marked in potentially sexist, racist, or homophobic characterizations in Shakespeare's texts. To paraphrase Cixous, Shakespearean character continues to serve an order which parades itself across the theatre of pedagogy.

Nor does this display go unnoticed and unchallenged. Our critical binary is alive and well. We can endlessly uncover the ideologically and professionally validated marginal identities in the plays and biased flaws in earlier readings. Or we can complain and explode the folly of invested current readings. We have Terry Hawkes and we have Richard Levin.[10] And we are undoubtedly destined to look as imbedded in our ideologies as earlier critics look to us, even after ninety percent of the astonishingly vast recent critical output has melted away like last night's dew burnt off the landscape by today's sun. As a recent graduate of the great American tenure machine and someone who is trying in some small way to work on historicism in its broadest sense, I find myself almost incapable of saying that the nineteenth-century critics are simply wrong – they are as right for their context as we are for ours. More important, their assumptions about Shakespeare are often still current in the biases of our students.

There is a fascinating disjunction between our students' investment in the idealized individual Shakespeare, as offered by the Romantics and the Victorians, and current critical investment in the fragmented self that Shakespeare's plays also seems to support. This difference arises because our approach to Shakespeare differs so radically from our students' view, founded in Shakespeare's manifest cultural currency in film and media. As critics, we often wrestle with historical differences, trying to acknowledge that the plays "mean" far differently now than they did in the sixteenth and seventeenth centuries. Moreover, as part of the twentieth-century education business, we enter an intellectual competition for new, difficult ideas, the most difficult of which challenge our own sense of a unified self; at the same time, job changes, tenure decisions, and most important an increasingly peripatetic adjunct professoriat amply prove how disjointed our own lives are. Moreover, the splintering of geographically continuous family identities and erosion of permanent career choices are not just professional experiences for academic faculty; these social changes extend throughout the future working lives of our students.

Our imperative to revisit character and explore its fragmentation is consequently an advantage since our students are just as likely to face competing professional and personal demands. However, when students first encounter Shakespeare in college classes, they are often most concerned with establishing a coherent persona – choosing a major, grooming an effective (i.e. coherent) vita, and deciding what they want from their education. As many students seek to manufacture distinctive selves at the demand of college curricula and future employers, Shakespeare and his characters, four hundred years old and going strong, can seem the epitome of a desirable stable continuity. As a result, while many students wholly embrace the core idea of Shakespeare's genius as well as the wholeness and continuity of character they want to see in his plays, I struggle to display how completely inflected character has become in Shakespeare studies.

This essay traces some strategies for opening up the idea of character, most particularly exploring and testing student investment in coherence and continuity in character. To this end, early textual variations, the critical history of character as a category and even current films serve as my means of exploring how character becomes a significant measure of Shakespeare's influence. My goal is two-fold: to develop my students' critical assessments (and, I hope, their writing) about how character functions and to explore the current renewed interest in character expressed by Maus, Sinfield and others. In my teaching I use many recent Shakespearean films – *Hamlet, Romeo and Juliet, Twelfth Night* and especially *Looking for Richard* – as both symptoms of renewed interest in Shakespearean character and useful arenas for interrogating our (re)constructions of it.

> I will believe thou hast a mind that suits
> With this, thy fair and outward character.[11]

Character initially seems to my students to be the interior self which drives them into action. This "outward character", the exterior which may or may not represent an interior show, thus comes as a bit of a shock. After all, "character" connotes identity and distinctiveness, both crucial to the emergent adults whom we teach. It also offers a reassuringly monolithic literariness: all veterans of high school English courses know about well-rounded characters and stereotypes. As a result, character is even more comfortable than identity, as familiar and stable as the author. The pedagogical challenge becomes how to exploit the appeal of Shakespearean character while helping students to interrogate the concept, to envision character in ways which sometimes run completely opposite to their ideas.

Like the author, so famously revealed by Foucault as historical and contingent, character is altogether too self-evident for most students. The best way I have found to rework and challenge the canonical solidity of Shakespearean character is to embrace an historicism which uses and goes beyond twentieth-century analyses of Early Modern performances as relational and the word "character" as ascribed to Early Modern writing. Recent readings explain the discontinuities of Shakespearean character through such seventeenth-century models of character; however, this strategy only represents the latest way Shakespearean character has commanded attention over the last four hundred years. Inevitably, we have vested interests in the seventeenth-century models that we uncover and embrace. My courses on Shakespearean character seek to examine the category through the histories of Shakespearean characters – along the model of Elaine Showalter's work with the history of Ophelia.[12] This seems to me the most visceral and best way to incorporate into my teaching the increasingly complex views of character which have emerged recently.

Whereas critics in the early twentieth century discarded character in favor of poetic and symbolic language, our more recent approaches have challenged character criticism on historicist and textual grounds. When students use current criticism as the window on past views of character, they discover a valuable unsettling of unified character in light of variant texts and terminology. The evaluations of crucial differences in characters as they appear in variant early texts ultimately challenge any character's singularity. Quite obviously if there are several distinct early texts, subtly different staged identities emerge. This argument underpins crucial collections like *The Division of the Kingdoms* which records a series of challenges to character in *Lear*. In the wake of *Division*, critics have taken up a number of early texts. When Stephen Urkowitz offers "Five Women Eleven Ways", singularity in those roles undergoes obvious erasure.[13] Students are often eager to take up the task of analyzing the alternative behavior and lines of characters who appear differently in the Quarto texts: Margaret in *Richard III*, Gertrude and Horatio in *Hamlet*, Albany and Cordelia in *Lear*. However, their readings, even when they differ from Urkowitz's or the *Division* essays, still assume a coherent character within a given early text, therefore enabling students to construct character as coherence – just multiple coherences.

Randall McLeod's reading of variable speech headings within single texts is a useful corrective, offering a reading of Shakespearean roles as constructed relationally through stage groupings.[14] Along with a variety of observations about Early Modern texts, MacLeod uses the shifting speech headings applied to the Countess in *All's Well that Ends Well* in order to show how her function in Act 1, Scene 2 varies with the entrances of different characters. His insight is useful in less obvious textual circumstances. For example, in *Twelfth Night*, Orsino's variable titles of Duke and Count as well as the considerable delay in giving the name "Viola" to the character identified as Sebastian's twin sister and self-identified as Cesario raises issues about characters and their distinctive identities. In *Henry IV, part 1*, the mind-bending array of personal names for everyone opens up still more elaborate possibilities for relational characterization, especially given the crucial significance of naming and renaming in *Richard II*. Consider not only Prince Hal, also known as Harry Monmouth, the Prince of Wales, the heir apparent, etc., but also Falstaff, identified as Oldcastle in speech headings. The variations within these texts not only move students beyond Shakespeare's total genius but also yield contrasting uses of persons staged within the plays.

In the face of the textual traces that MacLeod analyzes, it becomes tempting to consider stage groupings rather than individuals in order to explore apparent discontinuities in character. We could read the shifting misogyny of *As You Like It*'s doubly named heroine, Rosalind/Ganymede, as the register of how her character is constructed through context, be it the company of her female cousin, the presence of her besotted beloved, or the presence of the stereotypical shepherd and shepherdess. With such an approach, students can see an alternative to psychologized readings of Rosalind training her beloved in romantic realism. Or perhaps Portia's unexpected legal expertise in the stage space of Venice in contrast with her more submissive graciousness as a hostess in Belmont could be read not just as the result of the cross-dressing her character undergoes but as a function of stage groupings – as the epistolary presence of Antonio and his legal problems with Shylock give way to his physical presence and demands on Portia's husband in the trial scene. In this kind of reading, social and theatrical contexts mark character as potentially multiple rather than obviously unified.

Allied to these variations in characters registered in the Folio and Quarto scripts is recent work from critics like Jonathan Goldberg on inscription as the mark of "character". Embracing a deconstructive approach which announces its twentieth-century position, Goldberg nonetheless draws undergraduates into a more careful consideration of what the term "character" actually could have meant in the Early Modern period.[15] He emphasizes the significance of writing to plays wherein fathers believe daughters "are but as a form in wax/By him imprinted and within his power/To leave the figure or disfigure it" (*A Midsummer Night's Dream* 1.1.48-52) and sons are bid "these few precepts in thy memory/Look thou character" (*Hamlet* 1.3.58-59). The impress of the father's name, the power of exterior image and status to Early Modern characters foregrounds writing, even if writing were not constantly configured as the model for memory and identity.

Moreover, Goldberg suggests that "character" referred to in the Early Modern texts on handwriting encodes both individuality and conformity (p. 323). The practice of copying handwriting models, of writing clean, conformable script, actually blurs identity. As Hamlet celebrates his ability to turn his practice of handwriting in the deceptive penning of Claudius's order, Maria's trick in *Twelfth Night* turns upon the fact that, as Olivia notes at the end of the play, "Alas, Malvolio, it is not my writing/ Though I confess, much like the character" (5.1.344-45). Even the distinctiveness of a handwritten early copy of Shakespeare's text would not anchor unified, distinctive identity, either in Shakespeare or in his characters.

These recoveries of early textual and linguistic traces open issues of character construction which relate to Alan Sinfield's recent arguments. His explorations of "character effects" and "gestural continuity" ultimately insist on the ideological fissures which render characters – especially female characters – discontinuous. In one chapter, Sinfield concentrates on Shakespeare's female characters – Lady Macbeth, Desdemona, Olivia – in order to show the ways in which these characters in particular reveal ideological disruptions. They fall silent, he notes, when their ideological purposes have been exhausted. Students, predictably, often oppose this pessimistic reading with a celebration of the female characters reminiscent of Anna Jameson's nineteenth-century essays insisting on the value of Shakespeare's women.[16]

For example, my class was quite emphatic in resisting Sinfield's reading of Olivia. He notes that, "Like Desdemona and Lady Macbeth, Olivia capitulates; and the break in presentation is negotiated by silence and, all too often, the assumption that Olivia's subjection to a 'real man' is only right and proper" (p. 72). However her subjection seems less than complete given her behavior in the final scene. My students, at least, were inclined to argue that when Olivia offers to house the wedding celebration "At my house and my proper cost"(*TN* 5.1.308), she effectively keeps control of the fortune she has presumably ceded to Sebastian. They noted her lengthy discourse with Malvolio in adjudicating his complaint as further evidence that she is not silenced.

As a class we raised the additional issue of how male characters might also be equally vulnerable to the kinds of discontinuity which Sinfield seems to be examining. One provocative example of male discontinuity we found was Lord Capulet in *Romeo and Juliet*, whose complete about-face in his treatment of and concern for his daughter proves extreme enough to precipitate Juliet's false suicide and the tragedy that ensues. Juliet's father proved a very interesting test case.[17] About half the class offered intratextual explanations which demonstrated that his behavior could be construed as consistent: he is mild only when he getting his way, he is only irrational in his concern for his obsessively grieving daughter, he exercises excessive control because the death of his kinsman has set the world out of his control, and, most politically, he is desperate for a marriage which will ally his family with the Prince's and thus alleviate any blame that might accrue from Tybalt's killing of Mercutio. These reasons justify Capulet's shift from delaying the marriage to forcing it on Juliet; however, as the other half of the class pointed out, none of these plausible motivations truly explains why he forces the marriage so very quickly, in three days in fact. One student even raised the

Shakespeare and the Construction of Character

question of the mourning period for Tybalt; after all, even Claudius in Hamlet apparently waited two months before his excessively speedy wedding to Gertrude.

Acknowledging their own need to make sense of his behavior, others in the class turned to extratextual possibilities in order to justify rather than dissolve his discontinuities: his anger is required by the necessities of plot or his enraged rejection of his daughter is merely one paternal stereotype among several which Lord Capulet adopts (the Sinfield reading). Still others suggested that the coherence of his character could be attributed to any of the "internal" reasons offered by the other half of the class, but only performance choices in excess of the text could produce that continuity. The debate over this particular character brought to the forefront of our analysis the impulse to perceive or construct continuity, an impulse which is itself, according to Sinfield, ideological in foundation.

Such discussions mark the beginning of involvement with the larger issues of character. The radical disjunctions we read in the sixteenth and seventeenth-century characters point to the more significant problem of how we conceive character and how we imagine character as conceived in times other than our own. Even while current critical perspectives open up Shakespearean characters and suggest ways of understanding character that resist equating the term with distinct, autonomous identity, they are contemporary readings, often poststructuralist in their awareness of significant discontinuities in Early Modern characters. True, these approaches resist the totalizing efforts to psychologize Shakespearean speakers, efforts which function as the alternate twentieth-century model for reading character. However, such readings still depend on currently validated readings of past characterization which often elide the development of character as character as well as the changing ideological purposes which draw attention to some characters over others.

Without a genuinely historical context for these twentieth-century assessments of how character works, we merely embrace current readings of "Renaissance character", and we may fail to understand how thoroughly even those readings are ideological. Several eighteenth and nineteenth-century critics can help create crucial perspectives on the purposes of character analysis. Morgann's celebration of Sir John Falstaff also argues for character as a significant critical category.[18] Thomas Whateley's "Essay on Richard III and Macbeth" presents the "single predominant principle" organizing character (pp. 22-23) and the creation of the distinctive differences between the two tyrants as the measure of Shakespeare's genius. In response to Whateley, John Philip Kemble argues for the moral efficacy involved in audience identification with such characters as Shakespeare's truly valuable contribution to characterization.[19] More obviously invested readings are equally useful, especially Anna Jameson's *Some Characteristics of Women* and more shockingly Mary Cowden Clarke's *Girlhood of Shakespeare's Heroines*.[20] Their involvement with Shakespeare's female characters helps to emphasize our own increased attention to them. Sinfield's arguments, for example, revise the earlier analyses to explore Shakespeare's female characters through the failures of their coherence rather than the nineteenth-century efforts to show their value as objects of study.[21] Teasing out the agendas associated with these proto-feminist texts is somewhat more straightforward than, for example, exploring why Charles Cowden Clarke chooses to write on *Shakespeare-Characters: Chiefly Those Subordinate*.[22] Clarke's writings, however, do emphasize the hierarchies applied to character and, in light of current readings, how those hierarchies shift. Different Shakespearean characters seem most important at different times.

However, even prefaced with as useful a guide as Brian Vickers's work on the emergence of character criticism, the sheer quantity of eighteenth and nineteenth-century character criticism can prove more than a semester or an undergraduate could tolerate.[23] The variorum editions, examined for character's roles, offer a useful, focused layering of critical readings, but the excavation involved can prove difficult as can distinguishing between the particular voices recorded and superceded within its notes. Nonetheless, I am unwilling to sacrifice the broader historicism I want students to bring to bear on character. My solution to this dilemma is inspired equally by my colleague Elizabeth Sagaser and by Elaine Showalter.

Shakespeare and the Construction of Character

> I would like to propose that instead Ophelia does have a story of her own that feminist criticism can tell; it is neither her life story, nor her love story, nor Lacan's story, but rather the history of her representation.
> (Showalter, p. 79)

Taking Showalter's history of Ophelias as a model, students readily see that characters have histories beyond the confines of their careers within the plays. With very little urging they also realize that the feminist agenda is not the only one which can be served by exploring those histories: they offer access to histories of the concept of character. Students participate in these histories by constructing a character chronology, like the chronologies that students create in my colleague Elizabeth Sagaser's Renaissance poetry classes by setting major literary figures and events in the contexts of the histories associated with their own interests in music, golf, beer or fashion. The character chronology requires that they choose a personage from the plays we have read and track down his or her critical, theatrical and artistic incarnations – including silences and absences if necessary – through the four centuries which mark the evolution of character we are studying. This assignment appeals greatly to students still cherishing the uniqueness of Shakespearean character; they plan to prove the valuable, enduring unity of their characters. However, the chronology they develop soon reveals radical shifts in the treatment of ostensibly unified and distinctive characters as critics, artists and performers make sense of that character based on their society's assumptions.

The students' choice of characters often proves as revealing as the chronologies that they produce. Two of the most interesting chronologies that I have received addressed Rosaline in *Romeo and Juliet*, a character who is little more than a name at the beginning of the play but who has a varied textual and theatrical life. The students who chose to work on Romeo, Juliet, or Rosaline greeted with varying degrees of bemusement the debates on whether Rosaline's presence in the play diminished his love for Juliet and with outright amazement the revisions in the Garrick text's ending which dominated the stage for so long.[24] Although we had discussed Garrick's influential revision in class and reviewed several film versions, they were taken aback to realize that some of the theatrical critics who had seen only Garrick's version were not praising the play that they knew.

In general, the chronologies based on female characters challenged the assumptions that the class brought to those characters in a feminist era.[25] The student who worked on Mistress Ford ended up tracing the degree to which the wives were distinguished from each other or merely allied as "wives" through successive centuries. Her chagrin at the critical neglect of these title characters matched the dismay of students who examined Portia's extratextual history when they discovered that critics all but dismiss her energies and talents.

Several fascinating papers grew from this chronology assignment. One analysis of *The Merchant of Venice* extended a critical argument that Shylock's characterization on stage developed with emergence of capitalism; another argued that the play constructs the Jewish faith as the scapegoat for Shylock's unacceptable behavior. Inspired by her chronology of Rosaline, one student offered a very persuasive essay arguing that Rosaline is crucial to Romeo's genuine love for Juliet and in fact that Romeo's early interest in Rosaline offers a gendered parallel to Juliet's involvement with Paris. There were also a couple of provocative treatments of *The Merry Wives of Windsor* which analyzed how the issues of class vary through the centuries.[26]

In addition to placing specific characters in the context of their extratextual histories, the chronologies also set the current film versions as part of an historical spectrum of possibilities. To give just one example, Kenneth Branagh's production of *Hamlet* extends the scope of Showalter's analysis by re-creating Ophelia's significance in the representation of madness. With the nineteenth-century set and costumes comes the treatment of Ophelia's insanity: when mad, she first appears with her hair confined in white hospital-style helmet and completely bound in what appears to be a full-body straight jacket. Characterized in the screenplay as a "wriggling wreck", Ophelia makes the confinement of her attire very apparent.[27] After her song to Laertes, she also undergoes a thorough hosing down after which she produces from her mouth the key which enables her escape and watery death, only shown in a brief cut to "the drowned OPHELIA as she lies under the surface of the water. A beautiful, ghostly corpse" (Branagh, p. 141). These details present the brutality of Edwardian treatments for insanity and eschew the characteristic flower-bedecked Ophelia's of early productions up to Olivier's.[28] As Russell Jackson explains it in his film diary: "she is being treated with a mixture of shock treatment (using water) and fairly brutal confinement, partly in accordance with some nineteenth-century notions of how to deal with the insane, but also because she is a political threat that has to be contained" (Branagh, p. 180). Moreover, Branagh's Ophelia, unlike earlier ones, has consummated her relationship with Hamlet so that her sexuality becomes a vivid part of her madness.

Because its extensive film editing combines with a complete text, Branagh's *Hamlet* reveals to students the growing significance of the film cut as the twentieth-century cinematic convention for conveying and sustaining character. They begin to recognize how film editing creates character and perceive the constructedness of a character's coherence once they examine recent films closely in the context of the playtexts – *Romeo and Juliet*, *Twelfth Night*, *Othello*, and especially *Looking for Richard*..

Al Pacino's *Looking for Richard* offers students simultaneously the most elaborately discontinuous twentieth-century reading of character and the clearest quest for coherence. Fragmentation is its mode, both in the documentary-style of the film and in its exploration of Richard's character against the backdrop of rehearsal, snippets of Shakespeareana, and, most notably, Al Pacino's commentary on the action. The work on the play is laced with the deflating commentary of well-known actors who have played Shakespeare yet did not like him in school – Kevin Kline and Kenneth Branagh – and Richard's wooing of Anne is prefaced with a director raging at Pacino that Pacino himself knows more about the play than any dusty academic. The jaundiced perspective offered on academic Shakespeare is set deliberately against the vivid power of the scenes from the play itself. Yet even those sequences build character through the powerful editing strategies of film. Pacino, in looking for Richard, enacts for students a version of their own quest throughout the semester for Shakespearean character. And his film produces fragments of Richard in response.

These excursions into film and film editing often prove to students not only that character discontinuity is in the eye of the beholder but also that our ways of reading coherence in fact may depend on discontinuity and even fragmentation. As Lorne Buchman has suggested, the film audience dynamically participates in filling the gaps of film.[29] Film editing, set in the context of the textual changes of earlier productions and of the Early Modern textual and linguistic features affecting the plays, reveals dramatically how producing coherence in Shakespearean character has always depended on updating rather than eliminating discontinuities in character. With these examples in front of them, students begin to recognize that producing the appearance of continuity is an illusion in which they participate, often without realizing the interplay of fragments and their own willingness to assume a whole character. Cinema, carefully examined, offers students and teachers a workshop for understanding the interaction between our commitment to character as coherent unity and our experience of twentieth-century characters and selves as fragmented, provisional, and improvisational. Fragments of texts, scenes, motivations are writ large in Shakespearean film but still call forth critical responses based in assumptions that Shakespeare's characters particularly have stable identities – witness Pacino looking so earnestly for Richard, as if he were a single, discoverable individual.

As Alan Sinfield so cogently points out, our ability to read character as unified and persuasively coherent reflects our investment in the presumably obsolescent ideologies those characters continue to represent: our willingness to read Desdemona as continuous, for example, reveals the ongoing effects of a set of ideological stereotypes of women. More generally, we seek and produce continuities throughout the Shakespearean families of characters, often willing to ignore especially so-called minor characters whose motivations waver or collapse. Very likely even using the category of character, as I have done, ratifies an unavoidable investment in coherence which persists despite critical "advances" and demonstrable disjointedness in twentieth-century lives and jobs.

Equally, I would add, the discontinuities that we uncover and explain underscore emergent ideologies which we currently seek to embrace as truth. The conjunction of current film and criticism underscores our particular interests in discontinuities of character, in the distance between Early Modern ways of understanding what character might be and our own. Ironically, I find, like Hudson, that our study of Shakespearean character – criss-crossed by ideological disruptions and reworked for contemporary coherence – does lend some insight into contemporary character and its disruptions. The "transpirations of character" that Hudson affirms have their mirror in the discontinuities of characters in cinematic representations which we create, read, and make coherent. Once again the mechanical exists in tension with the organic, the device of the film cut in tension with the dynamic response of a creative audience. The multiple fragments of texts, revealed in both current criticism and current cinematic performance, acknowledge and represent our discontinuity with the past – and we continue to overcome that difference through our negotiations with character and with identity.

Notes

1. Henry Hudson, "How to Use Shakespeare in School", in *Essays on Education, English Studies and Shakespeare* (Boston: Ginn, Heath, & Co, 1882), p. xiii. All further references appear within the text of the essay.

2. Russell Jackson, "Victorian Editors of *As You Like It*", in *The Theory and Practice of Textual-editing: Essays in Honour of James T. Boulton*, ed. Ian Small and Marcus Walsh (Cambridge: Cambridge UP, 1991), p. 147. Jackson points out how thoroughly the editing practices of the late nineteenth-century school texts reveal the purposes to which Shakespeare's plays were being put in schools and links this editing to the bowdlerized texts which make Shakespeare's plays acceptable to female audiences in particular.

3. See the Introduction to Charles and Mary Lamb, *Tales from Shakespeare* (New York: Weathervane Books, 1975), in which the authors assert that "for young ladies, too, it has been the intention chiefly to write" (p. viii). They go on to suggest that young women, who have less access to their fathers' libraries than do their brothers, can be gradually introduced to Shakespeare's marvels through these tales.

4. Michel Foucault, "What is an Author?", in *Memory, Counter-Memory and Practice: Selected Essays and Interviews*, ed. and transl. Donald Bouchard (Ithaca, NY: Cornell UP, 1977), pp. 113-139.

5. Helene Cixous, "The Character of 'Character'", *New Literary History*, 5 (Winter 1974), p. 385.

6. Joseph Porter, "Character and Ideology", in *Shakespeare: Left and Right*, ed. Ivo Kamps (New York: Routledge, 1993), pp. 131-33.

7   Alan Sinfield, "When is a Character Not a Character?: Desdemona, Olivia, Lady Macbeth, and Subjectivity", in *Faultlines: Cultural Materialism and the Politics of Dissident Reading* (Berkeley: California UP, 1992), p. 62.

8   Katharine Eisaman Maus, *Inwardness and Theater in the English Renaissance* (Chicago: Chicago UP, 1995).

9   Thomas Whateley, *Remarks on Some of the Characters of Shakspeare*, 3rd. edn. rev. Richard Whateley (London: B. Fellows, 1839).

10 The collection in which Porter's essay appears, Ivo Kamps's *Shakespeare: Left and Right* (New York: Routledge, 1993), exemplifies these alternate views.

11 William Shakespeare, *Twelfth Night* 1.2.50-1. All further allusions to Shakespeare's plays will appear in the body of the essay and refer to The Norton Shakespeare, ed. Stephen Greenblatt et. al. (New York: W.W. Norton, 1997).

12 Elaine Showalter, "Representing Ophelia: Madness in the Nineteenth Century", in *Shakespeare and the Question of Theory*. Geoffrrey Hartman and Patricia Parker (Chicago: Chicago UP, 1990), pp. 77-94.

13 Stephen Urkowitz, "Five Women Eleven Ways: Changing Images of Shakespearean Characters in the Earliest Texts", in *Images of Shakespeare: Proceedings of the Third Congress of the International Shakespeare Association* (Newark: Delaware UP, 1988), pp. 292-304.

14 Random Cloud (Randall McLeod), "'The Very names of the Persons': Editing and the Invention of Character", in *Staging the Renaissance: Reinterpretations of Elizabethan and Jacobean Drama*, ed. David Scott Kastan and Peter Stallybrass (New York: Routledge, 1991), pp. 88-98.

15 Jonathan Goldberg, "Hamlet's Hand", *SQ*, 39 (Fall 1988), pp. 307-27.

16 Anna Jameson, *Characteristics of Women, Moral, Poetical, and Historical* (New York: John Wiley, 1850).

17 We also discussed Hamlet in these terms, but his madness, whether feigned or actual, provides a logic to his discontinuity. Moreover, as critics like Maus and Goldberg have suggested, Hamlet's role is so excessive that the surplus of characterization offered for him poses one of the greatest problems in pinning down character.

18 Maurice Morgann, *Shakespearian Criticism*, ed. Daniel A. Fineman (Oxford: Clarendon Press, 1972).

19 John Philip Kemble, *Macbeth and Richard the Third: An Essay* (London: John Murray, 1817), p. 3.

20 Mary Cowden Clarke, *The Girlhood of Shakespeare's Heroines: A Series of Fifteen Tales* (London: Bickers & Son, 1893).

21 See Georgianna Ziegler's *Shakespeare's Unruly Women* (Washington, DC: Folger Shakespeare Library, 1997) for a well-illustrated introduction to the efforts of nineteenth-century critics in claiming female characters as appropriate objects of study.

22 Charles Cowden Clarke, *Shakspeare-Characters: Chiefly Those Subordinate* (London: Smith, Elder, & Co., 1863).

23 Brian Vickers, "The Emergence of Character Criticism, 1774-1800", *SS,* 34 (1981), pp. 11-21.

24 David Garrick, *Romeo and Juliet* (London: Bell & Sons, 1777). See also Jill Levinson's "Changing Images of Romeo and Juliet, Renaissance to Modern", in *Images of Shakespeare: Proceedings of the Third Congress of the International Shakespeare Association* (Newark: Delaware UP, 1988), pp. 151-62.

James Nuzum, Alyssa Hughes, Caroline Macuga and Amanda Magary.

26 These students included James Nuzum, Jami Fisher, Ellen Pignatella, and Alyssa Hughes. As the duplication from the previous note suggests, interesting chronologies resulted in strong papers.

27 Kenneth Branagh, *Hamlet, by William Shakespeare: Screenplay, Introduction, and Film Diary* (New York: W. W. Norton, 1996), p. 126.

28 In *Hamlet* (*Shakespeare Bulletin* 15.1 [Winter 1997], Samuel Crowl notes the anti-Oedipal perspective of Branagh's production: "There is not a trace of the Oedipal subtext in this Hamlet's relationship with Gertrude" (p. 35). Yet this production does provide the sexual subtext of his relationship with Ophelia more explicitly than any other so far.

29 Lorne Buchman, *Still in Movement: Shakespeare on Screen* (Oxford: Oxford UP, 1991), pp.106-07.

"SUIT THE ACTION TO THE WORD, THE WORD TO THE ACTION": USING PERFORMANCE PEDAGOGY TO ACTIVATE MULTIPLE INTELLIGENCES

Joan Mento
(Westfield State College)

A few years ago I was sitting with one of my students in the theatre discussing *Macbeth*. "Do you understand what we are trying to do in this scene?" he asked as his group rehearsed on stage. The scene was the first in Act 4 where Macbeth visits the witches for the second time. The group's rescening was not a traditional one. The cavern had been transposed to a desolate subway, the cauldron a smoking trashcan, and three attractively clad streetwalkers chanted "Double, double" around their cauldron can.

No, our class is not Acting 1 or a directing workshop. It is a Shakespeare course for undergraduates. This project "Scenes from Shakespeare" we do at the end of the semester, which allows the students time to plan the performance of a short, memorized scene. For several years I have been emphasizing performance in my introductory and English major courses, now not merely as an adjunct to Shakespeare's text but as an integral part of the course.

Yet the more I used theatre-based strategies to teach Shakespeare's plays, the more feasible seemed the possibility that performance techniques were grounded in the theory of multiple intelligences. In theatre practices actors used various intelligences long before they were formulated into learning theories. Performance pedagogy, because of its student-centered and process approach, enables students to become actively involved in learning. They interact with the script by analyzing it from the 'inside out'. This approach makes students aware of the various nuances of language through close-reading and script analysis. By an oral rendering of the lines rather than a silent reading, students engage with the poetry placing themselves inside Shakespeare's words and actions and thereby enhance their understanding of a scene.

Multiple intelligences is a theory put forth by the psychologist Howard Gardner. Working on a project on human potential at the graduate school at Harvard University, Gardner developed his theory about multiple intelligences through research on cognitive psychology with gifted children in the arts (Project Zero), work on neurology and brain research at the Boston Medical Center, and extensive readings of cultural history, studying prodigies and idiot savants in different fields from several cultures. The result of this research culminated in *Frames of Mind: The Theory of Multiple Intelligences*, basically a report on human potential. When Gardner published *Frames of Mind* in 1983, he was not specifically addressing the educational community. As a neuropsychologist he was primarily interested in the diversity of brain functions that he had observed. He was intrigued with the capacity of the human brain to process information in a multitude of ways – through language, spatial relations, mathematical knowledge, art, music, self-awareness, and interpersonal relationships.

To Gardner, intelligence refers to the human ability to solve problems or make something that is valued in one's cultures. First, though, that ability must answer certain criteria: Is there a particular representation in the brain for the ability? Are there populations that are especially proficient or impaired in an intelligence? Can an evolutionary and developmental history of the intelligence be seen? Can the intelligence support psychometric and psychological findings?

In analyzing intelligence tests administered to students, Gardner realized that the importance attached to the score is not entirely appropriate to success in the future though it may predict one's ability to handle school subjects. He saw there must be more to intelligence than short answers to short questions given in a decontextualized setting. These tests basically measure verbal and analytical skills. Hence, individuals strong in these areas will perform well on intelligence tests. Education in the United States has traditionally emphasized linguistic and mathematical skills. Yet Gardner draws a scenario of other cultures that use different forms of intelligences. In *Frames of Mind* he tells of a twelve year-old Puluwat boy of the Caroline Islands who is being tutored to become a sailor. The boy has learned to combine his knowledge of sailing, stars and geography for successful navigation around the hundreds of islands. A fifteen year-old Iranian youth has committed to memory the entire Koran and mastery of the Arabic language whereas a fourteen year-old in Paris is programming computers and four year-olds play musical instruments and compose music.

Gardner and his team of Harvard researchers postulated the concept of many intelligences by which we know, understand, and learn. Most of these ways of knowing go beyond what standard IQ or SAT tests can measure. He originally proposed a schema of seven intelligences:

1. Verbal/linguistic intelligence is the ability to effectively use oral and written language. It entails poetry, humor, story-telling, grammar, metaphors, abstract reasoning, symbolic thinking, conceptual patterning, reading and writing.

2. Logical/mathematical intelligence deals with inductive and deductive reasoning, numbers, and relationships. It involves the ability to recognize patterns, to work with geometric shapes, to reason, categorize, infer, analyze, calculate, and hypothesize.

3. Visual/spatial intelligence includes being able to visualize in respect to image, shape, space, and color. It deals with the visual arts, navigation, and games such as chess.

4. Bodily/kinesthetic intelligence is related to physical movement, and the expressing of ideas, feelings, and emotions. It is the physical ability to play a game athletically or to interpret and evoke effective body language.

5. Musical/rhythmic intelligence includes the ability to recognize tonal patterns, rhythm and beats. It includes sensitivity to environmental sounds, the human voice, and musical instruments.

6. Interpersonal intelligence is used in person-to-person relationships. It includes the ability to communicate and empathize with others.

7. Intrapersonal intelligence is based on knowledge of the inner self. It includes knowledge of feelings, thinking processes, range of emotional response, self-reflection, and a sense of intuition about spiritual concepts.

Each of us possesses all of these intelligences, but not all of them are developed equally. Therefore, we may not know how to use them effectively. Usually one or two intelligences are more fully developed than the others. In ordinary life, says Gardner, these intelligences work in harmony; consequently, their autonomy may not be so visible.

Gardner points out that the idea of multiple intelligences is an old one. He underscores the word idea. It is not yet a scientific fact, but it an idea that has recently regained the right to be discussed seriously. And it is being discussed frequently by educators. When he first published his findings, Gardner intended to challenge the traditional view of intelligence as a single capacity, not to write a book about learning theory. But since then educators have embraced his theory and many have welcomed the concept that students have capacities for learning in different ways. Initially teachers of young children, the gifted and disabled, and students who spoke English as a second language found in Gardner's approaches new ways of reaching their students and maximizing their performance. Over the next ten years, Gardner expanded his approach and became involved in curriculum development and assessment. Instructional programs, from elementary to college, based on multiple intelligences now exist in schools throughout the United States.

The implementation of performance pedagogy in the Shakespeare classroom allows students to use a variety of intelligences which includes drama as a way of knowing. For instance, in performance pedagogy script analysis uses linguistic as well as analytical intelligence for a deeper understanding of characters, issues, and staging. Learning can also take place kinesthetically as the body puts into action the lines and poetry of Shakespeare. Rhythm of the lines can be incorporated through dance movement and musical beats. Blocking of scenes entails visual and spatial knowledge. Collaboration with others to solve problems enhances critical thinking as well as interpersonal skills, and introspection on the process of one's own learning leads to reflective thinking. Observing what was happening as I experimented with theatre-based exercises, I began to see that strategies I had developed teaching Shakespeare through performance were embedded in the concept of multiple intelligences. I hope to show that using performance techniques to teach Shakespeare's plays naturally employs strategies of multiple intelligences and thereby enhances the learning potential of both native and non-native speakers of English.

When Gardner spoke of dramatic intelligence at Harvard in 1985 at a symposium, entitled "Creative Drama in a Developmental Context", he stressed the interpersonal nature of drama for the actor. In that talk he discussed intrapersonal, mathematical, musical, and spatial intelligences as not primarily important for the actor (305-307). I propose that dramatic intelligence incorporates all seven of Gardner's original intelligences. Gardner does point out that kinesthetic learning is frequently undervalued in school, and he laments the loss of the Greek harmony between mind and body where the body "is trained to respond to the expressive power of the mind" (*Frames,* 207). Theatre practitioners, such as Laban in movement training and Stanislavski with muscle memory, have long known the body contains its own wisdom. And more recently Tina Packer's (the Artistic Director of Shakespeare & Company's) vocal training entails connecting the thought and image of Shakespeare's lines with the breath of the actor.

A full theatrical production, as well as a scene study in a classroom, involves an interaction of many intelligences. Script study entails linguistic and analytical abilities to solve problems, think critically and interpret. Enacting the script entails kinesthetic, interpersonal, and spatial abilities of the actor, director and designers. Musical ability is needed to interpret the rhythm in Shakespeare's lines, incorporate music, or perform a dance such as the Pavane. The actor enriches intrapersonal intelligence when he or she studies the role as it relates to the inward feeling of self and character.

In studying the script, how we view the text and what we consider performance depends on our theoretical attitude toward the script and our definition of performance. In the light of postmodern theory in addition to the author's words, the interaction of the reader and text are considered. In performance interpreter and viewer must be added to the relationship that exits between dramatic text and performance texts. Because of the proliferation of postmodern criticism, we understand that texts produce various readings. A performance is an interpretation or reading of a play, an interaction among actor, director, designers, and audience. Yet for teachers and students it may be more profitable to analyze how the process of metamorphosing the written script into a performance enhances learning. For most students the process of oral interpretation goes beyond a silent reading. First, students become aware of various nuances of the language through close reading and script analysis. Second, when students speak and enact the lines, they are working with language on a physical, emotional, and intellectual level. Yet using exercises grounded in multiple intelligences is not just performing scenes or plays. It is also using theatre-based activities in various constructs of pedagogy that inform performance, for example, the use of creative drama, improvisation, debate, oral interpretation, and role playing, such as in historical reenactments or mock trials. Drama, then, enables students to internalize what they are studying and forcefully brings academic content to life. As I moved more toward a performance pedagogy grounded in the theory of multiple intelligences, I found myself devising projects that would require the students not only to perform Shakespeare's lines, but to perform, from the inside out, knowledge of the subject matter. Now I would like to apply Gardner's theory by demonstrating how theatre-based exercises employ several intelligences and thereby aid in an interactive teaching of Shakespeare's plays.

To see some of the ways my students acted in and reacted to these projects, I return to the students rehearsing *Macbeth*. In this scene their vision of a desolate subway station perhaps strays farther from what purists envision as an Elizabethan performance. The other five scenes performed, though, fell more or less into a "traditional' rendering in that they were not modernized to underscore contemporary social and moral problems. Yet the group who worked on the scene in which Ariel tricks the inebriated Caliban, Trinculo, and Stephano costumed themselves as clowns. Four students in commedia dell'arte style performed in a lively, dance-like fashion.

In the 'Scenes' project my students become members of a performing group, work collaboratively, choose a scene, analyze lines, block movements, design minimal costumes and props. Most intelligences come into play. Even intrapersonal is tapped, for during this project the students reflect on the learning process by writing a response journal.

To accustom the students to performing scenes, I start with exercises in creative drama. These exercises are short, involve the class working as a group or groups, and are not memorized; consequently, they prove non-threatening. Student evaluations indicate that performance projects turn out to be a favorite method of instruction. At first some students may feel daunted when they consider doing a scene. Yet as they progress from creative drama through role play and readers' theatre to memorized scenes, they begin to prefer the performance approach. One student echoed the sentiment of others, "I understand the language, psychology and stage movement better, interact with classmates, and enjoy Shakespeare."

Often we start *Macbeth* with a sound and gesture exercise. It entails the lines of the sergeant's report to Duncan about the battle (1.2.7-23). First we stand in a circle. I then lead the class in a warm-up exercise of riding a horse at a trot, canter, and gallop, ending with an enthusiastic yell of triumph. This energetic use of the body generally breaks any inhibition ice. Second I hand out a typed sheet of the lines, divided into phrase images. The purpose of the exercise is twofold: 1) to perceive how imagistic Shakespeare's language is; 2) to understand that in addition to the words linguistically forming a picture image, the body through gesture and movement can shape the image kinesthetically, thereby forming a stage picture visually and spatially. The students pair with a person next to them. We go around the circle, each pair reading one line image. We repeat the process with the other person on the team reading the line. Next I ask the entire group to put down the typed script. I instruct each pair to spontaneously come up with a sound and gesture/movement for the image as I read the line. I want them to work from the body quickly and instinctively. I assure them there is no right or wrong, only an interpretation, an enacting of the image. Just this simple exercise entails verbal, spatial, kinesthetic, and interpersonal intelligences.

As I kept a journal on the intelligences I was using in my teaching exercises, I noted the absence of musical intelligence. When I taught *Macbeth*, I had often pointed out the tone of the lines and especially the sharp, staccato effect in the quick exchange between the Macbeths in the scene after Duncan's murder. I then devised an exercise that would work with the music of Shakespeare's lines in a section of that scene (2.2.1-47). I divided the segment into three sections, lines 1-14 in which Lady Macbeth is alone on stage, lines 15-33, ending with Macbeth's "God bless us", and lines 34-47, ending with "Macbeth shall sleep no more." The exercise consists of dividing the class into three groups of 3-5 students, using double groups for each section. In their groups the students analyze the words, rhythm, and mood of the lines. Then they have fifteen minutes to create and practice an interpretation of the development of the section as a musical score. Some of the rhythmic beats have included Gregorian chant, clapping, recitative, rap, humming, Greek chanting, and singing. Some have added further to the rhythmic interpretation with drum beats or a piston-like movement. Sometimes they speak in unison, sometimes alternate with a single voice or sound effects such as the owl and cricket. After the groups have performed for one another, they write in their journals, reflecting on the process, starting with the prompt, "What conclusions can you draw about the rate, rhythm, intensity, and mood of the scene from the musical scores of the sections?" We then discuss their observations. In this exercise students employ rhythm and vocal composition. It also uses interpersonal intelligence in the collaboration of the group, linguistic in the study of the words, kinesthetic for the movement of the body, mathematical in the analysis of the beats, and intrapersonal in the use of the reflective journal.

Feeding in is a process some actors use in rehearsal before lines have been memorized. The process involves a person repeating the lines and standing near the actor who is receiving the lines. Part of the purpose is to allow the actor to be free for bodily movement without being hindered by script in hand. Furthermore, reciting and repeating words conjure an association of images which aids the actor in memory and interpretation. Using the feeding in process I devised the following exercise which builds on the actor Michael Chekhov's technique of archetypal gestures. The purpose is to enhance the subtext with the mental imagery in the scene where Beatrice and Benedick first clash in *Much Ado About Nothing* (1.1.112-140). The objective is to demonstrate how their duel with words becomes their dominant mode of expression throughout the play. Previous to this scene Beatrice had referred to Benedick as "Signior Mountanto", a fencing term for upward thrust, implying braggart. First the class forms rows and practices some archetypal push-pull gestures. Then the students pair off and mime fencing moves, first as abstract, larger and slower movement to get the archetype into the body, and then at a regular pace. After a few minutes of practice, they reform into groups of five, a Beatrice and Benedick, two feeders and one director who observes the movements and gives suggestions for making the action suit the words. The first time the feeders say the lines, the actors only mime fencing with moves that suggest an interpretation of the lines. The actors may use sound but not dialogue. The next time the actors repeat the lines being fed while miming action. Finally the actors repeat the lines but are only mentally aware of the bodily mime. The student actors are by then working with the script on an instinctual and imaginative level of subtextual archetypes as well as on kinesthetic, spatial, interpersonal, and linguistic levels of intelligence.

Even when students understand the language of Shakespeare's plays, they may have difficulty fully understanding a scene. One reason is that a play relies on dialogue and action and does not describe the scene in detail the way fiction does. Stage directions are often implied in the lines. Students may need to be prompted to come up with strategies to help them understand how action revealed through the text is presented on stage. Action involves the characters' stage movements (blocking) as well as their individual action (stage business). One to two weeks in advance I assign *Othello*, 4.1. 59-196 to four students. The four act the parts of Othello, Iago, Cassio, and Bianca. The Bianca student has the fewest line so she may also direct, or an additional student may direct. Out of class the performers collaboratively analyze the scene, seek out clues of implied stage directions, consider its function in the scene, and practice their interpretation. For the class they perform (memorized or readers' theatre) what they have discovered. This exercise encourages students to read visually and imaginatively in order to see and hear the implied directions. The goal is to have them portray the scene with appropriate character business, blocking, physical and vocal expressions in order to comprehend the subtle nuances of the lines. In this section Iago is manipulating Othello with the handkerchief, trying to convince him that Desdemona has committed adultery with Cassio. The scene is fraught with textual as well as subtextual motivations for the actors. Othello thinks Cassio is speaking of Desdemona when he is really speaking of Bianca. Consequently, it is important for the students to visualize the stage action, imagine the placement of characters, and realize why one character's lines are so important to the actions of another character, such as beckoning Othello in so he can hear better or having Cassio laugh and hang about Iago's neck as he mimics Bianca. For the trick to work, Othello must be hidden at a distance close enough to hear, "Ply Desdemona well", but far enough away not to hear "Now if this suit lay in Bianca's hands." So simple a point like lowering the voice (set off in modern stage directions) is implied in the nuances of the scene. Furthermore, Iago's lowering his voice and probably moving closer to Cassio when he speaks of Bianca fit in with the two men treating her as a smutty joke.

In the *Othello* scene study, as in all scene studies we do, not only do the actors and director take part but the other students become the critic-directors. After the performance the critic-directors pair off, briefly analyze the performance considering 1) Which particular parts came alive and why? 2) What did not seem to work and why? 3) What implied stage directions were noted? 4) What may have been implied in the text but not the performance? Quickly the pairs jot down their reactions and any questions they may have for the actors. At the same time the actors are discussing what they learned during the rehearsal process, what decisions they had to make as they decided on an interpretation, and what problems they encountered and solved. Then the class discusses the project, with the actors starting. As previously mentioned many intelligences categorized by Gardner are used in a scene study. Yet the other students taking on the role of critic-directors have gone beyond silent spectator to active participant, collaborating also in the process and using analytical, linguistic, interpersonal intelligences whereas the actors have further added kinesthetic and spatial skills.

For the past nine years I have conducted a survey at the beginning of the semester in my Shakespeare courses. The greatest challenge to students is the language. Students enrolling in the last few years have read more of Shakespeare's plays as well as seen more, though film and video far outnumber stage performances. As far as the language challenge goes, I encourage the students by pointing out that the more one reads Shakespeare, the more familiar the language becomes. This observation proves true when I again question them on language toward the end of the semester. Still, language is a huge concern. Students often refer to early modern English as 'old' English. If language is difficult for native speakers, then it must be doubly so for non-native speakers. Yet I would like to propose that theatre-based exercises that rely on other intelligences in addition to linguistic may aid the non-native speakers of English in their understanding of Shakespeare's plays.

After researching methods used in the ESL classroom for older secondary and higher education students, I began to see certain teaching principles emerge. Ideally students in ESL and bilingual classes should also be mainstreamed in academic courses. "Unless students have been in content-based ESL classes or maintained their subject matter development through instruction in their own languages", say Chamot and O'Malley, "they can be expected to have significant gaps in content-area knowledge" (110). When the non-native speakers are older, they often have acquired academic knowledge in their own language which makes mainstreaming easier. Many teachers and theorists propose a literature-based instruction which is grounded in the framework of Dewey, Piaget and Vygotsky, who argue that students should be active participants in their education. Furthermore, literacy and language development are seen as a holistic process which advocates teaching activities that combine speaking, listening, reading, and writing. Research indicates that a whole language approach "applies to L2 learners as strongly as it does to native English speakers" (Custodio and Sutton 19). In "Drama and the Whole Language Classroom" Stewig points out that "creative drama is the perfect vehicle for enhancing language development" (96).

In their introduction to *When They Don't All Speak English*, Rigg and Allen contend that non-native learners need a language-rich environment, both oral and written. Speaking and reading aloud have a significant effect on literary acquisition and development. The use of cooperative groups that pair ESL students with native speakers is recommended. Also important is working on meaningful tasks while interacting with students of their own age. Finally Rigg and Allen recommend authentic writing and not merely worksheet drills for non-native speakers. Shakespeare's plays are certainly language-rich, and theatre-based activities allow students to work in cooperative groups to solve problems and effect authentic communication while developing interpersonal skills. Research on learning styles indicates that "ESL students strongly preferred kinesthetic and tactile learning" (Reid, 92). Kinesthetic activities of theatre comprise a total physical involvement of experiential learning. Also high on the preference scale were auditory and oral methods. Dramatization is an effective activity for practicing language skills since it naturally lends itself to listening and reading aloud. Finally, responding reflectively in the Shakespeare journal not only gives practice in authentic writing but also enhances intrapersonal intelligence.

In my review of articles on teaching ESL in the classroom, I have found a study that implements multiple intelligences strategies in lesson plans and assessment whereas another uses theatre techniques to teach a drama workshop to ESL students. Mary Ann Christison ensures that her lessons address different intelligences, and some tasks include role play. She also tries to use a different intelligence to assess from the one she used to teach the lesson. Maria Guida uses creative dramatics such as theatre games and improvisations. These theatre techniques stimulate creativity, decrease anxiety, develop emotional expression, enhance storytelling, provide tasks for problem solving, develop fluency, sensory awareness and powers of observation. However, neither course includes Shakespeare. One reason may be the difficulty of Shakespeare's language. Some courses taught on the college and secondary levels did teach Shakespeare to ESL students but did not mention multiple intelligences. Two studies use a simplified version of *Romeo and Juliet*. The university-level students in Susan English's class improvised scenes, derived from a plot summary, in contemporary English. The secondary students in Lori Owen's class read aloud a plot summary, viewed a video, and read an abbreviated text in contemporary English. Another study combined deaf, limited English proficient, and emotionally disturbed students. The students integrated literature, performance, technology and sign language in a ten-month study of *King Lear*. The text used was a modified teacher-prepared one, which the class read together, yet the performance of *Lear* used Shakespeare's language. 'Modified' may have meant the play was shortened for production. Though *King Lear* may be considered a difficult play, the teachers said, "If our students could learn and understand this play, they could learn and understand any of Shakespeare's plays"(Cambridge and Abdulezer, 22). The teachers went on to say that no reading gets teenagers as excited as Shakespeare. Even though plots are complex and the language difficult, they felt teachers should consider teaching Shakespeare's plays to special populations.

Before I explore theatre exercises that can be adapted for students with limited English proficiency, I would like to turn to an interesting point made in *When They Don't All Speak English*. Older ESL students have developed learning strategies attuned to their experiences in their own countries, and some of these educational systems place a high value on rote memory (116). Memorization is a useful skill for theatre. In "Drama Literacy" Branigan recounts reading specialist Carol Chomsky's answer in "After Decoding: What?" She noted that even after students had learned to decode, that is, had been successful with phonics in isolation, they still had trouble reading. Her advice is to memorize. George Branigan maintains if students were helped to memorize whole texts the way actors do, meaning would be encoded. Furthermore, "cognitive space could then be freed up to explore how the text said what it did. Thus any kind of re-construction could be built upon their prior knowledge of those texts" (123). This process, says Branigan, is similar to the attributes of self-taught readers, who often memorize whole texts. He goes on to speak of the advantage of learning to read as an actor – advantages not necessarily obtained by the solitary reader. Actors repeat the text over and over, discussing lines along the way. Lines are tried in different

Using Performance Pedagogy

renderings. Directors challenge the actor to make sense in the overall context of the play. Actors are also challenged by other actors to be responsive to meaning and tone. Consequently, meanings are arrived at collaboratively and interactively worked out (123). Similarly when students are memorizing scenes some of these same processes are taking place. Therefore, having non-native speakers resort to memorization of Shakespeare's lines and interacting with other student actors may be an effective task for them.

Since I am opposed to simplified versions of Shakespeare's plays, I would suggest that the higher education students of very limited proficiency read the plays first in their own language. Afterwards they might view a video performed in English. Then they can begin to work on Shakespeare's lines with mime and feeding-in exercises and gradually add theatre-based projects involving linguistic skills. Chamot and O'Malley claim: "Rather than watering down content for second-language students, teachers can make challenging content comprehensible by providing additional contextual support through demonstrations, visuals, and hands on experiences"(114). In order to make Shakespeare's challenging content comprehensible to non-native learners, I propose using the "demonstrations, visuals, and hands-on experiences" of performance pedagogy reinforced by the use of different intelligences.

The following exercises may work equally well for native and non-native speakers, yet exploring the Shakespeare text first through mime and feeding-in processes may be less intimidating for the non-native speaker instead of plunging directly into an analysis of Shakespeare's language. It may be more profitable to start *Macbeth* with the sound and gesture exercise of the sergeant's speech. In addition to demonstrating the images in a stage picture, the exercise could also serve as an introduction to the play, or an approach to the historical background of the battle, or insight into Macbeth's character as both brave and violent.

The second mime, adapted from Michael Tolaydo, builds on but goes beyond sound and gesture to add interpretive style. This exercise is the dumb-show of the Player King and Queen in Hamlet (3.2). The Narrator slowly reads the lines while a Player King, Queen, Poisoner, and Attendants mime the scene. Those performing bodily enact the words the Narrator describes. I break the class into four groups of six players. Then they have fifteen minutes to create and practice a way of presenting this dumb-show. Often I am working on style and periods. Therefore, I give each group a different period style, such as Greek classical, Elizabethan, Restoration, nineteenth-century melodrama, or twentieth-century naturalism. For just style we may include, robotic/futuristic, operatic or musical, fluid or dance-like. The point is to listen carefully to the words of the Narrator to make certain each detail is enacted fully and clearly. Students need to work not only with the vocabulary but also with the nuances of the scene. Sound effects are often performed musically by the Attendants thereby giving them a larger role.

In this exploration of Shakespeare's language, style has been added to the kinesthetics of sound and gesture to create a text that incorporates visual/spatial intelligence. When I taught Shakespeare's plays in the Elizabethan period of an Acting Styles and Periods course, the class was from the freshman core (a required choice in the arts from the general education sequence). This particular class consisted mainly of learning disabled students as well as some limited English proficiency students from the Urban Education Program. In that class I also gave the students a choice of coming up with their own styles. In addition to the period styles given, some groups collaborated to create country-western, soap opera, and gangster/cop genres. After the performances we discuss the various interpretations to see whether the objectives have been adhered to, especially the comprehension of the lines through clear enactment. If time remains, we run the scenes again, using the feedback to improve the detail. I have found that this exercise appeals to Shakespeare students at all levels from freshmen through to English majors and post-baccalaureate graduates. Mime exercises help students realize how Shakespeare's language is replete with images and action and how vital each word or phrase is for complete stylistic enactment.

The next exercise again involves feeding in. In my introductory Shakespeare course when we did comedies, I decided to start with *The Comedy of Errors*. I had read that *Errors* was not a favorite of some critics who, finding not much to say of it, dismissed it as shallow or an early imitative work of Plautus. Interestingly, it thrives theatrically, both actors and audiences enjoying the experience. I was working on the theory that farce depends as much on visual as verbal humor, and that *The Comedy of Errors*, though critics debate whether it is comedy or farce, does use both kinds of humor and draws on farcical elements in a commedia dell' arte style. The Door scene (3.1) is an effective one because it uses a large cast. When I first tried this exercise I had eight students go up on stage. They broke into teams of four, one team on one side of the imaginary door, the other on the other side. It is the scene where Antipholus of Ephesus has brought guests home to dinner. Adriana won't let him in because she thinks her husband is already dining with her. We performed the scene with four on one side reading the lines while the four on the other side acted out the physical movements, gestures, sounds, facial expression as they interpreted the lines. I had told the actors to instinctively come up with the action, but if the actor did not spontaneously mime the lines through the body, then I had instructed the feeders to forcefully repeat words, phrases or lines until the actor responded. Usually the actor got immediately on track. Half way through the scene we switched roles. The actors, then, became mirror images of their counterparts. As we urged the student-actors on to more and more physicalizations, students on and off the stage began to realize the importance of gesture, movement, and stage business to bring lines visually alive in a farce. The audience of critic-directors not only roared at the antics created by the students on stage but also discovered that making meaning involves the whole person instinctually, physically, and mentally.

This feeding-in exercise can be adapted to accommodate non-native speakers as actors who are mainstreamed with native speakers as feeders. Then the crew would be expanded to include feeders paired and standing near each actor. If Angelo's few lines are cut, three actors and three feeders would be on one side of the door and the same number on the other side. The group of twelve practice until the actors are energetically miming the action and coming up with stage business. Then the exercise can move on to the verbal stage as the actors repeat the lines given by the feeders. The third step is for the actor, while still being fed the lines, to try putting the movement to the lines being repeated. The final step would be to take away the feeders and see whether the second-language students could improvise the lines by using as much of the vocabulary of the original as they can remember while reinforcing the lines with action. Part of the rationale behind this last step is that actors often remember lines because of accompanying movements of the body, executing muscle memory as well as kinesthetic and visual/spatial intelligences.

In these exercises the non-native speakers have gradually been progressing toward more verbal encounters with Shakespeare's lines. In the next project I have added a written assignment to the oral memorization or readers' theatre. This exercise was devised for native speakers but can be adapted for second language learners. It is a parallel-scene project with Hamlet and Ophelia, 3.1.91-164. Students form groups of three students to play Hamlet, Ophelia, and a director. Outside of class the students individually study the essential conflicts, issues, and emotional rhythms of this section. Then the teams discuss their findings. As a team they practice performing the original scene. Then they try to improvise contemporary dialogue that captures the essence of the original. When the scenario is set, they collaborate on writing their own modern parallel to the scene. In class the teams act out both versions. If the team has not memorized the scenes, they must know the lines well so that vocal and facial expressions, emotions, movements and actions are clearly conveyed to the audience. The point of the parallel scene is to capture the emotional rhythm of Shakespeare's lines and through working on a modern parallel to reinforce these rhythms in both scenes. I adapted this idea from Michael Flackmann. The difference is Flackmann's was an immediate modern improvisation whereas I made a longer project by allowing students time to study the scene, write a scenario, and practice. I also added the director. Furthermore, my students do not always do a *modern* parallel, though the majority do.

In a recent Shakespeare class I had three groups performing. One group came up with the idea of fusing the scenes by performing Orphelia's lines in contemporary dialogue and keeping Hamlet's lines in Shakespearean language. They wanted to show a conflict based on woman's honor with Hamlet taking the

Renaissance view of female chastity and Ophelia showing the modern woman's view of love and sex. Stage movements worked well in this scene as if a circling Hamlet were stalking a bewildered Ophelia. The second group's parallel scene was not a modern one. They felt that the conflict, rhythm, and confusion of the Hamlet-Ophelia situation could be portrayed in a comparison with the Biblical Mary and Joseph when Joseph hears rumors that Mary is with child. Facial expressions and reactions of Mary's harsh treatment carried over to a fearful Ophelia, especially on her, "What means your lordship?" The third group decided to do the assignment as a modern improvisation. They took a boyfriend-girlfriend conflict, closely following the rhythms in the original Hamlet scene. They improvised, practiced, and basically wrote the scenario from the improvisational dialogue. What worked well in this scene was the intensity of passion played out between the two. Hamlet's angry tone appeared genuine. The force transferred to the original scene, down to the clutching of Hamlet's fists and the naïve expression on Ophelia's face.

To adapt the parallel-scene project for non-native speakers, I suggest teaming them with a student who speaks the same language. Then they can collaborate to write a modern parallel in their own language, taking into account their own culture as well as the issues in the original Shakespeare scene. Next they translate the parallel scene into English. The ESL students then act out the contemporary script in their own language. The English speakers act out the translated script. If possible the second language learners may memorize the original Hamlet-and-Ophelia scene in English. Western education tends to disparage rote memory as a teaching-learning tool. Yet research indicates that memorization is a learning technique for many foreign students in their own countries, and in acting, bodily and spatial intelligences may help linguistic memory. If the second-language students are not proficient enough in English, then they can memorize the Shakespeare scene in their own language. Later, as they progress, they memorize scenes in English.

Building on mathematical, visual/spatial, and musical intelligences is also important for the non-native speaker. For my class of learning disabled and urban education students, I devised topics for research papers and projects from the

Elizabethan period that would be demonstrated in an oral presentation. The following is a brief description of projects that could be adapted for second language learners.

1. Build a 3-D model of an Elizabethan stage. In your demonstration indicate how the dimensions are to scale and explain the various parts of the stage and their functions in your paper and oral report. (spatial, mathematical, verbal)
2. Make a blueprint of an Elizabethan stage. Take two scenes from any Shakespeare play and indicate how you would block the scenes with the Elizabethan stage space. Use drawings and a written report of the process in your paper and demonstration. (visual/spatial, mathematical, verbal)
3. Use an instrument or synthesizer to underscore musically some sections of either *Macbeth*, *Hamlet*, or any other Shakespeare play. Make an audio tape and write a brief report on the effect or mood you are trying to achieve. Use the audio tape in you oral report. (musical and verbal)
4. Research Renaissance music. Make an audio tape of different pieces. Show how, where, and why you might fit this music into various parts of a Shakespeare play. Both written and oral reports will demonstrate how the music chosen interprets the scenes. (musical and verbal)
5. Research costumes and masks for the Elizabethan era. Use pictures. Then draw costumes and masks for a few of the characters in the ball scene in *Much Ado About Nothing*. In both the written and oral report include the research on the era, the pictures of costumes, and your original costumes and masks. (visual and verbal)

Dance also encompasses musical, kinesthetic, and spatial intelligences through the counting out of beats and moving rhythmically in space. In order for students to experience iambic pentameter, one quick exercise is to have them dance out the rhythm in the lines. That way, like actors, they can get the rhythm into their body. We start with any iambic pentameter passage from Shakespeare. The students form two lines parallel to and facing one another. Two students from opposite sides dance to their opposite sides by merely starting on the right toe on the unstressed syllable and putting the whole foot down on the stressed syllable. Then on the next syllable the left toe starts, alternating feet on the iambic beat until the line is finished. The students not crossing clap or chant on the syllables. This exercise is just a simple one in understanding meter. Dance was a favorite activity of the learning disabled and urban education students. They enjoyed learning the formal Pavane, which some students later used in a scene from *Romeo and Juliet*. The Pavane became not only a dance lesson but also a cultural lesson about the late Middle Ages and the early Elizabethan era. The steps include a salute with arms extended upward to heaven, parallel to middle earth, and down to hell. A discussion on medieval theater, especially stage space and cosmology, ensued. We danced two versions of the Pavane. The first was slower and more stately as it came at the end of the Middle Ages. The second was faster, more rambunctious, as though the beginning of the Elizabethan era was in its adolescent stage. Since dance depends less on linguistic ability and more on kinesthetic, spatial, and musical skills, it can easily be adapted for ESL students.

Finally, theatre techniques which incorporate multiple intelligences are not just used in acting scenes but expand into various constructs of performance pedagogy such as the use of role-playing in a critical debate or a simulated trial. A critical debate project can help students understand the multiple readings of Shakespearean criticism. My class of English majors does a project on role-playing the critics. To prepare, we discuss the amount of controversy that Shakespeare's plays generate among critics. Then I give the students a handout that explains they will be working in teams for the next week in order to research some critical articles on the play assigned. Each team is to find a different critical approach, such as New Criticism, Marxism, Freudianism, Myth Criticism, Feminism, New Historicism, Deconstruction, Cultural Materialism, or Performance Criticism. The students are not just to report on the articles but to become the critics by assuming the author's position and forcefully expressing their viewpoints. On the day of the debate each team brings in a photocopy of the article and notes. Then they role-play as the author or advocate and debate. The first time I tried this project the students who started the debate sounded as if they were reporting rather than role-playing. Then one of the young men playing Sigmund Freud suddenly 'became' Freud in voice and stance, arguing vehemently for his position. The other students were so surprised that they started to imitate by speaking heatedly, calling each other by the critics' names, trying to persuade others to their interpretation. Students began to see not only the various readings the play generated but also that different readings could be valid depending on the stance one took. For this project they had to research and digest the material, know the play thoroughly, and debate as the critics, thereby employing verbal, analytical, and interpersonal intelligences.

For a final project in my introductory class, composed of many criminal justice majors, I experimented with role-playing a trial. I had used trial projects in other literature classes but not in Shakespeare because of the difficulty some had in dealing with Shakespeare's language, never mind building a law case from the text. Yet I knew from experience that a trial makes pedagogical sense, demanding close reading and critical decision-making. What gave me courage to attempt a trial with a Shakespeare play was a conference paper presented by Jane Carducci at the West Virginia Shakespeare and Renaissance Association in April of 1993. She had used *Measure for Measure* in a mock trial. Her instructions included a brief handout that basically stated the charges and what characters were to be witnesses. Her paper concentrated on the experience of team teaching with another English professor, who specialized in the Jacobean period and judged the trial.

Because of my former experience with mock trials, I revised and expanded Jane's concept. First my handout sheet was more detailed in order to include the entire class and have them work in small groups in the preliminary planning. Secondly we used the pretrial time to study the play as a class. The trial project took two weeks, some class time devoted to team work for trial preparation. Before we started the play, I instructed them to consider certain points as they read *Measure for Measure*. I asked them to note what the play said about marriage contracts and dowries in respect of two couples: Juliet and Claudio and Angelo and Mariana. I further urged them carefully to read the Isabella-Angelo scenes, noticing the language.

Once they read the play I conducted a lecture-discussion on various critical problems with this dark comedy. Then I had the students briefly write on any questions, insights, or puzzlements they had had when they read the play. After a discussion of the reactions to the play, we broke into groups. Each group chose a piece of paper that asked them to consider specific issues about certain scenes: Isabella pleads with Angelo; Angelo's threatens and sexual harasses; Isabella visits Claudio in prison; the Duke justifies the bed trick to Isabella; Isabella publicly accuses Angelo; and Mariana begs Isabella to plead for Angelo's life. Group members studied the scene, analyzed the issues and conflicts. Then each group reported its findings to the other groups. Questions and discussion followed. The preliminaries ended. We were ready to start pretrial negotiations.

In the first class I had handed out a procedure sheet on trials. The case called to trial reported that Isabella charged Angelo with sexual harassment. A real lawyer from the community would preside as judge. Students signed up for parts that interested them. Teams worked on strategies to build their respective cases. All evidence had to come from the text except for the research on marriage customs and concept of honor from the Elizabethan era. Eight students divided the roles of the prosecuting and defense attorneys. Those groups of four built a case, made an opening statement, called witnesses, offered evidence, and delivered a closing statement. One student played each witness (character). Two students were news journalists who wrote and graphically designed the *Venetian Times*. One played both the bailiff and the court stenographer. Two students were paralegal assistants, doing the research on the Elizabethan marriage customs and laws as well as that period's concept of honor. All students had to keep a reflective journal and write a paper on topics relevant to their function in the trial. For example, the witnesses kept actor journals and wrote character-analysis papers.

The first day I thought the trial was moving too slowly in the questioning, especially the prosecution whose attorneys seemed to be floundering by not asking pointed questions. The defense team, though, was cross-examining with pertinent points. Later I realized that this was the first time they had ever experienced a mock trial. About half way through class a prosecution counselor began to become more adept at asking quick, short-answer questions. Soon his partners followed suit. With difficult witnesses attorneys from both sides (often with text in hand) would say, "Let me refresh your memory"; or "In your deposition you said"; or "We submit this for evidence." Then they proceeded to quote the character's words from the play.

Various intelligences are at work when students become actively engaged in the process of learning with theatre-based exercises. Mock trials, for instance, encourage critical reading and deepen the study of character motivation through role-playing, analysis, and improvisation. Students take responsibility for the play. They must document the case, respond in character, find evidence and thus understand the text.

One way to meet the challenge of teaching Shakespeare's plays is to encourage students to use multiple intelligences. Since performance-centered learning employs strategies to activate these intelligences, the students' potential for understanding and enjoying Shakespeare's plays is expanded. Both native and non-native speakers of English may benefit by experiencing this method of teaching.

Works Cited

Branigan, George. "Dramatic Literacy: Center Stage". *Currents in Literacy* 2 (1999), pp. 122-5, 42.
Cambridge, Teresa and Abdulezer, Susan. "Sharing Shakespeare: Integrating Literature, Technology, and American Sign Language". *NASSP Bulletin* 82 (1988), pp. 19-23.
Chamot, Anna and J. Michael O'Malley. "The Cognitive Academic Language Learning Approach." In *When They Don't All Speak English*, ed. Pat Rigg and Virginia Allen (Urbana, IL: NCTE, 1989), pp.108-25.
Christison, Mary Ann. "Multiple Intelligences & Second Language Learners". *Journal of the Imagination in Language Learning* 3 (1996), pp. 8-13.
Custodio, Brenda and Marilyn Jean Sutton. "Literature-Based ESL for the Secondary Student". *TESOL Journal* 7 (Autumn 1998), pp. 19-24.
English, Susan. "Shakespeare Made Simple". *WATESOL* (Winter 1985), pp. 38-42.
Flackmann, Michael. "Teaching Shakespeare Through Parallel Scenes". *Shakespeare Quarterly* 35. 5 (1984), pp. 644-6.
Gardner, Howard. *Frames of Mind: The Theory of Multiple Intelligences.* New York: Basic Books, 1983.

Gardner, Howard. *Multiple Intelligences: Theory in Practice*. NY: Basic Books, 1993.
Gardner Howard. "Towards a Theory of Dramatic Intelligence." In *Creative Drama in a Developmental Context*, ed. Judith Kase-Polisini. New York: UP of America, 1985, pp. 295-312.
Guida, Maria. "Creating Theatre in the ESL Classroom". *Journal of the Imagination in Language Learning* 3 (1996), pp. 112-14.
Owen, Lori. "Teaching Shakespeare When They All Don't Speak English". *Notes Plus*. (March 1994), pp. 1-2.
Reid, Joy. "The Learning Style Preferences of ESL Students". *TESOL Quarterly* 21 (March 1987), pp. 87-111.
Rigg, Pat and Allen, Virginia. *When They Don't All Speak English: Integrating the ESL Student in the Regular Classroom*. Urbana, IL: NCTE, 1989.
Shakespeare, William. *The Complete Works of William Shakespeare*, ed. David Bevington. New York: HarperCollins, 1992.
Stewig, John. "Drama and the Whole Language Classroom". *New England Theatre Journal* 5 (1994), pp. 93-100.
Tolaydo, Michael. "Dumbshow Makes for Smart Move." *Shakespeare* 1 (1996), pp. 9-10.

EXAMINING *MEASURE FOR MEASURE* THROUGH PERFORMANCE

Edward L. Rocklin and Sarah Innerst-Peterson
(California State Polytechnic University, Pomona)

Prologue

Since 1980, those faculty regularly teaching Shakespeare's plays at California State Polytechnic University, Pomona, have experimented with a number of ways of realizing the potentials of a performance-oriented approach to Shakespeare. In the course of his experiments, Edward Rocklin has developed an argument which suggests how a performance approach may meet some of the needs of those teaching Shakespeare's plays around the globe. In particular, Rocklin has noted that performance approaches foreground the fact that teaching Shakespeare's plays to literature students is always an exercise in translation, even when those students are native speakers of English. For Shakespeare's plays are written in two languages that look like but are not identical with the language of a purely literary text: first, the language of the script, a special form of writing in which the words on the page serve both as speeches by characters and as instructions to actors; and second, the language of the stage, where the medium is the actor, not the text nor even solely the spoken word. In this sense, both the dramatic medium and the dialogue are "second languages" to our students, and teaching Shakespeare to these students, therefore, entails teaching them ways of using their minds and bodies not taught in most literature classes. In the present essay, we offer a model for one such class which, we hope, may also demonstrate the virtues of the approach for those facing the challenge of teaching the plays in translation to speakers for whom English is a second language.

In a recent experiment, Edward Rocklin decided to offer one upper division course, Shakespeare in Performance, in which students would focus on a single play and perform most, if not all, of the scenes. At the same time, because he wanted the course to include a theatrical dimension, he asked Sarah Innerst-

Peterson, who has had an extensive career as a professional actor and director, and who has developed a program for students ages 8 to 12 called "Sidewalk Shakespeare", to work with him, supplying the expertise of her model for teaching acting approaches to non-actors. Together, we taught the course in the spring quarter of 1999. There were 17 students, mostly English majors, and we met twice a week, each meeting running for one hour and fifty minutes, so that we had almost 40 hours of class time – and could easily have used 80 hours without coming near to exhausting the richness of this play's potentials.

A Measured Design: Course Objectives
If we had to put it in a single sentence, we would say that our primary objective was for students to develop as full and as disciplined an engagement with *Measure for Measure*, in both dimensions of text and performance, as they were capable of achieving; as well as the detachment to reflect on and learn from that engagement with the playtext, with each other, and with their performances.

In terms of the text, we designed a course that would enable students not only to become engaged with the content and style of the play but also with its editorial problems. To this end, students worked with the Folio text (1623) as well as with the modern editions established by N. W. Bawcutt (Oxford, 1998), Brian Gibbons (Cambridge, 1991), and Barbara Mowat and Paul Werstine (New Folger Library, 1997).

In terms of the theatrical dimension, we sought to enable students to experience the fundamental reality that the actor is the medium of drama by learning to use their voices and bodies as instruments for experiment. That is, we wanted them to gain some (greater) awareness of, and stretch the capacities of, their voices and bodies as instruments for experimenting with the text in action; and to use these capacities in collaborative performances. At the same time, although similarities exist between the work we undertook in this literature classroom and an acting workshop, there are some significant differences concerning the reasons for employing performance work and the nature of that work. Of course, in an acting classroom the students perform in order to explore and expand their potential as artists. Any performance work that they undertake, therefore, is followed by a critique that almost certainly addresses the consistency and effectiveness of the choices that they made and the control that they demonstrated over that performance. So acting students, in their training, focus primarily on honing their sensitivity to their art and developing the tools of their profession; their bodies, their voices, their imaginations. In a literature classroom, discussing performances in these terms would serve virtually no purpose at all because, in addition to possibly shutting down any spirit of adventure or eagerness these non-actors have brought to their performances, it would not further the main purpose for implementing performance work in a literature course – namely to increase the range of activities students can deploy in reading drama as partners to the playwright. In other words, in focusing on the quality of a performance instead of the potential of the text, students would miss out on honing their interpretive skills, a much more vital talent in the English classroom than learning to act well.

Given that Cal Poly Pomona is part of the California State University system, a system which produces 60% of the teachers in the state, we also hoped future teachers, of whom there were a substantial number, would benefit from the course, finding themselves able to offer a much wider array of activities to their students than are deployed in many traditional midde- and high-school classrooms. We have anecdotal evidence that at least four of these students are, in fact, using some elements of what they learned in their own classes.

In order to realize our primary objective, we designed the course so that as the quarter progressed the students would:

(1) Read several texts of *Measure for Measure*, exploring the play's design and what editors have made of that design.
(2) Learn to ask and answer some basic questions that guide a literary approach to the patterns of language and patterns of action that are embodied in the page.
(3) Develop an understanding of the basic theatrical structures and conventions that shaped the Renaissance English stage, and use this knowledge to deepen their grasp of performance possibilities.

(4) Rehearse a series of warm-up activities which would help them use their voices and bodies to experiment with what the playtext is designed to do and can be made to do.
(5) Rehearse and gain some mastery of theatrical practices by which actors and directors move from page to stage, learning to read the playtext as a score offering alternate realizations.
(6) Explore the performance potentials of each scene: working together, they would perform at least two, and sometimes more, alternate versions.
(7) Produce a major paper: this final paper was to be a synthesis of the many different approaches used throughout the term.

In short, we spent our ten weeks together exploring *Measure for Measure* with an equal emphasis on the text, and the multiple ways the text has been edited; and on the play and the multiple ways the play can be and has been performed.

Course Focus: Why *Measure for Measure*?

At first sight *Measure for Measure* might not seem an obvious choice for such intensive study. For example, throughout the period from the Restoration to about 1950, *Measure for Measure* was generally considered one of Shakespeare's wearker and less satisfying plays. For one thing, a comedy that centers on rampant sexual disorder; that jokes harshly about sexuality and venereal disease; that features a young man sentenced to death for impregnating a woman who is either his fiance or his wife; and that creates an apparently insoluble knot when the judge who imposes this death sentence attempts to extort sex from the young man's sister, herself a would-be nun – such a play hardly seems to be a comedy. Evidence of how problematic this play has appeared to be to earlier generations can be found in its performance and publication history: not only is it one of the less-frequently performed plays but, beginning in 1720 and even into the early twentieth century, when *Measure for Measure* was performed it was invariably produced with heavy cuts (mostly eliminating the bawdier, more obsence elements), and with one of three rewritten endings. Meanwhile, literary critics found the play extremely unsatisfactory in its plot, its characterization, its apparent shift from tragedy to comedy in Act 3, Scene 1, and its extraordinarily contrived ending.

But in the past 30 years, *Measure for Measure* has come to be seen, both in the theater and in the study, as an intriguing, powerful, and effective play. And effective not in spite of some of the features enumerated above but because of those features. For example, the interplay of sexuality, disease, and power has come to seem precisely one element that enables the play to explore profound issues with which our societies still have to grapple. And while many who now see the power of the play would acknowledge that it is still not wholly satisfying in its design, it has become a much more central play in our current perception of the canon.

Even more important for our course project, it has come to be seen as a play whose depth and power can best be grasped if we engage with it as a design for a performance event as well as a poetic drama on the page. To take what has become the most obvious example, it is through performance that we can best grasp the specifics of the four marriages with which the play ends, and which, until recently, seemed to ratify the Folio's placement of it among the comedies. Indeed, it is only when beginning to think about performance that most readers, certainly those trained in literary studies, will encounter the problem that productions from 1970 onward have made so inescapable for contemporary interpreters, namely the question of whether there are in fact four marriages or only three marriages at the end: that is, it is especially when rehearsing or imagining the staging that we must answer the question "Does Isabella accept either (or both) of the Duke's offers of marriage?" Taken together, these features make *Measure for Measure* a particularly rewarding focus for the type of performance-centered exploration in a university classroom that two generations of teachers have sought to foster at Cal Poly Pomona.

Thus we invited students to approach *Measure for Measure* as a script intended for performance on the stage; as a text which, whatever Shakespeare's intentions, has been more read as literature than performed in the theater; and as a venerated, reviled, revised, and restored text for study by scholars, critics, and students in the classroom. The classroom, we suggest, can be a place where literary and theatrical practices interact, and where each of us can create what might be thought of as a third version of the play, namely an imagined version in the theater of the mind.

We concluded our course introduction by saying "We can sum up this outline by saying that this is a class for participants, not spectators. However comfortable we may feel in the spectator role, the heat and light that comes from participating is worth the vulnerability it entails. We can all learn from each other, and the course is structured so as to make such learning possible. We look forward to our work together."

The Course in Action: Freeing Voices

As we planned the course, we discussed an issue we have both encountered, namely the resistance many non-theater students are likely to feel when they are first asked to perform in front of their classmates. Based on her experience with other non-actors, Sarah Innerst-Peterson proposed an elegant solution in which, during the first class meeting, each student walked up to a podium at the front of the room, placed his or her hands on the edges of the podium, looked at us, uttered the words "Thank you – and goodnight!" and returned to his or her seat. In many ways, this moment served as a miniature version of our practice during the quarter, in which we sought to simplify the initial risk-taking not to make things easy but rather to immerse students in a set of challenges whose demands steadily increased as their ability and willingness to experiment were widened and intensified.

After the first class, we began each class with Innerst-Peterson leading a sequence of activities. First, we performed body-stretches designed to enable participants to find their "neutral stance" – so that by the end of this activity they were standing tall, with an erect spine, shoulders pushed back, neck aligned, legs straight, knees unlocked, their feet about twelve inches apart, and their eyes facing forward. The objective in assuming a neutral stance was simply to create a wider range of potential movement as students began to transform the roles on the page into the characters on the stage. Second, we worked on centering their breathing. And third, we conducted vocal warm-ups, working, for example, with plosives and concluding with unison performance of a line such as "How sharper than a serpent's tooth it is to have a thankless child!" – a wonderful line that has the advantage of rehearsing the four plosives, "P", "T", "D", and "K"; or with a line (often the opening line) from the scene we were about to rehearse and perform.

We discerned four specific benefits from this initiating activity, even as we also noted the interesting ways students, despite our best efforts, nonetheless either resisted or sought to downgrade the importance of these activities. First, they freed the voice and prepared students to respond to the intellectual and emotional impulses elicited by the speeches in the play. Second, they helped students, for the most part not used to using their bodies as a medium of drama or, indeed, a medium of education, to discover the power latent in the effort to incarnate a text. Third, the act of standing together in a circle while concentrating on vocal and physical awareness helped create a sense of ensemble for our intense 110 minutes of work on the play. And fourth, and perhaps most important, these activities served to initiate the movement from page to stage, from text to performance that was the core of most class meetings. These warm ups, in other words, were one means to help our students learn to make informed vocal and physical choices and then to analyze the effects of these choices – including the surprising performance effects which in turn sometimes prompted unexpected insights.

This initiating work often led directly to work with a given scene, as the class was divided into groups and prepared alternative performances which enabled us to learn about the range of performance potentials offered by the text of that scene. As part of this model, we also suggested that students could begin looking at a specific scene with five directorial questions in mind.

1. What is the function of the scene?
2. What do we learn about the characters in this scene?
3. What are the functions of these characters?
4. What are the dynamics between the characters? And what is the nature of the relationships that result from these dynamics?

5. Are there any changes in the status of the characters within the scene? And what prompts these changes in status?

In passing, we would note that the first question is deeply recursive, and often took us back to a more deeply searching examination of the play's design. That is, in the first classes we asked students to come up with an initial reading of the design of the play as a whole. And this initial reading helped them compose a first hypothesis as to what function or functions a specific scene might perform. But in exploring that scene, the students would also discover or invent performance potentials they had not foreseen or suspected. And these realized potentials might compel at least some students to revise their formulation of the play's design. The most obvious instance, as already noted, is the question (interestingly nearly unthinkable or unaskable for most of the play's history), "Does Isabella accept either (or both?) of the Duke's two proposals of marriage?" For these students, as is true of almost all the literature students Rocklin has worked with over the past 15 years of teaching the play, and like generations of scholars, critics, directors, actors, and spectators before them, assumed that Isabella must accept the Duke's proposal. And this was true even of students, mostly women, who indignantly asked "Why does Isabella accept?" But the same recursive effect could also occur when we focused, as we both think it is vital and rewarding to focus, on "small" often ignored scenes. So when students read, rehearsed, and performed 2.3 – a 42-line scene in which the Duke makes his first appearance disguised as a Friar and, under the eye of the Provost of the prison, seeks to confess Juliet, the woman whose betrothal/marriage to Isabella's brother and pregnancy precipitate the play's potentially tragic situation – they discovered the quite surprising range of possible performances of Juliet, who can range from self-effacingly submissive to penitent yet courageously defiant. Similarly, they discovered the remarkable range of performances for the Duke-as-Friar, possibilities which can make him seem, for example, a deeply compassionate figure whom the spectators can trust to create a happy ending; or a self-centered role-player whose insensitive response to Juliet's suffering seems to portend a disastrous conclusion to his risky experiment. Even the Provost, they discovered, can be performed so as to suddenly shift our point of view on or interpretation of the action.

Early in the course, we recognized that because they were novices in translating the text into performance, students find it relatively easy to be strong in performing mandated language and movements, but may become lost or uncomfortable in between, often dropping their characterizations while waiting for their next line or action. We knew that this dropping in and out was not due to a lack of talent or even solely to the nervousness they felt in these early performances, but a direct outcome of their inexperience.

Thus in one of the early classes we decided to have Innerst-Peterson lead a fishbowl examination of Act 1, scene 2. The fishbowl is a quite useful way of modelling a process new to a class. While the rest of the class, including Rocklin, watched, Innerst-Peterson brought a few student volunteers to the center of the circle to work through the scene in the sort of exploration that she employs as she prepares a play for performance. At the close of this activity, the whole group discussed not only what had occurred during the activity but how the process had unfolded, and what seemed to be the key questions, interventions, and inventions – both from the participants' and the observers' points of view. We also discussed what principles we could articulate for the performance of the scene from this experience.

This scene features Lucio and the First and Second Gentlemen. Instead of first discussing where they were or who would enter from where, the team read through the scene once and began with the five questions enumerated above. The team concluded that the scene has three basic functions: first, to introduce the audience to Lucio; second, to demonstrate the bawdiness pervading the streets and taverns of Vienna; and third, to act as both a response to Scene 1 and a bridge-yet-contrast to Scene 3. The team noted that Lucio was intelligent, cocky, and, they thought, witty but a bit obnoxious. They decided that Lucio acted within the design of the play as a representative of depravity, albeit comic depravity; and that the First and Second Gentlemen acted as mirrors to Lucio, reflecting his behavior even as they also served as catalysts for it. And, finally, the team concluded that the characters' status shifted within the scene – a dynamic inherent in the nature of these insult exchanges – but that Lucio, despite such shifts, both begins and ends on top, in part because he throws the first and last insults.

This analysis gave the students cues as to how to perform the scene. First, they knew that the scene called for a rapid-fire pace and that, given the nature of the exchanges, the character who had hurled the most recent barb and scored was, therefore, at least momentarily on top in terms of status, hence would almost certainly act in a way that displayed his relish of the triumph. They also knew that the scene should be loud and lewd, in part to serve as a contrast to the Duke's formal transfer of power (where, we might add, there are also three figures concerned with power); and as a preparation for the third scene, where Claudio's mortal sentence would create a further contrast in pace and tone. So when they performed the scene, they attempted to create vocally the pace and bawdiness that would project Lucio's sense of superiority, the tone of the streets of Vienna, and the competitive dynamic of the friendship-rivalry between these three men.

What we were modeling here was not just the work on this scene but the core sequence of activities, including the physical and vocal warm ups followed by the form of close-reading that included both literary study of the text and what we called "tablework". The aim, particularly in the early fishbowl activity, was to enable students not only to expand their performance range but to begin articulating an understanding of what is involved in the process of creating a performance. As they worked with this model, students were also taught to ask further questions about action, acting, setting, the use of props, and movement. Thus before the students invented their performance they had a good understanding of what the scene can be made to do, hence made to mean for the spectators; of the dynamics, including tone, pace, and rhythm; of the characters' inferable motivations; and of the characters' relationships with one another. This knowledge, coupled with the preparation they engage in through their warm-up activities, creates a wider palette from which they can compose their performance, as well as helping them develop a more detailed and precise ability to discern the patterns and nuances of their classmates' performances.

The Course in Action: Making Choices

One of the central problems we found ourselves confronting was the ratio of choices and non-choices the students made during their performances. Making choices between alternate options is, of course, the very core of what actors and directors do as they attempt to produce their own unique incarnation of the playtext. The choices they make serve a dual role. On the one hand, these choices prompt the spectators to make sense of the character's – and the play's – actions and words; while at the same time these choices also provide the cues which prompt the other characters to make some of their subsequence choices. Because any physical action can and will be read by the spectators and other *dramatis personae* as the outward manifestation of interior motive, the greater the control the actor has over his or her body and voice, the more precise and legible his or her choices will be. Conversely, what we called non-choices tend to make the performances less legible or more ambiguous. By non-choices, we explained to the students, we were designating the vocal and physical actions that were (or seemed to be) random or unselfconscious – their unmonitored behavior – for example, the way they often shifted their weight or wandered as they spoke the lines. The point here was that such non-choices would still be noted and, in many cases, interpreted by their fellow actors and even more often by the rest of the class in their role as spectators. In working with the class, we realized (again) that these non-choices played a large role in the performances early in the quarter because these students did not have the training required to achieve the vocal and physical discipline by which actors can make or seek to make every choice deliberate and telling; and, conversely, that as amateurs, these students were often so self-conscious that they were inhibited from even seeking to perform every choice they could imagine. As a result, the students often seemed to drift in and out of character during the course of a scene, creating a composite of what the character was thinking and doing and what the student was thinking and doing. Again, this was a problem that we sought to learn from as we worked on a specific scene.

In this case, we chose to focus on the issue of non-choices as the students worked on Act 1, Scene 4, wherein Lucio enters the convent and interrupts Isabella and Francisca, a nun. Derek, the student performing Lucio entered with great hesitation, his back to Isabella and Francisca, cheating (in theater parlance) to stage left – that is, with his feet facing downstage, but his torso turned to his left. He peeked around his own shoulder and motioned Isabella to come closer.

One possible interpretation, of course, and an easy (and probably correct) assumption to make was that Derek was nervous: read as the deliberate choices of Derek-the-actor seeking to transform the role into the character of Lucio, that is, his body-language seemed to communicate his desire to exit as soon as possible; and his beckoning gesture to Isabella seemed designed to minimize the need for moving any further into the performing space. We realized, however, and suggested to the class, that it might be more useful for us to interpret his actions *as if* they were all intentional choices and did not indicate a break in character by Derek, but, rather, something about the character of Lucio. In short, we got at the issue of non-choices by asking students to focus on one such non-choice as a choice. We hoped that the benefits of introducing the topic indirectly might be two-fold. First, reading Derek's behavior as his character's choices emphasized the public nature of performance, and prompted students to consider the inescapability and implications of making choices – even when such choices were not consciously made. Second, this premise aimed to encourage students to let go of their fears that the audience will be looking at *them* – at Derek or Katy or Marta or John – demonstrating that audiences watch plays to see characters. The indirect lesson we sought to convey was simply that it is often, in a sense, *safer* to stay in character.

So in the model we proposed, Derek made a choice, probably unintentional in terms of his character but perhaps reflecting his own personal preference, which if interpreted by the spectators as the choice of Lucio – that is, as the character's rather than the student-actor's expressive behavior – might be read as "Lucio feels unworthy to enter such sacred ground", or "Lucio is uncomfortable around such obviously religious people", or even simply "Lucio does not want a witness to his conversation with Isabella". The point is that this assumption will open up discussion of Lucio's character; whereas interpreting his action as meaning "Derek is uncomfortable" does not advance our discussion.

Emerging Rewards

One thing we both remember vividly is the awkwardness of the early sessions, when students found the warm up activities strange and uncomfortable. As we gathered in our circle, some students shifted uncomfortably from one foot to the other, while other students giggled or made good-natured yet slightly disparaging remarks, communicating quite clearly that they had not expected to be doing quite this much physical activity, even in a performance-centered English drama classroom. But as the weeks progressed, and as we developed longer and steadier routines, the nervous fidgeting and comments began to be replaced by a focused silence.

Around the fifth week of the quarter, students began to share with us that they had begun to incorporate vocal and physical warm-ups in their routines in other spheres of their lives. Some students, speaking in a whispered, co-conspiratorial manner, confessed to Innerst-Peterson that they had taken to leading themselves through these warm ups during study breaks; and, they would add, sometimes seeming shocked, that the warm ups made them more alert and more focused. Sarah would smile and say "Good!" There was, furthermore, a wonderful public moment that we both noticed when, in the ninth week, at the start of class, one student, who was feeling especially wound up and energized, walked to the center of the classroom, took her place in the circle, and thereby commanded us, in action rather than in words, to get down to business – finally chiding us, the teachers, for not moving quickly enough into our proper roles as initiators of the action.

This vivid transfer of initiative seemed to operate as a cue for our work together on this day. The students, armed with the performance tools and knowledge they had acquired during the previous eight weeks, took over the class, guiding themselves through their work. We were working now on a major scene, Act 3, scene 1, in which the Duke-as-Friar seeks to prepare Claudio for his apparently inevitable and imminent execution through the great (although oddly lacking in any Christian consolation) speech which begins with "Be absolute for death", only to have his work undone (or rather his own vivid depiction of mortality come back to haunt Claudio in the form of a desperate desire to live) when Isabella confides Angelo's proposal that Claudio will live if Isabella submits to Angelo's sexual advances. The four groups assembled, rehearsed, and performed this powerful scene. But whereas performance work at the start of the quarter was often fueled by our prompts, these performances were almost solely fueled by the students' own imagination and energy. And where many of the choices made at the beginning of the quarter included significant and potentially distracting non-choices, these groups efficiently decided upon their interpretations and then used their emerging art to project the choices they had made with clarity. The Isabellas ranged from quietly to violently angry, and on to vengeful and self-righteous. The Claudio's ranged from desperate or terror-stricken pleading to resigned introspection. The students watched each others' scenes intently, writing in their notebooks; and when it came time to discuss the performances, hands flew up excitedly as each student eagerly awaited his or her turn to make an observation, share an insight, or ask a question. These dynamic performances, in short, prompted an excited, rapid-fire discussion of how making choices orchestrates a scene, both in terms of performing the actions so as to convey the motives and emotions of the characters; and in terms of signaling the shaped units of action to the audience. As one of us remarked, at the end of the day we both felt as if we had died and gone to Shakespeare Teacher Heaven.

Epilogue
Although some may feel that the moments of payoff we have described here are small compared to the time and energy invested, we continue to believe that moments or even whole classes like these are rarely isolated. We believe that the work these students did during the spring quarter of 1999 will feed the way they participate in and reflect on other creative acts and arts tomorrow. For us,

teaching through performance is like shooting an arrow: the greater the focused energy applied in pulling back the bowstring and the steadier the breathing, the farther and more true the arrow will fly.

In closing, we return to the point about reading which opens this essay. We suggest that just as one virtue of the performance approach is that it foregrounds the translation challenge of learning to speak the language of the page and the language of the stage, so it may also make central the challenge of speaking these languages for teachers working with second-language students of English. We hope that the model provided in our essay will encourage teachers around the globe to employ an approach which, by asking students to experiment with performing the language not only engages them with the sound as well as the sense but invites them to explore what these words do and what these words can be made to do. We certainly can testify to the fact that in such a class students discover not only the poetic beauty but the sonic and kinetic power of the language through which Shakespeare invited all subsequent readers to become recreators of speech-in-action. We believe that employing this approach presents students and teachers with a resource for a fuller, deeper, and more vivid engagement with these remarkable and remarkably protean play texts.

TEACHING SHAKESPEARE THROUGH PERFORMANCE – "I KNOW MY COURSE"

Mary Z. Maher
(University of Arizona)

One of the most important assumptions behind the teaching of Shakespeare through performance is a recognition that the teacher is teaching two things and both are equally commendable, attainable, capable of being assessed, and necessary for everyday life: 1) Shakespeare's plays, and 2) the performance of Shakespeare's plays. With subjects as rich and complex as these, it is impossible at times to discriminate between content areas. In practice, it is the very interaction of the two that allows the literature to yield up its dramatic secrets. Plot, character, dialogue, language become necessary components of fulfilling the task.

In order to enact Shakespeare, the student has to come to a conclusion about what the lines mean. Much of the process is exploratory, trial-and-error, critique and adjustment, re-discussion and re-performance. Students are mastering a language which belongs to another time, one so rich in texture, nuance, and creative energy that those who study it need a high tolerance for ambuigity and complexity. Along with analytical skills, experience in performance engenders tangible outcomes – an increased ability of expression and communication (improved technical skills with the use of voice and body); poise and confidence; a sense of what is aesthetically pleasing and what is not (the development of taste); and a growing knowledge of what works in performance and what does not (development of critical faculties vis-à-vis performance).

Along with deeper knowledge and penetration of a great literary work come the attendant advantages of that kind of study: vicarious experience; knowledge of another time and culture; values clarification through contact with great ideas; mastery of advanced and highly-wrought language skills; and a sense – sometimes an actual physicalization – of structure, unity and balance within great works of art.

The focus of such a course is enacting Shakespearean texts in order to identify the source and nature of their dramatic potential and to discover their specifically *theatrical qualities*. Playtexts are treated as scripts – not as metaphors, symbols, or themes. Such labels can be insightful and help to establish a common vocabulary, but the playscripts are more importantly seen as potential actions, as entities which will be fully realized once articulated through gesture, vocal production, movement, and the other aspects of staging.

Such learning is extremely valuable within a twenty-first century curriculum. For many years, practice in communication skills was built into the college curriculum in the United States, just as many performance exercises, including verse and poetry memorization, presentation of self, character construction, and vocal practice, were part of the curriculum in Great Britain, Canada, Australia and New Zealand. Sadly, these courses have declined and have been replaced with more theoretical (or even more computer-oriented) curricula. Nonetheless, role-playing, gestural systems, vocal production – in short, performance skills, are still an essential part of the education of the citizenry in every country, every language, every part of the global community. This course fulfills a number of these educational needs.

I have taught a course called "Shakespeare Through Performance" for 25 years. For the first dozen years, the course was housed within a speech communication department as a split-level offering for upper undergraduates and graduate students in a (then) practicum-oriented speech program. For the second half of my teaching career, it was located in a theater department, where it was offered as one of the 'general education' requirements. This meant that it drew from a hugely diverse group of majors from the liberal arts through a wide variety of sciences.

The course was best taught to advanced students, preferably with an interest in performance and in Shakespeare, an expectation important to emphasize within the orientation lectures so that the students understood that they would be memorizing and rehearsing classical literature and were somewhat familiar with stage practice and with creative work. (Such students, I found, were readily available in majors like arid land studies, computer science, physics and optics, law and medicine, as well as in fine arts.) Other necessaries included establishing a class size of 20 members or under, a class period that extended beyond 50 minutes, and a flexible classroom which allowed division into performance-space and audience-space. 'Perks' or 'frills' included having video-viewing equipment in the classroom, a simplified lighting rig for the performance space, and a few basic blocks or furniture pieces usable within the scenes. Although the teaching materials can be subdivided quite easily, I preferred to teach this course in a night class or a late afternoon three-hour block.

I usually began the course with *Hamlet*, and also included a history play or a dark comedy, plus a comedy: What I sacrificed in quantity, I gained in the students' ownership of these 3 plays. I used the Signet Classic editions because I felt the notes were generally helpful and there was not too much editorial addition to the dialogue. Students read portions of J. L. Styan's *Shakespeare's Stagecraft*, especially relevant for the history and language units at the beginning of the course. 'On reserve' in the library were *Variorum* editions of the plays, plus the optional text, C.T. Onions' *Shakespeare's Glossary*.

* * *

I begin the course with what I think of as 'the name game', an opening exercise which promotes socialization. Once the rules of behavior are laid out (I am especially demanding about attendance, because missing classes cuts into each student's individual development as well as creates chaos in the groupwork aspect of the course), I put students in pairs and have them interview each other 1) to discover one another's names, 2) to elicit a performance history (which includes anything from teaching a swimming class to performing Shakespeare – i.e., assuming a certain role in front of an audience), 3) to find out one another's 3 favorite Shakespeare plays (this last gives me some idea of how much background in Shakespeare each student has had). Then each person introduces his/her new friend and offers a way to remember that person's first and last name. By the end of the first class period, each student has been required to learn every first and last name in the room. I emphasize that if we are going to be working closely with self-images and egos, it is polite to know your colleagues' names. Unbeknownst to the students, they have just completed their first oral presentation and also achieved their first memory task. Also, the professor has obtained a kind of rough diagnostic of the skills levels in the class, discovering which ones can help to mentor the others performance-wise.

The first full unit is a brief one, the history unit, built on the supposition that context is needed to understand a language and a culture over 400 years old. I begin by giving a lecture called 'Playing Conditions in Shakespeare's Time', where I describe acting companies and the professional players, public and private theaters, audiences, theater traditions (the flag flying outside the each theater, methods of advertising plays), the position of playwrights in the culture, lore and other conventions. I then ask students to sign up for one of 20 topics that I have written on the board, including personalities such as Queen Elizabeth I and Edward Alleyn, historical objects like Henslowe's diary, the Rose theater, and the First Folio, as well as conceptual ideas like the authorship controversy and Shakespeare's education. These topoi are tightly controlled by a reading list of acceptable reference materials, and by the way the students have to deliver these class presentations. The materials are to be transformed into *timed* visual-aid speeches (7 minutes each), requiring an illustrative handout or a costume or some other device which helps the audience to remember the material. Students must *directly communicate* and not *read* their presentations. These tactics are urged to 1) earn a higher grade for the speaker, and 2) to enliven the class period for the auditors. Twenty reports in one class session can be pretty rough going without a little tweaking of the presentational style, but students are usually very inventive in this assignment. One woman came in a long gown, and began her report with "I am the Globe Theatre". Another man, playing Richard Burbage, was an interviewee on a radio program. At the end of the unit, students have now executed their second performance experience, albeit playing the role of compliant student as opposed to Juliet or Autolycus. I close this unit by showing a film (these have varied over the years), currently *Shakespeare: The Man and his Times*.[1]

The next unit is somewhat longer, the 'language unit'. It makes use of an assignment the students got during the opening ceremonies (on the first day) which was to memorize 20 verse lines of *Hamlet*. I begin with a long lecture, which comes complete with a worksheet that illustrates the quotations/examples I am referring to. In the lecture, I give a brief history of Elizabethan language; cover language conventions in Shakespeare's time (prologues, epilogues, tirades, soliloquies, rhyming couplets to close a scene, etc.); and provide a simple method of text-based character analysis. I offer some common-sense guidelines, such as using the punctuation as a rough aid in deciding where to take short and long pauses, watching out for monosyllabic lines, noting changes from verse to prose, and I illustrate the major literary/rhetorical devices of anthesis, parallelism, and repetition. I review certain ornamental devices such as metaphor and personification and suggest how the performer might use them. All of these are demonstrated, emphasizing that we do not learn about them to label them but to discover what one must do with the voice and the body to *perform* them. One must always ask WHY? and WHAT DOES IT DO TO THE PLAY AND THE CHARACTER? and finally HOW COULD I PERFORM THIS? Knowing about the language should bridge into the performance of it. Lastly, I deal with verse structure and have students very simply 'meter out' certain lines as well as suggest ways to to deal with shortened lines, run-on lines, and enjambement.

RULES I keep repeating are my own: 1) "Yes, dear, you have to read the *whole* play", and 2) "Read for the sense of the line, not the rhythm of the line." I do not prioritize iambic pentameter (and this is my own personal belief) – I spend the most time on emphasizing the operative word in each sentence as one speaks the lines. I feel, for their stage of the game, this skill of learning proper vocal emphasis is more important than learning the divine subtleties and multiple varieties of verse. I find especially useful Patsy Rodenburg's dictum about "Heightened Realism": Shakespearean characters have a larger scope and do not fit easily into one's livingroom, but they must seem as real as Kevin Kline does on screen.[2] I demonstrate how to divide a longer speech up into 'beats' or bits or paragraphs and to find the character's intention in each. I reiterate that there are several right ways and several wrong ways – acting is creative work and one has options and choices: The best are easily read by the audience and well-grounded in the text.

My feet always hurt after this lecture because it is top-heavy with data and larded over with advice, so we end with a group exercise. Inspired by a book called *Shakespeare's Insults*, I have compiled a 3-page worksheet of curses and ejaculations, many of them humorous in a modern context and from this, an ice-breaker exercise has emerged.[3] I have the students hurl phrases at one another (on their feet) in order to get some inhibitions broken down, and then I divide the class into groups of 4, each of which creates an improvised playlet using lines from the worksheet. Students choose various locations ("Eat my leek!" fits nicely into a restaurant setting) and, in 10-20 minutes of workshopping, are required to create their own plot and characters. I tried this assignment on a whim one day, and it has survived with the immediate result of producing (usually) one really inventive scene per period and a long-term result of lots of relaxed interaction communication within the class. It also forces students to learn a number of Shakespeare's lines in order to perform the improvisation.

For a homework assignment connected with the language unit, they must now type out (triple-spaced) the 20 lines of *Hamlet* they have memorized and then print out two copies. They are asked to look up every important word (whether they know its twentieth-century meaning or not) in the *Oxford English Dictionary*. On one of their printed copies, they write a close paraphrase directly under each line of dialogue *in the character's voice*. No fair skipping over undecipherable passages – for these, they must consult the *Variorum* edition. On the second print-out, they are asked to 'meter out' the passage, marking it for iambic pentameter. The final page is a short essay which incorporates other hints from the language lecture and synthesizes what they have now discovered about the memorized 20-line passage.[4]

One must guard the actor's right and obligation to remain open-minded during the rehearsal process, but at a certain point, even the Royal Shakespeare Company's chief tragedienne has to *choose how she will interpret the role*. At this point, I like to provide the students with a worksheet I have developed for all of my acting classes called "Rehearsal Strategies". It is a double-sided sheet of paper, easily foldable into a billfold or purse, to carry along to rehearsals. The sheet reinforces all I have talked about during the language lecture but in the form of questions that the students are supposed to ask one another (and of the scene assigned) during their out-of-class rehearsals.

I advise that three rehearsals are needed for full preparation of each scene to be performed in class: one to cast the scene, to roughly plan a 'traffic control' pattern (blocking), and to do a read-through of the scene with discussion; one to closely work out what every line means and what actions and reactions might be (for this, come to rehearsal MEMORIZED); and a final rehearsal to put the polish on it, solidifying character conceptions and making use of all costumes and properties. Costumes and props, by the way, are almost always borrowed or pilfered, highly imaginative, and a bit over the top. I tell students early on that the theater department will not provide them rehearsal space, props, nor costumes, so that places us on our own resources, our own wardrobes, even our own bedsheets. Students seem to adapt to this 'found art' principle and to become even more entrepreneurial because of it. I urge long skirts for women, to give them grace and authority, and I point out how shorts and tank tops really vie with the language and the character messages. Our city has plenty of thrift shops and used clothing places to help them fill in the blanks at under $5, but mostly they prefer to tap their own creativity. My classroom has one fake tree-like potted plant, donated from somewhere, that has hidden Beatrice, displayed sonnets and various plastic flowers, and been tempest-toss'd by angry heroes.

I next begin to prepare the students for the first of their three scenes. The initial performance schedule has been handed out on an assignment sheet during (roughly) the second or third week of the course, so that they have plenty of time to memorize. I cast the plays, attempting a balance of weak and strong performers. I hope to give women a chance to play women at least once during the semester, noting that we are reversing gender at times (as Shakespeare did – boy players were featured in one oral report earlier on in the course), and that I am doing my best to be equitable. Occasionally, I will cast an all-female Act 1, Scene 1 of *Hamlet*; other scenes that play well with all women are the Osric scene, the recorder scene, and the grave-digger scene. Today's women often express a wish to play the role of Hamlet. I encourage that.

I spend a little time in class talking about ways to memorize and soliciting further suggestions from some of the more experienced performers in class.[5] I like to perform the first scenes from *Hamlet* because 1) I have written a book about it and know it really well, 2) it is often the play the students have read, 3) students can often identify with the main character. So, I begin with a lecture about 'performance options' in *Hamlet*, noting the possibilities for almost all of the characters in production, emphasizing that there have been many different-aged and different-shaped (and very successful) Hamlets and Ophelias.[6] I tell them that 50% of the role comes from the text and 50% from their own personalities, the parts which should be highlighted to match the character qualities of the role.

I show one scene from 2 to 3 different filmed versions of *Hamlet* so as to point out the wide variety of character conceptions possible. We work on how these 'read' in performance, and we discuss how the directorial concept shapes or limits character conception. We also discuss production values and how those influence character. *Hamlet* 1.2. works well because a number of characters appear, and we get a first peek at where these interpretations are heading. The nunnery scene works well, and so does the duel scene – because there is not much dialogue in it and the director has usually added a great deal of performance text to the playscript. Occasionally, I will tell students that they are graded Pass/Fail on this first scene, because it takes the pressure off of them for their maiden performance, and it also relieves me of awarding a great many C's (or lower) to fairly naive performances.

Each scene has two performances, a 'workshop' performance, and a final performance – each performance gets a separate grade. Each scene and each performer is graded individually. Partial memorization of lines is unacceptable. (For me to work with these performances in class, the scenes must be fully memorized.)

After each workshop performance, I lead the oral critique and ask for class input. I stick with the basics at first: Who are you? Where are you? What are you doing there? What do you want? If the audience does not mention glaring problems, I might ask, "What one thing would you advise this group to do to really improve the scene?" Usually, very fundamental things need to be corrected: performers need to 'play front' (allow the audience to see their eyes and faces) more; they need to speak louder; they need to SLOW DOWN (I write this critique so often I should have a rubber stamp made); they need to find the 'beats' or paragraphs in a speech; they need to change vocal tone when the dialogue does; the group needs to use more of the playing space; the group needs to use the forward part of the playing space; all of the blocking needs work; a pair of shoes/costume/props should be added or discarded or adjusted; there needs to be less furniture in the playing space, and so on.

Here, of course, is where directing training or theater background comes in handy.[7] I do advise students to keep things simple: a few well-chosen moves will provide the variety the audience needs in a blocking scheme, for example. Furthermore, I say "the audience does not know who you are until you move", until the performer displays body language. If your students incline toward being wooden statues, stand back, encourage them more, go to an acting text or a colleague for some good 'theater games' that get students moving and playing with each other. It usually takes very little if you are positive and nurturing.

So, the scary bit – giving criticism – has begun. I start by telling them I used to 'audition' my convention papers in front of my students because I *sought* and *wanted* critique on my delivery; I wanted them (as audience) to write (unsigned) criticism for me so I would not look like a fool by doing something drastic or counter-productive during my presentation. I emphasize that they are all reaching that maturity level where they want to do things *right*. Good criticism is something one seeks, one wants, and one then uses to improve one's performance.

Each performance session also draws in written feedback from peers (each student selects an individual performer – one from each scene per class period, to write critiques about on half-sheets of paper). I request that students deliver both COMPLIMENTS (everyone needs to know what s/he has done *well*) and SUGGESTIONS FOR IMPROVEMENT – this is *balanced* criticism. I assert that every scene needs improvement; even Kenneth Branagh prefers having a director. Each critic signs the criticism s/he as written (takes responsibility for it); it is returned to the performer (after I have recorded it as part of the 'audience participation' grade) during the following class period, with my written 'master critique', with the grade on it, stapled on the top. This way, the student knows what criticisms to make use of, to improve, prior to the final performance.

During the oral critique following the scenes, I point out details that need work, offering a way to improve things or, I might articulate, from my experience, fundamental guidelines. For example, "Audience members need to be able to see and hear at all times. What can we do to make this possible – because right now, we are hearing most of the lines but not all of them. Does anyone have suggestions for the performers?"

The final performances (for a second grade) for each scene are considerably more polished. I tend to use my more advanced students (which one discerns, really, once the introductions and the oral reports are concluded) as standard-setters. They raise the bar for the others to reach, and they can also mentor less experienced students through a scene. They are occasionally mistaken for 'favorites of the teacher', however, I usually give them fairly challenging scenes to keep them on their toes. Also, I abjectly confess (somewhere during the semester) that I do indeed have favorites, and those are always the students that are putting in effort – not the most talented ones but the hardest workers.

On the second play we perform, I begin to fine-tune more on text. I have done an exercise which the more ambitious students really like but, frankly, not everyone does. At the end of the 'workshop scenes' for this play, I have the cast sit on blocks or tables with their backs to us. Then, they simply re-speak the lines. Often, there are wrong-emphasis problems. Instead of announcing, "You are saying it wrong", I might lead in sideways: "I think you will get more mileage out of that line if you emphasize who *exactly* did what", OR "It works better to say, 'You have *stayed* me in a happy hour', rather than 'You have stayed me in a *happy* hour'. Because, you see, Beatrice is saying she prefers to be 'stayed' in a happier time or memory rather than saying she wants to go have drinks in a bar." One learns, over the years, the tactful way to express criticism – one also learns that one is not perfect and cannot please all of the students all of the time.

The other two plays assigned for the course follow pretty much along the lines of the first one, so that the last two thirds of the course focus intensively on performance. About a week before the end of the semester, the 'staging paper' is due (I request a 'due date' ahead of time so that students are not working on these papers when their final scenes are due). The 'staging paper', described in the syllabus and referred to throughout the semester, requires that a student select either a scene s/he has performed in or another scene performed by colleagues: The assignment is to describe the growth of that scene from the page to the stage. The paper (4-5 pages) expands on insights and discoveries the student has collected from the first time the scene was performed to the present. Observations should include explorations from class performances, insights on characterization, inner or outer condition of character clarified, specific interpretations of words or lines, stage business, movement, blocking, or gesture discovered, messages/themes resonated, images understood afresh. The paper should focus on a class performance but can include other film/video performances the group saw and learned from (I use a number of scenes from films in class to help introduce each play, and recommend others to be seen out of class). I explain that we watch films not to copy a performance (why bother to do that in a creative art!) but to discover performance options.

The papers are very individual and insightful. Some need to focus on text more, but all detail leaps and bounds of self-discovery, which is a great deal of what performance is about. Students always refer to "my role" in the paper. The papers always astound me, but then, so does the perennial comment, "This is the best course I took in college."

Over the years, I relinquished giving a final written exam. Counting the final performance of the final scenes as a double grade, and adding in the work of the staging paper seemed totality enough for a course that was after all, about speaking the speech. I began to prefer *A Midsummer Night's Dream* as a concluding play more and more. The final play-within-the-play and the surrounding magical scenes sounded a celebratory note appropriate for ending our revels, as well as for my journey with each particular – and most certainly individual – group.

Notes

1. This film is available through Films in the Humanities, or CLEARVUE/eav, 1-800-253-2788, 6465 No. Avondale Ave., Chicago, IL 60631. It is 47 min. long and has three parts: *Shakespeare's Life, Shakespeare's Theatre, Shakespeare's Life and Times*. The narrators are British, the illustrations mostly from the period, and the information reinforces the students' reports.

2. A brief but commonsense explanatory statement of Patsy Rodenburg's ideas appeared in the Summer 1998 *Shakespeare Bulletin* entitled, "Acting the Words: An Interview with Patsy Rodenburg", by Margaret A. Varnell, pp. 29-30. Rodenburg was head of voice, at different times, at the Guildhall Drama School, the Stratford Festival, and the Royal National Theatre.

3. This is an imaginative giftbook, a collection of *Shakespeare's Insults: Educating Your Wit*, by Wayne F. Hill and Cynthia J. Ottchen, Cambridge: MainSail Press, 1992.

4. This exercise is based on one devised by Audrey Stanley. If there is time, I will occasionally use the 20 lines in a group-memorizing marathon, where they speak them on their feet and physically change directions as the beats in the speech change.

5. There are different ways of memorizing. Some people memorize by ear, as some musicians do. Others like to write out the passage and have a tactile involvement with the words. Still others simply repeat and repeat lines until these are memorized. Occasionally, a tape recording, played again and again, especially before one falls to sleep, is helpful. It helps to 'run the lines' with a friend or partner. Sometimes my students call each other and do this on the telephone.

6. For an article that helps teachers understand how to use film, read Sharon Beehler's essay, entitled "Making Media Matter in the Shakespeare Classroom", in *Teaching Shakespeare into the Twenty-first Century*, by Ronald E. Salamone and James E. Davis (Athens: Ohio UP, 1997).

7. Experience, as we know, is a great teacher. A basic course in acting and one in directing can add much expertise to a teacher's innate instinct to improve a scene.

Appendix
SHAKESPEARE THROUGH PERFORMANCE – THEATER ARTS 336 SYLLABUS

This course has as its goal the understanding of Shakespeare's plays through performance. It is founded on a method of performance-oriented analysis which compels a thorough comprehension of the language, ideas, emotions, attitudes and intentions of characters in the selected plays performed. The course provides historical backgrounds for the theatrical tradition in Shakespeare's time, critical and analytical tools with which to understand and speak the language of the plays, and performance experience in classical drama. There is ample use of video and film resources.

REQUIRED TEXTS: *Shakespeare's Stagecraft*, J.L. Styan
Signet Classic editions of *Hamlet, Prince of Denmark*; *Much Ado About Nothing*; *A Midsummer Night's Dream*

OPTIONAL TEXT: *A Shakespeare Glossary*, C.T. Onions

OUTSIDE READINGS: See last page.
Also "A Shakespeare Sampler", the bibliography hand-out.

TENTATIVE CALENDAR:
Week 1: Introductions and orientation to the course and course requirements – syllabus, outside reading list, plus General Policies sheet regarding attendance, papers & exams, rehearsal guidelines. Film about Shakespeare's England.
Read article in folder on reserve, "The World of Elizabeth I."

Week 2: Lecture on "Playing Conditions in Shakespeare's Time", an historical overview – what the theater and acting were like during this period. Viewing of films about Shakespeare stage and theatre practice. Assignment of topics for oral presentations (See topics list under "Paperwork"). READ CHAPTERS 1 *through* 3 in Styan's book prior to lecture.

Week 3: Assignment of oral presentations (see "Thinkwork and Paperwork".) These are critiqued and graded for content as well as delivery. Give the speech extemporaneously – do not read it to the audience. You may use notecards. YOU MUST BE READY ON YOUR ASSIGNED DATE.

Week 4: Finish oral presentations.

Week 5: Begin lecture/discussion on the use of language in Shakepearean plays – influences, patterns of usage, word order, idioms, elisions. Conventions in Shakespeare's include prologues, epilogues, soliloquies, tirades, persuasion speeches, ornamental speeches, gestic speech, spoken decor. Instruction and resources for finding word meanings; delivery of verse and prose. We will conclude with in-class exercises which aid in deciphering performance options.
READ CHAPTERS 6 and 7 in the Styan book on "Orchestration of Speech".
Possible quiz over the chapters so far.

Week 6: Preparation lecture on Shakespearean tragedy, specific to *Hamlet*. Discussion of comparative scenes from film/video versions of *Hamlet*. Performance options of major characters and performance issues in *Hamlet*. Assignment of scenes from *Hamlet*. BRING YOUR PLAYTEXT TO CLASS!

Weeks 7,8&9: "Performance sessions" * of selected scenes from *Hamlet*.

Week 10: Recap discussion on *Hamlet*, with focus on gains and losses, effective rehearsal strategies. Handing out of *Much Ado About Nothing* scene assignments.

Week 11: Preparation for *Much Ado,* including preparatory lecture on dark comedy and creating comic characters. Analysis of Benedick's soliloquies and the chapel scene from the film. Have the play very thoroughly read because we're going to discuss the structure of the play, the language in the play, and characterization. Also read Ch. 4

& 5, Styan book. BRING YOUR PLAYSCRIPT TO CLASS!

Week 12 & 13: Performance Sessions * on *Much Ado*.

Week 14: Recap comments on *Much Ado*. **"Staging papers" ARE DUE SOON. Begin preparation on final play, *A Midsummer Night's Dream*. Lecture about Shakespeare's invitation to comic invention in this play, discussion of the different worlds set up by the playwright; film showing of comparative versions of Pyramus and Thisby play inset. Exercise on handling strictly rhymed iambic pentameter.

Week 15 & 16: Performance sessions * on *A Midsummer Night's Dream*.

NOTE: "Performance sessions" are very important class periods. I will hand out schedules of when groups perform. They will include one-person, two-person and three-person scenes which have been rehearsed outside of class (at least 3 separate times for each scene) and for which lines *must be memorized*. When scenes are given a designated class day for showing, this class period becomes a "workshop" session. Scenes are performed, sometimes re-performed in part or in whole and very throughly discussed. Discoveries are made about the play and about each person's capacity for performance and process of performance. Individual grades are given for each person in each scene. Grades are based on the quality of preparation and rehearsal, on memorization, on the quality of performance, on your attitude toward performance, and on your contributions to the discussion. **IMPORTANT! FOR CLASS ATTENDANCE AND GRADING CRITERIA, BE THERE FOR MY LECTURE AND DISCUSSION ABOUT THE "GENERAL POLICIES" SHEET.** It contains the formal agreement (rules and regs) for the course.

PAPERWORK, THINKWORK:

1. The outside reading list, SHAKESPEARE SAMPLER, is comprehensive but was selected to feature *performed* Shakespeare.

2. The **oral presentation** is 7 min. (no longer) in length, on an historical topic from Shakespeare's time. It must include one handout/visual aid which supports, pictorializes, or clarifies the topic presented. Hand in one page of "bibliography" which gives outside resources (library books, video, film or interview) consulted. Presenters are encouraged to appear in costume or to devise a *persona* appropriate to the material. Both *content* and *delivery* will be part of your grade.

  Topics list includes but is not limited to: The First Folio and Shakespearean quartos; reconstructions and remains of the Globe Theatre; the Rose Theatre (an archaeological site); the Swan Theatre; Kempe, Armin and Tarleton, clowns in Shakespeare's company; Richard Burbage; Edward Alleyn; Elizabeth I; King James; Sir Francis Drake and exploration; boy actors; Children of the Revels; Clothing – daily wear; costumes in Shakespeare's theater; the organization and personnel of Shakespeare's acting company, the Lord Chamberlain's Men and the King's Men; Henslowe's Diary; the "new" Globe on Bankside in London; Shakespeare's audience; Shakespeare's education; the authorship controversy. (Let me know if you have a special interest in one of these topics or have other topics.) IMPORTANT NOTE: Consult your "Shakespeare Sampler", the longish bibliography handed out at the beginning of the course, for guiding you to the best books and sources to consult in constructing your speech.

3. **Text analysis** of lines in *Hamlet*, including scansion, paraphrastic via *OED* and *Variorum* searches, and summary essay on what these exercises revealed. 4 pages.

4. **Staging paper**. From any of the scenes presented in class (yours or another group's), compose a 5-page paper which expands on insights and discoveries you have collected from the first time you read the scene to the present. These should include explorations from class performances, insights on characterization, how verse or prose affects the delivery of the lines, specific interpretations of words or lines, stage business, movement or gestures discovered, blocking and stage movement; inner or outer condition of character clarified, messages or themes resonated, images understood afresh, etc. The paper should *focus* on a class performance but can include other film/video performances you have seen. Attach a xeroxed copy of the scene you write about. Due dates are TBA. LATE PAPERS ARE NOT ACCEPTED. EVER. ALL PAPERS MUST BE TYPED.

6. **Final Performance**

GRADING: Papers, oral presentation   40%
   Exams   10%
   Performances & class participation 50%

OUTSIDE READING

(On Reserve in the Reserve Book Room in the University Main Library)
Helge Kökeritz   *Shakespeare's Names: A Pronouncing Dictionary*
J.L. Styan   *Shakespeare's Stagecraft*
H.H. Furness   *Variorum* editions of *Hamlet; A Midsummer Night's Dream; Much Ado About Nothing*

FOLDERS ON RESERVE IN RESERVE BOOK ROOM, COMPILED BY DR. MAHER:
 − −"The World of Elizabeth I" (article in folder)

AN APPROACH TO TEACHING *ROMEO AND JULIET*

Michael J. Collins
(Georgetown University)

When I first taught *Romeo and Juliet,* some twenty-five years ago, I did in the classroom what I had recently been taught in graduate school to do: I looked closely at the script (although I would not then have called it a script) in an effort to explicate for my students its meaning. As I look back at the notes I wrote and the materials I gathered for those first classes on *Romeo and Juliet,* I recall that I hoped, as students put it in those days, to make that meaning 'relevant' to the lives of the men and women who listened to my lectures. Along with the reviews of productions I clipped from newspapers and journals, I find an article from *The Irish Echo* on the violence in Northern Ireland and another from *The New York Daily News* on two families, Montagues and Capulets in Brooklyn, whose argument over a wall between their properties ended in a shooting on a crowded city street.

Citing Hugh Richmond's description of Romeo as an "amatory Che Guevara, bringing death and destruction to his own cause and allies"[1] and another article in *The New York Daily News* about a jilted lover who stole an airplane and flew it into the house where he believed the woman who jilted him was sleeping ("Well, Juliet, I shall lie with thee tonight"), I asked my students a question which still seems to me significant, a question the play repeatedly asks but finally refuses to answer: is it only Romeo's richly poetic language that makes us feel his actions, in love and on the streets of Verona, are more noble, less violent than those we read about in Northern Ireland (or the Balkans or the Middle East) or in *The New York Daily News*?

Some ten years later, I had not only seen Michael Bogdanov's production of *Romeo and Juliet* (with Sean Bean and Niamh Cusack) at the Royal Shakespeare Theatre in Stratford, which gave the play a contemporary setting and put particular emphasis on the moneyed life style of the wealthy Capulets (the "old accustomed feast" became a pool-side party with a live rock band), but I had also discovered that I had, like Capulet, an adolescent daughter in the house. As a result of both the production and the daughter, I began to look more closely with my students at the role Juliet's mother and father play in the tragedy, focusing particularly on Act 3, Scene 5, where Capulet first berates Juliet because she will not marry Paris and where her mother then refuses to speak on her behalf.

Listening to Capulet was like listening to every father (my father, my daughter's father), for he says what fathers have apparently always said: "how can you act this way after all I have done for you" and "as long as you live in this house you will do what I tell you to do." Ignoring his earlier admonition to Paris ("But woo her, gentle Paris, get her love"), thinking (as parents often do) that his child is simply an extension of himself, Capulet, I proposed, becomes as violent and willful in his way as Romeo and Tybalt are and thus helps bring about the tragic deaths of his daughter and her husband. Teachers and students, parents and children, I suggested, seeing themselves in that scene, might somehow through it come to live more wisely and generously with one another.

Over time, however, I began to grow uneasy with my approach to *Romeo and Juliet*. Although I continued to look closely at the language and structure of the play, I felt myself too often in the end saying things about parents and children, about tribal hatreds and "civil brawls" that my students already knew. At the same time, I read an article by Stephen Booth that seemed written precisely to make me more uneasy. When students, Stephen Booth wrote, "are set to work their way through a long, difficult play in preparation for a lively discussion of issues raised in it, students are likely to guess that the virtue of the play is as an occasion for discussion; they can presumably sense that a plot outline or a case study from a law school would do all that the pedagogic strategy suggests the play can do".[2] As I often now remind my students, anything we might learn from *Romeo and Juliet* we have (as the recent film by Baz Luhrman made eminently clear) already learned in the lunch room when we were students in secondary school, in the staff room when we became teachers, at home when we became parents, or (alas) in virtually any newspaper we might read.

It needs no playwright, come some four hundred years ago from Stratford, to tell us about love, tribal violence in the streets, drugs and suicide among adolescents:

the newspaper articles, the talk shows, the books on parenting provide more than we need to know. At the same time, we implicitly patronize *Romeo and Juliet* when we say it is valuable because it in some way reminds us of the world in which we live, because the story it tells seems to reflect some contemporary public event or our own private experience. If, as Stephen Booth suggests, it were the story Shakespeare tells in *Romeo and Juliet* that made the play valuable, then we might as well (as students are sometimes asked to do) read *West Side Story* or a news report of the latest tragic love affair between a Serb and an Albanian in Kosovo or a Catholic and a Protestant in Northern Ireland, for both the musical and the report are set in worlds more immediately recognizable and written in idioms more easily accessible.

As I began to see more productions of Shakespeare, to read and think about the plays not as poems or stories to be explicated, but as scripts to be performed, and to team-teach several courses for secondary school teachers with Stephen Booth (who continued both to teach me and to make me uneasy about my own teaching), I found a different way of approaching *Romeo and Juliet*. What we value in *Romeo and Juliet*, I suggest to my students today, is not the story it tells, the meaning it might have, or the wisdom it might impart: what we value in *Romeo and Juliet* (as we do in any work of art) is our experience of it. While it is surely easier to talk about tribal violence and parenting than about our experience of *Romeo and Juliet*, the challenge for the teacher is to bring students to see that what makes *Romeo and Juliet* an enduringly popular and highly valued play in our culture is not the story Shakespeare tells, but the way he tells the story, the profoundly complex, richly patterned structure of vibrant words that actors and readers alike bring to engaging life through their own wit and imagination.

I now begin teaching *Romeo and Juliet* with an acting exercise on Act 3, Scene 5, starting with Capulet's "God's bread" and ending with the close of the scene (Juliet's "myself have power to die"). I divide the class into groups of five (four actors and a director) and ask each group, with the help of some questions, to rehearse the scene and then to act it (or at least walk through it) in the classroom, sometimes in two stages (stopping after Lady Capulet's exit) and sometimes in its entirety. (The list of questions appears in the Appendix). Once all the groups have completed their performances, the class watches several filmed versions of the scene. Finally, each student writes a short essay in which he or she suggests, with references to the entire script, why Capulet, Lady Capulet, and the Nurse act as they do in the scene.

The primary goal of the exercise is to help students experience the openness of the scene (and the play as a whole) to interpretation on the stage, and the seven or eight groups of students my class generally yields inevitably make different choices and come up with various actions and tones of voice for each of the four characters. But since they have been asked to read the play in its entirety before they begin the exercise, they are also expected to make choices that are consistent with their understanding of what has come before, and they thus begin to see some of the patterns in the script, some of the ways its various components talk back and forth to one another, reflect, echo, parallel, invert one another.

As they look back through the script to guide their choices in 3.5, students (like actors and critics) inevitably understand lines and scenes differently, and they therefore inevitably perform them differently. With Capulet, for example, they must try to reconcile his earlier concern for Juliet's happiness ("But woo her, gentle Paris, get her heart") with his now stubborn refusal to reconsider for a moment the proposed marriage, locating it ordinarily in his rash promise to Paris in the previous scene. At the same time, they find in his confrontation with Tybalt at the feast an ambiguous mixture of tolerance and restraint with anger and willfulness and thus struggle to understand behavior in 3.5. that seems at once utterly paradoxical and entirely predictable. Then, if their text follows the Second Quarto, they must also, as they work to create a plausible Capulet in the scene, consider his reasonable, even generous defense of Romeo before the Prince in 3.1 ("Not Romeo, Prince: he was Mercutio's friend;/His fault concludes but what the law should end,/The life of Tybalt"). As a result, Capulet is sometimes furiously angry, sometimes menacingly restrained, and sometimes, at least initially, simply exasperated at what seems his daughter's irrational refusal of marriage to Paris.

Lady Capulet ordinarily seems more puzzling to students than does her husband in 3.5. They inevitably recall at once her discussion with Juliet and the Nurse in 1.3. and try to imagine how she might be played there. Some conclude that Lady Capulet has long ago ceded to the Nurse the role of Juliet's mother: the Nurse's story of Juliet's fall sounds to them like the story a mother might remember as her daughter approaches marriage. Some go a step farther and find Lady Capulet cold, detached, frustrated in her marriage to an older man, understanding her lines, "I was your mother much upon these years/That you are now a maid," as an explanation of Capulet's comment to Paris in 1.2. about young mothers, "And too soon marred are those so early made." But others take Lady Capulet's lines in a different direction and, recognizing that she is probably only twenty-eight herself, imagine her happy, excited, exuberant at the prospect of Juliet's courtship and eventual marriage to so attractive and prominent a man as Paris.

No matter how they imagine her in 1.3, they must also consider Lady Capulet's violent grief at Tybalt's death and her cry for vengeance before the Prince in 3.1, particularly after I point out the recent stage tradition of suggesting that she and Tybalt are deeply and perhaps romantically attached to one another. When they finally act out the scene, Lady Capulet emerges either as a cold and sometimes bitter woman, frustrated in her marriage to Capulet, angered by her daughter's attempt to escape an arranged marriage to which she herself was subject, or as a loving mother who, pulled in two directions, shows some affection for Juliet but finally lacks the courage to confront her husband in her daughter's defense. In the second case, students often see the scene in patriarchal terms and so play it as an instance of a man threatening, bullying three women and finally intimidating two of them.

As is the case with audiences in the theatre and actors in the role, students find the Nurse both puzzling and disappointing. As they look back at her description of Romeo to Juliet in 2.5, most find that her enthusiasm for him there contradicts her opinion of him in 3.5. Others, in an attempt to reconcile the contradiction, read literally the lines in 2.5. where the Nurse seems to tease Juliet by telling her she knows "not how to choose a man." While students are not initially sensitive to their implications, I also point out both the Nurse's practical wisdom ("Ah sir, ah sir, death's the end of all") in 3.3. and the latent sexual connotations of "you no use of him" in 3.5. As a result, some students come to imagine a Nurse who is above all practical, pragmatic, a realistic survivor who finally reduces romantic love to copulation. In the end, as they try to explain the Nurse's advice to Juliet, they most often conclude that she is now afraid to disobey Capulet explicitly and thus to expose her own collusion in Juliet's marriage to Romeo. But either understanding, a frightened Nurse or a pragmatic Nurse (and they are not mutually exclusive), allows students to play her advice to Juliet with enthusiasm or with reluctance: they might suggest that the Nurse truly believes what she says or (with some hesitation and averted eyes) that she doubts the wisdom of her own advice or (more often) that she knows it will not give Juliet the comfort and counsel she desires.

When they finally watch the filmed versions of the play, the students are ready to recognize and understand not simply the different choices the actors in the films have made, but the way in which those choices reflect what has gone before (as well as what is to come). The easily available films differ sufficiently from one another to make clear the varied possibilities of the scene, to show students choices they might have either rejected or never considered, and to provoke discussion of the relation of the scene to other parts of the play. In the BBC version, for example, Capulet appears exasperated, in the Thames Television version quietly menacing, and in Baz Luhrman's brutal and violent. The Lady Capulet in the CBC film of a Stratford Festival production seems deeply sympathetic to Juliet but finally unable to find the courage to intercede for her, while Luhrman's Lady Capulet seems entirely detached, self-absorbed, utterly indifferent to her daughter, an enigmatic presence in the scene. Franco Zeffirelli's Nurse, removing the sheets from the bridal bed, unable to face Juliet as she speaks, seems to play against the lines she has to say ("I think it best you married with the County") and to let the audience know she speaks from neither heart nor soul.

The writing assignment that follows is designed to allow each student to articulate what he or she has discovered about *Romeo and Juliet* through the acting exercise. It begins by setting out the operative assumption of the exercise, that by the time actors, directors, or readers reach the scene in question, the play has already suggested ways of understanding the four characters, their actions, their motivations in the scene. While different actors, directors, or readers will inevitably interpret the suggestions differently, the choices they make in the scene will inevitably be shaped by their understanding of what the play has already told them about their characters. The assignment then asks students first to find those moments in the play that suggest ways of understanding Capulet, Lady Capulet, and the Nurse in 3.5 and next to make clear just what understanding they think those moments might suggest and how they might explain the actions and reveal the motivations of the three characters in the scene.

While students generally enjoy the process and learn a great deal about the openness of the script from interpreting the scene and articulating those interpretations in performance, the acting exercise has other goals as well. Since it is almost always assigned during the first two or three weeks of the class, the exercise also lessens their anxiety over Shakespeare's language and helps them to read it more easily, for the process of defining thoughts, feelings, motivations, and relationships among the characters and then choosing actions and tones of voice to articulate them inevitably asks that they read the text carefully, understand precisely what it says, and turn Shakespeare's verse into their own living speech. The refusal of the script to allow them a single reading, a single tone of voice, or a single motivation prepares them to recognize and accept the play's larger refusal to interpret its own action, its simultaneous celebration and fear, for example, of the lovers' unqualified, headlong commitment to one another.

At the same time, the decision of most modern editors (J.A. Bryant, Jr., in the Signet edition is a notable exception) to follow (in 3.1) the Fourth rather than the Second Quarto and thus ascribe the lines "Not Romeo, Prince: he was Mercutio's friend;/His fault concludes but what the law should end,/The life of Tybalt" to Montague rather than Capulet offers an opportunity not simply to consider the rationale for each ascription, but to discuss the transmission of Shakespeare's scripts and the creation of modern editions. Finally, the substance of the scene – parents and an adolescent daughter in conflict – makes it inevitable that, like working actors, students will draw on their own experience, on their own history (as well as on the script) to understand and act the scene. As a result, they come to recognize another important point not just about *Romeo and Juliet*, but about all of Shakespeare's plays: the theatrical questions about how to act the script become, in the process of answering them, human questions about the characters, their motivations, their values, their relationships.

As I reflect on the exercise and the assumptions about teaching Shakespeare that lie behind it, I inevitably recall a week in late February 2000 when I had the good fortune to attend a Salzburg Seminar on *Shakespeare around the Globe*. Approximately forty actors, directors, critics, and teachers, from virtually every nation under heaven, gathered in Salzburg to discuss the global significance of Shakespeare's plays at the beginning of the twenty-first century. The faculty was as diverse as were the participants, coming from England, America, China, India, South Africa, and the Czech Republic. Two troublesome truths soon emerged in both the plenary sessions and the smaller discussion groups: first, that Shakespeare, while honored around the globe, means many different things to many different people and, second, that those different people have strongly held opinions about the function and value of Shakespeare's plays in our time. In the end, the most vexed and divisive question to emerge from the Seminar remained the one that never was (and never could be) satisfactorily answered: to what degree can a play of Shakespeare be appropriated to a particular culture, to a particular time and place, and still be called a play of Shakespeare?

Although the question came forward repeatedly throughout the week, it was probably most clearly articulated in the varied responses to the lectures of Welcome Msomi, the creator of *Umabatha*, the Zulu *Macbeth*, and Richard Eyre, the former Director of The Royal National Theatre in London. At the beginning of the week, Welcome Msomi discussed with the group his world-renowned appropriation of *Macbeth* to Zulu history, culture, and traditions of performance. Here, some participants, while recognizing the theatrical power and imaginative range of the

Msomi's play, asked whether anything that might be considered essentially Shakespearean remained in the play, whether it did not finally stand in relation to *Macbeth* as *Macbeth* does to its own sources. Later in the week, when Richard Eyre spoke to the group about his production of *King Lear* with Ian Holm at The Royal National Theatre, he described the way in which he had understood the script and worked with his actors to bring that understanding to life on the stage. In the discussions that followed, other participants criticized Eyre for his conservative approach to the script, for grounding his reading entirely on its words and suppressing (as he admittedly did) the political implications of the play, turning *King Lear* into the story of a dysfunctional family. While most (but by no means all) of the participants recognized that any production of a play by Shakespeare (even one by The Royal National Theatre on a stage in London) is inevitably an appropriation to a particular culture, time, and place, they were all consistently unable to decide the precise point at which a performance ceases to be a performance of Shakespeare.

The questions that animated the discussions at the Salzburg Seminar relate to teaching as well as to performance. If students read or act Shakespeare in translation, if they read or act adaptions (or simplifications) in English, if they read or act appropriations of Shakespeare to their own cultures, are they reading or acting Shakespeare or something that simply uses Shakespeare to some degree or another as a point of departure? How do teachers around the globe make Shakespeare's words, Shakespeare's meanings accessible to their students, relevant to their students? What, to put it as simply as possible, makes Shakespeare Shakespeare? While answers to such questions are implicit in the reasons I have offered for using the acting exercise on *Romeo and Juliet* in the classroom, I realize that many of the participants in the Seminar might find those answers, if not mistaken, at least impractical or irrelevant to the world in which they live and work.

While I was both amazed and inspired to discover the varied uses to which Shakespeare's plays have been put around the globe, the varied ways in which diverse people have appropriated Shakespeare to their own cultures and to the social and political context of their own time and place, I remain convinced that the plays speak across culture, time, and place, not entirely, as some in Salzburg suggested, through Anglo-American cultural imperialism, but, paradoxically, through the precise ways in which Shakespeare's words and dramaturgy shape the sources he chose to adapt, the stories he chose to tell. If teachers in Kosovo, Northern Ireland, or the Middle East, for example, value *Romeo and Juliet* because it anticipates and therefore illuminates or at least provides an occasion to comment on their own 'local habitation', they have access to the play finally because it has over time been enduringly powerful and engaging on the stage. No matter what else teachers might want to say about *Romeo and Juliet*, no matter what their particular time and place might demand that they say, an acting exercise that allows students to bring its admittedly difficult language to life and to discover its compelling dramaturgy, also allows them to understand why *Romeo and Juliet* may still speak to them about their particular time and place and why Shakespeare's plays are still today read, performed, and valued around the globe.

The exercise and the writing assignment that follows it remain above all an occasion to illustrate and make felt through the process of exploring and acting the script the rich and intricate complexity of the play. And if the value of *Romeo and Juliet* is, as I have proposed here, neither in the story it tells nor in whatever meanings we might find in it or make from it, if the value of *Romeo and Juliet* lies in our experience of it, in the experience the play makes possible through its way of telling its story, then that rich and intricate complexity (which the students encounter in the exercise) is precisely what brings about the experience we value. As actors bring the script to life on the stage, they articulate some (but by no means all) of that complexity, choosing what to give prominence and what to let recede from awareness. But it is nonetheless the rich complexity, the intricate patterning that creates the experience we value, making the play feel at once hugely satisfying and profoundly significant, even if we are finally unable to articulate adequately what its significance is or just where it lies. Like all of Shakespeare's plays, *Romeo and Juliet* offers audiences and readers an experience they have valued for some four hundred years. The acting exercise I have described here allows students to gain some earned understanding of that experience and how it is created.

Notes

1. *Shakespeare's Sexual Comedy: A Mirror for Lovers* (Indianapolis: Bobbs-Merrill, 1971), p. 1.
2. "The Function of Criticism at the Present Time and All Others," *Shakespeare Quarterly,* 41 (1990), p. 266.

APPENDIX

Questions for Act 3, Scene 5, Lines 177 - 244

1. How is the stage set? What prop(s), if any, should be on the stage? How should they be positioned?
2. Where are the four actors on the stage (i. e., how are they positioned on the stage in relation to one another and the audience) at line 177?
3. To whom is Capulet speaking? Does he pause at any time during his long speech? At what point (or points) does he do so? What is his tone of voice? Does it ever change?
4. How violent, how restrained is Capulet? Does he strike Juliet, push her, or does he only assault her with words? Or does he speak to her deliberately, emphatically, keeping whatever anger he feels under control?
5. Where are Juliet, the Nurse, and Lady Capulet during the speech? What does each of them do?
6. How does Capulet make his exit?
7. How does Juliet speak to her mother? What is her tone of voice? How are they positioned on the stage relative to one another (and to the audience)?
8. What is the tone of Lady Capulet's reply to Juliet? How does she make her exit?
9. What, if anything, does Juliet do as she begins her questions to the Nurse? What are their positions on the stage relative to one another (and to the audience)?
10. Does Juliet pause at any time during the speech? At what point (or points) does she do so? What is her tone of voice? Does it ever change?
11. Does the Nurse pause at any time during her response to Juliet? At what point (or points) does she do so? What is her tone of voice? Does it ever change?
12. Why does the Nurse give Juliet the advice she does? What does the Nurse do during the speech? How does she feel about the advice she gives Juliet? How does she make those feelings clear to the audience?
13. How are Juliet and the Nurse positioned on the stage relative to one another (and to the audience) during the Nurse's speech? What does each of them (Juliet and the Nurse) do during the speech?
14. During the next four lines (i.e., 228-31) what do Juliet and the Nurse do? What

An Approach to Teaching *Romeo and Juliet*

moves, if any, do they make on the stage?

15. What is the tone of Juliet's voice in line 232 ("Well, thou hast comforted me marvelous much")?
16. How does the Nurse make her exit? What, if anything, does she do and what, if anything, does Juliet do as the Nurse makes her exit?
17. What is the tone of Juliet's voice in her last speech? Does her tone ever change during the speech?
18. How does Juliet make her exit? Does she make an exit? What are the possibilities? What are their effects?

SHAKESPEARE AND PEDAGOGY

Christopher L. Morrow
(Texas A & M University)

This bibliography consists of works, published from 1974-2000, that focus on Shakespeare and pedagogy. It includes studies devoted to teaching Shakespeare generally as well as individual plays. It also includes studies whose topics include curricular issues at all stages of education, the use of technology in the classroom and advice for teaching Shakespeare to students with special needs. This bibliography does not include unpublished dissertations, historical approaches to pedagogy or curriculum or works that demonstrate how to use Shakespeare in teaching other subjects such as business or political science.

General Studies

Adams, Richard, ed. *Teaching Shakespeare: Essays on Approaches to Shakespeare in Schools and Colleges*. London: Robert Boyce, 1985.
Aers, Lesley and Nigel Wheale, ed. *Shakespeare in the Changing Curriculum*. London and New York: Routledge, 1991.
Ahrens, Rüdiger. *Shakespeare im Unterricht*. Anglistik und Englischunterricht 3. Trier: Volksfreund-Druckerei, 1977.
---. *William Shakespeare: Didaktisches Handbuch*. 3 vols. Munich: Fink, 1982.
Allen, Bob. "A School Perspective on Shakespeare Teaching". *Shakespeare in the Changing Curriculum*. Ed. Lesley Aers and Nigel Wheale (London and New York: Routledge, 1991), pp. 40-57.
Allen, John Alexander. "Students, Stereotypes, and Shakespeare". *Hollins* (Hollins College) 40:1 (1989), pp. 30-2.
Anderegg, Michael A. "Shakespeare on Film in the Classroom". *Literature/Film Quarterly* 4 (1976), pp. 165-75.
Andreas, James R. "Silencing the Vulgar and Voicing the Other Shakespeare". *Nebraska English Journal* 35 (Spring-Summer 1990), pp. 74-88.
Barber, C. L. "On the Use of Talking Passages". *Shakespeare Newsletter* 25 (1975), p. 11.
Barry, Jackson G. "Shakespeare with Words: The Script and the Medium of Drama". *Shakespeare Quarterly* 25 (1974), pp. 161-71.
Bartenschlager, Klaus. "Shakespeares Dramen und ihr Publikum". *William Shakespeare: Didaktisches Handbuch*. Ed. Rüdiger Ahrens. 3 vols (Munich: Fink, 1982), II, pp. 617-41.
Bates, Laura Raidonis. "The Bard on Spring Break: Using Shakespeare as a Composition Model". *Shakespeare and the Classroom* 6:2 (1998), pp. 24-6.
---. "'I have been studying how I may compare this prison where I live': Teaching Shakespeare in Prison". *Shakespeare* (Georgetown University) 3:1 (1999), pp. 23-7.
Béchervaise, Neil, ed. *Shakespeare on Celluloid*. Rozelle, New South Wales: St. Clair Press, 1999.
Beehler, Sharon A. "Censorship and the Teaching of Shakespeare". *Ideological Approaches to Shakespeare: The Practice of Theory*. Ed. Robert P. Merrix and Nicholas Ranson (Lewiston, Queenston, and Lampeter: Mellen, 1992), pp. 215-28.
---. "Making Media Matter in the Shakespeare Classroom". *Teaching Shakespeare into the Twenty-First Century*, ed. Richard E. Salomone and James E. Davis. Athens: Ohio UP, 1997), pp. 247-54.
---. "'Such Impossible Passages of Grossness': Education and the Censoring of Shakespeare". *Nebraska English Journal* 35 (Spring-Summer 1990), pp. 16-31.

Beneke, Jürgen. "Das elisabethanische Englisch im vergleich zum heutigen Englisch". *William Shakespeare: Didaktisches Handbuch*. Ed. Rüdiger Ahrens. 3 vols (Munich: Fink, 1982), I, pp. 145-80.
---. "Möglichkeiten der Schulaufführung". *William Shakespeare: Didaktisches Handbuch*. Ed. Rüdiger Ahrens. 3 vols (Munich: Fink, 1982), I, pp. 293-311.
Berry, Siobhan, and Mary Pitman-Jones. "Students Publish Shakespeare Periodicals". *Shakespeare* (Georgetown University) 4:2 (2000), p. 13.
---. "Getting Shakespeare Right in the Middle". *Shakespeare* (Georgetown University) 1:3 (1997), p. 16.
Bevington, David, and Gavin Witt. "Working in Workshops". *Teaching Shakespeare through Performance*. Ed. Milla Riggio. Modern Language Association of America Options for Teaching (New York: Modern Language Association of America, 1999), pp. 169-83.
Blackburn, Thomas H. "Shakespeare in the Electronic Classroom". *Shakespeare and the Classroom* 4:1 (1996), pp. 15-17.
Blaicher, Günther. "'Time for Comedy': Für die Behandlung englischer Komödien im Oberstufenunterricht". *Literaturwissenschaft. Literaturdidaktik. Literaturunterricht: Englisch*. Ed. Hans Hunfeld (Königstein: Scriptor, 1982), pp. 149-59.
Blake, Norman Francis. "Shakespeare, Discourse, and the Teaching of English". *Text – Culture – Reception: Cross-Cultural Aspects of English Studies*. Forum Anglistik New Series 8 (Heidelberg: Winter, 1992), pp. 431-45.
Blumenfeld, Odette-Irenne. "What Do/Can We Teach in a Shakespeare Class?" *Shakespeariana* (University of Galati, 1996), p. 2.
Boltz, Ingeborg. "Shakespeare: The Animated Tales: Vom Trickfilmstudio in die Schule". *Shakespeare Jahrbuch* 133 (1997), pp. 118-33.
Booth, Stephen. "The Function of Criticism at the Present Time and All Others". *Shakespeare Quarterly* 41 (1990), pp. 262-68.
Boris, Edna Zwick. "Teaching Shakespeare: Non-Traditional Research Topics". *Shakespeare Newsletter* 42 (1992), p. 41.
Bowden, William R. "Four More Tips on Teaching Shakespeare". *Teaching Shakespeare Bulletin* 1 (1976).
Boxleitner, Linda. *Reading Emily's Mail and Two More Thematic Thinking and Writing Units*. Portland, ME: Walch, 1994.
Breen, Kathleen. "A Festive Scene". *Teaching Theatre* 8.3 (1997), pp. 10-14.
Brimer, Alan. "Approaches to the Teaching of Shakespeare". *Crux: A Journal on the Teaching of English* 12 (January 1978), pp. 41-5.
---. "Shakespeare and South African Politics". *Shakespeare in Southern Africa* 6 (1993), pp. 29-44.
Buhler, Stephen M. "Introducing Stage History to Students". *Teaching Shakespeare through Performance*. Ed. Milla Riggio. Modern Language Association of America Options for Teaching (New York: Modern Language Association of America, 1999), pp. 220-31.
Bulman, James C. "The BBC Shakespeare and 'House Style.'" *Shakespeare Quarterly* 35 (1984), pp. 571-81.
Burkman, Katherine H. *Literature through Performance*: Shakespeare's Mirror *and* A Canterbury Caper. Athens: Ohio UP, 1978.
Burnett, Rebecca E. "Persona as Pedagogy: Engaging Students in Shakespeare". *Ideological Approaches to Shakespeare: The Practice of Theory*. Ed. Robert P. Merrix and Nicholas Ranson (Lewiston, Queenston, and Lampeter: Mellen, 1992), pp. 243-55.
Burns, Jean. "Shakespeare without Reverence". *Indiana English* 5.1-2 (1982), pp. 37-9.
Burr, Suzanne. "Students Write about Shakespeare: The 'Triple Play' in the College Classroom". *Shakespeare and the Triple Play: From Study to Stage to Classroom*. Ed. Sidney Homan (Lewisburg: Bucknell UP; London and Toronto: Associated UPs, 1988), pp. 207-14.
Bursey, Jane. "Communicative Shakespeare: Democracy in the Classroom". *Occasional Papers and Reviews, Shakespeare Society of Southern Africa* 9:1-2 (1994), pp. 16-23.
Busacker, Klaus. "Aufführungsrezensionen als Interpretationshilfen bei der Behandlung von Shakespeares Dramen im Unterricht". *Shakespeare-Jahrbuch* (Bochum, 1983), pp. 193-9.

---. "Zum Einsatz deutscher Übersetzungen im Englischunterricht". *Literatur in Wissenschaft und Unterricht* 15 (1982), pp. 307-19.
Cabat, Joshua. "'And here remain with your uncertainty': Teaching Shakespeare's Politics without *Julius Caesar*". *Shakespeare* (Georgetown University) 2:3 (1998), pp. 13-14.
---. "Beyond *West Side Story*: The Problem of Shakespearean Modernizations on Film". *Shakespeare* (Georgetown University) 3:2 (1999), pp. 19-20.
Capey, A. C. "Confessions of a Practical Critic". *Use of English* 36:1 (1984), pp. 17-21.
Carpenter, Christina B. "Where There's a Will, There's a Way". *Shakespeare* (Georgetown University) 4:2 (2000), pp. 12-13.
Carroll, Aileen M. *Here's Shakespeare: Study Guides, Activities, and Quizzes*. Portland, ME: J. Weston Walch, 1985.
Carroll, D. Allen. "The Presentation of Shakespeare". *Teaching Shakespeare*. Ed. Walter Edens, Christopher Durer, Duncan Harris, Keith Hull, and Walter F. Eggers, Jr. (Princeton: Princeton UP, 1978), pp. 48-63.
Cavazos-Kottke, Sean. "Shakespeare Plugged-In: Teaching the History Plays with Modern Technology". *Shakespeare* (Georgetown University) 4:1 (2000), pp. 13, 15.
Ceruzzi, Frank. "Alternative Shakespeare: Screenplays in the Classroom". *Shakespeare* (Georgetown University) 2:2 (1998), pp. 22-23.
Cohen, Ralph Alan. "Original Staging and the Shakespeare Classroom". *Teaching Shakespeare through Performance*. Ed. Milla Riggio. Modern Language Association of America Options for Teaching (New York: Modern Language Association of America, 1999), pp. 78-101.
---. "Teaching Shakespeare's Early Comedies". *Shakespeare's Sweet Thunder: Essays on the Early Comedies*. Ed. Michael J. Collins (Newark: Delaware UP; London: Associated UPs, 1997), pp. 228-44.
Collins, Michael J. "For World and Stage: An Approach to Teaching Shakespeare". *Shakespeare Quarterly* 41 (1990), pp. 251-61.
---. "Love, Sighs, and Videotape: An Approach to Teaching Shakespeare's Comedies". *Teaching Shakespeare Today: Practical Approaches and Productive Strategies*. Ed. James E. Davis and Ronald E. Salomone (Urbana: National Council of Teachers of English, 1993), pp. 109-16.
---. "Using Films to Teach Shakespeare". *Shakespeare Quarterly* 46 (1995), pp. 228-35.
---. "'You can never bring in a wall': Some Thoughts on Teaching Shakespeare". *Shakespeare Bulletin* 7:2 (1989), pp. 25-6.
Cookson, Linda. "Knowing Hawks from Handsaws". *Teaching Shakespeare: Essays on Approaches to Shakespeare in Schools and Colleges*. Ed. Richard Adams (London: Robert Boyce, 1985), pp. 170-83.
Coursen, H. R. "The New Historicism and the Teaching of Shakespeare". *Shakespeare and the Classroom* 2:1 (1994), pp. 24-6.
---. *Teaching Shakespeare with Film and Television: A Guide*. Westport and London: Greenwood, 1997.
---. "Uses of Media in Teaching Shakespeare". *Teaching Shakespeare into the Twenty-First Century*. Ed. Richard E. Salomone and James E. Davis (Athens: Ohio UP, 1997), pp. 193-200.
Cummings, Scott T. "Interactive Shakespeare". *Theatre Topics* 8:1 (1998), pp. 93-112.
Cunningham, Karen. "Having Our Literature and Seeing It Too: The Actors-in-Residence Program". *Shakespeare Bulletin* 3:2 (1985), pp. 5-6.
D'Aeth, Eve, and Linda Costain. *Shakespeare Teaches*. Ottawa: Longparish, 1989.
Dabbs, Thomas. "Shakespeare and the Department of English". *English as a Discipline: Or, Is There a Plot in This Play?* Ed. James C. Raymond (Tuscaloosa and London: Alabama UP, 1996), pp. 82-98.
Davis, James E. and Ronald E. Salomone. *Teaching Shakespeare Today: Practical Approaches and Productive Strategies*. Urbana: National Council of Teachers of English, 1993.
Dessen, Alan C. "Shakespeare's Theatrical Vocabulary and Today's Classroom". *Teaching Shakespeare through Performance*. Ed. Milla Riggio. Modern Language Association of

America Options for Teaching (New York: Modern Language Association of America, 1999), pp. 63-77.
Dickenson, Mavis. "Buckets of Blood: It Is Possible for Children of All Ages to Enjoy Shakespeare". *Times Educational Supplement* 24 May 1991, p. 40.
Dionne, Craig. "Point and Click Shakespeare". *Shakespeare and the Classroom* 7:1 (1999), pp. 50-3.
D'Lima, Fiona. "Studying Shakespeare in the Twentieth Century". *Shakespeare in the Twentieth Century.* Ed. N. M. Aston (New Delhi: Prestige Books, 1997), pp. 32-3.
Donawerth, Jane. "Teaching Shakespeare in the Context of Renaissance Women's Culture". *Shakespeare Quarterly* 47 (1996), pp. 476-89.
Doss, Ellen. "Rehearsing 'most obscenely and courageously': An English Teacher Directs Shakespeare". *Shakespeare* (Georgetown University) 1:3 (1997), p. 15.
Dow, Marguerite R. "The Shakespearean Play as a Theatrical Event in the Classroom". *English Quarterly* 17:4 (1984), pp. 16-22.
Draheim, Joachim. "Shakespeares Dramen in der Musik". *William Shakespeare: Didaktisches Handbuch.* Ed. Rüdiger Ahrens. 3 vols (Munich: Fink, 1982), II, pp. 693-727.
Dyer, M. "'Alas, I took great pains to study it': Examining Shakespeare in Schools". *Crux: A Journal on the Teaching of English* 11 (April 1977), pp. 43-50.
Edens, Walter, Christopher Durer, Duncan Harris, Keith Hull, and Walter F. Eggers, Jr, ed. *Teaching Shakespeare.* Princeton: Princeton UP, 1978.
Edgecombe, David. *Theatrical Training during the Age of Shakespeare.* Studies in Theatre Arts 2. Lewiston, Queenston, and Lampeter: Mellen, 1995.
Edmonds, John. "The Dramatic Image in the Initial Teaching of Shakespeare". *English in Education* 16 (1982), pp. 2-7.
Einenkel, Robert, and Bernice W. Kliman. "Team Teaching Shakespeare: Breaking Barriers to the Bard". *Teaching Shakespeare through Performance.* Ed. Milla Riggio. Modern Language Association of America Options for Teaching (New York: Modern Language Association of America, 1999), pp. 266-76.
Elith, Kim, Judy Embrey, and Paul Hicks. *Studying Shakespeare Today.* Melbourne: Oxford UP, 1997.
Erickson, Peter. "Rita Dove's Two Shakespeare Poems". *Shakespeare and the Classroom* 4:2 (1996), pp. 53-4.
Erickson, Peter, and William Collins Watterson. "Shakespeare in the 21st Century: Two Views". *Shakespeare and the Classroom* 2:1 (1994), pp. 7-8.
Erickson, Peter. "Start Misquoting Him Now: The Difference a Word Makes in Adrienne Rich's 'Inscriptions.'" *Shakespeare and the Classroom* 5:1 (1997), pp. 55-6.
Feitelberg, Doreen. "Shakespeare Lives". *Crux: A Journal on the Teaching of English* 23:4 (1989), pp. 32-6.
Ferguson, Chris. "Modern Art Gives Clues to Early Modern Characters". *Shakespeare* (Georgetown University) 2:3 (1998), pp. 21-2.
Flachmann, Michael. "Changing the *W*'s in Shakespeare's Plays". *Teaching Shakespeare Today: Practical Approaches and Productive Strategies.* Ed. James E. Davis and Ronald E. Salomone (Urbana: National Council of Teachers of English, 1993), pp. 99-106.
---. "Professional Theater People and English Teachers: Working Together to Teach Shakespeare". *Teaching Shakespeare into the Twenty-First Century.* Ed. Richard E. Salomone and James E. Davis (Athens: Ohio UP, 1997), pp. 57-64.
---. "Teaching Shakespeare through Parallel Scenes". *Shakespeare Quarterly* 35 (1984), pp. 644-6.
Flannagan, Roy. "Beyond the Gee Whiz Stage: Computer Technology, the World Wide Web, and Shakespeare". *Teaching Shakespeare into the Twenty-First Century.* Ed. Richard E. Salomone and James E. Davis (Athens: Ohio UP, 1997), pp. 262-70.
---. "Shakespeare Enters the Electronic Age". *Teaching Shakespeare Today: Practical Approaches and Productive Strategies.* Ed. James E. Davis and Ronald E. Salomone (Urbana: National Council of Teachers of English, 1993), pp. 151-8.

Foakes, R. A. "Cutting the Bard Down to Size". *Teaching with Shakespeare: Critics in the Classroom*. Ed. Bruce McIver and Ruth Stevenson. Newark: Delaware UP; London and Toronto: Associated UPs, 1994), pp. 60-77.

Francoz, M. J. "The Logic of Question and Answer: Writing as Inquiry". *College English* 41 (1979-80), pp. 336-9.

Franek, Mark. "Producing Student Films: Shakespeare on Screen". *English Journal* 85:3 (1996), pp. 50-4.

Freedman, Barbara. "Pedagogy, Psychoanalysis, Theatre: Interrogating the Scene of Learning". *Shakespeare Quarterly* 41 (1990), pp. 174-86.

Freeman, Sara E. "Make Friends with Shakespeare". *Schooldays* 17:4 (1998), pp. 61-8.

Frey, Charles H. "Making Sense of Shakespeare: A Reader-Based Response". *Teaching Shakespeare into the Twenty-First Century*. Ed. Richard E. Salomone and James E. Davis. (Athens: Ohio UP, 1997), pp. 96-103.

---. "Making Sense of Shakespeare: Thought and Feeling in Reading the Plays". *Shakespeare and the Classroom* 4:2 (1996), pp. 42-7.

---. "Shakesperience! What to Teach? What to Learn?" *Shakespeare and the Classroom* 2.2 (1994), pp. 66-9.

---. "Teaching Shakespeare in America". *Shakespeare Quarterly* 35 (1984), pp. 541-59.

Gibbs, G. L. "Introducing Shakespeare in Schools". *Use of English* 36:2 (1985), pp. 67-73.

---. "Why Teach English Literature?" *The Use of English* 28:1 (1976), pp. 25-8.

Gibson, Rex. "Owning Shakespeare: Teaching His Plays by Performance". *International Schools Journal* 18:1 (1998), pp. 9-21.

---. "Teaching Shakespeare through Film and Video". *As You Like It: AudioVisual Shakespeare*. Ed. Cathy Grant (London: British Film and Video Council, 1992), pp. 1-5.

Gilbert, Miriam. "Teaching Shakespeare through Performance". *Shakespeare Quarterly* 35 (1984), pp. 601-8.

---. "Writing about Performance: Writing as Performance". *Teaching Shakespeare through Performance*. Ed. Milla Riggio. Modern Language Association of America Options for Teaching (New York: Modern Language Association of America, 1999), pp. 307-17.

Glaap, Albert-Reiner. "Das englische Drama bis Shakespeare: Gattungen und Formen in der unterrichtlichen Präsentation". *William Shakespeare: Didaktisches Handbuch*. Ed. Rüdiger Ahrens. 3 vols (Munich: Fink, 1982), I, pp. 199-217.

Gokhale, Shridhar. "Teaching Shakespeare in India: Ripeness Is All". *Shakespeare in the Twentieth Century*. Ed. N. M. Aston (New Delhi: Prestige Books, 1997), pp. 28-31.

Goodall, J. E. "Shakespeare Match". *ELTIC Reporter* (English Academy of South Africa) 12:2 (1987), pp. 28-40.

Goodman, Lizbeth. "Creative Imagination and Media-Assisted Learning: Shakespeare in Performance". *Literary and Linguistic Computing* 12 (1997), pp. 259-68.

Gowda, H. H. Anniah. "Research in English: Language and Literature; Language or Literature?" *Indian Writing in English*. Ed. Ramesh Mohan (Bombay: Orient Longman, 1978), pp. 221-33.

Graham, Arthur. *Shakespeare in Opera, Ballet, Orchestral Music, and Song: An Introduction to Music Inspired by the Bard*. Studies in the History and Interpretation of Music 57. Lewiston, Queenston, and Lampeter: Mellen, 1997.

Green, Mary. *Coursework: Shakespeare*. Specials! Dunstable: Folens, 1999.

Griffin, C. W. "Interrogative Assignments". *Shakespeare and the Classroom* 6:1 (1998), pp. 38-40.

---. "Students Reading Shakespeare". *Shakespeare and the Classroom* 7:2 (1999), pp. 35-9.

---. "Teaching Shakespeare on Video". *English Journal* 78:7 (1989), pp. 40-43.

---. "Teaching Shakespeare: A Report". *Shakespeare and the Classroom* 5:1 (1997), pp. 44-52.

---. "Textual Studies and Teaching Shakespeare". *Teaching Shakespeare into the Twenty-First Century*. Ed. Richard E. Salomone and James E. Davis (Athens: Ohio UP, 1997), pp.. 104-11.

Haas, Rudolf. "Shakespeare als pädagogische Herausforderung". *Shakespeare-Jahrbuch* (Bochum) 112 (1976), pp. 128-53.

Habicht, Werner. "Die 'Shakespearebühne.'" *William Shakespeare: Didaktisches Handbuch.* Ed. Rüdiger Ahrens. 3 vols (Munich: Fink, 1982), I, pp. 181-98.

---. "Zum Shakespeare-Bild heute – Tendenzen und Impulse neuerer Shakespeare-Forschung". *Shakespeare im Unterricht.* Ed. Rüdiger Ahrens. Anglistik und Englischenunterricht 3 (Trier: Volksfreund-Druckerei, 1977), pp. 39-52.

Haddon, John. "Who's Listening: Stage Picture and Dramatic Meaning in Shakespeare". *Use of English* 47 (1995-96), pp. 97-115.

Hale, David G. "More than Magic in the Web: Plagiarism for the Shakespeare Class". *Shakespeare and the Classroom* 6:1 (1998), pp. 30-3.

Halio, Jay L. "'This wide and universal stage': Shakespeare's Plays as Plays". *Teaching Shakespeare.* Ed. Walter Edens, Christopher Durer, Duncan Harris, Keith Hull, and Walter F. Eggers, Jr. (Princeton: Princeton UP, 1978), pp. 273-89.

Hall, Kim F. "Uses for a Dead White Male: Shakespeare, Feminism, and Diversity". *New Theatre Quarterly* 11 (1995), pp. 55-61.

Hallett, Charles A. "Scene versus Sequence: Distinguishing Action from Narrative in Shakespeare's Multipartite Scenes". *Shakespeare Quarterly* 46 (1995), pp. 183-95.

Hamilton, Donna B. "Shakespeare's Romances and Jacobean Political Discourse". *Approaches to Teaching Shakespeare's* The Tempest *and Other Late Romances.* Ed. Maurice Hunt. Approaches to Teaching World Literature 41 (New York: Modern Language Association, 1992), pp. 64-71.

Hamilton, Sharon. *Shakespeare: A Teaching Guide.* Portland, ME: Walch, 1993.

Hansen, Niels Bugge. "Teaching Shakespeare in the Nineties". *Literary Pedagogics after Deconstruction: Scenarios and Perspectives in the Teaching of English Literature.* Ed. Per Serritslev Petersen. Dolphin 22 (Aarhus: Aarhus UP, 1992), pp. 26-32.

Hart, Francis Russell. *Beyond the Books: Reflections on Learning and Teaching.* Columbus: Ohio State UP, 1989.

Hassel, R. Chris, Jr. "'Fatal Vision?'" *Shakespeare and the Classroom* 3:2 (1995), pp. 42-4.

---. "Teaching the Christian Scene in Shakespeare". *Shakespeare and the Classroom* 2:1 (1994), pp. 12-13.

Healey, Sister Dolores. "On 'Teaching' Shakespeare". *Commentary* (National University of Singapore) 5:3-4 (1982), pp. 119-20.

Heilman, Robert B. "Shakespeare in the Classroom: Scientific Object vs. Immediate Experience". *Teaching Shakespeare.* Ed. Walter Edens, Christopher Durer, Duncan Harris, Keith Hull, and Walter F. Eggers, Jr. (Princeton: Princeton UP, 1978), pp. 3-26.

Hellenga, Robert R. "Shakespeare: Our Contemporary or His?" *Teaching Shakespeare Bulletin* 1 (1976).

Hicks, Paul, and Angela Cairns. *Introducing Shakespeare: Learning about His Life and Work.* Melbourne: Oxford UP, 1995.

Hilton, Julian. "Practising Shakespeare". *Shakespeare-Jahrbuch* (Bochum, 1986), pp. 147-54.

Hiramatsu, Hideo. "Shakespeare and the Japanese: Translation and Teaching". *Shakespeare Worldwide* 14-15 (1995), pp. 147-68.

Hirschfeld, Heather A., and A. Leigh DeNeef. "Collaborative Pedagogy: An Experiment in Team-Teaching Shakespeare". *Renaissance Papers 1997*, pp. 75-85.

Hirsh, James E. "Picturing Shakespeare: Using Film in the Classroom to Turn Text into Theater". *Teaching Shakespeare Today: Practical Approaches and Productive Strategies.* Ed. James E. Davis and Ronald E. Salomone (Urbana: National Council of Teachers of English, 1993), pp. 140-50.

---. "Teaching Paradoxes: Shakespeare and the Enhancement of Audience Skills". *Shakespeare Quarterly* 41 (1990), pp. 222-9.

Holland, Norman N. "Reading Readers Reading". *Researching Response to Literature and the Teaching of Literature: Points of Departure.* Ed. Charles R. Cooper. Norwood, NJ: Ablex, 1985.

Holmer, Joan Ozark. "Sparking: A Methodology to Encourage Student Performance". *Teaching Shakespeare Today: Practical Approaches and Productive Strategies.* Ed. James E. Davis and Ronald E. Salomone (Urbana: National Council of Teachers of English, 1993), pp. 90-8.

Holzer, Madeleine, and Robert Price. "CD-ROMs in the Classroom: Collaboration, Individualization, Imagination". *Shakespeare* (Georgetown University) 1:2 (1997), p. 19.
Homan, Delmar C. "The Journal as Performance Explicator of Shakespeare". *Kansas English* 76:1 (1990), pp. 20-5.
---. "Shakespearean Festivals: The Popular Roots of Performance". *Teaching Shakespeare Today: Practical Approaches and Productive Strategies*. Ed. James E. Davis and Ronald E. Salomone (Urbana: National Council of Teachers of English, 1993), pp. 117-22.
Homan, Sidney. "Minimalist Theatre and the Classroom: Some Experiments with Shakespeare and Beckett". *CEA Critic* 53:1 (1990), pp. 7-15.
Hortmann, Wilhelm. "Literaturunterricht zwischen Wissenschaft und Didaktik: Exempel Shakespeare". *Praxisbezüge der Anglistik*. Ed. K. Schuhmann and K. Maroldt (Grossen-Linden: Hoffmann, 1980), pp. 87-114.
---. "Shakespeare-Unterricht zwischen Text und Theater". *Shakespeare im Unterricht*. Ed. Rüdiger Ahrens. Anglistik und Englischenunterricht 30 Trier: Volksfreund-Druckerei, 1977. 101-32.
---. "Theaterschocks bei avantgardistischen Shakespeare- Inzenierungen". *William Shakespeare: Didaktisches Handbuch*. Ed. Rüdiger Ahrens. 3 vols (Munich: Fink, 1982), I, pp. 313-42.
Houliston, Victor. "Shakespeare Not Our Contemporary: Classical Rhetoric and the Teaching of Shakespeare". *Shakespeare in Southern Africa* 3 (1989), pp. 67-77.
Howe, Allie, and Robert A. Nelson. "The Spectogram: An Exercise in Initial Analysis". *Shakespeare Quarterly* 35 (1984), pp. 632-41.
Hunt, Maurice. "Strengthening Thinking Skills through Reading Shakespeare's Plays". *ISDA Journal* (Intellectual Skills Development Association) 4:1 (1991), pp. 15-24.
Hunter, Lauren. "Teaching Shakespeare through Performance, or Name That Tune". *Shakespeare and the Classroom* 7:2 (1999), pp. 5-10.
Huston, J. Dennis. "The Shakespearean Scholar and Teacher on Stage: Double Identity or Split Personality?" *CEA Critic* 51.1 (1988), pp. 67-72.
Inglis, Fred. "Recovering Shakespeare: Innocence and Materialism". *Shakespeare in the Changing Curriculum*. Ed. Lesley Aers and Nigel Wheale (London and New York: Routledge, 1991), pp. 58-73.
Jaccariro, Victor. "What's in a New Name? Collaborative Learning and Shakespeare". *English Journal* 82:3 (1993), pp. 64-6.
Jacques, Jill. "Teaching the Literature Essay". *Crux: A Journal on the Teaching of English* 25:2 (1991), pp. 27-35.
Jennings, Caleen Sinnette. "Exploring Shakespeare's Texts with Neutral Masks". *Shakespeare* (Georgetown University) 1:2 (1997), p. 13.
Jones, Peter, ed. *Shakespeare Workshop: Photocopiable Workshop Approaches to* Hamlet, Julius Caesar, Macbeth, The Merchant of Venice, Romeo and Juliet. Portland, ME: Calendar Island in association with St. Clair Press, 1999.
Jones, Rhodri. *An ABC of English Teaching*. London and Exeter, NH: Heinemann Educational Books, 1980.
Keating, Keith. "Notes Towards the Development of a Poetics of the English Class". *Journal of Comparative Literature and Aesthetics* 4:1-2 (1981), pp. 81-110.
Kelly, Philippa. "Shakespeare in Prison". *Meanjin* 58 (1999), pp. 122-30.
Kennedy-Manzo, Kathleen. "The Play's the Thing: Teachers Try Livelier Ways to Bring the Bard to Life for the MTV Generation". *Education Week* 8 April 1998, pp. 29-32.
Knight, G. Wilson. "The Teacher as Poetic Actor". *Teaching Shakespeare*. Ed. Walter Edens, Christopher Durer, Duncan Harris, Keith Hull, and Walter F. Eggers, Jr. (Princeton: Princeton UP, 1978), pp. 290-304.
Knight, Stephen. "In the Golden World: Shakespeare and the Pedagogy of Power". *Shakespeare's Books: Contemporary Cultural Politics and the Persistence of Empire*. Ed. Philip Mead and Marion Campbell. Melbourne University Literary and Cultural Studies Series 1 (Melbourne: Department of English, University of Melbourne, 1993), pp. 113-24.
Kranz, David. "Cinematic Elements in Shakespearean Film: A Glossary". *Teaching Shakespeare through Performance*. Ed. Milla Riggio. Modern Language Association of America Options for Teaching (New York: Modern Language Association of America, 1999), pp. 341-60.

Krieger, Elliot. "Shakespearean Crossroads: Teaching Shakespeare through Induction". *College English* 39 (1977), pp. 286-9.
Ledebur, Ruth Freifrau von. "Der Shakespeare-Unterricht muss umkehren!" *Schreibfest: Modisches und Methodisches aus englischen Gefilden. Fur Helmut Jochems zum 60. Geburtstag.* Ed. Ruth Freifrau von Lebedur and Reimer Jehmlich (Siegen: Universität Siegen, 1987), pp. 97-103.
---. "Teaching Shakespeare in America: Anregungen für den Shakespeare-Unterricht". *Shakespeare-Jahrbuch* (Bochum, 1987), pp. 124-33.
Leech, Carolyn. "Shakespeare for the Post Modern Age: On Reading Aloud to Your Students". *Vital Speeches of the Day* 62:7 (1996), pp. 205-9.
Lemmer, André. "Responding to Shakespeare". *Crux: A Journal on the Teaching of English* 26.3 (1992), pp. 24-35.
Liston, William T. "Paraphrasing Shakespeare". *Teaching Shakespeare into the Twenty-First Century.* Ed. Richard E. Salomone and James E. Davis (Athens: Ohio UP, 1997), pp. 11-17.
Livesey, Robert. *Creating with Shakespeare: Shakin' with Willie.* Mississauga, Ontario: Little Brick Schoolhouse, 1988.
Loehlin, James N. "On Your Imaginary Forces Work: Shakespeare in Practice". *Teaching Shakespeare through Performance.* Ed. Milla Riggio. Modern Language Association of America Options for Teaching (New York: Modern Language Association of America, 1999), pp. 286-94.
LoMonico, Michael. "Using Computers to Teach Shakespeare". *English Journal* 84:6 (1995), pp. 58-61.
Longhurst, Derek. "Reproducing a National Culture: Shakespeare in Education". *Red Letters* 11 (1981), pp. 3-14.
Lynch, James. "Archetypaling in the Classroom, with Special Reference to Shakespeare". *English in Texas* 8:2 (1977), pp. 42-4.
MacIsaac, Warren J. "Viva Voce: On Speaking and Hearing Shakespeare's Sentences". *Shakespeare Quarterly* 25 (1974), pp. 172-87.
Malcolm, Ann, and Peter Traves. *Teaching Shakespeare.* n.p.: Shropshire County Council, n.d.
Mallick, David. *How Tall Is This Ghost, John?* Adeliade: Australian Association for the Teaching of English, 1984.
---. "Shakespeare and Performance". *Use of English* 38:2 (1987), pp. 33-7.
---. "What Could Be on the Left Hand Page?" *English in Australia* 64 (June 1983), pp. 59-68.
Marathe, Sudhakar. "Shakespeare Criticism via Theatre". *Shakespeare in Indian Languages.* Ed. D.A. Shankar (Shimla, India: Indian Institute for Advanced Study, 1999), pp. 186-208.
Marcus, Leah S. "Disestablishing Shakespeare". *Teaching with Shakespeare: Critics in the Classroom.* Ed. Bruce McIver and Ruth Stevenson (Newark: Delaware UP; London and Toronto: Associated UPs, 1994), pp. 98-114.
Marder, Louis. "Audio-Visual Teaching and Electronic Software". *Shakespeare Newsletter* 40 (1990), pp. 41, 45.
---. "Do's and Dont's of Shakespeare Teaching: Experimental List". *Shakespeare in the Classroom: Resources and Media Aids* (Kenosha: University of Wisconsin-Parkside, 1977), pp. 51-5.
---. "On Teaching Shakespeare and the Shakespeare Data Bank". *Shakespeare Newsletter* 42 (1992), p. 44.
---. "Shakespearean Drama: Literature or Performance". *Shakespeare Newsletter* 29 (1979), p. 39.
---. "A Working Method for Teaching Shakespeare". *Shakespeare Newsletter* 25 (1975), p. 10.
Markel, Michael H. "Why Hermione Lives but Desdemona Dies: An Approach to Shakespearian Genre Definition". *Publications of the Arkansas Philological Association* 4:2 (1978), pp. 50-6.
Matchinske, Megan. "Credible Consorts: What Happens When Shakespeare's Sisters Enter the Syllabus?" *Shakespeare Quarterly* 47 (1996), pp. 433-50.
Mazer, Cary M. "Playing the Action: Building an Interpretation from the Scene Up". *Teaching Shakespeare through Performance.* Ed. Milla Riggio. Modern Language Association of

America Options for Teaching (New York: Modern Language Association of America, 1999), pp. 155-68.

McCloskey, Susan. "Teaching Dramatic Literature". *College English* 46 (1984), pp. 385-91.

McEvoy, Sean. "The Politics of Teaching Shakespeare". *English in Education* 25:3 (1991), pp. 71-8.

McFeely, Maureen Connolly. "'That's the scene that I would see': Videos in the Shakespeare Classroom". *Shakespeare and the Classroom* 2:1 (1994), pp. 38-9.

McIver, Bruce and Ruth Stevenson. *Teaching with Shakespeare: Critics in the Classroom*. Newark: Delaware UP; London and Toronto: Associated UPs, 1994.

McLean, Andrew M. "Teaching Shakespeare as a Foreign Language Text". *Shakespeare Newsletter* 41 (1991), pp. 35, 39.

---. "Teaching Shakespeare". *Shakespeare Newsletter* 29 (1979), p. 39.

---. "Teaching Shakespeare". *Shakespeare Newsletter* 30 (1980), p. 46.

McManus, Eva B. "'But can you teach all this you speak of?': Using Technology in the Shakespeare Classroom". *Shakespeare and the Classroom* 7:1 (1999), pp. 57-61.

---. "Shakespeare Festivals: Materials for the Classroom". *Teaching Shakespeare into the Twenty-First Century*. Ed. Richard E. Salomone and James E. Davis (Athens: Ohio UP, 1997), pp. 232-44.

McMurtry, Jo. *Shakespeare Films in the Classroom: A Descriptive Guide*. Hamden: Archon-Shoe String, 1994.

Meszaros, Patricia K. "Notes on a Workshop Approach to Shakespeare". *Shakespeare Quarterly* 25 (1974), pp. 188-97.

Michaels, Wendy. *Playbuilding Shakespeare*. Cambridge and New York: Cambridge UP, 1996.

---. *When the Hurly Burly Is Done*. [Epping, New South Wales: St. Clair Press,] 1986.

Miller, Mark. "Shakespeare's Languages, Whole and Unspoiled". *Use of English* 32:3 (1981), pp. 30-41.

Mitchell-Dwyer, Barbi. "'Are We Gonna Do Anything Fun?'" *English Journal* 70:6 (1981), pp. 24-5.

Molony, Rowland. "Sh . . . You Know Who!" *Times Educational Supplement* 13 November 1992, p. xii.

Morris, Muriel J. *Shakespeare Goes to the Dogs: Cartoon Synopses and Quizzes*. Portland, ME: Walch, 1990.

Morton, C. "A Case against Shakespeare". *Crux: A Journal on the Teaching of English* 15:3 (1981), pp. 33-5.

Much Ado about Shakespeare. [Armdale, Nova Scotia:] Nova Scotia Teachers Union for the Association of Teachers of English of Nova Scotia, [1981?].

Muir, Kenneth. "The Wrong Way and the Right". *Shakespeare Quarterly* 35 (1984), pp. 642-3.

Mullin, Michael. "Interactive Shakespeare Communities on the Web". *Shakespeare and the Classroom* 7.1 (1999), pp. 53-6.

---. "Problems of the Teaching and Criticism of Shakespeare on Film". *Shakespeare Newsletter* 26 (1976), p. 4.

Murphy, Georgeann. "*Commedia* in the Classroom: *Commedia dell'arte* Performance, Shakespearean Pedagogy, and Popular Culture". *Theatre Symposium* 1 (1993), pp. 135-41.

Murphy, Peter E. "Poems and Poetry: Writing Useful for Teaching Shakespeare". *Shakespeare Quarterly* 35 (1984), pp. 647-52.

Murray, Braham. "On Your Imaginary Forces at Work". *Teaching Shakespeare: Essays on Approaches to Shakespeare in Schools and Colleges*. Ed. Richard Adams (London: Robert Boyce, 1985), pp. 41-56.

Nagarajan, S. "The Teaching of Shakespeare in India". *Indian Writing in English*. Ed. Ramesh Mohan (Bombay: Orient Longman, 1978), pp. 239-51.

Neely, Carol Thomas. "Feminist Criticism and Teaching Shakespeare". *ADE Bulletin* 87 (1987), pp. 15-23.

Nelson, George D., and David Morgan. "Unlocking the Secrets of Will's World". *Drama/Theatre Teacher* 6:2 (1994), pp. 26-8.

Newman, David. "Teaching Shakespeare". *Curriculum Review* 30 (December 1990), pp. 7-11.

Nicholl, James R. "Another Time, Another Place: Imagination and Shakespearean Drama". *Exercise Exchange* 24:2 (1980), pp. 15-17.
Noling, Kim H. "Reconstructing Shakespeare's Company: Liberal Learning through Playing". *Shakespeare and the Classroom* 4:2 (1996), pp. 65-7.
Nünning, Ansgar. *Uni-Training englische Literaturwissenschaft: Grundstrukturen des Fachs und Methoden der Textanalyse*. Stuttgart: Klett for Wissen und Bildung, 1996.
O'Brien, Ellen J. "Inside Shakespeare: Using Performance Techniques to Achieve Traditional Goals". *Shakespeare Quarterly* 35 (1984), pp. 621-31.
O'Brien, Peggy. "Doing Shakespeare: 'Yo! A hit! A very Palpable hit!'" *English Journal* 82:4 (1993), pp. 40-5.
O'Brien, Veronica. *Teaching Shakespeare*. Teaching Matters. London: Arnold, 1982.
O'Connor, Teresa, and Susan Brock. "Teacher Resources at the Shakespeare Birthplace Trust". *English Association Newsletter* 157 (1998), pp. 5-6.
Oldrieve, Susan. "On Technology: Making Use of Educational Technology in the Shakespeare Course". *Shakespeare and the Classroom* 8:1 (2000), pp. 19-24.
Olive, David. "Videos and the Teaching of Shakespeare in Performance". As You Like It: *AudioVisual Shakespeare*. Ed. Cathy Grant (London: British Film and Video Council, 1992), pp. 6-9.
Oppel, Horst. "Shakespeares Dramen in der Bildkunst". *William Shakespeare: Didaktisches Handbuch*. Ed. Rüdiger Ahrens. 3 vols (Munich: Fink, 1982), II, pp. 667-91.
Orgel, Stephen. "Why Did the English Stage Take Boys for Women?" *Teaching Shakespeare through Performance*. Ed. Milla Riggio. Modern Language Association of America Options for Teaching (New York: Modern Language Association of America, 1999), pp. 102-13.
Orme, David. *Shakespeare*. Press for Action. Dunstable: Folens, 1991.
Ozanne, Christine. "Teaching Shakespeare the *Original* Way". *Speech and Drama* 43:1 (1994), pp. 16-21.
Pafford, Michael. "Shakespeare Rules, O.K.?" *Use of English* 36:3 (1985), pp. 49-52.
Peat, Derek. "Looking Up and Looking Down: Shakespeare's Vertical Audience". *Shakespeare Quarterly* 35 (1984), pp. 563-70.
---. "Teaching through Performance: An Interview with J. L. Styan". *Shakespeare Quarterly* 31 (1980), pp. 142-52.
Pechter, Edward. "Teaching Differences". *Shakespeare Quarterly* 41 (1990), pp. 160-73.
Pellikka, Paul. "ACTER, Actors, and Teaching Shakespeare through Performance". *Studies in Medieval and Renaissance Teaching* 7:1 (1999), pp. 75-86.
Petronella, Vincent F. "Teaching Shakespeare's Development as Poetic Dramatist". *Indirections* (Ontario Council of Teachers of English) 1:3-4 (1976), pp. 37-41.
Plasse, Marie A. "An Inquiry-Based Approach". *Teaching Shakespeare into the Twenty-First Century*. Ed. Richard E. Salomone and James E. Davis (Athens: Ohio UP, 1997), pp. 120-6.
Potter, Alex. "The Concept of Context in the Teaching of Shakespeare". *Occasional Papers and Reviews, Shakespeare Society of Southern Africa* 3:2 (1988), pp. 6-9.
Potter, Lois. "Teaching Shakespeare: The Participatory Approach". *Teaching Shakespeare through Performance*. Ed. Milla Riggio. Modern Language Association of America Options for Teaching (New York: Modern Language Association of America, 1999), pp. 235-43.
Pritchard, William H. "Shakespeare Alive and Well". *Shakespeare and the Classroom* 6:1 (1998), pp. 34-5.
Rainwater, Lynne. "Wall to Wall: Production History Leads to Production". *Shakespeare* (Georgetown University) 1:3 (1997), pp. 14-15.
Rao, Adapa Ramakrishna. "Teaching Shakespeare: The Indian Context". *Indian Journal of Shakespeare Studies* 1 (1985), pp. 41-6.
Rao, T. V. Subba. "Shakespeare and the Indian Reader". *Indian Journal of Shakespeare Studies* 1 (1985), pp. 7-27.
Reeves, Barbara. "*Mr. William Shakespeare and the Internet*". *School Library Media Activities Monthly* 16:9 (2000), pp. 20-22, 27.
Reich, Sabine. "The Bard in the Movies: Vorschläge zum Einsatz von Shakespeareverfilmungen im Unterricht". *Fremdsprachenunterricht* 5 (1998), pp. 336-42.

Reinsberg, Carol L. "Conning Shakespeare". *English Journal* 70:5 (1981), pp. 54-6.
Rempe, Robert H. "Using the Poem 'The Little Boy' in Shakespeare Class". *Shakespeare and the Classroom* 8:1 (2000), pp. 28-9.
Reynolds, Peter. "Active Reading: Shakespeare's Stagecraft". *Teaching Shakespeare: Essays on Approaches to Shakespeare in Schools and Colleges.* Ed. Richard Adams (London: Robert Boyce, 1985), pp. 118-32.
---. *Practical Approaches to Teaching Shakespeare.* London: Oxford UP, 1991.
Reynolds, Peter. "Unlocking the Box: Shakespeare on Film and Video". *Shakespeare in the Changing Curriculum.* Ed. Lesley Aers and Nigel Wheale (London and New York: Routledge, 1991), pp. 189-203.
Richmond, Hugh. "Teaching Shakespeare in Performance at the Restored Shakespeare Globe Theatre at Bankside, London". *Studies in Medieval and Renaissance Teaching* 7:2 (1999), pp. 61-6.
Riggio, Milla, ed. *Teaching Shakespeare through Performance.* Modern Language Association of America Options for Teaching. New York: Modern Language Association of America, 1999.
---. "The Universal Is the Specific: Deviance and Cultural Identity in the Shakespeare Classroom". *Shakespeare Quarterly* 46 (1995), pp. 196-209.
Roberts, Jeanne Addison. "Making a Woman and Other Institutionalized Diversions". *Shakespeare Quarterly* 37 (1986), pp. 366-9.
Rocklin, Edward L. "'An Incarnational Art': Teaching Shakespeare". *Shakespeare Quarterly* 41 (1990), pp. 147-59.
---. "Performance Is More Than an 'Approach' to Shakespeare". *Teaching Shakespeare through Performance.* Ed. Milla Riggio. Modern Language Association of America Options for Teaching. New York: Modern Language Association of America, 1999), pp. 48-62.
Rocklin, Edward L. "Shakespeare's Script as a Cue for Pedagogic Invention". *Shakespeare Quarterly* 46 (1995), pp. 135-44.
Roets, Ninon. *Literature-Based Listening Comprehension.* Johannesburg: Language Service RAU, 1987.
Rooks, John. "Shakespeare in a West African Context: Boundaries and Points of Access". *Nebraska English Journal* 35 (Spring-Summer 1990), pp. 116-29.
Rostron, David. "Some Approaches to Teaching Shakespeare". *The Use of English* 26:3 (1974-75), pp. 222-8.
Rothwell, Kenneth S. "Segmentation and De-Segmentation: A Semiological Approach to Shakespeare on Screen". *Shakespeare and the Classroom* 2:2 (1994), pp. 74-7.
Rovine, Harvey. "Shakespeare as a Theatrical Event". *The Practical Bard.* Ed. Cher Stempler (Orlando: Shakespeare Institute, University of Central Florida, 1979), p. 157.
Rozett, Martha Tuck. "Creating a Context for Shakespeare with Historical Fiction". *Shakespeare Quarterly* 46 (1995), pp. 220-27.
---. "Holding Mirrors Up To Nature: First Readers as Moralists". *Shakespeare Quarterly* 41 (1990), pp. 211-21.
---. "Shakespeare the Survivor: Or, Shakespeare and the Politics of the Curriculum". *Upstart Crow* 18 (1998), pp. 20-26.
---. *Talking Back to Shakespeare.* Newark: Delaware UP; London and Toronto: Associated UPs, 1994.
Rozett, Martha Tuck. "When Images Replace Words: Shakespeare, Russian Animation, and the Culture of Television". *Teaching Shakespeare into the Twenty-First Century.* Ed. Richard E. Salomone and James E. Davis (Athens: Ohio UP, 1997), pp. 208-14.
"S/F in Classrooms: A Preliminary Report". *Shakespeare on Film Newsletter* 2:2 (1978), pp. 4-5, 7.
Saeger, James P. "The High-Tech Classroom: Shakespeare in the Age of Multimedia, Computer Networks, and Virtual Space". *Teaching Shakespeare into the Twenty-First Century.* Ed. Richard E. Salomone and James E. Davis (Athens: Ohio UP, 1997), pp. 271-83.
Salomone, Richard E. and James E. Davis, ed. *Teaching Shakespeare into the Twenty-First Century.* Athens: Ohio UP, 1997.

---, ed. "Teaching Shakespeare, II". *Focus: Teaching English Language Arts* 12:1 (1985), pp. 1-93.
Saraswati, V. "Teaching Shakespeare". *Journal of English and Foreign Languages* 6 (December 1990), pp. 47-52.
Sauer, David Kennedy. "'Speak the speech, I pray you,' or Suiting the Method to the Moment: A Theory of Classroom Performance of Shakespeare". *Shakespeare Quarterly* 46 (1995), pp. 173-82.
Sauer, David Kennedy, and Evelyn Tribble. "Shakespeare in Performance: Theory in Practice and Practice in Theory". *Teaching Shakespeare through Performance*. Ed. Milla Riggio. Modern Language Association of America Options for Teaching (New York: Modern Language Association of America, 1999), pp. 33-47.
Saunders, J. G. "Circe and the Cyclops: A Shakespearean Adventure". *Teaching Shakespeare: Essays on Approaches to Shakespeare in Schools and Colleges*. Ed. Richard Adams (London: Robert Boyce, 1985), pp. 97-117.
Scanlan, David. *Reading Drama*. Mountain View, CA: Mayfield, 1988.
Schabert, Ina. "Der werkgenetische Aspekt: Shakespeares Dramen im Vergleich zu ihren Quellen". *William Shakespeare: Didaktisches Handbuch*. Ed. Rüdiger Ahrens. 3 vols (Munich: Fink, 1982), III, pp. 761-78.
Schechner, Richard. "Re-Wrighting Shakespeare: A Conversation with Richard Schechner". *Teaching Shakespeare through Performance*. Ed. Milla Riggio. Modern Language Association of America Options for Teaching (New York: Modern Language Association of America, 1999), pp. 127-41.
Schiff, Peter. "Shakespeare Cereals: A Popular Culture Exercise". *Exercise Exchange* 43 (Fall 1997), pp. 8-9.
Schott, Penelope Scambly. "The Student Director". *Teaching Shakespeare Bulletin* 1 (1976).
Schroenn, Manfred. "The Abiding Relevance of Shakespeare". *Crux: A Journal on the Teaching of English* 28:1 (1994), pp. 53-8.
Schwartz, Murray M. *A Thematic Introduction to Shakespeare*. Saratoga Springs: Empire State College, State University of New York, 1974.
Scolnicov, Hanna. "An Intertextual Approach to Teaching Shakespeare". *Shakespeare Quarterly* 46 (1995), pp. 210-19.
Sedlak, Werner. "Der politisch-kulturelle Hintergrund der Dramen Shakespeares". *William Shakespeare: Didaktisches Handbuch*. Ed. Rüdiger Ahrens. 3 vols (Munich: Fink, 1982), I, pp. 113-44.
Sell, Roger D. "Teaching Shakespeare on Literary Pragmatic Principles". *Literary Pedagogics after Deconstruction: Scenarios and Perspectives in the Teaching of English Literature*. Ed. Per Serritslev Petersen. Dolphin 22 (Aarhus: Aarhus UP, 1992), pp. 9-25.
Shafer, Ronald G. "The Triple Stage and the National Endowment Shakespeare Institute". *Shakespeare and the Triple Play: From Study to Stage to Classroom*. Ed. Sidney Homan (Lewisburg: Bucknell UP; London and Toronto: Associated UPs, 1988), pp. 215-21.
Shakespeare and Schools (1986-1994)
  Devoted specifically to Shakespeare and pedagogy, this journal contains a series of short articles, ranging from general teaching strategies to approaches for specific plays as well as accounts of school productions and other educational projects. Due to the space limitations, these articles are not listed individually in this bibliography.
Shakespeare im Unterricht. Begleitpapier zu einer Ausstellung der Amerika-Gedenkbibliothek/Berliner Zentralbibliothek. Berlin, 1988.
The Shakespeare Plays: A Study Guide. San Diego: University of California, San Diego, 1978.
The Shakespeare Plays: A Study Guide for the Second Season. Dubuque, IA: Kendall-Hunt, 1980.
"Shakespeare's Language: A Teacher's Toughest Task and Greatest Pleasure". *Shakespeare* (Georgetown University) 2:1 (1998), pp. 3-10.
Shand, G. B. "Reading Power: Classroom Acting as Close Reading". *Teaching Shakespeare through Performance*. Ed. Milla Riggio. Modern Language Association of America Options for Teaching (New York: Modern Language Association of America, 1999), pp. 244-55.

Shapiro, Michael. "Improvisational Techniques for the Literature Teacher". *Teaching Shakespeare through Performance.* Ed. Milla Riggio. Modern Language Association of America Options for Teaching (New York: Modern Language Association of America, 1999), pp. 184-95.

Shea, Michael. "The Value of not Teaching[:] Literary Theory in the Shakespeare Classroom". *Shakespeare and the Classroom* 4:1 (1996), pp. 35-41.

Shepherd, Simon. "Acting against Bardom: Some Utopian Thoughts on Workshops". *Shakespeare in the Changing Curriculum.* Ed. Lesley Aers and Nigel Wheale (London and New York: Routledge, 1991), pp. 88-107.

Simone, R. Thomas. "Shakespeare and a New Pedagogy: A Report on Computer/Laserdisc Technology and the Teaching of Shakespeare on Film". *Shakespeare and the Classroom* 5:1 (1997), pp. 68-73.

Sinfield, Alan. "Drama Teaching and the Politics of Plausibility". *Use of English* 41:3 (1990), pp. 41-7.

---. "Give an Account of Shakespeare and Education, Showing Why You Think They Are Effective and What You Have Appreciated about Them. Support Your Comments with Precise References". *Political Shakespeare: New Essays in Cultural Materialism.* Ed. Jonathan Dollimore and Alan Sinfield (Manchester: Manchester UP, 1985), pp. 134-57.

Slagle, Patti. "Learning Logs Lead to Discoveries about Women's Issues and Give Rise to Writing". *Shakespeare* (Georgetown University) 2:2 (1998), pp. 19-20.

Slover, George W. "Video versus Voice: Teaching Students and Teachers Shakespeare". *Nebraska English Journal* 35 (Spring-Summer 1990), pp. 32-53.

Smallwood, Robert. "Shakespeare at Stratford: Text and Theatre". *European English Messenger* 2:1 (1993), pp. 68-9.

Smith, Barbara A. "Why I Teach Shakespeare". *Shakespeare Newsletter* 43 (1993), pp. 51, 55.

Sousa, Geraldo U. de. "Paradigm Lost? The Fate of Literature in the Age of Theory". *Shakespeare Quarterly* 48 (1997), pp. 449-64.

Spencer, Jeff. "Drawing Students into Shakespeare". *English in Texas* 26:1 (1994), pp. 30-3.

Starr, Robert J., and Evelyn Wofford. "The Development of a Teaching Strategy Utilizing Formulae to Teach Shakespeare". *First Language* 5 (1984-85), p. 232.

Staton, Shirley F. "Shakespeare Redivivus: Supplementary Techniques for Teaching Shakespeare". *Literature/Film Quarterly* 5 (1977), pp. 358-61.

Stempler, Cher. "Botticelli, a.k.a. Essences". *The Practical Bard.* Ed. Cher Stempler. Orlando: Shakespeare Institute, University of Central Florida, 1979), pp. 163-65.

---. "'We're Gonna Do WHAT??' Improvisation in the Classroom". *The Practical Bard.* Ed. Cher Stempler (Orlando: Shakespeare Institute, University of Central Florida, 1979), pp. 158-60.

Stibbs, Andrew. "Between Desk, Stage, and Screen: 50 Years of Shakespeare Teaching". *Educational Review* 50:3 (1998), pp. 241-8.

Stodder, Joseph H. "Teaching Shakespeare through Play Production". *Journal on Excellence in College Teaching* 6:2 (1995), pp. 31-46.

Strickland, Ronald. "Teaching Shakespeare against the Grain". *Teaching Shakespeare Today: Practical Approaches and Productive Strategies.* Ed. James E. Davis and Ronald E. Salomone (Urbana: National Council of Teachers of English, 1993), pp. 168-78.

Styan, J. L. "Direct Method Shakespeare". *Shakespeare Quarterly* 25 (1974), pp. 198-200.

---. "Shakespeare Teaches Shakespeare". *Shakespeare Newsletter* 25 (1975), p. 16.

---. "Shakespeare's Use of His Stage". *Shakespeare and English History: Interdisciplinary Perspectives.* Ed. Ronald G. Shafer (Indiana: Indiana University of Pennsylvania, 1976), pp. 29-44.

---. "'Show and Tell' in the Shakespeare Classroom". *Teaching Shakespeare Bulletin* 1 (1976).

---. "The Writing Assignment: The Basic Question". *Teaching Shakespeare into the Twenty-First Century.* Ed. Richard E. Salomone and James E. Davis (Athens: Ohio UP, 1997), pp. 3-10.

Sullivan, Theresa. *Getting into Shakespeare.* The English Collection. Harlow, Essex: Longman, 1992.

Suvin, Darko. "A Modest Proposal for the Semi-demi Deconstruction of (Shakespeare as) Cultural Construction". *Semeia: Itinerari per Marcello Pagnini.* Ed. Loretta Innocenti, Franco Maurcci and Paola Pugliatti (Bologna: Il Mulino 1994), pp. 67-76.

Swander, Homer. "In Our Time: Such Audiences We Wish Him". *Shakespeare Quarterly* 35 (1984), pp. 528-40.
---. "Teaching Shakespeare as Performance". *Shakespeare Newsletter* 25 (1975), p. 19.
---. "Teaching Shakespeare: Tradition and the Future". *William Shakespeare: His World, His Work, His Influence.* Ed. John F. Andrews. 3 vols (New York: Scribner's, 1985), pp. 873-87.
Szilassy, Zoltán. "Some New Trends and Practices in Hungarian Shakespeare Studies". *Shakespeare Yearbook* 7 (1996), pp. 235-48.
Taft-Kaufman, Jill. "A Rhetorical Perspective for Teaching the Solo Performance of Shakespearean Dramatic Literature". *Communication Education* 29:2 (1980), pp. 112-24.
Tales of Shakespeare. Mt. Prospect, IL: Learning Quest, 1986.
Tate, Joseph M. "The Motion of Emotion: Physical Responses of Early Modern Playgoers". *Shakespeare and the Classroom* 6:2 (1998), pp. 41-5.
Taylor, Barry. "Academic Exchange: Text, Politics, and the Construction of English and American Identities in Contemporary Renaissance Criticism". *Discontinuities: New Essays on Renaissance Literature and Criticism.* Ed. Viviana Comensoli and Paul Stevens. Theory/Culture (Toronto and Buffalo: Toronto UP, 1998), pp. 181-200.
Teaching Shakespeare News: A Publication of the Teaching Shakespeare Resource Center. Kenosha: University of Wisconsin-Parkside, 1989- .
Terkelson, Care, Sue Perona, and Wendy Manker. "Feelin' Free with Shakespeare". *English Record* 17 (Winter 1977), pp. 2-4.
Thompson, Ann. "Does It Matter Which Edition You Use?" *Shakespeare in the Changing Curriculum.* Ed. Lesley Aers and Nigel Wheale (London and New York: Routledge, 1991), pp. 74-87.
Thwaytes, Joy. *Shakespeare's England.* London: Philip, 1975.
Timm, Norbert. "Shakespeare audiovisuell". *Der Fremdsprachliche Unterricht* 20 (1986), pp. 143-7.
Toms, Caroline. *Themes in Shakespeare: Set A.* Cambridge, England: Pearson, 1992.
Tretler, Lawrence J. "Literature and Playscript: A Primer for English Teachers Who Teach Drama". *English Journal* 70:2 (1981), pp. 45-7.
Tropea, Silvana. "Shakespeare on Page and Stage at the RSC". *Theater* 23:2 (1992), pp. 44-7.
Tucker, Patrick, ed. *Shakespeare Cue Script Scenes for the Classroom: General Selections [; Duologues].* 2 vols. London: London Academy of Music and Dramatic Art and Original Shakespeare Company, 1998.
---. "Teaching and Acting Shakespeare from Cue Scripts". *Shakespeare Bulletin* 8:3 (1990), pp. 25-9.
Velz, John W. "Performing Shakespeare in a Humanities Course: The Scope and the Focus". *Shakespeare and the Classroom* 3:2 (1995), pp. 28-9.
---. "Shakespeare Inferred". *Teaching Shakespeare.* Ed. Walter Edens, Christopher Durer, Duncan Harris, Keith Hull, and Walter F. Eggers, Jr. (Princeton: Princeton UP, 1978), pp. 27-47.
Voth, Grant L. *Five Shakespeare Plays: Third Season Study Guide.* Palo Alto, CA: Bay Area Community College Television Consortium, 1980.
Wade, Barrie. "The Play's the Thing!" *Language and Learning* 9-10 (1995), pp. 31-3.
Wagner, Joe. "Shakespeare Students: On Their Feet and on Camera, Too". *Shakespeare and the Classroom* 5:2 (1997), pp. 49-52.
Wain, John. "The Nature of Shakespeare's Realism". *Teaching Shakespeare: Essays on Approaches to Shakespeare in Schools and Colleges.* Ed. Richard Adams (London: Robert Boyce, 1985), pp. 16-40.
Walker, Lewis. "Using Comic Strips to Teach Shakespeare". *North Carolina English Teacher* 51:4 (1994), pp. 12-19.
Waller, Gary F. "Decentering the Bard: The BBC-TV Shakespeare and Some Implications for Criticism and Teaching". *Shakespeare on Television: An Anthology of Essays and Reviews.* Ed. James C. Bulman and H. R. Coursen (Hanover and London: New England UP, 1988), pp. 18-30.

---. "The Late Plays as Family Romance". *Approaches to Teaching Shakespeare's* The Tempest *and Other Late Romances*. Ed. Maurice Hunt. Approaches to Teaching World Literature 41 (New York: Modern Language Association, 1992), pp. 57-63.

Walton, W. G., Jr. "Bringing Performances into Classrooms through Multiple Media". *Teaching Shakespeare through Performance*. Ed. Milla Riggio. Modern Language Association of America Options for Teaching (New York: Modern Language Association of America, 1999), pp. 321-40.

Warner, Christine D. "Building Shakespearean Worlds in the Everyday Classroom". *Teaching Shakespeare into the Twenty-First Century*. Ed. Richard E. Salomone and James E. Davis (Athens: Ohio UP, 1997), pp. 147-53.

Watson, Robert N. "Teaching 'Shakespeare': Theory versus Practice". *Teaching Literature: What Is Needed Now*. Ed. James Engell and David Perkins. Harvard English Studies 15 (Cambridge and London: Harvard UP, 1988), pp. 121-50.

Weitzel, Roy L. "Trying for the Apprehension of Literature: Shakespeare and Uses of Our Imagination". *College English* 37 (1975), pp. 294-306.

Wells, Randall A. "The Rolling Start: Helping the Novice Begin a Shakespeare Play". *Shakespeare Newsletter* 25 (1975), p. 52.

West, Gilian. *An Approach to Shakespeare*. London and New York: Cassell, 1995.

Wheale, Nigel. "Scratching Shakespeare: Video-Teaching the Bard". *Shakespeare in the Changing Curriculum*. Ed. Lesley Aers and Nigel Wheale (London and New York: Routledge, 1991), pp. 204-21.

Wheeler, Richard P. "Psychoanalytic Criticism and Teaching Shakespeare". *ADE Bulletin* 87 (1987), pp. 19-23.

Widmann, R. L. "From a Student's Point of View". *On Teaching. Volume 1*. Ed. Mary Ann Shea. Boulder: Faculty Teaching Excellence Program (University of Colorado at Boulder, 1987), pp. 87-114.

Wilcock, Erik, Patrick Redsell, and Robin Little. *The Shakespeare File: New Teaching Strategies*. London: Heinemann Educational, 1987.

Williams, Jason. "Teaching the Students How to Speak the Speech". *Shakespeare and the Classroom* 5:2 (1997), p. 52.

Williamson, David. "English Children Are too Sophisticated for Shakespeare". *Use of English* 38:2 (1987), pp. 27-32.

Willinsky, John. "From Feminist Literary Criticism: Certain Classroom Splendours". *English Quarterly* 18 (1985), pp. 35-43.

Willson, Robert F., Jr. "Bardic Bricolage: Tracing the Playtext in Hollywood Offshoots". *Shakespeare and the Classroom* 2:1 (1994), pp. 37-8.

---. "Why Teach Shakespeare? A Reconsideration". *Shakespeare Quarterly* 41 (1990), pp. 206-10.

Wilson, John Howard. "A World Ransomed: Shakespeare on Video". *Proceedings of the First Dakotas Conference on Earlier British Literature*. Ed. Jay Ruud (Aberdeen: Northern State UP, 1993), pp. 12-21.

Wilson, Michael, ed. *Scenes from Shakespeare: Fifteen Cuttings for the Classroom*. Colorado Springs, CO: Meriwether, 1993.

Winslow, Moira. "Thinking about Shakespeare in the School". *Johannesburg Shakespeare Quarterly* 1:3 (1994), pp. 1-4.

Wishoff, Robert. "Who's the Fruit with the Ring in His Ear? Or, a Devil's Advocacy of William Shakespeare's Plays". *The Practical Bard*. Ed. Cher Stempler (Orlando: Shakespeare Institute, University of Central Florida, 1979), pp. 154-6.

Worrall, Patricia B. "Technology Rescues Shakespeare". *Shakespeare and the Classroom* 2:1 (1994), p. 35.

Worthen, Helena, and Julian Levy. "Waking up the Storyteller inside Us: Three Writing Exercises". *Teachers and Writers* 24:3 (1993), pp. 10-15.

Wray, Ramona. "Shakespeare and the Sectarian Divide: Politics and Pedagogy in (Post) Post-Ceasefire Belfast". *Shakespeare and Ireland: History, Politics, Culture*. Ed. Mark Thornton Burnett and Ramona Wray (Basingstoke: Macmillan; New York: St. Martin's Press, 1997), pp. 235-55.

Wright, Laurence. "William Shakespeare's African Future". *Shakespeare Society of Southern Africa Newsletter, Incorporating Occasional Papers and Reviews* 14 (1999), n.p.

Wright, Laurence, and Jane Bursey. "The L2 Learner versus Shakespeare's Editors: An Aspect of the SSOSA/ISEA Shakespeare Text Development Project". *Crux: A Journal on the Teaching of English* 25:2 (1991), pp. 39-53.

Yandell, John. "Reading Shakespeare, or Ways with Will". *Changing English* 4.2 (1997), pp. 277-94.

Yogev, Michael. "'How shall we find the concord of this discord?': Teaching Shakespeare in Israel, 1994". *Shakespeare Quarterly* 46 (1995), pp. 157-64.

Young, Michael W. "All the Class' a Stage: Connecting Shakespeare with the Student's World through Performance". *Shakespeare and the Classroom* 3:2 (1995), p. 31.

Zahorski, Kenneth J. "The Next Best Thing: Shakespeare in Stereo". *College English* 39 (1977), pp. 290-3.

Zimmerman, Hester. "All Right, Shakespeare Fans, On Your Feet". *English Journal* 77:7 (1988), pp. 20-1.

General Studies: Primary and Middle Schools

Aagesen, Colleen, and Margie Blumberg. *Shakespeare for Kids: His Life and Times: 21 Activities.* Chicago: Chicago Review Press, 1999.

Ackroyd, Judith, Jonothan Neelands, Michael Supple, and Jo Trowsdale. *Key Shakespeare 1: Teaching Shakespeare to 10-14 Year Olds*. London: Hodder and Stoughton, 1998.

---. *Key Shakespeare 2: Teaching Shakespeare to 14-16 Year Olds*. London: Hodder and Stoughton, 1998.

Beaumier, Tony. "A Shakespeare Festival for the Middle Grades". *English Journal* 82:4 (1993), pp. 49-51.

Bevington, Frances A. "Learning to Love the Language of Shakespeare". *Learning* 22:6 (1994), pp. 60-1.

Burr, Constance. "Shakespeare for Kids". *Humanities* 17:3 (1996), pp. 14-17.

Burson, Linda. *Play with Shakespeare: A Guide to Producing Shakespeare with Young People.* Charlottesville, VA: New Plays Books, 1992.

Carlson, Susan, and Ann Messier. "Where There's a Will, There's a Play". *Voices from the Middle* 4:2 (1997), pp. 11-15.

Carter, Candy. "Move Over, Marva, or How 35 Students Learned 'To Be or not to Be.'" *English Journal* 72:3 (1983), pp. 27-9.

Cecil, Lynn A. "Profile: Lois Burdett". *Canadian Children's Literature* 85 (1997), pp. 41-4.

Church, Laura E. "Turned On to Shakespeare". *Shakespeare and the Classroom* 3:2 (1995), pp. 32-8.

Ciabotti, Patricia A. *Gaming It Up with Shakespeare: A Combined Study of Drama and Theatre.* Triad Prototype Series. Mansfield Center, CT: Creative Learning Press, 1980.

Cox, Carole. "Shakespeare and Company: The Best in Classroom Reading and Drama". *Reading Teacher* 33 (1980), pp. 438-41.

---. "Stirring Up Shakespeare in the Elementary School". *Literature – News That Stays News: Fresh Approaches to the Classics*. Ed. Candy Carter (Urbana: National Council of Teachers of English, 1985), pp. 51-8.

Coxwell, Margaret J. "Shakespeare for Elementary Students". *Teaching Pre-K-8* 27:6 (1997), pp. 40-2.

Cullum, Albert, ed. *Shakespeare in the Classroom: Plays for the Intermediate Grades*. Carthage, IL: Fearon Teacher Aids-Paramount Supplemental Education, 1995.

DeFord, Andrea. "To Like or not to Like: A Shakespeare Encounter". *English Journal* 84:3 (1995), pp. 85-6.

Deveson, Tom. "Sharp and Subtle Perceptions". *Around the Globe* Winter 1998, pp. 18-19.

Egan, Penny. "An RSA Assessment of the Wider Issues". *Shakespeare for All, Volume 1: The Primary School: An Account of the RSA Shakespeare in Schools Project*. Ed. Maurice Gilmour (London: Cassell, 1997), pp. 100-103.

Engen, Barbara, and Joy Campbell. *Elementary, My Dear Shakespeare: Producing a Shakespearean Festival in the Elementary Schools.* Revised edition. Salt Lake City: Market Master, 1995.

Foster, Cass, and Lynn G. Johnson. *Shakespeare: To Teach or not to Teach.* Fourth edition. Chandler, AZ: Five Star Publications, 1998.

Gilmour, Maurice, ed. *Shakespeare for All, Volume 1: The Primary School: An Account of the RSA Shakespeare in Schools Project.* London: Cassell, 1997.

Huggins, Cynthia. "Shakespeare in the Middle School?" *The Practical Bard.* Ed. Cher Stempler (Orlando: Shakespeare Institute, University of Central Florida, 1979), pp. 150-1.

Isaac, Megan Lynn. *Heirs to Shakespeare: Reinventing the Bard in Young Adult Literature.* Young Adult Literature Series. Portsmouth, NH: Boynton/Cook-Heinemann, 2000.

Kameenui, Edward J. "Shakespeare and Beginning Reading: 'The readiness is all.'" *Teaching Exceptional Children* 28:2 (1996), pp. 77-81.

King, Neil. "Starting Shakespeare". *Teaching Shakespeare: Essays on Approaches to Shakespeare in Schools and Colleges.* Ed. Richard Adams (London: Robert Boyce, 1985), pp. 57-76.

Langley, Joan. "The Exalting Possibilities of Shakespeare". *Drama/Theatre Teacher* 6:2 (1994), pp. 13-16.

Long, Bob. "The Shakespeare Year in Southern California". *Social Studies Review* 21:1 (1981), pp. 35-7.

McGonigal, James. "Unsettling the Set Text: Reading as Writing Poetry". *Young Readers, New Readings.* Ed. Emrys Evans (Hull: Hull UP, 1992), pp. 124-44.

Misenheimer, Carolyn. "The Pleasures of Early Enlightenment: The Lambs' *Tales from Shakespeare*". *Charles Lamb Bulletin* 67 (1989), pp. 69-82.

Neumark, Victoria. "Where There's a Will". *Times Educational Supplement* 19 March 1993, p. xi.

Pienaar, Oonagh. "Shakespeare in the Primary School". *Crux: A Journal on the Teaching of English* 23:1 (1989), pp. 16-17.

Richardson, Cheryl. "As They Like It: Shakespeare in the Elementary School". *The Active Learner* 2:2 (1997), pp. 14-15, 38.

Rosenfeld, Judith B. "An Elizabethan Interlude: A Course for Middle Schoolers". *English Journal* 76:8 (1987), pp. 49-51.

Ryniker Bashian, Kathleen. "Playing Shakespeare". *Momentum* 24:1 (1993), pp. 67-8.

Sands, Alyce. "Using Shakespeare in the Elementary School". *The Practical Bard.* Ed. Cher Stempler (Orlando: Shakespeare Institute, University of Central Florida, 1979), pp. 152-3.

Schoon, Marilyn J. "Shakespeare in the 7th Grade? It Works". *Arizona English Bulletin* 25:2 (1983), pp. 92-7.

Schultz, Lois V. *The Bard for Beginners.* [Middletown, Ohio]: Globe-Three, 1985.

Sedgwick, Fred. *Shakespeare and the Young Writer.* London and New York: Routledge, 1999.

Sewlall, Haripersad. "Shakespeare in the Classroom". *Crux: A Journal on the Teaching of English* 27:3 (1993), pp. 40-3.

Smith, Mike. *Introducing Children to Shakespeare.* North Humberside, England: Working with Your Children, 1994.

Stephenson, Cherry. "The RSA Shakespeare Project in Leicestershire". *Speech and Drama* 43:1 (1994), pp. 1-6.

Stidolph, Sherry. "Shakespeare in the Yard". *Shakespeare* 1:1 (1996), pp. 3-5.

Thompson, Mike, Linda Weir, Sue Freeman, Ann Palmer, Anne Watts, Janet Thomas, Sue Gammon, Lynne Grindlay, Juliet Gasser, Elspeth Myles, Sue Trigg, Katherine Liggins, Clare Mulholland, and Patsy Ryder. "The Shakespeare Project: A Whole School Approach". *Shakespeare for All, Volume 1: The Primary School: An Account of the RSA Shakespeare in Schools Project.* Ed. Maurice Gilmour (London: Cassell, 1997), pp. 44-50.

Walker, Muriel. "A Primary Teacher's View of the Project". *Shakespeare for All, Volume 1: The Primary School: An Account of the RSA Shakespeare in Schools Project.* Ed. Maurice Gilmour (London: Cassell, 1997), pp. 70-2.

Ward, David, Valerie Grosvenor Myer, and Eric Dehn. "2B or not 2B: Should the Bard Be Obligatory?" *Guardian* 7 May 1991, p. 21.

Wellborn, Linda. "Teaching Shakespeare in the Elementary Classroom". *Shakespeare and the Classroom* 2:2 (1994), pp. 78-9.
Wood, Robin H. "Shakespeare in an Elementary School Setting: A Unique and Inspiring Educational Experience". *Phi Delta Kappan* 78 (1996-97), pp. 457-9.

General Studies: Secondary School

Adams, Richard. "Shakespeare in School: The State of Play". *Teaching Shakespeare: Essays on Approaches to Shakespeare in Schools and Colleges.* Ed. Richard Adams (London: Robert Boyce, 1985), pp. 1-15.
Aers, Lesley. "Shakespeare in the National Curriculum". *Shakespeare in the Changing Curriculum.* Ed. Lesley Aers and Nigel Wheale (London and New York: Routledge, 1991), pp. 30-9.
Alkire, Nancy L. "Shakespeare for Freshmen". *Shakespeare Newsletter* 42 (1992), p. 41.
Anderson, Sexton G. "Counselor and Teacher Together in the Classroom: 'Character is fate,' or Is It?" *School Counselor* 34 (1987), pp. 392-5.
Armstrong, Donna. "Alternative Uses for Shakespeare in the High School English Class". *The Practical Bard.* Ed. Cher Stempler (Orlando: Shakespeare Institute, University of Central Florida, 1979), pp. 148-9.
Baines, Lawrence. "The Shakespeare Frolic Project: Massaging Shakespeare through Multimedia". *Clearing House* 70:4 (1997), pp. 194-8.
Barker, Simon. "Bard or Bored? Shakespeare's Place in the Curriculum and the Academy". *Speech and Drama* 43:1 (1994), pp. 30-2.
---. "Re-Loading the Canon: Shakespeare and the Study Guides". *Shakespeare and National Culture.* Ed. John J. Joughin (Manchester: Manchester UP, 1997), pp. 42-57.
Batho, Rob. "Shakespeare in Secondary Schools". *Educational Review* 50 (1998), pp. 163-72.
Bauer, Hannspeter. "Statistische Untersuchung zur Praxis der Shakespeare-Lektüre: Plädoyer für eine Neuorientierung". *Praxis des neusprachlichen Unterrichts* 39 (1992), pp. 250-9.
Beehler, Sharon A. "'That's a Certain Text': Problematizing Shakespeare Instruction in American Schools and Colleges". *Shakespeare Quarterly* 41 (1990), pp. 195-205.
Bernstein, Abraham. "The Full Treatment". *English Record* 29 (1978), pp. 6-7.
Blackmore, John. "A Practical Approach to Shakespeare's Language". *Shakespeare for All, Volume 2: The Secondary School: An Account of the RSA Shakespeare in Schools Project.* Ed. Maurice Gilmour (London: Cassell, 1997), pp. 21-6.
Boone-Grubbs, Chris. "It Was Greek to Me: Teaching Shakespeare to General Education Students". *Indiana English* 9:3 (1985), pp. 4-6.
Bottoms, Janet. "Playing with Shakespeare: Or, 'Where there's a will there's a way.'" *English in Education* 28:3 (1994), pp. 25-33.
---. "Representing Shakespeare: Critical Theory and Classroom Practice". *Cambridge Journal of Education* 25 (1995), pp. 361-73.
Breen, Kathleen T. "Taking Shakespeare from the Page to the Stage". *English Journal* 82:4 (1993), pp. 46-8.
Brown, John, and Terry Gifford. *Teaching A Level Literature: A Student-Centered Approach.* London: Routledge, 1989.
Burnett, Rebecca E., and Elizabeth Foster. *Shakespeare Persona: A Creative Approach to Writing.* Littleton, MA: Sundance, 1988.
---. "'The *role's* the thing': The Power of Persona in Shakespeare". *English Journal* 82:6 (1993), pp. 69-73.
Christel, Mary T., and Ann Legore Christiansen. "Where There's a 'Will,' There's a Way!" *Teaching Shakespeare Today: Practical Approaches and Productive Strategies.* Ed. James E. Davis and Ronald E. Salomone (Urbana: National Council of Teachers of English, 1993), pp. 197-204.
Clemen, Wolfgang. "Die Fortbildungsseminare für Gymnasiallehrer an der Shakespeare-Bibliothek München". *Shakespeare im Unterricht.* Ed. Rüdiger Ahrens. Anglistik und Englischunterricht 3 (Trier: Volksfreund-Druckerei, 1977), pp. 173-80.

Condee, Ralph Waterbury. "Goneril without a White Beard". *Shakespeare on Film Newsletter* 1:1 (1976), pp. 1, 5, 7.
Cox, J. F. A. "Criticism and Creativity in the Sixth Form". *Critical Quarterly* 26:1-2 (1984), pp. 175-80.
Derricott, Christopher. *Introducing Shakespeare*. Warwick, England: Econ-o-Text, [2000?]. 17 + 5 + 8 + 5 leaves.
Doyle, Brian, and Derek Longhurst. "The Cultural Production of Shakespeare in Education". *Australian Journal of Cultural Studies* 3:1 (1985), pp. 40-61.
Edwards, Angela. "Encounters with Shakespeare: His Life and Work". *Shakespeare for All, Volume 2: The Secondary School: An Account of the RSA Shakespeare in Schools Project*. Ed. Maurice Gilmour (London: Cassell, 1997), pp. 27-36.
Eggert, Hartmut. "25 Schüler und ein Lehrer suchen ein Stück: Erfahrungen zum Nachahmen und Abwandeln (9./10. Klasse)". *Der Deutschunterricht* 34:2 (1982), pp. 18-24.
Finkenstaedt, Thomas. "Shakespeare zwischen Wissenschaft und Unterricht – echs Fragen an die Schule". *Shakespeare im Unterricht*. Ed. Rüdiger Ahrens. Anglistik und Englischenunterricht 3 (Trier: Volksfreund-Druckerei, 1977), pp. 53-62.
Freeman, John. "Filling in the Margins of Shakespeare's Texts: The New Historicism in the Classroom". *Nebraska English Journal* 35 (Spring-Summer 1990), pp. 108-15.
Gathergood, William J. "Computers in the Secondary Shakespeare Classroom". *Teaching Shakespeare into the Twenty-First Century*. Ed. Richard E. Salomone and James E. Davis (Athens: Ohio UP, 1997), pp. 255-61.
Gibson, Rex, ed. *Secondary School Shakespeare: Classroom Practice*. "Shakespeare and Schools" Project. Cambridge: Cambridge Institute of Education, 1990.
---. "Shakespeare on Film and the National Curriculum". *Use of English* 42:2 (1991), pp. 43-9.
---. *Teaching Shakespeare*. Cambridge School Shakespeare. Cambridge and New York: Cambridge UP, 1998.
---. "Teaching Shakespeare in Schools". *Teaching English*. Ed. Susan Brindley. Open University Postgraduate Certificate of Education Series (London and New York: Routledge in association with the Open University, 1994), pp. 140-8.
Gibson, Rex, and Janet Field-Pickering. *Discovering Shakespeare's Language: 150 Stimulating Activity Sheets for Student Work*. Cambridge School Shakespeare. Cambridge and New York: Cambridge UP, 1998.
Gilmour, Maurice, ed. *Shakespeare for All, Volume 2: The Secondary School: An Account of the RSA Shakespeare in Schools Project*. London: Cassell, 1997.
---. "Shakespeare in a Society of Diverse Cultures". *Shakespeare for All, Volume 2: The Secondary School: An Account of the RSA Shakespeare in Schools Project*. Ed. Maurice Gilmour (London: Cassell, 1997), pp. 88-148.
---. "Shakespeare in the Secondary School". *Shakespeare for All, Volume 2: The Secondary School: An Account of the RSA Shakespeare in Schools Project*. Ed. Maurice Gilmour (London: Cassell, 1997), pp. 5-8.
Gleaves, David B., Patricia A. Slagle, and Kay E. Twaryonas. "Shakespeare and the At-Risk Student". *Teaching Shakespeare Today: Practical Approaches and Productive Strategies*. Ed. James E. Davis and Ronald E. Salomone (Urbana: National Council of Teachers of English, 1993), pp. 179-89.
Gocke, Rainer. *Highlights of Shakespearean Comedy: Unterrichtsmodelle für die Sekundarstufe II*. Frankfurt am Main: Hirschgraben, 1989.
---. *Shakespeare's Tragedies. Unterrichtsmodell für die Sekundarstufe II*. Second revised edition. Frankfurt am Main: Hirschgraben, 1988.
Green, Michael. "Sixth Form and Pressure: Why Teach Shakespeare at A-Level?" *Reclamations of Shakespeare*. Ed. A. J. Hoenselaars. DQR Studies in Literature 15 (Amsterdam and Atlanta: Rodopi, 1994), pp. 281-302.
Griffith, Peter. "'Art Made Tongue-Tied by Authority.'" *Who Owns English?* Ed. Michael J. Hayhoe and Stephen Parker (Buckingham: Open UP, 1994), pp. 33-42.
Haddon, John. "'I was Macbeth's kilt-maker': or, What Are We Making of Shakespeare?" *Use of English* 44 (1993), pp. 122-31.

Häublein, Ernst. "Shakespeare und die hermeneutische Erziehung". *Shakespeare im Unterricht.* Ed. Rüdiger Ahrens. Anglistik und Englischenunterricht 3 (Trier: Volksfreund-Druckerei, 1977), pp. 93-100.

Hermes, Liesel. "Shakespeare-Ausgaben für die Schule: Eine didaktische Analyse". *William Shakespeare: Didaktisches Handbuch.* Ed. Rüdiger Ahrens. 3 vols (Munich: Fink, 1982), I, pp. 87-110.

Herz, Sarah K., with Donald R. Gallo. *From Hinton to Hamlet: Building Bridges between Young Adult Literature and the Classics.* Westport and London: Greenwood Press, 1996.

Hise, Jesse. *Shakespeare Festival: A Notebook Program That Enlivens Shakespeare's Works.* Lakeside, CA: Interact, 1990.

Holderness, Graham, and Andrew Murphy. "'Shakespeare Country': The National Curriculum and Literary Heritage". *Critical Survey* 7 (1995), pp. 110-15.

Holderness, Graham, and Andrew Murphy. "Shakespeare's England: Britain's Shakespeare". *Shakespeare and National Culture.* Ed. John J. Joughin (Manchester: Manchester UP, 1997), pp. 19-41.

Hollindale, Peter. "Approaches to Shakespeare at A Level". *Teaching Shakespeare: Essays on Approaches to Shakespeare in Schools and Colleges.* Ed. Richard Adams (London: Robert Boyce, 1985), pp. 77-96.

Hombitzer, Eleonore. "Shakespeare- Lektüre in der reformierten gymnasialen Oberstufe--unter besonderer Berücksichtingung von Grundkursen". *Shakespeare im Unterricht.* Ed. Rüdiger Ahrens. Anglistik und Englischenunterricht 3 (Trier: Volksfreund-Druckerei, 1977), pp. 77-92.

Hopkins, Lisa. "Teaching the Government's Texts: Official Shakespeare". *Shakespeare and the Classroom* 1:2 (1993), pp. 27-9.

Hornbrook, David. "'Go play, boy, play': Shakespeare and Educational Drama". *The Shakespeare Myth.* Ed. Graham Holderness. Cultural Politics (Manchester: Manchester UP, 1988), pp. 145-59.

James, Daniel F. "L'étude des textes classiques doit-elle être bannie de l'enseignement des langues vivantes?" *Les langues modernes* 75 (1981), pp. 354-60.

Jobson, Susan. "Shakespeare – the Cultural Weapon". *Scrutiny2* 1:1-2 (1996), pp. 112-18.

Johnson, Linda. "Shakespeare Is not Just for Eggheads: An Interview with Two Successful Teachers". *Teaching Shakespeare Today: Practical Approaches and Productive Strategies.* Ed. James E. Davis and Ronald E. Salomone (Urbana: National Council of Teachers of English, 1993), pp. 161-7.

Kahn, Coppélia. "'Brush up your Shakespeare, and they'll all kow-tow.'" *Shakespeare and the Classroom* 1:2 (1993), p. 4.

Kiester, Jane Bell. *The Chortling Bard: Caught'ya! Grammar with a Giggle for High Schools.* Gainesville, FL: Maupin House, 1998.

Klaw, Luisa. "Why Shakespeare in the High Schools?" *English Quarterly* 16:1 (1983), pp. 13-15.

Leach, Susan. *Shakespeare in the Classroom: What's the Matter?* English, Language, and Education Series. Buckingham and Philadelphia: Open UP, 1992.

Ledebur, Ruth Freifrau von. "Die Shakespeare-Lektüre in den Curricula der reformierten Oberstufe". *Shakespeare im Unterricht.* Ed. Rüdiger Ahrens. Anglistik und Englischenunterricht 3 (Trier: Volksfreund-Druckerei, 1977), pp. 63-76.

Lee, Rick. "An Approach to Shakespeare through Role Play". *Shakespeare for All, Volume 2: The Secondary School: An Account of the RSA Shakespeare in Schools Project.* Ed. Maurice Gilmour (London: Cassell, 1997), pp. 66-70.

Leithart, Peter J. *Brightest Heaven of Invention: A Christian Guide to Six Shakespeare Plays.* Moscow, ID: Canon, 1996.

Lemmer, André. "'The Play's the Thing': Some Thoughts on the Teaching of Shakespeare at School". *Occasional Papers and Reviews, Shakespeare Society of Southern Africa* 1:1 (1986), [2-7].

---. *Upgrading the Study of Shakespeare in Southern African High Schools: An Interim Report.* Grahamstown: Institute for the Study of English in Africa, Rhodes University, 1988.

---. "Teaching in the 'New South Africa': Shakespeare in the Heterogeneous Classroom". *Occasional Papers and Reviews, Shakespeare Society of Southern Africa* 9:1-2 (1994), pp. 7-15.

Long, Bob. "The Shakespeare Year in Southern California". *Social Studies Review* 21:1 (1981), pp. 35-7.

McCray, Nancy. "Animating Shakespeare (or, Celing the Bard)". *Booklist* 89 (1993), p. 1870.

McCullough, Christopher J., interviewer. "John Hodgson". *The Shakespeare Myth*. Ed. Graham Holderness. Cultural Politics (Manchester: Manchester UP, 1988), pp. 160-5.

McDonald, Russ. "Shakespeare Goes to High School: Some Current Practices in the American Classroom". *Shakespeare Quarterly* 46 (1995), pp. 145-56.

Mellor, Bronwyn, and Annette Patterson. "Critical Practice: Teaching 'Shakespeare.'" *Journal of Adolescent and Adult Literacy* 43 (2000), pp. 508-17.

Mintz, Anita. "Shakespeare's Scripts". *Humanities* (National Endowment for the Humanities) 4:1 (1983), pp. 17-18.

Orkin, Martin R. "Possessing the Book and Peopling the Text". *Post-Colonial Shakespeares*. Ed. Ania Loomba and Martin Orkin. New Accents (London and New York: Routledge, 1998), pp. 186-204.

Perrin, Judith. "Shakespeare's Language Explained to the Natives". *Indiana English* 11 (Fall 1987), pp. 15-17.

Pienaar, Peter. "Spotlight on the Bard, Restored (to Pristine Health in EL 2 Classrooms throughout the Sub-Continent)". *Crux: A Journal on the Teaching of English* 21:4 (1987), pp. 68-71.

Pinder, Brenda. *Shakespeare: An Active Approach*. Unwin Hyman Skills and Resources Series. London: Unwin Hyman, 1990.

Rempe, Robert H. "Playing All Parts: A Compendium of Theoretical Roles and Responsibilities for Readers of Shakespeare's Plays in High School Classrooms". *Shakespeare and the Classroom* 5:1 (1997), pp. 66-7.

---. "These Kids Are Just Acting Out Most of the Time". *Shakespeare and the Classroom* 3:2 (1995), p. 30.

Robbins, Mari Lu. *Interdisciplinary Unit: Shakespeare*. Huntington Beach, CA: Teacher Created Materials, 1995.

Roberts, Peter. *Shakespeare and the Moral Curriculum: Rethinking the Secondary School Shakespeare Syllabus*. New York: Pripet Press, 1992.

Robinson, Randal F. "Improvisation and the Language of Shakespeare's Plays". *Nebraska English Journal* 35 (Spring-Summer 1990), pp. 54-64.

---. *Unlocking Shakespeare's Language: Help for the Teacher and Student*. Urbana, IL: National Council of Teachers of English, 1989.

Rowan, Nicole. "Academic Shakespeare versus Classroom Shakespeare". *Folio: Shakespeare-Genootschap van Nederland en Vlaanderen* 3:2 (1996), pp. 5-11.

Rygiel, Mary Ann. *Shakespeare among Schoolchildren: Approaches for the Secondary Classroom*. Urbana: National Council of Teachers of English, 1992.

Schlusberg, Julian S. "Shakespeare on the High School Stage". *Secondary School Theatre Journal* 20:2 (1981), pp. 2-5.

Schott, Penelope Scambly. "The Chronicle of Wasted Time: Some Observations on Shakespeare in High Schools and How to Recover". *CEA Forum* 6 (December 1975), pp. 2-3, 10-11.

Schuhmann, Kuno. "Ausstellung 'Shakespeare im Unterricht' in Berlin". *Shakespeare-Jahrbuch* (Bochum), 1989, pp. 406-7.

Shakespeare Study Kit: The Shakespeare Plays. Los Angeles: Tel-Ed, 1978.

Sherman, Joseph. "No Literature for Anybody: A Stronger Case against Shakespeare". *Crux: A Journal on the Teaching of English* 18:2 (1984), pp. 3-9.

Smith, Edward B. "Fresh Fish or More Shakespeare?" *American Secondary Education* 21:3 (1993), pp. 15-18.

Stritmatter, Roger. "Teaching the Next Generation That Oxford Was Shakespeare". *Shakespeare Oxford Newsletter* 34:4 (1999), pp. 1, 10-13.

Stuart, Jan. "Classroom Calibans: The Bard Is Winning New Friends in New York City Schools". *American Theatre* 2:9 (1985), pp. 36-7.

Swerdlow, Alan. "Shakespeare in Jeans". *Johannesburg Shakespeare Quarterly* 1:1 (1993), pp. 19-28.
Tempera, Mariangela. "Shakespeare for Everybody: The Ferrara Project". *European English Messenger* 8:2 (1999), pp. 20-21.
"Text Alive!" *Asides: A Quarterly Publication of the Shakespeare Theatre* Winter 1991: 3.
Ungerer, Friedrich. "Der Shakespeare-Kanon für den Schulunterricht". *William Shakespeare: Didaktisches Handbuch.* Ed. Rüdiger Ahrens. 3 vols (Munich: Fink, 1982), I, pp. 219-39.
---. "Fragen der kursorischen und statarischen Lektüre bei der Shakespeare-Behandlung". *William Shakespeare: Didaktisches Handbuch.* Ed. Rüdiger Ahrens. 3 vols (Munich: Fink, 1982), II, pp. 371-92.
Veidemanis, Gladys V. "Some 'Basics' in Shakespearean Study". *Teaching Shakespeare Today: Practical Approaches and Productive Strategies.* Ed. James E. Davis and Ronald E. Salomone (Urbana: National Council of Teachers of English, 1993), pp. 3-13.
Wade, Barrie, and John Sheppard. "How Teachers Teach Shakespeare". *Educational Review* 46:1 (1994), pp. 21-8.
Wadhwa, Kamal. "Why Read Shakespeare in India?" *Indian P.E.N.* 47:1-2 (1985), pp. 11-14.
Ward, David, Valerie Grosvenor Myer, and Eric Dehn. "2B or not 2B: Should the Bard Be Obligatory?" *Guardian* 7 May 1991: 21.
Williams, Deborah A. "Shakespeare in the High School Classroom". *Shakespeare Quarterly* 25 (1974), pp. 263-4.
Wilson, Kate. "Make It Real: How to Get Shakespeare Across: A Guide for English Teachers". *Teaching Theatre* 1:3 (1990), pp. 7-9.
Wilson, Richard. "NATO's Pharmacy: Shakespeare by Prescription". *Shakespeare and National Culture.* Ed. John J. Joughin (Manchester: Manchester UP, 1997), pp. 58-80.
Woodbridge, Linda. "Presidential Address". *Shakespeare and the Classroom* 1:2 (1993), pp. 2-3.

General Studies: Colleges and Universities

Baker, Kay. "Modeling Shakespeare". *Teaching English in the Two-Year College* 20:1 (1993), pp. 38-9.
Berger, Thomas L. "Small-Time Shakespeare: The Politics of the Curriculum at a Liberal Arts College". *Shakespeare and the Classroom* 7:1 (1999), pp. 13-17.
Berkowitz, Gerald M. "Teaching Shakespeare to Today's College Students – Some Heresies". *Shakespeare Quarterly* 35 (1984), pp. 560-2.
Berry, Edward. "Teaching Shakespeare in China". *Shakespeare Quarterly* 39 (1988), pp. 212-16.
Brantlinger, Patrick. "Who Killed Shakespeare? An Apologia for English Departments". *College English* 61 (1999), pp. 681-90.
Charney, Maurice. "The Shakespeare Seminar as Pedagogical Entertainment". *Teaching Shakespeare through Performance.* Ed. Milla Riggio. Modern Language Association of America Options for Teaching (New York: Modern Language Association of America, 1999), pp. 256-65.
Cunningham, Karen. "Shakespeare, the Public, and Public Education". *Shakespeare Quarterly* 49 (1998), pp. 293-8.
Drew-Bear, Annette. "Using Improvisational Exercises to Teach Shakespeare". *Teaching Shakespeare Today: Practical Approaches and Productive Strategies.* Ed. James E. Davis and Ronald E. Salomone (Urbana: National Council of Teachers of English, 1993), pp. 79-84.
Egan, Catherine. "Putting the Bard on the Small Screen". *Sightlines* 11:1 (Fall 1977), pp. 8-13.
Freeman, John. "Filling in the Margins of Shakespeare's Texts: The New Historicism in the Classroom". *Nebraska English Journal* 35 (Spring-Summer 1990), pp. 108-15.
Frey, Charles H. "Teaching Shakespeare's Romances". *College Literature* 4 (1977), pp. 252-6.
Friedlander, Larry. "The Shakespeare Project: Experiments in Multimedia Education". *Academic Computing* 2:7 (1988), pp. 26-9, 66-8.
Friedman, F. Richard. "On Dramatizing the Script in the Classroom". *Teaching English in the Two-Year College* 10 (Spring 1984), pp. 261-3.

Gaskill, Gayle. "Performance Theory and Research in the Undergraduate Shakespeare Survey". *Studies in Medieval and Renaissance Teaching* 8:1 (2000), pp. 35-44.
Graham, Arthur. "Shakespeare and Music: An Undergraduate Class". *Shakespeare Newsletter* 45 (1995), pp. 65, 70.
Halio, Jay L. "Team Learning". *Shakespeare Quarterly* 41 (1990), pp. 230-4.
Haresnape, Geoffrey. "Teaching Shakespeare at University: Shakespeare for Africa". *Occasional Papers and Reviews, Shakespeare Society of Southern Africa* 6:1 (1991), pp. 3-5.
Hartshorn, Margaret P. "Shakespeare for Life: Teaching Shakespeare in General Education Courses to the Non-Traditional Student". *Ideological Approaches to Shakespeare: The Practice of Theory*. Ed. Robert P. Merrix and Nicholas Ranson (Lewiston, Queeston, and Lampeter: Mellen, 1992), pp. 257-64.
He Qixin. "Teaching Shakespeare in Chinese Universities". *Zhongguo Shaxue nianjian 1994 [Chinese Shakespeare Yearbook 1994]*. Ed. Xianqiang Meng (Changchun: Northeast Normal UP, 1995), pp. 211-24.
Henley, W. V. "Our Readers Write. . . ". *Occasional Papers and Reviews, Shakespeare Society of Southern Africa* 6:1 (1991), pp. 6-8.
Hotchkiss, Wilhelmina, and Elizabeth V. Young. "Engendering Response: Staging and Sexual Identity in an Introductory Shakespeare Course". *Proceedings of the First Annual CSU Shakespeare Symposium*. Ed. Kay Stanton (Fullerton: California State University at Fullerton Repro Graphics Center, 1991), pp. 11-19.
Huffman, Clifford. "The RSC *Playing Shakespeare* Tapes in a College Classroom". *Shakespeare on Film Newsletter* 14:2 (1990), p.3.
Jamison, William A. "The Case for a Compleat Shakespeare". *Shakespeare Quarterly* 25 (1974), pp. 258-9.
Johnson, Robert Carl. "Decentering the Instructor in Large Classes". *Teaching Shakespeare Today: Practical Approaches and Productive Strategies*. Ed. James E. Davis and Ronald E. Salomone (Urbana: National Council of Teachers of English, 1993), pp. 190-6.
Jones, Gordon Pryce. "Long-Distance Shakespeare". *Shakespeare Quarterly* 35 (1984), pp. 590-6.
---. "Televising Shakespeare: A Video Paper". *Proceedings: Communications Technology in Higher Education/Actes du colloque: Technologie des communications et éducation supérieure*. Ed. Jocelyne Picot (Moncton, New Brunswick: Université de Moncton, 1986), pp. 195-203.
Klingspon, Ron. "Teaching Shakespeare to Undergraduates: The Professor as Practiser". *English Quarterly* 17:2 (1984), pp. 16-26.
Küpper, Reiner. *Shakespeare im Unterricht: Geschichte, Konzeptionen, Tendenzen*. Epistemata. Würzburger Wissenschaftliche Schriften: Reihe Literaturwissenschaft 11 (Würzburg: Königshausen und Neumann, 1982), p. 460.
Lewis, Cynthia. "Performing Shakespeare: The Outward Bound of the English Department". *Teaching Shakespeare through Performance*. Ed. Milla Riggio. Modern Language Association of America Options for Teaching (New York: Modern Language Association of America, 1999), pp. 295-306.
Long, Cynthia D. "The Bard of Bakersfield: Professor of the Year Brings Shakespeare to Life". *Academe* 82:1 (1996), pp. 36-9.
Loomba, Ania. "Teaching the Bard in India". *Journal of English and Foreign Languages* 7-8 (1991), pp. 147-62.
Maher, Mary Z. "Shakespeare in Production". *Teaching Shakespeare into the Twenty-First Century*. Ed. Richard E. Salomone and James E. Davis (Athens: Ohio UP, 1997), pp. 35-42.
---. "The Value of the Actors in the Classroom". *Shakespeare Quarterly* 35 (1984), pp. 616-20.
Martin, Jerry L., Anne D. Neal, and Michael S. Nadel. *The Shakespeare File: What English Majors Are Really Studying*. Washington: National Alumni Forum, 1996.
McDermott, Kristen. "Staging the Classroom". *Shakespeare* (Georgetown University) 2:2 (1998), pp. 5-6.
Millard, Barbara C., Georgianna Ziegler, and Geraldine R. Custer. "'Playing Out the Play': Actors, Teachers, and Students in the Classroom". *Shakespeare Quarterly* 35 (1984), pp. 609-15.
Milward, Peter. "Teaching Shakespeare in Japan". *Shakespeare Quarterly* 25 (1974), pp. 228-33.

Neumann, Anne Waldron. "Should You Read Shakespeare?" *Meanjin* 56 (1997), pp. 17-25.
Nicholl, James R. "The In-Class Journal". *College Composition and Communication* 30 (1979), pp. 305-7.
Omans, Stuart E., and Patricia A. Madden. "Shakespeare – Dull and Dusty? Some Revolutions in Central Florida". *Shakespeare in the South: Essays on Performance.* Ed. Philip C. Kolin (Jackson: Mississippi UP, 1983), pp. 278-91.
Orkin, Martin R. *Shakespeare against Apartheid.* Craighall, South Africa: Ad. Donker, 1987.
Pendleton, Thomas A. "Testing for Visual Details in Shakespeare Films". *Shakespeare on Film Newsletter* 4:2 (1980), pp. 2, 6-7.
Pinti, Daniel J. "Introducing Shakespeare with First Folio Advertisements". *Teaching Shakespeare Today: Practical Approaches and Productive Strategies.* Ed. James E. Davis and Ronald E. Salomone (Urbana: National Council of Teachers of English, 1993), pp. 123-9.
Rabkin, Norman. "Shakespeare and the Graduate English Curriculum". *Teaching Shakespeare.* Ed. Walter Edens, Christopher Durer, Duncan Harris, Keith Hull, and Walter F. Eggers, Jr. (Princeton: Princeton UP, 1978), pp. 67-78.
Richmond, Hugh M. "Shakespeare at the University of California". *Shakespeare and the Classroom* 1:1 (1993), pp. 1-2.
---. "Shakespeare College at Berkeley". *Shakespeare Newsletter* 25 (1975), p. 19.
---. "Teaching Shakespeare: The Shakespeare Program at Berkeley". *Shakespeare Newsletter* 33 (1983), p. 18.
Robinson, Randal F. "Improvisation and the Language of Shakespeare's Plays". *Nebraska English Journal* 35 (Spring-Summer 1990), pp. 54-64.
---. *Unlocking Shakespeare's Language: Help for the Teacher and Student.* Urbana, IL: National Council of Teachers of English, 1989.
Rowan, Nicole. "Academic Shakespeare versus Classroom Shakespeare". *Folio: Shakespeare-Genootschap van Nederland en Vlaanderen* 3:2 (1996), pp. 5-11.
Salvaggio, Ruth. "Shakespeare in the Wilderness; or Deconstruction in the Classroom". *Demarcating the Disciplines: Philosophy, Literature, Art.* Ed. Samuel Weber. Glyph Textual Studies new series 1 (Minneapolis: Minnesota UP, 1986), pp. 95-102.
Serotte, Brenda. "The Human Experience in Shakespeare: A Multicultural Approach". *Shakespeare Newsletter* 43 (1993), p. 51.
Shafer, Ronald G. "Film and the Interdisciplinary Shakespeare Course". *Shakespeare on Film Newsletter* 2 (December 1977), p. 6.
Shaw, Patricia. "Estudio y docencia de Shakespeare en la universidad española". *Shakespeare en España: Crítica, traducciones y representaciones.* Ed. José Manuel González Fernández de Sevilla (Alicant: Universidad de Alicante; Zaragoza: Pórtico, 1993), pp. 95-117.
"The Teaching Shakespeare Resource Center". *Shakespeare and the Classroom* 2:1 (1994), p. 36.
Thompson, Torri. "Studies in Shakespeare: Strategies for a Feminist Pedagogy". *Feminist Teacher* 8:2 (1994), pp. 67-74.
---. "Transformative Teaching of Renaissance Literature through Intertextual Discursive Constellations". *Transformation* 10:1 (1999), pp. 12-25.
Tippens, Dora. "Crossing the Cirriculum with Shakespeare". *Shakespeare Quarterly* 35 (1984), pp. 653-6.
Woodbridge, Linda. "Presidential Address". *Shakespeare and the Classroom* 1:2 (1993), pp. 2-3.

General Studies: Special Needs

Abdulezer, Susan, and Terry Cambridge. "Shakespeare in Speech, Sign, and Cyberspace". *NECC '96* (Eugene, OR: International Society for Technology in Education, 1996), pp. 1-3.
Anderson, Peggy L. "Using Literature to Teach Social Skills to Adolescents with LD". *Intervention in School and Clinic* 35:5 (2000), pp. 271-9.
Cambridge, Theresa, and Susan Abdulezer. "Sharing Shakespeare: Integrating Literature, Technology, and American Sign Language". *NASSP Bulletin* 82 (January 1998), pp. 19-22.
Checkley, Rebecca. "Building Links with the Bard". *Times Educational Supplement* 3 February 1995, sec. 2: 6.

Collie, Joanne, and Stephen Slater. *Literature in the Language Classroom: A Resource Book of Ideas and Activities*. Cambridge: Cambridge UP, 1987.

Cowgill, Terry D. "On Teaching Shakespeare to Students with LD". *Their World: National Center for Learning Disabilities* 1996-97, pp. 31-3.

Eidenier, Betty. *Warp Zone Shakespeare! Active Learning Lessons for the Gifted, Grades Six through Twelve*. Manassas, VA: Gifted Education Press, 1990.

Geller, Conrad. "Classics in the Remedial Classroom". *English Journal* 78:4 (1989), pp. 25-6.

Halkitis, Perry N., and Mala Hoffman. "Applying Literature in the Elementary School: Shakespeare in the Intermediate Grades". *Gifted Child Today* 15:6 (1992), pp. 2-6.

Johnson, Kathryn King. "Teaching Shakespeare to Learning Disabled Students". *English Journal* 87:3 (1998), pp. 45-9.

Kester, Ellen S. *Word Magic: Shakespeare's Rhetoric for Gifted Students*. Bellingham, WA: Pickwick, 1985.

Kincaid, Arthur. "International Teaching: The Shakespeare Experience in Teaching Foreign Speakers". *Shakespeare and the Classroom* 8:1 (2000), pp. 15-19.

Kujawinska-Courtney, Krystyna. *English 321: Shakespeare: Selected Plays*. 2 vols. Austin: University of Texas at Austin, Extension Instruction and Materials Independent Learning, 1990.

Lentz, Alyce Slater, and Deirdre Kennedy Ritter. "Shakespeare Lives at CSD!" *Post Milan ASL and English Literacy: Issues, Trends, and Research*. Ed. Bruce D. Snider (Washington: Continuing Education and Outreach, Gallaudet University, 1994), pp. 263-6.

Lewis, Susan. "Shakespeare Made Simple". *WATSOL Working Papers* 2 (1984-85), pp. 38-41.

Marcus, Karen. "All You Need Is Love: Using Shakespeare to Build Community". *English Journal* 85:3 (1996), pp. 58-60.

Péchou, Anne, and Madeleine Achard. "Contributions du jeu dramatique et du théâtre à l'apprentissage d'une langue étrangère: Une expérience d'anglais dans une école d'ingenieurs". *Les langues modernes* 88:2 (1994), pp. 25-33.

Rothenberg, Sally Sue, and Susan M. Watts. "Students with Learning Difficulties Meet Shakespeare: Using a Scaffolded Reading Experience". *Journal of Adolescent and Adult Literacy* 40 (1997), pp. 532-9.

Thorson, Sue. "*Macbeth* in the Resource Room: Students with Learning Disabilities Study Shakespeare". *Journal of Learning Disabilities* 28 (1995), pp. 575-81.

Walters, Michael E. *Teaching Shakespeare to Gifted Students, Grades Six through Twelve: An Examination of the Sensibility of Genius*. Manassas, VA: Gifted Education Press, 1990.

General Studies: Bibliographies

Boltz, Ingeborg. "Bibliographie zu Shakespeare im Unterricht". *Shakespeare im Unterricht*. Ed. Rüdiger Ahrens. Anglistik und Englischenunterricht 3 (Trier: Volksfreund-Druckerei, 1977), pp. 181-9.

---. "Didaktische Bibliographie". *William Shakespeare: Didaktisches Handbuch*. Ed. Rüdiger Ahrens. 3 vols (Munich: Fink, 1982), III, pp. 1037-81.

Hacksley, Malcolm. "Shakespeare in *Crux*, 1967-1991: An Overlooked Resource for Teachers of Shakespeare?" *Occasional Papers and Reviews, Shakespeare Society of Southern Africa* 7:1 (1992), pp. 14-20.

Kliman, Bernice W. "Shakespeare on Video: Good News for Teachers". *Shakespeare on Film Newsletter* 8:2 (1984), pp. 1, 8-10.

LaRose, Joseph A. "Teaching Shakespeare: A Multilevel Bibliography". *Bulletin of Bibliography* 54 (1997), pp. 67-76.

Macklin, Susan. "Teaching Shakespeare: A Survey of Recent Useful Publications". *Teaching Shakespeare: Essays on Approaches to Shakespeare in Schools and Colleges*. Ed. Richard Adams (London: Robert Boyce, 1985), pp. 151-69.

McLean, Andrew M. "Annotated Bibliography". *Teaching Shakespeare*. Ed. Walter Edens, Christopher Durer, Duncan Harris, Keith Hull, and Walter F. Eggers, Jr. (Princeton: Princeton UP, 1978), pp. 317-33.

---. "Audio-Visual Resources for the Teaching of Shakespeare". *Shakespeare in the Classroom: Resources and Media Aids* (Kenosha: University of Wisconsin-Parkside, 1977), pp. 56-82.
---. *Shakespeare: Annotated Bibliographies and Media Guide for Teachers.* Urbana, IL: National Council of Teachers of English, 1980.
---. "Teaching Shakespeare on Film: A Checklist". *Shakespeare in the Classroom: Resources and Media Aids* (Kenosha: University of Wisconsin-Parkside, 1977), pp. 31-5.
O'Brien, Peggy. "'And gladly teach': Books, Articles, and a Bibliography on the Teaching of Shakespeare". *Shakespeare Quarterly* 46 (1995), pp. 165-72.
Riggio, Milla. "Annotated Guide to Classroom Editions of Shakespeare". *Teaching Shakespeare through Performance.* Ed. Milla Riggio. Modern Language Association of America Options for Teaching (New York: Modern Language Association of America, 1999), pp. 442-53.
Smolka, Dieter. "Homepages für den Englischunterricht: Shakespeare im Internet". *Fremdsprachenunterricht* 5 (1998), pp. 383-4.

Individual Plays:

Antony and Cleopatra

Böhm, Rudolf. "Die fächerübergriefende Erhellung: Shakespeare und Corneille". *William Shakespeare: Didaktisches Handbuch.* Ed. Rüdiger Ahrens. 3 vols (Munich: Fink, 1982), II, pp. 643-64.
Earthman, Elise Ann. "Shakespeare in the City". *Teaching Shakespeare through Performance.* Ed. Milla Riggio. Modern Language Association of America Options for Teaching (New York: Modern Language Association of America, 1999), pp. 277-85.
Feuerstein, Phyllis A. "Shakespeare's Dysfunctional Families". *School Librarian's Workshop* 17:5 (1997), pp 5-6.
Gardner, Mary. "Teaching *Antony and Cleopatra* (A Personal Impression)". *Occasional Papers and Reviews, Shakespeare Society of Southern Africa* 2:2 (1987), pp. 11-12.
Kelley, Brian J. "See the Light through *Antony and Cleopatra*". *Shakespeare* (Georgetown University) 2:3 (1998), p. 15.
Male, David A., ed. *Antony and Cleopatra.* Shakespeare on Stage. Cambridge: Cambridge UP, 1984.
Michaels, Wendy. *Gaze on Cleopatra: A Workshop Approach to* Antony and Cleopatra. Shakespeare. Workshop Series. New Rozelle, New South Wales: St. Clair Press, 1992.

As You Like It

Collins, Michael J. "Do Women in the Comedies Get Married and Live Happily Ever After? Act It Out and See". *Shakespeare* (Georgetown University) 2:2 (1998), pp. 20-1.
Funke, Peter. "Der Dramentext und seine Aufführung, dargestellt an *As You Like It*". *William Shakespeare: Didaktisches Handbuch.* Ed. Rüdiger Ahrens. 3 vols (Munich: Fink, 1982), I, pp. 261-92.
Haddon, John. "Shakespeare: Exploring the Idea of Love in *As You Like It*". *English in Practice: Literature at "A" Level.* Ed. Roger Knight (Edinburgh: Scottish Academic Press, 1989), pp. 25-34.
Heck, DeAnn M., and Sheryl Lee Hinman. As You Like It: *Curriculum Unit.* Rocky River, OH: Center for Learning, 1993.
Hobby, Elaine. "'My affection hath an unknown bottom': Homosexuality and the Teaching of *As You Like It*". *Shakespeare in the Changing Curriculum.* Ed. Lesley Aers and Nigel Wheale (London and New York: Routledge, 1991), pp. 125-42.
Powell, Neil. "Liking It". *Use of English* 26 (1974), pp. 3-8.
Robinson, Dennis, and Ken Watson. *Love's Keen Arrows: A Workshop Approach to* As You Like It. Rozelle, New South Wales: St. Clair Press, 1998.

Coriolanus

George, David, and Kent Burnside. "Shakespeare in the Classroom, Then and Now: The Case of *Coriolanus*". *Shakespeare and the Classroom* 4.1 (1996), pp. 29-32.
Hunfeld, Hans. "Shakespeare – Brecht – Grass: Die kontrastive Analyse am Beispiel des *Coriolanus*". *William Shakespeare: Didaktisches Handbuch*. Ed. Rüdiger Ahrens. 3 vols (Munich: Fink, 1982), III, pp. 933-52.
Otten, Kurt. "Politische Rhetorik als kommunikationstheoretisches Problem. Eine Darstellung anhand der Tragödien *Julius Caesar* und *Coriolanus*". *William Shakespeare: Didaktisches Handbuch*. Ed. Rüdiger Ahrens. 3 vols (Munich: Fink, 1982), II, pp. 517-59.
Pols, Robert. "Cartoon Criticism". *English Review* 4:2 (1993), p. 31.
Vickers, Brian. "Teaching *Coriolanus*: The Importance of Perspective". *Teaching Shakespeare*. Ed. Walter Edens, Christopher Durer, Duncan Harris, Keith Hull, and Walter F. Eggers, Jr. (Princeton: Princeton UP, 1978), pp. 228-70.

Cymbeline

Kehler, Dorothea. "Teaching the Slandered Women of *Cymbeline* and *The Winter's Tale*". *Approaches to Teaching Shakespeare's* The Tempest *and Other Late Romances*. Ed. Maurice Hunt. Approaches to Teaching World Literature 41 (New York: Modern Language Association, 1992), pp. 80-6.
Lewis, Cynthia. "Teaching 'A Thing Perplex'd': Drawing Unity from the Confusion of *Cymbeline*". *Approaches to Teaching Shakespeare's* The Tempest *and Other Late Romances*. Ed. Maurice Hunt. Approaches to Teaching World Literature 41 (New York: Modern Language Association, 1992), pp. 72-9.

Hamlet

Alsup, Andrea. "Taking Poetic License with Shakespeare: Companion Poems for Four Plays". *English Journal* 82:5 (1993), pp. 66-8.
Askew, Kay. Hamlet: *Teacher's Notes*. Shakespeare 16-19: Teaching Strategies for Advanced Level. London: Arnold, 1989.
Barbieri, Richard E., and Richard Lederer. *Hamlet*. Insight: Literary Analysis Activities Program. Littleton, MA: Sundance, 1988.
Baumlin, James S., and Tita French Baumlin. "Knowledge, Choice, and Consequence: Reading and Teaching *Hamlet*". *CEA Critic* 52.1-2 (1989-90), pp. 13-30.
Beckerman, Bernard. "Some Problems in Teaching Shakespeare's Plays as Works of Drama". *Teaching Shakespeare*. Ed. Walter Edens, Christopher Durer, Duncan Harris, Keith Hull, and Walter F. Eggers, Jr. (Princeton: Princeton UP, 1978), pp. 305-16.
"Best of the Best: Veteran Teachers Tell How They Teach *Hamlet*". *Shakespeare* 1:1 (1996), pp. 8-11.
Boch, Gudrun and Annette Rothenberg-Joerges. "*Hamlet* in der Sekundarstufe II: Vorschläge zu einer Unterrichtseinheit". *Gulliver: Deutsch-Englische Jahrbücher/German-English Yearbook* 6 (1979), pp. 48-65.
Bronson, Daniel R. "The Claudius Cover-up: A Psychology of Politics in *Hamlet*". *English in Texas* 8:2 (1977), pp. 45-6.
Carter, Dennis. "A Country Discovered: Upper Juniors Explore Meanings in *Hamlet*". *Cambridge Journal of Education* 19 (1989), pp. 333-50.
Collins, Mary B. Hamlet: *A Unit Plan*. Berlin, MD: Teacher's Pet, 1994.
Costello, Mary Enda, Stephen L. Jacobs, and Mary Neelan. Hamlet: *A Teacher Resource Unit*. Villa Maria, PA: Center for Learning, 1988.
---. *Experiencing Shakespeare II: An Introductory Approach to* Hamlet *and* Julius Caesar. Dubuque, IA: Center for Learning, 1983.

Dean, J. S. "What's the Matter with *Hamlet* in the Schools?" *Shakespeare in the Classroom: Resources and Media Aids* (Kenosha: University of Wisconsin-Parkside, 1977), pp. 16-30.

Devoe, Thelma. *Hamlet*. Ed. Lois A. Markham. REACT: Reading and Critical Thinking. Littleton, MA: Sundance, 1991.

Felter, Douglas P. "Exploring Shakespeare through the Cinematic Image: Seeing *Hamlet*". *English Journal* 82:4 (1993), pp. 61-4.

Gavin, Rosemarie. "*The Lion King* and *Hamlet:* A Homecoming for the Exiled Child". *English Journal* 85:3 (1996), pp. 55-7.

Giese, Loreen L. "Images of *Hamlet* in the Undergraduate Classroom". *Teaching Shakespeare into the Twenty-First Century*. Ed. Richard E. Salomone and James E. Davis. Athens: Ohio UP, 1997. 172-76.

Hapgood, Robert. "Hamlet's First Soliloquy: An Exercise". *Shakespeare and the Triple Play: From Study to Stage to Classroom*. Ed. Sidney Homan (Lewisburg: Bucknell UP; London and Toronto: Associated UPs, 1988), pp. 197-200.

Harrison, Bernard T. "A Sense of Worth: Seven Days with *Hamlet*". *Use of English* 35:3 (1984), pp. 21-34.

Helphinstine, Frances L. "Using Playgrounding to Teach *Hamlet*". *Teaching Shakespeare into the Twenty-First Century*. Ed. Richard E. Salomone and James E. Davis (Athens: Ohio UP, 1997), pp. 50-6.

Herold, Niels. "Pedagogy, *Hamlet*, and the Manufacture of Wonder". *Shakespeare Quarterly* 46 (1995), pp. 125-34.

Johnson, Robert Carl. "What Happens in the Mousetrap: Versions of *Hamlet*". *Teaching Shakespeare into the Twenty-First Century*. Ed. Richard E. Salomone and James E. Davis (Athens: Ohio UP, 1997), pp. 177-81.

Kamm, Jay D. "How Now, Hamlet?" *English Journal* 71:7 (1982), pp. 52-5.

Kanakaraj, S. "Transnational Implications of Tamil *Hamlet*s". *Perspectives: Studies in Translatology* 2 (1994), pp. 219-23.

Keller, Karen Faith. "'A happiness that often madness hits on': Teaching *Hamlet* to Undergraduates". *CCTE [Conference of College Teachers of English of Texas] Studies* 49 (1984), pp. 73-9.

Knapp, Peggy Ann. "'Stay, Illusion,' or How to Teach *Hamlet*". *College English* 36 (1974), pp. 75-85.

Knoblock, Jennifer. *A Literature Guide for William Shakespeare's* Hamlet. San Antonio: ECS Learning Systems, 1994.

Levine, Gloria. Hamlet *by William Shakespeare: Teacher Guide*. Palatine, IL: Novel Units, 1992.

Lillich, Helen M. "Hooked on *Hamlet*". *Indiana English* 7:1 (1983), pp. 25-7.

López Román, Blanca. "Multicritical Introduction to Shakespeare Television Adaptations and the BBC *Hamlet* (1980, 1990)". *Actas del III congreso internacional*. Ed. María Luisa Dañobeitia (Granada: SEDERI, 1992), pp. 159-69.

Marshall, Sarah. "Behind the Scenes". *2D* 8.2 (1989), pp. 50-8.

McKenna, John J. "Using Learning Styles to Put Hamlet on Trial". *Contemporary Education* 61 (Winter 1990), pp. 81-6.

McKenna, Michael. "Shakespeare in Grade 8". *Journal of Reading* 19 (1975), pp. 205-7.

Müller-Schwefe, Gerhard. "Shakespeares Dramen in der Filmkunst". *William Shakespeare: Didaktisches Handbuch*. Ed. Rüdiger Ahrens. 3 vols (Munich: Fink, 1982), II, pp. 729-56.

Nathan, Gay T. "Hamlet's Letters". *English Journal* 66.7 (1977), pp. 60-1.

Nettles, John. "Customary Suits of Solemn Black Rubber: Hamlet as Contemporary Action Hero". *Shakespeare and the Classroom* 7:2 (1999), pp. 44-7.

O'Brien, Peggy, general ed. *Shakespeare Set Free: Teaching* Hamlet *and* Henry IV, Part 1. New York: Washington Square Press, 1994.

Pfister, Manfred. "Moderne *Hamlet*-Bearbeitungen im Spannungsfeld aktueller Dramaturgien". *William Shakespeare: Didaktisches Handbuch*. Ed. Rüdiger Ahrens. 3 vols (Munich: Fink, 1982), III, pp. 953-84.

Pinder, Brenda. *A Workshop Approach to* Hamlet. Ed. Peter Jones. Rozelle, New South Wales: St. Clair Press, 1990.

Potter, A. M. "A Confrontation with the Text". *Crux: A Journal on the Teaching of English* 20:1 (1986), pp. 19-36.
Roark, Chris. "Hamlet, Malcolm X, and the Examined Education". *CEA Critic* 57:1 (1994), pp. 111-22.
Rock, Andrea W. "Mock Trials and Shakespeare: From Advocacy to Meaning". *Shakespeare and the Classroom* 2:2 (1994), pp. 69-74.
Rozakis, Laurie E. *A Teaching Portfolio for* Hamlet. Cliffs Teaching Portfolios. Lincoln, NE: Cliffs Notes, 1987.
Schlösser, Anselm. "Über das Herangehen an *Hamlet*". *Shakespeare-Jahrbuch* (Weimar) 120 (1984), pp. 103-12.
Semple, Hilary. "Teaching Image Patterns in *Hamlet*". *Crux: A Journal on the Teaching of English* 27:2 (1993), pp. 8-16.
Sherlock, Stafford. "An Approach to *Hamlet*". *Use of English* 37:2 (1986), pp. 43-6.
Sowder, Wilbur H., Jr. "The Thing's the Play: Doing *Hamlet*". *English Journal* 82:4 (1993), pp. 65-7.
Study Guide to Hamlet *by William Shakespeare*. Strategies for Teaching. Evanston, IL: McDougal, Littell, 1989.
Swart, Marieken. "Cracking the Code: Approaches to the Teaching of *Hamlet*". *Crux: A Journal on the Teaching of English* 22:4 (1988), pp. 31-43.
Swope, John Wilson. *Ready-to-Use Activities for Teaching* Hamlet. Shakespeare Teachers Activities Library. West Nyack, NY: Center for Applied Research in Education, 1994.
Teng I-lu. "Shakespeare in a Chinese Class: With Some Observations on *Hamlet*". *Sino-American Conference on Shakespeare*. Taipei: Crane, 1991.
Ulen, Amy, and Joe Bonfiglio. "'Enterprises of great pitch and moment' – Using the Internet to Teach *Hamlet*". *Shakespeare* 1:1 (1996), pp. 12-13.
Van der Mescht, Hennie. "To See or Not to See: Zeffirelli and the Teacher of *Hamlet*". *Crux: A Journal on the Teaching of English* 26:2 (1992), pp. 17-22.
Walizer, Marue E. "Adolescent Experience as Shakespearean Drama". *English Journal* 76:2 (1987), pp. 41-3.
Whitesides, Nigel, and Adrian G. Packer. *Primary Shakespeare: An Introductory Drama Scheme*: Hamlet. Strood, England: P.S. Publishers, 1999.
Wilson, Diane. "The Misfit in Literature: A Course That Links Some Interesting Classics". *Literature – News That Stays News: Fresh Approaches to the Classics*. Ed. Candy Carter (Urbana: National Council of Teachers of English, 1985), pp. 9-10.

1 Henry IV

Alsup, Andrea. "Taking Poetic License with Shakespeare: Companion Poems for Four Plays". *English Journal* 82:5 (1993), pp. 66-8.
Costello, Mary Enda. Henry IV, Part I: *Curriculum Unit*. Rocky River, OH: Center for Learning, 1995.
Darrell, Sherry Bevins. "If Only One, then *Henry IV, Part 1* for the General Education Course". *Teaching Shakespeare Today: Practical Approaches and Productive Strategies*. Ed. James E. Davis and Ronald E. Salomone (Urbana: National Council of Teachers of English, 1993), pp. 263-9.
Earthman, Elise Ann. "Enter the Madcap Prince of Wales: Students Directing Henry IV, Part I". *English Journal* 82:4 (1993), pp. 54-60.
Hawkins, Sherman. "Teaching the Theatre of Imagination: The Example of *1 Henry IV*". *Shakespeare Quarterly* 35 (1984), pp. 517-27.
Hays, Irene de La Bretonne. "Using Semantic Clues to Get at Meaning in *Henry IV, Part I*". *Exercise Exchange* 29:1 (1983), pp. 7-12.
Hinman, Myra. "Teaching *1 Henry IV* to Beginning College Students". *Shakespeare Quarterly* 25 (1974), pp. 153-60.
Meyer, Herbert M., and Lee Thomsen. "Actively Experiencing Shakespeare: Students 'Get on their feet' for *Henry IV, Part One*". *English Journal* 88:5 (1999), pp. 58-61.

Michaels, Wendy. *The Theme of Honour's Tongue: A Workshop Approach to* Henry IV Part 1. Ed. Peter Jones. Shakespeare Workshop Series. Rozelle, New South Wales: St. Clair Press, 1991.

Newlin, Louisa Foulke. "Nice Guys Finish Dead: Teaching *Henry IV, Part I*". *Humanities* 17:3 (1996), pp. 22-5.

O'Brien, Peggy, general ed. *Shakespeare Set Free: Teaching* Hamlet *and* Henry IV, Part 1. New York: Washington Square Press, 1994.

Timm, Norbert. "'The better part of valour is discretion': Shakespeares *Henry IV Part 1* in einem Leistungskurs der Sekundarstufe II". *Praxis des neusprachlichen Unterrichts* 36 (1989), pp. 137-47.

Whitesides, Nigel, and Adrian G. Packer. *Primary Shakespeare: A Drama Scheme for Primary Schools*: Henry IV Part One. Strood, England: P. S. Publishers, 1996.

2 Henry IV

Weeks, Watson. "Genesis of a School Play". *Use of English* 36:2 (1985), pp. 57-65.

Henry V

Barker, Simon. "'But you must learn to know such slanders of the age': Literary Theory in the Study of Shakespeare". *Bridging the Gap: Literary Theory in the Classroom*. Locust Hill Literary Studies 17 (West Cornwall, CT: Locust Hill Press, 1994), pp. 219-44.

Blumrich, Ann Nord. "Into the Past through the Future: Captain Picard Meets Henry V". *English in Texas* 25:4 (1994), pp. 5-6.

Brent, Harry. "Versions of *Henry V*: Laurence Olivier versus Kenneth Branagh". *Teaching Shakespeare Today: Practical Approaches and Productive Strategies*. Ed. James E. Davis and Ronald E. Salomone (Urbana: National Council of Teachers of English, 1993), pp. 130-9.

Buhler, Stephen M. "Text, Eyes, and Videotape: Screening Shakespeare Scripts". *Shakespeare Quarterly* 46 (1995), pp. 236-44.

Costello, Mary Enda. Henry V: *Curriculum Unit*. Rocky River, OH: Center for Learning, 1993.

Hale, David G. "Video in the Shakespeare Class: *Henry V* 5.2". *Shakespeare and the Classroom* 3:1 (1995), pp. 21-3.

Howlett, Kathy M. "Team-Teaching Shakespeare in an Interdisciplinary Context". *Teaching Shakespeare into the Twenty-First Century*. Ed. Richard E. Salomone and James E. Davis (Athens: Ohio UP, 1997), pp. 112-19.

Kissler, Linda. "Teaching Shakespeare through Film". *Teaching Shakespeare into the Twenty-First Century*. Ed. Richard E. Salomone and James E. Davis (Athens: Ohio UP, 1997), pp. 201-7.

Nibbs, Joanne. *We Happy Few: A Workshop Approach to* Henry V. Rozelle, New South Wales: St. Clair Press, 1992.

Orme, David. *Shakespeare*, Henry V. Specials! Dunstable: Folens, 1998.

Page, Philip, and Marilyn Pettit. *William Shakespeare's* Henry V: *Teacher's Resource Book*. Livewire Shakespeare. London: Hodder and Stoughton Educational in association with the Basic Skills Agency, 2000.

Patterson, Annabel. "'A political thriller': The Life and Times of Henry V". *Teaching with Shakespeare: Critics in the Classroom*. Ed. Bruce McIver and Ruth Stevenson (Newark: Delaware UP; London and Toronto: Associated UPs, 1994), pp. 222-53.

Reynolds, Peter. "Shakespeare and Image Theater: *Henry V*". *Teaching Shakespeare through Performance*. Ed. Milla Riggio. Modern Language Association of America Options for Teaching (New York: Modern Language Association of America, 1999), pp. 361-72.

Robinson, Marsha S. "*Henry V* as Monumental History". *Nebraska English Journal* 35 (Spring-Summer 1990), pp. 98-107.

I Henry VI

Sexton, Elizabeth Ann. "When Is a Witch not a Whore? Historical Heresy, Pedagogical Practice, and Shakespeare's Joan de Pucelle". *Shakespeare and the Classroom* 7:1 (1999), pp. 24-6.

Julius Caesar

Barbieri, Richard E., and Richard Lederer. *Julius Caesar*. Insight: Literary Analysis Activities Program. Littleton, MA: Sundance, 1982.
Barry, Arlene L. "Visual Art Enhances the Learning of Shakespeare". *Education* 117 (1997), pp. 632-9.
Bonfiglio, Joseph. "Et tu, Plutarch". *Shakespeare* (Georgetown University) 2:3 (1998), pp. 9-10.
Bredella, Lothar. "Shakespeares *Julius Caesar* im Englischunterricht: Ein hermeneutisches Modell". *William Shakespeare: Didaktisches Handbuch*. Ed. Rüdiger Ahrens. 3 vols (Munich: Fink, 1982), II, pp. 561-93.
Busacker, Klaus. *Shakespeares* Julius Caesar: *Vorschläge zur Behandlung des Dramas in einem Leistungkurs*. Epistemata: Würzburger Wissenschaftliche Schriften 8. Würzburg: Königshausen und Neumann, 1982.
Christel, Mary T., and Christine Heckel-Oliver. "Role-Playing: *Julius Caesar*". *Teaching Shakespeare into the Twenty-First Century*. Ed. Richard E. Salomone and James E. Davis (Athens: Ohio UP, 1997), pp. 18-24.
Costello, Mary Enda, Stephen L. Jacobs, and Mary Neelan. Julius Caesar: *A Teacher Resource Unit*. Villa Maria, PA: Center for Learning, 1988.
---. *Experiencing Shakespeare II: An Introductory Approach to* Hamlet *and* Julius Caesar. Dubuque, IA: Center for Learning, 1983.
Crowl, Samuel. "'Our lofty scene': Teaching Modern Film Versions of *Julius Caesar*". *Teaching Shakespeare into the Twenty-First Century*. Ed. Richard E. Salomone and James E. Davis (Athens: Ohio UP, 1997), pp. 222-31.
Fleissner, Robert F. "The Meditations of *Julius Caesar*: Some Stoical Considerations of Shakespeare's". *Shakespeare and the Classroom* 7:2 (1999), pp. 29-34.
Forgy, Una. "Hi, Yo, Silver, Or Julius Caesar Rides Again". *English in Texas* 18:1 (1986), p. 23.
Friedman, Audrey A. *Julius Caesar*. Ed. Brian K. McLaughlin. REACT: Reading and Critical Thinking. Littleton, MA: Sundance, 1991.
Glanvill, André. "Brutus on Trial". *Educamus* 35:5 (1989), pp. 27-9.
Gless, Darryl J. "*Julius Caesar*, Allan Bloom, and the Value of Pedagogical Pluralism". *Shakespeare Left and Right*. Ed. Ivo Kamps (New York and London: Routledge, 1991), pp. 185-203.
Harrison, Myra. "Communicative Activities for *Julius Caesar*". *ELTIC Reporter* (English Academy of South Africa) 9:2 (1984), pp. 30-5.
Häublein, Ernst, and Edelbert Weinig. *Shakespeare's* Julius Caesar. A Teacher's Guide. Berlin: Cornelsen-Velhagen und Klasing, 1984.
Hombitzer, Eleonore. "Die Shakespeare-Verfilmung im Englischunterricht der gymnasialen Oberstufe". *William Shakespeare: Didaktisches Handbuch*. Ed. Rüdiger Ahrens. 3 vols (Munich: Fink, 1982), III, pp. 987-1013.
Johannessen, Larry R. "Digging into *Julius Caesar* through Character Analysis". *Teaching Shakespeare Today: Practical Approaches and Productive Strategies*. Ed. James E. Davis and Ronald E. Salomone (Urbana: National Council of Teachers of English, 1993), pp. 207-17.
Kennedy, Jo-ann. Julius Caesar *Today*. CELs 1992: S101.71. Saskatchewan: Teaching Materials Centre, Saskatchewan Teachers' Federation, [1992].
Lemmer, André. "Teaching *Julius Caesar* in 1993". *Crux: A Journal on the Teaching of English* 27:3 (1993), pp. 43-8.
McMurtry, Jo. "Teaching *Julius Caesar* with Film Bits". *Shakespeare on Film Newsletter* 16:2 (1992), p. 7.

Michaels, Wendy, and Ken Watson. *The Dogs of War: A Workshop Approach to* Julius Caesar. Rozelle, New South Wales: St. Clair Press, 1991.
Orme, David. *Shakespeare,* Julius Caesar. Specials! Dunstable: Folens, 1995.
Perret, Marion D. "Teaching Shakespeare on Video". *Shakespeare on Film Newsletter* 7:1 (1982), pp. 1, 6.
Potter, Alex. "Approaches to the Teaching of *Julius Caesar*". *Occasional Papers and Reviews, Shakespeare Society of Southern Africa* 2:2 (1987), pp. 6-11.
Potter, Sally, and Sue Welshman. *"The Play's the Thing!"* Julius Caesar: *Resources for Practical Group Work.* Tarvin, England: Cheshire Drama Resource Centre, [1994].
Rebbeck, Barbara. "'How Many Ages Hence.'" *Gifted Child Today* 16:4 (1993), pp. 20-4.
Rock, Andrea W. "Mock Trials and Shakespeare: From Advocacy to Meaning". *Shakespeare and the Classroom* 2:2 (1994), pp. 69-74.
Rode, Anne E. "Reflective Teaching: Governing the 'Tragic Absolutism' in Our Profession". *English Record* 44:3 (1994), pp. 8-14.
Ruggieri, Colleen A. "Laugh and Learn: Using Humor to Teach Tragedy". *English Journal* 88:4 (1999), pp. 53-8.
Snodgrass, Mary Ellen. *A Teaching Portfolio for* Julius Caesar. Cliffs Teaching Portfolios. Lincoln, NE: Cliffs Notes, 1986.
Swope, John Wilson. *Ready-to-Use Activities for Teaching* Julius Caesar. Shakespeare Teachers Activities Library. West Nyack, NY: Center for Applied Research in Education, 1993.
"Upstairs, Downstairs with Shakespeare's Irony". *Shakespeare* (Georgetown University) 2:3 (1998), p. 24.
Utley, Katherine. "The Sculpture Garden". *Shakespeare* (Georgetown University) 2:3 (1998), pp. 8-9.
Waters, Jane, and Malcolm Burgess. *Shakespeare Survival Pack*: Julius Caesar. Milton Keynes: Chalkface Project, 1996.
Wilders, John. "Dramatic Structure and Dramatic Effect in *Julius Caesar*". *Teaching with Shakespeare: Critics in the Classroom.* Ed. Bruce McIver and Ruth Stevenson (Newark: Delaware UP; London and Toronto: Associated UPs, 1994), pp. 142-51.
Wright, Laurence, and Jane Bursey. "Page-to-Stage: Teaching *Julius Caesar*". *Crux: A Journal on the Teaching of English* 28:1 (1994), pp. 28-36.

King Lear

Berger, Thomas L. "The (Play) Text's the Thing: Teaching the Blinding of Gloucester in *King Lear*". *Teaching Shakespeare through Performance.* Ed. Milla Riggio. Modern Language Association of America Options for Teaching (New York: Modern Language Association of America, 1999), pp. 196-219.
Biglin, Trevor. *King Lear.* Shakespeare 16-19: Teaching Strategies for Advanced Level. London: Arnold, 1988.
Boose, Lynda E. "An Approach through Theme: Marriage and the Family". *Approaches to Teaching Shakespeare's* King Lear. Ed. Robert H. Ray. Approaches to Teaching World Literature 12 (New York: Modern Language Association, 1986), pp. 59-68.
Cambridge, Theresa, and Susan Abdulezer. "Sharing Shakespeare: Integrating Literature, Technology, and American Sign Language". *NASSP Bulletin* 82 (January 1998), pp. 19-22.
Carter, Dennis. "*King Lear* in the Junior Classroom". *English in Education* 29 (1986), pp. 44-7.
Collins, Michael J. "Teaching *King Lear*". *Teaching Shakespeare into the Twenty-First Century.* Ed. Richard E. Salomone and James E. Davis (Athens: Ohio UP, 1997), pp. 166-71.
Driver, Martha, and Jeanine Meyer. "*Beowulf* to *Lear*: Text, Image, and Hypertext". *Literary and Linguistic Computing* 14 (1999), pp. 223-35.
Guido, Maria Grazia. *King Lear Workshop.* Galatina: Congedo, 1992.
Harcourt, John B. "A Theatrical Approach: Readers' Theater". *Approaches to Teaching Shakespeare's* King Lear. Ed. Robert H. Ray. Approaches to Teaching World Literature 12 (New York: Modern Language Association, 1986), pp. 119-24.

Hirsh, James E. "An Approach through Dramatic Structure". *Approaches to Teaching Shakespeare's* King Lear. Ed. Robert H. Ray. Approaches to Teaching World Literature 12 (New York: Modern Language Association, 1986), pp. 86-90.

Hunt, Maurice. "'Mapping' *King Lear* in a Drama Survey Course: A Guide in an Antiformalist Terrain". *Approaches to Teaching Shakespeare's* King Lear. Ed. Robert H. Ray. Approaches to Teaching World Literature 12 (New York: Modern Language Association, 1986), pp. 91-7.

Imbrie, Ann E. "An Archetypal Approach". *Approaches to Teaching Shakespeare's* King Lear. Ed. Robert H. Ray. Approaches to Teaching World Literature 12 (New York: Modern Language Association, 1986), pp. 69-74.

John, Peter. "Lear's Dance of Death". *Shakespeare for All, Volume 2: The Secondary School: An Account of the RSA Shakespeare in Schools Project.* Ed. Maurice Gilmour (London: Cassell, 1997), pp. 17-20.

Johnsen, William A. "Elementary English". *Centennial Review* 34 (1990), pp. 457-83.

Joyce, Anne. "*King Lear*: Making Shakespeare Relevant". *Shakespeare for All, Volume 1: The Primary School: An Account of the RSA Shakespeare in Schools Project.* Ed. Maurice Gilmour (London: Cassell, 1997), pp. 51-61.

Klene, Jean, C.S.C. "An Approach through Visual Stimuli and Student Writing". *Approaches to Teaching Shakespeare's* King Lear. Ed. Robert H. Ray. Approaches to Teaching World Literature 12 (New York: Modern Language Association, 1986), pp. 125-9.

Kranz, David L. "'Is This the Promis'd End?' Teaching the Play's Conclusion". *Approaches to Teaching Shakespeare's* King Lear. Ed. Robert H. Ray. Approaches to Teaching World Literature 12 (New York: Modern Language Association, 1986), pp. 136-41.

Leonarder, Rod. "Radical Experiment". *English in Australia* 70 (1984), pp 53-5.

Mallick, David, and Michelle Sims. "Writing about a Shakespeare Scene". *English in Australia* 70 (1984), pp. 42-52.

Matoba, Junko. "Shakespeare in the Classroom". *Shakespeare Translation* 10 (1984), pp. 63-72.

Michaels, Wendy. *The Natural Fool of Fortune:* King Lear: *A Teacher's Handbook.* Double Bay, Australia: Shakespeare Globe Centre Australia, 1993.

Neel, Jasper. "Plot, Character, or Theme? *Lear* and the Teacher". *Writing and Reading Differently: Deconstruction and the Teaching of Composition and Literature.* Ed. Douglas G. Atkins and Michael L. Johnson (Lawrence: Kansas UP, 1985), pp. 185-205.

Neelan, Mary. King Lear: *A Teacher Resource Unit.* Villa Maria, PA: Center for Learning, 1988.

Paton, Ann. "*King Lear* in a Literature Survey Course". *Approaches to Teaching Shakespeare's* King Lear. Ed. Robert H. Ray. Approaches to Teaching World Literature 12 (New York: Modern Language Association, 1986), pp. 75-9.

Petronella, Vincent F. "An Eclectic Critical Approach: Sources, Language, Imagery, Character, and Themes". *Approaches to Teaching Shakespeare's* King Lear. Ed. Robert H. Ray. Approaches to Teaching World Literature 12 (New York: Modern Language Association, 1986), pp. 38-49.

Pinder, Brenda. *Sharper than a Serpent's Tooth: A Workshop Approach to* King Lear. Ed. Peter Jones. Shakespeare Workshop Series. Rozelle, New South Wales: St. Clair Press, 1991.

Ramm, Hans-Christoph. "'Lear's shadow' – Zugänge zu Shakespeare's Drama *King Lear* im Englischunterricht der Sekundarstuff II". *Neusprachliche Mitteilungen aus Wissenschaft und Praxis* 48 (1995), pp. 228-34.

Ray, Robert H. *Approaches to Teaching Shakespeare's* King Lear. Approaches to Teaching World Literature 12. New York: Modern Language Association, 1986.

Richmond, Hugh M. "*King Lear* in a Course on Shakespeare and Film". *Approaches to Teaching Shakespeare's* King Lear. Ed. Robert H. Ray. Approaches to Teaching World Literature 12 (New York: Modern Language Association, 1986), pp. 130-5.

Robinson, J. W. "A Course Devoted Exclusively to *King Lear*". *Approaches to Teaching Shakespeare's* King Lear. Ed. Robert H. Ray. Approaches to Teaching World Literature 12 (New York: Modern Language Association, 1986), pp. 142-6.

Rothwell, Kenneth S. "Teaching a Plural Work Pluralistically". *Approaches to Teaching Shakespeare's* King Lear. Ed. Robert H. Ray. Approaches to Teaching World Literature 12 (New York: Modern Language Association, 1986), pp. 50-8.

Shurgot, Michael W. "'Passing the hat': A Teaching Strategy for *King Lear*". *Shakespeare and the Classroom* 6:1 (1998), pp. 36-7.
Styan, J. L. "A Theatrical Approach: *King Lear* as Performance and Experience". *Approaches to Teaching Shakespeare's* King Lear. Ed. Robert H. Ray. Approaches to Teaching World Literature 12 (New York: Modern Language Association, 1986), pp. 111-18.
Thompson, Ann. "*King Lear* and the Politics of Teaching Shakespeare". *Shakespeare Quarterly* 41 (1990), pp. 139-46.
Urkowitz, Steven. "Drama and Composition in the Classroom". *Teachers and Writers* 9:3 (1978), pp. 24-8.
Warren, Michael. "Teaching with a Proper Text". *Approaches to Teaching Shakespeare's* King Lear. Ed. Robert H. Ray. Approaches to Teaching World Literature 12 (New York: Modern Language Association, 1986), pp. 105-10.
Whittle, Peter. "Two School Drama Projects". *The Use of English* 27:3 (1976), pp. 18-23.
Young, Bruce W. "Shakespearean Tragedy in a Renaissance Context: *King Lear* and Hooker's *Of the Laws of Ecclesiastical Polity*". *Approaches to Teaching Shakespeare's* King Lear. Ed. Robert H. Ray. Approaches to Teaching World Literature 12 (New York: Modern Language Association, 1986), pp. 98-104.

Love's Labour's Lost

Bergeron, David M. "Plays within Plays in Shakespeare's Early Comedies". *Teaching Shakespeare*. Ed. Walter Edens, Christopher Durer, Duncan Harris, Keith Hull, and Walter F. Eggers, Jr. Princeton: Princeton UP, 1978. 305-16.

Macbeth

Ahrens, Rüdiger. "Jan Kotts Analyse von *Macbeth*: Drama und kritischer Text". *William Shakespeare: Didaktisches Handbuch*. Ed. Rüdiger Ahrens. 3 vols (Munich: Fink, 1982), III, pp. 885-909.
Alsup, Andrea. "Taking Poetic License with Shakespeare: Companion Poems for Four Plays". *English Journal* 82:5 (1993), pp. 66-8.
Benecke, Ingrid. *Stundenblätter* Macbeth. Stuttgart: Klett, 1985.
---. "Zum Einsatz von Filmmaterial bei der Behandlung von *Macbeth*". *Shakespeare-Jahrbuch* (Bochum) (1990), pp. 171-82.
Berry, Boyd M. "King James and the Weird Sisters". *Shakespeare* (Georgetown University) 1:4 (1997), pp. 18-19.
Breen, Kathleen T. "Found Poetry in *Macbeth*". *Shakespeare* (Georgetown University) 1:4 (1997), pp. 4-5.
Brent, Harry. "Different Daggers: Versions of *Macbeth*". *Teaching Shakespeare into the Twenty-First Century*. Ed. Richard E. Salomone and James E. Davis (Athens: Ohio UP, 1997), pp. 215-21.
Briggs, Martyn. "'It's mad this, sir.'" *Creative Drama* (Birmingham) 4:8 (1976), pp. 23-6.
Brindley, D. J. "*Macbeth* as Evidence of Shakespeare's Dramatic Genius". *Crux: A Journal on the Teaching of English* 15:1 (1981), pp. 34-41.
Burke, Adrian, and Gill Ager. "*Macbeth*: The Final Frontier!" *English in Education* 19 (1984), pp. 49-54.
Callahan, Colleen. "To be or not to be': The Place of Shakespeare in the English Curriculum for Secondary Education in South Africa of the 1900s [that is, 1990s]". *Shakespeare Society of Southern Africa Newsletter, Incorporating Occasional Papers and Reviews* 13 (1998), pp. 9-16.
Collins, Mary B. Macbeth: *A Unit Plan*. Berlin, MD: Teacher's Pet, 1994.
Costello, Mary Enda, Stephen L. Jacobs, Mary Neelan, and Gary Tutty. Macbeth: *Curriculum Unit*. Rocky River, OH: Center for Learning, 1988.

Dennis, Mary L., and Maureen Kirchhoefer. Macbeth: *Teacher Guide*. Palatine, IL: Novel Units, 1993.
Devoe, Thelma. *Macbeth*. REACT: Reading and Critical Thinking. Littleton, MA: Sundance, 1990.
Edmunds, Karl. *Kursmodell Englisch. Shakespeares* Macbeth. *Grundkurse, Leistungskurse*. 2 vols. Munich: Langenscheidt-Longman, 1983.
Figgins, Margo A., and Alan Smiley. "Building a Bridge to Shakespeare's *Macbeth* with Cormier's *The Chocolate War*". *Teaching Shakespeare Today: Practical Approaches and Productive Strategies*. Ed. James E. Davis and Ronald E. Salomone (Urbana: National Council of Teachers of English, 1993), pp. 241-9.
Flickstein, Dan. *Teaching* Macbeth *and More: Better Planning, Better Learning*. Thousand Oaks, CA: Corwin Press, 1996.
Geraths, Armin. "Shakespeare und die Historie: *Macbeth* als Geschichtsdrama". *William Shakespeare: Didaktisches Handbuch*. Ed. Rüdiger Ahrens. 3 vols (Munich: Fink, 1982), II, pp. 595-616.
Gibson, Rex. "Shakespeare's Rhetoric in Action". *Rebirth of Rhetoric: Essays in Language, Culture, and Education*. Ed. Richard Andrews (London and New York: Routledge, 1992), pp. 156-71.
Gillen, Jay M. "A Lesson from *Macbeth*". *English Journal* 81:3 (1992), pp. 64-6.
Gilmour, Maurice. "Keystage Theatre in Education: *Macbeth* for Primary Schools". *Shakespeare for All, Volume 1: The Primary School: An Account of the RSA Shakespeare in Schools Project*. Ed. Maurice Gilmour (London: Cassell, 1997), pp. 73-84.
Gordon, Richard. "'Why do you dress me in borrowed robes?' *Macbeth*: An Excursion into Video Scripting". *Crux: A Journal on the Teaching of English* 25:2 (1991), pp. 18-21.
Gordon, Sarah, and Christopher Geelan. *IBM Young Shakespeare* Macbeth: *Practical Approaches to* Macbeth *in the Primary School*. London: English Shakespeare Company, 1993.
Grindhammer, Lucille. "An Animated *Macbeth* in the Intermediate-Advanced English Language Classroom". *Praxis des neusprachlichen Unterrichts* 41 (1994), pp. 264-70.
Hasler, Jörg. "Methoden des inszenierenden Lesens: Interpretation der Aufführungssignale im Text". *William Shakespeare: Didaktisches Handbuch*. Ed. Rüdiger Ahrens. 3 vols (Munich: Fink, 1982), I, pp. 243-60.
Hattatt, Lance, and James Sale. *Macbeth*. Q series. London: Hodder and Stoughton, 1987.
Hayhoe, Michael J. *Creative Work Ideas for* Macbeth. Rozelle, New South Wales: St. Clair Press, 1988.
---. "Drama as Gaming: 'To bestir and busily occupy.'" *English Journal* 78.4 (1989): 54-58.
Hinkle, Doug. "*Macbeth*: From Picture Book to Rave Reviews". *Teaching Pre-K-8* 29.6 (1999): 50-52.
Hombitzer, Eleonore. "Die Shakespeare-Verfilmung im Englischunterricht der gymnasialen Oberstufe". *William Shakespeare: Didaktisches Handbuch*. Ed. Rüdiger Ahrens. 3 vols (Munich: Fink, 1982), III, pp. 987-1013.
Kearney, John. "The Relevance of *Macbeth*". *Crux: A Journal on the Teaching of English* 15:2 (1981), pp. 43-56.
Knoblock, Jennifer. *A Literature Guide for William Shakespeare's* Macbeth. San Antonio, TX: ECS Learning Systems, 1994.
Kovacs, Mary Anne, Dennis P. Meier, and Gary A. Tutty. Macbeth: *A Teacher Resource Unit*. Rocky River, OH: Center for Learning, 1988.
Lemmer, André. "Starting *Macbeth*". *Crux: A Journal on the Teaching of English* 25:2 (1991), pp. 22-7.
Lomonico, Michael. "'To th' amazement of mine eyes': *Macbeth* on Video". *Shakespeare* (Georgetown University) 1:4 (1997), p. 14.
Lusardi, James P. "Shakespeare's Performed Words: *Macbeth* and Improvisation in the Classroom". *CEA Critic* 54:2 (1992), pp. 21-9.
Macbeth *and the Dark Ages*. Special issue of *Nexus*, 1998.
"*Macbeth*". *The Practical Bard*. Ed. Cher Stempler (Orlando: Shakespeare Institute, University of Central Florida, 1979), pp. 105-23.

Shakespeare and Pedagogy: A Bibliography

Makua, A. M. "Taking the Fear out of Shakespeare: Approaches to the Teaching of *Macbeth*". *Educamus* 36:6 (1989), pp. 18-20.

Male, David A. *Macbeth*. Shakespeare on Stage Series. Cambridge: Cambridge UP, 1984.

Marchand, Marion. "Using Visual Media to Introduce *Macbeth*". *Crux: A Journal on the Teaching of English* 25:2 (1991), pp. 12-17.

Oakes, Elizabeth. "Enacting Shakespeare's Language in *Macbeth* and *Romeo and Juliet*". *Teaching Shakespeare Today: Practical Approaches and Productive Strategies*. Ed. James E. Davis and Ronald E. Salomone (Urbana: National Council of Teachers of English, 1993), pp. 85-9.

O'Brien, Peggy, general ed. *Shakespeare Set Free: Teaching* Romeo and Juliet, Macbeth, A Midsummer Night's Dream. New York: Washington Square Press, 1993.

O'Connor, John S. "Playing with Subtext: Using Groucho to Teach Shakespeare". *English Journal* 88:1 (1998), pp. 97-100.

Orme, David. *Shakespeare*, Macbeth. Specials! Dunstable: Folens, 1997.

Page, Philip, and Marilyn Pettit. *William Shakespeare's* Macbeth: *Teacher's Resource Book*. Livewire Shakespeare. London: Stodder and Houghton in association with the Basic Skills Agency, 1999.

Peeling, Michelle. "Wake Duncan with Thy Knocking – An Improvisation". *Shakespeare* (Georgetown University) 1:4 (1997), pp. 6-7.

Purves, Alan. "The State of Research in Teaching Literature". *English Journal* 70:3 (1981), pp. 82-4.

Reisin, Gail. "Experiencing *Macbeth*: From Text Rendering to Multicultural Performance". *English Journal* 82:4 (1993), pp. 52-3.

Robinson, Chris, and Jane Carducci. "'Herein I teach you': Shakespeare's *Macbeth* in the Middle School Classroom". *Shakespeare and the Classroom* 6:1 (1998), pp. 40-4.

Robinson, Lee Bolton, and E. Morrison. *Teaching Literature through Drama*: Macbeth. North Vancouver, Canada: Creative Curriculum, 1991.

Rothenberg, Sally Sue, and Susan M. Watts. "Students with Learning Difficulties Meet Shakespeare: Using a Scaffolded Reading Experience". *Journal of Adolescent and Adult Literacy* 40 (1997), pp. 532-9.

Rubano, Gregory L., and Philip M. Anderson. "'Sleep that knits up the raveled sleave of care': Responding to *Macbeth* through Metaphorical Character Journals". *Teaching Shakespeare Today: Practical Approaches and Productive Strategies*. Ed. James E. Davis and Ronald E. Salomone (Urbana: National Council of Teachers of English, 1993), pp. 231-40.

Schröder, Gottfried. "Polanski's *Macbeth* im Englischunterricht". *Literatur und Film: Studien zur englischsprachigen Literatur und Kultur in Buch und Film II*. Ed. Paul G. Buchloh, Jens Peter Becker, and Ralf J. Schröder. Kieler Beiträge zur Entwicklung der englischen Philologie 4 (Kiel: Kieler Verlag Wissenschaft und Bildung, 1985), pp. 113-31.

Shields, Julia. "Fair Is Foul". *English Journal* 70:3 (1981), pp. 54-5.

---. "*Macbeth*: The Love Story". *Shakespeare* (Georgetown University) 1:4 (1997), pp. 10-11.

Skill, Elaine Strong. *A Teaching Portfolio for* Macbeth. Cliffs Teaching Portfolios. Lincoln, NE: Cliffs Notes, 1986.

Spurlock, Ken. "Three Writing Activities to Use with *Macbeth*". *Teaching Shakespeare Today: Practical Approaches and Productive Strategies*. Ed. James E. Davis and Ronald E. Salomone (Urbana: National Council of Teachers of English, 1993), pp. 250-3.

Stables, Andrew. "English and Environmental Education: The Living Nation in *Macbeth*". *Use of English* 44 (1993), pp. 218-25.

Sullivan, Paul. "Murdering *Macbeth*: The Education of a Schoolteacher". *Shakespeare* (Georgetown University) 1:4 (1997), pp. 12-13.

Swope, John Wilson. *Ready-to-Use Activities for Teaching* Macbeth. Shakespeare Teachers Activities Library. West Nyack, NY: Center for Applied Research in Education, 1994.

Taylor, Joanne. "Drama in the Classroom: Lady Macbeth Comes to Life!" *Exercise Exchange* 34:2 (1989), pp. 24-6.

Walatara, Douglas. "F. R. Leavis: Educationist: A Sri Lanka View". *Literary Criterion* 14:2 (1979), pp. 52-61.

Wertheim, Albert. "'Things climb upward to what they were before': The Reteaching and Regreening of *Macbeth*". *Teaching Shakespeare*. Ed. Walter Edens, Christopher Durer, Duncan Harris, Keith Hull, and Walter F. Eggers, Jr. (Princeton: Princeton UP, 1978), pp. 114-37.
Whitesides, Nigel, and Adrian G. Packer. *Primary Shakespeare: An Introductory Drama Scheme: Macbeth*. Strood, England: P. S. Publishers, 1996.
Wiest, Don. "*Macbeth* for the Reluctant Student". *Virginia English Bulletin* 36:2 (1986), pp. 156-8.
Williams, Michael. "Re-Teaching Shakespeare (1): *Macbeth* and the 'Witchcraft' Question [(2): The Shrew Oppressed; (3): Zeffirelli's *Romeo and Juliet*]". *Use of English* 41:1 (1989), pp. 37-45; 41:3 (1990), pp. 31-40; 42:2 (1991), pp. 50-8.
Zunin, Hilary Stanton. "'Give sorrow words': Shakespearean Lessons on Loss". *Shakespeare* (Georgetown University) 1:4 (1997), pp. 8-9.

Measure for Measure

Carducci, Jane and Victoria Boynton. "'Let my trial be mine own confession': Angelo and the Mock Trial Experience in the College Classroom". *Shakespeare and Renaissance Association of West Virginia: Selected Papers* 17 (1994), pp. 104-11.
Hamilton, A. C. "On Teaching the Shakespeare Canon: The Case of *Measure for Measure*". *Teaching Shakespeare*. Ed. Walter Edens, Christopher Durer, Duncan Harris, Keith Hull, and Walter F. Eggers, Jr. (Princeton: Princeton UP, 1978), pp. 95-113.
Hapgood, Robert. "Listening for the Playwright's Voice: Rehearsing through Class Discussion the 'Kill Claudio' Episode". *Teaching Shakespeare through Performance*. Ed. Milla Riggio. Modern Language Association of America Options for Teaching (New York: Modern Language Association of America, 1999), pp. 145-54.
Hogan, Patrick Colm. "Reading for Ethos: Literary Study and Moral Thought". *Journal of Aesthetic Education* 27:3 (1993), pp. 23-34.
Melanaphy, Pat. "*Measure for Measure* with a Mixed-Ability Group". *Shakespeare for All, Volume 2: The Secondary School: An Account of the RSA Shakespeare in Schools Project*. Ed. Maurice Gilmour (London: Cassell, 1997), pp. 9-17.
Simmons, John S. "*Measure for Measure*: Links to Our Time". *Teaching Shakespeare Today: Practical Approaches and Productive Strategies*. Ed. James E. Davis and Ronald E. Salomone (Urbana: National Council of Teachers of English, 1993), pp. 281-7.

Merchant of Venice

Ahrens, Rüdiger. "Das Thema des Wuchers in *The Merchant of Venice* and in F. Bacons 'Of Usury.'" *William Shakespeare: Didaktisches Handbuch*. Ed. Rüdiger Ahrens. 3 vols (Munich: Fink, 1982), III, pp. 829-50.
Blocksidge, Martin. "Shakespeare at 'A' Level II: *The Merchant of Venice*". *Use of English* 51 (1999-2000), pp. 133-40.
Bousted, Mary. "Praising What Is Lost: The Demise of Coursework in GCSE Literature". *Use of English* 44:1 (1992), pp. 15-24.
Brown, Ted. "The Merchants of Venice and Their Lessons for High School Students". *Nebraska English Journal* 35 (Spring-Summer 1990), pp. 89-97.
Cohen, Derek. "Shylock in 'Berlin.'" *Shakespeare and the World Elsewhere*. Studies in Shakespeare 2 (Adelaide: Australian and New Zealand Shakespeare Association, 1993), pp. 89-95.
Costello, Mary Enda. *The Merchant of Venice: Curriculum Unit*. Villa Maria, PA: Center for Learning, 1990.
Dachslager, E. L. "To Teach or Not to Teach Antisemitism". *Sh'ma* (Port Washington, NY) 24 December 1976, pp. 25-6.
Ellie, Bethine. *The Merchant of Venice: Study Guide*. Eau Claire, WI: Progeny Press, 1993.

Gellert, James. "Shylock, Huckleberry, and Jim: Do They Have a Place in Today's High Schools?" *Children's Literature Association Quarterly* 12:1 (1987), pp. 40-3.

Kehler, Dorothea. "Shakespeare, Okada, Kingston: The First Generation". *Comparatist* 22 (1998), pp. 110-22.

Ledebur, Ruth Freifrau von. "*The Merchant of Venice*: Drama – Bühnengeschichte – Theaterrezension". *William Shakespeare: Didaktisches Handbuch*. Ed. Rüdiger Ahrens. 3 vols (Munich: Fink, 1982), III, pp. 852-83.

---. "Reading Shakespeare's *The Merchant of Venice* with German Students". *Reading Plays: Interpretation and Reception*. Ed. Hanna Scolnicov and Peter Holland (Cambridge and New York: Cambridge UP, 1991), pp. 123-39.

Lee, Rick. "The Casket Makers: *The Merchant of Venice*: An Account of Advisory Work at St. Peter's Church of England Primary School, Market Bosworth". *Shakespeare for All, Volume 1: The Primary School: An Account of the RSA Shakespeare in Schools Project*. Ed. Maurice Gilmour (London: Cassell, 1997), pp. 62-9.

McKendy, Thomas. "Gypsies, Jews, and *The Merchant of Venice*". *English Journal* 77:7 (1988), pp. 24-6.

The Merchant of Venice. Perma-Guides to Literature. Jacksonville, IL: Perma-Bound, 1996.

Michaels, Wendy. "Raising Awareness of Fathers and Daughters". *Shakespeare* (Georgetown University) 2:2 (1998), p. 21.

Orme, David. *Shakespeare*, Merchant of Venice. Specials! Dunstable: Folens, 1999.

Photocopiable Resources in Support of The Merchant of Venice. Halifax, England: B and D Publishing, 1998.

Roy, David M. S. *Drama*: The Merchant of Venice: *Learning and Teaching Guide*. Dundee, Scotland: Scottish Consultative Counsil on the Curriculum, 1998.

Russell, Ben. "Teachers Defend Role of Shakespeare's 'anti-Semitic' Play". *The Independent* 14 March 1998, p. 7.

Seach, Gregory. *Let Him Look to His Bond: A Workshop Approach to* The Merchant of Venice. Ed. Peter Jones. Shakespeare Workshop Series. Rozelle, New South Wales: St. Clair Press, 1991.

Stock, Freda. *The Merchant of Venice*. Model Essays. Lutterworth, England: Tynron Press, 1992.

Veidemanis, Gladys V. "Reflections on 'The Shylock Problem.'" *Censored Books: Critical Viewpoints*. Ed. Nicholas J. Karolides, Lee Burress, and John M. Kean (Metuchen and London: Scarecrow, 1993), pp. 371-8.

Wilson, Robert J. "Censorship, Anti-Semitism, and *The Merchant of Venice*". *English Journal* 86:2 (1997), pp. 43-5.

Wright, Nancy Glass. "Changing 'Bored' to 'Bard': Adolescents Meet Shakespeare's *Merchant*". *English in Texas* 25:3 (1994), pp. 34-8.

Yandell, John. "'Sir Oracle': *The Merchant of Venice* in the Classroom". *Changing English* 4:1 (1997), pp. 105-21.

Merry Wives of Windsor

Kindler, Michael, and Andrew Lasaitis. *Moonshine Revellers: A Workshop Approach to* The Merry Wives of Windsor. Rozelle, New South Wales: St. Clair Press, 1998.

Parker, Patricia. "Interpreting through Wordplay: *The Merry Wives of Windsor*". *Teaching with Shakespeare: Critics in the Classroom*. Ed. Bruce McIver and Ruth Stevenson (Newark: Delaware UP; London and Toronto: Associated UPs, 1994), pp. 166-204.

Midsummer Nights Dream

Beehler, Sharon A. "Teaching Shakespeare's Dramatic Dialogue". *Teaching Shakespeare Today: Practical Approaches and Productive Strategies*. Ed. James E. Davis and Ronald E. Salomone (Urbana: National Council of Teachers of English, 1993), pp. 14-23.

Bergeron, David M. "Plays within Plays in Shakespeare's Early Comedies". *Teaching Shakespeare*. Ed. Walter Edens, Christopher Durer, Duncan Harris, Keith Hull, and Walter F. Eggers, Jr. (Princeton: Princeton UP, 1978), pp. 305-16.

Bharathi, V., and A. Giridhar Rao. "Text into Performance". *Provocations: The Teaching of English Literature in India.* Ed. Sudhakar Marathe, Mohan Ramanan, and Robert Bellarmine. Hyderabad: Orient Longman in association with the British Council, 1993.

Catt, Robert, and Tom Sweeney. "'In very likeness of a roasted crab': Shakespeare, Drama, and Text – *A Midsummer Night's Dream* in Maryland". *Maryland English Journal* 31:1 (1996), pp. 7-15.

Chirinian, Alain. A Midsummer Night's Dream: *A Practical Guide for Teaching Shakespeare in the Middle Grade Classroom*. Torrance, CA: Good Apple, 1997.

Collins, Michael J. "*A Midsummer Night's Dream*: An Exercise in Interpretation". *Shakespeare* (Georgetown University) 3:2 (1999), p. 15.

Farrow, Ed. "*A Midsummer Night's Dream* in a Multi-Cultural Context". *Shakespeare for All, Volume 1: The Primary School: An Account of the RSA Shakespeare in Schools Project.* Ed. Maurice Gilmour (London: Cassell, 1997), pp. 20-3.

Findlay, Alison. "'Linguistic flesh': A Feminist Approach to *A Midsummer Night's Dream*". *Folio: Shakespeare-Genootschap van Nederland en Vlaanderen* 4:1 (1997), pp. 5-20.

Hakaim, Charles J., Jr. "A Most Rare Vision: Improvisations on *A Midsummer Night's Dream*". *English Journal* 82:11 (1993), pp. 67-70.

Hilliard, Barbara. "Confronting Shakespeare's Language in *A Midsummer Night's Dream*". *Literature—News That Stays News: Fresh Approaches to the Classics*. Ed. Candy Carter (Urbana: National Council of Teachers of English, 1985), pp. 84-5.

Hübler, Axel. "Die Einbeziehung deutscher Vers- und Prosaübersetzungen bei der Behandlung von Shakespeare-Dramen, dargestellt am Beispiel von *A Midsummer Night's Dream* ". *William Shakespeare: Didaktisches Handbuch*. Ed. Rüdiger Ahrens. 3 vols (Munich: Fink, 1982), II, pp. 393-420.

Jardine, Laurie. "Making Connections through Drama Education". *English Quarterly* 25 (1993), pp. 14-16.

Johnson, Kathryn King. "Teaching Shakespeare to Learning Disabled Students". *English Journal* 87:3 (1998), pp. 45-9.

Kappe, Gerhard. "Dramenbehandlung auf der Mittelstufe: Shakespeares *A Midsummer Night's Dream* als Puppentheater". *Praxis des neusprachlichen Unterrichts* 35 (1988), pp. 148-59.

Lob, Heinz Peter. "'Is there no play to ease the anguish of a torturing lesson?' Anregungen zu Shakespeares *A Midsummer Nights Dream* im Unterricht". *Deutsche Shakespeare-Gesellschaft/Deutsche Shakespeare-Gesellschaft West Jahrbuch 1994*, pp. 149-57.

McDonald, Irene Brezinsky. *A Teaching Portfolio for* A Midsummer Night's Dream. Cliffs Teaching Portfolios. Lincoln, NE: Cliffs Notes, 1989.

McFadden, Mark. *The Course of True Love: A Workshop Approach to* A Midsummer Night's Dream. Shakespeare Workshop Series. Rozelle, New South Wales: St. Clair Press, 1992.

"*A Midsummer Night's Dream*". *The Practical Bard*. Ed. Cher Stempler (Orlando: Shakespeare Institute, University of Central Florida, 1979), pp. 1-28.

Miltner, Robert. A Midsummer Night's Dream: *Curriculum Unit*. Rocky River, OH: Center for Learning, 1993.

O'Brien, Peggy, general ed. *Shakespeare Set Free: Teaching* Romeo and Juliet, Macbeth, A Midsummer Night's Dream. New York: Washington Square Press, 1993.

Ochs, Heinz-Dieter. "'Oh Pyramus, get up, arise!': Schülerder Klasse 7 spielen *A Midsummer Night's Dream*". *Praxis des neusprachlichen Unterrichts* 33:2 (1986), pp. 135-40.

Orme, David. *Specials! Shakespeare:* A Midsummer Night's Dream. Dunstable, England: Folens, 1995.

Potter, Sally, and Sue Welshman. *"The Play's the Thing!"* A Midsummer Night's Dream: *Resources for Practical Group Work*. Tarvin, England: Cheshire Drama Resource Centre, [1994].

Putnam, Lynne. "Reading Program Decisions: The Connection between Philosophy and Practice". *Childhood Education* 62 (1986), pp. 330-6.

Richmond, Hugh M. "The Centrality of *A Midsummer Night's Dream*". *Teaching Shakespeare Today: Practical Approaches and Productive Strategies.* Ed. James E. Davis and Ronald E. Salomone (Urbana: National Council of Teachers of English, 1993), pp. 254-62.

Sandvoss, Ernst. "'Pyramus und Thisbe' bei Ovid und Shakespeare: Ein motivegeschichtlicher Vergleich". *William Shakespeare: Didaktisches Handbuch.* Ed. Rüdiger Ahrens. 3 vols (Munich: Fink, 1982), III, pp. 779-99.

Shurgot, Michael W. "'So quick bright things come to confusion': Shakespeare in the Heterogeneous Classroom". *Teaching Shakespeare into the Twenty-First Century.* Ed. Richard E. Salomone and James E. Davis (Athens: Ohio UP, 1997), pp. 139-46.

Smith, Joyce. "Shakespeare through Story-Telling with Year 6". *Speech and Drama* 43:1 (1994), pp. 6-9.

Snodgrass, Mary Ellen. A Midsummer Night's Dream: *Teacher's Guide.* Living Literature Series. Jacksonville, IL: Perma-Bound, 1986.

Swope, John Wilson. *Ready-to-Use Activities for Teaching* A Midsummer Night's Dream. West Nyack, NY: Center for Applied Research in Education, 1997.

---. "A Whole Language Approach to *A Midsummer Night's Dream*". *Teaching Shakespeare into the Twenty-First Century.* Ed. Richard E. Salomone and James E. Davis (Athens: Ohio UP, 1997), pp. 127-36.

Ulen, Amy. "Kids Just Wanna Have Fun: Teaching *A Midsummer Night's Dream* through Adolescent Issues". *Shakespeare* (Georgetown University) 3:2 (1999), pp. 17-18.

Walker, Muriel. "*A Midsummer Night's Dream* as Enjoyed by One Mixed-Ability Class of 8-10-Year-Olds in a Small Village School". *Shakespeare for All, Volume 1: The Primary School: An Account of the RSA Shakespeare in Schools Project.* Ed. Maurice Gilmour (London: Cassell, 1997), pp. 6-19.

Much Ado about Nothing

Andreas, James R. "Writing Down, Speaking Up, Acting Out, and Clowning Around in the Shakespeare Classroom". *Teaching Shakespeare into the Twenty-First Century.* Ed. Richard E. Salomone and James E. Davis (Athens: Ohio UP, 1997), pp. 25-32.

Collins, Michael J. "Sleepless in Messina: Kenneth Branagh's *Much Ado about Nothing*". *Shakespeare Bulletin* 15:2 (1997), pp. 38-9.

Dionne, Craig. "The Conjuring of Renaissance Social Relations in *Much Ado about Nothing*". *Shakespeare and the Classroom* 4:2 (1996), pp. 48-51.

Figgins, Margo A. "Mirrors, Sculptures, Machines, and Masks: Theater Improvisation Games". *Teaching Shakespeare into the Twenty-First Century.* Ed. Richard E. Salomone and James E. Davis (Athens: Ohio UP, 1997), pp. 65-77.

Levine, Marilyn. "Teaching *Much Ado about Nothing* and *Othello*: Comedy and Tragedy". *Shakespeare* (Georgetown University) 3:3 (1999), pp. 7-9.

"*Much Ado about Nothing*". *The Practical Bard.* Ed. Cher Stempler (Orlando: Shakespeare Institute, University of Central Florida, 1979), pp. 49-71.

Much Ado about Nothing. Perma-Guides to Literature. Jacksonville, IL: Perma-Bound, 1996.

Peters, Denise Wright. Much Ado about Nothing: *Curriculum Unit.* Rocky River, OH: Center for Learning, 1997.

Pope, Jan. "Beginning *Much Ado about Nothing*". *Shakespeare* (Georgetown University) 1:3 (1997), p. 13.

Schulz, Volker. "*Much Ado About Nothing*: Ein Unterrichtsmodell". *Shakespeare im Unterricht.* Ed. Rüdiger Ahrens. Anglistik und Englischenunterricht 3 (Trier: Volksfreund-Druckerei, 1977), pp. 133-60.

Seach, Gregory. *A Skirmish of Wit: A Workshop Approach to* Much Ado about Nothing. Shakespeare Workshop Series. Rozelle, New South Wales: St. Clair Press, 1992.

Skrebels, Paul. "Transhistoricizing *Much Ado about Nothing*: Finding a Place for Shakespeare's Work in the Postmodern World". *Teaching Shakespeare into the Twenty-First Century.* Ed. Richard E. Salomone and James E. Davis (Athens: Ohio UP, 1997), pp. 81-95.

Swope, John Wilson. *Ready-to-Use Activities for Teaching* Much Ado about Nothing. West Nyack, NY: Center for Applied Research in Education, 1997.
Tranter, Humphrey. "What to Do about William Shakespeare's *Much Ado about Nothing*". *Making Connections, Part 2: Introducing Eight Texts for Senior English Studies.* Ed. Annie Greet (Adelaide: FUED; Trinty Gardens: SAETA, 1991), pp. 62-8.

Othello

Bache, William B. "A Procedure for Teaching a Shakespeare Play". *Shakespeare Newsletter* 28 (1978), p. 17.
Blocksidge, Martin. "The Two Languages of *Othello*: An Approach for 'A' Level". *Use of English* 49 (1998-99), pp. 223-9.
Christenbury, Leila. "Problems with *Othello* in the High School Classroom". *Teaching Shakespeare into the Twenty-First Century.* Ed. Richard E. Salomone and James E. Davis (Athens: Ohio UP, 1997), pp. 182-90.
Costello, Mary Enda. Othello: *Curriculum Unit.* Villa Maria, PA: Center for Learning, 1990.
Elstein, Judith. "*Othello* Boggle". *Shakespeare* (Georgetown University) 3:3 (1999), p. 9.
Ffolliott, Daphne. "Introductory Assignments for Group Discussions on *Othello*". *Crux: A Journal on the Teaching of English* 24:3 (1990), pp. 16-23.
Gardner, Colin. "A Class on *Othello*". *Shakespeare Society of Southern Africa Newsletter, Incorporating Occasional Papers and Reviews* 12 (1997), pp. 12-15.
Gardner, Mary. "Some Notes on *Othello*". *Crux: A Journal on the Teaching of English* 15:3 (1981), pp. 37-40.
Habicht, Werner. "Alte und neue Zugänge zu Shakespeare am Beispiel des *Othello*". *Literatur in Wissenschaft und Unterricht* 24 (1991), pp. 149-60.
Harris, Martha. "Some Whys and Hows for Teaching *Othello*". *Shakespeare* (Georgetown University) 3:3 (1999), pp. 6-7.
Iyasere, Simon O. "Teaching *Othello* in a Class of Multi-Racial Students". *Shakespeare and the Classroom* 1:2 (1993), pp. 14-15.
Kass, Sarah. "The Trials of Othello". *Journal of Education* 176 (1994), pp. 85-100.
Kearney, J. A. "On Teaching *Othello*". *Crux: A Journal on the Teaching of English* 21:1 (1987), pp. 55-63.
Lee, Elizabeth M. "From Basic Skills to *Othello*". *Teaching English in the Two-Year College* 12 (1985), pp. 307-11.
Levine, Marilyn. "Teaching *Much Ado about Nothing* and *Othello*: Comedy and Tragedy". *Shakespeare* (Georgetown University) 3:3 (1999), pp. 7-9.
Nunez, Elizabeth. "Could Shakespeare Have Known". *Journal of Negro Education* 45:2 (1976), pp. 192-6.
O'Brien, Peggy, general ed. *Shakespeare Set Free: Teaching* Twelfth Night *and* Othello. New York: Washington Square Press, 1995.
Peim, Nick, and Gerry Elmer. "*Othello*: A Drama Approach to 'A' Level English". *2D* 3.3 (1984), pp. 82-7.
Rozett, Martha Tuck. "Talking Back to Shakespeare: Student-Reader Responses to *Othello*". Othello: *New Perspectives.* Ed. Virginia Mason Vaughan and Kent Cartwright (Rutherford: Fairleigh Dickinson UP; London and Toronto: Associated UPs, 1991), pp. 256-72.
Salway, John. "Veritable Negroes and Circumcised Dogs: Racial Disturbances in Shakespeare". *Shakespeare in the Changing Curriculum.* Ed. Lesley Aers and Nigel Wheale (London and New York: Routledge, 1991), pp. 108-24.
Snodgrass, Mary Ellen. *Othello.* Perma-Guides to Literature. Jacksonville, IL: Perma-Bound, 1997.
Study Guide for Othello *by William Shakespeare.* Strategies for Teaching the Play. Evanston, IL: McDougal, Littell, 1990.
Sullivan, Theresa. *Othello.* Shakespeare 16-19: Teaching Strategies for Advanced Level. London: Arnold, 1988.

Thomas, Peter. "Shakespeare Page to Stage: An Active Approach to *Othello*". *English in Education* 28:1 (1994), pp. 45-52.
Watson, Ken, and Stuart Wilson. *The Green-Ey'd Monster: A Workshop Approach to* Othello. Shakespeare Workshop Series. Rozelle, New South Wales: St. Clair Press, 1991.

Pericles

Campbell, Kathleen. "Reviving *Pericles*". *Shakespeare and the Classroom* 4:1 (1996), pp. 32-5.

Richard II

Radcliffe, Catherine, David Nicholson, and Ken Watson. *Bitter Bread: A Workshop Approach to* Richard II *and* The Winter's Tale. Shakespeare Workshop Series. Rozelle, New South Wales: St. Clair Press, 1997.
"*Richard II*". *The Practical Bard*. Ed. Cher Stempler (Orlando: Shakespeare Institute, University of Central Florida, 1979), pp. 29-48.

Richard III

Borgmeier, Raimund. "Shakespeare als Landeskunde? Staat und Gesellschaft des elisabethanischen England im Spiegel von Shakespeares Historien dargestellt am Beispiel von *Richard III*)". *Neusprachliche Mitteilungen aus Wissenschaft und Praxis* 36 (1983), pp. 216-23.
Costello, Mary Enda. Richard III: *Curriculum Unit*. Rocky River, OH: Center for Learning, 1994.
Durrant, Clavin. *To Prove a Villain: A Workshop Approach to* Richard III. Shakespeare Workshop Series. Rozelle, New South Wales: St. Clair Press, 1994.
Gocke, Rainer. "Laurence Oliviers *Richard III*: Motivationsförderung durch den *sound track* eines Filmklassikers". *William Shakespeare: Didaktisches Handbuch*. Ed. Rüdiger Ahrens. 3 vols (Munich: Fink, 1982), III, pp. 1015-33.
Kleine-Horst, Dieter. "Anforderungen an eine didaktische Shakespeare-Ausgabe". *William Shakespeare: Didaktisches Handbuch*. Ed. Rüdiger Ahrens. 3 vols (Munich: Fink, 1982), II, pp. 347-70.
Oberdorfer, Richard. "Pursuing the White Boar: Approaches to Teaching *Richard III*". *Studies in Medieval and Renaissance Teaching* ns 6:1 (1998), pp. 67-85.
Quilliam, Faith. "Shakespeare's Villains: *Richard III*". *Shakespeare for All, Volume 2: The Secondary School: An Account of the RSA Shakespeare in Schools Project*. Ed. Maurice Gilmour (London: Cassell, 1997), pp. 45-65.
Rice, Michael. "*Richard III* for Standard 10". *ELTIC Reporter* 11:1 (1986), pp. 12-15.

Romeo and Juliet

Adams, Jeff. "The Play's the Thing". *Vocational Education Journal* 67:8 (1992), pp. 32-3.
Adams, Pamela E. "Teaching *Romeo and Juliet* in the Nontracked English Classroom". *Journal of Reading* 38 (1995), pp. 424-32.
Alsup, Andrea. "Taking Poetic License with Shakespeare: Companion Poems for Four Plays". *English Journal* 82:5 (1993), pp. 66-8.
Bailey, Paul. "An Approach to Shakespeare through Drama". *Use of English* 36. 2 (1985), pp. 47-56.
---. "Not so Bard after All! Some Approaches to Shakespeare". *2D* 4:1 (1984), pp. 64-79.
Bashian, Kathleen Ryniker. "The Dialogue of Disciplines: An Arts Approach to Shakespeare". *Momentum* 27:3 (1996), pp. 56-8.
Béghin, Janie and Geneviève Sabiron. "*Roméo et Juliette* en class de troisième: Une approche interdisciplinaire (français-anglais)". *Les langues modernes* 90:3 (1996), pp. 49-55.

Billings, Denise. "Romeo and Juliet Resurrected!" *English in Texas* 24:4 (1993), p. 3.
Brown, Verna. "*Romeo and Juliet* for Relevance: Suggestions for Group Work Discussion". *Crux: A Journal on the Teaching of English* 26:1 (1992), pp. 37-8.
Christ, Jim. "Exploring Emotion through *Romeo and Juliet*". *Literature – News That Stays News: Fresh Approaches to the Classics.* Ed. Candy Carter (Urbana: National Council of Teachers of English, 1985), pp. 66-9.
Collins, Mary B. Romeo and Juliet: *A Unit Plan.* Berlin, MD: Teacher's Pet, 1994.
Collins, Michael J. "Teaching *Romeo and Juliet*: 'the change of fourteen years.'" *Critical Survey* 3 (1991), pp. 186-93.
Evans, Robert C. "Teaching Literary Structure: Episodic Parallels in the Design of *Romeo and Juliet*". *CEA Critic* 46:1-2 (1983-84), pp. 2-8.
Feuerstein, Phyllis A. "Shakespeare's Dysfunctional Families". *School Librarian's Workshop* 17:5 (1997), pp. 5-6.
Gibson, Rex. "'O, what learning is!' Pedagogy and the Afterlife of *Romeo and Juliet*". *Shakespeare Survey* 49 (1996), pp. 141-52.
Glaap, Albert-Reiner. "Von Romeo zu Romanoff: Moderne Adaptationen von *Romeo and Juliet* im Englischunterricht". *William Shakespeare: Didaktisches Handbuch.* Ed. Rüdiger Ahrens. 3 vols (Munich: Fink, 1982), III, pp. 913-32.
Goldfarb, Liz, and Terry Cambridge. "Signing Shakespeare: Romeo Loves Juliet". *Perspectives in Education and Deafness* 13:3 (1995), pp. 12-15.
Guinhawa, Wilhelmina. "Studying Characters in *Romeo and Juliet*". *English in Texas* 25:4 (1994), pp. 47-8.
Guntner, John, and H. Ohlendorf. *Die Behandlung von Shakespeare in der Sekundarstufe II: Ein Erfahrungsbericht über ein Versuch.* Braunschweig: Privately Printed, 1979.
Guntner, Lawrence. "Shakespeare im Leistungskurs: Ein Erfahrungsbericht". *Shakespeare-Jahrbuch* (Bochum) (1981), pp. 211-15.
Hager, Alan, ed. *Understanding* Romeo and Juliet: *A Student Casebook to Issues, Sources, and Historical Documents.* Greenwood Press Literature in Context Series. Westport and London: Greenwood, 1999.
Haroutunian-Gordon, Sophie. *Turning the Soul: Teaching through Conversation in the High School.* Chicago and London: Chicago UP, 1991.
Hogge, Quentin. "Gallop Apace, You Fiery-Loined Teenagers". *Crux: A Journal on the Teaching of English* 27:3 (1993), pp. 33-7.
Holmer, Joan Ozark. "'O, what learning is!': Some Pedagogical Practices for *Romeo and Juliet*". *Shakespeare Quarterly* 41 (1990), pp. 187-94.
Jarman, F., G.-D. Kämmer, and D. Whybra. *Not Only in Verona: Variations on the* Romeo and Juliet *Theme.* Patterns – Materialien für den Sekundarbereich II mit Lehrerheft. Hannover: Schoedel, 1988.
Johannessen, Larry R. "Enhancing Response to *Romeo and Juliet*". *Teaching Shakespeare into the Twenty-First Century.* Ed. Richard E. Salomone and James E. Davis (Athens: Ohio UP, 1997), pp. 154-65.
Knoblock, Jennifer. *A Literature Guide for William Shakespeare's* Romeo and Juliet. San Antonio: ECS Learning Systems, 1993.
Kovacs, Mary Anne, Dennis P. Meier, and Gary A. Tutty. Romeo and Juliet: *A Teacher Resource Unit.* Villa Maria, PA: Center for Learning, 1988.
Lambert-Scronce, Kathy. *A Teaching Portfolio for* Romeo and Juliet. Cliffs Teaching Portfolios. Lincoln, NE: Cliffs Notes, 1988.
LaRocque, Geraldine E. "Shall We Dance? An Approach to *Romeo and Juliet*". *English Journal* 77:7 (1988), pp. 22-3.
Leach, Susan. Romeo and Juliet: *Approaches and Activities.* Exploring Shakespeare. Oxford: Oxford UP, 1994.
Levenson, Jill L. "*Romeo and Juliet* on the Stage: 'It is a kind of history.'" *Teaching Shakespeare through Performance.* Ed. Milla Riggio. Modern Language Association of America Options for Teaching (New York: Modern Language Association of America, 1999), pp. 114-26.
Lorenz, Sarah L. "*Romeo and Juliet*: The Movie". *English Journal* 87:3 (1998), pp. 50-51.

McRoberts, Valerie. *A Wizard Lit Master to William Shakespeare's* Romeo and Juliet. Ballarat, Australia: Wizard Books, 1998.
Morgan, Terry. *Activity Book*: Romeo and Juliet. Thornhill, England: Tynron Press, 1989.
Morrison, Evlyn, and Lee Bolton Robinson. *Teaching Literature through Dramatic Experiences*: Romeo and Juliet. Vancouver: Creative Curriculum, 1992.
Newlin, Louisa Foulke. "DeLantae's Kiss, or Teaching *Romeo and Juliet* in High School". *Nebraska English Journal* 35 (Spring-Summer 1990), pp. 65-73.
Oakes, Elizabeth. "Enacting Shakespeare's Language in *Macbeth* and *Romeo and Juliet*". *Teaching Shakespeare Today: Practical Approaches and Productive Strategies*. Ed. James E. Davis and Ronald E. Salomone (Urbana: National Council of Teachers of English, 1993), pp. 85-9.
O'Brien, Peggy, general ed. *Shakespeare Set Free: Teaching* Romeo and Juliet, Macbeth, A Midsummer Night's Dream. New York: Washington Square Press, 1993.
O'Connor, Kevin, and Jennifer Stehn. *English*: Romeo and Juliet. Carlton, Victoria: Curriculum Corporation, 1997.
Ohly, Werner. "Schüler erleben Literatur: Textanalyse und generative Verfahren im Englischunterricht: Ein Modell". *Die neueren Sprachen* 94 (1995), pp. 132-53.
Orme, David. *Shakespeare*, Romeo and Juliet. Specials! Dunstable: Folens, 1995.
Peer, Willie van. "Paraphrase as Paradox in Literary Education". *Poetics* 21 (1993), pp. 443-59.
Peitz, Mary. *William Shakespeare's* Romeo and Juliet: *A Study Guide*. Ed. Joyce Friedland and Rikki Kessler. Novel-Ties. New Hyde Park, NY: Learning Links, 1997.
Potter, Sally, and Sue Welshman. *"The Play's the Thing!"* Romeo and Juliet: *Resources for Practical Group Work*. Tarvin, England: Cheshire Drama Resource Centre, [1994].
Rampone, William K. "Teaching Feminist Criticism to Freshmen". *Shakespeare and the Classroom* 1:2 (1993), p. 16.
Rempe, Robert H. "Connecting Shakespeare with the Writing Process, and the Pros and Cons of Sanitization". *Shakespeare and the Classroom* 4:2 (1996), pp. 51-2.
Robbins, Mari Lu. *A Literature Unit for* Romeo and Juliet. Huntington Beach, CA: Teacher Created Materials, 1997.
Robinson, Lee Bolton. "Some Days Are Golden". *English Quarterly* 25 (1993), pp. 8-13.
Romeo and Juliet *and the Renaissance*. Special issue of *Nexus*, 1995.
"*Romeo and Juliet*". *The Practical Bard*. Ed. Cher Stempler (Orlando: Shakespeare Institute, University of Central Florida, 1979), pp. 73-104.
Romeo and Juliet. Perma-Guides to Literature. Jacksonville, IL: Perma-Bound, 1992.
Sandvoss, Ernst. "'Pyramus und Thisbe' bei Ovid und Shakespeare: Ein motivegeschichtlicher Vergleich". *William Shakespeare: Didaktisches Handbuch*. Ed. Rüdiger Ahrens. 3 vols (Munich: Fink, 1982), III, pp. 779-99.
Scheidler, Katherine P. "*Romeo and Juliet* and *The Glass Menagerie* as Reading Programs". *English Journal* 70:1 (1981), pp. 34-6.
Scoble, Fran Norris. "In Search of the Female Hero: Juliet Revisited". *English Journal* 72:2 (1986), pp. 85-7.
Sheaffer, Lloyd E. "'Music with her silver sound': An Introduction to *Romeo and Juliet*". *English Journal* 81:1 (1992), pp. 68-71.
Shrubb, Gordon, and Ken Watson. *Star-Cross'd Lovers: A Workshop Approach to* Romeo and Juliet. Second edition. Shakespeare Workshop Series. Rozelle, New South Wales: St. Clair Press, 1998.
Straughan, June. "*Romeo and Juliet* and the ESL Classroom". *English Journal* 85:8 (1996), pp. 52-4.
Stupple, Donna-Marie. "Rx for the Suicide Epidemic". *English Journal* 76:1 (1987), pp. 64-8.
Swope, John Wilson. *Ready-to-Use Activities for Teaching* Romeo and Juliet. Shakespeare Teachers Activities Library. West Nyack, NY: Center for Applied Research in Education, 1993.
Swope, John Wilson. "A Whole Language Approach to *Romeo and Juliet*". *Teaching Shakespeare Today: Practical Approaches and Productive Strategies*. Ed. James E. Davis and Ronald E. Salomone (Urbana: National Council of Teachers of English, 1993), pp. 218-30.

Whitesides, Nigel, and Adrian G. Packer. *Primary Shakespeare: An Introductory Drama Scheme*: Romeo and Juliet. Strood, England: P. S. Publishers, 1996.
Williams, Michael. "Re-Teaching Shakespeare (1): *Macbeth* and the 'Witchcraft' Question [(2): The Shrew Oppressed; (3): Zeffirelli's *Romeo and Juliet*]". *Use of English* 41:1 (1989), pp. 37-45; 41:3 (1990), pp. 31-40; 42:2 (1991), pp. 50-8.
Willinsky, John, and Jim Bedard. *The Fearful Passage:* Romeo and Juliet *in the High School: A Feminist Perspective*. CCTE Monographs and Special Publications. [Ottawa?]: Canadian Council of Teachers of English, 1989.

Sonnets

Burke, Kate. "From Page to Stage: The Use of Shakespeare's Sonnets in Introducing Intimidated Students to His Drama". *Iowa State Journal of Research* 62 (1988), pp. 347-50.
Coryell, Susan M. "Shakespeare in a Fishbowl". *Exercise Exchange* 40:1 (1996), pp. 3-6.
Dulek, Ron. "A Device for Teaching Shakespeare's Sonnets". *CEA Forum* 9 (April 1979), pp. 7-9.
Freese, Peter. "Zur Einbeziehung von Quellen und Nachdictungen in die Textarbeit, dargestellt am Beispiel von Shakespeares Sonnett LX". *William Shakespeare: Didaktisches Handbuch*. Ed. Rüdiger Ahrens. 3 vols (Munich: Fink, 1982), II, pp. 421-45.
Gaskill, Gayle. "Reading Shakespeare's Sonnets in the Contexts of His Plays". *Shakespeare and the Classroom* 3:2 (1995), pp. 39-41.
Hebbert, Deanna. "A Sonnet Concertina". *Shakespeare* (Georgetown University) 2:1 (1998), pp. 17-18.
Klautsch, Ann. "Defining Shakespearean Sonnets through Acting Vocabulary". *Ideological Approaches to Shakespeare: The Practice of Theory*. Ed. Robert P. Merrix and Nicholas Ranson (Lewiston, Queenston, and Lampeter: Mellen, 1992), pp. 265-72.
Koon, William J. "Using the Macintosh for Teaching and Research in Shakespeare". *Proceedings of the First Annual CSU Shakespeare Symposium*. Ed. Kay Stanton (Fullerton: California State University at Fullerton Repro Graphics Center, 1991), pp. 1-10.
Ledebur, Ruth Freifrau von. "Einzelgedicht und Zyklus: Shakespeares Sonette". *Shakespeare-Jahrbuch* (Bochum) 1984, pp. 168-77.
Newlin, Louisa. "Experiencing a Sonnet". *Shakespeare* (Georgetown University) 2:1 (1998), pp. 19-20.
Pierce, Robert B. "Teaching the Sonnets with Performance Techniques". *Teaching Shakespeare into the Twenty-First Century*. Ed. Richard E. Salomone and James E. Davis (Athens: Ohio UP, 1997), pp. 43-9.
Slogsnat, Helmut. "Eine Sonettfolge als Index epochaler Prozesse". *Anglistik und Englischunterricht* 11 (1980), pp. 115-64.
Wiener, Monica. "Strip Sonnets: An Introduction to Shakespeare". *Shakespeare* (Georgetown University) 4:2 (2000), pp. 14-15.

Taming of the Shrew

Aronowitz, Beverly Lynne. "Playing Tricks and Proving Love in *The Taming of the Shrew*". *Exercise Exchange* 32:1 (1986), pp. 3-6.
Bergeron, David M. "Plays within Plays in Shakespeare's Early Comedies". *Teaching Shakespeare*. Ed. Walter Edens, Christopher Durer, Duncan Harris, Keith Hull, and Walter F. Eggers, Jr. (Princeton: Princeton UP, 1978), pp. 305-16.
Costello, Mary Enda, Paulette S. Goll, Stephen L. Jacobs, and Eileen K. Maloney. *Shakespearean Comedies*. Dubuque, Iowa: Center for Learning, 1984.
Geimer, Roger. "Shakespeare Live – on Videotape". *Shakespeare and the Triple Play: From Study to Stage to Classroom*. Ed. Sidney Homan (Lewisburg: Bucknell UP; London and Toronto: Associated UPs, 1988), pp. 201-6.
Giese, Loreen L. "Teaching *The Taming of the Shrew*: Kate, Closure, and Eighteenth-Century Editions". *Teaching Shakespeare Today: Practical Approaches and Productive Strategies*.

Ed. James E. Davis and Ronald E. Salomone (Urbana: National Council of Teachers of English, 1993), pp. 270-80.
Guelcher, William C. *William Shakespeare's* The Taming of the Shrew. Strategies-in-Teaching Series. Eagan, MN: Idea Works, 1989.
Heese, M. "Teaching in the Real World". *Crux: A Journal on the Teaching of English* 23:1 (1989), pp. 21-3.
Kliman, Bernice W. "Writing Dialogue to Argue Interpretations: Bianca in *Shrew*". *Shakespeare and the Classroom* 2:2 (1994), pp. 60-2.
Levine, Gloria. The Taming of the Shrew *by William Shakespeare: Student Packet*. Palatine, IL: Novel Units, 1996.
Mastrandrea, Mary. "Slang Opens Our Eyes to Attitude about Kate". *Shakespeare* (Georgetown University) 2:2 (1998), pp. 18-19.
Parry, Sally E. "Is the Shrew Tamed? Interpretation and Performance in *The Taming of the Shrew*". *Exercise Exchange* 39:1 (1993), pp. 16-19.
Ramm, Hans-Christoph. "'She hath prevented me.' Zur Problematik der Geschlechterbeziehung in Shakespeares Komödie *The Taming of the Shrew*: Ein didaktischer Versuch". *Shakespeare Jahrbuch* 135 (1999), pp. 100-116.
Snodgrass, Mary Ellen. *The Taming of the Shrew*. Living Literature Series. Jacksonville, IL: Perma-Bound, 1995.
Sutton. R. B. "*A Taming of the Shrew*: Adapting the Deconstruction". *Studies in Theatre Production* 8 (1993), pp. 63-75.
Watson, Ken. *Such a Bad Marriage: A Workshop Approach to* The Taming of the Shrew. Sydney: St. Clair Press, 1993.
Williams, Michael. "Re-Teaching Shakespeare (1): *Macbeth* and the 'Witchcraft' Question [(2): The Shrew Oppressed; (3): Zeffirelli's *Romeo and Juliet*]". *Use of English* 41:1 (1989), pp. 37-45; 41:3 (1990), pp. 31-40; 42:2 (1991), pp. 50-8.

The Tempest

Aercke, Kristiaan P. "'An odd angle of the isle': Teaching the Courtly Art of *The Tempest*". *Approaches to Teaching Shakespeare's* The Tempest *and Other Late Romances*. Ed. Maurice Hunt. Approaches to Teaching World Literature 41 (New York: Modern Language Association, 1992), pp. 146-53.
Carey-Webb, Allen. "Shakespeare for the 1990s: A Multicultural *Tempest*". *English Journal* 82:4 (1993), pp. 30-5.
Cavecchi, Mariacristina, and Nicolette Vallorani. "Teaching Shakespeare through Cinema: A Didactic Approach". *Moving the Borders: Papers from the Milan Symposium, Varenna – September 1994*. Ed. Marialuisa Bignami and Caroline Patey. Biblioteca di anglistica: Collana di testi e studi 5 (Milan: Unicopli, 1996), pp. 417-26.
Coursen, H. R. "Using Film and Television to Teach *The Winter's Tale* and *The Tempest*". *Approaches to Teaching Shakespeare's* The Tempest *and Other Late Romances*. Ed. Maurice Hunt. Approaches to Teaching World Literature 41 (New York: Modern Language Association, 1992), pp. 117-24.
Fawcett, Margot, Frank Gallagher, Carol James, Ian North, and Dorothy Waite. "'Be not afeard': Producing *The Tempest* with Juniors". *Shakespeare for All, Volume 1: The Primary School: An Account of the RSA Shakespeare in Schools Project*. Ed. Maurice Gilmour (London: Cassell, 1997), pp. 34-43.
Gordon, Sarah, and Christopher Geelan. The Tempest: *Active Approaches to Shakespeare for the Under Twelves*. London: Buttonhole Press, 1994.
Herold, Niels. "Yet More New Uses of Adversity in Teaching *The Tempest*". *Shakespeare and the Classroom* 5:1 (1997), pp. 57-9.
Higgins, Victoria. "Bringing Shakespeare to Life through *The Tempest*". *Shakespeare for All, Volume 1: The Primary School: An Account of the RSA Shakespeare in Schools Project*. Ed. Maurice Gilmour (London: Cassell, 1997), pp. 24-33.

Hunt, Maurice, ed. *Approaches to Teaching Shakespeare's* The Tempest *and Other Late Romances*. Approaches to Teaching World Literature 41. New York: Modern Language Association, 1992.

---. "Materials". *Approaches to Teaching Shakespeare's* The Tempest *and Other Late Romances*. Ed. Maurice Hunt. Approaches to Teaching World Literature 41 (New York: Modern Language Association, 1992), pp. 3-22.

Hyler, Rebecca. "Teaching *The Tempest* to Third Graders". *Shakespeare and the Classroom* 5:1 (1997), pp. 64-6.

Jones, Dan C. "Anticipating Reader Response: Why I Chose *The Tempest* for English Literature Survey". *Teaching English in the Two-Year College* 11:3 (1985), pp. 32-8.

Juszkiewicz, Victor. "*The Tempest*". *Shakespeare for All, Volume 2: The Secondary School: An Account of the RSA Shakespeare in Schools Project*. Ed. Maurice Gilmour (London: Cassell, 1997), pp. 39-44.

Kinney, Arthur F. "Teaching *The Tempest* as the Art of 'If.'" *Approaches to Teaching Shakespeare's* The Tempest *and Other Late Romances*. Ed. Maurice Hunt. Approaches to Teaching World Literature 41 (New York: Modern Language Association, 1992), pp. 153-9.

Kory, Fern. "Shakespearean Drama: A Pair of Writing Assignments". *Exercise Exchange* 40:1 (1996), pp. 13-17.

Mangan, Michael. "Theory, Practice, Theatre Praxis: Shakespeare and Practical Drama Work". *Studies in Theatre Production* 9 (1994), pp. 38-49.

McNee, Lisa. "Teaching in the Multicultural Tempest". *College Literature* 19.3-20.1 (1992-93), pp. 195-201.

Morse, William R. "A Metacritical and Historical Approach to *The Winter's Tale* and *The Tempest*". *Approaches to Teaching Shakespeare's* The Tempest *and Other Late Romances*. Ed. Maurice Hunt. Approaches to Teaching World Literature 41 (New York: Modern Language Association, 1992), pp. 133-8.

Niggemann, Heinz. "Unterrichtsreihen Englisch: Shakespeares *The Tempest* im Unterricht". *Anglistik und Englischunterricht* 34 (1988), p. 147-65.

Nunez, Elizabeth. "Could Shakespeare Have Known". *Journal of Negro Education* 45:2 (1976), pp. 92-6.

Oakes, Elizabeth. "Writing Shakespeare: Some Pre-Play Exercises for *The Tempest*". *English Journal* 82:4 (1993), pp. 36-8.

Pinder, Brenda. *Full Fathom Five: A Workshop Approach to* The Tempest. Shakespeare Workshop Series. Rozelle, New South Wales: St. Clair Press, 1991.

Rempe, Robert H. "Collaboration in the Midst of the Storm: Teaching *The Tempest*". *Shakespeare and the Classroom* 3:1 (1995), pp. 51-2.

Richmond, Hugh M. "Teaching *The Tempest* and the Late Plays by Performance". *Approaches to Teaching Shakespeare's* The Tempest *and Other Late Romances*. Ed. Maurice Hunt. Approaches to Teaching World Literature 41 (New York: Modern Language Association, 1992), pp. 125-32.

Stockholder, Kay. "Shakespeare's Magic and Its Discontents: Approaching *The Tempest*". *Approaches to Teaching Shakespeare's* The Tempest *and Other Late Romances*. Ed. Maurice Hunt. Approaches to Teaching World Literature 41 (New York: Modern Language Association, 1992), pp. 160-7.

Stoll, Karl-Heinz. "Wortfelduntersuchungen zu Shakespeares *The Tempest*". *William Shakespeare: Didaktisches Handbuch*. Ed. Rüdiger Ahrens. 3 vols (Munich: Fink, 1982), II, pp. 473-91.

"*The Tempest*". *The Practical Bard*. Ed. Cher Stempler (Orlando: Shakespeare Institute, University of Central Florida, 1979), pp. 125-46.

Van Eeden, Janet. "The Monastery Months". *Crux: A Journal on the Teaching of English* 21:1 (1987), pp. 22-5.

Whitesides, Nigel, and Adrian G. Packer. *Primary Shakespeare: An Introductory Drama Scheme*: The Tempest. Strood, England: P. S. Publishers, 1996.

Titus Andronicus

Young, Robert. "In Defense of *Titus Andronicus*". *Shakespeare* (Georgetown University) 4:1 (2000), p. 12.

Troilus and Cressida

Davis, Boyd H. "Cressida in Conversation: Introducing Novice Readers to Shakespeare and Chaucer". *Sino-American Conference on Shakespeare* (Taipei: Crane, 1991), pp. 79-92.

Twelfth Night

Bergeron, David M. "Plays within Plays in Shakespeare's Early Comedies". *Teaching Shakespeare*. Ed. Walter Edens, Christopher Durer, Duncan Harris, Keith Hull, and Walter F. Eggers, Jr. (Princeton: Princeton UP, 1978), pp. 305-16.
Boone, Ann. "An On-Your-Feet Introduction to *Twelfth Night*". *Shakespeare* (Georgetown University) 1:3 (1997), pp. 12-13.
Collins, Jane. "'Boy Actresses' in the Classroom". *Shakespeare* (Georgetown University) 3:1 (1999), pp. 19-20.
Costello, Mary Enda, Paulette S. Goll, Stephen L. Jacobs, and Eileen K. Maloney. Twelfth Night: *Curriculum Unit*. Rocky River, OH: Center for Learning, 1998.
Jeffcoate, Robert. "Introducing Children to Shakespeare: [1] Some Conclusions; [2] *Twelfth Night* in Years 5 and 6". *Use of English* 48 (1996-97), pp. 122-33; 216-26.
Metham, Patricia. "Teaching Shakespeare with Years 7 and 8". *Speech and Drama* 43:1 (1994), pp. 22-5.
O'Brien, Peggy, general ed. *Shakespeare Set Free: Teaching* Twelfth Night *and* Othello. New York: Washington Square Press, 1995.
Orkin, Martin R. "Right-Seeing and the Matriculation *Twelfth Night*". *Crux: A Journal on the Teaching of English* 18:2 (1983), pp. 40-9.
Orme, David. *Shakespeare,* Twelfth Night. Specials! Dunstable: Folens, 1998.
Page, Philip, and Marilyn Pettit. *William Shakespeare's* Twelfth Night or "What You Will": *Teacher's Resource Book*. Livewire Shakespeare. London: Stodder and Houghton in association with the Basic Skills Agency, 1999.
Watson, Ken. *The Food of Love: A Workshop Approach to* Twelfth Night. Shakespeare Workshop Series. Rozelle, New South Wales: St. Clair Press, 1991.

The Winter's Tale

Campbell, Kathleen. "Making the Statue Move: Teaching Performance". *Approaches to Teaching Shakespeare's* The Tempest *and Other Late Romances*. Ed. Maurice Hunt. Approaches to Teaching World Literature 41 (New York: Modern Language Association, 1992), pp. 109-16.
Coursen, H. R. "Using Film and Television to Teach *The Winter's Tale* and *The Tempest*". *Approaches to Teaching Shakespeare's* The Tempest *and Other Late Romances*. Ed. Maurice Hunt. Approaches to Teaching World Literature 41 (New York: Modern Language Association, 1992), pp. 117-24.
Forker, Charles R. "Negotiating the Paradoxes of Art and Nature in *The Winter's Tale*". *Approaches to Teaching Shakespeare's* The Tempest *and Other Late Romances*. Ed. Maurice Hunt. Approaches to Teaching World Literature 41 (New York: Modern Language Association, 1992), pp. 94-102.
Hurd, Myles. "Shakespeare's Paulina: Characterization and Craftsmanship in *The Winter's Tale*". *CLA Journal* 26 (1982-83), pp. 303-10.
Kehler, Dorothea. "Teaching the Slandered Women of *Cymbeline* and *The Winter's Tale*". *Approaches to Teaching Shakespeare's* The Tempest *and Other Late Romances*. Ed. Maurice

Hunt. Approaches to Teaching World Literature 41 (New York: Modern Language Association, 1992), pp. 80-6.
Lenig, Stuart. "A Community College *Winter's Tale*". *Shakespeare and the Classroom* 4:1 (1996), pp. 42-5.
Male, David A. *The Winter's Tale*. Shakespeare on Stage Series. Cambridge: Cambridge UP, 1984.
Morse, William R. "A Metacritical and Historical Approach to *The Winter's Tale* and *The Tempest*". *Approaches to Teaching Shakespeare's* The Tempest *and Other Late Romances*. Ed. Maurice Hunt. Approaches to Teaching World Literature 41 (New York: Modern Language Association, 1992), pp. 133-8.
Radcliffe, Catherine, David Nicholson, and Ken Watson. *Bitter Bread: A Workshop Approach to Richard II and* The Winter's Tale. Shakespeare Workshop Series. Rozelle, New South Wales: St. Clair Press, 1997.
Slights, William W. E. "Trusting Shakespeare's *Winter's Tale*: Metafiction in the Late Plays". *Approaches to Teaching Shakespeare's* The Tempest *and Other Late Romances*. Ed. Maurice Hunt. Approaches to Teaching World Literature 41 (New York: Modern Language Association, 1992), pp. 103-8.
Stodder, Joseph. "Teaching Shakespeare through Play Performance: A Folio Production of *The Winter's Tale*". *Performance Practice* 3 (1997), pp. 26-30.
Young, Bruce W. "Teaching the Unrealistic Realism of *The Winter's Tale*". *Approaches to Teaching Shakespeare's* The Tempest *and Other Late Romances*. Ed. Maurice Hunt. Approaches to Teaching World Literature 41 (New York: Modern Language Association, 1992), pp. 87-93.

TWO TEXTUAL NOTES ON
THE TAMING OF THE SHREW

Rodney Stenning Edgecombe
(University of Cape Town)

I. THE 'ROPE-TRICKS' IN 1.2

Commentators have long been baffled – if only partly – by Grumio's reference to "rope-tricks" in Act 1, Scene 2 of *The Taming of the Shrew*. Boasting about Petruchio's mastery of verbal abuse, and his ability to trump Katherina's skill in this regard, he remarks that: "and he begin once, he'll rail in his rope-tricks. I'll tell you what, sir, and she stand him but a little, he will throw a figure in her face, and so disfigure her with it that she shall have no more eyes to see withal than a cat" (1.2.110-14). Although many tantalizing contemporary near-analogues for 'rope-tricks' have been unearthed over time, none has proved close enough to establish a definitive reading. The Arden editor thus sums up the debate: "Probably, then, the nonce-word 'rope-tricks' is Grumio's perversion of 'rhetorics', or 'rope-rhetoric' (meaning 'rhetoric for which the author deserved hanging'), or 'tropes of rhetoric', or, as Hibbard suggests) 'trope-tricks' (though the word is not known to exist). Or it may be a confused recollection of all of these" (189). Even allowing for that tactful preface of probability, none of these readings strikes me as very convincing, if only because in the Latin lesson in *The Merry Wives of Windsor* (another occasion on which 'learned' terms are corrupted by an ignorant spectator), Shakespeare makes the phonetic connections between source and analogue much more plausible. In "hang hoc" we have a Welsh corruption of "hanc hoc", from which one moves effortlessly to "'Hang hog' is Latin for bacon, I warrant you" (Oliver, 4.1.40-1). The same may be said of "Genitive case" = "Ginny's case" and *horum* = "whore" (4.1.50-3). Turning from this to the loose aphasia that aligns 'rope-tricks' and 'rhetorics', one cannot help feeling that the joke is feebler for being less clearly delineated. The mismatched diphthong and vowel in 'rope' and 'rhetoric', the syllabic inequality and the phonetic distance between P and T all serve to undermine the parallel. 'Genitive' and 'Ginny' are, admittedly, almost as far apart, but, in that instance, 'case' provides the unequivocal bridge between the original word and the misprision, and a clear line of connection is evident at this and all other points where Mistress Quickly's literal-minded analogues jostle the pedant's words aside.

I would therefore suggest a different line of approach to 'rope-tricks'. It is clear from the context that Grumio has an extremely violent conception of language, and that, in his book, words can be thrown to wound. The disfiguring force of a 'figure' is proof of that. Would it not therefore be better to assume that 'rope-tricks' is a misprint for 'rope-bricks', and that 'rope-bricks' is Grumio's Quickly-esque stab at 'rubrics', which he breaks down into rope that linguistically trusses up the victim and bricks for hurling at her (as brickbats often were in violent confrontations). The phonetic connection of the /uː/ in 'rubric' with the terminal /u/ of the diphthong glide ('rope') is much closer than that between that same /u/ and the /e/ of 'rhetoric'. Furthermore, b and p are both bilabial plosives, whereas the alveolar t of 'rhetoric' occurs further back in the mouth than the p it is meant to displace in the 'rope-tricks' reading. Then again, 'rope-bricks' matches 'rubrics' syllable for syllable, and 'rhetorics' has one left over.

Works Cited

Shakespeare, William. *The Merry Wives of Windsor*. Ed. H.J. Oliver. London: Methuen, 1971.
——. *The Taming of the Shrew*. Ed. Brian Morris. London: Methuen, 1981.

II. THE "HUMOUR OF FORTY FANCIES" IN 3.2

In Act 3, Scene 2 of *The Taming of the Shrew*, Biondello lists Grumio's nuptial motley as including an "old hat, and the humour of forty fancies pricked in't for a feather" (Morris, ll. 66-7). Scholars have frankly confessed their bafflement about that 'humour', from the earlier Cambridge edition ("In short, no one knows what it means" – Quiller-Couch and Wilson, 157) to the later ("The exact meaning is obscure" – Thompson, 103). The Arden editor provides a survey of various readings, some of which suggest that Shakespeare had something showy and elaborate in mind: "a parcel of forty ribbons tied together instead of a feather" (Halliwell); "some fantastical ornament comprising the humour of forty fancies" (Malone) (229) – a conception that also informs Ann Thompson's interpretation of the phrase ("some excessively elaborate decoration is implied" – 103).

Adding my five cents' worth to these conflicting visions of Grumio's hat, I would suggest that something dowdy would better accord with the grotesque, improvisatory quality of his costume, and would argue that Shakespeare might well have had a simple goose quill in mind. If we take 'humour' to be a misreading of the agent noun 'humourer', then a quill pen would be the *humourer* of forty fancies to the extent that it indulged them ('fancies' being both Grumio's many erotic attractions and the lyrics that embodied them) and also to the extent that it brought them into being with the 'humour' (= moisture) of its ink. So, instead of a rich Tudor plume, Grumio is wearing a blunted, soiled, ink-stained, chewed-at-the-tip quill that has done service in the laborious production of no fewer than forty love lyrics.

Works Cited

Shakespeare, William. *The Taming of the Shrew*. Ed. A. Quiller-Couch and John Dover Wilson. Cambridge: Cambridge UP, 1928.
—————. *The Taming of the Shrew*. Ed. Brian Morris. London: Methuen, 1981.
—————. *The Taming of the Shrew*. Ed. Ann Thompson. Cambridge: Cambridge UP, 1984.

REVIEWS

Lorna Flint, *Shakespeare's Third Keyboard: The Significance of Rime in Shakespeare's Plays*. Newark: University of Delaware Press/London: Associated University Presses, 2000. pp. 208. ISBN 0-87413-692-X

This book has a common assumption to correct: that rhymed verse, "Shakespeare's third keyboard", is diminishingly present and diminishingly significant as his dramatic output unfolds. Lorna Flint thinks otherwise: "Shakespeare's correlation of perfect and imperfect rime throughout each play demonstrates the dramatic significance he never ceased to attach to it" (7). Flint also has quarrels with assessments of rhyme which confine themselves to end-rhyme, and to 'standard' rhyme; but it should be said that her excursions into the analysis of freer conceptions of acoustic patterning are modest, and necessarily so, since too great an extension of parameters would undermine the declared project itself, and one might begin to wonder why the negative rhymes, or anti-rhyming, of blank verse had not also been considered.

Part One deals with rhyme in all its many masks and manifestations, without, for all that, addressing exit/entrance couplets. This investigation is prefaced by a chapter (Two) devoted to critical background, which traces the attitudes to rhyme of Shakespeare's contemporaries (Puttenham, Campion, Daniel, etc.) and subsequent critical responses to rhyme in Shakespeare's plays. This exercise, while strengthening Flint's own case, is curiously unfruitful, and the chapter might have been better devoted to the dramatic functions of rhyme in sixteenth-century theatre more generally, or indeed to textual problems relating to rhyme created by discrepancies between Quartos and Folio (as an anticpation of Chapter Nine), or by editorial and directorial decisions.

In guiding us through the Prologues, Choruses and Epilogues (Chapter Three), Flint has very helpful parallels to draw between the 'lyric' structures of these speeches and the dramatic structure of the corresponding whole play. This is a point at which Bakhtin's distinction between the monologic and the dialogic might have usefully been invoked. Does rhymed verse present itself as a truth 'officialised', to be swallowed whole, as utterance totally in possession of itself? Is it the task of blank verse and prose constantly to re-instal the dialogic, the heteroglossic, to relativise reality? Or is the position of blank verse altogether more ambiguously poised between the monologic and dialogic?

And there is still research to be done into the relation of rhyme to enjambement and endstopping, this cross-patterning which so affects the pacing of language and the way in which a text is vocally delivered (see Time's mid-play chorus in *The Winter's Tale*). Enjambement tends to make the caesura, mobile though it is, the major lineal juncture, and thus sets up an alternative structure of endings where potential rhymes or strategies of anti-rhyming become part of a speech's plot. Flint's own fascinating findings would tend to suggest that the more the caesura becomes fixed, that is, a structural given, the more it is likely to attract to itself rhyming effects, as in Biron's sonnet in alexandrines from *Love's Labour's Lost* (Chapter Four).

Defining verse structure is an important undertaking if one is to identify the voice with which rhyme is speaking. Flint reads Timon's epitaph (Chapter Four) as printed in the 1623 Folio, that is, as an alexandrine followed by a line in poulter's measure (a misidentification?), followed by two "jogging fourteeners"; this strategy leads to the persuasive discovery of caesuras in unorthodox places and consequent effects of dislocation and harshness. But lineal re-arrangement is not unexpected in early Shakespearean editions, and one can imagine this long-line presentation as a printer's device for saving space. At all events, read as laid out in the Oxford or Norton Shakespeares, for example, that is, as a pair of ballad stanzas, these lines shake off caesural irregularity, and add a certain ironic vulgarity to the bitterness of the words, seasoned with a dash of poignancy provided by the silent foot of the first line ("Here lies [x /] a wretched corpse").

An absorbing analysis of the three casket poems from *The Merchant of Venice* brings to a close a chapter (Four) in which we have been shown how inserted poems, through the isolation imposed by endrhyming, act as fixed points amidst the flux of an action they sometimes check, sometimes appraise and sometimes instigate. In similar fashion, songs (Chapter Five), whether a love song from *The Two Gentlemen of Verona* ("Who is Silvia?"), or a drinking song from *Antony and Cleopatra* ("Come, thou monarch of the vine"), and whatever diversionary relief they momentarily provide, are "so placed, so measured, so worded, that [they become] a touchstone, a crucible, in which the characterization, atmosphere, tone and themes of the play work on the audience at a deeper level than is immediately apparent" (56). Rhyme is full of insinuations and subliminal promptings, and Flint's analyses in these chapters are compelling explorations of acousticity's guileful innocence.

A problem similar to the one encountered with Timon's epitaph recurs with Posthumus's rhymed vision of the Ghosts in *Cymbeline*, which the Folio again presents as fourteeners rather than as flexible ballad stanzas. But the high point of this chapter on rhymed verse as the vehicle for visions, masques and plays within plays (Chapter Six) is the closing consideration of *The Murder of Gonzago*, which deftly shows how the style of the inset performance and the style of the dramatic context are interwoven in a complex dialogue of similarities and differences, with Hamlet himself as the essential negotiator between the two.

Chapter Seven examines "Unpredictable Rime": the disconcerting occurrence of sonnets, more or less submerged in the text, particularly in the early lyrical plays; the use of couplets in soliloquy, where rhyme may screw up the will of protagonists, or generate moments of peculiar autonomy or psychic distance, or act as an instrument of exposition, drawing the map of dominant issues in mnemonic form; and other episodes, such as the Talbot scenes in *1 Henry VI*, or the appearances of the Weird Sisters in *Macbeth*, or the bout of forensic sententiousness between the Duke and Brabantio in *Othello*, where rhyme operates as an immobilising, transfixative force, simultaneously damping down and damming up inner vehemences.

Part Two undertakes the extensive analysis of two plays, *All's Well That Ends Well* and *King Lear*. The opportunity to track the developing interplay of the three keyboards – prose, blank verse, rhymed verse – in *All's Well* (Chapter Eight) is the opportunity to vindicate a play that critics and public alike have tended to disparage on account of its stylistic heterogeneity and muddled disunity. Flint's illuminating commentary tenaciously searches out the underlying and cohesive roles played by each medium: "The overall impression is that the blank verse steadily carries the main weight of the narrative and of the characters' expansive, considered reflections. The prose contributes two contrasting elements: it is the chief vehicle for varied types of humor, ranging from verbal wit to farce, but also for the low-key, spontaneous, yet thoughtful dialogue between intimates. And the free-ranging rhyme, sometimes unobtrusively and briefly, sometimes ostentatiously and at length, controls the dramatic effect from the beginning to the end of the play" (140). This control of dramatic effect is multiform in its operation, and to Flint's impressive array of identified functions – developing theme, personality, mood; creating or maintaining suspense; dictating exits and entrances, gestures, groupings, axioms, volubility and silence; etc. – one might add that rhyme establishes a different mode of ironic cognition, that it generates or registers compulsions and obligations of various kinds, and that, being line-transcendent, it is susceptible to the beckonings of the metaphysical. The final chapter (Nine), which reviews textual additions and subtractions as between the 1608 Quarto *King Lear* and its 1623 Folio twin, is a fitting culmination to the enquiry as a whole, and underlines what profit is to be gained from reading Shakespeare with the perceptivity, the 'listening' sympathy, but, above all, with the subtle sense of the dramatic interactivity of formal variation, that Flint brings to bear on her chosen task.

University of East Anglia, Norwich   Clive Scott

Michele Marrapodi and Giorgio Melchiori. *Italian Studies in Shakespeare and his Contemporaries.* Newark: University of Delaware Press; London: Associated University Press, 1999. pp. 299. ISBN 0 87413 666 0; and Michele Marrapodi, A. J. Hoensellars, Marcello Cappuzo and L. Falzon Santuzzi, editors. *Shakespeare's Italy: Functions of Italian Locations in Renaissance Drama.* Manchester: Manchester University Press, 1977. pp. X +326. ISBN 07190 5220 3

In a sense these two volumes appear to complement each other: *Italian Studies in Shakespeare and his Contemporaries* is a collection of fourteen essays by Italian scholars, all translated from Italian and most of them reprinted from Italian collections or journals, which gives a picture of the current state of Italian scholarship in this area, while *Shakespeare's Italy*, a collection of seventeen essays by scholars from many countries, many already in print elsewhere, focuses specifically on the representation of Italy in criticism of the drama. In fact, although there is some overlap of personnel, the interest of the two collections is rather different: *Shakespeare's Italy* would be useful to the student and general reader who wants to know more about the "most significant case of appropriation of an alien culture" that the Italianate drama of early modern England represents, whereas *Italian Studies in Shakespeare* offers more to the specialist concerned with the cultural codes whereby non-English critics interpret this drama.

Italian Studies in Shakespeare is a very disparate collection in terms of the critical methodologies represented. Marrapodi in his introduction draws attention to the emergence of criticism in Italy from "largely idealistic and post-Crocean roots" into the worlds of cultural materialism and of semiotics, a process demonstrated here. Some of the essays (for example, those by Vito Amoruso and the late Fernando Ferrara) are almost belle-lettristic in manner, others, particularly those in the third section entitled "Language and ideology" are densely theoretical and jargon-ridden, and still others, like Marcello Pagnini's "*A Midsummer Night's Dream*: An Example of Shakespeare's Specularity", filled with diagrams and formulae. In his introduction Marrapodi calls Pagnini the "introducer of post-structuralism in Italy", and his method of structural analysis is demonstrated in this essay. Alessandro Serpieri's "Bonds of Love and Death in *The Merchant of Venice*" is another neatly schematic essay, not particularly original as a reading, but useful for the analytical model it proposes. One of the best essays is Angela Locatelli's "Shakespeare's Discursive Strategies and Their Definitions of Subjectivity", an ambitious and all-too-short piece which approaches the definition of subjectivity through a theory of "double enunciation" whereby the speech of an individual character is counterbalanced against the value-system created by the text as a whole. In her brief but suggestive account of *The Merchant of Venice* (a play with which Italian critics seem to be especially preoccupied) she applies the theory to Portia showing how "we have the illusion of subjectivity [...] while the dissolution of the (female) subject is carried out almost completely". Roberta Mullini throws light on a relatively neglected play in "'But thou didst understand me by my signs': The Instability of Signs in *King John*", convincingly discovering evidence in the play for a "crisis of the sign system through the lack of correspondence between expression and content". Mullini is interested in the relation of the play's ambiguities to the role of its subject in Reformation politics: the role of Protestantism in the formation of early modern English culture is a concern of many of these essays, and this, along with a commitment to detailed linguistic analysis, gives the collection a kind of unity.

According to Manfred Pfister in an Afterword, *Shakespeare's Italy* as a collection aims to avoid the problem often encountered with the 'conjunctive genre' of Shakespeare studies, whereby "Shakespeare and ..." studies fail to utilise the information gathered to generate new interpretations of Shakespeare. This collection, published in the wake of two book-length studies of Shakespeare's relation to Italy, needed to justify its appearance. It is evident, particularly in the several essays devoted to Venice, that these books (Murray J. Levith, *Shakespeare's Italian Settings and Plays* and David C. McPherson, *Shakespeare, Jonson, and the Myth of Place*) cast something of a shadow over the enterprise. As in *Italian Studies in Shakespeare*, these essays are critically and stylistically diverse; there are really too many of them, and some are too short to achieve much, though Giorgio Melchiori's "'In fair Verona': *Commedia Erudita* into Romantic Comedy" manages to make illuminating points about the native origins of love comedy as well as to suggest a source for Falstaff's character in Munday's *Fedele and Fortunio*, in only a few pages. Sergio Rossi's "Duelling in the Italian Manner: the Case of *Romeo and Juliet*" is another effective short piece, but in this instance more of an extended footnote on Shakespeare's use of Italian duelling manuals. Avraham Oz's "Dobbin on the Rialto: Venice and the Division of Identity" is a longer essay, which focusses on the relation of identity and property, mainly in *The Merchant of Venice*, and defines Shylock interestingly as a "legal terrorist". Oz explores the usefulness of Italy for Shakespeare and the "token reality" he accords it, in terms of the representation of 'otherness' in Shakespeare, a subject of several essays. Angela Locatelli in "The Fictional World of *Romeo and*

Juliet: Cultural Connotations of an Italian Setting" similarly sees Italy as a convenient "cultural space" for Shakespeare in which meanings and values may be established, and also a way of mirroring his own culture through the depiction of another. For Leo Salingar, in "The Idea of Venice in Shakespeare and Ben Jonson" Venice becomes " refracted projection of London" for both dramatists.

In this collection, unlike the other, several good essays concern dramatists other than Shakespeare. A. J Hoensellars's "Italy Staged in English Renaissance Drama" surveys the devices used by a range of dramatists for creating the illusion of Italy (rather than England) as the place of the dramatic action; again, it is all too short; he has a second short essay on the language of Italy in the drama, which explores the idea (elaborated in his recent book) that Italian settings served to rehearse concerns about the still lowly status of English as an international language. Mariangela Tempera writes at greater length on "The Rhetoric of Poison in John Webster's Italianate plays", and , like Zara Bruzzi and A. A. Bromham, in "The soil alters [...]: Multiple Perspectives and Political Resonance in Middleton's *Women Beware Women*", shows how a dramatist can use Italy to depict a world of courtly corruption in a way that might have been dangerous with an English setting.

It is striking that some of the longer and better essays in this collection were specially written for it, whereas the majority in both are reprints. While students may find library copies useful in order to consult individual essays, it is hard to imagine who would want to buy either collection for itself.

Birkbeck College, University of London   Sandra Clark

Andrew Gurr and Mariko Ichikawa, *Staging in Shakespeare's Theatres*. Oxford Shakespeare Topics, Oxford: Oxford University Press. 2000. pp. vi +181. ISBN 0 -19 -871159 - X

This slim volume on Elizabethan/Jacobean staging forms part of a series (ed. Holland and Wells) whose full range of titles is set to include topics guaranteed to figure on any self-respecting modern academic course in Shakespeare Studies:

Shakespeare and Women, Shakespeare and Masculinity, Shakespeare and Race and *Shakespeare and Film*, for example. Within the scope of such a series, however, it was also clearly necessary to devote some attention to historical context and the way the writer's works were originally performed; and who better to provide a *resumé* of this background than Professor Andrew Gurr, who has been so closely associated with the Globe reconstruction project? Surprisingly, though, little direct reference is made to the Bankside Globe, except as a "laboratory in which some of the theories set out here will be tested". But some lively details noted – such as the worst place to stand in the playhouse courtyard during a rainstorm and the fact that spoken cues onstage are difficult to hear from behind the scenic doors – while clearly based on observation in the new Globe Playhouse, are not actually acknowledged as such.

Gurr, with the co-author Professor Mariko Ichikawa, has produced a broad survey, designed for students and teachers, of the London theatres in Shakespeare' day (not, for the record, just those with which Shakespeare was personally associated), covering audience, companies, buildings, acting styles, costumes, scenery, properties and stage practice; a wide remit for a relatively short work. Information is derived mainly from the standard works of Bentley and Chambers, but much useful material is drawn from a comparison of the Folio and Quarto texts and from primary sources such as Henslowe's famous bizarrely-spelled diary entries. Illustrations are regrettably few, comprising only the inevitable de Witt sketch, an Inigo Jones theatre plan, a plan of the new Globe and two stage blocking diagrams.

The focus of the work varies considerably. Relatively accessible and circumstantial accounts of the theatres of the day are interspersed with some rather laborious line-counting exercises to establish exactly how long it took to make an entrance (and identifying a category of entrance pattern as "*Exiting to Fetch Something and Re-enter with It*" is symptomatic of this sometimes overly methodical approach). Much time is devoted, too, to considering how the flow of stage action was managed and establishing the convention of scene changes. To a public once more accustomed to open-stage presentation, some of these points seem rather self-evident and it is surely perversely conservative to insist that, for modern theatre audiences, the proscenium arch and cinematic realism are still the perceived norm. The experiments of Granville Barker, Poel and Nugent Monck demonstrated, early on, the merits of 'authentic' Shakespeare staging: pace, fluency and independence from scenic spectacle.

Given the size of the repertoire and the regular introduction of new plays, a principal problem for the companies must surely have been the plotting of a performance. It is suggested that, with only a very brief time available for staging a production, some convention must have been adopted to facilitate movement over the stage. The Beckerman theory, that one door was used only for entrances while the other was reserved for exits, in the manner of a restaurant kitchen, has to be rapidly abandoned, however, when tested against the practical requirements of the plays. There is also an (uncredited) glance at Leslie Hotson's theory that performances were directed towards the lords' room above the stage, but this notion is likewise not pursued.

It almost goes without saying that, for depth and detail, the students and teachers at whom this series is aimed would be better directed to Gurr's own earlier work *The Shakespearean Stage 1574 -1642*. Gurr opens that study with some observations on Osric's excessive deference in not replacing his hat in Hamlet's presence, but in the present work, this exchange seems to have gone on to generate something of a bee in the writer's own bonnet: Osric has apparently interpreted (as we should also) Hamlet's graveside cry of "This is I, *Hamlet* the Dane!" as a mad delusion that he is indeed King, or his father, or both – a nuance of interpretation which is distractingly reintroduced on several further occasions.

Some other slightly idiosyncratic views crop up repeatedly in this otherwise uncontroversial work with the insistence of *idées fixes*: Fortinbras, being (presumably) armoured, is a visual co-relative of the Ghost and thus embodies the spirit of Revenge; Fortinbras does *not* pursue personal revenge, whereas Hamlet and Laertes do and are ultimately damned for it; Ophelia definitely *does* commit suicide. All these claims, made within the space of a few pages, are far from being beyond debate, and one grows warier of trusting such pronouncements on reading, for example, in the section on stage fights, that Macduff could be armed with a battle-axe at Dunsinane – in spite of the fact that a sword is specified no fewer than three times in the text. Furthermore, any summer-season Fluellen could testify that the availability of property leeks is not as stated here.

Hamlet looms large in this study, since the final chapter is a scene-by-scene account of how the play might have originally been presented. Chosen as an exemplar partly by virtue of being so well known, it helpfully illustrates the use of many features of the Globe Theatre. The authors bear in mind the conditions of staging in the Globe, the manners, costumes and conventions of the time. Their account is full of valuable performance detail, yet it is impossible not to feel that most of this commentary would be appropriate to any halfway competent production of Shakespeare's play and that in some ways it is an attempt to direct by proxy. Why, for instance, are we told that, in her mad scene, Ophelia walks "with short stabbing steps"? On what authority is the student, Horatio, "dressed as a gentleman, in a velvet doublet and cloak"? Do Ophelia's remembrances *have* to be "wrapped in a small fabric package"? Such speculative points are clearly visualised, but can be irritating when given equal weight with details that are textually justified. For a thorough, practical (if non-Globe-specific) account of this play's implications for performance, the student would be far better advised to consult Michael Pennington's fascinating *Hamlet: A User's Guide*.

Staging in Shakespeare's Theatres serves to fill a niche in a uniform series for reference and fulfils its purpose in providing a convenient study guide. All aspects considered, however, its format and approach do not always seem particularly attractive or appropriate to those who might be expected to find it most beneficial.

Norwich   David Gwyn Harris

Charles Edelman, *Shakespeare's Military Language: A Dictionary*. London and New Brunswick, NJ: Athlone, 2000. pp. xvii + 423. ISBN 0 485 11546 8 HB

First impressions are highly favourable. Running from "Admiral" (for Edelman covers maritime affairs as well as land warfare and, entirely correctly for ancient, medieval and early modern times, declines to draw a hard-and-fast distinction between merchant shipping and men-o'-war) and "Yeoman", this dictionary of militaria in Shakespeare provides great quantities of information. It does so in an attractive form. The volume is stoutly bound to withstand the hard usage that inevitably awaits reference works, and the temptation of presenting masses of information in small print on crowded pages has been resisted, which both facilitates rapid consultation and encourages browsing. A few of the entries are laconic, but many occupy a good page while others are more extensive still: this allows for quite full treatment without any undue rush or compression, and the system of reference that has been adopted spares readers the dispiriting sense of needing to crack an enigma before being granted access to further information.

Whether or not Shakespeare served in the Low Countries, as William J. Thomas surmised, or rose, as Duff Cooper less seriously suggested, to the rank of sergeant, *arma virumque cano* would have made a suitable epigraph to the dramatist's work at a time when Plutarch and Holinshed provided plots for tragedies and when soldiers from the wars returning risk challenging "Cupid in the fight" in comedies from *Much Ado about Nothing* to *The Merry Wives of Windsor*. The check-list of citations reveals that reference is made both to a score of other Elizabethan and Jacobean plays and also to the entire Shakespeare canon, save *The Winter's Tale*. Though *Sir Thomas More* is not mentioned, *Edward III* is covered, yielding particularly interesting points on naval topics, with intiguing parallels drawn between the Battle of Sluys and the defeat of the Great Armada.

A mere list of Shakespeare's plays and a little reflection on their dates and on the periods they depict with their author's celebrated tendency to conflate his vision of the past with his responses to his own time will give some measure of dimension of Edelman's task. To assist modern readers, who are not without some knowledge of the past, though it must always be shaped by the prejudices and convictions of their own age, he seeks to elucidate Shakespeare's interpretations of warfare and his use of the language of war in myth and history, in distant lands and also near to home in accounts of struggles that still had marked current resonances. Many of the campaigns to which he refers had, moreover, been fought in an era when tactics and equipment employed were similar, to but by no means identical with, those that his first audience knew from first-hand experience. In other words, the natural urge to note what appears to us now in the twentieth century to be the truth about the various issues has to be balanced with the obligation of giving enough weight to Elizabethan views and opinions. Very largely Edelman succeeds. The result is a work of surprisingly wide range that will be of value, not only to those particularly interested in the evolution of war, but to all who enjoy reading Shakespeare or watching performances of his plays.

Not everyone will, however, agree with Edelman on every point or every editorial decision. To begin with a detail, is it really correct to suppose that in *Twelfth Night*, 2.3, Sir Toby Belch is making ironic reference to Maria's smallness of stature by calling her "Penthesilea" (or "Penthesilia", as Edelman has it)? Though Mahood remarks that "Maria's spirit is out of all proportion to her size", there is no implication that the classical allusion is prompted by her stature rather than her feistiness. As for the line "to take up arms against a sea of troubles", Pope's uncomprehending emendation is less to the point than the relationship between Shakespeare's collocation and a classical tag so stale as probably to have loss its salty savour.

Every reader will be grateful for the conscientious explanations of various types of arms and equipment. All the same, when, after explaining just what a 'falchion' is, Edelman goes on to note that on occasion the term may be employed just as a metrical variant of 'sword', he appears, so to speak, to cut the ground from under his feet and leaves us with the question of the extent to which Elizabethan playgoers cared about terminological accuracy in such matters. Though Edelman's descriptions of weapons, for instance, and various types of helmet are clear, line illustrations would undoubtedly have been a help. It is a pity too that Edelman, who regrets the fewness and the poor quality of the maps provided by Oman (p.40), does not make exemplary use of them himself. Graphic methods have many advantages for the presentation of complex material, and many readers will regret that details of campaigns and battles are not in this way presented as well as being frequently referred to in passing in other articles.

There are instances when the dictionary method, despite generally serving well, leads to unfortunate fragmentation when a more determined strategy of cross-referencing to major articles might have been more satisfactory. Giving 'Arthur's Show' individual treatment appears reasonable, but the entry on 'Archer' might well have begun with the account of the archer's weapon found under 'Bow' and gone on by linking the discussion of archery legislation with Elizabethan arguments for and against reliance on England's traditional weapon. Some consolidation of the entries dealing with sieges might likewise have been helpful; at least a cross-reference from 'forlorn hope' might have been included, and the allusion to 'the Harfleur breech' (p.392) is unfortunate. The articles on 'gun powder', 'saltpetre' and the international arms trade are, however, fascinating.

Edelman has clearly taken great pains to collect information and gives a full biography. It might, however, have been a service to complement the slightly wayward discussion offered under 'theoric' by including within the alphabetical sequence brief notes on the historians and military writers, such as Roger Ascham, with whose works Shakespeare is known or may be assumed to have been acquainted. Whether Montaigne, whose earliest essays were, of course, on soldierly topics, should be counted among them might merit further investigation. At times, too, some readers may be a little disconcerted on finding, printed after author's names, dates that for a moment seem to make no sense, especially as recourse is often had to the present tense (as, e.g., in "Digges adds"). Edelman does explain at the outset that these references should be taken as applying to the modern reprint that is being quoted. All the same, some alternative convention of citing the date of first publication would be advantageous.

Shakespeare's Military Language is a reference book that will do yeoman service, elucidating a great number of topics that were far clearer to Shakespeare's first audiences than to his readers today. As Sandra Clark remarks in her Series Editor's Preface, the present volume is one of a number that will each focus on a single important aspect of Shakespeare's work, illuminating it in the light of recent scholarship. Edelman does not quite hit the bull's eye every time, but he is never far off target.

University of East Anglia, Norwich   Christopher Smith

Romeo and Juliet, 1597, ed. Jill L.Levenson and Barry Gaines. The Malone Society Reprints, No. 163 (Oxford: Oxford University Press, for the Malone Society, 2000). pp.xv + 91. ISBN 0 19 729039 6

Once again, as it has been doing since 1907, the Malone Society renders a service to scholarship. This edition of the 1597 first, or 'Bad', quarto of *Romeo and Juliet* makes available to all a photographic facsimile of the Stace-Kemble-Devonshire copy; once owned by John Philip Kemble, it is now preserved at the Henry E. Huntington Library, San Marino, California. An appendix provides nine pages – $C1^v$, C3, $C4^v$, $F4^v$, $H2^v$, $I4^v$, $K1^r$, $K1^r$ and $K2^v$ – from the Edward Capell copy at Trinity College, Cambridge, because, though generally not so suitable for reproduction, this volume has not suffered so much from injudicious cropping and is less impaired by shine-through at these particular points. Though the pale grey of the photographed pages is not particularly attractive, the text is generally quite easy to read. The Librarian of Trinity College, Dr David McKitterick, very kindly allowed me to examine the copy of the Quarto in the Capell collection. Its paper is certainly lighter in colour than the pages as presented in the facsimile; stains that were only quite light-brown, almost opaque patches have come out black in the reproduction, where the effects of show-through are, moreover, somewhat more pronounced. All the same, the facsimile will serve its purposes well, the more so since scholars will be able to keep it by them in their studies for consultation and not need to treat it with the respect due to a rare and precious sixteenth-century book. Line-numbers are inserted in the ample margins of the pages in which the reproductions are set; in the outer margins another set of figures facilitates comparisons with the 1623 Folio, as given by Charlton Hinman in *The Norton Facsimile*.

Only three other copies of the first quarto of *Romeo and Juliet* are known to exist; one is held by the British Library, and another by the Folger: the third, at the Bodleian, was part of the collection owned by none other than Edmond Malone. Collation of all five extant copies has revealed no variants, which does not surprise the editors who, in a succinct but thoroughly documented and energetically argued introduction, go on to discuss the interpretation of this 'Bad' Quarto. They are disinclined to be over-impressed by the reputation from which it has suffered for the last century and a half. An initial observation is that Q1 has fewer typesetting errors than Q2, and the editors show exemplary caution towards disparaging suppositions about Danter's right to print and publish the play. Harry R. Hoppe's suggestion, in *The Bad Quarto of 'Romeo and Juliet'* (1948), that Allde finished a task Danter could not complete after the seizure of his presses, is set aside in favour of the view that the two printers worked, not consecutively, but concurrently on what is seen as simply "a typical printing job shared by two London printing houses".

Doubts about memorial reconstruction are certainly in order, as David Farley-Hills shows in his article "The 'Bad' Quarto of *Romeo and Juliet*" (*Shakespeare Survey*, 49 (1996), pp.27-44). But the editors may appear, at least to some, to be embracing a methodology of scepticism when they opine that "the printed reference to Lord Hunsdon's Servants on the Q1 title page need have no implications for dating its printing. The information may have been inaccurate, or the reference may have been up-to-date when written but out of-date when the book was printed some months later." The Introduction ends with the remark that it is "unlikely that Q1 will ever give an unambiguous account of the play's early text career". It will be interesting to see whether Shakespeare bibliographical criticism will rise to the challenge implied by this somewhat dispiriting conclusion.

Members of the Malone Society receive its publications, including this edition of *Romeo and Juliet*, at an advantageous rate. Details may be found on www.sbu.ac.uk/malone.

University of East Anglia, Norwich   Christopher Smith

The Cambridge Companion to Shakespeare on Film. Edited by Russell Jackson. Cambridge: Cambridge University Press, 2000. pp. xiv + 342. ISBN 0-521-63975-1 (paperback); 0-512-63023-1 (hardback)

The *Cambridge Companion to Shakespeare on Film* joins the list of *Cambridge Companions to Literature*, and counterpoints to volumes in the series which address Shakespeare, in particular (*The Cambridge Companion to Shakespeare Studies*) and in context (*The Cambridge Companion to English Renaissance Drama* and *The Cambridge Companion to Ben Jonson*). Readers familiar with the series will have certain expectations of its contents: a collection of scholarly essays which address the broad range of critical issues pertaining to the topic, juxtaposed with exemplary close textual readings, edited and given a keynote introduction by a high-profile specialist. It will be accessible to a broad readership, eschewing the more arcane areas of literary criticism and jargon, framing its intellectual arguments in clear, direct and ordinary language which appeals primarily to students and scholars, but does not necessarily alienate the non-academic.

In this volume, the ability to address both the academic and non-academic constituencies is a particular requirement, given the recent flurry of Shakespeare films which have targeted a younger and more mainstream audience. For this group, whose first positive encounter with Shakespeare may well be through Leonardo di Caprio in Baz Luhrmann's *Romeo + Juliet*, Mel Gibson's *Mad-Max*-inflected *Hamlet*, or *10 Things I Hate about You*, a collection such as this needs to be able to bridge the gap between simply watching a Shakespeare film and beginning to think critically about it.

Editor Russell Jackson sets both the tone and the scope of the volume in his Introduction and in his subsequent essay, "From play-script to screenplay". The films are placed within the sweep of national and international cinema history, *as* films, and also in relation to the theatrical origins of the play texts. The tension (sometimes productive, sometimes reductive) between those two media – film and theatre – is a constant thread which runs through the seventeen essays and gives the volume coherence.

The volume is organised into four parts: "Adaptation and its Contexts", "Genres and Plays", "Directors", "Critical Issues", each part containing four or five essays. This organisation is very clear, and allows the reader to 'cherry-pick' a particular selection: useful, in particular, to the student reader who may be researching a class paper. Within the four parts, the sections on play genres and directors are more predictably organised: comedies/tragedies/histories; Olivier/Welles/Kosintsev/Zeffirelli/Branagh. The other two sections, on adaptation and critical issues, are more eclectic: Michèle Williams on the impact of video technology, Harry Keyishian on movie genre (adaptation); Carol Chillington Rutter on female characters, Neil Taylor on national and racial stereotypes (critical issues). for example.

Personally I found the most stimulating essay within these two looser groupings; not least because of what the choice of topics excluded, as well as the prominence given to those which were included. Rutter's and Taylor's topics, for example, foreground the impact upon Shakespeare criticism of gender and sociopolitical issues, while absent is any sustained discussion of the impact of 'queer' politics (or indeed politics *per se*) or of the ongoing 'high art v. popular culture' debate which results in accusations of 'dumbing down'. In this sense, the volume offers not only a direct discussion of Shakespeare films, but also an indirect commentary on Shakespeare criticism itself.

Barbara Freedman's "Critical junctures in Shakespeare screen history: the case of *Richard III*" and Neil Forsyth's "Shakespeare the illusionist: filming the supernatural" are absorbing essays. Freedman's benefits from detailed research into early U.S. film versions, the link to stage productions, and to film economics and reception issues, anchored by the focus on one particular play. Forsyth, on he other hand, organises his essay around a recurring problem for the cinema: how to treat the supernatural – ghosts, apparitions, spirits, magic – in a predominantly realistic medium, and uses close textual reading to build a persuasive discussion.

Jackson chooses not to discuss Shakespeare on television in this volume; though there is an essay on the impact of video technology and the ubiquity of the videotape, this is a collection about Shakespeare in the cinema. It is an understandable choice, as it sets clear limits to the scope of material covered, but it does lead to some duplication: the same plays and films are treated multiple times. There is a benefit, in that the reader can locate different critical approaches; but there is also a feeling of repetitiveness, and a consequent narrowing of the range. I would have liked to see at least one essay tackling television versions, or explicitly comparing the production and reception issues of the same play in the cinema and on television. One or two essays do allude to such issues, and point to a very large area of significant debate, which I missed here.

Opening up the field in this way would also have brought more of Shakespeare's plays, or more unusual treatments thereof, within the scope of the essays; for example, the English Shakespeare Company's *Wars of the Roses* cycle, or Babakhine's animated versions. If there is one major criticism I would make of this collection it would be that is rather conservative, centred as it is on Anglo-American productions, the majority of them drawn from earlier epochs of cinema. Many of these have been fairly exhaustively covered elsewhere, in books written, in some cases, by essayists represented here. This is not in itself a bad thing, since it may encourage the reader to refer outwards, either to the essayists' own books, or to several others featured in the very useful chapter notes.

However, there is precisely lacking in the collection the kind of energy I alluded to earlier, which has re-ignited the cinema industry's interest in filming Shakespeare for a new, young and/or mainstream audience. The absence of any sustained discussion of more radical – if, in terms of market penetration, marginal – productions or production strategies, gives the collection a rather familiar, even slightly routine, feel. I am thinking of the potential benefits, in terms of inter-essay dialogue, of treating at lengths such difficult works as Peter Greenaway's *Prospero's Books*, Derek Jarman's *The Tempest*, or Coronado's *Hamlet* and *A Midsummer Night's Dream*.

Though these are not part of the most recent wave of Shakespeare films, they would have reacted well within the essay which seemed to me to possess something of the necessary kind of freshness and energy: Tony Howard's "Shakespeare's cinematic offshoots". Howard looks at a range of films which either work directly from Shakespeare originals (such as *West Side Story* or *Joe Macbeth*) or borrow and transform elements of those originals *Jubal, My Private Idaho, Forbidden Planet*). He succeeds not only in uncovering a (loose) continuity of Shakespearean influence upon a huge range of films and genres – westerns, gangster, sci-fi, domestic melodrama – but also in opening up the breadth of strategic responses to the Shakespeare texts themselves. Particularly for a younger, highly cinema-literate readership also well versed in the creative strategies of, for examples, the music industry, this critical approach is well placed to fire their imagination and engagement.

The Cambridge Companion to Shakespeare on Film is a well-priced, intelligently-written collection which brings together familiar strands of critical analysis; as such, it is a valuable addition to a library collection. It sits well within the *Cambridge Companion* series, and may owe some of its conservatism to the series brief. I liked it, but still hankered somewhat for a collection which would have moved the debate further on.

University of East Anglia, Norwich   Val Taylor

Reviews

William Shakespeare, *King Henry VIII, OR ALL IS TRUE*. Edited by Jay L. Halio. Oxford World's Classics. Oxford: Oxford University Press. 1999. pp. ix + 230. ISBN 0-19-284036-3
William Shakespeare, *King Henry VIII (ALL IS TRUE)*. Edited by Gordon McMullan. The Arden Shakespeare. London: Thomson Learning. 2000. pp. xxiii + 506. ISBN 1-903436-24-9

The status of Shakespeare's works within the curriculum of literary study has often been debated; there has been less recognition of a canon existing within his works. Yet, as admirers of *King John* and *Timon of Athens* can testify, critical understanding of Shakespearean tragedy or of the history play is often grounded upon a narrow selection of texts. Despite evoking a rich tradition of critical responses, *Henry VIII* has never enjoyed a substantial presence in the teaching syllabus and its theatrical fortunes have declined sharply in the twentieth century. Its stature has been impeded by doubts concerning the extent of Shakespeare's authorship and the play's thematic and formal coherence – should it be conceived as a romance, a history play, or a 'last play'? *Henry VIII* certainly offers some additional interpretative conundrums – its historical emphases are surprising. The schism with Rome, the central event of Henry VIII's reign and of the sixteenth century, is only referred to obliquely. Instead, the play narrates, in the manner of a *de casibus* tragedy, the successive falls from power of Buckingham, Wolsey and Queen Katherine and the corresponding rise in fortune of Anne Boleyn. Throughout, the character of the king is enigmatic and his role in these events proves difficult to evaluate; generally, political and personal sympathies are far from clear-cut. Yet, these uncertainties are better seen as integral to the play's fascination. For anyone interested in Shakespeare's continuing reflection upon the Tudor world, or in his depiction of female protagonists, or in his relationship with collaborators, or in his concern with history, statecraft, and religion – that is, anyone with an informed interest in Shakespeare at all – *Henry VIII* should be of central concern.

An opportunity to consider again the play's significance has been offered by its publication in two new editions. Jay L. Halio's Oxford edition is clear, economical and modestly conceived. In a brief introduction, Halio surveys the historical events with which Shakespeare was concerned and notes his modifications of sources. He does not consider, in any depth, how the writer's own Jacobean context might have affected his viewpoint. There follows a narrative commentary upon the action that emphasises its balanced, or complementary, perspectives. Halio touches lightly upon the contentious issue of the interrelationship between the play's discrete episodes. Here, he identifies two predominant themes: the use and abuse of power and self-knowledge – he concludes that Henry VIII grows in self-awareness to achieve a new authority. There is also a useful section on the contrasting linguistic registers of the play – a formal and courtly language is juxtaposed against more colloquial forms of political commentary – and a detailed consideration of its stage history. This is a convenient and modestly priced edition for new readers. Yet, its critical commentary is suggestive rather than analytical and some crucial issues, such as the play's genre, are noted rather than explored. Similarly, there is a neglect of some significant critical work by, among others, Ivo Kamps and Pierre Sahel. A fuller sense of the critical tradition would have been helpful as well as a more thoroughly developed interpretation. Halio's textual commentary is informative and unfussy.

The impression of thinness created by the Oxford text is further emphasised by Gordon McMullan's edition for the third series of the Arden Shakespeare. The length of this makes it a substantial undertaking. As McMullan's introduction runs to over two hundred pages, one might have wished for a more rigorous application of his critical interest in moderation – especially with regard to some rather copious acknowledgements. Yet, this would be ungenerous: this edition is a major contribution to scholarship of *Henry VIII*. It offers not only a lucid and comprehensive introduction to the play, but develops a sophisticated argument that suggests new contexts for its interpretation. McMullan has also included far more detailed commentary on the text and he draws, throughout, on an impressive range of cultural sources. This can make the edition appear complex. Yet, his textual comments are illuminating and follow the practice of Arden3 by including quotations from sources. This directs attention towards authorial decisions as the play proceeds, rather than allowing source materials to languish (often unread) in a subordinate space at the end.

In his critical introduction, McMullan structures his account around one of *Henry VIII*'s keywords: 'truth'. He presents a detailed survey of how critical and theatrical traditions have attempted to uncover the truth of the play, predominantly by presenting it as a royalist and patriotic spectacle. Yet, as this edition suggests, *Henry VIII* asks some difficult questions about truth – a category prone to bewildering mutation in post-Reformation England – especially in its foregrounding of contradictory testimony. The anxiety the play generates concerning truth is attributed to two sources. First, the unstable political mood that arose in 1612-13, after the shocking death of Henry, Prince of Wales, alongside the more auspicious marriage of his sister Elizabeth. Second, McMullan assumes, despite his scepticism concerning author-centred criticism, that Shakespeare (and Fletcher) – harboured largely ironic attitudes towards the Henrician reformation and its consequences. The play is seen as both utilising and qualifying a providential, Protestant interpretation of the reign. McMullan identifies rhetorical ambiguities in its most propagandistic speeches, and further ambiguities derive from *Henry VIII*'s subtle exploitation of retrospect. We cannot help but be aware of the fate awaiting Cranmer, Anne Boleyn, and Thomas Cromwell. History is revealed as desperately unpredictable and even those who make the most authoritative attempts to master it can be outwitted. Such ironic awareness is further augmented by the play's fondness for reported action. This allows competing judgements to be expressed with regard to all of the protagonists and their actions. The admission of varying reactions affects responses to the king, who emerges, in this account, as a more complex and culpable figure than Halio's presentation of a monarch slowly reaching maturity. The editor stresses that Protestant evaluations of Henry VIII were mixed and notes the play's interest in his flawed masculinity, with its constant potential for immoderation. Typically, the audience has to qualify its judgement of the king and, in the broader sweep of the play, the auditor has to become, in effect, an historian, testing alternative explanations and sifting equivocal evidence. Truth may be glimpsed, but its credibility has to be appraised carefully from moment to moment.

This is a subtle and persuasive reading of *Henry VIII*'s equivocal sense of history. Its implications are pursued in a wide-ranging account that is full of fresh suggestion. If the play explores the ways in which truth is debated and established, rather than confirming a received version of events, this also affects its genre. McMullan argues the play is Terentian in conception – that is, it presents a providential outcome from unpromising circumstances – but that the expectations this form arouses are often displaced by its action. Perhaps the edition's most radical argument for the duality inherent in *Henry VIII* derives from seeing it as a fully-fledged collaboration between Shakespeare and Fletcher. This argument stems partly from the editor's own previous study of Fletcher and partly from Jonathan Hope's recent work on the authorship of Shakespeare's plays. This has the salutary consequence of reminding us that *Henry VIII* is the 'late' work for only one author and an early experiment for a second. McMullan concludes by urging us to recognise how the early modern theatrical world thrived upon a constant process of imaginative and material exchange.

Perhaps an interpretation of the play that emphasises its self-consciousness could have reflected more consistently on its own critical premises and historical context. Shakespeare and Fletcher are presented here as largely post-structuralist in temper with an advanced sense of historical contingency, the inaccessibility of truth and of the past as being constituted by multiple narratives. The 'oppositional' spirit of *Henry VIII* is largely detected in its sense of political futility. Whether such a thorough going relativism wholly encompasses the play's meaning – or, if it does, whether this is ethically or politically desirable – is open to question. Other critical readings might well decipher more explicit religious or ethical commitments in *Henry VIII*. McMullan assumes that it is the product of a wholly Protestant mentality. It would be interesting to see how a critic engaged by Shakespeare's (possible) Catholic affiliation might challenge this view. Still, McMullan's edition ensures that such a debate be conducted with a new range and seriousness; admirers of *Henry VIII* are in his debt.

University of Northumbria   Dermot Cavanagh

Lawrence Danson, *Shakespeare's Dramatic Genres*. Oxford Shakespeare Topics. Oxford: Oxford University Press, 2000. pp. vi + 160. ISBN 0-19-871173-5

This work is part of a series that aims to provide students and teachers with short books on important aspects of Shakespeare criticism and scholarship. The 'students' intended are presumably university undergraduates, but the book would also justify its place on the shelves of a school library as a reference book for pre-university study.

Lawrence Danson, Professor of English at Princeton University, writes with a light touch. For example, he makes his initial point about how assumptions about genre can affect the reading of a work by referring to the Thurber story of the tourist looking for some easy reading at a hotel who finds *Macbeth* on the Mystery shelves and proceeds to interpret it according to the conventions of the detective novel. The style is free of critical jargon in a way that would make it quite accessible to pre-university students, and in places it does seem to have been written for students with very little knowledge of literary criticism, as when the author explains that random death beneath a passing bus is not a tragedy in the literary sense of the word. Nevertheless, such students would experience some difficulties with a book that makes reference to the entire Shakespearean corpus and to contemporary playwrights. Such quibbles apart, this is a book which gives a helpful introductory survey of Shakespeare's plays for the student who is beginning a serious study of Shakespeare, and the discussion of genre helps to provide both a cultural context and an instrument for analysing not only what each play has in common with others of the same genre, but also what makes it distinctive.

If we assume that the study of genres is not just a necessary preliminary to arranging books correctly on library shelves, nor simply a way of passing judgment on how successful a writer has been in observing immutable rules (as Pope seems to be in danger of assuming), then we may well, like Lawrence Danson, quote Samuel Johnson with approval: "every genius produces some innovation, which, when invented and approved, subverts the rules which the practice of foregoing authors had established" (*The Rambler*, 125). Hence part of Danson's purpose is to study the ways in which Shakespeare's plays are "endlessly invoking and endlessly complicating the genres they simultaneously inherit and make".

In an opening section entitled 'The Genres in Theory' Danson sketches in the background information on Aristotle and Horace necessary for an understanding of the late sixteenth-century view of tragedy (although his fleeting references to Philip Sidney may not mean much to the average first-year student). He also explains the theory of comic types and the generality of comedy as opposed to the particularity of tragedy, referring to Donatus. Most helpful of all to the student is his excellent exposition of the title page of Jonson's *Works* (1616), with its figures of comedy and tragedy below, separated from each other, but also separated from the figures of satire and pastoral above by the Horace quotation, *Singula quaeque locum teneant sortita decenter* (Let each kind stay in its own appropriate place), while tragicomedy is perched precariously over the top. Danson makes good use of the apparently abstruse visual imagery of the title page to clarify the contemporary understanding of critical theory.

For the purposes of his own study Danson chooses to adhere to the categories of comedy, history and tragedy found in the 1623 *Folio*. He accepts the value of the term romance, but prefers to consider the comic and tragic elements in the late play under those two headings. As for the expression 'problem play', he considers it to have outlived its usefulness, being too vague to be helpful, quite apart from the fact that it is obviously not a genre.

He uses comparisons with other playwrights of the period to bring out the way in which variations from a generic norm can emphasise the distinctive qualities of a particular author or play. Thus the typically Shakespearean ending of comedy in marriage is put into focus by comparison with Jonson's *Epicoene*, ending as it does in a divorce, or with *Volpone*, in which Celia and Bonario are still separated at the end. Equally the comic types of Jonsonian comedy highlight the greater individuality of Shakespeare's creations, for although the lovers can be seen as types ("Lord, what fools these mortals be" – *Midsummer Night's Dream*; "More sacks to the mill" – *Love's Labours Lost*), the women above all are seen to establish their identities and strength of personality by their use of language. When Rosalind criticises Orlando's poor love verses we have no difficulty in endorsing her judgment, and when she tells Orlando to woo her, albeit that she is disguised as a boy, he obeys her. Danson does not, however, only stress variety from one author to another, but also the variety within Shakespeare's own use of each genre. In *Measure for Measure* Isabella does not share Rosalind's success in the use of language, for she provokes a quite different response from Angelo from that which she intended, while at the end of the play she is given no words to respond to the Duke's proposal of marriage.

It is not only within a genre that Danson makes comparisons. He considers not only the expressiveness of a Rosalind, but also the pathos of a Desdemona, whose failure to understand the cause of her husband's anger prevents her finding words to defend herself, and the paradoxical ability of Lavinia with her tongue cut out to express without speech the otherwise inexpressible horror of her fate. (He also points to the importance of being aware of the fashion for Senecan tragedy that made *Titus Andronicus* more highly regarded by its first audiences than any since.)

In tragedy Danson points to Marlowe's influence as the creator of a character who appears to be morally reprehensible, Faustus, and yet for whom the audience may feel sympathy. Such an extension of the concept of tragedy from the mere narrative of the fall of a great man makes possible the subtleties of a Macbeth, a ruthless murderer in whose feelings of terror, grief and disillusion we can nevertheless share. Danson also argues that Marlowe's *Edward II*, with its more complex characterization, contributed to the widening of Shakespeare's vision in the history plays from *Richard II* onwards.

In considering *The Winter's Tale* and *The Tempest* Danson makes a convincing case for seeing a blending of genres, in which "impossibly demanding protagonists", comparable to Lear and Othello, are "given a kind of second chance: comedy finds them in the midst of their tragic quests". Prospero's island is the site for either "comic forgiveness or tragic revenge", but recognising that "The rarer action is / In virtue than in vengeance" he opts for the former.

In his epilogue Danson observes that recent historicist criticism "tends to seek out the heterodox or the exceptional in culture; it can find the idea of genre too normalizing for its purposes". But he goes on to point out that "that same historicism must also lead us back to the Renaissance idea of dramatic genre" and that is precisely what Danson's book sets out to do. In doing so he surveys Shakespeare's work in a way that offers insights that will be helpful for those students who have already read many of Shakespeare's plays, but who need an appropriate understanding of Shakespeare's cultural context to help them form their own views.

Dixie Grammar School, Market Bosworth   Richard Willmott